I0836590

C. C. Dawson

A COLLECTION

OF

FAMILY RECORDS,

WITH

BIOGRAPHICAL SKETCHES

AND OTHER MEMORANDA OF VARIOUS FAMILIES AND INDIVIDUALS BEARING THE NAME

DAWSON,

OR ALLIED TO FAMILIES OF THAT NAME.

COMPILED BY

CHARLES C. DAWSON.

"FOR A MEMORIAL."—Ex. xvii, 14.

ALBANY, N. Y.:
JOEL MUNSELL, 82 STATE STREET.
1874.

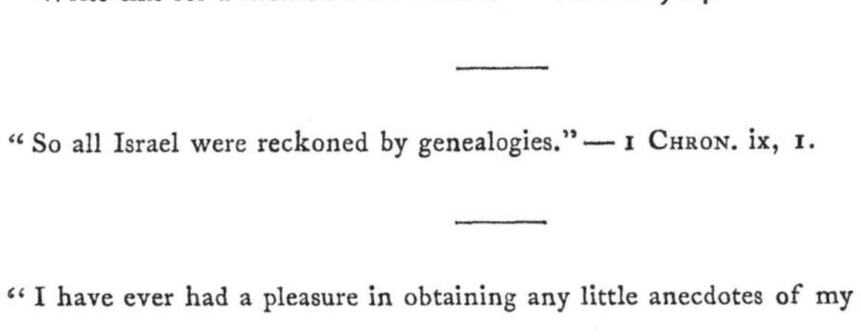

"Write this for a memorial in a book." — Ex. xvii, 14.

"So all Israel were reckoned by genealogies." — 1 CHRON. ix, 1.

"I have ever had a pleasure in obtaining any little anecdotes of my ancestors."
FRANKLIN.

"The dry branches of genealogical trees bear many pleasant and curious fruits for those who know how to search after them." — BEECHER.

"He only deserves to be remembered by posterity who treasures up and preserves the history of his ancestors." — BURKE.

PREFACE.

This book had its origin in the desire of the compiler to know something of his own family history. The purpose of compiling it was formed in boyhood, after his father's death; and the first crude notes which he committed to paper, containing the facts which had been treasured up in his mother's very retentive memory, are yet preserved. The occasion of meeting with any aged relative was always improved to add something to the information already secured, and the swelling bulk of the carefully kept "notes," when further interlineations and additions seemed inadmissible, made repeatedly necessary the task of transcribing and reärranging them, each time in a new and larger volume. The series of books which have been thus laboriously filled finds an end in the volume which is now presented.

The family name, common and widely disseminated as it is known to be now, was, in the early days of this enterprise, rarely met with and scarcely known outside of a few nearly related families. It was natural to suppose that all of the name, at least in this country, must be descended from a common ancestor, discoverable by genealogical researches. How far this early belief was from the truth, this collection of records will bear but partial evidence.

Records, more or less nearly complete, of a large number of families, the descendants of different American ancestors, not known to be otherwise connected than by identity of family name, are here presented. These are generally classified according to the states in which the ancestors first settled or chiefly resided. Of some families, believed to be quite considerable in point of numbers, records are almost entirely wanting. Greater fullness and accuracy would gladly have been secured, but it was impossible to publish information which those who were applied to for it, failed, for various reasons, to furnish.

To such as have kindly responded to his inquiries, the compiler would tender his grateful acknowledgments.

C. C. D.

EXPLANATION.

The plan adopted in the arrangement of the following records differs from that of any similar work known to the compiler as well as from any system recommended by either of the Genealogical Societies. It has seemed to the compiler to be convenient and reasonably simple, and for these reasons, as well as because of the difficulty of recasting these records to conform them to any other plan, it is retained. By means of the marginal numbering, merely, the inquirer may readily trace the lineage of any individual of a family either in the ascending or descending line, and the necessity of the insertion of figures in parenthesis for purposes of reference is avoided; thus dispensing with what seems usually a complicated and difficult feature of publications of this character.

The compiler's plans will be found to differ from those of most genealogists, also, in the fact that he has paid more attention to the descendants of female children than is common, often tracing them through several generations, and under various changes of names. In England, where the law of primogeniture prevails, genealogies have little regard except for the descendants of the eldest male child in each generation. In this country it has been common to preserve the record of the descendants of all the male children, but to disregard those of the female. Latterly a better fashion has been introduced of recording the descendants of *all* the children, though naturally the difficulty of tracing the descendants of female children, in consequence of changes of name, prevents the extending of such records in most cases as far as those of the descendants in the male lines. This feature will be noticed more especially in two of the most extended of the records which follow, viz. those commencing respectively at pages 21 and 411.

In another respect the plan of the compiler differs from that pursued in most works of this nature, in the fact that he has attempted to give, by means of copious foot notes, the genealogical history of those who have come into the Family, or rather various Families, by marriage. Thus, where the plan has been successfully carried out, the lineage of any one ranking as a descendant of the ancestor first named may be traced back on *both* sides — in the case of the parent, whether father or mother, who was also a descendant, by means of the marginal numbers, and in the case of the other parent, by means of the foot notes. It seems to the compiler that a study of the ancestral qualities on both sides, and equally on one side with the other, is indispensable in the case of every one who would obey the injunction, *Know Thyself*.

It has been attempted, also, herein, to render the record of each single family or household complete in itself, to the extent of presenting the history of the parents as fully as practicable, and of the children sufficiently to indicate their names, dates and places of births and deaths, whether married or single, and, if living, generally the place of residence. If a child dies unmarried, the biographical sketch of same, if any, is usually introduced in this connection; if the child marries, the facts, beyond those of birth, marriage, and death, or place of residence, are reserved to be stated in connection with the re-appearance of the name as that of the head of a family. In such case all these facts are restated, and the biographical sketch receives such amplification as the circumstances may warrant. Though thus involving the necessity of a repetition of certain facts, the very desirable object is accomplished of presenting the family group — the single household — before the eye, upon a single page, or as concisely as practicable, yet with all the facts essential to show what has been its history as to numbers and members, ages, marriages and locality.

In these records two columns of marginal numbers are used. The left-hand figures are intended to indicate the particular *generation* to which each individual belongs, and in the right-hand column the members of each generation are separately numbered in consecutive order. The head of the family, founder, first known ancestor or original emigrant, receives, however, merely the number *one* (**1**.), which indicates that, for the purposes of this work, he is regarded as alone of the first generation. His children are numbered 2–1, 2–2, 2–3, etc., which indicates that they are of the second generation, and the *first*, *second*, *third*, etc., of that generation in chronological order. The children of such of these as become heads of families are numbered 3–1, 3–2, 3–3, etc., the numbering in the right-hand column being consecutive as to all the individuals of that generation. The children of those who were of the third generation receive the numbers 4–1, 4–2, 4–3, etc., consecutively through the entire generation, and the same plan is continued through all the generations which follow. This plan does not admit of numbering the children of each separate household in chronological order, as is done in most similar works. In general, however, this special numbering is more ornamental than useful — the number of children in any given family being easily ascertained at a glance — and as the separate chronological numbering would involve the necessity of a third column of figures, it is dispensed with.

The numbers attached to the names of HEADS OF FAMILIES are in larger type than those which stand against the names of *children*.

In the records of each family let the following particulars be noticed:

The name of the father is printed in CAPITALS.

The maiden name of the mother is in *italics*.

The letter *m*. placed after a son's name, indicates that he has married, and that the record of his family is to be looked for further on.

If a *daughter* has married, the name acquired by marriage is placed in CAPITALS after her own, thus also indicating that the record of her family is to be looked for *forward*.

To find the son's or daughter's family record, notice the numbers opposite his or her name, and look *forward* to where they appear in larger type opposite the same name introduced as that of the head of a family. In this method any particular line of descent may be followed throughout the work.

To trace *back* the line of an individual's ancestors, find (by the proper index) where his name appears in the record, notice the figures opposite the name of his father or mother, refer *back* to where the same figures appear in smaller type opposite the name of a child; notice again the numbers opposite the name of the parent there mentioned, and refer back as before. This method, repeated, will bring the enquirer back to the original ancestor.

Abbreviations are used as follows:

Ae. or a.	for	age, aged.	gt.	for	great.
abt.	"	about.	m.	"	married.
b.	"	born.	mo.	"	month.
bapt.	"	baptized.	res.	"	reside, resides, resided, residence.
bro.	"	brother.			
bur.	"	buried.	Rev., rev.	"	Revolution, revolutionary; Reverend.
ch., chn.	"	child, children.			
d.	"	died.	unm.	"	unmarried.
dau.	"	daughter.	w.	"	wife.
gr.	"	grand.	wid.	"	widow.
grad.	"	graduate, graduated.	y.	"	young.

C. C. D.

PORTRAITS.

ADDITIONAL ILLUSTRATIONS

IN THIS COPY.

CONTENTS.

OF THE NAME.

The desire to know something of the origin, significance and history of one's name is no mean or idle curiosity.

All names are said — and doubtless in some sense truly — to have been originally significant; yet their signification, in many cases, can have been but slight or fanciful, and cannot always have been considered in their selection or bestowal.

The sources from which names have been derived are many. These include manifold forms of human pursuits, almost all varieties of bodily and mental characteristics, and a multitude of localities, events and objects in nature.

Names, thus variously derived, have changed with languages and customs, and have, in process of time, undergone such modifications and corruptions that, in many instances, as we are assured by diligent students, the originals cannot be traced.

However significant and appropriate they may have been originally, names which have descended through several generations are likely to have lost their special fitness to those who bear them; and as we daily meet with individuals bearing names descriptive of bodily peculiarities the opposite of those which they possess, so it is common to find like disagreements between the names of persons and their mental or moral qualities. We may, therefore, well conclude with Camden,[1] that "no name whatever is to be disliked in respect either of originall or of signification; for neither the good names doe disgrace the bad, neither do evil names disgrace the good. If names are to be accounted good or bad, in all countries both good and bad have been of the same surnames, which, as they participate one with the other in glory, so sometimes in shame .... Time hath confused and intermingled all."

---

[1] William Camden, "Prince of English Antiquaries," author of *Britannia*.

Surnames (*over* names, for so they were originally written), as now used, and transmitted to succeeding generations, are of modern invention. At the beginning of the Christian era, and for many centuries after, they were unknown; for although surnames were used by the Romans to some extent, they had not, among them, the inheritable quality by which they are now distinguished. The early converts to Christianity in Europe, in laying aside their Pagan names, received such as were conferred upon them by the missionaries who instructed and baptized them — names derived from the Scriptures or from church history. Their example was followed by others, until the ancient Pagan names were almost universally supplanted. With a few exceptions, a single name sufficed for each person, and in some cases it is said that a whole company would be baptized by the same name to save trouble. Thus such names as John, James, Matthew, David, Mark, Luke, Peter, Joseph and the like, became extremely common. Then came surnames by way of distinction: among the higher classes at first, finally among all. These were formed by adding the name of the parent to the personal name, or by adding some name suggested by anything peculiar to the person, his residence, condition or estate. Camden tells us that surnames began to be settled or hereditary in France about the year 1000, and in England about the date of the Conquest (1066) or a little before; also, that the Scots claim a like or even greater antiquity for their surnames, although he doubts if any have descended to posterity of a date earlier than the Conquest. In Ireland and Wales surnames were not adopted until long after this time, but were in process of introduction in the fifteenth and sixteenth centuries. In all Great Britain they remained irregular and unfixed among the common people throughout a great portion of the middle ages. After the Reformation the introduction of parish registers of births, marriages and deaths in England, greatly contributed towards giving them permanence.

As well before as after the introduction of hereditary surnames, the name of the father was used as a surname by the child — either with a prefix denoting son, as *Fitz* (Norman), *Ap* (Welsh), *Mac* (Irish), or with the addition of *son* (English), or *s* merely, which is Welsh. The Scotch used both the Irish and English forms.[1] Thus, instead of John the son of John, or John *John's son*, the name became, by a slight abbreviation, John *Johnson*, or the Welsh *Johns*, and from this *Jones;* and these latter came finally to be transmitted as family names. Thus, also, were formed the names of Davidson or Davids, instead of the son of David, or *David's son;* Matthewson or Matthews, instead of *Matthew's son*, and so on; and these, with like names, constitute a class of surnames of the most obvious origin. The diminutives or nicknames of these same originals furnish other forms of surnames. The son of one whose name was Robert, but nicknamed Rob, might be called *Rob's son* or *Robson;* the son of Walter, nicknamed Wat, *Watson;* and thus, by various forms of prefixes and suffixes to the same Christian or baptismal name, and its several nicknames and diminutives, a considerable variety of surnames may have been formed from the same original. McWilliams, Williamson, Willson, Wills, and no less than twenty-five other surnames are formed by Lower[2] from the name of William. The name of David[3] affords, according to the same author, a variety of surnames almost as great and equally as diverse, and among these is reckoned by Camden, Arthur,[4] Lower, and other authors, the name of DAWSON. "Though of ancient standing in Wales," says Lower, "this Christian name scarcely appears in England before the Conquest. Modified in various forms, it has since produced many family names, some of which are among the commonest in use, as Davids, Davidson, Davidge; Davey, Davy, Davie; Davies, Davis, Davison. From Daw,[5] the nickname, come Daws, Dawes, DAWSON, Dawkins[6], Dawkes, Dawkinson; and from another form of the nickname, according to Camden, we

---

[1] The prefix *O'* in Irish names denotes not the son, but a grandson or descendant.

[2] *Patronymica Britannica*, A Dictionary of the Family Names of the United Kingdom, by MARK ANTONY LOWER.

[3] A Hebrew word signifying *Beloved*.

[4] *An Etymological Dictionary of Family and Christian Names*, by WILLIAM ARTHUR.

[5] Da (Daw) being a contracted pronunication of *Daibhidh*, the Gaelic form of the name. Some infer from this derivation of the name that the DAWSONS were originally a Lowland offshoot from some clan of the Gaels of the Scottish Highlands. It is suggested that if they were English their surname would be more likely to be Davidson.

[6] The nickname *Daw*, and diminutive *kin*, or little.

get Day, Dayes, Days, Dakin." Of Dow, he remarks that it is "probably a corruption of the Gaelic *Dhu*—i.e. *black*; but *dow* or *doo*, the Scottish for dove or pigeon, may be the origin. It also appears to have been a personal name, and to have given rise to Dowson, Dowse, Dowsing and Dowsett." "DOSSON," he says, is "the same as DOWSON"; but it will be seen hereafter that both these names, as well as Dorson, Dolson and Dauson, are sometimes at least merely corruptions, or perhaps only misprints, of the name DAWSON.

Truly, if, as Lower tells us, we are descendants of some early worthy named, and haply baptized, DAVID, and if from the same source comes that great array of families which he enumerates, the name of our kindred must be legion! But if the name is thus derived, is it to be supposed that we are all descended from one original? Why not many different stocks from as many originals so named? [1] It is evident that there may have been numerous founders of the name. So, also, of those surnames which were derived either from some peculiarity in the characters or the persons of the originals, or were suggested by occupation or place of residence—as, for instance, the Smiths, the Clarks, the Farmers—the Browns and Whites—the Hills, Woods and Vales—all of which might originate in a great number of separate parishes, as they doubtless did. "There is," says Whitmore,[2] "one popular fallacy into which too many of

---

[1] From the account of the Anglo-Irish Dawsons which follows in this chapter it will be seen that the name was introduced into Ireland about 1600. It is said to be a fact, however, that some Irish families who are now known in English as Dawsons are really sprung from septs of much more ancient date. During the time when the Penal Laws against Irishmen and Catholics were in force, it was not unusual for members of the prescribed race and creed to adopt such English surnames as came near to their own either in significance or sound. Thus Dawson is said to be a rather frequent surname of the very Gaelic county of Donegal, for families who call themselves in their vernacular either O'Dorrian or MacDavett. Both these names belong to different and very ancient septs. No reason whatever appears why an O'Dorrian should call himself Dawson, in English, though it is asserted such is the case; but Dawson is an exactly literal translation of *Mac Daibhidh* (MacDavett or MacDevitt), and the facts stated are interesting in connection with the suggestion of a multiplicity of original or distinct founders of the family name. (It may be here mentioned, also, that the name is borne by sundry "American citizens of African descent," former slaves, who adopted their name after that of their late masters on being emancipated. A Mr. Dawson is a colored member of the Arkansas state senate, Feb. 1873; and Lawrence Dawson, colored, was recently proposed as a candidate for Holy Orders in the Episcopal Church of South Carolina.)

[2] *The American Genealogist*, by WILLIAM H. WHITMORE.

our genealogists have fallen, and that is the supposition that all the bearers of a given name are descended from a common stock." Identity of name, therefore, does not always imply identity of origin. It is, however, the first token of kinship, and as such is not to be lightly esteemed; though the fact that it does not furnish positive evidence of that relation is not to be forgotten.

In regard to the termination "son," which belongs to our name in common with a great number of English, Scotch and other surnames, Lower remarks that "a popular but very erroneous notion prevails that it indicates a Danish extraction." In fact, no evidence as to race can be educed from it.

According to Burke [1] and other writers on the British Peerage, the founder of the DAWSON family in England was Sir Marmaduke D'Ossone (Marmaduke *of Ossone*). He was one of the Norman noblemen who accompanied William the Conqueror into England in 1066, and for services rendered in battle is said to have received a grant of an estate from his successful leader, and to have remained in England during the rest of his life. It is said that the original seat of the family was in the county of York. The descendants of Sir Marmaduke intermarried with many ancient and some noble families, and the name, by an easy process, became changed, *Anglicised*, to DAWSON. Several of the family have been elevated to the British Peerage, and the books of heraldry mention no less than fifteen coats of arms belonging to individuals and families of this name. These are described in the *Encyclopedia of Heraldry* (Burke, London, 1844), in the following order: 1. That of the Earl of Portarlington, whose motto was as noble as his rank: *Vitæ via virtus*—Virtue is the way of life; 2. Viscount Cremorne: motto, *Toujours propice*—Always propitious; 3. Family of Penrith, county of Cumberland, 1761; 4. Of Ireland and London; 5. Thomas Dawson, Esq., Grasmere, county Westmoreland; 6. James Dawson, Esq., Sutterby, county Lincoln, 1664; 7. James Dawson, Esq., of Low Wray, near Hawkshead, a Justice of the Peace for Lan-

[1] *Dictionary of the Peerage and Baronetage of the British Empire.* By JOHN BURKE, an author whose works on heraldry and family history are said to be "the first authority."

cashire, President of Liverpool Medical Institution, etc, of the same family as the Dawsons of Sutterby: motto, *Deeds, not words;* 8. Castle Dawson, county Londonderry, as borne by Rt. Hon. Geo. Robert Dawson, descended from Thomas Dawson, Esq., who purchased Castle Dawson in 1663,[1] and was of a Westmoreland family; 9. London; 10. Newcastle;[2] 11. Spaldington, county of York; 12. Wharton, county of Lancaster; 13. Yorkshire; 14. Dawson; 15. Dawson. (The localities of the two last named families not stated).

The pedigree of the late Earl of Portarlington, (John Dawson) an Irish peer, was, according to Burke, as follows: From Sir Marmaduke D'Ossone lineally sprang (being the twentieth in descent), Richard Dawson, of Spaldington, in the county of York, who married Anne, daughter of Sir Henry Lowther, Knight, of Westmoreland county. "From this marriage descended William Dawson, Esq., the first member of the family whom we find in Ireland, a collector of the revenue for the counties of Down and Antrim, and the port of Carrickfergus, in the reign of Charles the Second.[3] His son, "Ephraim Dawson, Esq., having purchased the Portarlington and other estates in the Queen's county, took up his residence there, and represented the same in Parliament in the reigns of George the First and George the Second." His son, William Henry Dawson, Esq., also M. P. for Queen's county, was made Baron Dawson, 1770, Viscount Carlow, 1776; and was succeeded by his son John, second Viscount, made Earl of Portarlington, 1785, in whose family the title and estates remain. The pedigree of this Peer as given by Stockdale,[4] differs considerably from the above, but he also states that the family is of Norman extraction, and claims a lineal descent from Sir Marmaduke D'Ossone. The descent is traced from Alexander Dawson, of Spaldington, county of York, 1584.

---

[1] In 1633, according to the same author's *Landed Gentry*, a later publication.

[2] The representation of *daws* in this coat of arms suggests the possibility of the name having originated, in one family, at least, from some fancied resemblance in the founder of it to this bird. Perhaps he was a boisterous talker:

"The loud daw, his throat displaying, draws
The whole assembly of his fellow daws."

But possibly the *name* may have suggested the device.

[3] 1660–1685.

[4] STOCKDALE'S *Peerage of the United Kingdom.*

Of another Irish peer, Viscount Cremorne, (Thomas Dawson, created Baron Dartry), of Dawson Grove, in the county of Monaghan, grandson of Walter Dawson, who died in 1718, it is stated by Stockdale that his family, which was originally of Yorkshire, settled in Ireland in the reign of James the Second.[1] But according to Burke's *Peerage*, the ancestor of this peer in Ireland was Thomas Dawson, who removed from York (Westmoreland ?)towards the close of the reign of Queen Elizabeth,[2] and became in the succeeding reign[3] a burgess of Armagh. The viscounty became extinct in 1813, but the barony of Cremorne descended to Richard Thomas Dawson, of Castle Dawson, Monaghan, grand-nephew of the above-named viscount. It may be noted in passing that the second wife of Viscount Cremorne was Philadelphia Hannah Freame, of Philadelphia, a grand-daughter of William Penn.[4] One of the sons of Walter Dawson, above-named, was Richard Dawson, an eminent banker in Dublin, 1723–1776, and other members of the family, being excluded from succession to their ancestors' titles and estates through the operation of the law of primogeniture, entered the army or navy, or took holy orders; while the same law which forced them into these professions must have carried their de-

---

[1] 1685–1688.

[2] She died in 1603. In Burke's *Genealogical and Heraldic Dictionary of the Landed Gentry of Great Britain and Ireland* (1868) it is stated that the family was long seated at Acornbank, in the parish of Sowery, Westmoreland, and became established in Ireland at the opening of the 17th century, when Thomas and Robert Dawson, sons of Christopher Dawson, Esq., of Acornbank, settled in that kingdom. The younger of the two, Dr. Robert Dawson, was consecrated Bishop of Clonfert in 1627; the elder, Thomas Dawson, went to Ireland in 1601, from Temple Sowerby, *Westmoreland*, and purchased the lands of Castle Dawson, 1633. By another line of descent from him, we have the lineage of Robert Peel Dawson, Esq., M.P. from Londonderry, 1868, as follows: 1. Thomas Dawson, above named. 2. His son Thomas Dawson, commissary of the musters of the army in Ireland, died 1683. 3. His son, Thomas Dawson Esq., of Castle Dawson, M. P. for Antrim. 4. His brother and successor, Joshua Dawson, Esq., of same, M.P. for Londonderry, one of the barons of the Exchequer, 1742. 6. His nephew and successor, Arthur Dawson, Esq., of same, M.P., died 1822. 7. His son, Rt. Hon. Geo. Robert Dawson, of same, M.P. for Londonderry, 1815–1833, under Secretary of State for the Home Department, 1823, Secretary of the Treasury, 1828, Privy Councillor, 1830, Secretary of the Admiralty, 1834, son-in-law to Sir Robert Peel, and father of Robert Peel Dawson, Esq., above named.

[3] James I, 1603–1625.

[4] An accomplished lady, b. 1740, m. 1770, d. 1826. She was dau. of Thomas Freame and Margaret, fourth ch. of William Penn, by his second w., Hannah Callowhill. — Watson's *Annals of Philadelphia*, p. 108; *Am. Hist. Record*, vol. 1, p. 455.

scendants back into the common walks of life. The descendants of these, as well as of the minor branches of the Earl of Portarlington's family, must be numerous. There are or have been other families of our name in Great Britain possessing hereditary titles, but it will not serve any useful purpose in this connection to inquire further into their origin or history. The above facts have been referred to simply as furnishing data by which to trace the rise and spread of the family name, and without any intention on the part of the compiler hereof of claiming connection for any American Dawsons with the noted families of our name in Great Britain. Among the younger branches of those families, constituting the gentry of the country,[1] very many cases must have occurred where individuals became tradesmen and yeomen, losing all recollection of their connection, not even preserving the family arms or other memorials. It is not improbable that some of this class may have emigrated to this country. "None are so apt to seek foreign shores as those deprived by fortune of the position of their ancestors;" but where there is no evidence from records or other contemporary writings of descent from illustrious families, it will be most reasonable to conclude that no such relationship exists.

That the name, however it may have originated, is an ancient and highly respectable one, no other evidence need be adduced than the foregoing. Of other English bearers of it may be men-

---

[1] One of the ancestors of George Pelsant Dawson, Esq., of Osgodby Hall, co. York, barrister, &c., had *eleven sons*. The lineage of this gentleman, condensed from Burke's *Landed Gentry*, is as follows: 1. Bertram Dawson, the seventh in lineal descent from Archibald Dawson, of Greystock, in Cumberland, recorded as having been with Edward the *Black Prince* in France, 1345–1356. 2. His son, Simon Dawson. 3. His son, Sir Roger Dawson, Knt. of Dalstone. 4. His son, Bertram Dawson, father of eleven sons, of whom Gilbert, the ninth, was the ancestor of the Dawsons of Azerley. 5. The fourth son, Richard Dawson, Esq., of Heworth, county York, living 1588, was followed by two Richards of same, these by two Williams of same, the last of whom was succeeded by his son George Dawson, Esq., of North Ferriby, county York, major in the army, born 1689, killed at Carthagena, 1741, father of George Dawson, Esq., of same county, b. 1739, d. 1811, governor of Masulipitan and member of council at Madras. His son, George Dawson, Esq., of same, b. 1763, d. 1832, lieut. 1st royals, father of George Pelsant Dawson, Esq., above named, b. 1802. It is easy to see how the minor branches of such a prolific family should become so numerous as to be practically untraceable in the course of a few generations. The English books record only the main stem of each family. Another extensive family is descended from Henry Dawson, of Breedon, county of Leicester, where he died in 1577. The present representative of this family is Edward Finch Dawson, Esq., of Launde Abbey, in that county, whose ancestors for many generations have held successively the office of high sheriff. *Vide* Burke's *Landed Gentry*.

tioned John Dawson, of the county of Lancaster, who went a pilgrim from England to Rome in 1504;[1] also two early printers, John Dawson, of London, 1639, in which year he printed (and *sold*, for the printers of those days corresponded to our modern publishers) a work entitled *New England's Prospect*, esteemed a rare and valuable book now; and Thomas Dawson, of London, 1652, who printed in that year another important work relating to America, entitled *Divers Voyages touching the Discovery of America and the Islands adjacent unto the same*, etc. (Perhaps it was the same Thomas Dawson, possibly another, who, in 1613, then "dwelling near *The Three Cranes in the Vinetree*," London, printed "*The Excellency of Good Women. The honor and estimation that belongeth unto them*"). Henry Dawson, who died in 1653, was, in that year, the first representative of the county of Durham in the House of Commons.[2] This was the Parliament called "Barebone's," and prepared the way for the Protectorate. The name of the member for Durham has sometimes been printed dubiously "Davison,"[3] but all doubt as to the true name has been removed by the discovery of a monumental inscription upon a tablet affixed to the northern wall of the church of St. Mary Abbotts, Kensington.[4] "It has been said that fame is but a name. It was not even that, hitherto, with the first member for the county of Durham; for Henry Dawson had to share his

---

[1] "1504, 25 Nov., venit Jhes Dauson scholare de coitatu Lancastrie Lichfeldes Dioces." [Names of Pilgrims from England to Rome.] *Collectanea Topographica et Genealogica*, vol. 5, p. 60.

[2] "Being a county palatine, Durham was formerly 'exempt from the burden of representation.' The Bishop of Durham, as we read in Surtees, levied taxes within the bishopric by virtue of his palatine jurisdiction, his Council (and not Parliament) granting consent; and although the question of a representation of the county had repeatedly been brought before the House of Commons in the reigns of Elizabeth, James and Charles, it was not until the time of Cromwell that a member for the county palatine had a seat."—*Notes and Queries*, 3d. ser., XI, 20, 21.

[3] The name does not appear in the *Parliamentary History*, but that of Henry *Davison* figures as member for Durham. In the list, however, of members for the "Four Northern Counties" in that Parliament given in Burton's *Diary*, Henry Dawson is named as one of them.—*Parl. Hist.*, III, 1407; Burton, II, 499.

[4] "Neere this piller lieth the body of HENRY DAWSON, Esq., Alderman of Newcastle-upon-Tyne, who was twice Maior of the said town, and a member of the present Parliament, who departed this life Augst ye 2, 1653."—*Notes and Queries*, 3d ser., X, 474. This tablet is supposed to have been first put up inside the old church, and to have been removed to the wall when the church was rebuilt, about 1694. A writer in *Notes and Queries* pleads for its better present protection, because of its "interest, not only heraldic, but as an instance of a monument to one of the rebel Parliament."

seat with a possible Davison.[1] But the name is at last established; and the member is identified with a mayor of Newcastle." He was deputy-mayor of that city, 1646–47, and mayor 1652–53, dying during his incumbency of the office. Two other Dawsons held the same office — *William*, 1649–50, and *George*, 1650–51, and a second time 1657, besides completing Henry's year of office in the borough, from his death, in August, to the appointment of a new mayor in October, 1653. The Dawsons who thus held the office of mayor five times between the siege of Newcastle and the restoration, "were evidently of the commonwealth party."[2] Ambrose Dawson,[3] a native of Yorkshire, became an eminent physician in London, and died in 1794, aged 88; and his son, Pudsey Dawson, Esq.,[4] who died in 1816, aged 64, was mayor of Liverpool, and founder of a school there for the indigent blind. Peter Dawson was vicar of Cumberland, Surrey, England, from 1618 to 1643. He was also rector of Carshalton. John Dawson, a collector of the customs at Yarmouth (Norfolk county, England), died there in 1679, aged 56. He was a native of Loughborough, to which town he bequeathed £100, and the same sum to the corporation of Yarmouth, for the payment of £5 yearly "for teaching poor children arithmetic and the mathematics."[5] Another John Dawson was a noted English mathematician and teacher of mathematics, 1734–1820.

The virtues of one Mr. Robert Dawson, who was buried at

---

[1] Many a Dawson can no doubt recall instances in which he has figured as "a possible Davison." The name, if at all carelessly written, is very apt to be thus misprinted.

[2] For an interesting discussion of the Heraldic emblems engraven upon the tablet at St. Mary Abbotts, see *Notes and Queries*, 3d ser., x, 475; xi, 22, 23, 47, 166.

[3] He was son of William Dawson, Esq., of Landcliffe Hall, Yorkshire, a justice of the peace for that county, and a personal friend of Sir Isaac Newton, who is said to have paid him frequent visits. From him also descend the Dawsons of St. Leonard's Hill, county Berks. His father was Christopher, eldest son of Joseph, eldest son of Christopher Dawson, Esq., who was of the parish of Arncliffe, in Yorkshire, about 1600.

[4] His eldest son, Pudsey Dawson, Esq., inherited Hornby Castle, county Lancaster, 1840, was high sheriff of Lancaster, 1845, and was succeeded at his decease by his nephew, Richard Pudsey Dawson, Esq., b, 1821, capt. 1st Royal Lancashire militia, &c.

[5] He was ancestor of Dawson Turner, Esq., the botanist and author, who has preserved some account of him in the work entitled *Sepulchral Reminiscences of a Market Town*. This family became extinct by the death of Mr. James Dawson, uncle to the botanist's father, in 1792.

Ripon, Yorkshire (probably before 1750), were celebrated in a neat epitaph, as follows:

"His Nature mild, his Mind devout,
His Wealth the Poor well fed:
Tho' dead, he lives in Spite of Death,
And Grave, his fatal Bed;
Whom lately Sheriff, Merchant free,
York's wealthy City had;
And Farmer chief of Rippon church,
Now Rippon Mould hath clad.[1]

Within the recollection of many persons now living was a celebrated Wesleyan Methodist preacher in England named William Dawson, a very entertaining sketch of whom may be seen in *Pulpit Portraits*, by John Ross Dix. He was better known as the Yorkshire farmer — a sturdy, rough man, wholly unprofessional in appearance, but gifted with eloquence so remarkable, such a fertile imagination and power of language, and endowed with such fervent piety and untiring zeal, that thousands were attracted to his ministrations from miles around, and were moved in a most unwonted manner by his wonderful oratory.[2] George Dawson, another noted English divine, was a native of the parish of St. Pancras (1821) where his father conducted an extensive academy. He was graduated at the University in Glasgow, and has since been distinguished as an Independent minister at Birmingham, but has been more widely known as a literary lecturer, in which capacity he attained the highest popularity. Benjamin Dawson, LL.D., Rector of Burgh, Suffolk, son of a dissenting minister at Halifax, and living in

---

[1] Choir of Ripon Church. *A New Select Collection of Epitaphs*, by T. Webb, London, 1775. Another epitaph in this collection is as follows:

"On Anne Dawson.
"In Bloom, the tender, faithful Wife
Expir'd in bringing forth a son;
Both the same Moment gave up Life,
And lie lamented in this Tomb."
[Ewall, Surry, England, 1755.]

[2] A more elaborate account of him, with numerous anecdotes illustrative of his wit, courage and piety, may be seen in Wakeley's *Heroes of Methodism*, pp. 355–380. A biography has also been published. He was b. at Goforth, near Leeds, in 1773, and d. suddenly, July 3, 1841. He received a good English education. His father, Luke Dawson, occupied a small farm and tenanted a colliery under the late Sir Thomas Gascoigne.

1812, at an advanced age, was the author of a volume of *Sermons on the Divinity of Christ*, 1765, *Free Thoughts on the Subject of a further Reformation of the Church of England*, 1771, a *Dictionary of the English Language*, 1806, and other works. Of other early English authors the compiler has seen the names of Thomas, author of *The Good Houseuive's Jewell*, 1596–7; John, "minister of the word of God, at Mayden-head, in Berkshire, sometimes of Christ Church in the University of Oxford,"[1] *Eighteen choice sermons preached upon the Incarnation and Nativity of our Lord and Savior Jesus Christ*, posthumously printed, at London, 1642; George, a *Treatise on the Origin of Laws*, 1694; John, author of a *Greek and English Lexicon*, 1709; Thomas, *Memoirs of St. George, the English Patron, and of the Order of the Garter*, 1714; William, author of *The Atheist, a Philosophical Poem*, 1723,[2] Thomas, author of sundry dissertations on Biblical subjects, 1727; Ambrose, M.D. and Thomas, M.D., authors of professional treatises, 1744–82; Rev. Abraham, a Biblical translator, 1763–86; and others. Since 1800, the name, although not very prominent in literature, has afforded too many authors for enumeration here.

It may be safely asserted that there is no English speaking country or colony where the name is not found, and the commercial enterprise and religious zeal of individuals have carried it far beyond these limits—into nearly all lands, indeed, Christian and heathen.[3]

---

[1] Anthony a Wood says that he was "a most eminent preacher of his time;" he was vicar of Maidenhead; "died in the prime of his years, in 1641."—*Collectanea Top et Gen.*, VI, 172.

[2] Perhaps this author was the Rev. William Dawson, "Minister of the Gospel at Newcastle-upon-Tyne," who, in 1732, was appointed Professor of Hebrew and other Oriental languages in the University of Edinburgh. "He is supposed to have been descended from the Irish family of Cremorne."— *Notes and Queries*, 1st ser., v, 396.

[3] The names of many Dawsons in Foreign parts have been seen by the compiler, but not preserved. The following may be noted: Dr. J. Dawson and wife were American Baptist Missionaries at Avah, Burmah, in 1850; J. Dawson, Gold Coast, Africa, 1849, was a Life Member of the British and Foreign Bible Society; Colwell, Dawson & Co., merchants, 1869, at Callao, Peru; R. Dawson, Vice Commercial agent of the U. S., 1871, at Ceylon, India; Geo. B. Dawson, U. S. Vice Consul, Cork, Ireland. The *Commercial Directory* of London, 1867, contains the names of 86 Dawsons, and the *Court Directory* of that year the addresses of 38 persons of the same name. The *Directory* of Liverpool, England, for 1871, contains the addresses of 105 persons of the name, that of Glasgow, 16, and that of Edinburgh some half dozen only. The name is much more common in England than in Scotland, although by no means rare there.

The name of Dawson is borne by an important river in East Australia, by a lake in Canada,[1] by an island in the Pacific,[2] by a street and a place in London, a street in Dublin,[3] by several counties,[4] and numerous post-offices[5] in the United States; and as a personal name is not always a surname, being not unfrequently found as another part of the individual cognomen.[6]

---

[1] In Ottawa county, Lower Canada.

[2] "*Dawson Island*, a considerable island of Terra del Fuego, in the middle of the Strait of Magellan, intersected by the parallel of 54° S. and by the meridian of 70° 30′ W."— *Cyclopedia.*

[3] "Ireland claims a passing allusion. If its literary localities are less numerous, they are scarcely less interesting. To begin with the Metropolis......How many a one — even the admirer of her poetry — passes 20 DAWSON street, without thinking of Mrs. Hemans; yet in that house the 'falcon-hearted dove' folded its wing and fell asleep, and in the vaults of St. Ann's church, hard by, her mortal remains are laid."— *Salad for the Solitary*: chap: "The Shrines of Genius."

[4] In Georgia, Nebraska, Texas.

[5] *Dawson*, Terrill Co., Georgia; Sangamon Co., Illinois; *Dawson's*, Alleghany Co., Maryland; *Dawsonburgh*, Fremont Co., Iowa; *Dawsonville*, Dawson Co., Georgia; Montgomery Co., Maryland; Green Co., Virginia; *Dawson's Mills*, Richardson Co., Nebraska; *Dawson's Prairie*, Kaufman Co., Texas; *Dawson's Station*, Fayette Co., Pennsylvania. *Dawson's Bridge*, a small hamlet, and *Dawson Castle*, a post-office and castle, are situated in the county of Londonderry, province of Ulster, Ireland.

[6] The names of the English botanist and author, Dawson Turner, F. R. S., the Hon. Dawson A. Walker, who was the Republican candidate for governor of Georgia, 1872, the late commander Dawson Phenix, of the United States navy, and Charles Dawson Shanly, the popular magazinist, are examples.

NEW ENGLAND:

NOTES RELATING TO EARLY SETTLERS, AND RECORDS OF SEVERAL FAMILIES OF NEW ENGLAND ORIGIN.

EARLY MENTION.

Perhaps the first of the name in New England was HENRY DAWSON, of Boston, admitted a freeman 2 June, 1641,[1] having joined the church on the 16th of May preceding, to qualify him for admission as freeman.[2] In the same year in which he was admitted freeman, a will was executed at Roxbury, and "Goodman Dawson" received a small bequest.[3] This may have been N. DAWSON, of Charlestown, 1648, in which year Robert Saltonstall conveyed to him by deed a house in Windsor, Conn.[4]

---

[1] In the list of freemen of this date the name is spelled DAUSON. — *N. E. Hist. & Gen. Reg.*, vol. III, p. 188; Farmer's *Genealogical Register*.

[2] Drake says he was admitted an inhabitant 25 Jan., 1641. — *Hist. and Antiq. of Boston*, 259, *note*. He was in the employment of William Hudson, jun., who went to England about 1643, to serve in the army of parliament against the king, having committed the care of his family and business to Dawson, "a young man of good esteem for piety and sincerity," whose wife was in England. During the two years of Hudson's absence Dawson was exposed to such temptation as brought him and the wife in peril of their lives. — (Winthrop's *History of New England*, II, 249). He was, in 1645, when the case was investigated, cast out of the church; but next year, on penitent acknowledgement, was restored. — (Savage's *Genealogical Dictionary*). It does not appear that his wife ever came to this country.

[3] This was the will of John Tey, probated 7th 10th mo. (*O. S. Jan.*), 1641, and the bequest was "To Goodman Dawson 10*s.* besides satisfaction for his labor." — *N. E. Hist. & Gen. Reg.*, vol. II, p. 105, Art: *Abstract of the earliest wills upon record in the county of Suffolk, Mass.*

[4] Suffolk deeds, Boston, Mass., 22d 9th Mo., 1648. "House in Windsor, Conn., formerly of Francis Stiles, of Seabrook, now in occupancy of Thomas Gilbert and John Bancroft." But the "N. Dawson" here mentioned may be the same resident of Charlestown who is called Nicholas *Davison* by Savage. Another "possible Davison!" THOMAS DAWSON, of Morley, county York, England, had certain "land and housing" in Windsor, 1697. — Trumbull's *Colonial Records of Conn.*, vol. IV, 206.

The name of HENRY DAWSON occurs in "A list of Capt. William Turner's men, as they came from Boston, taken at Medfield," Feb. 1675–6,[1] and on Conn. river, April, 1676, under Capt. Pierce.[2] This could hardly have been the freeman of 1641, because of age; yet the same Capt. Turner was a freeman of Dorchester, 1643. The name again occurs in a list of Boston freemen, 8 May, 1678; [3] at which time it appears he had two children; [4] and HENRY DAWSON was a freeman of Boston, 15 May, 1690,[5] where he had baptized at the Second church, Thomas, 22 Nov., 1691; James, 9 Feb., 1695-6; Hannah, 20 March, 1698; Elizabeth, 31 March, 1700.[6] JAMES DAWSON (probably the same who was baptized 1695–6), had baptized at this church, Mary, Nov. 1, 1719; Samuel, Feb. 16, 1723–4; Henry, April 2, 1727.[7] MARY DAWSON was admitted a member of the Second church Jan. 5, 1728–9, and had baptized Elizabeth, March 14, 1731; Abigail, March 10, 1734; Abigail, Feb. 1, 1735–6.[8] There was also baptized in the New Brick church, Boston, BENJAMIN DAWSON, Feb. 22, 1740–1; Hannah, Oct. 17, 1742.[9]

There was a member of the Society of Friends, named GEORGE DAWSON, at Boston, July, 1677.[10] It was during the time of the Quaker persecution. In this month one Margaret

---

[1] Drake's *Boston*, 418.

[2] Savage's *Gen. Dict.* Art: DAWSON. He says of Capt. Turner, that he had command on the upper waters of the Conn. river; on the 18th May, (1641) surprised the Indians at the place where the falls have since borne his name, giving them a signal defeat; but on the return was surrounded at Green river, and the next day after the Falls fight, was killed, with eighteen of his men.

[3] DAWSON or DOSSON, Henry, admitted member of Second church, Boston (which was Increase Mather's), April 14, 1678, probably to qualify him for admission as freeman in the month following, as above.— See *History of the Second Church*, by Chandler Robbins, *appendix*.

[4] The name is again written DAUSON in the list of freemen.—*N. E. Hist. & Gen. Reg.*, vol. 3, 244.

[5] *Ibid*, p. 350. At a town meeting in Boston, Sept. 16, 1689, Henry Dawson was appointed one of the "overseers of woodcorders."— Drake's *Boston*, 487.

[6] Savage's *Gen Dict.*

[7] Robbins's *Hist. Second Church*, appendix.

[8] *Ibid.*

[9] *N. E. Hist. & Gen. Reg.*, vol. 18, p. 339; names of parents not stated.

[10] Probably the same "George Dauson" who was of "Middlebury" (Middleborough?) 1674, and was, 27 October, of that year, "for doeing servill worke on the Lord's day," fined forty shillings; the court consisting of Gov. Winslow, with John Alden, Wm. Bradford, and other assistants. As late as July 13, 1677, this fine had not been paid, the Colonial Treasurer reporting it "still due to the country," as he had done each year previously since it was imposed.—*Plymouth Colony Records*, vol. v.

Brewster, a Quaker, for "making a horrible disturbance on the Lord's day," was "whipped at a cart's tail up and down the town, with twenty lashes." On the same day that Margaret and her companions were apprehended, three other women and eleven men, one of whom was George Dawson, were taken up at a Quaker meeting, and all but two of them (Miles Foster and Thomas Scott, whose fines were paid by some person, against their wishes), were publicly whipped.[1] At the next meeting several of the same company (including GEORGE DANSON, as printed, though undoubtedly written DAUSON), were again arrested and whipped.[2] The same George Danson (Dauson) was one of three "loaf bread bakers" in Boston, who petitioned the general court, Oct. 29, 1679,[3] for relief from the "intolerable burdens" which they alleged were imposed upon them "by reason of ye deffect of ye assize given in ye law." They observed that their calling was a lawful one, to learn which they had "served long and hard apprenticeships," and added, "wee conceive wee have a just right to live by itt."[4]

In an attack on Middleborough, Mass., by Indians, 1675, a man named DAWSON [5] was shot from his horse near the house of

---

1 Drake's *Boston*, 429.

2 *Ibid.*

3 *Ibid*, 437. Mr. Savage says GEORGE DAWSON, a Quaker, was at or of Boston, 1679.—*Gen. Dict.* Another instance of Danson misprinted for Dauson or Dawson occurs in *N. E. Hist. and Gen. Reg.*, vol. 3, *Index.*

4 Probably the same George Dauson (misprinted Danson) removed to Barnstable within a year or two after the date of this petition; one of this name was in possession of the house and land comprising the estate of Nicholas Davis, deceased, of Barnstable, seized by the "chief marshall" of the colony, by order of the court, as per return made 7 July, 1681.—*Plymouth Colony Records*, vol. 6. One of this name, had been, also, prior to 14 May, 1684, a petitioner, with others, for certain lands which they claimed to have purchased from Wampas, an Indian. The court made answer at this time that it knew not "of any land that Wampas, Indian, had any true or legal right to, he being no Sachem, but a common person; if the persons can find any lande that was his, and withheld from them, the law is open where they may obteyne their right, if they can make any such appear."—*Plymouth Colony Records*, vol. 5, 442. In his will, 1692, his trade (that of a baker) is stated, and he is again described as "of Boston." The will mentions his w. Elizabeth, and gr. chn. George, Charles and Elizabeth *Crossweight*. A representation of his seal is to be found in the *Heraldic Journal*, vol. II, p. 181. Art: Suffolk Wills. He obtained, about 1686, a grant of 200 acres of land at Worcester, and it would seem that he built a house there, and occupied it (either by himself or some representative) for three years.— Lincoln's *History of Worcester*, 36, 37.

5 *N E. Hist. and Gen. Reg.*, vol. 15, p. 267: Art: *Notes on the Indian Wars in New England.*

John Thompson, as he stopped to let his horse drink at a brook."

In a list of early settlers of Essex and Old Norfolk, Mass.,[1] occurs the name of MARGARET DAWSON, relict of DANIEL, late of Ipswich, 1693.[2]

It appears that there were persons of the name at Hull, Mass., about 1750–60; one MARY DAWSON having become the second wife of Joseph Spear, a lighterman of that place, some time after 1743;[3] and one JOSEPH DOSSON having been listed as one of a foot company of militia in the town of Hull, under command of John Gould, jun., as appears by a list "taken at Weymouth, March 22, 1759."[4]

JOHN DAWSON, of Salem, was taken a prisoner and carried to Canada, at the surrender of Fort William Henry, in 1757;[5] and TIMOTHY DAWSON was a school teacher at Salem in 1781.[6]

At Marlborough, Mass., WILLIAM DAWSON, by wife Sophia, had Darius, born March 8, 1780.[7] Of him or his family nothing more has been learned, nor is it known whence any of the persons above mentioned came to this country. "It is not common to learn that interesting fact concerning more than one in ten of our early settlers."[8]

The above are the only early references to the name in New England that have come to the compiler's knowledge, except

---

1 *N. E. Hist. and Gen. Reg.*, vol. 5, p. 250.

2 There was a Daniel Davison, at Ipswich, aged 40, in 1670. — *Ibid*, vol. 6, p. 250. Probably the correct name, and the above a misprint, as might easily be the case. If so, she was the second wife and widow of this Daniel. See Savage's *Gen. Dict.*, Arts: DAWSON and DAVISON.

3 *N. E. Hist. and Gen. Reg.*, vol. 18, p. 158. Art: *Spear Family Record.* Their children were, Barney, Joshua, 1749, Joseph, 1747, died 1794, was a surveyor, and had been a soldier of the Rev. By Boston overseers' records it appears that Joseph Spear, wife and three children, of Hull, Aug. 3, 1758, time of residence in Boston six months, were warned out of town by Abijah Adams, constable; it having been an annual custom for many years in that pious and prudent city to warn several thousand of the poorer inhabitants, as a *matter of form*, so that in case of extreme poverty happening to them afterwards, the town might not be legally bound to support them!

4 *Ibid*, vol. 4, p. 75.

5 "Among those of Salem carried prisoners to Canada were John Oakman, JOHN DAWSON, Peter Smith, Moses Atwood, John Knapp and Jonathan Morrison." — *Annals of Salem*, vol. 2, p. 513.

6 "1781, Dec. 12, TIMOTHY DAWSON teaches one of the public schools. He appears to have taken the place of Mr. Ford, who died the preceding June 27." — *Ibid*, vol. 1, p. 452.

7 Hudson's *History of Marlborough*, *p.* 354.

8 Hon. John Savage, letter, May 12, 1855.

such as relate to the persons and families below mentioned, whose records follow in this work in the order named:

I. ROBERT DAWSON, a resident at East Haven, 1682-3, and probably in or near there some years earlier. He had two sons, whose descendants are very numerous.

II. THOMAS DAWSON, who, in a deed to his son Job, describes himself as "late of Newport in the province of Road Island," was at New Haven, 1721-2.

III. JOHN DAWSON, an Englishman, who had deserted the British service in this country towards the close of the war of the revolution, and married at Philadelphia, removed shortly after to Connecticut, and settled at Monroe, in Fairfield county. His descendants are also quite numerous.

IV. PETER DAWSON, a native of Linlithgow, near Edinburgh, Scotland, emigrated thence about 1800, and settled in Barnet, Caledonia county, Vermont. He had three sons and six daughters, some of whom had issue.

Of many other families of the name originally established in this country, in other than the New England States, such information is given in the following pages, as the compiler hereof, after diligent efforts, (by means of an extensive correspondence and otherwise), has been able to obtain.[1]

Concerning the many imperfections in the records which follow he craves the indulgent judgment of his readers. Those alone who have had some experience in attempting the compilation of records of this nature, can appreciate the difficulties which beset the work.

---

[1] The following memoranda are added for preservation and future reference: "Eunice Eggleston, b. May 1, 1779, m. 1, JOHN DAWSON; 2, Stafford; 3, Fuller; removed to Wheatland, N. Y., and lives in Holly, N. Y." — Stiles's *History of Ancient Windsor*, 1859. (*Quere*: what *John Dawson*? Samuel Eggleston, father of the above named Eunice, lived in Northeast, Dutchess Co., N. Y., and d. Jan. 25, 1822, aged 84. Eunice, his ninth child, was probably born there, and John Dawson, her first husband, probably *not* of New England origin.)

In a list of Emigrants from Gravesend to the Barbadoes, April 3, 1635, per the "Peter Bonaventure," is found the name RICHARD DAWSON, aged 28. — Drake's *Result of Researches*, etc., 102; *N. E. His. and Gen. Reg.* vol. 14, p. 349. The same name in a list of passengers for Virginia, 20 June, 1635, per the "Philip," Richard Morgan, master. The men had been examined, as certified, by the minister of the town of Gravesend, "of their conformitie to the orders and discipline of the Church of England," and had taken the oath of allegiance. — *Ibid*, vol. 3, p. 184.

A list of passengers for the Barbadoes from Gravesend, 20 November, 1635, contains the name of HUGH DAWSON, aged 18. — Drake's *Result of Researches*, 112.

A RECORD

OF THE

DESCENDANTS OF ROBERT DAWSON OF EAST HAVEN, CONNECTICUT;

ALSO

Records of the Families

OF

THOMAS DAWSON, OF NEW HAVEN, CONN.,
JOHN DAWSON, OF MONROE, CONN.,
PETER DAWSON, OF BARNET, VT.,
HENRY DAWSON, OF MILLBURY, MASS. AND BROAD BROOK, CONN.

FAMILY OF ROBERT DAWSON,

OF EAST HAVEN, CONN., 1682–1718.

The township of East Haven, in Connecticut, forms a part of New Haven county, and consists of a tract of land about seven miles long from north to south, and from two to three or four miles wide, lying between the townships of Branford and North Branford on the east, and New Haven township and harbor on the west. On the north it is bounded by the township of North Haven, and on the south by Long Island sound. The population is largely agricultural.

The central portion of the township is divided from Branford by a beautiful sheet of water called Saltonstall lake (formerly locally known as *the pond*) which, besides being the scene in recent times of gay regattas of the college students from New Haven, is the source from which that city is principally supplied with ice. The lake is about three miles in length, but quite narrow, being nowhere, perhaps, more than one-third of a mile in width. The East Haven, or west, shore of the lake consists of a high rocky ridge, formerly known as *the Pond Rock* or *Pond Rocks*, and which, though " the pond " has now a nobler designation, is still called by its ancient name. On the northwesterly side of the lake and rock (being in the northerly part of the township) is a fertile plain, on some portion of which it is supposed that an Indian sagamore named Foxon had his residence at an early day. The plain was called *Foxon's Farms* from this circumstance, and the farms there lying are still so designated. The name is on record of the date of 1644.[1] Through this plain, and coursing thence along the foot of the rock in a southwesterly direction, flows a small stream called Stoney river, which, turning to the southeast below the rock, flows thence into the sound, forming, in its lower portion, the boundary line between Branford and East Haven.

This township was formerly a part of the ancient colony of New Haven, and was connected with that colony and town, in all its domestic and foreign concerns, about one hundred and forty years. It was in part originally purchased of Momauguin, then sachem of that part of the country, and his counsellors, by Theophilus Eaton, Rev. John Davenport, Thomas Gregson, Edward Hopkins, and other English planters,[2] on the 24th Nov., 1638. These persons had arrived in Boston the previous year, where they were strongly urged to continue, but came to this wilderness in accordance with their design of founding a new colony, a New Haven for their persecuted brethren of the mother country. To this, their first purchase, they shortly after added another large tract, three miles long north and south, and thirteen miles in breadth ; the two tracts costing the purchasers altogether twenty-five coats of English cloth, and a few articles of merchandise of small value.

This was probably the most opulent company of adventurers which had come into New England. Mr. Davenport had been

---

[1] The people of Branford complained that the Indians set traps in the cattle's paths ; and a marshall was sent from New Haven "to warn *Uncas*, or his brother, or *Foxon*, to come and speak to the Governor about it." — *East Haven Register*, p. 18. In 1658 the inhabitants of the village petitioned the town "that a line might be run from the rear corner of Mr. Davenport's farm towards the town, to *Foxon's Weekwam*, and so Stoney river be their bounds on the east." — *Ibid.*

[2] So called because *planters* of a colony.

a celebrated minister in the city of London, and Mr. Eaton and Mr. Hopkins had been merchants in that city, possessed great estates, and were men of eminence for their ability and integrity.

Early after their arrival the planters entered into covenant, binding themselves, in all civil and religious concerns, to "be regulated by the rules which the Scriptures held forth to them." The next year they formed their constitution.[1] They were men loving power, their community was small, and their laws, if scriptural, were often severe and arbitrary.

For many years public worship in the colony was attended solely at New Haven, but to the inhabitants on the east side of the Quinipiack,[2] with great inconvenience, labor and danger. "They were obliged," says the author of the *East Haven Register*,[3] "to leave home early in the morning, travel through the woods on unmade roads, and then cross the ferry, which was often dangerous. During the Indian wars and commotions the women and children, on the sabbath, were collected together at one house in the neighborhood, under the protection of a guard, while some part of the families attended public worship at New Haven. And for many years the men were required by law, under the penalty of a fine, to appear at meeting with their arms ready for battle." It was not until 1680 that the people of East Haven obtained liberty to become a distinct society.[4] This was greatly to their relief and satisfaction, and they proceeded at once to "invite and settle an orthodox minister amongst them," in accordance with the grant and stipulation of the court.

Their meetings were warned

"By sound of horn
Or beat of drum."[5]

---

[1] This provided that church members only should be "free Burgesses," and that they alone "should have power of transacting all publique civil affairs of the plantation, of making and repealing laws, dividing of inheritances, deciding of differences that may arise, and doing all things or business of like nature." — *E. H. R.*, p. 10.

[2] The Quinipiack river separated East Haven parish from New Haven.

[3] The Rev. STEPHEN DODD. He died at East Haven 5 Feb., 1856, aged 79.

[4] The records of the village of East Haven commence in this year, but they are imperfect. The records of the church, prior to 1755, are lost. — *E. H. R.*, p. 6.

[5] In 1707 one Austin was granted a piece of land "for beating the drum for public worship and other occasions." — *E. H. R.*, 47.

Their dwellings were mostly plain structures of one story, and their means were generally small. They had not the same facilities for education that the people of New Haven enjoyed. They were obliged to endure all the hardships and privations of a frontier life — literally a life in the wilderness — and, particularly of the generation immediately succeeding the first settlers, it must be remarked that their deficiency, even in regard to a common education, was very great. Experience taught them the necessity of paying more attention to the education of their children, and advantage was taken of the earliest opportunity offered for the establishment of schools in the township. The first school appears to have been established in 1707, and was taught by their first minister, the Rev. Mr. Hemingway, then recently graduated from Yale College, and the first from this township who had enjoyed this honor. Prior to this time the people of East Haven had been dependent for educational facilities, of course available to but a limited extent, on the schools established at New Haven. A free school had been opened and taught there as early as 1641.

In the fall of 1655 the General Court of New Haven, which then had jurisdiction over East Haven in civil as well as ecclesiastical affairs, was informed [1] that there was a purpose "that an *Iron Worke* should be set up beyond the farmes at Stoney river." Liberty was given for the *Worke* to go on, and it was accordingly established; being the first of the kind within the present bounds of the state. Branford appears to have been jointly concerned with New Haven in this enterprise, or at least "was treated as having some interest in the Iron Works," pending a neighborly controversy as to the ownership of certain territory adjoining the Furnace pond, the right to which was claimed by both townships. The land was afterwards relinquished by Branford to East Haven, and is referred to in the records as "the half mile." Some of the workmen employed here were probably brought from similar works in Massachusetts [2] — others perhaps came direct from English furnaces. The furnace was

---

[1] By Mr. Goodyear, who "declared that Mr. Winstone and himself did intend to carry it on." — *N. H. Records*, 12 Nov., 1655.

[2] The Russells were from Taunton, Pinion from Lynn, &c. — Savage's *Gen. Dict.*

supplied with bog ore from North Haven. Of so much consequence was this establishment considered that after the union of New Haven with Connecticut a special grant was made (1669) to the people employed in the work to free them from taxes for seven years; yet the population thereby introduced brought in some disorderly elements, requiring the occasional interposition of the civil authority. There was great mortality in the village in the year 1679, and the business was about this time (1679 or '80) relinquished — for what reason cannot now be satisfactorily ascertained. Probably it had not been very profitable, and the loss by death of some of the principal workmen, which happened just then, may have hastened its discontinuance. The Iron Works farm, after one or two changes, passed into the hands of William Rosewell, of Branford, formerly an extensive merchant at New Haven, whose only daughter and heir married Gurdon Saltonstall, afterwards governor of Connecticut, in honor of whom Saltonstall lake was named. In 1681 a grist-mill was set up at the furnace dam, and though at this time some reservations were made in the grant of the dam for the mill, with a view to the possible reëstablishment of iron works here, and though some years later (1692) a bloomary furnace was erected on one of the small brooks running into Stoney river, the business never subsequently attained to much importance, and was soon permanently abandoned. Thus the town returned to the quiet pursuits of a farming population. Of the people at the works, thrown out of employment by the discontinuance of the business, it is probable that some, receiving no encouragement to remain, removed to other parts — while others, of the sort better calculated to live in a farming community, and better esteemed by the townspeople, received grants of land, and made their homes permanently in the township.

It is possible that among those who were thus graduated from the Furnace to the Farms, was ROBERT DAWSON,[1] founder of the family whose records are herein given. East Haven had then established, or at least asserted, for itself a semi-

[1] In a list of "The proprietors of New Haven, Conn., in 1685," prepared by Hon. C. W. Bradley, Secretary of State of Conn., 1847, the name is printed ROBERT DAUSON.—*N. E. Hist. and Gen. Reg.*, vol. 2, p. 157.

independence in civil as well as ecclesiastical affairs (though under a certain bondage to New Haven in township concerns for a hundred years after), and at a village meeting, May 17, 1682, Thomas Pinion, William Roberts, Robert Dawson and William Luddington, propounded for land to be assigned to each of them on Stoney river. Of these persons one, Thomas Pinion, had certainly been engaged at the Iron Works. Luddington's father had died there in 1662, and without doubt he had been employed about the same business. (His daughter subsequently married the eldest son of Robert Dawson).

At the next division of land, which was made in 1683, and was the third in which the first inhabitants of New Haven had participated, Pinion, Dawson, Roberts, Joseph Abbott and James Tailor, being evidently partial to the Stoney river land, and apparently desirous of having their farms constitute adjoining tracts, were, on their own motion, excepted from the regular division — which if made as usual by lot would leave their location subject to chance — and it was accordingly ordered that they should have their land next to that which the town had obtained from Branford, thirty acres each being allotted to the three first named in consideration of their being married men, and twenty each to the others, on condition that each of the five should build on his land a tenantable house within three years. This land was afterwards surveyed to them in a body, and was described as lying "about 30 rods eastward about ye place where Foxon's wigwam was," they being left, "for their five p'ticular parts," after making sufficient allowance for "cartwaies between ye Pond Rock and their land," "to lay out and to bound as they will agree upon among themselves."[1] The grants made by the village to these men were confirmed by a town vote of New Haven, and their land was afterwards referred to in the records as "the five men's land at Foxon's."

It had been laid out to them by Matthew Moulthrop, whose father had been by appointment conservator of the morals of the people about the Iron Works, and by Sergt. John Potter, who was by trade a blacksmith, and had been concerned in the Iron

[1] *N. H. Records*, vol. 1, p. 403.

Works property. He and Pinion were the ones who petitioned the town for the privilege of the bloomary which was built in 1692. Concerning Roberts, Abbott and Tailor, little is known; certainly nothing to discredit the supposition that they were Iron Works men.

Dawson made record of his land 17th March, 1683, it being described as "lying half a mile in length and thirty rods in breadth, east and west, with the river running [through] the middle, and is bounded by Thomas Pinion's on the east [and the] highway on the west."[1] Pinion was thus his nearest neighbor. It is probable that he built and occupied immediately. Dodd makes the following record:

"ROBERT DAWSON settled at Foxon's in 1683. He then had John, born in 1677. After this he married widow Hannah Russell, and had Thomas, 1693."[2]

Her maiden name is not known. John Russell, her former husband, had been a potter in the furnace at the Iron Works, and died there in 1681.[3] His brother Ralph, one of the principal workmen, had died there during the great sickness, two years previously.[4]

In regard to the former wife of Robert Dawson, no information can be obtained. If they were living at the Iron Works — as may be surmised from his having been so curiously connected with the furnace people — it is not unlikely that she may have fallen a victim to the prevailing sickness in 1679, leaving him with one child, John, born 1677, as stated by Dodd. If this was the case, the marriage of Robert Dawson and widow Russell must have occurred *before* the settlement at Foxon's, he having been a married man at the time the grant of this land was made to him. And this would explain the fact that in this year (1683) his family is "listed" as consisting of six persons. His son John was then about six years of age; the other five were himself

---

[1] *E. H. Records.*— It was near the upper or north end of the Pond Rock. "At a village meeting 15th Feb., 1709, agreed to sell all the undivided lands on the Pond Rock *to the upper end. Thence* south of a line from the south corner of Robert Dawson's home lot, a strait line to the northeast corner of Davenport's farme," &c.

[2] *E. H. Register*, p. 115.

[3] *Ibid*, 146. First there about the year 1664.

[4] *Ibid*, 27.

and wife, and probably her three children by her former husband.[1]

As to the date of birth of Robert Dawson's son Thomas, it is probable that the date above given (1693) is erroneous; for at his death, Jan. 12, 1759, he was said to be 72 yrs. of age,[2] which would make the date of his birth, 1687.

It has been erroneously supposed that Robert Dawson married, first, Sarah Tuttle,[3] daughter of William Tuttle, one of the first settlers of the colony. A copy of the *East Haven Register*, in the possession of William H. Dawson, Esq., of Westville, Conn., contains a marginal note, supposed to be in the handwriting of the author of that work, which states that Robert Dawson and Sarah Tuttle were married Nov. 17, 1663. The error is referred to by Savage in his *Genealogical Dictionary*. It appears that she really married John Slawson, of Stamford, Nov. 12, 1663. In the original record,[4] his Christian name is not given — a very unusual circumstance — and the surname was so illegibly written that it might easily have been mistaken for Dawson. (The initial letter has been over-written *Sl* by a modern hand). These circumstances, and the fact that Slawson was not a New Haven or East Haven name, may account for the error by which her name has been connected with that of Robert Dawson.

---

[1] Hannah, b. 1670, m. Joseph Grannis, Nov. 3, 1702; William, b. Sept., 1676; John, Nov. 1, 1680.— *E. H. R.*, 146.

[2] *Ibid*, 171.

[3] Concerning her there is a curious chapter on record, which, as illustrating the character of those times, is here briefly referred to. All intercourse of society was very formal, and especial pains were taken that there should be no disorderly conduct among "the young men and maidens." At a court held May 1, 1660, Jacobeth Murline (Melyen) and Sarah Tuttle were prosecuted "for setting down on a chest together, his arme about her waiste, and her arme upon his shoulder, or about his necke, and continuing in yt sinfull posture about half an hour, in which time he kyssed her and she kyssed him, as ye witnesses testified." Mr. Tuttle alleged that Jacob had endeavored to steal away his daughter's affections, "but yt Sarah denied, and it did not appear to ye courte." They were sentenced to pay each of them 20s. to the treasurer.—Lambert's *History of New Haven*. But one half of her fine was subsequently remitted, at her father's request.—*N. H. Records*, March 4, 1661–2. Jacob Melyen removed to Elizabeth, N. J., where, and in New York, he was a prominent citizen.—Hatfield's *History of Elizabeth*. There was also a sad and tragical chapter in her history, for thirteen years after she became the wife of John Slawson, and when she was the mother of three little children, she was killed with an ax by her brother Benjamin, who, *though probably insane*, was executed for it, 13 June, 1677.—Savage's *Gen. Dict.* Huntington's *History of Stamford*.

[4] New Haven Records of births, marriages, &c.

Whence or when Robert Dawson came to this country is uncertain. Speculation on the subject is of little avail. That he was English or of English parentage is undoubted.[1]

The township and parish records afford but scanty information.

In 1683 his name occurs in a catalogue of donors to a fund "for building the minister's house, and fencing the home lot." His contribution was £2.[2] He had a house to build for himself that year.

The privilege which the inhabitants of East Haven had obtained in 1680 of becoming a distinct society, was understood by them as conveying a larger liberty in local affairs — especially in the disposal of the public lands — than the people at New Haven were willing to sanction. The danger of more serious difficulties with their neighbors appears to have been apprehended, and it may have been questioned whether, in order to avoid controversy, they should not return to their former status. At a meeting of the village, therefore, March 29, 1684, the question

---

[1] On the Branford *Town Records*, under date of 14 July, 1680, (nearly two years prior to the date of his appearance as a propounder for land in East Haven), his name occurs as a witness to a deed of William Rosewell and others, agents for and all at that time of the town of Branford, of a parcel of land which they had sold on behalf of the town. The other witness was Katherine Rosewell, wife of the said William Rosewell, and this being the very earliest record of the name of Robert Dawson which has been discovered,* though of slight importance in itself, suggests speculations as to his origin in another direction. Rosewell's wife having signed as witness to the deed in question indicates that the instrument was executed at his house, as would have been natural, he having been the chief agent of the township in the matter. The other most convenient witness would naturally be some person employed about the premises, and (though the circumstances are slight on which to base a theory) it is surmised that Rosewell (who, it will be remembered, was the purchaser of the Iron works farm) had, on the discontinuance of the business at the Furnace, taken Dawson into his employ. But it is possible that Dawson came to Branford or New Haven originally in Rosewell's service, and had not been at the Iron works at all. Rosewell had come into the colony some fifteen years before from Charlestown, in the colony of Massachusetts, and his father-in-law, Hon. Richard Russell, had resided there until his death in 1676. The surmise that Dawson may have come from thence receives some slight support from the fact that one N. Dawson was a resident of Charlestown — the purchaser, it will be remembered, from Robert Saltonstall of a house in Windsor — possibly related to the Thomas Dawson, of Morley, Co. York, England, who afterwards claimed property there. But these are the merest hints. Can any clue be got from them as to R. D's history prior to 1680? Was Russell, whose widow he married, in any way related to the family to which Mrs. Rosewell belonged?

[2] *E. H. Register*, p. 61.

*Dodd records birth of John, son of R. D., 1677,— three years earlier than any date seen by the compiler. If he did not find this date in original records, how did he obtain it? He may have done so by deducting 55 (alleged age) from 1732 (year of J. D.'s death, as he has it) though the latter date is certainly erroneous.

was stated whether they "should go on or not with [carrying on] of the village." The people were "desired to declare their minds by speech." Nineteen men, one of whom was Robert Dawson, being present, they all "declared for carrying on ye village."[1] And with what tenacity some of them clung to the privileges held by them to be conveyed by the original concessions from New Haven will be seen by what follows. In 1707, the general assembly, on the petition of the villagers, who sought thereby to end disputes, ordered that "they should be a village distinct from the towne of New Haven," with all proper "immunities and privileges" necessary for the "upholding of the public worship of God, as also their own civil concerns," with the "libertie to have a school amongst themselves," and freedom "from paying any taxes to the towne of New Haven."[2] Articles of agreement between East Haven and New Haven under this act being proposed at a village meeting, Oct. 25, 1708, "Capt. Alling Ball, Robert Dawson, John Hemingway, William Roberts, Geo. Pardee, Joseph Grannis and Henry Luddington," entered "*their protest* against any propositions being offered that may," says the record, "be a wrong to our old grants."[3] The pertinency of the protest is explained by the fact that New Haven denied that the assembly's act conferred full township privileges, as claimed by East Haven, and persisted in asserting the same right of control over the common lands there as before. Two years later — the legislature sitting that year in New Haven — they succeeded in getting the assembly to so explain its former act as to neutralize its effects, though not in form to revoke it.[4] Nevertheless, the people of

---

[1] *E. H. Village Records.*

[2] *Colonial Records,* quoted in *E. H. Register,* p. 41.

[3] *E. H. Village Records,* p. 34. One article of the "grants" from New Haven was as follows: "That when they are settled in a village way with ministry, they have liberty to admit their own inhabitants, for the future, but to attend to such cautions and considerations for the regulation of their settlement as may consist with the interest of religion, and the congregational way of the churches, provided for to be upheld." Another gave them permission to purchase land of the Indians, and the whole would seem designed to set them at liberty to control their own affairs.— *E. H. R.,* 57.

[4] "New Haven, Oct. 1710. This assembly taking into consideration an act passed in the general court held at Hartford, 8 May, 1707, granting several privileges to the village called (in the said act) East Haven, do declare upon the same that there is nothing contained in the said act that concerns property of lands, or that

East Haven, though overreached, were not defeated. They had not much influence in the "general court," but they had a certain dogged perseverance that was better than wit. They relied on their "old grants," and quietly pursued their course. New Haven threatened and prosecuted, but East Haven sold land to defray the expenses of its lawsuits, to maintain its minister, and for its other occasions, and in process of time it disposed of every acre within its limits. The last regular division was made in 1715, and the Indian reservation [1] was sold some fifteen years later; but the vexed controversy in regard to their township privileges was not settled until 1785, when they procured a new charter from the assembly, constituting them in express terms "a distinct and separate town by themselves." The first town meeting under this act was opened with prayer by Rev. Mr. Street, and a sermon from a text in Psalms cxxii: "For my brethren and companions' sakes I will now say, *Peace be within thee.*"

From the date of his settlement at Foxon's onward for more than thirty years, R. D. continued to participate in the divisions of the town lands, in which the inhabitants shared — not equally, but equitably — upon the basis of their estates, and the number of persons in their several families.[2]

In 1702 his family was "listed" as consisting of four persons,[3]

---

excludes the said village from being within the township of New Haven, nor that intends to give the said village the liberty of choosing deputies distinct from the town of New Haven." — [*Colonial Records.*] *E. H. R.*, p. 43.

[1] "Near Mr. Gregson's," which was at Solitary Cove.— *E. H. R.*, 57.

[2] As, in 1704, when what was styled a "half devissyon" was made, and they agreed to draw lots "who should pich (*pitch, i. e.* select) first and next and soe on." R. D. received 13½ acres at this time, which he sold in 1711 to Samuel Russell. In 1708 the division was made "after much discors how to pay ye charges of building oure meeting hous and some reariges of rates to mister Hemingway." Each man was required to pay on the land he received "one shilling and eight pence per acre to cleare ye aforesaid debts." In 1709, the undivided lands on the Pond Rock were ordered to be sold (see p. 27, n. 1) and in March, 1714–15, a sort of clearing up distribution was ordered, which included the unsold lots on the Pond Rock, a "half division" at Piper's brook, and sundry parcels of broken land, as to which latter, if not yet laid out, "the proprietors to have liberty to pitch a half division where they please."— *E. H. R.*, pp. 38, 45, 47, and *E. H. Village Records.* R. D. owned land at Piper's brook in 1709, which he sold to Henry Luddington, and in 1713 he sold land near Foxon's to widow Elizabeth Potter. In his deeds he is described as "a husbandman" or "yeoman."

[3] His son John was now 25 years of age, while his wife's second child, William, was dead, and her eldest, Hannah, was this year married. Hence it is inferred that his family consisted, besides himself and wife, of her youngest child by her former

and in Feb. 1708-9 of two only.[1] In this month he executed a deed of gift[2] to his eldest son, John, married the preceding summer, of a house and home lot of five acres at Foxon's; reserving to himself, however, liberty of half the fruit of the orchard, then standing, yearly, and of *planting tobacco* as long as he should live, "in ye yard for that use." It is pleasant to find the words "for ye love I beare" in the ancient records. As to the donor's further intent in the gift of the homestead,[3] the deed recites as follows: "I give ye aforesaid land to my aforesaid son and to his first son if he live, and if he die before possessed, then to ye next son, and soe forth, and for want of male heirs to female, beginning at ye oldest," etc. The land is described as bounded on the north "by land I have given to Joseph Grannis." The deed to Grannis bears a later date — the next month — and conveys to him a small tract of about two acres. He had married, seven years before, R. D's step-daughter, Hannah Russell, and was a farmer of average estate. Probably it was expected or hoped he would occupy the two acres as a home lot. The consideration of love, as expressed, seems to have more than a formal significance, in this quaintly worded instrument. "For ye love I beare to my son-in-law Joseph Grannis and to his present wife Hannah.........as also ye grate afection I beare to their oldest child Joseph," so says the record,[4] "I doe make over a certain trackt of upland lying on ye bounds of East Haven aforesaid, at a place called Foxon's, by estimation two acres, be

---

husband, and their one child, Thomas, then probably fifteen years of age. Or, if the daughter was not married until after this "listing," she may have been reckoned as one of R.D's family, and his wife's youngest son by her former husband, being then just of age, not reckoned. Or, it may be that R. D. *had another child by his second wife*, living at this time, but who died young and unrecorded. After his death his sons John and Thomas described themselves as his *only surviving children.*

[1] Thomas being at this time separately listed as a single man proves that he must have been of age this year, and consequently born in 1687, as before suggested, instead of in 1693, as Dodd states. He and John (who, having married in 1708, was set down as having two persons in his family) both participated in the division of land this year, as also in the later distributions.

[2] Feb. 6, 1708-9. — *E. H. Village Records*, p. 79.

[3] Feb. 25, 1708-9, it was agreed on and voted to "lay out the rest of ye land" .... "from ye corner southward of Robert Dawson's home lot, where his house stood, now made over to his son John Dawson, thence to Mr. Davenport's northeast corner," etc. — *E. H. V. R.*, p. 58.

[4] March, 11, 1708-9. — *E. H. V. R.*, p. 80. The *child Joseph* was lost at sea about twenty years after this date. — *E. H. Register*, p. 122.

it more or less, bounded.........by ye land of Thomas Pinion ....Robert Dawson.........ye highway, and.........ye land of John Dawson.........to J. G. and H. his wife during their life, and at their death I give it to their oldest child Joseph aforesaid, and if he die before possessed then it shall be to the next of my son Joseph Grannis children," &c.

Thirty years after the settlement of Robert and Hannah Dawson at Foxon's she died, said by Dodd to be "aged 49",[1] an impossible age, as her eldest child (Hannah Russell Grannis) was born in 1670, and was therefore about forty-three years of age when the mother died. The record states neither name nor age, but this only: "The second wife of Robert Dawson deceased the 30th day of January, 1713–14."[2] In the March following — "a valuable," but unexpressed, "consideration" him "thereunto moving"— he gave their son-in-law Joseph Grannis — son to him however only by adoption — a deed of his second "home lot" at Foxon's.[3] This contained eight acres of land, with dwelling-house thereon, and adjoined the lot of land which he had previously given Grannis, as mentioned above.

He was still living in 1717,[4] but the date of his death does not appear. It is certain, however, that it occurred before the 17th March, 1718, his sons John and Thomas joining in a deed of that date in which they describe themselves as "sons of Robert Dawson deceased."[5] By this instrument, upon consideration that their father had bargained and sold "all his right to land in a place called ye Pond Rock" to Ebenezer Chedsey, and had "received satisfaction for the same," but had not "made it over to him," they confirm to said Chedsey "all ye right that did belong to our aforesaid father in said rockey land called Pond Rock, according as his lot was drawn by East Haven," though "not yet laid out," &c.

By another instrument,[6] their father having evidently died intestate, these sons enter into an agreement for the settlement of

---

1 *E. H Register*, p. 164.
2 *E. H. V. Records*, p. 114.
3 4 March, 1713–14. — *E. H. V. R.*, p. 163.
4 See location of his residence this year described.— *E. H. R.*, p. 47.
5 *E. H. V. R.*, p. 137.
6 15 June, 1719.— *E. H. V. R.*, p. 247.

his estate. It recites that they, being the sole surviving children of their deceased father, the movable estate being already divided, are to pay debts and receive dues of the estate equally, Thomas Dawson to have a certain home lot of five acres, and also a piece of lowland and upland (the quantity not expressed) and John Dawson to have the house and homestead which R. D. lived in, then in J. D.'s possession, containing about five acres, and a piece of lowland and upland of about twenty acres ; all the remaining undivided land to be divided in equal shares between them, their heirs and assigns.

The age of Robert Dawson at his death was probably from 65 to 70 years ; and his record may be briefly restated as follows :

1. ROBERT DAWSON, farmer, received grant of land at Foxon's, East Haven, 1683, on condition of building a tenantable house thereon within three years ; was living, 1717 ; died there before 17 March, 1718, aged near 70 years. Had by his first wife, name unknown, one son :

2–1. John, born 1677, died 1737 or later ; *m.*

He married, second, 1683 or earlier, widow Hannah Russell, who died in East Haven, 30 Jan., 1713–14. They had :

2–2. Thomas, born 1687, d. Jan. 12, 1759 ; *m.*

2–1. JOHN DAWSON, farmer, b. 1677, eldest son of Robert Dawson, also resided at Foxon's, in East Haven. He shared in various divisions of the common lands after he became of age, and also received land from his father's estate before and after the death of the latter.[1] He was chosen one of the "Listers" of Estates, 13 Dec., 1714.[2] In 1737 he and his wife were parties to a sale of land of her late father, William Luddington, sold to pay the debts of his estate.[3] In the same year,

---

[1] See the preceding account of R. D., and *notes.* J. D. sold small tracts of land, to Joseph Grannis, 8 Jan., 1711–12 ; Joseph Tuttle, 29 Mar., 1714; Moses Mansfield, 5 Feb., 1716–17 ; Jeremiah Atwater, 13 Jan., 1719–20; Samuel Russell jr., 7 Mar., 1721–22; Joseph Grannis sr., house and two parcels of land, 20 April, 1724; Samuel Smith jr., 29 Jan., 1728–29.—*E. H. V. R.*, pp. 164, 197, and *N. H. Records*, vol. 5, pp. 530, 379; vol. 6, p. 29; vol. 7, p. 91; vol. 8, p. 44. In 1710 a highway was laid out "from Matthew Moulthrop's home lot westward of the river lots until you come to John Dawson's home lot of four rods wide."—*E. H. Register*, 87.

[2] *E.H. V. R.*, 120.

[3] June 21, 1737.—*N. H. R.*, vol. 10, p. 366.

it having been voted in a village meeting "to sell the parsonage and constitute a permanent fund with the avails," he and a few others entered their protest against the sale of the property.[1] Dodd states that he died Aug. 28, 1732, aged 55.[2] As to the *year* the error is manifest; it may have been 1737, but could not have been earlier.[3] He married, 1st. July 1, 1708, *Sarah Chedsey*,[4] b. Dec. 8, 1689, d. May 22, 1709. 2d. 1715, *Mary Luddington*,[5] b. May 31, 1691, d. "of fever and dysentery," Oct. 11, 1742. She was the mother of his children. They had:

3-1. Timothy, b. April 27, 1716, d. May 15, 1740; *m*?[6]
3-2. Robert, b. March 2, 1718, d. Jan. 26, 1799; *m.*
3-3. Anna, b. 1720, d. young.
3-4. Titus, b. 1722, d. "of fever and dysentery," Sept. 28, 1742; *unm.*
3-5. John, b. , d. May 19, 1787; *m.*

2-2. Thomas Dawson, farmer, b. 1687, son of Robert and Hannah Dawson, resided at Foxon's;[7] purchased tracts of land[8]

---

[1] *E. H. R.*, p. 66.

[2] *Ibid*, p. 166.

[3] The original record, which Dodd must have seen but incorrectly transcribed, as to *date*, and perhaps as to *age*, has not been found by the compiler hereof, and the discrepancies here apparent cannot at present be explained. (See p. 29, sub-note *) It is not impossible that J. D. was son of the *second* wife of R. D., since 1683+55=1738.

[4] Her father was Ebenezer Chedsey, shoemaker, township clerk for 24 years, b. Feb. 10, 1665, d. Sept. 26, 1726, son of John Chedsey, farmer, deacon of the first church in N. Haven, and "father of all the Chedsey family." He signed the Colony Constitution in 1644, being then about 23 years of age; removed to Stoney river 1681, and d. there Dec. 31, 1688, aged 67.

[5] She was eldest ch. of Wm. Luddington jun., (d. Feb. 3, 1737, aged abt. 80) farmer, of considerable estate, and his second w. Mercy Whitehead (b. Jan. 10, 1668, d. Nov. 23, 1743, dau. of John and *Martha Bradfield* Whitehead, of Branford). They were m. 1690. Previous to their marriage it was stipulated by written covenant that the first child which she might have should be made equal in heirship with his first ch. which he had by his first w., he being entitled to a double share, and that her other chn. should be made equal to his other chn. Wm. Luddington sen., of Charlestown or Malden, Mass., 1642, d. at the Ironworks, 1662.

[6] Dodd says he d. *unm.*, but it is supposed it was his widow, *Margaret Dawson*, who m. Richard Darrow, 6 Nov., 1759.—*E. H. Church Records.* If not so, who was she?

[7] See description of highways laid out, 1734, through and along his land.—*E. H. R.*, pp. 90, 91. "Jan. 22, 1739-40. Voted that Caleb Palmery shall have liberty to shut up the highway between his own land and Thomas Dawson's land from the Pond Rock to the river during the pleasure of the proprietors."—*E. H. Proprietors' Records*, vol. 2, p. 3.

[8] From Jacob Mallory, 21 Aug., 1713; Thomas Robinson, 20 May, 1723; both "at Foxon's." From Benj. and Mabel Utter moiety of seven acres salt meadow land she received from estate of her father, Capt. John Russell (16 Oct., 1728). From Joseph Mallory (13 Nov., 1727) a right of land which belonged to his

there of various parties; sold some;[1] shared in divisions of the common lands from 1708 onward;[2] also in the division of his father's estate.[3] He was one of three chosen by vote to take care of the school in the Foxon district.[4] He and his w. Hannah joined (Sept. 30, 1736), with other heirs of her grandfather, Eliakim Hitchcock, deceased, in a deed to her uncle John Hitchcock of all lands belonging to the estate of said E. H. lying in East Haven; and (12 Oct. same year) the same to same released and quit claimed all right in the personal estate of Matthias and Hannah Hitchcock, late of E. Haven, deceased.[5] He died Jan. 12, 1759, aged 72,[6] having married, 1st. *Mehitabel* ...., who d. Oct. 25, 1723.[7] 2d. *Hannah Robinson*,[8] b. Feb. 24, 1698, bapt. June 13, 1756, d. a wid. July 7, 1781, aged 82.[9] He had, by first w.:

3–6. Sarah, b. 1723, d. "of throat ail," 1736, a. 13.

By his second w. he had:

"father Pinion," called in *E. H. Records* "the pitch lots." From Joseph Abbott, land at Foxon's, 8 May, 1731; Samuel Russell, ditto, 21 Sept., 1731; Joseph Abbott, two other tracts at Foxon's, 12 Nov., 1733 and 18 Jan., 1733–34; Benj. and Dorothy Mallory, 16 acres at Foxon's, 12 July, 1740.— *E. H. V. R.*, 150; *N. H. R.*, vol. 6, p. 280; vol. 7, pp. 56, 121, 333; vol. 9, pp. 81, 372, 454; vol. 11, p. 406.

1 To Richard Darrow, 4 Feb., 1711–12; John Robinson, 4 Mar., 1713–14; Thomas Carns, 27 Mar., 1718; Jos. Grannis jun., 18 Jan., 1733–34; Daniel Hitchcock, 1 Dec., 1741; and to Stephen Grannis, consideration of £195, "equal half part of land in parish of East Haven, lying at a place called Foxon's, containing in the whole 13 acres," 17 May, 1754. The last-named grantee was his son-in-law.— *E. H. V. R.*, pp. 143, 150, 252; *N. H. R.*, vol. 9, p. 510; vol. 11, p. 382; vol. 19, p. 272.

2 See p. 32, n. 2.

3 See p. 33.

4 Dec. 4, 1732, "At a Society Meeting, Lt. Samuel Smith, Matthew Roe and Thomas Dawson were chosen by vote to take care of the school in those parts where they live, and take their orders from the school committee."— *E. H. V. R.*

5 *N. H. R.*, vol. 10, pp. 268, 448.

6 *E. H. R.*, p. 171. His will, dated 22 March, 1756, probated 20 June, 1759, mentions his w. Hannah, "eldest daughter Hannah Grannis," daughter Lydia Grannis, and "two youngest daughters, Sarah and Mary."

7 The name occurs only in the record of deaths: "1723. Oct. 25, Mehitabel, w. of Thomas Dawson."— *E. H. R.*, p. 165.

8 Dau. of Jacob Robinson, weaver, who m. Sarah Hitchcock, 1690. His w. was b. Oct. 16, 1669, and was dau. of Eliakim (farmer, of good estate) and *Sarah Merrick* Hitchcock, m. Nov. 4, 1667; gr. dau. of Matthias Hitchcock, who came to Boston from London, in the "Susan and Ellen," 1635, aged 25, signed the Plantation Covenant at New Haven, 1639, and was one of the purchasers of Southend Neck, East Haven. He d. 1669.

9 "On motion of Israel Potter, of Litchfield, husband of Mary Potter, who was Mary Dawson, daughter of Thomas Dawson, late of New Haven, deceased," the Court of Probate appointed (30 Oct., 1781,) persons to divide her dower estate, which was given to Hannah and Lydia Grannis, and the heirs of Sarah Smith, deceased.

3–7. Mary, b. 1726, d. "of throat ail," Nov. 9, 1736, a. 10.
3–8. Hannah, b. abt. 1727. GRANNIS.
3–9. Lydia, b. 1729, d. a wid. Dec. 7, 1789, a. 60. GRANNIS.
3–10. Joseph, b. 1735, d. "of throat ail," Feb. 8, 1737, a. 2.
3–11. Mary, b. 1736, d. "of throat ail," Feb. 9, 1737, *infant.*
3–12. Sarah, b. 1737, d. Oct. 23, 1764, a. 28. SMITH.
3–13. Mary, b. abt. 1740. POTTER.

3–2. ROBERT DAWSON was a farmer at Foxon's, East Haven, b. Mar. 2, 1718, d. in same township, "of a pleurisy," Jan. 26, 1799, aged 81.[1] He shared in the division of his father's estate; also bought land there of his brother John;[2] and from his uncle William Luddington, who lived in Waterbury, he purchased the right to "a certain lottment" which had been his grandfather Luddington's.[3] He sold small tracts at Foxon's to Levi Bradley[4] and Asher Moulthrop.[5] He m. 1st. wid. Thankful Grannis,[6] who d. "of consumption," June 29, 1787, aged 60. She was "admitted to communion," Aug. 4, 1757, and was mother of all his children. He m. 2d. Dec. 6, 1787, *Mary Russell*,[7] b. April 20, 1732, d. May 13, 1824, aged 92. He had six children:

4–1. Desire, d. young.
4–2. Abigail, b. abt. 1743, d. Dec. 15, 1766, aged 23. WAY.
4–3. Mary, b. abt. 1745, d. "in child-bed" Jan. 26, 1773, aged 28. SMITH.
4–4. Susan, m. DAVID DOWNS, Feb. 9, 1768. No further record.
4–5. Huldah.
4–6. Joel, abt. 1754, d. Nov. 4, 1801, aged 46; *m.*

---

[1] His will, dated Nov. 22, 1796, probated Feb. 21, 1799, gave to his w. Mary all his personal estate, and the use for life of all his real estate; after her use, all the real estate to his son Joel.

[2] A home lot of three acres adjoining land of John Dawson and Josiah and Matthew Moulthrop, 12 Jan., 1740–41.—*N. H. R.*, vol. 11, p. 245. And another similar tract from Asaph Hotchkiss and w. and Mary Russell, 25 July, 1795.—*E. H. R.*, vol. 2, p. 96. His wid. purchased several parcels of land after his death.—*E. H. R.*, vol. 2, pp. 277, 310; vol. 3, pp. 103, 189.

[3] Nov. 28, 1744.—*N. H. R.*, vol. 12, p. 364.

[4] Seven and a half acres at Foxon's, 11 June, 1755.—*N. H. R.*, vol. 21, p. 431.

[5] About three acres at Foxon's, 26 March, 1759.—*N. H. R.*, vol. 21, p. 494.

[6] She was wid. of William Grannis, son of Joseph and gr. son of Edward Grannis, of N. Haven. Her maiden name was *Allen.*

[7] After Robert Dawson's death, she, being then 67, m. Ebenezer Chedsey, whom she survived 18 yrs., he having d. in 1806. She was dau. of Edward (b. Apl. 19, 1698, d. Apl. 21, 1773) and *Catherine Utter* Russell. Her father was son of Capt. John (b. Dec. 14, 1664, d. Feb. 13, 1724), and *Hannah Moulthrop* Russell, m. April 17, 1687; gr. son of Ralph (d. 1679) and *Mary Hitchcock* Russell, m. Oct. 12, 1663. Ralph was bro. of John Russell, whose wid. was 2d. w. of the first Robert Dawson.

3-5. JOHN DAWSON JUN., farmer, b. in East Haven, d. in New Hartford, Conn., May 19, 1787, aged abt. 68 years.[1] Some say that he was a ship-carpenter and mariner. It is probable that he went on several voyages, principally to trade in the West Indies; but his occupation was properly that of a farmer.[2] He was a person of considerable estate.[3]

In 1741 he, with three others, obtained liberty from the East Haven proprietors to set up a "Sabba-day house" for each of them, near the meeting-house.[4]

---

[1] This information from his gt. gr. dau., Mrs. Emily Worden, of Danby, N. Y., whose accuracy as to dates has been remarkably verified in several cases by reference to original records. She states that he was 68 yrs. of age when he d., which would make the date of his birth 1719. If so, his place in his father's record should be next after Robert, though he is named last by Dodd. From the fact that he executed a conveyance of land to his brother in Jan., 1740-41, it is inferred that he was of age that year, which would confirm Mrs. W's. statement.

[2] Stories of his capture and maltreatment by pirates, at one time in the course of his seafaring life, are traditional in the family. He doubtless had some experience of that sort. In his old age he resided with his son Titus, in New Hartford. The late Mr. John Dawson, of Spencer, N. Y., son of Titus, was 8 yrs. of age when the gr. father d., and in 1870 told the compiler hereof he had often heard his gr. father relate the story of his capture by the pirates, and remembered that he would always appear excited and angry when he referred to the outrages they had committed. He was a man of medium height, thick set, and very sprightly in step and manner. Though nearly 70 yrs. of age, his hair and beard, which were naturally dark, retained their original color.

[3] Several deeds of sale of his lands in East Haven are on *N. H. Records*. To Isaac Grannis, 3 March, 1745-6; to Russell Grannis jun., 31 May, 1748; to Stephen Grannis, 11 Jan., 1748-9; same, 4 Jan., 1749-50; Timothy Jones, 5 Jan., 1761.— *N. H. R.*, vol. 12, p. 156; 14, p. 339; 15, pp. 157, 358; 24, p. 95. He afterwards owned and sold land in Southington. See deed to Eber Merriam, consideration £90, tracts of 30 acres and 2 acres, 22 Jan., 1784.— *South'n. Records*, vol. 1, p. 331. He received from Farmington town commissioners deed of land in consideration of land taken for highway, 24 May, 1764; from Barnabas Dunham half of house, barn, 91 acres, and "one piece more of ye little plain," 17 Dec., 1767. Sold, with son Timothy, 16 acres to Samuel and Oliver Smith, of North Haven, 3 June, 1773; and to Gamaliel Cowles, of Farmington, two small tracts, 21 May, 1777.— *Farmington Records*, vol. 15, p. 352; 19, p. 441; 22, p. 54.

[4] "Jan. 18, 1741-42, voted that Lt. John Russell and John Dawson, and Matthew Moulthrop and Asher Moulthrop shall have liberty for each of them to set up a Sabaday house as near the meeting house as may be convenient."— *E. H. Prop. Rec.*, vol. 2, p. 2. The Sabbaday or noon houses then common were rendered necessary from the fact that the meeting houses were destitute of the modern conveniences for warming. They usually consisted of four rooms, with a fire place in each, and were generally built at the united expense of four or more persons, to be occupied only on the sabbath by their respective families, and such guests as they invited to join with them. "On the morning of the sabbath, the owner of each room deposited in his saddle bags the necessary refreshments for himself and family, and took an early start for the sanctuary. He first called at his noon-house, built a fire, deposited his luncheon, warmed himself and family, and at the hour of worship they were all ready to sally forth and to shiver in the cold during the morning service. At noon they returned to their noon-house, where a warm room received them. The refreshments, consisting of bread and cheese, doughnuts, apples, cider, and perhaps cold meat or chicken, were

He m. *Mary Moulthrop*,[1] who was "admitted to communion," March 7, 1757,[2] and d. before 1778.[3] They removed to Southington, then a parish of the town of Farmington, about 1762; after her death he lived with his son Titus in New Hartford.

Their children, probably all b. in E. Haven, were:

4–7. Mary, b. about 1742, d. *nnm.*
4–8. Timothy, b. abt. 1743, d. June, 1828, aged 85; *m.*
4–9. Titus, b. Jan. 13, 1748, d. March 14, 1840, aged 92; *m.*
4–10. Sarah, b. Feb. 2, 1750, d. Dec. 1838, aged 88. FULLER.
4–11. Polly, b. abt. 1757, d. abt. 1785, aged 28. BARNES.
4–12. Martha, d. when abt. 17.[4]

3–8. *Hannah Dawson*, b. abt. 1727, m. her cousin STEPHEN GRANNIS,[5] abt. 1745, farmer, of East Haven; afterwards resided at Southington.

They had six children:

4–13. Joel.
4–14. Stephen.
4–15. Jacob.
4–16. Mabel.
4–17. Lydia.
4–18. Jerusha.

---

then brought forth, and after all had partaken, thanks being returned, the remaining time was spent in conversation, or reading a chapter from the Bible or some religious book, or discussing the morning's sermon; and not unfrequently prayer was offered before returning again into the sanctuary for afternoon worship. At the close of the service of the afternoon, if the weather was severely cold, the family returned to the noon house to warm themselves, after which the fires were extinguished, the saddle bags gathered up, the house locked, and all returned home."

[1] Dau. of John jun. (b. March 17, 1696, d. 1727), and Sarah Moulthrop; gr. dau. of Sergt. John (b. Feb. 5, 1667, d. Feb. 14, 1713), and *Abigail Bradley* Moulthrop, m. June 29, 1692. The last named J. M. was son of Matthew jun., (d. Feb. 1, 1691, aged 53), and *Hannah Thompson* Moulthrop, m. 2 June, 1662, in which year M. M. sen., removed from New Haven to Stoney river. He signed the Colony Constitution, 1639; participated in the first division of land, and became a man of some prominence. He was appointed conservator of the morals of the people about the Iron Works. He d. Dec 22, 1668; his wid. Jane, d. May, 1672.

[2] *E. H. Church Records*, which also contain the following: "Molly, Timothy, Titus and Sarah, children of John Dawson, were bapt. June 10, 1757."

[3] So states Mrs. Worden.

[4] The names of Polly and Martha from Mrs. E. Farnsworth, Spencer, N. Y., gr. dau. of Titus; the other names from *East Haven Register*, p. 115; also from Church Record above quoted.

[5] Her father, Thomas Dawson, and his mother, Hannah Russell, had the same mother. He was son of Joseph Grannis, of North Haven, (b. Mar. 12, 1677), and w. Hannah, dau. of John Russell, m. Nov. 3, 1702; gr. son of Edward and *Elizabeth Andrews* Grannis, m. 3 May, 1655.

3-9. *Lydia Dawson*, b. abt. 1729, m. abt. 1750, her cousin's son, SAMUEL GRANNIS,[1] and d. a wid., Dec. 7, 1789, aged 60. He was a farmer, of East Haven, and d. abt. 1765.[2] They had:

4-19. Russell.
4-20. Lydia, who d. May 23, 1797, aged 41. SMITH ; MOULTHROP.
4-21. Samuel.

3-12. *Sarah Dawson*, b. 1737, "baptized on owning covenant," June 27, 1756, became the second w. of Capt., afterwards Deacon, STEPHEN SMITH, Nov. 20, 1760, and d. Oct. 23, 1764. He was b. Nov. 28, 1724, d. Jan. 22, 1816, aged 92.[3] They had:

4-22. Thomas, b. Nov. 29, 1761 ; *m.*

3-13. *Mary Dawson*, b. abt. 1740, m. Feb. 4, 1761, ISRAEL POTTER,[4] of E. Haven and Litchfield. They had seven chn.:

4-23. Sarah. LUDDINGTON.
4-24. Hannah.
4-25. Anna, d. young.
4-26. Joel.
4-27. Asahel.
4-28. Anna.
4-29. Enos.

4-2. *Abigail Dawson*, b. abt. 1743, d. Dec. 15, 1766, aged 23 ; m. TIMOTHY WAY,[5] October 2, 1765, and had:

5-1. Abigail, b. Dec. 7, 1766.

---

[1] He was son of Russell Grannis (bro. of Stephen, above named) and w. Lydia Forbes, who d. a wid., 1761.

[2] Administration on his estate was granted to his wid. Lydia Grannis, Sept., 1765, and in October of same year she was appointed guardian of their three minor children, Russell, Lydia and Samuel Grannis.

[3] He was one of the committee of East Haven men selected to procure separation from New Haven, and was appointed by the General Assembly to preside at the first town-meeting held under the act providing for the separation, July, 1785.— *Village Soc. Rec.*, vol. 2, p. 153; *E. H. R.*, p. 53. He was son of Thomas Smith 3d and w. Abigail Goodsell; gr. son of Thomas jun., and w. Sarah Howe; gt. gr. son of Thomas and *Elizabeth Patterson* Smith, m. 1662.

[4] Son of Enos and *Sarah Hemingway* Potter; gr. son of John 3d and *Elizabeth Holt* Potter, m. Feb. 23, 1692. John 3d was son of Sergt. John jun., and *Hannah Cooper* Potter, m. 1661 ; gr. son of John Potter, who signed the Plantation Covenant, June 4, 1639. Sarah Hemingway was dau. of Abraham Hemingway, and gr. dau. of Samuel and *Sarah Cooper* Hemingway, of E. Haven, m. 1662. Elizabeth Holt was dau. of John and *Elizabeth Thomas* Holt, gr. dau. of William and Sarah Holt, of New Haven. Hannah Cooper was dau. of John Cooper, who removed from N. Haven to Stoney river "about the time the Iron Works was established." He was agent of the Works, and also, 1664-67, representative in the general court.

[5] By his second w. Timothy Way had 13 chn., 8 of whom d. young, and his third

4-3. *Mary Dawson*, b. 1745, d. in childbed, Jan. 26, 1773, aged 28; m. SAMUEL SMITH jun., April 11, 1765, and had:

5-2. Samuel.
5-3. Jared, d. at sea, May 6, 1796, aged 24; *unm.*
5-4. Lydia, b. Jan., 1773, m. ISAAC CHEDSEY,[1] 1791. No further record.

4-6. JOEL DAWSON, farmer, b. abt. 1754, d. Nov. 4, 1801, aged 46. He m. abt. 1778, *Sybil Luddington*,[2] b. June 18, 1758, d. March 6, 1823, aged 65. Both b. in E. Haven, d. in Schodack, N. Y., to which latter place — *then* in Albany county, *now* in Rensselaer county — they removed from Connecticut between 24 Sept., 1783,[3] and 8 Nov., 1785.[4] They had five children:

5-5. Huldah, b. in E. Haven, Nov. 5, 1779, d. in Schodack, Oct. 29, 1871, a. 92. CARPENTER.
5-6. Mary, b. in E. Haven, April 28, 1782, d. in Castleton, N. Y., May 2, 1835, a. 53. SMITH.
5-7. Thankful, b. in Schodack, July 11, 1786, d. in Greenbush, N. Y., Aug. 26, 1853, a. 67. FULLER.
5-8. Amy, b. in Schodack, May 8, 1790, d. in Schodack, March 2, 1833, a. 43. VAN VALKENBURGH.
5-9. Joel, b. in Schodack, March 3, 1793, res. 1873, South Schodack, N. Y.; *m.*

4-8. TIMOTHY DAWSON, farmer, b. in E. Haven, abt. 1743, d. in New Hartford, Conn., June, 1828, aged 85. He resided in Southington (then a parish of the township of Farmington) from about 1772 to 1795.[5] He rendered some service as a

---

w. had 6 more. He was b. March 16, 1745, d. 1814, aged 59; son of James Way, sexton, who m. Dorcas Luddington, b. July 16, 1704, youngest sister of Mercy Luddington, 2d w. of John Dawson (2-1).

[1] Eldest son of Ebenezer Chedsey (d. July 9, 1806, a. 69) and w. Elizabeth Grannis (d. July 9, 1803, a. 62), m. June 26, 1761; gr.. son of Capt. Isaac Chedsey (b. June 3, 1710, d. Aug. 12, 1793) and w. Mary Pardee, (who d. Dec. 23, 1789, a. 77). Capt. Isaac was a bro. of Sarah Chedsey, who m. John Dawson (2-1), 1708.

[2] Eldest ch. of Amos Luddington, who m. Mercy Thompson, June 7, 1757; son of Eliphalet Luddington and w. Abigail Collins. E. L. was b. April 28, 1697, and was bro. of Mercy L., the second w. of John Dawson (2-1).

[3] In a deed of this date conveying land in E. Haven, they describe themselves as "of New Haven."—*N. H. R.*, vol. 40, p. 204.

[4] Joined with other heirs of her gr. father Eliphalet Luddington in conveyance to Ebenezer Holt of land in township of New Haven; now described as "of Scodack, in Albany Co., N. Y."—*E. H. V. R.*, 305.

[5] Deeds in Southington: *From* Solomon Cowles, two pieces of land, 54 acres, 28 Sept., 1772. *To* Earles Sharp of Farmington, 1½ acres, 11 Feb., 1777; to Oliver and Mary Smith, of New Haven, 10 acres, 4 March, 1777; to Gamaliel Cowles, two lots, quantity not stated, "lying undivided with land of my honored father, John Dawson," 14 March, 1777. With his father, to Samuel and Oliver Smith of North Haven, 16 acres, 3 June, 1773.—*Farmington Records*, vol. 19, pp. 104, 441; 22, pp. 47, 107; 21, p. 495.

Revolutionary soldier, but the particulars are not known. He was of a merry, jocular disposition, and is reputed to have been a man of great physical strength, which he was fond of displaying in feats of lifting, etc.[1]

He married, 1st. Jan. 2, 1772, *Anna Holt*,[2] who was b. in E. Haven, March 14, 1752, d. Oct., 1776, aged 24. She had 3 chn. He married,

2d. 1777, *Abigail Winston*,[3] of Southington; b. in Southington parish (Farmington), Nov. 6, 1754, d. in New Hartford, June, 1816, aged 62. She had eight children. He married,

3d. 1818, *Lucina Marsh*,[4] who was b. in New Hartford,

---

[1] Many anecdotes are told of his achievements of this sort. One which illustrates his character as well as his strength is as follows: A neighbor, somewhat below him in stature, angered by some fancied wrong, attempted an assault on him, but he, holding the assailant for a moment at arms' length, and innocent of any wish to injure him, said, with a good natured smile, "Why, neighbor J.——,I would scorn to strike you!" at the same time lifting him from his feet, and, with extended arms, holding him in that position until his anger had time to cool. He was a large, broad shouldered man, and somewhat noted as a perpetrator of practical jokes, and the promoter of harmless pleasantries of all sorts.

[2] Dau. of Daniel (b. Sept. 6, 1711, d. June 11, 1756), and *Anna Smith* Holt. Her father was one of the prominent men in E. Haven, and took much interest in public affairs. He was 3d son of Joseph (b. June 23, 1680), and *Abigail Hemingway* Holt, m. Feb. 28, 1705–6; gr. son of John (b. 1645, d. June 16, 1733), and *Elizabeth Thomas* Holt, m. Jan., 1673; gt. gr. son of William Holt (b. probably in England, 1610, d. 1683), who signed the Colony Constitution of New Haven, 1 July, 1644.— *E H. R.*, 127; Durrie's *History of the Holt Family*.

[3] Dau. of John and *Lydia Bristow* Winston, m. in New Hartford, March 12, 1752. Her father, who had been in early life a school teacher, was a farmer in Farmington, much respected, and owned a considerable property in Southington parish — now Southington township — a part of which, for "consideration of parental love," &c., was deeded to him by his father. He d. in E. Haven abt. 1789, aged abt. 60. He was son of Daniel Winston, of same township, formerly of Wallingford, twin bro. of Stephen, b. 18 Aug., 1690; gr. son of Sergt. John (b. N. Haven, 21 April, 1657), and *Elizabeth Daniel* Winston, m. 9 May, 1682. Sergt. J. W., was repeatedly appointed commissary for county of New Haven (1690 to 1704), in connection with the fitting out of expeditions for the king's service against the enemy — French and Indians — at Albany, etc.— His father, also named John Winston (sometimes written Winstone, Wenston, Wenstone), was recorded a freeman of New Haven colony, March 7, 1647; purchased house and home lot in New Haven, of Samuel Whitehead, 1651; was concerned with Stephen Goodyear in establishing the Iron Works at E. Haven, 1655, the first in Conn.; commissioner on the part of New Haven to fix the bounds of Wallington, 1673; d. probably 1697; held in good esteem by his fellow citizens.— Savage's *Gen. Dict.*; Hoadley's *Colonial Records*; *E. H. Register*. Elizabeth Daniel, above named, was dau. of Stephen Daniel and w. Anna or Hannah, dau. of Thomas Gregson, who was a principal man in the colony, and the first white settler at E. Haven. He was appointed agent of the colony to the parliament in England to obtain a patent, and was lost at sea, on the voyage over, 1647. See story of the *Phantom Ship*, Mather's *Magnalia*; also *E. H. Register*.

[4] She was a maiden lady, having a small property in her own right. She was dau. of John Marsh (d. in Whitestown, N. Y., 1805, aged 78), and his 2d w. *Sarah Nash* (b. 26 April, 1738, d. in New Hartford, 17 July, 1775), m. 17 June, 1763;

June 15, 1764, and d. a wid. in that township, abt. Oct. 1831,[1] aged 67. No chn.

The chn. of Timothy and *Anna Holt* Dawson, were:

5–10. Holt, b. probably in Southington, Jan. 5, 1773, d. in New Hartford, Aug. 25, 1825, aged 52; *m.*

5–11. Thomas, b. in Southington, July 28, 1775, d. in New Haven, Jan. 18, 1835, aged 60; *m.*

5–12. Mary, *twin sister of Thomas*, d. in E. Haven, July 31, 1870, aged 95. TUTTLE.

The chn. of Timothy and *Abigail Winston* Dawson, were:

5–13. Abigail, b. 1778, d. young.

5–14. Anna, b. in Southington, Aug. 7, 1779, d. in Union, N. Y., Feb. 26, 1858, a. 79. MELOY.

5–15. Eunecia, b. in Southington, Dec. 26, 1781, d. in Dunkirk, N. Y., March 4, 1855, a. 73. PRESCOTT; ALDRICH.

5–16. Bristol, b. in Southington, June 12, 1785, d. in Meriden, Ct., Feb. 25, 1859, a. 74; *m.*

5–17. Timothy John, b. in Southington, Aug. 13, 1788, d. in Cazenovia, N. Y., March 2, 1843, a. 55; *m.*

5–18. Lydia, b. in Southington, Feb. 10, 1791, d. in Ellicottville, N. Y., June 29, 1835, a. 44. BEECHER.

5–19. Seth, b. in Southington, 1795, d. in Nelson, N. Y., Sept. 16, 1835, a. 40; *m.*

5–20. Elizur Andrus, b. in New Hartford, March 18, 1798, res. 1873, Northampton, Mass.; *m.*

4–9. TITUS DAWSON, farmer, b. in E. Haven, Jan. 13, 1748, d. in Danby, N. Y., March 14, 1840, aged 92. He served as a soldier in the Revolutionary war, and was a half-pensioner. He m. in Cheshire, Conn., Aug. 26, 1778, *Sybil Dennison*,[2] who was b. in E. Haven, Oct. 14, 1746, and d. in Danby, N. Y., Aug. 14, 1837, aged 91, having been blind for some years previously. They resided in East Haven, Southing-

---

first b. after the death of his first w. who was *Lusina Seymour*, (m. 2 Feb., 1758, d. 14 May, 1762).

[1] The *Nash Family* record says she d. in N. Hartford "about 1847," but the above is believed to be very nearly the correct date.

[2] Eldest dau. of James and *Sarah Smith* Denison. Her father was son of James jun., (b. Jan. 5, 1683), and gr. son of James Denison, who m. Bethiah, dau. of Jarvis Boykim, Nov. 25, 1662, d. 8 May, 1719. He was a farmer, of good estate. The catalogue of donors to the fund for building the minister's house, 1683, was headed by his name, and a subscription of £20. The w. of Titus Dawson, and *Anna Holt*, first w. of Timothy Dawson (4–8) were cousins, their mothers having been sisters, daus. of Samuel and *Anna Morris* Smith, m. 1708, gr. daus. of Thomas and *Elizabeth Patterson* Smith, m. 1662, of E. Haven.

ton [1] and New Hartford, and removed from Conn., to Oneida county, N. Y., about 1788 ; thence to Lenox, Madison county, 1807 ; thence to Danby, Tompkins county, 1813. Their chn., all b. in Conn., were :

5–21. John, b. in E. Haven, July 27, 1779, bapt. Oct. 30, 1779,[2] d. in Spencer, N. Y., March 15, 1872, a. 93 ; *m.*
5–22. Martha, b. in New Hartford, Dec. 16, 1781,[3] d. in Cortland Centre, Mich., Sept. 19, 1861, a. 80. BARNES.
5–23. Titus, b. in New Hartford, March 5, 1785, d. in Spencer, N. Y., Sept. 30, 1859, a. 74 ; *m.*
5–24. Sybil, *twin sister of Titus,* d. in Oswego, N. Y., April 15, 1846, a. 61. DOOLITTLE.
5–25. James Denison, b. in New Hartford, Feb. 25, 1788, d. in Fowler, O., July 18, 1845, a. 57 ; *m.*

4–10. *Sarah Dawson*, b. in E. Haven, Conn., Feb. 2, 1750, m. ABEL FULLER, 1783, removed from Conn. to New Hartford, Oneida Co., N. Y., about 1790, and thence to Caroline, Tompkins Co., N. Y., where she d. Dec. 1838, aged 88. They had :

5–26. Martin, b. in New Milford, Ct., June 18, 1784, d. in Barton, N. Y., April 14, 1864, a. 80 ; *m.*
5–27. Marvin, b. in Litchfield or Southington, Ct., April 13, 1786, d. July 17, 1805, a. 19.
5–28. Polly, b. in Litchfield, Ct., Sept. 3, 1789, d. in Springfield, Ill., 1863, a. 74. HAGAR.
5–29. Abel Burton, b. in Oneida Co., N. Y., July 10, 1792, d. in Candor, N. Y., Sept. 24, 1870, a. 78 ; *m.*

4–11. *Polly Dawson*, b. in East Haven abt. 1757, m. NATHANIEL BARNES, d. abt. 1785, aged 28. They res. in Southington, and had :

5–30. Nathaniel Day.
5–31. Lucy.

4–20. *Lydia Grannis*, b. in E. Haven, 1756, married,

1st. JOSEPH SMITH, Feb. 4, 1777. He d. "of small pox, at sea," Oct. 20, 1784, a. 36. They had :

5–32. Samuel, who lost his life at sea.
5–33. Lydia.
5–34. Nancy.
5–35. *An infant* of Jos. Smith, d. April 8, 1783, aged 4 weeks.

---

[1] In a deed of land to her brother, Jesse Denison, of New Haven, they describe themselves as "of Southington," 27 April, 1781.— *E. H. Records*, vol. 1, 325.

[2] *E. H. Church Record.*

[3] This date is from New Hartford township Records of births, &c. Her family had the record "May 16, 1782."

She m. 2d. JOSIAH MOULTHROP,[1] July 4, 1792. They had:

5–36. Desire, b. April 16, 1793, d. May 10, 1824, a. 31; *unm.*
5–37. Jared, b. Mch. 9, 1795.
5–38. Samuel Russell, b. May 5, 1797. The mother d. 23d of same month, aged 41.

4–22. THOMAS SMITH, b. Nov. 29, 1761, m. *Desire Thompson*, Oct. 16, 1792. They had eleven children:

5–39. Stephen, b. Sept. 18, 1793.
5–40. Samuel, b. Oct. 21, 1795.
5–41. Warren, b. Sept. 9, 1798, lost at sea in a gale, between Sept. 18 and 25, 1819.
5–42 Willard, b. Sept. 12, 1800.
5–43. Aaron, b. Nov. 17, 1802.
5–44. Caleb Alfred, b. March 9, 1805.
5–45. Sarah.
5–46. Thomas.
5–47. Merwin.
5–48. Charlotte.
5–49. Nancy.

4–23. *Sarah Potter*, b. abt. 1761, m. June 9, 1777, ELIPHALET LUDDINGTON.[2] They had five children:

5–50. Jairus.
5–51. Sarah, m. JOSEPH HOWD, of Branford, March 2, 1796.
5–52. Eunice.
5–53. Lois, *twin sister of Eunice.*
5–54. Eliphalet.

5–5. *Huldah Dawson*, b. in East Haven, Nov. 5, 1779, d. in Schodack, N. Y., Oct. 29, 1871, aged 92. She m. in Schodack, 1806, JOHN CARPENTER, a native of that place, b. Aug. 15, 1786, d. there Aug. 26, 1849. They had seven children, all b. in Schodack:

6–1. Walter, b. Nov. 26, 1807, res. 1873, Schodack; *m.*
6–2. Mary Ann, b. May 26, 1809, d. Jan. 20, 1813, a. 4.
6–3. Joel, b. June 5, 1812, d. Dec. 17, 1870, a. 58; *m.*
6–4. Mary Ann, b. March 11, 1814, d. Sept. 9, 1870, a. 56.
6–5. Elizabeth, b. Aug. 6, 1817, d. March 2, 1836, a. 19.
6–7. Isaac, b. Feb. 17, 1821, res. 1873, Schodack; *m.*
6–8. Lucas S., b. Nov. 10, 1822, res. 1873, Schodack; *m.*

---

[1] He was b. May 30, 1754, eldest son of Samuel and *Sarah Denison* Moulthrop; gr. son of Israel (b. June 7, 1706) and *Lydia Page* Moulthrop; gt. gr. son of John (b. Feb. 5, 1667) and *Abigail Bradley* Moulthrop, m. June 29, 1692. The last named was gr. father of Mary Moulthrop, w. of John Dawson jun. (3–5).

[2] Son of Jesse and *Mehitable Smith* Luddington; gr. son of Eliphalet (b. April 28, 1697) and *Abigail Collins* Luddington. She d. a wid. Dec. 12, 1790, aged 90. E. L. was bro. of Mercy, second w. of John Dawson (2–1).

5-6. *Mary Dawson*, b. in E. Haven, April 28, 1782, d. in Castleton, N. Y., May 2, 1835,[1] aged 53. She m. JOHN DANIEL SMITH, a native of Dutchess Co., N. Y., who d. in New York city, March 22, 1832. They had:

6-9. Sarah, b. in Schodack, Jan. 24, 1804, d. Sept. 3, 1856, a. 52. PECK; WARNER.
6-10. Joel Dawson, b. in Schodack, Nov. 12, 1810, res. 1873, Castleton, N. Y.; *m.*

5-7. *Thankful Dawson*, b. in Schodack, N. Y., July 11, 1786, d. in Greenbush, N. Y., Aug. 26, 1853, aged 67, m. WARREN FULLER, who d. in Albany, N. Y., abt. 1865. They had ten children:

6-11. Mary, b. Dec. 1, 1812, m. WARREN HYDE, res. 1870, in New York city.
6-12. Amy, b. June 14, 1814, res. 1870, Virginia.
6-13. Chauncey, b. March 23, 1816, d. May 10, 1844.
6-14. Amanda, b. March 4, 1819, d. in Castleton, N. Y., Nov. 15, 1870, m. PETER H. VAN SLYKE, who d. before 1870.
6-15. Joel, b. June 24, 1821, res. 1870, Virginia.
6-16. Warren, b. March 23, 1824.
6-17. Sarah, b. Jan. 14, 1826.
6-18. Christina, b. Sept. 11, 1828, m, —— WORLEY, res. Virginia.
6-19. Lewis, b. Nov. 26, 1830, m. ——— res. Oregon.
6-20. Lucinda, *twin sister of Lewis*, m. ISAAC BARTON, res. New York city.
No further records of this family.

5-8. *Amy Dawson*, b. in Schodack, N. Y., May 8, 1790, d. there March 2, 1833, aged 43, m. JEREMIAH VAN VALKENBURGH, who d. in Schodack, abt. 1845. They had:

6-21. Jeremiah, b. abt. 1831, res. 1870, Castleton, N. Y.; *unm.*

5-9. JOEL DAWSON, farmer, b. in Schodack, N. Y., March 3, 1793, m. there Nov. 29, 1821, *Levina Schermerhorn*, a native of same place, b. Aug. 13, 1802, d. in Schodack, Jan. 27, 1871, aged 68. He res. 1873, in South Schodack. They had seven children, all b. in Schodack:

6-22. Joel J., b. Dec. 15, 1822, res. 1873, Castleton, N. Y.; *m.*
6-23. Lucas, b. Dec. 4, 1824, d. Schodack, Jan. 31, 1843, a. 18.
6-24. Henry, b. Feb. 24, 1827, res. Castleton; *m.*
6-25. William, b. May 29, 1829, res. South Schodack; *m.*
6-26. Smith, b. April, 23, 1832, res. Castleton; *unm.*
6-27. Mary Helen, b. Sept. 12, 1836, res. Schodack. VAN HOESEN.
6-28. James Monroe, b. March 11, 1840, res. Castleton; *m.*

[1] One correspondent wrote date of her death 1839, but this from her son.

5-10. HOLT DAWSON, farmer, b. Jan. 5, 1773, d. in New Hartford, Aug. 25, 1825, aged 52. He "took the Freeman's oath in open Freemen's meeting," in East Haven, Sept. 17, 1804,[1] and owned lands there, but removed to New Hartford before 1812, where he was made one of the surveyors of highways, 9th November of that year.[2] His widow made a deed of land in New Hartford to A. Abernethy and Solomon Johnson, administrators of his estate, April 27, 1827.[3] He married *Irene Shepard*, May 20, 1793.[4] She was born in East Haven, 1769, and died in West Haven, Oct. 6, 1846, aged 76. They had six children:

6-29. Anna, b. in E. Haven, July 31, 1794, d. in Westfield, Ct., Dec. 3, 1862, a. 68. DOUGLASS.
6-30. Eliza Teresa, b. in E. Haven, 1796, d. in Orange, Ct., Feb. 1, 1840, a. 44. JOHNSON.
6-31. Mary Leonora, b. in E. Haven, Oct. 9, 1798, d. in Saybrook, O., June 10, 1843, a. 45. CALAWAY.
6-32. Jennette, b. in E. Haven, April 25, 1805, res. 1873, in West Haven, Ct. MORSE.
6-33. William Holt, b. in N. Guilford, Ct., Aug. 16, 1809, res. 1873, Westville, Ct.; *m.*
6-34. Henry Shepard, b. in New Hartford, Ct., July 3, 1813, res. 1873, New Haven; *m.*

5-18. THOMAS DAWSON, farmer and shoemaker, b. in Southington, Ct., July 28, 1775, d. in New Haven, of a cancer, Jan. 18, 1835, aged 60. He m. in Northford, Ct., Chloe, wid. of Sylvester Howd. Her maiden name was *Linsley* or *Lindsley*. She d. in Northford, of lung fever, Sept. 29, 1833, aged 61. They had three chn.:

6-35. Holt, b. abt. 1805, d. young.
6-36. Thomas Holt, b. Dec. 7, 1807, d. in Licking Co., Ohio, June 7, 1847; *m.*
6-37. Mary Adaline, b. April 25, 1810, d. in Northford, Ct., July 2, 1837, aged 27. SMITH.

---

[1] *E. H. Proprietors' Records*, vol. 2, p. 274.
[2] *N. Haven Township Records.*
[3] *New Haven Township Records.*
[4] The date otherwise communicated by the family, but this from E. Haven Church Records, and the date of her death and age from grave stone in Old Cemetery at New Haven. She was one of nine chn. of John (b. Oct. 27, 1743) and *Elizabeth Bradley* Shepard, m. April 18, 1765. He was son of John and *Sarah Russell* Shepard; gr. son of Thomas and Hannah Shepard, who became members of the Church in Branford, 1709, and removed to E. Haven, 1717. Thomas had removed from Charlestown, Mass., to Bristol, before 1700, and thence to Branford. He was son of Thomas Shepard, b. in England, who was at Charlestown, 1657, and m. Nov. 19, 1658,

5-12. *Mary Dawson*, twin sister of Thomas, above named, m. May 1, 1815, CHRISTOPHER TUTTLE,[1] farmer, b. in E. Haven, Sept. 26, 1759. They resided in the Foxon district, in that township, where he d. June 29, 1839, aged 80, and she July 31, 1870, having just completed her 95th year, and being at the time of her decease the oldest person in the township. She had been a remarkably active, industrious woman, and had enjoyed almost uninterrupted health. They had one child only:

6-38. Sarah Smith, b. in E. Haven, Nov. 4, 1816, res. 1873, in E. Haven. JACOBS.

5-14. *Anna Dawson*, b. in Southington, Ct., Aug. 7, 1779,[2] d. in Union, N. Y., at the residence of her son-in-law, Charles E. Keeler, Feb, 26, 1858, aged 79. She m. in Southington, March 25, 1798, HENRY MELOY, who survived her. The term of their married life lacked only one month of sixty years. They had five children, all born in New Haven, and removed thence to Broome county, N. Y., residing for many years, and until within a few months prior to her decease, at Chenango Forks. Mr. Meloy was b. at North Branford, Ct., March 25, 1778, and d. suddenly in Union, March 8, 1860, aged 82. He learned the cooper's trade in Conn., and carried on the coopering business at various places in that state, but chiefly at New Haven, where he was also a merchant. He spent a part of the year 1807 on the Island of Trinidad, where he employed workmen

---

Hannah Ensign, dau. of Thomas Ensign, of Scituate, who was killed by Indians at the Rehoboth fight, March 26, 1676.

[1] His second marriage. By his first w., Abigail Luddington, he had 7 chn. He was youngest son of Joel (b. Oct. 28, 1718, d. June 30, 1789) and *Rebekah Rowe* Tuttle, (d. Jan. 7, 1806, aged 87), m. Feb. 1743; gr. son of Capt. Joseph (b. Nov. 10, 1692, d. Jan. 16, 1761), and *Mercy Thompson* Tuttle. The last named was son of Joseph (b. March 18, 1668), and *Elizabeth Sanford* Tuttle, m. Nov. 10, 1691; gr. son of Joseph (bapt. in New Haven, 22 Nov., 1640), and *Hannah Munson* Tuttle, m. May 2, 1667; gt. gr. son of William and Elizabeth Tuttle, who came to Boston in the "Planter," 1635, removed to New Haven 1639, and settled at Stoney river about 1645. William Tuttle was a man of consequence in the colony, and much employed in public affairs.

[2] The notice of her death, published in the *Cattaraugus Freeman*, says she d. at Union "after a lingering and painful illness, on the 26th day of February [1858] aged 78 yrs. 7 mos. 12 days." If so, the date of her birth must have been July 14, 1779, but the date above given was communicated by her grandson, and he received it from her own lips. Her disease was a neuralgic affection. She was a very motherly, amiable and pious woman, universally beloved.

in making hogsheads, which he exchanged for molasses. A cargo of that commodity he took back with him to New Haven. He continued trading in the West Indies for years after, carrying on at the same time his business in New Haven. He was one of a company who fitted out a privateer in the war of 1812. The vessel was lost in Charleston harbor. On his removal to Broome county, he purchased a tract of timber-land, and carried on the combined business of merchant and cooper for many years. He was a man of exemplary piety, and of excellent natural abilities,[1] improved by experience and observation. He was highly esteemed by his fellow citizens. They had five children:

6–39. Harriet Lewis, b. Jan. 4, 1799, d. in Chenango Forks, N. Y., Feb. 22, 1873, aged 74. ROGERS.
6–40. Henry, b. March 9, 1801, res. 1873, Ellicottville, N. Y.; *m.*
6–41. Frederick William, b. Feb. 26, 1805,[2] res. 1873, Ellicottville, N. Y.; *m.*
6–42. Julia Anna, b. Nov. 12, 1810, res. 1873, Chattanooga, Tenn. RICHMOND.
6–43. Grace Amelia, b. July 4, 1813,[3] res. 1873, Union, N. Y. KEELER.

5–15. *Eunecia Dawson*, b. in Southington, Conn., Dec. 26, 1781, d. in Dunkirk, N. Y., March 4, 1855, aged 73. She m. in Batavia, N. Y.,

---

[1] He left in Ms. an interesting autobiographical sketch, which is now in possession of his grandson, W. A. Meloy, Esq., of Washington, D. C. His father, Edward Meloy, was b. in Dungannon, county Tyrone, Ireland, May 16, 1734; emigrated to New Haven when 16 years of age, where he learned the shoemaking trade. After completing his apprenticeship, he bought out the business of his employer, but shortly after abandoned this, and engaged in the shipping business, in which he amassed a large property. He traded in the Mediterranean and W. Indies, and when the Revolutionary war broke out was owner of several vessels, and part owner of others. The war occasioned him the loss of a considerable part of his property, in consideration of which the state of Connecticut granted to his heirs a large and valuable tract of land in Ohio. He was a man of piety, and zealously devoted to the American cause. He was one of about one hundred citizens of New Haven who petitioned the governor and council of Conn., Sept. 17, 1776, complaining of some half dozen residents of that town as being unfriendly to the cause of the country. See Hinman's *Part Sustained by Conn.*, etc., pp. 566–7. He m. 1758, Mary Parmalee (b. Oct. 29, 1739, d. Feb. 1800, or 1801), dau. of Jeremiah Parmalee and w. Mary Beecher, dau. of Joseph ancestor of Moses Beecher (see 5–18, note). He contributed £19 towards building a Pier at New Haven on the site of the present Long Wharf. He paid £10 "in rum," money being then very scarce, and barter the order of the day. This was in 1771.— *N. Haven His. Society's Papers*, 1, pp. 92, 96.

[2] In Henry Meloy's family record, now in possession of Theodore Rogers, Esq., of Binghamton, N. Y., the year is 1803; but this date communicated by F. W. M.

[3] A different day of the month communicated, but this from the family record.

1st. JOHN PRESCOTT,[1] 1820, b. in Sanbornton, N. H., March 28, 1787.

2d. SIMEON ALDRICH, 1826. Her only child was:

6–44. Harriet Mead *Prescott*, b. in Batavia, June 25, 1821, res. 1873, East Otto, N. Y. DRESSER.

5–16. BRISTOL DAWSON, farmer, b. in Southington, Ct., June 12, 1785, d. in Meriden, Ct., Feb. 25, 1859, aged 74.[2] He m. *Sybil Merrill*, March 1, 1813. She was b. in New Hartford, July 1, 1789, and d. at the residence of her son-in-law, Joseph Sigourney, Esq., in Bristol, Ct., July 27, 1871, aged 82. They had eight children, all b. in New Hartford:

6–45. Elliott Marshall, b. Jan. 22, 1814, res. 1873, Waterville, Ct.; *m.*
6–46. Mary Ann, b. May 14, 1816, res. 1873, Broad Brook, E. Windsor, Ct. PARSONS; BISSELL.
6–47. Eveline Abigail, b. April 26, 1818, res. 1873, Meriden, Ct. PERKINS.
6–48. Minerva, d. young.
6–49. Juliette, b. March 18, 1821, res. 1873, Broad Brook, E. Windsor, Ct. BISSELL.
6–50. Sybil, d. young.
6–51. Sybil, b. Nov. 21, 1825, res. 1873, Bristol, Ct. SIGOURNEY.
6–52. Marilla Elizabeth, b. Oct. 31, 1828, res. 1873, Bristol, Ct. EVANS.

5–17. TIMOTHY JOHN DAWSON, farmer and innkeeper, b. in Southington, Conn., Aug. 13, 1788, d. in Cazenovia, N. Y., of bilious fever, March 2, 1843. He was a plain, unpretending private citizen, whose character alone distinguished him from the mass of men occupying a similar station in life. He was eminently a good citizen, giving no offense, promoting good order by counsel and example, obedient to the laws, but never holding or seeking any public office, small or great. In the community where he lived he enjoyed a degree of regard that was

---

[1] His second marriage. By his first w., Rebecca George, he had four chn. He was elder bro. of Dr. Wm. Prescott of Concord, N. H., author of the *Prescott Memorial;* son of Capt. William (b. in Hampton Falls, N. H., Oct. 14, 1762, d. in Northfield, N. H., Oct. 17, 1845) and *Deborah Welch* Prescott; gr. son of Major William, (b. in Hampton Falls, July 28, 1728, d. Sept. 28, 1811, captain in Rev. war), and *Susannah Sanborn* Prescott; gt. gr. son of Samuel (b. March 14, 1697, d. June 12, 1769), and *Mary Sanborn* Prescott. Samuel was son of Deacon James jun., (b. Sept. 1, 1671) and *Maria Marston* Prescott; gr. son of James sen., (b. 1643), and *Mary Boulter* Prescott. James Prescott sen., emigrated from England to Hampton, N. H., about 1665, and d. there, Nov. 25, 1728.

[2] Admitted an Elector at New Hartford, April 5, 1819.— *Township Records.*

more than respect and neighborly good will, though including both of these; it was positive affection — such only as a simple-hearted, genial, honest and truthful man could inspire. He was something above the medium stature, and possessed a good degree of physical vigor; and, with his father's peculiar tendency to humor, he had an almost womanly sensitiveness and tenderness of character — qualities which were perhaps traceable to his mother.

He m. in Windsor, Conn., Feb. 8, 1813, *Ruhamah Roberts*,[1] who was b. in Windsor, Oct. 22, 1792. She now (1873), resides in Clarendon, Orleans Co., N. Y. A few months after their marriage they removed to Canton, in Conn., where they owned a small homestead, and where they remained until October, 1815. From this place they removed to the town of Cazenovia, Madison Co., N. Y., where they settled upon a farm situated on the eastern boundary of that township, on the line of the turnpike between the villages of Cazenovia and Nelson. He had purchased the farm while on a journey through the state some months previously. About the year 1822 they removed to Nelson village in the same county, where they occupied and kept a public house for many years. This little village was then, before the era of railroads, a place of considerable business. It was a station on the chief thoroughfare for eastern and western

[1] Dau. and eldest ch. of Oliver Roberts, farmer (b. in Windsor, July 25, 1754, d. in Cazenovia, N. Y., Jan. 14, 1818), and w. Anna Bunce (b. May 13, 1772, d. in Pompey, N. Y., Sept. 5, 1854), m. Jan. 1792; gr. dau. of John (d. Dec. 11, 1775, aged 62) and *Mary Allyn* Roberts, m. Oct. 22, 1734; gt. gr. dau. of John and Ruhamah Roberts, or, as some say, De Roberts.*— Oliver Roberts was a soldier of the Revolution, and a man of good education for the times in which he lived. His brother, Peletiah Roberts, was a physician. His mother, Mary Allyn, above named, was dau. of Capt. Peletiah Allyn (b. May 3, 1689, d. Nov. 3, 1766) and w. Mary Stoughton (dau. of Thomas and *Abigail Edwards* Stoughton) m. Aug. 26, 1711; gr. dau. of Hon. Col. Matthew Allyn, "many years one of the council, and judge of the Superior court for the colony of Connecticut," who was b. Jan. 5, 1660, m. Elizabeth Wolcott (gr. dau. of Hon. Henry Wolcott, from whom she inherited an estate in England) Jan. 5, 1686; d. Feb. 17, 1758, in his 98th year. She d. June 4, 1734, aged 69. He was son of Capt. Thomas Allyn and w. Abigail Wareham (dau. of Rev. John Wareham), m. Oct., 1658; gr. son of Hon. Matthew Allyn, b. in England, d. in Windsor, Feb, 1, 1670, prominent in the early history of that place and of Hartford.

*There is a tradition that the last named John Roberts, or perhaps his father of same name, was a Huguenot, coming from France in consequence of the revocation of the edict of Nantes. Oliver Roberts, above named, fully believed this to have been the fact, and sought repeatedly to impress it upon the minds of his children. In their day it was generally believed in the family. The evidences on which their faith was based, if such existed, seem to have faded out; but it appears certain that this was a family distinct from all others of the name, Roberts, in Connecticut, and the compiler has learned nothing tending to disprove the theory of the Huguenotic origin.

travel through the state, and in those days the "way-side inns" were often thronged to their utmost capacity. From Nelson he removed, about the year 1838, to the village of Cazenovia, where he also kept a public house, in which he remained until his decease.

He had great fondness for company, and was noted for his hospitality, kindness of heart, and practical benevolence. These qualities rendered him a popular landlord, while a remarkably keen insight into human nature, and a conscientious and faithful devotion to business, contributed to render him a successful one.[1]

---

[1] It is said that he could never listen to any tale of suffering unmoved, and his charities were numerous and wholly unostentatious. After the war of 1812-14, while he was living on the farm, and when the country was overrun by poor wayfarers, beggared by the evil fortunes of the times, many a poor but worthy person, who had been refused admittance to other doors, found shelter and good cheer under his roof. To such as were really needy and deserving, his benefactions were not limited by a meal or a night's lodging. He nursed the sick, kept the footsore till they were healed, helped the destitute to clothing or shoes, assisted them on in some way towards their destination, or found them employment and the means of self help. Many a grateful "God bless you!" was spoken at his door in those early and troubled times, as well as often in later days. The sick and poor of his neighborhood were not forgotten, and he had a sympathetic, helpful manner that seemed to be peculiarly encouraging and comforting. His charities were not large, but they were frequent and discriminating, and he had always the co-operation of a wise and frugal help-meet who was never weary in well doing.

One of his daughters writes as follows: "He was very fond of pets, and had the art of making every helpless and dependent creature love him. For years before his death he had for proteges a flock of birds, which came daily, during the summer, around the piazza, to be fed from his hand.........

"He used to say that whatever bills he might yet quarrel with he should never quarrel with a school bill.........

"......... Charitable as he was in his acts, he was not less so in his judgments. He rarely censured any person, and he permitted no approach to gossiping or censorious conversation among his children. 'If you have nothing good to say, don't say anything,' was his motto.

"He had great store of wit and humor, and of the most amusing anecdotes. His temperament was very cheerful, yet he sometimes suffered from extreme depression of spirits. The shadows were short-lived, however, and the sun soon shone again.

"He had strong kindred affection .... I have seen him greet absolute strangers, who came to him recommended only by identity of family name, and a very remote common ancestry, as if they had been the friends of a life time. And he never forgot them afterwards."

Another writes: "He was the truest of friends, the most genial of companions. He enjoyed a good joke as much as any man I ever saw, and had a quick and ready wit, especially in repartee. He was dignified in manner, yet one of the most loving and indulgent of parents. His word was law with his family, yet spoken so mildly and reasonably we never wished it otherwise."

"*His life was gentle*, and the elements
So mixed in him that Nature might stand up
And say to all the world, 'This was a man!'"

Timothy J. and *Ruhamah Roberts* Dawson had eight children :

6–53. Lucia Eunecia Amelia, b. in Canton, Ct., Nov. 18, 1813, d. in Bloomingdale, Ill., Aug. 20, 1852, aged 39. KINNEY.

6–54. Lucius Roberts, b. in Canton, Ct., March 15, 1815, res. 1873, Binghamton, N. Y. ; *m.*

6–55. Rollin Laureat, b. in Cazenovia township, N. Y., Feb. 16, 1817, d. Nov. 5, 1821, a. 4.

6–56. Maria Louisa, b. in Cazenovia township, Sept. 7, 1819, res. 1873, Addison, N. Y. BATES ; COBURN.

6–57. Oliver Winston, b. in Cazenovia township, Feb. 1, 1821, res. 1873, Toledo, O. ; *m.*

6–58. Edward Sebried, b. in Nelson, N. Y., July 22, 1822, res. 1873, Syracuse, N. Y. ; *m.*

6–59. Mary Anne Augusta, b. in Nelson, N. Y., April 7, 1826, res. 1873, Toledo, O. ; *unm.*[1]

6–60. Charles Carroll, b. in Nelson, N. Y., Feb. 4, 1833, res. 1873, Plainfield, N. J. ; *m.*

5–18. *Lydia Dawson*, b. in Southington, Conn., Feb. 10, 1791, d. in Ellicottville, N. Y., June 29, 1835, aged 44. She m. in New Hartford, Jan. 4, 1813, MOSES BEECHER, who was b. in Hartford,[2] May 5, 1791. About the year 1814 they removed from Connecticut to Batavia, N. Y., where for some time he carried on business as a merchant. Afterwards he became engaged as an accountant in the Land Office of the Old Holland Land Company, and in 1827, he was transferred to a similar position in the Company's Land Office at Ellicottville. In this very responsible situation some twenty years of his life in Ellicottville were spent. Subsequently he was engaged in a manufacturing business, which he carried on until within a short period of his death.

He possessed cultivated literary tastes, and not a little literary skill, was specially fond of music and poetry, and was withal a person of great integrity and moral worth, taking rank as an influential and useful citizen of his town and county. He received from the governor of the state, as early as 1830, the appointment of surrogate of that county, which office he held for eight years, and he was repeatedly appointed by the same authority to

---

[1] A gifted and accomplished lady, to whom the compiler hereof is largely indebted for aid in the collection of materials for these records.

[2] This information from his daughter Mary, and is believed to be correct. In an Obituary, written by Rev. Mr. Kidder, it is stated that he was born in New Haven. Perhaps it was New Hartford.

the offices of loan commissioner and notary public, which latter he held at the time of his decease. He was a most genial friend, a pleasant companion, a kind neighbor, and ever ready to promote the welfare of all among whom he lived. He was a communicant of the Episcopal church in Ellicottville for many years. He died in Dunkirk, N. Y., while making a visit to his daughters, Feb. 14, 1867, aged 76.[1]

Moses and *Lydia Dawson* Beecher had ten children :

6–61. Sophia Mersena, b. in New Hartford, Ct., Oct. 5, 1813, d. in Dunkirk, N. Y., Sept. 30, 1867, aged 54. COLMAN.

6–62. Harriet Winston, b. in Batavia, N. Y., Aug. 16, 1816, res. 1873, Ellicottville. SILL.

6–63. Emily Frances, b. in Batavia, March 3, 1818, res. 1873, Dunkirk. COLMAN.

6–64. Juliette, b. in Batavia, Feb. 18, 1820, res. 1873, Ellicottville. SKINNER.

6–65. William Henry, b. in Batavia, Dec. 24, 1821, res. 1873, La Salle, Ill. ; *m.*

6–66. Mary Jane, b. in Batavia, August 31, 1824, res. 1873, Ellicottville ; *unm.*

6–67. Moses, b. in Ellicottville, July 26, 1827, res. 1873, Warren, Pa. ; *m.*

6–68. Charles Mortimer, b. in Ellicottville, Jan. 31, 1829, res. 1873, Wellsville, N. Y. ; *m.*

6–69. Lydia, b. in Ellicottville, Dec. 27, 1831, d. March 3, 1832.

6–70. Lucia Annette, b. in Ellicottville, Dec. 27, 1833, d. in Dunkirk, N. Y., May 7, 1866, a. 32. CARY.

5–19. SETH DAWSON, b. in Southington, Conn., 1795, d. in Nelson, N. Y., Sept. 16, 1835, aged 40 ; m. *Lydia Bates*, who d. in Nelson, July 5, 1846. They had :

6–71. Charles, b. in Nelson, about 1825, d. in infancy.

---

[1] He m. a second w. *Emma Newcomb*, May 26, 1841. She was b. at Windhill, Vt., Dec. 1808, and survives him. They had three chn., all b. in Ellicottville : Asher George, Nov. 1, 1842; Arthur Herbert, Nov. 28, 1844; Walter Henry, May 5, 1848. His father, also named Moses Beecher, d. Feb. 1852, aged 86. He was b. at New Haven, and was a shipmaster; son of Moses Beecher; son of Joseph Beecher ;* son of John Beecher; son of Mrs. Beecher, who came to New Haven with the Davenport colony. She received a tract of land by vote of the colonists as a testimonial of their appreciation of her services as a midwife. The deed is on New Haven Records. Her descendants are now very numerous. The celebrated Rev. Dr. Lyman Beecher was the son of David Beecher, blacksmith; son of Nathaniel Beecher, son of Joseph Beecher, above named. "John Beacher" (father of Joseph) was one of the party sent out by the colony from Boston to explore the country of the Quinepiack, in the autumn of 1637. Seven men remained at New Haven through the winter. He was one of the number. Lambert's *History of the Colony*, etc., p. 42.

*He was a clock maker ; built the first town clock of New Haven, which clock was put in the tower of Yale College, and used for more than half a century.— Ms. of Henry Meloy (5–14).

5–20. Elizur Andrus Dawson, farmer, b. in New Hartford, Ct., March 18, 1798, res. 1873, in Northampton, Mass. He m. 1st., in Nelson, N. Y., Sept. 4, 1823, *Cynthia Roberts*, b. in Windsor, Ct., April 4, 1804, d. in Pompey Hill, Onondaga Co., N. Y., Aug, 30, 1849, aged 45, youngest sister of Ruhamah, w. of Timothy John Dawson (5–17). They had six children. He m. 2d, in Northampton, Mass., May 12, 1859, *Mary* (maiden name *Hagar*) wid. of James Baker. She was b. in Rockingham, Vt., June 8, 1805.

The children of Elizur A. and *Cynthia Roberts* Dawson were:

6–72. Rollin Laureat, b. in Nelson, N. Y., March 25, 1825, d. in Haydenville, Mass., Aug. 24, 1857, a. 32; *m.*

6–73. Lucien Augustus, b. in Nelson, N. Y., Aug. 10, 1826, res. 1873, Springfield, Mass.; *m.*

6–74. David Derastus, b. in Pompey, N. Y., Aug. 13, 1828, d. in Chicago, Ill., Sept. 20, 1864, a. 36; *m.*

6–75. Frederick DeForest, b. in Pompey, N. Y., Dec. 1833, d. March 12, 1841, a. 7.

6–76. James O'Donnell, b. in Pompey, N. Y., Jan. 1841, res. 1858, Barrington, Ill.; went south; not since heard from.

6–77. Mary Diane, b. in Pompey, N. Y., Aug. 11, 1848, res. 1873, Springfield, Mass.; *unm.*

5–21. John Dawson, farmer, b. in East Haven, Conn., July 27 (bapt. Oct. 30) 1779,[1] d. at the residence of his son, Nelson Dawson, Esq., in Spencer, N. Y., March 15, 1872, being in his 93d year.

His parents removed from Connecticut to Oneida county, N. Y., about 1788. He m. there, and five of his chn. were b. in that county, and an equal number in Tompkins county, in same state, to which he removed in 1813. In subduing the wilderness of that then new country he spent the most active years of a remarkably laborious and useful life. He had been during life strictly temperate, abstaining from the use both of spirituous liquors and tobacco. He was noted as a very successful hunter and trapper, in early life, and excelled as a marksman even when past his "three score years and ten." He

[1] The baptism is recorded on *E. Haven Church Records*; but shortly after this date his parents removed to New Hartford, in the same state, and the date of his birth was recorded on the Records of that township, probably placed there at the time the birth (1781), of the next child was recorded.

married, 1st. in Paris, N. Y., Jan. 6, 1803, *Thankful Warren*,[1] who was b. in Gostown, Vt., May 14, 1785, d. in Danby, N. Y., Nov. 20, 1830, aged 45. She was the mother of all his chn. 2d. in Danby, Dec. 29, 1831, *Betsey Elizabeth Cooper*, b. in Gostown, Vt., June 16, 1781, d. in Danby, Nov. 15, 1868, aged 87. He had ten chn.:

6–78. Morris, b. in Paris, N. Y., Nov. 26, 1803, res. 1873, Wellsboro, Pa., *m.*

6–79. Harman, b. in Paris, N. Y., March 12, 1806, d. June 19, 1826, a. 20.

6–80. Almira, b. in Paris, N. Y., Jan. 9, 1805, d. in Wabash Valley, Ind., Oct. 1, 1834, a. 29. HOBART.

6–81. Emily, b. in Paris, N. Y., Nov. 8, 1807, res. 1873, Danby, N. Y. BUTTON; WERDON.

6–82. Samantha, b. in Utica, N. Y., June 27, 1811, res. 1871, Mungersville, Mich. FOX; VROOMAN.

6–83. Nelson, b. Danby, N. Y., June 8, 1813, res. 1873, Spencer, N. Y.; *m.*

6–84. Chester, b. Danby, N. Y., April 7, 1815, res. 1873, Spencer, N. Y.; *m.*

6–85. Mary Ann, b. Danby, N. Y., May 20, 1817, res. 1871, Mansfield, O. GERMAN.

6–86. Milton, b. Danby, N. Y., March 28, 1821, d. in Spencer, N. Y., July 27, 1865, a 44; *m.*

6–87. Harriet Eliza, b. Danby, N. Y., June 3, 1826, res. 1873, Ithaca, N. Y. MORSE; MASTIN.

5–22. *Martha Dawson*, b. in New Hartford, Ct., Dec. 16, 1781,[2] d. in Cortland Centre, Kent Co., Mich., Sept. 19, 1861, aged 80, having been blind during the five years preceding. She m. in Paris, N. Y., April 10, 1805, ABEL BARNES,[3] who was b. in Farmington, Conn., Dec. 5, 1775, d. in Cortland, Mich., Feb. 7, 1865, aged 89. He was a farmer. They resided in Oneida county, N. Y., until 1845, when they removed to Grand Rapids, Mich., and thence to Cortland, in the same state, where they resided as early as 1855. They had ten children, all b. in Paris, N. Y.:

---

[1] Dau. of Lt. Ephraim Warren, a farmer of Oneida county, N. Y., who served with credit in the Rev. war. (The date of her death has also been communicated Nov. 29, 1830.)

[2] This date is from New Hartford township Records of births, etc. Her family had the record "May 16, 1782."

[3] Son of James (d. in Paris, N, Y., abt. 1830, aged abt. 70) and *Sarah Dickenson* Barnes, who d. in Westmoreland, N. Y., abt. 1840, aged abt. 80. Both b. in Conn.

6–88. [BARNES.] Iram, b. Dec. 9, 1806, res. 1870, Cortland Centre, Mich.; *m.*
6–89. Seth, b. Nov. 20, 1807, res. 1870, McConnellsville, N. Y.; *m.*
6–90. James Titus, b. Feb. 11, 1810, d. aged abt. 3 mos.
6–91. Milton, b. Jan. 22, 1811, d. in Cortland, Mich., March 24, 1863, a. 52; *m.*
6–92. Mary Sophia, b. Aug. 29, 1813, res. 1870, Grand Ledge, Eaton Co., Mich. WOODRUFF.
6–93. Sybil Amanda, b. Sept. 16, 1815, d. April 23, 1851, a. 36.
6–94. James, b. July 28, 1817, res. 1870, Plainfield, Kent Co., Mich.; *m.*
6–95. Pitt Dawson, b. Feb. 7, 1820, res. 1870, in Wis., said to be *m.* but no chn.
6–96. Sylvia Ann, b. Sept. 29, 1822, d. Sept. 23, 1856, a. 34.
6–97. Abel, b. Oct. 23, 1824, d. April 27, 1860, a. 36.

5-23. TITUS DAWSON, farmer, b. in New Hartford, Conn., March 5, 1785, d. in Spencer, Tioga Co., N. Y., Sept. 30, 1859, aged 74. He m. in Lenox, Madison Co., N. Y., Sept. 1, 1811, *Lucy Lockwood*,[1] who was b. in Lenox, Aug. 25, 1792, and d. in Spencer, Nov. 4, 1868, aged 76. They had seven children, all b. in Danby, Tompkins Co., N. Y.:

6–98. A *daughter*, b. Feb. 18, 1816, d. same day.
6–99. A *son*, b. April 13, 1816, d. same day.
6–100. Sally Eleanor, b. Aug. 3, 1818, res. 1873, in Spencer, N. Y.[2] FARNSWORTH.
6–101. Edward Riley, b. Sept. 18, 1820, d. in Spencer, Sept. 19, 1845, a. 25; *unm.*
6–102. Martha Maria, b. Feb. 4, 1822, res. 1873, Milwaukee, Wis. HOMISTON.
6–103. Phebe Isabella, b. June 10, 1824, res. 1873, Spencer, N. Y. STEPHENS; JUDD.
6–104. Hermon Frederick, b. April 30, 1826, res. 1873, Ithaca, N. Y.; *m.*

5-24. *Sybil Dawson*, twin sister of Titus, above named, (5–23), m. in Lenox, N. Y., Dec. 21, 1809, ELIHU DOOLITTLE,[3] farmer, who was b. Nov. 4, 1786. They removed from Madison county to Danby, in Tompkins county, N. Y.,

---

[1] Dau. of Job Lockwood, a soldier of the Revolution, (b. on Long Island, Oct. 6, 1755, d. in Danby, N. Y., March 20, 1841) and w. Irena Tolles (b. in Lenox, N. Y., Jan. 5, 1764, d. in Danby, Feb. 13, 1851), m. Dec. 15, 1781.

[2] She m. Oct. 27, 1842, EDGAR FARNSWORTH, who was b. in Leominster, Mass., Jan. 13, 1821. They res. 1873, in Spencer, N. Y. No issue.

[3] Bro. of Hon. Sylvester Doolittle, Oswego, N. Y.; son of Major Joel Doolittle (b. March 2, 1764, d. in Sodus, N. Y., Oct. 23, 1814) and w. Millie Wetmore (b. Oct. 17, 1766, d. Dec. 5, 1834, in Pompey, N. Y.), m. March 23, 1786.

in 1813, and resided there until 1843, when they went to reside in Oswego, N. Y., where she d. April 15, 1846, aged 61, and he d. Feb. 25, 1806, aged 69.

Elihu and *Sybil Dawson* Doolittle had nine children:

6–105. Lucy Maria, b. in Lenox, N. Y., Nov. 24, 1810, d. in Danby, Oct. 8, 1830, a. 20; *unm.*
6–106. William Young, b. in Lenox, Jan. 19, 1813, res. 1873, in Candor, Tioga Co., N. Y.; *m.*
6–107. Joel Carolus, b. in Danby, N. Y., May 23, 1815, d. at Horicon, Wis., Sept. 6, 1856, a. 41; *m.*
6–108. Eli Barnard, b. in Danby, June 13, 1817, d. at Oswego, N. Y., July 24, 1846, a. 29; *unm.*
6–109. Samuel Woodworth, b. in Danby, July 9, 1819, d. in Danby, Nov. 14, 1819, a. 4mos.
6–110. James Austin, b. in Danby, Nov. 1, 1820, res. 1873, Delavan Walworth Co., Wis.; *m.*
6–111. Egbert Denison, b. in Danby, June 29, 1823, d. in St. Louis, Mo., Aug. 16, 1863, a. 40; *m.*
6–112. Julia Antoinette, b. in Danby, July 17, 1825, d. in Oswego, Aug. 5, 1844, a. 19. FULLER.
6–113. Wealthy Melissa, b. in Danby, Sept. 9, 1828, d. in Oswego, May 5, 1844, a. 16.

5-25. JAMES DENISON DAWSON, farmer, b. in New Hartford, Conn., Feb. 25, 1788, in which year, probably, his parents removed to Oneida county, N. Y. They removed thence to Lenox, Madison county, in the same state, 1807, where he m. Oct. 10, 1811, *Charlotte Rhoads.*[1] They removed to Danby, Tompkins county, N.Y., 1813, and thence, in 1816, to Fowler, Trumbull Co., Ohio, where he d. July 21, 1865, aged 77. She was b. in Barrington, Berkshire county, Mass., Jan. 31, 1790, and d. Jan. 11, 1871, aged 81, at the old homestead in Fowler, which she had occupied ever since their first residence in that place. They had nine children:

6–114. Julia Esther, b. in Lenox, N. Y., Jan. 11, 1813, res. 1873, Freedom, Portage Co., O. DOUD.
6–115. Lorenzo, b. in Danby, N. Y., Oct. 18, 1815, d. in Newville, DeKalb Co., Ind., June 4, 1870, a. 55; *m.*

---

[1] Dau. of John Rhoads, farmer, (b. March 20, 1747, d. June 24, 1819, in Fowler, O., one of the first settlers of that place), and w. Hannah Graves (b. Dec. 14, 1752, d. 1835), m. abt. 1769 or '70. When Mr. R. went to Fowler he bought a large tract of land; and all his children being married and settled in life, he induced them to follow him by the offer of 100 acres of land to each of his three sons, and fifty acres to each of his three daughters.

6–116. Angeline, b. in Fowler, O., July 15, 1817, res. 1873, New Bedford, Lawrence Co., Pa. JACKSON.
6–117. Emeline, b. in Fowler, O., Dec. 28, 1818, res. 1873, Bazetta, Trumbull Co., O. WALKER.
5–118. Maria, b. in Fowler, June 30, 1820, d. Dec. 16, 1829, a. 9.
6–119. Rodolphus, b. in Fowler, March 27, 1822, res. 1873, Linwood, Butler Co., Neb.; *m.*
6–120. Addison, b. in Fowler, May 21, 1825, res. 1873, Fowler, O.; *m.*
6–121. Pembroke, b. in Fowler, Feb. 7, 1828, res. 1873, Fowler, O.; *m.*
6–122. James Harmon, b. in Fowler, Nov. 22, 1822; m. *Ann Hathaway;* res. 1873, Gustavus, Trumbull Co., O.; no issue.

5–26. MARTIN FULLER, farmer, b. in New Milford, Conn., June 18, 1784, d. in Barton, N. Y., April 14, 1864, aged 80. He m. *Sally Lockwood*, b. in Lenox, N. Y., May 6, 1800, d. in Barton, March 4, 1862, aged 62, sister to Lucy Lockwood, w. of Titus Dawson (5–23). They had seven children:

6–123. Cyrus, b. in Danby, N. Y., Feb. 14, 1819, d. in Barton, N. Y., Jan. 14, 1837, a. 18.
6–124. Clark, b. in Danby, June 8, 1822, d. in Barton, March 16, 1843, a. 21.
6–125. Edward Allen, b. in Danby, Sept. 1, 1825; m. *Sally Ann Hamilton*, 1845; res. in Mich., 1870.
6–126. Ruth Ann, b. in Caroline, N. Y., July 30, 1827; m. in Barton, JOHN SEVERN; res. in Mich., 1870.
6–127. Lucy Keziah, b. in Barton, N. Y., Feb. 20, 1834; m. in Barton, ISAAC MANNING, res. 1870, in Spencer, N. Y.
6–128. Esther, b. in Barton, May 6, 1837, d. in Barton, Sept. 6, 1849, a. 12.
6–129. Sarah, b. in Barton, May 5, 1840, d. June 5, 1842, a. 2.

5–28. *Polly Fuller*, b. in Litchfield, Conn., Sept. 3, 1789, d. in Springfield, Ill., 1863, aged 74; m. in Danby, N. Y., 1812, JOSEPH HAGAR, who d. in Springfield, Ill., Sept. 21, 1839. They had:

6–130. Julius, b. in Danby, N. Y., 1813, res. 1870, in Springfield, Ill.
6–131. Myron, b. in Danby, 1820, res. 1870, in Missouri.

5–29. ABEL BARTON FULLER, farmer, pensioner for service in war of 1812, b. in Oneida Co., N. Y., July 10, 1792, d. in Candor, Tioga Co., N. Y., Sept. 24, 1870, aged 78; m. in Danby, N. Y., Nov. 1, 1827, *Elizabeth Cornwell*, who survives him. She resides, 1870, in Candor. They had eleven children:

6–132. [FULLER.] Marvin, b. in Danby, N. Y., Nov. 24, 1828, res. 1870, in Candor; *m.*

6–133. Jacob Cornwell, b. in Danby, Jan. 9, 1830, res. 1870, in Candor; *m.*

6–134. John Stubbs, b. in Caroline, N. Y., Oct. 22, 1831, res. 1870, in Greene Co., Pa.; *m.*

6–135. Alexander, b. in Caroline, Sept. 18, 1833, d. abt. 1863; *m.*

6–136. Sarah Jane, b. in Caroline, N. Y., June 30, 1835, res. 1870, in Tioga Centre, N. Y. SPEAR; RICE.

6–137. Phebe Martha, b. in Caroline, Aug. 25, 1837, res. 1870, in Ithaca, N. Y. RHOADS.

6–138. Robert Cornwell, b. in Caroline, July 16, 1839, res. 1870, Waverly, N. Y.; *m.*

6–139. Alvah Bogardus, b. in Caroline, Nov. 21, 1841, res. 1870, Candor, N. Y.; *m.*

6–140. Charles Clapp, b. in Caroline, Oct. 15, 1844, res. 1870, Green Co., Pa.; *m.*

6–141. Mary Elizabeth, b. in Caroline, Oct. 31, 1846, res. 1870, Fayette Co., Pa. FRANKS.

6–142. James Williams, b. in Candor, Oct. 2, 1851.

6–1. WALTER CARPENTER, b. in Schodack, N. Y., Nov. 26, 1807, m. Dec. 31, 1835, *Christina Miller.* They res. 1873, in Schodack. Two children, b. in Schodack:

7–1. John W., b. Oct. 14, 1836, res. 1873, Schodack; *m.*

7–2. Catharine Elizabeth, b. Nov. 8, 1841, res. 1873, Schodack. SMITH.

6–3. JOEL CARPENTER, b. in Schodack, N. Y., June 5, 1812, d. Dec. 17, 1870; m. Sept. 12, 1844, *Albertine Van Hoesen*, who d. April 25, 1847. One child:

7–3. John DeWitt, b. April 13, 1846.

6–7. ISAAC CARPENTER, b. in Schodack, N. Y., Feb. 17, 1821, m. in Schodack, June 9, 1858, *Caroline Van Dyck*, who was b. in Schodack, March 12, 1839, dau. of Dr. Cornelius P. and Mary Ann Van Dyck. They res. 1873, in Schodack. Three children:

7–4. Mary Loise, b. April 9, 1859, d. Nov. 20, 1862.

7–5. DeWitt, b. Oct. 25, 1866.

7–6. Mary, b. Sept. 12, 1869.

6–8. LUCAS S. CARPENTER, b. in Schodack, N.Y., Nov. 10, 1822, m. 1st, Nov. 15, 1854, *Elizabeth Kittle*, who was b. in Schodack, April 4, 1832, and d. Dec. 16, 1863. He m. 2d, June 28, 1871, *Mary Van Dyck*, who was b. in Schodack, Nov. 14, 1825. They res. in Schodack. Three children:

7-7. [CARPENTER.] Chester, b. Aug. 28, 1855.
7-8. Anna M., b. Oct. 7, 1862, d. April 17, 1863.
7-9. Jennie B., *twin sister of above*, d. May 26, 1863.

6-9. *Sarah Smith*, b. in Schodack, N. Y., Jan. 24, 1804, d. in Castleton, N. Y., Sept. 3, 1856, aged 52. She m. 1st, in Albany, N. Y., Nov. 16, 1822, JOHN PECK, who d. in New York, March 2, 1825. 2d, in New York city, 1827, ELIAS WARNER. Children:

7-10. William John *Peck*, b. Sept. 14, 1823, d. in Aspinwall, Sept. 1, 1852, a. 29.
7-11. Elizabeth *Warner*, b. in New York, April 12, 1828.

6-10. JOEL DAWSON SMITH, b. in Schodack, N. Y., Nov. 12, 1810, m. in Castleton, N. Y., Nov. 23, 1836, *Hannah Esluch Stearns*, who was b. in Castleton, Jan. 10, 1820. He was formerly a forwarding and commission merchant, and steamboat proprietor: now, 1873, President of the First National Bank of Castleton, where they reside. They have three children, all b. in Castleton:

7-12. John Daniel, b. Dec. 27, 1837.
7-13. William Peck, b. May 23, 1846.
7-14. Charles Hyde, b. Nov. 2, 1848.

6-22. JOEL J. DAWSON, farmer, b. in Schodack, N. Y., Dec. 15, 1822, m. in Schodack, Feb. 23, 1853, *Lucretia Kittle.* They reside, 1873, in Castleton, N. Y. They have two children:

7-15. Mary Jane, b. in Toneka, Ill., Feb. 1, 1859.
7-16. Amy S., b. in Schodack, N. Y., May 12, 1866.

6-24. HENRY DAWSON, merchant, b. in Schodack, N. Y., Feb. 24, 1827, m. in Mitcheskill, N. Y., Sept. 3, 1851, *Lany E. Folmsbee*, who was b. in Schodack, Aug. 1, 1833. They reside in Castleton, N. Y. Two children, both b. in Schodack:

7-17. Eldores J., b. Dec. 21, 1852.
7-18. Lucas Henry, b. Dec. 25, 1865.

6-25. WILLIAM DAWSON, farmer, b. in Schodack, N. Y., May 29, 1829, m. March 14, 1858, *Rebecca Hyck.* They reside, 1873, in South Schodack, N. Y. One child:

7-19. Charles, b. in Schodack, Jan. 29, 1859.

6-27. *Mary Helen Dawson*, b. in Schodack, N. Y., Sept. 12, 1836, m. in same place, Nov. 25, 1857, T. REILY VAN HOESEN. They res. 1873, in Schodack. Two children:

7-20. Mary Elvina, b. in Schodack, Dec. 4, 1858.
7-21. Minnie, b. in Schodack, Oct. 6, 1866.

6-28. JAMES MONROE DAWSON, b. in Schodack, N. Y., March 11, 1840, m. in Castleton, N. Y., Dec. 24, 1865, Miss *Kate Hudson*. They res. 1873, in Castleton. Two children:

7-22. Levina, b. in Castleton, Nov. 26, 1867.
7-23. Helen, b. in Castleton, May 29, 1870.

6-29. *Anna Dawson*, b. in East Haven, Conn., July 31, 1794, d. in Westfield (Middletown) Conn., Dec. 3, 1862, aged 68. She m. Feb. 15, 1814, CHESTER DOUGLASS,[1] who was b. in New Hartford, Conn., Dec. 25, 1785, and d. in Westfield, Dec. 22, 1861, aged 76. He had learned the cooper's trade, but followed the occupation of a farmer through life. They had eight children, all b. in New Hartford:

7-24. Emily Cyrene, b. Nov. 5, 1815, res. 1873, in New Haven, Ct. FOWLER.[2]
7-25. Benajah Hervey, b. Oct. 6, 1817, res. 1873, New Haven, Ct.; *m.*
7-26. Sarah Ann, b. Sept. 13, 1819, res. 1873, Durham, Ct. ALLING; WAY.
7-27. Lloyd Waldo, b. June 17, 1821, res. 1873, in New Haven, Ct.; *unm.*
7-28. Chester Holt, b. June 25, 1823, res. 1873, Norwalk, Ct.; *m.*
7-29. Eliza Henrietta, b. Dec. 17, 1825, res. 1873, Meriden, Ct. ROBERTS.
7-30. William Bradley, b. Nov. 10, 1828, res. 1873, New Haven, Ct.; *m.*
7-31. Solomon Johnson, b. Oct. 3, 1834, res. 1873, New Haven, Ct.; *m.*

6-30. *Eliza Teresa Dawson*, b. in East Haven, Conn., 1796, a member of the First Church of the United Society, New

---

[1] Son of Moses (d. abt. 1827, aged abt. 86) and *Anne Spencer* Douglass, m. in New Hartford, Ct., June 28, 1781; gr. son of Samuel Douglass, who was b. in Plainfield, Ct.; gt. gr. son of Samuel Douglass, who was "born in Scotland." So says Mr. Riverius Douglass, brother of Chester, above named; but the compiler hereof thinks that investigation would show that the Samuel Douglass last above named was not the original emigrant.

[2] ELISHA FOWLER, merchant, m. *Emily Cyrene Douglass*, March 26, 1838. He was b. in North Branford, Ct., July 27, 1810, and d. in New Haven, June 7, 1862 aged 52. They had no issue.

Haven, Feb. 1821, d. in Orange, Conn., Feb. 1, 1840, aged 44. She m. Sept. 30, 1822, SOLOMON JOHNSON,[1] farmer and teacher, who was b. Feb. 9, 1786, and d. at Orange, Ct., June, 16, 1843, aged 57. She was his second w. They had four children, all b. in Orange:

7–32. Solomon, b. April 1, 1824, res. 1870, in Washoe City, Nevada.
7–33. David Alling, b. Feb. 14, 1826, d. in New Haven, Ct., Aug. 6, 1864.[2]
7–34. William Holt, b. Oct. 19, 1828, res. 1873, in New Haven ; *m.*
7–35. A *daughter*, d. in infancy.

6–31. *Mary Leonora Dawson*, b. in East Haven, Ct., Oct. 9, 1798, d. in Saybrook, Ashtabula Co., Ohio, June 10, 1843, aged 45 ; m. in New Hartford, Ct., Dec. 1, 1819, JAMES CALAWAY,[3] farmer, who was b. in Harwinton, Ct., Feb. 27, 1796, d. in Kingsville, O., July 26, 1870, aged 74. They had ten children:

7–36. James, b. in New Hartford, Ct., July 24, 1819, res. 1871, in Ashtabula, O. ; *m.*
7–37. William Holt, b. in New Hartford, Sept. 30, 1821, res. 1871, in Ashtabula, O. ; *m.*
7–38. Fayette, b. in Austinburg, O., Dec. 17, 1823, d. in Austinburg, Aug. 26, 1828, a. 5.
7–39. Mary Jane, b. in Austinburg, July 9, 1826, res. 1871, in Geneva, O. WILLIAMS.
7–40. Sarah, b. in Austinburg, July 18, 1828, d. in Madison, O., Feb. 18, 1847, a. 19.
7–41. Lucretius Bissell, b. in Austinburg, July 8, 1831, d. in same place, 1832.

---

[1] Seventh ch. of Ebenezer and *Esther Punderson* Johnson, m. Jan. 4, 1769; gr. son of Stephen Johnson, of W. Haven, b. 1704, d. 1797, a descendant of John Johnson, one of the original settlers of New Haven, 1643. Esther Punderson was dau. of Thomas Punderson, b. Aug. 24, 1713, d. Feb. 22, 1781, and w. Mary Miles, b. Dec. 18, 1719, dau. of Joseph Miles, mariner, and w. Elizabeth Trowbridge, b. March 29, 1693, d. Jan. 23, 1783, m. March 20, 1718. Thomas Punderson was son of John Punderson, for forty years deacon, and gr. son of John Punderson, one of the original "seven pillars," of the First Church of New Haven. Elizabeth Trowbridge was the dau. of Thomas Trowbridge, planter and merchant, of large estate, b. Feb. 14, 1664, d. Sept. 15, 1704; and w. Mary Winston, m. Oct. 16, 1685; gr. dau. of Thomas Trowbridge, a large W. India merchant, Justice of the Quorum, etc., b. in England, 1632, d. Aug. 22, 1702, and w. Sarah Rutherford; gt. gr. dau. of Thomas Trowbridge, who emigrated from Taunton, Somersetshire, England, abt. 1636. See "*Trowbridge Family*." Mary Winston was dau. of John Winston, of New Haven, 1647, concerning whom see n. 3, p. 42.

[2] He was a private in company E. of the 43d N. Y. Rgt. of Infantry, enlisted about Sept., 1861; died from wounds received at Rappahannock Station, Va., in engagement of Nov. 9, 1863.

[3] Son of William Calaway (b. in England, d. in Conn.), and w. Sarah Collier (b. in Barkhamstead, Ct., d. in Illinois).

7–42. [CALAWAY.] Orestes Hawley, b. in Austinburg, May 16, 1833, res. 1871, in Saybrook, O.; *m.*

7–43. Henry Dawson, b. in Austinburg, Jan. 6, 1837, d. at Chancellorsville, Va., May 3, 1863, a. 26.[1]

7–44. Eliza, b. in Austinburg, Sept. 25, 1839, res. 1871, at Geneva, O. BRETT.

7–45. Emily Irene, b. in Saybrook, O., April 24, 1841, res. 1873, at Tittabawassee, Mich. STONE.

6–32. *Jennette Dawson*, b. in East Haven, Ct., April 25, 1805, res. 1873, in West Haven, Ct. She m. in New Hartford, Ct., Aug. 28, 1824, BARZILLIA MORSE,[2] farmer, b. in Litchfield, Ct., April 9, 1801, d. in West Haven, June 14, 1863, aged 62. They had three children:

7–46. Henry Shepard, b. in Austinburg, O., April 9, 1827; d. July 27, 1872, in Olney, Ill.; *m.*

7–47. Elizabeth Jennette, b. in Vienna, Oneida Co., N. Y., Sept. 29, 1833, res. 1873, in West Haven, Ct. CATLIN.

7–48. Adelaide Theresa, b. in Orange, Ct., March 5, 1840, res. 1873, in Southington, Ct. NEALE.

6–33. WILLIAM HOLT DAWSON, formerly merchant in New York city, now (1873) proprietor of the Rockview vineyards and fruit farm, at Westville, Ct., was b. in North Guilford, Ct., Aug. 16, 1809. He m. in Orange, Ct., May 11, 1834, *Martha Wilmot*,[3] who was b. in Milford, Ct., Dec. 9, 1816.

---

[1] He was a private in Company D., 11th N. Y. Infantry, enlisted 23 Sept., 1862. He was killed in battle.

[2] Eldest son of Elihu (b. July 16, 1774) and *Abigail Barber* Morse, res. Litchfield, Ct., Wolf Lake, Ind., and Panaka, Wis.; gr. son of Solomon (b. Feb. 18, 1749, d. June 4, 1820) and *Mary Spellman* Morse, m. March 23, 1770, res. Wallingford, Ct.; gt. gr. son of David (b. May 15, 1716, d. May 16, 1766) and Mindwell Morse, m. Oct. 7, 1737, res. at Wallingford. The last named was son of Solomon, (b. July 9, 1690, d. Oct. 10, 1752), and *Ruth Peck* (d. March 29, 1728) Morse or Moss, m. June 28, 1714, res. Wallingford; gr. son of John (b. Oct. 12, 1650, d. March 31, 1717) and *Martha Lathrop* (d. Sept. 21, 1719) Moss, m. Dec. 12, 1677, res. New Haven and Wallingford; gt. gr. son of John Moss, of New Haven, b. in England abt. 1619, res. at New Haven 1639–70, Wallingford 1670–1708. He was a member of the General Court, and a prominent, influential man. See sketch of him and an account of his descendants: — *Memorial of the Morses*, p. 144, appendix, XCVII.

[3] Dau. of Walter Wilmot (b. in Bethany, Ct., Jan. 5, 1782, d. in West Haven, May 12, 1854, a. 72) and w. Sarah Clark, (b. in Milford, Feb. 14, 1781, d. in West Haven, May 12, 1832, dau. of Elisha and *Sarah Beach* Clark) m. June 24, 1802; gr. dau. of Walter Wilmot, (b. in Woodbridge, d. in Bethany, Ct., July, 1824, a. 69) and w. Hannah Johnson, who d. in Waterbury, May 8, 1833, a. 71. The last named W. W. was a soldier in Rev. war; a gunner in Fort Montgomery, which he was one of the last to leave when it fell into the hands of the British, he and three others making their escape by swimming the Hudson river; he was a son of Valentine Wilmot (b. and d. in Southold, L. I.); gr. son of Alexander Wilmot

H. S. Dawson

They reside, 1873, in Westville. Seven children, all b. in New Haven:

7–49. William Henry, b. Sept. 10, 1835, d. in Westville, May 9, 1865, a. 30; *m.*
7–50. Frances Emma, b. June 28, 1838, d. Dec. 21, 1841, a. 3.[1]
7–51. Edward Walter, b. Nov. 20, 1840, res. 1873, in New Haven; *m.*
7–52. George Wallace, b. Oct. 9, 1842, res. 1873, in New Haven; *m.*
7–53. Franklin Tuttle, b. July 15, 1844, res. 1873, in Westville; *m.*
7–54. Caroline Ives, b. Aug. 9, 1846, res. 1873, in Westville.
7–55. Ella Anzonetta, b. Aug. 3, 1849, res. 1873, in Westville.

6–34. Henry Shepard Dawson, b. in New Hartford, Conn., July 3, 1813, m. in Orange, Ct., June 4, 1839, *Elizabeth Alling*,[2] who was b. in Orange, Feb. 17, 1817. They reside, 1873, in New Haven, where he was for many years a merchant and manufacturing confectioner. He was, until recently, president, and is now a director and vice-president, of the New Haven and Derby R. R. Company. He is also a director of the Yale National Bank, of New Haven, and president of the New Haven City Water Works Company, with which company he has been prominently connected from the date of its organization, about 1859. He early recognized, as few at that time did, the necessity and advantages to New Haven of an abundant supply of pure water, and to his sound judgment and indomitable energy it now largely owes the distinction which it enjoys of being among the most favored of our cities in this respect. Much of the recent rapid increase of that city, in business, wealth and population, is due to the numerous manufacturing establishments removed to or originating in New Haven since the introduction of water, and impossible there before for lack of it; while the benefits of its introduction, as regards health, comfort, security from fires, and domestic con-

also of Southold — the place where, it is said, the ancestors of this family "settled when they emigrated from England to America." Sarah Beach, above named, was dau. of Leander Beach (d. in Orange, Dec. 28, 1823, aged 96), and w. Abigail Baldwin (d. in Orange, Feb. 25, 1824, aged 97) m. in Milford, lived together over 60 years, and left living descendants, 7 children, 72 gr. children, 192 gt. gr. children and 17 gt. gt. gr. children.

[1] The date of her death copied from the family record, but the grave-stone says Dec. 20.

[2] Dau. of Gilead Alling (b. in Orange, d. in New Haven, May 25, 1844), and w. Mary Smith, b. in Milford, April, 1792 — dau. of Thomas and *Mary Lambert* Smith, m. in Orange; gr. dau. of John and *Lydia Hall* Alling, of West Haven.

venience, are almost incalculable. In connection with many other enterprises for the benefit of the "city of Elms," Mr. Dawson's name might be honorably mentioned. He is one of its most active, public spirited and useful citizens. Mr. and Mrs. Dawson have had nine children, all b. in New Haven:

7–56. Henry Shepard, b. Aug. 22, 1841, d. in New Haven, Dec. 3, 1867, a. 26; *unm.*
7–57. Sidney Holt, b. Oct. 27, 1842, res. 1873, in New Haven; *m.*
7–58. Augustus Edward, b. Feb. 20, 1844, res. 1873, in New Haven; *m.*
7–59. David Alonzo, b. Jan. 11, 1846, d. April 2, 1861, a. 15.
7–60. Theodore Shepard, b. May 15, 1847, d. April 14, 1861, a. 14.
7–61. Mary Elizabeth, b. Jan. 15, 1849, d. March 20, 1861, a. 12.
7–62. Charles Albert, b. March 31, 1853, d. Feb. 1, 1854, a. 1.
7–63. Florence Irene, b. Nov. 10, 1854, d. May 27, 1861, a. 7.
7–64. Charles Herbert, b. Nov. 16, 1857, d. Feb. 16, 1861, a. 3.[1]

6–36. THOMAS HOLT DAWSON, school teacher and farmer, b. in Northford, Ct., Dec. 17, 1807, d. in Licking county, Ohio, June 7, 1847, aged 40. He m. in Caldwell, N. J., Nov. 27, 1833, *Abigail Jacobus*, of Caldwell, who was b. March 28, 1813. They removed the same year to Northford, returned to Caldwell in April, 1836, and removed thence to Hartford-town, Licking county, O., in 1840, her parents having gone thither a short time before. She m. again, and res. 1873, at Condit P. O., Delaware Co., O. They had five children:

7–65. Stephen V., b. Nov. 10, 1834, d. Aug. 15, 1855, aged 21; *unm.*
7–66. Mary Adaline, b. Jan. 28, 1839, d. May 21, 1868; was m. but d. without issue.
7–67. Reuben Thomas, b. April 10, 1841, d. June 7, 1847.
7–68. Fanny, b. Jan. 7, 1845, res. 1873, Condit, O. HUFF.
7–69. Chloe, b. Jan. 14, 1848, res. 1873, Condit, O. WILSON.

6–37. *Mary Adaline Dawson*, b. in Northford, Conn., April 25, 1810, m. in Northford, April 25, 1833, HORACE SMITH, farmer, b. in North Haven, Jan. 20, 1811, res. 1871, in Wallingford. She d. in Northford, July 2, 1837, aged 27, leaving one child, then three weeks old, viz:

7–70. Merit Dawson, b. June 11, 1837, res. 1871, in Wallingford; *m.*

[1] The five interesting children whose deaths occurred, as appears by the above melancholy record, within the space of about ten weeks in the early months of 1861, were victims to that dread scourge *diptheria*, then very fatally prevalent in the country. A similar instance appears to have occurred in the family of Thomas Dawson, 1736–37 (2–2).

6-38. *Sarah Smith Tuttle*, b. in East Haven, Nov. 4, 1816, m. in same town, Feb. 10, 1835, George Henry Jacobs, who was b. in North Haven, Sept. 27, 1813, and d. in Sacramento, Cal., Oct. 30, 1850, aged 37. She res. 1873, in East Haven. One child:

7-71. Hiram, b. in East Haven, Jan. 22, 1836, res. 1873, in East Haven; *unm.*

6-39. *Harriet Lewis Meloy*, b. in New Haven, Conn., Jan. 4, 1799, m. in Chenango, N. Y., Jan. 4, 1820, John Barker Rogers, who was b. in Lisle, N. Y., May 6, 1796. He resides 1873, in Chenango Forks, N. Y., where he has been for many years in active business as a merchant, miller, and extensive dealer in dairy products, which commodities he purchases in large quantities for eastern markets. He was postmaster at Chenango Forks, by appointment of several different administrations, but, having acted prominently with the whig party, was removed for political causes during the presidency of James K. Polk. He was a member of the state assembly in 1844, and has repeatedly served as county supervisor, to which office he continued to be elected so long as he would consent to accept it. Probably to him more than to any other man is due the business prosperity of the village and vicinity where he resides, and he enjoys in a high degree the confidence and esteem of the community.

Mr. and Mrs. Rogers celebrated the fiftieth anniversary of their marriage at their pleasant home on the fourth of January, 1870. Besides a very large attendance of friends from near and far, the *family* gathering numbered over fifty, including seven children, eighteen grand-children, and three great grand children; and it was remarked of the groom and bride that they received and entertained their friends with a cordiality and ease which would have graced a much earlier anniversary of their wedded life. They were made the recipients of very many elegant and costly gifts, as well as of letters from numerous friends in distant places, expressive of the utmost good will and best wishes.[1]

[1] Mr. R. is a son of Simeon Rogers, farmer and inn keeper (b. in Guilford, Ct., Aug. 1762, d. in Barker, N. Y., March 27, 1856, aged 94), and w. Mary Barker, (b. in Branford, Ct., d. in Barker, 1858, aged 86) m. in town of Lisle, N. Y., abt.

Mrs. Rogers d. at Chenango Forks, Feb. 22, 1873, aged 74. "For half a century she was identified with the social and religious history of this village. Of the Congregational church, during the half century of its existence, it is not too much to say that Mrs. Rogers was 'the strongest soul.' In this community, for the same period, alike in her social standing and her Christian example, she was 'a shining light.' Of the many women whose social and Christian influence has been a blessing to this place, the general verdict would promptly give to Mrs. Rogers a representative place."......"Where there was good work to be done, there she was to be found, and always among the foremost. Surely hers was a worthy life."[1] They had nine children:

7–72. Henry Augustus, b. in Chenango Forks, April 30, 1821, res. 1873, in Chenango Forks; *m.*

7–73. Theodore Simeon, b. in Chenango Forks, Oct. 14, 1824, res. 1873, Binghamton, N. Y.; *m.*

7–74. Mary Ann, b. in Greene, N. Y., April 17, 1826, res. 1873, Dunkirk, N. Y. FULLAGER.

7–75. Norman Stevens, b. in Chenango Forks, Oct. 3, 1828, res. 1873, Chenango Forks; *m.*

7–76. Julia Eliza, b. in Chenango Forks, Oct. 30, 1830, res. 1873, Chenango Forks. HAGAMAN.

7–77. William, b. in Chenango Forks, Dec. 4, 1832, d. May 5, 1837.

7–78. Caroline Harriet, b. in Chenango Forks, Feb. 16, 1835, res. 1873, Chenango Forks, N. Y.

7–79. George William, b. in Chenango Forks, Oct. 14, 1838, res. 1873, Binghamton, N. Y.; *m.*

7–80. Catharine Juliett, b. in Chenango Forks, June, 1844, d. Sept. 23, 1848.

1790. She was a dau. of John Barker, a pioneer settler in the Chenango Valley country. See interesting anecdotes of her early life and adventures among the Indians, *Annals of Binghamton*, pp. 160–163. Simeon Rogers was a "minute-man" at New Haven, when sixteen years old; served for six months at one time, and for shorter periods on other occasions. He opened in 1795, "the first inn, kept the first store, and built the first mill" in the town of Barker. His marriage was also the first in the township. He was appointed, under President Jefferson, the first postmaster at Chenango Forks, which office he resigned after a few years in favor of his son, who held it continuously until removed as above stated, by Pres. Polk.* Of Simeon Rogers it was said that "he had been in the enjoyment of remarkably good health all his long life, and he possessed unusual mental and physical activity and energy. Intelligent, patriotic and kind hearted, he was respected and beloved by all who knew him." — *Obituary:* Binghamton paper.

[1] From *Obituaries.*

*About a year after his removal, his son Theodore was made postmaster, and the office is now held by another son, Henry, having been out of the family only one year since it was established.

6-40. Henry Meloy jun., b. in New Haven, Ct., March 9, 1801, m. in Greene, N. Y., Feb. 17, 1828, *Nancy Waterman*, who was b. in Otsego, N. Y., July 13, 1801, and d. at Linden, Orleans Co., N. Y., July, 1855, aged 54. He res. 1873, at Ellicottville, N. Y. They had one child:

7-81. Catharine, b. in Union, N. Y., March 9, 1842, d. at Linden, Aug. 27, 1856, a. 14.

6-41. Frederick William Meloy, merchant, b. in New Haven, Conn., Feb. 26, 1805, m. 1st. in Greene, N. Y., Dec. 8, 1830, *Martha Emilia Willard*,[1] who was b. at Stafford Springs, Conn., Nov. 16, 1808, d. in Ellicottville, N. Y., March 11, 1868, aged 59; mother of all his children. He m. 2d. in West Haven, Ct., Oct. 21, 1869, wid. Susan Frances Meloy McCarthy,[2] b in Orange, Ct., Aug. 27, 1834. They

[1] Third child and only dau. of Dr. Samuel Willard (b. at Stafford Springs, Ct., Dec. 26, 1766, d. at Cincinnati, O., Feb. 16, 1820), and w. Abigail Perkins (b. at Chaplin, Ct., abt. 1773, d. at Greene, N. Y., Feb. 22, 1839, dau. of Isaac and *Tamisen Chaplin* Perkins, of Ashford, Ct.), m. Aug. 1798; gr. dau. of Rev. Dr. John Willard (b. in Biddeford, Me., Feb. 8, 1733, d. at Stafford Springs, Ct., Feb. 16, 1807), and w. Lydia Dwight (b. Brookfield, Mass., Jan. 14, 1732, d. Jan. 23, 1798, dau. of Joseph Dwight), m. Nov. 24, 1758. Rev. Dr. J. W. was son of Rev. Dr. Samuel Willard (b. at Kingston, Jamaica, abt. Sept. 1705, d. at Kittery, Me., Oct. 25, 1741), and w. Abigail Wright (b. at Sudbury, Mass., Feb. 19, 1708-9, d. at Scarborough, Me., aged 70, dau. of Capt. Samuel and *Mary Stephens* Wright, of Rutland), m. Oct. 29, 1730; gr. son of Major John Willard, (b. at Groton, Mass., Sept. 8, 1673, d. at Kingston, Jamaica, abt. 1710-20), and w. Frances Sherburne, of Jamaica, (d. at Kingston, 1733), m. 1703 or '04. Major J. W. was son of Rev. Dr. Samuel Willard (b. at Concord, Mass., Jan. 31, 1639-40, d. at Boston, Sept. 12, 1707), and his first w. Abigail Sherman, (b. 1647, d. abt. 1677, dau. of Rev. John and *Mary Launce* Sherman,) m. Aug. 8, 1664; gr. son of Major Simon Willard, (b. at Horsmonden, Kent, England, 1605, d. at Charlestown, Mass., between 1675 and 1680), and his first w. Mary Sharpe, (bapt. at Horsmonden, Oct. 16, 1614, dau. of Henry and *Jane Feylde* Sharpe). Major Simon W. emigrated to Boston 1634, became a prominent military officer of the Colony, and a member of the governor's council. He was son of Richard Willard (d. at Horsmonden, Feb. 1617), and his second w. Margery (d. at Horsmonden, Dec. 1608). Rev. Dr. Samuel W., above named, son of Major Simon W., was a grad. of Harvard College, 1659; pastor of Old South Church, Boston, 1678; and president of Harvard, 1701–7. Other graduates of that Institution, above named, were Major John W., 1670, merchant, of Kingston, Jamaica; Rev. Dr. Samuel W., 1723, pastor of church at Biddeford, Me., 1730, "an earnest, zealous, and affectionate preacher;" Rev. Dr. John W., 1751, "a venerable servant of God, faithful and devoted in his station as a Christian minister for a term of nearly fifty years;" and Dr. Samuel W., 1787. *Willard Memoir*, by Joseph Willard, Boston, 1858.

[2] Wid. of Sergt. Thomas McCarthy, of Co. I., 16th Regt. Conn. Vols., killed in battle, of Antietam, Sept., 7, 1862, dau. of Falama Meloy, (b. in Orange, Ct., March 25, 1792,) and w. Amarilla Richards, (b. in Orange, March 4, 1800, d. June 3, 1862,) m. May 28, 1820; gr. dau. of John Meloy, (Dec. 4, 1766, d. in West Haven, Ct., aged 74,) and w. Esther Umberville. Her gr. father was a bro. of Henry Meloy, (5-14).

reside, 1873, in Ellicottville. He has had nine children:

7–82. [MELOY.] William Augustus, b. in Chenango Forks, N. Y., Aug. 26, 1832, res. 1873, Muirkirk Station, Md.; *m.*

7–83. John Willard, b. in Chenango Forks, Sept. 8, 1834, res. 1873, Portville, Cattaraugus Co., N. Y.; *m.*

7–84. Samuel Henry, b. in Chenango Forks, Sept. 8, 1836, res. 1873, Washington, D. C.; *m.*

7–85. Abigail, b. in Greene, N. Y., Dec. 9, 1838, res. 1873, Ellicottville, N. Y.

7–86. Anna, b. in Chenango, N. Y., Aug, 8, 1841, res. 1873, Great Valley, N. Y. RIDER.

7–87. Charles Frederick, b. in Barker, N. Y., Dec. 17, 1843, res. 1873, Cuba, N. Y.; *m.*

7–88. Edward Richmond, b. in Barker, N. Y., June 12, 1846, res. 1873, Corsicana, Navarro Co., Texas; *unm.*

7–89. Theodore Dwight, b. in Barker, N. Y., April 18, 1849, d. in Ellicottville, April 3, 1858, a. 9.

7–90. Martha Emilia, b. in Greene, N. Y., May 26, 1854, res. 1873, Ellicottville.

6–42. *Julia Anna Meloy*, b. in New Haven, Conn., Nov. 12, 1810, m. at Union, N. Y., June 21, 1833, Rev. JUDAH L. RICHMOND, who was b. in Durham, Schoharie Co., N. Y., April 17, 1807, and d. in Sheffield, Ashtabula Co., Ohio, May 14, 1868, aged 61. He was a Baptist minister, graduate of Hamilton College.[1] She resides, 1873, with her son, in Chattanooga, Tenn. They had six children:

---

[1] Son of Rev. Edmund Richmond, also a Baptist minister (b in Berkshire county, Mass., March 16, 1780, d. at Sheffield, O., Jan. 24, 1862), and w. Ruth Leaming (b. in Farmington, Conn., abt. 1782, d. in Sheffield, O., Feb., 1838, dau. of Judah Leaming, of Bristol, Ct.), m. in Bristol, N. Y., Dec. 1, 1801; gr. son of Gideon Richmond (d. in Berkshire, 1800, a soldier of the Revolution) and w. Hannah Richmond (d. in Berkshire, 1780), dau. of John Richmond, of Taunton, Mass. The father of Gideon Richmond was Nathaniel, who also lived at Taunton. The Richmonds are of English descent. They were at Taunton as early as 1640. Rev. Edmund Richmond was "for sixty years a worthy member of the Baptist church, and for above fifty years a faithful and successful preacher of the Gospel. He was pastor of the Baptist church in Milford, Otsego Co., N. Y., more than twenty years, during which time a church of 14 members increased to 144, and erected a good House of Worship, which still remains. Thence he removed to Rome, Ashtabula Co., O., where he gathered a small church, which increased to 50 members, and erected a House of Worship, during his pastorate of seven years. The last twenty-three years of his pastoral life he devoted to the Baptist church in Sheffield, to which he gave a lot of ground for a meeting house, towards the erection of which he was also the principal donor. He had eight sons and four daughters. Of these, all but two sons survived him, besides whom he left a posterity of 67 grand children and 27 great grand children." — *Obituary.* In September, 1853, one hundred of his children and children's children met him on a visit. Several large general gatherings of the Richmonds have taken place, and it is understood that a book of Records of the family is in course of preparation.

7–91. [RICHMOND.] Theodore, b. in Jefferson, O., March 2, 1837, res. 1873, in Chattanooga, Tenn.; *m.*
7–92. Amelia, b. in Stockton, N. Y., June 5, 1840, res. 1873, in Goshen, Ind. THOMAS.
7–93. Charles Henry, b. in Fredonia, N. Y., Dec. 14, 1842, res. 1873, in Brighton, Lorain Co., O.; *m.*
7–94. Grace Adelia, b. in Warsaw, N. Y., April 13, 1846, res. 1873, in Ai, Fulton Co., O. BARTHOLOMEW.
7–95. Frederick Meloy, b. in Warsaw, N. Y., March 27, 1848, res. 1873, in Cleveland, O.; *m.*
7–96. Katherine, b. in Deposit, N. Y., Dec. 25, 1850, res. 1873, in Goshen, Ind. POOLEY.

6–43. *Grace Amelia Meloy*, b. in New Haven, Ct., July 4, 1813, m. Nov. 1, 1831, CHARLES EGBERT KEELER, merchant, b. in Binghamton, N. Y., April 4, 1806, d. at the residence of her son in-law, Dr. Johnson, in Greene, N. Y., Nov. 2, 1872, aged 66.[1] They resided many years in Union, N. Y., and had two children., both b. in that place:

7–97. Julia Anna, b. Jan. 12, 1833, res. 1873, Fulton, Ill. MERCEREAU.
7–98. Adelaide Amelia, b. Aug. 20, 1836, res. 1873, Greene, N. Y. JOHNSON.

6–44. *Harriet Mead Prescott*, b. in Batavia, N. Y., June 25, 1821, m. July 31, 1841, DR. ELIJAH DRESSER,[2] allopathic physician, who was b. in Paris, Oneida Co., N. Y., Sept. 15, 1810. They reside, 1873, in East Otto, Cattaraugus Co., N. Y., and have had five children, all b. in E. Otto:

7–99. Harlan Cephas, b. Sept. 2, 1843, res. 1871, Dunkirk, N. Y.; *m.*
7–100. Emily Eunecia, b. Jan. 2, 1849, d. Nov. 2, 1849.
7–101. Moses Beecher, b. Jan 4, 1851.[3]
7–102. Charles Corydon, b. March 20, 1853.
7–103. Laura Prescott, b. March 28, 1858.

---

[1] Son of Lewis Keeler, who went from Norwalk, Ct., and kept a public house and carried on the hatting business at Chenango village (near where Binghamton now stands) for some years prior to 1800. He built in Binghamton, 1801, the first tavern in that place.—*Annals of Binghamton*, 176–177. His son Lewis Keeler, of Greene, N. Y., m. Mary, sister of John B. Rogers (6–39). They celebrated the fiftieth anniversary of their marriage, Feb. 1869. (Ralph Keeler, at Hartford, 1640, was one of the first settlers of Norwalk; freeman there, 1668.—Savage's *Gen. Dict.*).

[2] Son of Elijah Dresser (b. in Wendall, Mass., d. in Geneseo, N. Y., abt. 1822, aged 52) and w. Amelia Beach (d. in Geneseo, N. Y., abt. 1818, aged 44) m. in Paris, Oneida Co., N. Y. (Probably a descendant of John Dresser, of Rowley, Mass., 1643).

[3] In *Prescott Memorial* the date of his birth is erroneously given "*June* 4, 1851," and date of Emily's birth is also erroneously printed "*June* 2, 1849."

6-45. ELLIOTT MARSHALL DAWSON, painter, b. in New Hartford, Conn., Jan. 22, 1814, m. 1st. Oct. 1, 1838, *Esther Smith*, b. in Harwinton, Ct., May 11, 1817, d. in Bristol, Ct., Aug. 25, 1842. No children. 2d. Jan. 4, 1846, *Rosetta Norton*, b. in Plymouth, Ct., Nov. 10, 1819. They res. 1873, in Plymouth, Ct., and have had five children, all b. in that state:

7-104. Marshall, b. in New Haven, Sept. 20, 1846, d. in New Haven, Oct. 4, 1846.

7-105. Helena, b. in Fair Haven, June 9, 1850, res. 1873, Plymouth, Ct. ROSSITER.

7-106. Millard Elliott, b. in Ansonia, Sept. 21, 1852, d. in Ansonia, Sept. 21, 1853.

7-107. Fred Elliott, b. in Meriden, Feb. 15, 1857, d. in Hartford, Feb. 6, 1860.

7-108. Fred Millard, b. in Waterville, Sept. 7, 1862.

6-46. *Mary Ann Dawson*, b. in New Hartford, Ct., May 14, 1816, m. 1st. Sept. 3, 1837, NORTON C. PARSONS, who was b. in Enfield, Ct., Aug. 18, 1810, d. of lung fever, at Broad Brook, East Windsor, Conn., June 6, 1855, aged 45. They had two children, both b. in East Windsor:

7-109. Clifford Dawson, b. Nov. 14, 1838, res. 1873, Bristol, Ct.; *m.*

7-110. Arthur, b. Aug. 28, 1840, res. 1873, Bristol, Ct.; *m.*

She m. 2d., Dec. 14, 1858, ORRIN BISSELL, b. in E. Windsor, Dec. 1, 1792, d. of lung fever, at Broad Brook, Jan. 8, 1873. She res. 1873, at Broad Brook.

6-47. *Eveline Abigail Dawson*, b. in New Hartford, Ct., April 26, 1818, m. May 2, 1841, Dea. RUSSELL B. PERKINS, who was b. in West Springfield, Mass., April 10, 1817. They reside, 1873, in Meriden, Ct. Three children:

7-111. Charles Russell, b. in New Hartford, Jan. 25, 1844, res. 1873, Meriden; *m.*

7-112. George Willard, b. in Meriden, Aug. 11, 1850.

7-113. Judson Norton, b. in Meriden, Dec. 7, 1852.

6-49. *Juliette Dawson*, b. in New Hartford, Ct., March 18, 1821, m. Oct. 14, 1841, HENRY W. BISSELL,[1] who was

[1] Son of Lawrence (b. March 11, 1772, d. Feb. 7, 1853), and *Jane Wolcott* Bissell, m. Feb. 28, 1805; gr. son of Roswell (b. May 3, 1755), and *Olive Stoughton* Bissell; gt. gr. son of William (b. Sept. 15, 1725, d. June 22, 1796), and *Jemima Skinner* Bissell, m. June 4, 1754. The last named was son of Ensign Nathaniel jr., (b. Jan. 7, 1665, d. March 4, 1752), and *Sarah Gaylord* Bissell, m. July 8, 1714; gr. son of Nathaniel (b. Sept. 24, bapt. Sept. 27, 1640, d. March 12, 1713-14), and *Mindwell*

b. in East Windsor, Dec. 23, 1818. They res. 1873, at Broad Brook, E. Windsor. Five children, all b. in that town:

7–114. Elizabeth E., b. Aug. 8, 1841, res. 1873, Broad Brook. DAVENPORT.
7–115. Lucius H., b. Jan. 29, 1845, res. 1873, Broad Brook.
7–116. Juliette, b. April 30, 1848, res. 1873, Broad Brook.
7–117. Mary M., b. Jan. 27, 1853, res. 1873, Broad Brook.
7–118. Katie J., b. Sept. 30, 1857, d. at Broad Brook, April 6, 1869.

6–51. *Sybil Dawson*, b. in New Hartford, Ct., Nov. 21, 1825, m. June 9, 1845, JOSEPH SIGOURNEY, merchant, b. in Spezia, Italy, Feb. 17, 1821. They res. 1873, in Bristol, Conn.; have two children, both b. in Bristol:

7–119. Albert Marshall, b. Aug. 1, 1850, res. 1873, in Bristol; *m.*
7–120. Frank Willard, b. Oct. 25, 1856.

6–52. *Marilla Elizabeth Dawson*, b. in New Hartford, Ct., Oct. 31, 1828, m. in Bristol, Nov. 15, 1848, GEORGE HOSFORD EVANS, who was b. in Chatham, Conn., Nov. 4, 1824, son of George and Esther Evans. They res. 1873, in Bristol. Nine children:

7–121. William Henry, b. in Bristol, Sept. 9, 1849.
7–122. Mary Esther, b. in Bristol, Dec. 15, 1854, res. Bristol. WOODRUFF.
7–123. George Burdett, b. in Burlington, Ct., Oct. 14, 1857.
7–124. Harriet Nina, b. in Bristol, Feb. 9, 1860.
7–125. Harry, b. in Bristol, July 8, 1863, d. Aug. 13, 1865.
7–126. Anna Elizabeth, b. in Bristol, Aug. 17, 1865.
7–127. Nellie Marilla, b. in Bristol, Jan. 27, 1867.
7–128. Harry, b. in Bristol, Jan. 17, 1870.
7–129. Sybil, b. in Bristol, March, 1872.

6–53. *Lucia Eunecia Amelia Dawson*, b. in Canton, Ct., Nov. 18, 1813, d. at "Lone Oak Farm," Bloomingdale, Du Page Co., Ill., Aug. 20, 1852, aged 39; m. in Nelson, N. Y., Jan. 2, 1832, FREDERICK AVERY KINNEY,[1] and removed to Bernadotte, Ill., about 1837. He was b. in Nelson, N. Y., Nov. 4, 1807, and d. in Bloomingdale, July 19, 1859, aged 52.

Moore Bissell, m. Sept. 25, 1662; gt. gr. son of John Bissell sen., who d. Oct. 3, 1667, aged 86. He was b. in England: "came to Windsor about 1640; was the first white settler [in Windsor] on the East side of the Connecticut, and the founder of a numerous, energetic and honorable family."— Stiles' *History of Ancient Windsor*.

[1] Son of Ezra Kinney (b. in Dutchess county, N. Y., Aug. 25, 1776, d. in Nelson, N. Y., Jan. 2, 1836) and w. Matilda Langworthy (b. in Stonington, Ct., Oct. 18, 1782) m. Nov. 23, 1800.

Mr. and Mrs. Kinney were greatly esteemed in the community where they lived. They would hardly have been selected, perhaps, as suitable pioneers to the then "far west," whither they so early emigrated. In point of education and refinement they were superior to the majority of the early settlers of those western wilds; but all their resources, mental and physical, were devoted to the developing and upbuilding of their chosen home, shared with their less fortunate neighbors, and made instrumental of good in numerous ways, such as only the truly charitable, laboring in the spirit of genuine Christianity, can devise and adopt. Their influence was widely felt and gratefully acknowledged. They were Universalists in religious faith and by church membership. They had five children:

7–130. Timothy Lee, b. in Erieville, N. Y., April 23, 1834, d. in Erieville, Sept. 30, 1834.

7–131. Frederica Grace, b. in Erieville, Dec. 5, 1835, res. 1873, in Grouse, Kane Co., Ill. GOODWIN.

7–132. Kate Eugenia, b. in Bloomingdale, Ill., March 25, 1848, res. 1873, Grouse, Ill.

7–133. May Augusta, b. in Bloomingdale, June 24, 1852, d. Aug. 20, 1850.

7–134. Fred Dean, b. in Bloomingdale, June 24, 1852, d. in Aurora, Ill., June 14, 1866. He was run over by railroad cars, losing both legs, and survived but a few hours.[1]

6–54. LUCIUS ROBERTS DAWSON, house and bridge carpenter and builder, b. in Canton, Ct., March 15, 1815, m. in Cazenovia, N. Y., *Julia Emeline Blackman*,[2] March 5, 1838. She was b. in Linklean, Chenango Co., N. Y., April 4, 1820.

---

[1] He was a pupil in the Clark Seminary, at Aurora, and was a lad of great promise. For some years he had been living at Aurora, in the family of his brother-in-law and sister, Mr. and Mrs. Goodwin, who supplied as far as possible the place of parents to him during his orphanage. "He was kind and amiable in disposition, genial and gentlemanly in manners, respectful and dutiful to teachers. He was sincere, outspoken and upright, uniform in temper and spirit, determined in purpose. He was without reproach, so far as we know, in words, habits and morals.........In some departments of study he ranked among the best in his classes......On his way home [from school] he was crushed beneath the cars. His fellow pupils, from their windows in the seminary, witnessed his misfortune, and hastened to his presence, and attended him, so far as their services were needed, to the last. He exhibited unusual presence of mind and fortitude. Much more calm than any about him, he gave directions as to taking him home, and continued quiet and self possessed as long as he lived. From time to time he ministered words of comfort to his deeply afflicted and sorrowful friends. He was buried at Bloomingdale."— *Obituary.*

[2] Dau. of Roswell Blackman (b. Oct. 22, 1791) and w. Lorinda Haywood (b. Aug. 21, 1799) m. April 29, 1819; gr. dau. of Enoch Blackman (b. Sept. 15, 1760) and w. Abigail Clark (b. Sept. 22, 1760) both of Conn.

He enlisted, May, 1863, in the Construction Corps, U. S. Volunteers, and was for some months in service in Virginia, until the company to which he belonged was disbanded. He reënlisted in December, 1863, in the same service, under Major E. L. Wentz, and was stationed in Tennessee, in charge of a party of men who were employed in cutting and dressing timber for the rebuilding of bridges destroyed in the war; afterwards built a shingle-mill for the government at Lenoir, Tenn., of which he had charge about one year.

They res. 1873, in Binghamton, N. Y., and have had five children:

7–135. Lucia Diane, b. in Cazenovia, N. Y., July 9, 1839; res. 1873, in Binghamton. GRAY.
7–136. Frances Mary, b. in Linklaen, N. Y., June 26, 1841, d. in Chenango, N. Y., Jan. 23, 1860. PARKER.
7–137. Lee De Forest, b. in Linklaen, Aug. 22, 1843, res. 1873, Binghamton; *m.*
7–138. Charles Edward, b. in Chenango Forks, N. Y., Feb. 28, 1846, d. at Yorktown, Va., June 16, 1864.[1]
7–139. Florence Marie, b. in Chenango Forks, July 28, 1853, d. Nov. 20, 1853.

6–56. *Maria Louisa Dawson*, b. in Cazenovia township, N. Y., Sept. 7, 1819, m. 1st. in Cazenovia, Oct. 29, 1839, EMILIUS AHIRA BATES,[2] farmer, b. in Nelson, N. Y., Feb. 9, 1811, d. in same place, Dec. 8, 1853, aged 42. He was some time a student at Hamilton College, Madison, N. Y. In his youth he was a skeptic on religious subjects, but for nearly twenty years prior to his decease he was a devoted member and local preacher of the Methodist Episcopal Church. He had a good degree of literary skill, with refined and cultivated tastes; and even in failing health, and through a long, weary

[1] Private in 27th Regt. N. Y. S. Vols., enlisted Sept. 15, 1863, transferred to the 168th Regt., and d. in the military hospital at Yorktown after only five days' illness. "His regiment was to be disbanded about the eighteenth of June, and I suppose the dear boy's mind turned often to that hope. His last words were, 'I am mustered out of service — I am going home.' He was a brave lad. His letters were full of the true soldierly spirit." — *Extract from a letter.*

[2] Son of Rufus Bates (b. in Pownal, Vt., Nov. 1, 1788) and w. Sally Marshall, (b. in Tolland, Mass., May 30, 1788, d. in Wampsville, N. Y., Aug. 11, 1873), m. in Nelson, N. Y., April 5, 1810, where they res. 1871; gr. son of Archibald Bates, (b. in Rhode Island, March 15, 1763, d. Jan. 11. 1838,) and w. Hannah Wever, m. in Vt., Nov. 8, 1787. (2d. w. Hannah Dorrence Coman, m. Aug. 29, 1808.)

illness, maintained a cheerful spirit until the last. They had three children:

7–140. [BATES]. Edward Francis, b. in Cazenovia tp., Dec. 30, 1840, d. in Washington, D. C., March 6, 1864, aged 23 ; *m.*

7–141. William Rufus, b. in Cazenovia tp., June 28, 1845, res. 1873, at Saginaw, Mich. ; *m.*

7–142. Florence Maria, b. in Nelson, N. Y., April 30, 1852, d. April 21, 1853, aged 1 year.

She m. 2d. in Cazenovia, N. Y., Jan. 18, 1859, LEMAN DAVID COBURN, merchant, b. in Truxton, N. Y., April 22, 1817. He was agent, by governor's appointment, 1865, for the state of New York, to care for the sick and wounded soldiers of the state, and for the exchanged prisoners of war ; with headquarters at Annapolis, Md. They reside, 1873, at Addison, N. Y. A very pleasant celebration of their "tin wedding" occurred on the evening of Jan. 18, 1869 — a large company being present, some of whom had journeyed long distances for the purpose of attending.

6–57. OLIVER WINSTON DAWSON, b. in Cazenovia township, Madison Co., N. Y., Feb. 1, 1821. Before he was 13 years of age he engaged as a clerk in the store of his cousin, F. W. Meloy (6–41 of this record), at Chenango Forks, N. Y., remaining there about one year, and he was afterwards similarly employed for longer periods at Pompey Hill and Salina, N. Y. On the death of his father, in March, 1843, he succeeded to the charge of the business and family. He removed to Syracuse, N. Y., in 1845 ; became landlord of the Fayette House in that city, and subsequently of hotels in Oran and Delphi, N. Y., selling out the three latter establishments, however, in each instance, within one year after commencing business. He spent about two years in the service of the saddlery hardware house of C. Pope & Co., of Syracuse, as traveling agent for the sale of their goods, and for some years was also employed as traveling agent for the sale of drugs and patent medicines. In 1853, he removed to Adrian, Mich., and accepted a clerkship in the General Ticket office of the Michigan Southern and Northern Indiana Railroad, being the chief clerk of the "Local Ticket" Department of that office, which position he has ever since held. The office, however, has been

Eng^d by H B Hall & Sons, 62 Fulton St N Y

E. J. Dawson

several times removed, being successively, after leaving Adrian, at Toledo, O., Chicago, Ill., and at present (since the consolidation with the Lake Shore R. R.) at Cleveland, Ohio. The changes in administration of this great railway interest have been still more frequent, but under all changes his valuable services have been retained, he having occupied the same desk for a period of over nineteen years. He possesses an organizing mind, and conducts the complicated business of his office with admirable system and efficiency. He m. in Cazenovia, Jan. 28, 1845, *Sarah Adaline Long*,[1] who was b. in Hartsville, town of Pompey, N. Y., Sept. 19, 1822. They resided, from about 1858 to 1872 in Toledo, O., removed in 1872, to Cleveland, in that state, and returned to Toledo, 1873. They have had five chn.:

7–143. Sarah Elizabeth, b. in Cazenovia, Dec. 17, 1846, res. 1873, in Toledo.[2]

7–144. Timothy John, b. in Oran, N. Y., Nov. 21, 1849, res. 1873, in Toledo.[3]

7–145. Oliver James, b. in Cazenovia, Jan. 18, 1853, d. in Adrian, Mich., Jan. 9, 1855.

7–146. Mary Louisa, b. in Adrian, Mich., Aug. 28, 1856, d. Sept. 15, 1856.

7–147. Henry Hobart, b. in Toledo, O., Sept. 18, 1860.

6–58. Edward Sebried Dawson, b. in Nelson, N. Y., July 22, 1822. From his twelfth year until he became of age he was employed as a clerk in country stores, of which time the last seven years were spent in the service of Mr. Horace Wheaton, at Pompey Hill, N. Y. On leaving the service of Mr. Wheaton, he devoted a few months to acquiring a knowledge of dentistry, which profession, however, he abandoned in favor of a mercantile career. In 1844 he removed to Syracuse, N. Y., to take the position of bookkeeper for the firm of

---

[1] Dau. of Nehemiah Benjamin Colbay Long, merchant tailor (b. in Va., Oct. 29, 1782, d. in Oran, N. Y., July 31, 1828,) and w. Sarah Rouse, (b. in West Greenwich, Kent Co., R. I., Jan. 27, 1793, res. 1871, Elmwood, Peoria Co., Ill.; dau. of Benj. and *Ruth Gorton* Rouse, both natives of West Greenwich), m. Dec. 17, 1812; gr. dau. of Benjamin Long and w. Mary Colbay, who was Dutch or of Dutch descent. The gr. parents moved to Schenectady, N. Y., in 1796, where they resided several years, and kept a hotel, and where Benj. Long died. After his death his wid. lived with a son, Moses Long, printer, in Albany, N. Y. He dying, she removed to Va., where she had other children living, and where she died.

[2] An accomplished and successful teacher, in one of the public schools of Toledo.

[3] Telegraph operator. Formerly, for more than two years, assistant, and since 1871, chief, train despatcher for the Eastern and Southern Divisions of the Lake Shore and Michigan Southern Railway.

Wheaton & Robinson, dealers in general hardware, with whom he remained three years, which were succeeded by two years in the service, in a similar capacity, of Messrs Charles Pope & Co., dealers in and manufacturers of saddlery hardware. He became a partner in this firm March 1, 1849, and continued in the same establishment and business under the different firm names of Charles Pope & Co., Pope & Dawson, Wheaton & Dawson and E. S. Dawson & Co., until Dec. 1, 1856, when he retired from the business. From the first of January following he was engaged in the business of Insurance, until Oct. 1, 1858, when he reëntered the saddlery hardware trade under the firm name of E. S. Dawson & Co. In this business he continued, conducting an extensive trade and a large manufacturing establishment, until Jan. 1, 1869, when he accepted the position of treasurer of the Onondaga County Savings Bank, which position he still occupies. This bank, of which he had been, for many years previously, a trustee, is the oldest institution of the kind in Syracuse, and one of the largest in the state. He is the inventor and patentee of several valuable improvements in saddlery and harness hardware, as also of other useful inventions, and possesses business qualifications of a high order.

He m. in Pompey Hill, N. Y., Sept. 18, 1849, *Clarissa Hannah Marsh*,[1] who was b. in Pompey, Dec. 19, 1825. They res. 1873, in Syracuse, and have had four children, all b. in that city:

7–148. Flora Marsh, b. June 3, 1850.
7–149. Edward Seymour, b. Sept. 29, 1852.
7–150. Homer Wheaton, b. March 6, 1856.
7–151. John Barker, b. Jan. 13, 1863.

6–60. Charles Carroll Dawson, compiler of these records, was b. in Nelson, N. Y., Feb. 4, 1833. When in

[1] Dau. of Moses Seymour Marsh (b, at New Milford, Ct., Dec. 28, 1792, d. at Syracuse, Oct. 12, 1843) and w. Flora Wheaton (b. at New Milford, July 23, 1799, d. at Syracuse, Sept. 17, 1847), m. at Pompey, N. Y., Aug. 19, 1820. He was a merchant at Pompey, afterwards cashier for many years and president of the Onondaga County Bank, at Syracuse; son of Rev. Truman and *Clarissa Seymour* Marsh. Flora Wheaton, above named, was dau. of Augustus Wheaton, farmer, one of the early settlers of the town of Pompey, to which he removed from Dutchess county, N. Y., about 1810 or '12. Rev. Truman Marsh was rector for many years (from 1809 or earlier) of the Episcopal church in Litchfield, Conn., where he d. April, 1851, aged about 80 years. Clarissa Seymour, sister of the late Henry Seymour (father of Ex. Gov. Horatio Seymour, of New York), d. at Litchfield, Sept. 2, 1865, aged 93 years, 1 month.

his thirteenth year he became a clerk in the bookstore of L. W. Hall & Co., of Syracuse, with whom he remained something more than a year, leaving their service to accept a clerkship in the general country store of Camp and Stone, at Trumansburg, N. Y. Two years later he returned to Syracuse, and became a clerk in the book establishment of Wynkoop & Brother, successors to his former employers. After about two years spent in their employ he became bookkeeper to Mr. Ezra Towne, grocer and insurance agent, in whose service he remained until 1853, when he removed to New York city, to fill the position of bookkeeper and cashier in the book publishing house of Daniel Burgess & Co., then leading school book publishers in that city. With this firm he remained until its dissolution in 1856, which occurred in consequence of the death of Mr. Daniel Burgess. In the fall of that year he made a collecting tour through the western states as representative of the administrator of Mr. B.'s estate. As a result of this trip came his removal to Des Moines, Polk county, Iowa, in the month of January following, where, as one of the firm of Redhead & Dawson, he engaged in business as a bookseller, publisher and stationer. In this business he continued until the winter of 1859–60, when, having been elected superintendent of Public Schools for that county, he disposed of his interest in the book business and devoted himself to the duties of his office, in connection with the business of a real estate and insurance agency, which he established about this time. He also became assistant state agent of the Aetna Insurance Company, of Hartford, Conn., traveling extensively for the purpose of adjusting losses, appointing local agents, inspecting the condition of various local agencies, and performing other like duties. At this time also he occasionally wrote for the papers and magazines in prose and verse,[1] wrote and delivered various lectures and addresses, and served as permanent secretary of sundry literary, social and church organizations. In the second year of his term of office as school superintendent he resigned the same in favor of his deputy and friend Dr. Wilmot H. Dickinson; and a little time after received the appointment of deputy clerk of the United

[1] Of his effusions in verse, a portion have been collected and "PRINTED FOR PRIVATE USE" in a volume entitled "*Occasional Thoughts and Fancies*, by C. C. D."

States Circuit Court of the District of Iowa,[1] which office he held about two years, meanwhile continuing his business as a Real Estate and Insurance agent, and also at the same time as for some years previously, serving as secretary of the City School District. In the spring of 1863 he was appointed chief clerk in the office of the provost marshal[2] for the fifth congressional district of Iowa, and assisted in organizing the provost service in that extensive district, then comprising twenty-three counties.[3] In this very laborious position he remained nearly two years, conducting also, during a part of the time, the agencies before mentioned, which, however, he surrendered early in 1864. In the fall of the same year considerations of health, and the desire of availing himself of certain advantages of study and instruction, with change of air and scene, and relief from business cares, induced him to resign his clerkship in the provost service, and remove with his family to Ann Arbor, Michigan, where he became a student in the State University. He remained there in that capacity during the residue of that year and all of the year following, graduating in the Law Department of the University in the spring of 1866. While making arrangements to return to Iowa for the purpose of engaging there in the practice of law, he was offered, during a visit to New York in the summer of 1866, and accepted, the position of corresponding and advertising clerk to the parties then controlling by contract the sale of the Congress and Empire spring waters.[4] In 1869 he became a member of the board of trustees of the company owning the

---

[1] The clerk at that time was the Hon. W. G. Woodward, of Muscatine, formerly chief justice of the Supreme Court of Iowa.

[2] Capt. S. C. Brownell, one of the most genial of men, and best of officers. He now resides at Medina, N. Y.

[3] The provost service was the great system by means of which the army of the Union was continually reinforced. There were then no railroads in the district, and the District Headquarters were 180 miles from the General Rendezvous of the state, to which all recruits and arrested deserters were required to be forwarded. The providing of transportation, clothing and subsistence, under these circumstances, for large numbers of men, was attended with peculiar difficulties, and involved a multiplicity of accounts, and the necessity of a large correspondence.

[4] Messrs. HOTCHKISS SONS, 58 Cliff St., connected with which establishment was their wholesale hardware house, 92 Beekman street, chiefly for the sale of goods produced at their extensive factory at Bridgeport, Conn. A portion of Mr. D.'s time was devoted to similar duties connected with the hardware establishment, and he also had charge, for about six months, Mr. B. B. Hotchkiss being in Europe, of a factory in New York, belonging to the latter, for the manufacture of iron wheels and of solid shot and shell for rifled cannon.

spring property at Saratoga, and manager of the company's business in New York city, which positions he still retains.[1]

He m. in Brooklyn, N. Y., according to the order of the Society of Friends, May 21, 1856, *Jeannette Margaret Simonson*, who was b. in Westfield township, Staten Island, March 19, 1829.[2] They reside, 1873, in Plainfield, N. J., and have had five children:

7–152. Howard, b. in Des Moines, Iowa, May 26, 1857.
7–153. Colman, b. in Des Moines, May 7, 1859.
7–154. Robert, b. in Des Moines, Aug. 14, 1861, d. of scarlet fever and diphtheria, in Des Moines, July 16, 1863.
7–155. Charles Wilmot, b. in Plainfield, N. J., Dec. 10, 1867.
7–156. Catharine Ruhamah, b. in Plainfield, Nov. 21, 1870.
They have also an adopted daughter,
Mary Hill Dawson, b. in Brooklyn, N. Y., Nov. 21, 1853.[3]

---

[1] Since 1866, he has made several extended trips through the western and southern states: also, in the fall of 1871, a visit to Europe — the former on business, the latter chiefly for health and pleasure.

[2] Prior to her marriage a teacher in the Packer Collegiate Institute, Brooklyn, N. Y.; dau. of John Simonson (b. at Freshkill, near Richmond, Staten Island, Feb. 3, 1803, d. June 25, 1857), and w. Catharine Ann Harned (b. in Woodbridge, N. J., Nov. 23, 1805), m. in Woodbridge, June 26, 1824. She now, 1873, res. in Plainfield, N. J., wid. of Stephen Vail. John Simonson was son of John Simonson (b. at Richmond, S. I., May 24, 1764, d. April 9, 1854, aged 90, farmer, and tanner and currier), and w. Margaret Swaim (b. S. I., Aug. 21, 1782, d. Sept. 29, 1845), m. about 1800; gr. son of Arthur Simonson (d. Feb. 26, 1808), and w. Elizabeth Egbert, whose ancestors were Huguenots. The ancestors of Arthur Simonson were from Holland, and among the first settlers of Staten Island. Margaret Swaim was dau. of Benj. Swaim, farmer, of Staten Island, and w. Martha, dau. of John Marshall. Catharine Ann Harned was dau. of Jacob Harned (b. 7 mo. 9, 1769, d. 9 mo. 5, 1828), and w. Catharine Potter (d. Oct. 7, 1815, aged about 46) m. 1794; gr. dau. of Phinneas Potter and w. Elizabeth Hampton; gt. gr. dau. of Andrew Hampton (b. 12 mo. 10, 1722), and w.——Mercereau. Jacob Harned was son of Jonathan Harned (b. 2 mo. 18, 1746, d. 1811), and w. Sarah Laing (dau. of David and *Anna Randolph* Laing, of Woodbridge), m. 7 mo. 16, 1766. Jonathan Harned was son of Nathaniel Harned (b. 10 mo. 3, 1716), and w. Anna Clawson, (dau. of John Clawson, of Woodbridge), m. 4 mo. 17, 1742. Nathaniel, Jonathan and Jacob Harned were all members of the Society of Friends, all b. and d. at Woodbridge, where they carried on successively the same business — that of tanners and curriers — in connection with the farm, which was the family estate. Nathaniel Harned suffered notably in person and estate during the Revolutionary war on account of his strict adherence to his principles as a non-combatant — being plundered and oppressed in turn by both parties, American and British, as were many others of his sect. Andrew Hampton, above named, was a quaker of wealth and

---

[3] Her only bro., Warren Burleigh Hill, (b. in Brooklyn, Aug. 15, 1850), d. of diphtheria, at Mr. D.'s residence in Des Moines, May 29, 1863. Their parents were John Warren Hill (b. in Portsmouth, N. H., June 20, 1819, d. while acting assistant paymaster, U. S. Navy, at Pensacola, Fla., Sept. 26, 1863), and w. Mary Augusta Simonson (b. in Rahway, N. J., Oct. 17, 1825, d. in Brooklyn, Sept. 29, 1856, sister to Mrs. Dawson), m. Nov. 14, 1849.

6-61. *Sophia Mersena Beecher*, b. in New Hartford, Conn., Oct. 5, 1813, d. in Dunkirk, N. Y., Sept. 30, 1867, aged 54. Her death was justly regarded as "a bereavement of the whole community," which had "long felt the influence of her practical virtues and unostentatious charities." She m. April 21, 1831, TRUMAN ROWLEY COLMAN, who was b. in Coventry, Conn., Nov. 9, 1809, and resides, 1873, in Dunkirk.[1] His parents removed to Madison county, N. Y., in his boyhood. At the age of twelve he left home, and thenceforth not only supported himself independently, but assisted, to some extent, his father's family. He first lived two years with the Hon. Gerrit Smith, who, discerning in him capacity superior to his position, procured for him a clerkship in Peterboro, in the store of his brother-in-law, Mr. Backus. In 1826, his employer discontinuing business, he went to Utica, where he found a situation with a mercantile firm whose business was transferred to Rochester in 1828, and to Ellicottville in 1829, he going with it, and remaining as clerk in the establishment until 1832, when he became a partner. The next year he became sole owner. The stock consisted of dry goods, groceries, drugs and medicines, and a large variety of miscellaneous goods, including, as was common in the country stores of the time, spirituous liquors. He signalized his new position by discontinuing wholly the sale of the latter, thus becoming the first merchant in the county to adopt this reform. He has ever since been a consistent and influential advocate of the temperance cause. He continued in the mercantile business

---

prominence in Elizabeth, as early as 1688; appointed deputy to the colonial legislature, 1698; d. Jan., 1738-9. He built a brick house on the site of the present parsonage of St. John's church in Elizabeth. A portion of the original house still remains, in which is seen the old corner stone, inscribed with name and date—[1697—Andrew Hampton and Margret.] His w. was Margaret Cummin. They had 8 children, who were bapt. by Rev. Geo. Keith (an Episcopal missionary, formerly a quaker preacher), in Nov. 1703, himself and w. having, so writes Keith, "come over from Quakerism to the Church." His son Andrew, however, though probably one of the children bapt. by Keith, was a quaker. A. H., the deputy, supposed a son of James Hampton, who emigrated from Salem, Mass., to Southampton, L. I., about 1652.

[1] Son of Asa Colman (b. in Coventry, Ct., Nov. 7, 1785, d. in Dunkirk, N. Y., July 19, 1859), and w. Betsey Trapp (b. July 17, 1787, d. April 30, 1833, dau. of William Trapp, of Coventry), m. in Coventry, Oct. 17, 1804; gr. son of Asa Colman (d. in Logan Co., O., about 1845, aged 87) and w. Hannah Babcock (d. about 1847, aged 87), m. in Coventry about 1775, moved thence to Cazenovia, N. Y., about 1811, and thence to Logan Co., O., about 1817. The father of the last named Asa Colman, lived to be over 90 years of age. The Colmans were at Coventry as early as 1713, and probably earlier.—See *Records*, town clerk's office.

at Ellicottville until 1844, when he became agent for the proprietors of extensive tracts of lands in western New York, known as the "Holland Land Purchase." Three years later he purchased a large interest in the property, to the management and sale of which he afterwards devoted several years. In 1854 he removed to Dunkirk, and established the Lake Shore Bank, of which he is now president. Mr. Colman is distinguished for his liberality and public spirit. That "the liberal hand maketh rich" has been abundantly verified in his case. His charities are manifold and ungrudging.[1] They had seven children, all b. in Ellicottville:

7–157. Charles Henry, b. July 5, 1832, d. Aug. 19, 1832.
7–158. Emily, b. July 3, 1833, d. Dec. 9, 1833.
7–159. Albert Emilius, b. Feb. 8, 1835, res. 1873, in Dunkirk; *m.*
7–160. Lydia Beecher, b. June 8, 1837, d. in Dunkirk, Oct. 8, 1872, aged 35. VAN BUREN.
7–161. Ellen Sophia, b. Aug. 25, 1840, res. 1873, in Dunkirk. BARRETT.
7–162. Mary Melissa, b. Dec. 31, 1842, res. 1873, in Dunkirk. GIFFORD.
7–163. William Truman, b. Feb. 18, 1845, res. 1873, in Dunkirk; *m.*

6–62. *Harriet Winston Beecher*, b. in Batavia, N. Y., Aug. 16, 1816, resides, 1873, in Ellicottville. She m. in Ellicottville, Dec. 24, 1833, DELOS ENOCH SILL,[2] who was b. in Cooperstown, N. Y., April 13, 1811, and d. in Ellicottville, Feb. 12, 1869, aged 58. He was well known for many years as a prominent and influential editor and politician. He was for twenty-five years publisher of the *Cattaraugus Freeman*; twice candidate for presidential elector;[3] messenger, in 1848, to convey the vote of the Electoral College of New York to Washington; agent for the New York Indians, by appointment of President Lincoln, 1861–64. Of commanding presence and winning address, ardent in his attachments, impulsive and enthusiastic in his nature, and untiring in his energies, he wielded an influence in political affairs which was hardly second

[1] He was candidate for presidential elector on the Liberal Republican and Democratic state ticket, fall of 1872.

[2] Son of Enoch Sill (b. in Saybrook, Conn., 1782, d. in Springville, N. Y., Aug. 1850) and w. Mary Potter (dau. of Evans Potter, Cooperstown), m. in Cooperstown, 1805; gr. son of Ezra Sill (b. in Silltown, Lyme, Ct., abt. 1753, d. at Saybrook) and w. Charity Pratt.

[3] Elected to the office on each occasion, voting, in 1848, for Zachary Taylor; in 1856, for John C. Fremont.

to that of any other man in his county or district. "As a man he was just and upright; as a citizen, liberal and public spirited; as a neighbor, kind, sympathizing and obliging; as a husband and father, affectionate and indulgent." He was "a kind, tender-hearted, faithful friend; a pleasant, genial, original, witty companion." They had two children, both b. in Ellicottville:

7–164. Charles Delos, b. Aug. 28, 1843, res. 1873, in Ellicottville; *m.*
7–165. Harriet Beecher, b. May 14, 1853, res. 1873, in Ellicottville.

6–63. *Emily Frances Beecher*, b. in Batavia, N. Y., March 3, 1818, m. June 3, 1838, HARLAN COLMAN, merchant, who was b. in Cazenovia, N. Y., Feb. 9, 1816; brother to Mr. Truman R. Colman, who m. Sophia M. Beecher (6–61). Mr. C. commenced a business life as a clerk in a country store at the age of fifteen. He removed to Ellicottville about the year 1834, and to Dunkirk in 1852. Since residing in Dunkirk he has been engaged as a Forwarding and Commission Merchant, also in the grain and milling business, and in the hardware trade, and more recently has been largely interested in the oil business of Western Pennsylvania. His enterprises are extensive, and his business ability of a high order. They reside, 1873, in Dunkirk, N. Y., and have had five children, all b. in Ellicottville:

7–166. Frances Emily, b. March 22, 1839, res. 1873, in Dunkirk. WHITTLESEY.
7–167. Juliette Clarissa, b. Oct. 28, 1843, res. 1873, in Dunkirk. ALLING.
7–168. Grace Eunecia, b. Aug. 1, 1845, res. 1873, in Dunkirk. CANDEE.
7–169. Harriet Sophia, b. July 6, 1847, d. in Ellicottville, April 13, 1848.
7–170. Charles Harlan, b. Aug. 13, 1849, d. in Ellicottville, Nov. 22, 1849.

6–64. *Juliette Beecher*, b. in Batavia, N. Y., Feb. 18, 1820, m. Oct. 9, 1848, PETER VAN RENSSELAER SKINNER,[1] merchant, who was b. in Redding, Steuben Co., N. Y., Jan. 7, 1815. They res. 1873, in Ellicottville, where their two children were born:

---

[1] Son of Addi Skinner (b. in Conn. abt. 1783, d. April 1832) and w. Mary Van Zandt (b. abt. 1786, d. in Van Buren Co., Iowa, 1862, dau. of Peter Van Zandt) m. in Ovid, N. Y., abt. 1806; gr. son of Wait Skinner, d. at Skinner's Eddy, Pa.

7–171. [Skinner.] Florence, b. July 25, 1849, d. Dec. 3, 1850.
7–172. Sophie, b. July 22, 1851, res. 1873, in Ellicottville. Smith.

6–65. William Henry Beecher, b. in Batavia, N. Y., Dec. 24, 1821; editor and proprietor of *The Whig and Advocate*, at Angelica, N. Y., 1853–1856, and connected with other newspaper enterprises, at Ellicottville and Dunkirk, N. Y., and in Illinois. He is the author of many graceful poems. He res. 1873, at La Salle, Ill. He m. in Hamburgh, N. Y., *Helen M. White*, Feb. 23, 1852.[1] One child:

7–173. Eva, b. in Angelica, N. Y., March 15, 1854, res. 1873, Buffalo, N. Y.

6–67. Moses Beecher, b. in Ellicottville, N. Y., July 26, 1827; hardware merchant; also cashier of the First National Bank of Warren, Pa.: elected to that position on the organization of the Bank, in August, 1864 — a very popular and efficient officer. He m. 1st. in Fredonia, N. Y., Oct. 22, 1851, *Sarah Taylor*,[2] who was b. in Norwalk, Ct., Aug. 28, 1831, and d. in Ellicottville, July 9, 1853, aged 22, leaving one child:

7–174. Jessie Cumming, b. in Ellicottville, April 7, 1853, res. 1873, in Warren.

He m. 2d. in Utica, N. Y., Aug. 2, 1855, *Emily E. Downer*,[3] b. in Utica, Feb. 27, 1831. They res. 1873, in Warren, Pa., and have had five children:

7–175. Charles Emerson, b. in Dunkirk, N. Y., Oct. 9, 1856.
7–176. Richard Cary, b. in Warren, Pa., Sept. 5, 1860.
7–177. Truman Colman, b. in Warren, April 7, 1862.
7–178. Harry Downer, b. in Warren, Feb. 26, 1844, d. in Warren, April 22, 1865.
7–179. Mary Esther, b. in Warren, May 30, 1865.

6–68. Charles Mortimer Beecher, b. in Ellicottville, N. Y., Jan. 31, 1829; a practical printer; has been editor and publisher of newspapers at Ellicottville, N. Y., Sabula, Iowa, Dunkirk, Hornellsville and Corning, N. Y., and is now, 1873, editor and publisher of *The Genesee Valley Free Press*, at Wellsville, N. Y. He m. in Cuba, N. Y., Dec. 22, 1852, *Amelia Elizabeth Hastings*,[4] who was b. in Rush, Monroe Co., N. Y., Feb. 7, 1832. They have had five children:

---

[1] Or March 23, 1853, as communicated by another.
[2] Dau. of Abijah Fitch Taylor, Fredonia.
[3] Dau. of Andrew Otis and *Esther McLeod Emerson* Downer, of Detroit, Mich.
[4] Dau. of Warner and *Elizabeth Fisher* Hastings.

7–180. [BEECHER.] Lucia Emily, b. in Ellicottville, Jan. 23, 1854.
7–181. Charles Moses, b. in Ellicottville, March 10, 1855.
7–182. Susan Juliette, b. in Bellevue, Iowa, Jan. 3, 1859, d. in Almond, Alleghany Co., N. Y., May 20, 1867.
7–183. Guy Stone, b. in Dunkirk, Sept. 3, 1865, d. in Warren, Pa., March 12, 1866.
7–184. Elizabeth Fisher, b. in Hornellsville, July 30, 1869.

6–70. *Lucia Annette Beecher*, b. in Ellicottville, N. Y., Dec. 27, 1833, d. in Dunkirk, N. Y., May 7, 1866, aged 33. She m. in Ellicottville, April 9, 1851, RICHARD CARY,[1] merchant, b. in Boston, Erie Co., N. Y., Feb. 11, 1827, res. 1873, in Dunkirk, of which place he was postmaster, by appointment of President Lincoln, from March 25, 1861, until his removal, for political causes, by President Johnson, Jan. 24, 1866. They had four children:

7–185. Richard Lincoln, b. in Ellicottville, July 1, 1854.
7–186. Eugene Charles, b. in Dunkirk, Nov. 21, 1857.
7–187. Philip, b. in Dunkirk, May 4, 1864.
7–188. Lucia Beecher, b. in Dunkirk, May 6, 1866.

6–72. ROLLIN LAUREAT DAWSON, b. in Nelson, N. Y., March 25, 1825, d. in Haydenville, Mass., Aug. 24, 1857, aged 32. He was one of the earliest manufacturers of gold pens at Syracuse, N. Y.; removed to Haydenville about 1846, and in connection with Mr. Hayden, a button manufacturer, and the founder of the place, established there the manufacture of gold pens, and gold and silver pen and pencil cases. This business became very extensive and profitable, its success being largely due to his ingenuity and inventive skill in the adaptation and production of machinery suited to the various processes of

---

[1] Son of Luther Harvey Cary (b. in Williamsburgh, Mass., Feb. 19, 1800), and w. Lucy Doolittle (b. in Wallingford, Vt., April 25, 1794, dau. of Calvin Doolittle) m. at Little Valley, N. Y., Dec. 16, 1821; gr. son of Richard Cary (b. in Mansfield, Ct., Jan. 15, 1759, d. in Boston, N. Y., Dec. 1841), and w. Susannah Ford, m. in Williamsburgh, Mass., about 1782-3; gt. gr. son of Joseph Cary (b. in Windham, Ct., Sept. 28, 1723), and w. Phebe Mack; m. 1747, lived in Mansfield, Ct. The last named Joseph Cary, was son of Jabez Cary (b. in Windham, Ct., July 12, 1691), and w. Hannah Hendee, m. Nov. 15, 1722; gr. son of Dea. Joseph Cary (b. 1663, d. Jan. 10, 1722), and w. Hannah ———, m. 1688, removed to Windham, 1689; gt. gr. son of John Cary, a "Plymouth Pilgrim" — so described by his distinguished descendant, Gen. S. F. Cary, of Cincinnati, O., but not so recognized by *Savage*, who styles him *of Bridgewater*, "said to have come from neighborhood of Bristol, England, at the age of 25, and set down first, 1637, at Duxbury." He m. June, 1644, Elizabeth, dau. of Francis Godfrey; "was the first town clerk, and early his name was written *Carew*, but as the English pronounce that name *Cary*, spelling soon followed sound."— Savage's *Gen. Dict.*, art: Cary.

manufacture. He established, 1851, the firm of Dawson, Warren and Hyde, in New York city.

He m. March 23, 1847, *Jane Elizabeth Lewis*, who was b. in Middletown, Ct., Oct. 6, 1825, and res. 1873, in Northampton, Mass. They had one child:

7–189. Mary Isabella, b. in Haydenville, Aug. 9, 1855.

6–73. LUCIEN AUGUSTUS DAWSON, b. in Nelson, N. Y., Aug. 10, 1826, m. Oct. 10, 1855, *Ellen Eliza Pierce*,[1] who was b. in Peru, Mass., Aug. 28, 1838. He is a broker and capitalist; place of business, Northampton. They reside in Springfield, Mass., and have had three children, all b. in that place:

7–190. Lute Elizur, b. June 24, 1866, d. June 25, 1866.
7–191. Clara Eliza, b. Feb. 23, 1867.
7–192. Greta Cynthia, b. July 5, 1871.

6–74. DAVID DERASTUS DAWSON, b. in Pompey, N. Y., Aug. 13, 1828; farmer; was quarter-master's sergeant, 1861, in 13th Illinois Cavalry, (Col. Theodore Hartman), and served about one year — discharged on account of sickness; d. in Chicago, Ill., Sept. 20, 1864 — buried in Barrington. He m. Nov. 7, 1860, *Electa Chase*, who was b. in Bridgeway, Orleans Co., N. Y., Dec. 13, 1842, and d. in Chicago, Aug. 18, 1866. They had two children:

7–193. Henry, b. in Barrington, Ill., April 9, 1862, d. April 17, 1862.
7–194. Nellie L., b in Barrington, Aug. 29, 1864, d. Feb. 23, 1865.

6–78. MORRIS DAWSON, farmer, was b. in Paris, Oneida Co., N. Y., Nov. 26, 1803, m. in Danby, N. Y., Oct. 7, 1827, *Sophia Smith*, who was b. in Aurelius, Cayuga Co., N. Y., Oct. 6, 1806. They res. 1873, in Wellsboro, Tioga Co., Pa. Seven children, all b. in Danby, N. Y.:

7–195. Amanda, b. Aug. 6, 1828, res. 1873, Wellsboro, Pa. HART.
7–196. Harmon Jackson, b. April 13, 1830, res. 1873, Wellsboro; *m.*
7–197. Charles Ryle, b. July 31, 1832, res. 1873, Wellsboro; *m.*

---

[1] Dau. of Isaac S. Pierce, stone mason (b. 1802), and w. Eliza H. Thomson; gr. dau. of Ebenezer Pierce, of Peru, Mass. (b. 1770), who m. a dau. of John and Hepsibah Leland. Ebenezer Pierce (whose name, in the *Pierce Family Record* is printed *Eber*) was son of Shadrach Pierce jr., (b. 1750), and w. Anna Bridges; gr. son of Shadrach Pierce (b. 1717), and w. Abigail Hoskins; gt. gr. son of Thomas Pierce and w. Naomi Booth. Thomas Pierce was son of Isaac Pierce (b. about 1661); gr. son of Abraham Pierce, who was of Plymouth colony, 1623.

7–198. John James, b. April 29, 1834, d. at Clarksburg, W. Va., Aug. 14, 1865, aged 31 ; *m.*
7–199. Wealthy, b. June 21, 1836, d. in Charleston, Pa., Jan. 30, 1863, aged 27. NICKERSON.
7–200. Ruth, b. May 10, 1843, d. Sept. 3, 1844, aged 1.
7–201. George Smith, b. Sept. 15, 1845, res. 1873, Wellsboro ; *m.*

6–80. *Almira Dawson*, b. in Paris, Oneida Co., N. Y., Jan. 9, 1805, d. in Wabash Valley, Indiana, Oct. 1, 1834, aged 29 ; m. in Danby, N. Y., March 19, 1824, JOHN HOBART, who d. in Indiana about 1860. They had seven children :

7–202. *A daughter*, b. about Dec., 1824, d. in infancy.
7–203. Walter, b. April, 1826, res. 1860, Indiana.
7–204. } *Twins*, b. about 1828, d. young.
7–205. }
7–206. Ophelia, b. about 1830, d. 1843.
7–207. Edmund, b. about 1832, d. young.
7–208. *A daughter*, b. 1834, d. in infancy.

6–81. *Emily Dawson*, b. in Paris, Oneida Co., N. Y., Nov. 8, 1807, res. 1873, Danby, N. Y. She m. 1st. in Danby, June 23, 1833, ASA PHELPS BUTTON, (son of Asa and *Sarah Luce* Button), b. in Mass., March 19, 1808, d. in Danby, June 4, 1834 ; farmer. They had one son :

7–209. Asa Wesley, b. in Danby, March 15, 1834, res. 1873, in Danby ; *m.*

She m. 2d. in Danby, April 14, 1838, HOWLAND SHERMAN WERDON, who was b. in Pauldingstown, Dutchess Co., N. Y., April 3, 1807, d. in town of Newfield, Tompkins Co., N. Y., Oct. 10, 1848 ; farmer. They had three children :

7–210. Lucinda, b. in Danby, Jan. 27, 1839, d. May 25, 1841.
7–211. Chester Lorenzo, b. in Newfield, Oct. 20, 1840, res. 1872, Ulysses, Tompkins Co., N. Y. ; *m.*
7–212. Ophelia A., b. in Newfield, Oct. 11, 1844, res. 1872, Sullivanville, N. Y. SLOCUM.

6–82. *Samantha Dawson*, b. in Utica, N. Y., June 27, 1811, m. 1st., in Danby, N. Y., Nov. 16, 1829, CRAWFORD FOX, who was b. in Otsego Co., N. Y., July 15, 1808, d. in Michigan, March 11, 1856. They had eight children :

7–213. Emeline Adams, b. in Caroline, Tompkins Co., N. Y., Aug. 11, 1832, res. 1870, Owasso, Mich. FULLER.
7–214. William John, b. in Addison, Steuben Co., N. Y., March 2, 1834, res. 1870, Venice, Mich. ; *m.*

7–215. [Fox.] Chester Dawson, b. in Erwin, Steuben Co., N. Y., Dec. 18, 1835, res. 1870, Shiawassee Co., Mich.; *m.*
7–216. Angeline S., b. in Southfield, Mich., Nov. 29, 1838, res. 1870, Owasso, Mich. HALL.
7–217. Crawford Samuel, b. in Brighton, Mich., Jan. 30, 1842, d. in U. S. Army, of typhoid fever, at Munfordsville, Ky., Nov. 3, 1862, aged 20.
7–218. *A twin brother* of Crawford — d. in infancy.
7–219. Milton Dawson, b in Brighton, Mich., Dec. 8, 1844, res. 1870, Duplain, Mich.; *m.*
7–220. Casandra A., b. in Cahocta, Mich., Dec. 14, 1850, res. 1870, Venice, Mich. GAINER.

Mrs. Fox m. 2d. Sept. 11, 1859, PETER VROMAN, b. in Herkimer county, N. Y., Feb. 4, 1813. They res. 1871, in Mungersville, Shiawassee Co., Mich.

6-83. NELSON DAWSON, farmer, b. in Danby, N. Y., June 8, 1813, m. in Spencer, N. Y., Nov. 5, 1835, *Lorena Cowell*, who was b. in Spencer, Feb. 23, 1818. They res. 1873, in Spencer. Five children, all b. in Spencer:

7–221. Myron Havillah, b. March 24, 1837, d. in U. S. Hospital, Beltsville, Md., Nov. 1, 1862, a. 25; *m.*
7–222. Almira, b. Nov. 21, 1841, d. of consumption, July 2, 1861, a. 20.
7–223. John, b. Dec. 19, 1842, res. 1873, Spencer, N. Y.; *m.*
7–224. Ruth Diana, b. Feb. 23, 1847, res. 1873, Spencer, N. Y. PERRIN.
7–225. Nancy Delphine, b. Dec. 18, 1853, m. at Spencer, March 13, 1873, ABRAM DORN.

6-84. CHESTER DAWSON, farmer, b. in Danby, N. Y., April 7, 1815, m. Sept. 1, 1840, *Margaret McKnight*, who was b. in New York city, May 10, 1820. Three children, all b. in Spencer:

7–226. Seth Warren, b. Dec. 16, 1841, res. 1873, Spencer; *m.*
7–227. William A., b. June 14, 1845, d. in Spencer, Sept. 2, 1872, a. 27; *m.*[1]
7–228. Elizabeth Thankful, b. Oct. 14, 1848, res. 1873, Spencer.

6-85. *Mary Ann Dawson*, b. in Danby, N. Y., March 20, 1817, m. in Caroline, N. Y., Sept. 22, 1838, ISAAC GERMAN, farmer, who was b. in Charleston, Montgomery Co., N. Y.,

[1] He m. in Vanettenville, Chemung Co., N. Y., Oct. 30, 1870, *Mary Margaret Goodsell*, who was b. in Cameron, Steuben Co., N. Y., Nov. 5, 1840. No issue.

July 6, 1804. They res. 1872, in Mansfield, Richland Co., O. Five children:

7–229. [GERMAN.] Isabel, b. in Ithaca, N. Y., May 27, 1840, res. 1872, in Mansfield. KEYSER.
7–230. Horace, b. March 20, 1843, d. Nov. 26, 1855.
7–231. Lydia Ann, b. in Danby, Oct. 22, 1845, res. 1872, in Mansfield. GATES.
7–232. Zachary, b. in Danby, Nov. 22, 1848, res. 1872, in Mansfield.
7–233. Edward Dawson, b. in Peru township, Huron Co., O., April 1, 1850, res. 1872, in Mansfield.

6–86. MILTON DAWSON, farmer, b. in Danby, N. Y., March 28, 1821, d. in Spencer, N. Y., July 27, 1865, aged 44. He m. March 4, 1849, *Mary Ann Schofield*, who was b. in Spencer, June 15, 1826, where she res. 1873. They had two children, both b. in Spencer:

7–234. Amoretta Gertrude, b. May 15, 1858.
7–235. Minnie, b. Oct. 25, 1864.

6–87. *Harriet Eliza Dawson*, b. in Danby, N. Y., June 3, 1826, m. 1st. in Spencer, N. Y., Feb. 27, 1848, EDGAR LORAINE MORSE, who was b. in Vermont, Aug. 8, 1828, son of John Tilman Morse. They had two children:

7–236. Wallace Adelbert, b. in Spencer, N. Y., June 6, 1851, res. 1873, Chicago, Ill.; *m.*
7–237. Francis Wheeler, b. in St. Johnstown, Lake Co., Ind., Aug. 16, 1855, enlisted 1872, private U. S. Army.

Mrs. Morse m. 2d. in Danby, N. Y., June 28, 1863, LUCIUS MASTIN, who was b. in Richford, Broome county, N. Y., Oct. 5, 1838. They res. 1873, in Ithaca, N. Y.

6–88. IRAM BARNES, farmer, b. in Paris, Oneida Co., N. Y., Dec. 9, 1806, m. in same town, Nov. 18, 1830, *Juliet Austin*, who was b. in Paris, Sept. 25, 1803. They res. 1870, in Cortland Centre, Kent Co., Mich. Ten children:

7–238. Iram, d. in infancy.
7–239. Martha Maria, b. in Paris, N. Y., Oct. 27, 1833, res. 1870, Mich. DAVIS.
7–240. Mary Jane, b. in Paris, March 2, 1835, res. 1870, Mich. TUTTLE.
7–241. Horace Lamotte, b. in Sharon, Mich., March 27, 1836, res. 1870, Mich.; *m.*
7–242. James, b. in Sharon, d. aged 4 mos.

7-243. [BARNES.] John Milton, b. in Cortland, Mich., March 27, 1839, res. 1870, Mich. ; *m.*
7-244. Milo, } twins, b. in Cortland, both d. in infancy.
7-245. Milan, }
7-246. Eliza, b. in Cortland, Sept. 17, 1844 ; m.— DAVIS ; res. 1870, Iowa ; three children, no records.
7-247. Lucien Denison, b. in Cortland, April 11, 1847, res. 1870, Mich. ; *m.*

6-89. SETH BARNES, farmer and shoemaker, b. in Paris, Oneida Co., N. Y., Nov. 20, 1807, m. 1st. in Camden, Oneida county, March 12, 1836, *Amelia Tuttle*, who d. without issue, Oct. 5, 1863, aged about 52. He m. 2d. in Taburg, N. Y., May 5, 1864, *Maria Barnes* Wheeler, widow of Charles Wheeler, and dau. of Heulet and Cynthia Barnes. She was b. in Annsville, Oneida Co., N. Y., April 7, 1833. They res. 1870, in McConnellsville, same county. Two children, both b. in McConnellsville :

7-248. Archus Pitt, b. Feb. 5, 1865.
7-249. Cynthia Amelia, b. Nov. 22, 1866.
They have, also, an adopted son, Frederick, b. June 1, 1856.

6-91. MILTON BARNES, farmer, b. in Paris, Oneida Co., N. Y., Jan. 22, 1811, d. in Cortland, Mich., March 24, 1863, aged 52. He m. at Oriskany Falls, N. Y., Jan. 1, 1834, *Laura Barnes*, who was b. in Farmington, Hartford Co., Ct., May 16, 1810, dau. of Thomas Barnes. She res. 1870, in Cortland Centre, Mich. They had six children :

7-250. Edwin Woodbury, b. in Verona, Oneida Co., N. Y., Nov. 4, 1834, res. 1870, Big Prairie, Newaygo Co., Mich. ; *m.*
7-251. Augustus Milton, b. in Verona, Sept. 16, 1836, res. 1870, Grattan, Kent Co., Mich. ; *m.*
7-252. Lucy Jane, b. in Verona, Jan. 8, 1839, d. in Davis Co., Mo., Aug. 14, 1859, aged 20. PRENTICE.[1]
7-253. Iram Curtis, b. in Verona, April 15, 1843, res. 1873, Cortland, Mich. ; *m.*
7-254. Frances Amanda, b. at Chemung Creek, Chautauque Co., N. Y., April 30, 1846, res. 1870, Cortland, Mich.
7-255. Charles Spencer, b. at Chemung Creek, June 23, 1852, res. 1870, Cortland.

---

[1] She m. in Cortland, Mich., April 17, 1855, CHESTER PRENTICE ; only child d. when 3 months old.

6-92. *Mary Sophia Barnes*, b. in Paris, Oneida Co., N. Y., Aug. 29, 1813, m. Feb. 24, 1835, JOHN WOODRUFF, who was b. in Mass. They res. 1870, in Oneida, Eaton Co., Mich. Two children:

7-256. Mary Delica, b. in Westmoreland, Oneida Co., N. Y., March 19, 1838.
7-257. Jane Amanda, b. in Spencer, Tioga Co., N. Y., July 24, 1840.

6-94. JAMES BARNES, hotel-keeper, b. in Paris, N. Y., July 28, 1817, m. 1st. Oct. 23, 1845, *Silence Woodruff*, who was b. in Spencer, N. Y., Feb. 28, 1823, d. in Plainfield, Mich., Jan. 17, 1852. They had two children, b. in Plainfield:

7-258. Tryphena Elizabeth, b. July 3, 1849.
7-259. Uriel, b. Dec. 19, 1851.

Mr. Barnes m. 2d. Dec. 24, 1853, *Mahala Haines*, who was b. in Lawrence, Otsego Co., N. Y., July 22, 1819. They res. 1870, in Plainfield.

6-102. *Martha Maria Dawson*, b. in Danby, Tompkins Co., N. Y., Feb. 4, 1822, m. Sept. 14, 1843, FORBES HOMISTON,[1] railroad policeman, who was b. in Great Barrington, Berkshire Co., Mass., Sept. 28, 1820. They res. 1873, at Milwaukee, Wis. Two children, both b. in Fond du Lac, Wis.:

7-260. Edward Ray, b. Jan. 8, 1845, res. 1873, Faribault, Rice Co., Minn., telegraph operator.
7-261. Eunice Rebecca, b. Jan. 16, 1847, res. 1873, Winona, Minn. JOHNSON.

6-103. *Phebe Isabella Dawson*, b. in Danby, N. Y., June 10, 1824, m. 1st. June 30, 1842, WILLIAM STEPHENS. They had two children:

7-262. Eleanora, d. at age of 3 years.
7-263. Lucy Maria.

She m. 2d. June 19, 1849, JEROME JUDD, who was b. in Naugatuck, Ct., Aug., 1823, d. in Grafton, Mass., June 23, 1867. They had two children:

7-264. Charles Edward, b. in Auburn, N. Y., Feb. 6, 1850, res. 1870, Worcester, Mass.
7-265. Caroline Isabel, b. in Naugatuck, Ct., Jan. 26, 1856.

She res. 1871, in Spencer, N. Y.

[1] Son of Dea. Jerre Homiston (b. in Hamden, Ct., March 19, 1790, d. Dec. 29 1872), and w. Mary Ray, (b. in Great Barrington, Mass).

6-104. HERMON FREDERICK DAWSON, carriage maker, b. in Danby, N. Y., April 30, 1826, m. in Southport, N. Y., Dec. 31, 1855, *Sarah Jane Quick*, who was b. in the town of Hunter, Greene Co., N. Y., Nov. 12, 1833. They res. 1873, in Ithaca, N. Y. No children.

6-106. WILLIAM YOUNG DOOLITTLE, farmer, b. in Lenox, Madison Co., N. Y., Jan. 19, 1813, m. 1st. in Candor, N. Y., Nov. 2, 1837, *Cinderella Holmes*, who was b. in Rensselaerville, N. Y., April 17, 1813, d. in Candor, Feb. 2, 1861. They had three children:

7-266. Lucy Maria, b. in Candor, Aug. 17, 1838, res. 1870, Warrensburg, Johnson Co., Mo. MARTIN; FLANINGDON.[1]

7-267. Eugene DeAlton, b. in Candor, Nov. 25, 1839, d. in Candor, Oct. 29, 1862.

7-268. Susan Delphine, b. in Bradford, Rock Co., Wis., Aug. 24, 1847, res. 1873, Candor. HOLLY.

Mr. Doolittle, m. 2d. in Candor, N. Y., Aug. 4, 1861, *Caroline Holmes*, b. in Rensselaerville, Dec. 17, 1815. They res. 1873, in Candor.

6-107. JOEL CAROLUS DOOLITTLE, lumber merchant, b. in Danby, Tompkins Co., N. Y., May 23, 1815, d. at Horicon, Wis., Sept. 6, 1856, aged 41. He m. Sept. 14, 1837, *Palmyra Stephens*,[2] who was b. in Bridgewater, Pa., Aug. 1, 1815. She res. 1873, at Horicon. They had eight children:

7-269. Elbert Curtis, b. in Danby, N. Y., Aug. 28, 1838, d. Dec. 18, 1840.

7-270. Wealthy Josephine, b. in Danby, March 25, 1842, res. 1873, Horicon, teacher.

7-271. Sylvester Legrand, b. in Danby, Jan. 21, 1845, res. 1873, Oshkosh, Wis.

7-272. Floyd Legranson, b. in Horicon, Wis., April 20, 1847, res. 1873, Horicon.

7-273. Frances Adalene, b. in Dekorra, Wis., Oct. 14, 1849, res. 1873, Horicon.

7-274. Emma Elizabeth, b. in Dekorra, April 15, 1851, res. 1873, Horicon.

7-275. Charles Elihu, b. in Dekorra, Sept. 13, 1853, d. March 16, 1855.

7-276. Hubert Joel, b. in Horicon, Dec. 14, 1855, d. Dec. 6, 1856.

---

[1] She m. 1st., GEORGE MARTIN; one child, Cinderella, b. in Spencer, N. Y., June 9, 1861, d. in Spencer, Aug. 5, 1862. She m. 2d. WILLIAM FLANINGDON. No issue.

[2] Dau. of William and *Sarah Plumb* Stephens.

6-110. James Austin Doolittle, foundry pattern maker, b. in Danby, N. Y., Nov. 1, 1820, m. in Oswego, N. Y., July 12, 1846, *Frances Eliza Thorp*,[1] who was b. in Oswego, March 22, 1825. They res. 1873, in Delavan, Walworth Co., Wis. Five children, all b. in Oswego:

7-277. Eli Barnard, b. Nov. 12, 1847, res. 1873, in Brooklyn, N. Y.; *unm.*
7-278. Mary Elizabeth, b. Jan. 18, 1850, res. 1873, in Delavan, Wis. Allyn.
7-279. Florence Adelaide, b. July 26, 1852, res. 1873, Walworth, Wis. Rector.
7-280. Anna Raynor, b. July 28, 1853, d. Delavan, Wis., March 7, 1869.
7-281. Frederick Truman, b. May 12, 1855, res. 1873, Delavan.

6-111. Egbert Denison Doolittle, farmer, b. in Danby, N. Y., June 29, 1823, enlisted Aug. 15, 1862, as a private in Co. F., 38th Reg't. Iowa Infantry Volunteers, participated in the siege of Vicksburg, d. of chronic dysentery, at Benton Barracks, St. Louis, Aug. 16, 1863, aged 40. He m. 1st. in Bradford, Rock Co., Wis., Oct. 13, 1847, *Diana House*,[2] who was b. in the town of Stirks, Herkimer Co., N. Y., June 25, 1820, d. at West Union, Fayette Co., Iowa, Dec. 23, 1860. They had seven children:

7-282. Selba Austin, b. in Bradford, Wis., Aug. 5, 1848, d. at West Union, Iowa, March 2, 1856.
7-283. Julia Josephine, b. in Bradford, Dec. 2, 1849, res. 1870, West Union, teacher.
7-284. James Fenimore Cooper, b. in Dover, Fayette Co., Iowa, April 3, 1851.
7-285. Wealthy Albertina, b. in Clayton Co., Iowa, Oct. 23, 1852, d. in West Union, Aug. 9, 1853.
7-286. Albert Elihu, b. in West Union, Jan. 20, 1855, d. in West Union, March 8, 1865.
7-287. Ida Caroline, b. in West Union, Jan. 8, 1857.
7-288. Adah Lemira, b. in West Union, Jan. 18, 1859.

Mr. Doolittle m. 2d. in West Union, Sept. 1, 1861, *Delia Louisa Davis*, who was b. in Springfield, Mass., Oct. 29, 1827, and res. a wid. at West Union.

---

[1] Dau. of Truman and Mabel Thorp.
[2] Dau. of Abram Isaac House and w. Rachel Putnam — both b. in Stirkville, N. Y., where they were m. and where she d.; he d. in West Union, Iowa.

6-112. *Julia Antoinette Doolittle*, b. in Danby, N. Y., July 17, 1825, d. in Oswego, N. Y., Aug. 5, 1844, aged 19. She m. WILLIAM FULLER, ship carpenter, b. in England, res. 1870, in New York city. They had two children:

7-289. George, res. 1870, New York city.
7-290. William, res. 1870, Oswego, N. Y., adopted son of his mother's uncle, Hon. Sylvester Doolittle.

6-114. *Julia Esther Dawson*, b. in Lenox, Madison Co., N. Y., Jan. 11, 1813, m. in Fowler, O., Aug. 1, 1830, AHIMAS DOUD,[1] who was b. in Canton, Hartford Co., Conn., July 11, 1811, farmer. They res. 1873, in Freedom, Portage Co., O. Two children, both b. in Freedom:

7-291. Edwin Garrit, b. Dec. 17, 1831; res. 1873, Vassar, Tuscola Co., Mich.; *m.*
7-292. Henry Rhoads, b. June 30, 1833; res. 1873, Freedom, O.; *m.*

6-115. LORENZO DAWSON, farmer, b. in Danby, N. Y., Oct. 18, 1815, d. in Newville, De Kalb Co., Ind., June 4, 1870, aged 55. He m. 1st. Oct. 10, 1839, *Emeline Case*, dau. of Ira Case. She was b. in Vernon, O., July 12, 1819, and d. in Newville, Ind., Feb. 27, 1860, aged 41. They had seven children:

7-293. Julia Maria, b. in Vernon, O., Oct. 8, 1840, d. Feb. 7, 1860. WANENAKER.
7-294. Albert Addison, b. in Fowler, O., Jan. 4, 1842, res. 1870, Concord, Ind.; *m.*
7-295. Ursula Amelia, b. in Concord, Ind., Dec. 20, 1845, res. 1870, Concord. HAMILTON.
7-296. Philetus P., b. in Concord, June 3, 1848, res. 1870, Newville.
7-297. Viola S., b. in Concord, Jan. 11, 1855, d. Sept. 11, 1860.
7-298. Clarence, b. in Newville, Ind., May 20, 1858, d. Nov. 15, 1860.
7-299. Florence C., *twin sister of Clarence.*

Mr. Dawson m. 2d., Feb. 14, 1861, *Catharine Augusta Headley*, dau. of Joseph Headley. She was b. in Bazetta, O., March 9, 1819, and res. 1870, in Newville.

6-116. *Angeline Dawson*, b. in Fowler, O., July 15, 1817, m. in Fowler, March, 1, 1838, JOHN JACKSON, grocer and

[1] Son of Samuel Doud, farmer (b. in Burlington, Conn., Dec. 1, 1781, d. in Vienna, Trumbull Co., O., July 24, 1849), and w. Lois Garrit (b. in Canton, Conn., Feb. 17, 1779, d. in Fowler, O., Feb. 25, 1861), m. in Canton, Jan. 1, 1800; gr. son of Ezra Doud.

farmer, b. July 15, 1810. They res. 1873, in New Bedford, Lawrence Co., Pa. Two children, both b. in Bazetta, O.:

7–300. Charlotte, b. Jan. 21, 1839, res. 1870, Pittsburg, Pa. SCOTT.
7–301. John, b. Feb. 2, 1849, res. 1870, New Bedford, Pa.

6–117. *Emeline Dawson*, b. in Fowler, O., Dec. 28, 1818, m. in Freedom, O., Jan. 8, 1840, GILBERT BUCHANAN WALKER, farmer, who was b. in Knox, Jefferson Co., O., Dec. 1, 1816. They res. 1873, in Bazetta, Trumbull Co., O. Six children, all b. in Bazetta:

7–302. Margaret, b. May 31, 1841, d. in Bazetta, Nov. 1, 1862, a. 21.
7–303. Ira Rhoads, b. Sept. 19, 1842.
7–304. William Breedon, b. March 7, 1845.
7–305. Gilbert Dawson, b. April 18, 1852.
7–306. Charlotte Elizabeth, b. May 19, 1856.
7–307. James Addison, b. Feb. 20, 1858.

6–119. RODOLPHUS DAWSON, b. in Fowler, O., March 27, 1822, m. in Fowler, May 3, 1855, *Adaline Charlotte Hill*, who was b. in Harwinton, Conn., Nov. 4, 1828. They res. 1873, in Linwood, Butler Co., Nebraska. They have had six chn.:

7–308. Charlotte Clarissa, b. in Macomb, McDonough Co., Ill., April 13, 1856.
7–309. Daniel Gaius, b. in Macomb, Ill., June 26, 1858.
7–310. Estella Maria, b. in Macomb, Feb. 13, 1860.
7–311. Mary Eliza, b. in Macomb, May 25, 1862.
7–312. Alvaretta V., b. in Lucas Co., Iowa, Dec. 7, 1863.
7–313. Benjamin Franklin, b. in Smyrna, Clark Co., Iowa, Feb. 5, 1869, d. in Smyrna, April 6, 1869.

6–120. ADDISON DAWSON, farmer, b. in Fowler, O., May 21, 1825, m. in Fowler, June 18, 1862, *Catharine Rhoads*,[1] who was b. in Fowler, Feb. 4, 1833. They res. 1873, in Fowler. Three children, all b. in that place:

7–314. Florence Adele, b. Aug. 31, 1864.
7–315. Frank Eugene, b. Jan. 16, 1866.
7–316. Edward Everett, b. Nov. 16, 1869.

6–121. PEMBROKE DAWSON, farmer, b. in Fowler, O., Feb. 3, 1828, m. in Fowler, Oct. 24, 1850, *Marinda Sigler*,[2] who

---

[1] Dau. of Neeham Cushing Rhoads, farmer, (b. in Cazenovia, N. Y., April 13, 1806, res. 1870, in Fowler, O.), and w. Elizabeth White Campbell (b. in Sadsbury, Crawford Co., Pa., Nov. 6, 1809, d. in Fowler, July 25, 1850), m. in Sadsbury, Feb. 23, 1831; gr. dau. of Jonathan Rhoads, farmer, (b. June 5, 1771, d. in Pa.,); gt. gr. dau. of John Rhoads (see 5-25, n. 1).

[2] Dau. of Uriel Sigler, farmer, one of the first settlers of Fowler, O. (b. in Tyring-

was b. in Fowler, Dec. 21, 1827. They res. 1873, in Fowler. Two children, both b. in that place:

7–317. Isabel, b. April 14, 1852.
7–318. Arturo, b. Jan. 15, 1857.

6–132. MARVIN FULLER, farmer, b. in Danby, N. Y., Nov. 24, 1828, m. in Candor, N. Y., Dec. 30, 1850, *Agnes Horton*, who was b. in Otsego Co., N. Y., 1826. He was three years in the U. S. army (volunteer service), during the civil war, and was several times wounded, though not severely. They res. 1870, in Candor, N. Y. One child:

7–319. George Burton, b. in Wilseyville, N. Y., Jan. 1, 1852.

6–133. JACOB CORNWELL FULLER, farmer, b. in Danby, N. Y., Jan. 9, 1830, m. *Lydia Jane Whitley*, who was b. in Ulysses, N. Y., April 3, 1833. They res. 1870, in Candor, N. Y.

6–134. JOHN STUBBS FULLER, farmer, b. in Caroline, N. Y., Oct. 22, 1831, m. in Green Co., Pa., May, 1851, wid. Sarah Jane Rhineheart, maiden name *Armstrong*, who was b. Feb. 14, 1816. They res. 1870, in Greene Co., Pa.

6–135. ALEXANDER FULLER, b. in Caroline, N. Y., Sept. 18, 1833, was in the Confederate army, and d. in that service about 1863. He m. *Sarah Jane Paget* (or *Patchin*) who res. 1869, in Ralph, Pulaski Co., Mo. Two children:

7–320. John Burton, b. about 1859.
7–321. Martha.

6–136. *Sarah Jane Fuller*, b. in Caroline, N. Y., June 30, 1835, m. 1st. in Danby, N. Y., Dec. 17, 1856, TUNIS SPEAR, who d. Jan. 1857; 2d. in Candor, N. Y., May 1858, STEPHEN RICE. They res. 1870, in Tioga Centre, N. Y., and have two children:

7–322. Charles Burton, b. in Ithaca, N. Y., July 10, 1859.
7–323. Elizabeth, b. in Spencer, N. Y., July 2, 1867.

6–137. *Phebe Martha Fuller*, b. in Caroline, N. Y., Aug. 25, 1837, m. in Little Meadows, Pa., May 29, 1858, WILLIAM

---

ham, Berkshire Co., Mass., June 28, 1794, d. Fowler, O., May 11, 1854), and w. Isabel Hall, (b. in Granville, Hampden Co., Mass., July 10, 1799, d. in Fowler, July 22, 1858), m. in Fowler, Nov. 20, 1817.

FREDERICK RHOADS, who was b. in Ulysses, N. Y., March 4, 1824. Four children, all b. in Ithaca, N. Y.:

7–324. Ann Eliza, b. May 29, 1859.
7–325. George Burton, b. April, 1861.
7–326. Myron Jones, b. March, 1863.
7–327. Harriet Van Order, b. — 1865.

6–138. ROBERT CORNWELL FULLER, b. in Caroline, N. Y., July 16, 1839, m. 1st. in Farmer, N. Y., Jan. 12, 1863, *Julia Arnee*, b. July 4, 1835, d. —; 2d. in Owego, N. Y., Sept. 12, 1869, *Mary Brink*, b. 1851. They res. 1870, in Waverly, N. Y. He was in the U. S. Army (volunteer service) three years during civil war; was severely wounded in the foot, and permanently crippled.

6–139. ALVAH BOGARDUS FULLER, b. in Caroline, N. Y., Nov. 21, 1841, m. in Enfield, N. Y., April 18, 1869, *Cornelia Lamera Newman*, b. Nov. 9, 1834. They reside, 1870, in Candor, N. Y. He was three years in the U. S. army (109th Regt. N. Y. Vols.) during the civil war; was severely wounded in the leg, and permanently crippled.

6–140. CHARLES CLAPP FULLER, b. in Caroline, N. Y., Oct. 15, 1844, m. in Brownsville, Pa., Dec. 29, 1867, *Mary Ann Davidson*, b. in Greene Co., Pa., Feb. 29, 1844. He served three years in the U. S. army (volunteer service) during the civil war. They res. 1873, in Cumberland township, Greene Co., Pa. Two children, b. in that township:

7–328. Elizabeth Lucinda, b. Aug. 29, 1868.
7–329. Rose Ella, b. Oct. 28, 1870.

6–141. *Mary Elizabeth Fuller*, b. in Caroline, N. Y., Oct. 31, 1846, m. in Brownsville, Pa., Aug. 19, 1865, WILLIAM FRANKLIN FRANKS, b. in Fayette Co., Pa., Aug. 16, 1838, where they res. 1873. He served four years and two months in the Union army during the civil war, and was some time a prisoner at Andersonville. Three children:

7–330. Ulysses Grant, b. May 29, 1867.
7–331. Nelson Isaac, b. May 15, 1870.
7–332. Eli, b. Sept. 29, 1872.

7–1. JOHN W. CARPENTER, b. at Schodack, N. Y., Oct. 14, 1836, m. Nov. 27, 1861, *Caroline S. Huyck*, who was b.

at Coeymans, Feb. 26, 1836. They res. 1873, at Schodack. Three children :

8–1. [CARPENTFR.] Mary Kate, b. Jan. 12, 1863.
8–2. Christina Louise, b. April 17, 1865, d. Oct. 21, 1870.
8–3. Walter J., b. Aug. 23, 1871.

7–2. *Catharine Elizabeth Carpenter*, b. at Schodack, N. Y., Nov. 8, 1841, m. ISAAC N. SMITH, who was b. at Schodack, Jan. 26, 1835. They res. at Schodack. Four children :

8–4. Elva C., b. Oct. 13, 1861.
8–5. Georgiana, b. July 3, 1864, d. Feb. 6, 1871.
8–6. Hattie, b. Dec. 24, 1866.
8–7. John N., b. Dec. 23, 1871.

7–25. BENAJAH HERVEY DOUGLASS, b. in New Hartford, Conn., Oct. 6, 1817, m. in New Haven, April 15, 1840, *Decia Diana Wilmot*, who was b. in Milford, Ct., Feb. 21, 1818, a sister of Martha Wilmot, w. of William H. Dawson (6–33). He is a manufacturing confectioner and merchant, of firm of B. H. Douglass & Sons, New Haven. They res. 1873, in New Haven, and have had six chn., all b. in that city :

8–8. George Walter, b. April 2, 1841, d. in New Haven, April 11, 1870, a. 29 ; *m.*[1]
8–9. John Francis, b. May 18, 1844, res. 1873, in New Haven ; *unm.*
8–10. Frederick Fowler, b. April 5, 1847, res. 1873, in New Haven ; *unm.*
8–11. Anna Amanda, b. June 19, 1850, d. in Aiken, S. C., Dec. 17, 1869, a. 19.
8–12. Benajah Holt, b. Nov. 28, 1857.
8–13. Henry Wilmot, b. Nov. 23, 1859, d. abt. Jan. 25, 1860, a. 9 wks.

7–26. *Sarah Ann Douglass*, b. in New Hartford, Conn., Sept. 13, 1819, m. 1st. April 24, 1848, VINUS ALLING (his third w.). He was b. in Hamden, Ct., Aug. 24, 1819, and d. in Westville, Ct., Sept. 30, 1860, aged 41. They had one ch. :

8–14. Jennie Lind, b. in Westville, July 23, 1856.

Mrs. Alling m. 2d. April 18, 1867, JEROME WAY, farmer, b. in New Milford, Ct., Jan. 14, 1807, son of Jared Way. They res. 1873, in Durham, Ct. No children.

7–28. CHESTER HOLT DOUGLASS, confectioner, b. in New Hartford, Ct., June 25, 1823, m. in Westville, Ct., Dec. 12,

[1] He was in the U. S. service during the civil war — a private in 15th Regt. Conn. Inf. vols. ; m. Aug. 17, 1862, *Emma Ward Rodgers*, b. in Meriden, Ct., Nov. 30, 1843, dau. of Wm. Rodgers. No issue.

1847, *Eliza Ann Alling*, who was b. in Westville, Feb. 6, 1830, dau. of Vinus Alling (7–26). They res. 1873, in Norwalk, Ct. Four children, all b. in New Haven:

8–15. [DOUGLASS.] Caroline Adelia, b. Jan. 6, 1849.
8–16. Emily Frances, b. Feb. 12, 1851, d. in New Haven, Jan. 11, 1856.
8–17. Mary Eliza, b. Sept. 18, 1852.
8–18. Frank Spencer, b. June 6, 1855, d. in Norwalk, May 20, 1872.

7-29. *Eliza Henrietta Douglass*, b. in New Hartford, Ct., Dec. 17, 1825, m. in Meriden, Ct., April 4, 1852, BENJAMIN HULBERT ROBERTS, manufacturer of Britannia ware, son of Elijah Roberts. They res. 1873, in Meriden, Ct. Three children, all b. in Middletown, Ct.:

8–19. Emily Munroe, b. Jan. 25, 1853.
8–20. Willie Benjamin, b. Dec. 16, 1858.
8–21. Burton Douglass, b. June 24, 1863.

7-30. WILLIAM BRADLEY DOUGLASS, b. in New Hartford, Ct., Nov. 10, 1828, m. in New Haven, Oct. 28, 1850, *Martha Horton*,[1] who was b. in Bristol, Ct., April 12, 1830. They res. 1873, in New Haven; two children, both b. in that city:

8–22. Charles Alfred, b. Aug. 29, 1852.
8–23. Burritt Horton, b. Nov. 30, 1857.

7-31. Rev. SOLOMON JOHNSON DOUGLASS, b. in New Hartford, Ct., Oct. 3, 1834. He entered Yale College in 1853, after pursuing a preparatory course under direction of Rev. Samuel H. Eliot, in Westville, graduating at Yale in 1857, after which he studied in Yale Theological Seminary. He was licensed to preach by the New Haven West Association, and was ordained and installed pastor of the Congregational church in Sherman, Conn., Oct. 14, 1863. He resigned his charge, on account of impaired health, July, 1867, since which time he has resided in New Haven. He m. in New Haven, Oct. 6, 1863, *Mary Elliot*,[2] who was b. in Brattleboro, Vt., Sept. 20, 1835. They have two children:

8–24. Eliot Chester, b. in Sherman, July 19, 1864.
8–25. Anna Sophia, b. in New Haven, March 21, 1870.

---

[1] Dau. of Alfred Horton (b. in Wolcott, Ct., Dec. 3, 1803, d. in New Haven, April 26, 1858), and w. Julia Ann Norton (b. in Bristol, April 8, 1807), m. in Bristol, July 7, 1828.

[2] Dau. of Samuel Elliot (judge of Probate and associate judge of County Court) and w. Sophia Flint.

7-34. William Holt Johnson, b. in Orange, Ct., Oct. 19, 1828, manufacturer of carriage trimmings. He served nearly four years in the Union army, during the civil war, having enlisted Sept. 7, 1861, in Co. E., 7th Conn. Inf. Vols., was promoted sergeant 17th of same month, and made first sergeant, Sept. 1, 1862. He was discharged Dec. 21, 1863, by reason of reënlistment as a veteran volunteer, was commissioned 1st lieutenant March 10, 1865, and finally discharged at the close of the war, July 20, 1865. He participated in engagements at Port Royal, Pulaski, James Island, St. John's Bluff, Pocotaligo, Morris Island, Fort Wagner, Drury's Bluffs, Bermuda Hundred, Fort Fisher, and the capture of Wilmington, N. C., besides numerous minor engagements. In the battle of Bermuda Hundred he was severely wounded in the side. He m. in New Haven, Dec. 5, 1855, *Hannah Jerusha Shew*,[1] who was b. in Utica, N. Y., Jan. 13, 1834. They res. 1873, in New Haven. They have had four children:

8-26. William Arthur, b. in New Haven, Feb. 26, 1856, d. Aug. 16, 1856.
8-27. Mary Teresa, b. in New Haven, July 27, 1859.
8-28. Lillian Estelle, b. in Wallingford, Oct. 25, 1860.
8-29. Charles Stone, b. in New Haven, July 22, 1869, d. Sept. 5, 1869.

7-36. James Calaway, b. in New Hartford, Ct., July 24, 1819, m. in Ashtabula, O., Sept. 30, 1840, *Rebecca Fitz Gerald*,[2] who was b. in Austinburg, O., July 4, 1817. They res. 1871, in Ashtabula, and have had four children:

8-30. Hester Ann, b. Feb. 5, 1842, d. May 21, 1849.
8-31. James Wilson, b. Jan. 22, 1844.
8-32. Henry Fayette, b. Sept. 20, 1847.
8-33. Carrie Eliza, b. July 16, 1850, d. Sept. 8, 1865.

7-37. William Holt Calaway, b. in New Hartford, Ct., Sept. 30, 1821, m. in Medina Co., O., July 15, 1850, *Helen Mar Tefft*, who was b. in Monroe Co., Mich., July 26, 1833. They res. 1871, in Ashtabula, O. Two children, both b. in Saybrook, O.:

8-34. Mary Josephine, b. Feb. 4, 1853.
8-35. Effie Amanda, b. Aug. 30, 1863.

---

[1] Dau. of Jacob Shew and his w. Betsey Minerva Stone.

[2] Dau. of Edmond Fitz Gerald, one of the first settlers in Austinburg, O., (b. in Saybrook, Ct., July 10, 1779, d. in Waterford, Pa., 1829), and w. Mindwell Humphrey (b. in Barkhamstead, Ct., Oct. 6, 1779, d. in Austinburg, O., Feb. 10, 1849), m. in Barkhamstead, 1801; gr. dau. of Ambrose and *Rebecca Chub* Humphrey, both b. in Barkhamstead, m. there, and d. in Austinburg, O.

7-39. *Mary Jane Calaway*, b. in Austinburg, O., July 9, 1826, m. in Geneva, O., March 1, 1846, HARDEN CHAUNCEY WILLIAMS, b. in Mendon, Monroe Co., N. Y., Jan. 28, 1823. They res. 1871, in Geneva, Ashtabula Co., O. Two children, both b. in Geneva:

8-36. Sarah C., b. April 25, 1847. STONE.
8-37. Albert C., b. Aug. 5, 1848.

7-42. ORESTES HAWLEY CALAWAY, b. in Austinburg, O., May 16, 1833, m. in Ashtabula, O., Aug. 14, 1862, *Mary Jennette Thayer*, who was b. in Ashtabula, Sept. 6, 1840. They res. 1871, in Saybrook, O. Two children, both b. in Saybrook:

8-38. Etta Louisa, b. Aug. 8, 1864.
8-39. Henry Edward, b. March 19, 1866.

7-44. *Eliza Calaway*, b. in Austinburg, O., Sept. 25, 1839, m. in Jefferson, O., April 14, 1856, JOSEPH BRETT, who was b. in Geneva, O., May 14, 1826. They res. 1871, in Geneva, and have three children:

8-40. Harriet, b. in Lodi, Wis., Aug. 12, 1858.
8-41. Abbie, b. in Geneva, O., March 4, 1861.
8-42. Bertha, b. in Geneva, July 2, 1869.

7-45. *Emily Irene Calaway*, b. in Saybrook, O., April 24, 1841, m. in Jefferson, O., Oct. 26, 1859, WILLIAM STONE, who was b. in Evans, Erie Co., N. Y., Aug. 13, 1836. They res. 1871, at Tittabawassee (Jay P. O.) Saginaw Co., Mich., and have one child:

8-43. Ida, b. in Evans, N. Y., July 3, 1861.

7-46. HENRY SHEPARD MORSE, joiner, b. in Austinburg, O., April 9, 1827, d. July 27, 1872, in Olney, Ill., m. in Homer, N. Y., June 11, 1852, *Martha Sophia Stewart*, who was b. in Homer, Dec. 3, 1826. She res. 1873, in Olney. Five children:

8-44. Walter Stewart, b. in Macon, Geo., March 26, 1853.
8-45. Anna Jennette, b. in Lexington, Geo., April 8, 1855.
8-46. Henry Irving, b. in Lincoln Co., Geo., June 1, 1857.
8-47. Martha Elliot, b. in Lincoln Co., Geo., Aug. 30, 1858.
8-48. Clara Minnie May, b. in Olney, Ill., Aug. 30, 1863.

7-47. *Elizabeth Jennette Morse*, b. in Vienna, Oneida Co., N. Y., Sept. 29, 1833, m. in New Haven, Ct., May 17, 1860,

JOHN WOODRUFF CATLIN,[1] who was b. in Harwinton, Ct. Dec. 30, 1832. They res. 1873, in West Haven, Ct., and have one child:

8–49. Jennie Dawson, b. in West Haven, July 14, 1863.

7-48. *Adelaide Theresa Morse*, b. in Orange, Ct., March 5, 1840, m. in West Haven, Ct., April 25, 1872, ROLLIN W. NEALE, b. in Southington, Ct., Dec. 7, 1828, son of Jeremiah and *Charlotte Hills* Neale, now of Plainville, Ct. They res. 1873, in Southington.

7-49. WILLIAM HENRY DAWSON, b. in New Haven, Ct., Sept. 10, 1835, m. in Troy, N. Y., May 1859, *Antoinette Pierce*, and d. in Westville, Ct., May 9, 1865. They had one child:

8–50. William Henry, b. in Brooklyn, N. Y., March, 1863, d. Nov. 1863.

7-51. EDWARD WALTER DAWSON, lawyer, b. in New Haven, Ct., Nov. 20, 1840. He graduated at Washington Institute, in the town of Orange, Ct., and pursued his legal studies in Milford and Westville, while teaching school, and also in the Law Department of Yale College. During the second year of his attendance at the law school, he entered the law office of the Hon. Luzon B. Morris, with whom he remained until admitted to the bar.

To his efforts in the years 1868, 1869, and subsequently, are largely due the introduction and growth of the Order of the Knights of Pythias in New England. He was elected, in 1869, grand chancellor of the Order in Connecticut, and deputy grand chancellor for New England. The second lodge of the Order organized in his native state (the Dawson lodge, Fair Haven, Dec. 17, 1868), was named in his honor. He has also been prominently identified with Odd Fellowship and Masonry, being, in 1869, W. M. of Hiram Lodge No. 1, of New Haven (Masonic), said to be "the oldest lodge in the United States, save one."[2] He has recently made a trip to Europe for the benefit of his health, spending some months in Italy. Since his

---

[1] Son of Lewis and *Anna Catlin* Catlin.

[2] See sketch and portrait in *The Knight's Armor: a History of the Early Origin of the Order of the Knights of Pythias, and Review of its Principles.* By H. K. Shackleford, New Haven: 1869, pp. 173.

return he has published *The Castle of the Three Mysteries*, a translation, by himself, of an Italian historical romance of the seventeenth century.[1] He has also published an entertaining volume of travel, entitled *Benedict's Wanderings*.[2]

He m. in New Haven, Jan. 30, 1865, *Alice Augusta Smith*, who was b. in New Haven, Aug. 15, 1846, dau. of Willis M. Smith, Esq., of New Haven. They res. 1873, in New Haven, and have two children, both b. in that city:

8–51. Mary Lilia, b. Aug. 7, 1865.
8–52. Howard Park, b. July 2, 1869.

7–52. GEORGE WALLACE DAWSON, professor of music (pianist), b. in New Haven, Oct. 9, 1842, m. in New York city, Feb. 5, 1866, *Julia A. Ackerman*, who was b. in Windsor Locks, Ct., 1845. One child:

8–53. Geneva Ernestine, b. in New Haven, Feb., 1868.

7–53. FRANKLIN TUTTLE DAWSON, b. in New Haven, July 15, 1844, fruit farmer and manufacturer of domestic wines; served six months in the civil war as a private in Company A, of the 27th regiment Conn. Vols. He m. in Westville, Ct., Nov. 6, 1872, *Nellie Peck*, dau. of L. W. Peck, of that place. They reside at Westville.

7–57. SIDNEY HOLT DAWSON, merchant, b. in New Haven, Oct. 27, 1842, m. in New Haven, Oct. 10, 1871, *Sophie L. Pierce*. They res. 1873, in New Haven. One child:

8–54. Henry Shepard, b. in New Haven, June 22, 1872.

7–58. AUGUSTUS EDWARD DAWSON, b. in New Haven, Ct., Feb. 20, 1844, m. in that city, Aug. 25, 1873, *Katie J. Guay*. They res. in New Haven.

7–68. *Fanny Dawson*, b. in Licking county, Ohio, Jan. 7, 1845, m. Jan. 6, 1862, LAWRENCE HUFF, who was b. Nov. 6, 1837. They res. 1873, Condit, O. Two children:

8–55. Nellie D., b. Nov. 21, 1868.
8–56. Frank, b. May 28, 1870.

---

[1] New Haven: C. C. Chatfield and Co.: 1872.

[2] *Benedict's Wanderings in Ireland, Scotland, Italy and Sicily*, by Edward W. Dawson. New Haven: George H. Richmond and Co., 442 Chapel St. 1873. 12 mo, pp. 566.

7-69. *Chloe Dawson*, b. in Licking county, Ohio, Jan. 14, 1848, m. Sept. 11, 1869, ALLEN WILSON, who was b. April 23, 1844. They res. 1873, Condit, O. One child:

8-57. Inah Delle, b. Sept. 15, 1870.

7-70. MERIT DAWSON SMITH, b. in Northford, Ct., June 11, 1837, m. *Lucy C. Wright*, May 18, 1857. She was b. in Winton, Ct., Aug. 7, 1840. They res. 1871, in Wallingford, Ct. Three children, all b. in Wallingford:

8-58. Charles Luzerne, b. Sept. 24, 1859.
8-59. William Henry, b. Oct. 3, 1861.
8-60. Mary Ruth, b. Oct. 3, 1864.

7-72. HENRY AUGUSTUS ROGERS, b. in Chenango Forks, N. Y., April 30, 1821, m. 1st. Jan. 5, 1842, *Emma Willard*, who was b. in Chenango Forks, March 19, 1821, and d. in Albany, N. Y., April 17, 1865, aged 44. They had three children, all b. in Chenango Forks:

8-61. Harriet Eliza, b. May 9, 1843, res. 1873, in Chenango Forks. ELY.
8-62. Helen Mary, b. Nov. 8, 1845, res. 1873, Newark Valley, N. Y. LANDFIELD.
8-63. Grace Meloy, b. Jan. 28, 1848, res. 1873, Hornellsville, N. Y. JILLSON.

Mr. Rogers m. 2d. Feb. 8, 1866, *Harriet A. Ells*. They res. 1873, in Chenango Forks, of which place he is postmaster.

7-73. THEODORE SIMEON ROGERS, merchant, b. in Chenango Forks, N. Y., Oct. 14, 1824, m. in Chenango Forks, Sept. 10, 1851, *Harriet Nacissa Johnson*,[1] b. in Manchester, Vt., Dec. 31, 1827, d. on board the steamer Arctic, on Lake Superior, Sept. 16, 1871, aged 44. They had five children, all b. in Chenango Forks, where Mr. R. was formerly postmaster and merchant. He res. 1873, in Binghamton, N. Y.

8-64. Charles Hatch, b. June 21, 1853, d. in Chenango Forks, Aug. 29, 1853.
8-65. George Tracy, b. July 9, 1854.

---

[1] Dau. of Rev. Leonard Johnson, who officiated at her marriage; sister of Dr. L. M. Johnson (7-98). Rev. L. J. was b. in Chester, Vt., Nov. 9, 1798; graduated at Amherst College; some time a resident of Binghamton, N. Y., afterward stated supply of the Congregational church at Chenango Forks, then at Triangle; died Aug. 21, 1858. He m. March 18, 1827, Harriet N. Hatch, who was b. in Cavendish, Vt., March 25, 1807.

8–66. [ROGERS.] Frederick Theodore, b. April 11, 1857, d. in Chenango Forks, Jan. 27, 1859.
8–67. Chittenden Hatch, b. June 25, 1859.
8–68. John Barker, b. April 14, 1865.

7–74. *Mary Ann Rogers*, b. in Greene, N. Y., April 17, 1826, m. in Chenango Forks, N. Y., Aug. 16, 1846, LANGLEY FULLAGER, who was b. in Kent, England, Sept. 11, 1817. He is cashier of the Lake Shore Bank, Dunkirk, N. Y., where they reside (1873). They have four children :

8–69. Elizabeth Kate, b. in Chenango Forks, July 14, 1848.
8–70. Mary Langley, b. in Chenango Forks, March 29, 1854.
8–71. Hattie Carrie, b. in Dunkirk, July 2, 1860.
8–72. Guy Kent, b. in Dunkirk, Aug. 7, 1870.

7–75. NORMAN STEVENS ROGERS, merchant, express agent, etc., b. in Chenango Forks, N. Y., Oct. 3, 1828, m. Aug. 31, 1852, *Eliza Thomas*, who was b. in Norwich, N. Y., April 10, 1831. They res. 1873, in Chenango Forks, and have five children :

8–73. Anna Carrie, b. in Chenango Forks, July 26, 1853.
8–74. William Thomas, b. in Lisle, N. Y., June 5, 1856.
8–75. Henry Martin, b. in Carbon Cliff, Ill., Feb. 14, 1860.
8–76. Lida Reed, b. in Chenango Forks, Feb. 14, 1865.
8–77. Hattie Meloy, b. in Chenango Forks, Jan. 5, 1869.

7–76. *Julia Eliza Rogers*, b. in Chenango Forks, N. Y., Oct. 30, 1830, m. Sept. 18, 1849, JAMES HAGAMAN, farmer, who was b. in Greene, N. Y., Dec. 11, 1819. They res. 1873, in Chenango Forks. Five children, all b. in that place :

8–78. Mary Diana, b. March 21, 1851, d. in Chenango Forks, July 21, 1852.
8–79. John Barker, b. April 2, 1852.
8–80. Julia Rogers, b. Nov. 9, 1855.
8–81. Judith Birdsall, b. Nov. 1, 1863.
8–82. Langley Fullager, b. March 7, 1867, d. in Chenango Forks, March 13, 1871.

7–79. GEORGE WILLIAM ROGERS, railway conductor, b. in Chenango Forks, N. Y., Oct. 14, 1838, m. 1st, April, 1854, *Zane Knapp*, who d. March 4, 1864. No children. He m. 2d, Sept. 21, 1864,. *Lida Jane Reed*, who was b. in Wolcott, N. Y., Oct. 28, 1843. They res. 1873, Binghamton, N. Y. One child :

8–83. George Worthy, b. in Unadilla, N. Y., Feb. 19, 1868.

Mr. and Mrs. Rogers have, also, an adopted son:

Charles Augustus, b. Jan. 6, 1867.

7-82. WILLIAM AUGUSTUS MELOY, lawyer, b. in Chenango Forks, N. Y., Aug. 26, 1832, graduated at Yale College, New Haven, 1854, and for some years past has been successfully engaged in the practice of his profession at Washington, D. C. He m. in Washington, Dec. 16, 1868, Mrs. Emily Josepha Steuart, who was b. in Washington, July 2, 1841.[1] They res. 1873, at "Brookland," near Muirkirk Station, Md. Two children:

8-84. Edith Willard, b. in Washington, D. C., Oct. 8, 1869.
8-85. Isabella Rittenhouse, b. at "Brookland," April 15, 1871.

7-83. JOHN WILLARD MELOY, merchant, b. in Chenango Forks, N. Y., Sept. 8, 1834, m. in Ellicottville, N. Y., *Frances Abigail Williams*,[2] who was b. in Ellicottville, Sept. 19, 1835. They res. 1873, in Portville, Cattaraugus Co., N. Y. Four children:

8-86. Frances, b. in Ellicottville, April 4, 1863.
8-87. Frederica, b. in Ellicottville, Dec. 8, 1864.
8-88. Mary, b. in Portville, Aug. 12, 1866.
8-89. John Earl, b. in Portville, June 14, 1871.

7-84. SAMUEL HENRY MELOY, b. in Chenango Forks, N. Y., Sept. 8, 1836, m. in Washington, D. C., Oct. 11, 1870, *Anna Isabella Nourse*, who was b. in Washington, Nov. 2, 1852, sister of Emily, wife of Wm. A. Meloy (7-82). They res. 1873, in Washington, where he occupies a responsible clerkship in the U. S. Treasury. One child:

8-90. Arthur Nourse, b. in Washington, March 8, 1872.

7-86. *Anna Meloy*, b. in Chenango, N. Y., Aug. 8, 1841, m. in Ellicottville, N. Y., Nov. 30, 1865, GEORGE MIL-

---

[1] Wid. of Alex. S. Steuart, dau. of William and *Isabella Bond* Nourse, of Washington.

[2] Dau. of Dr. Thomas Jones Williams (b. in Middlefield, N. Y., April 29, 1806) and w. Abigail Perkins Day (b. in Providence, R. I., Aug. 4, 1813) m. in Ellicottville, April 20, 1831, where they res. 1871; gr. dau. of Evander Williams (b. in Brooklyn, Ct., Oct., 1782, d. in Ellicottville, N. Y., Feb., 1857) and w Abigail Jones (b. in Middlefield, N. Y., 1786, d. in La Crosse, Wis., 1857) m. in Middlefield, 1805. Abigail Perkins Day was the dau. of Israel Day (b. in Killingly, Ct., May 29, 1783, d. in Ellicottville, May 4, 1852), and w. Mary Perkins (b. in Ashford, Ct., March 5, 1790), m. in Ashford, June 21, 1809.

FORD RIDER,[1] who was b. in Trenton, N. Y., Sept. 15, 1844. They res. 1873, at Ellicottville, N. Y. Two children:

8–91. Charlotte Christiana, b. in Ellicottville, Nov. 10, 1866.
8–91*b*. Milford Willard, b. in Ellicottville, Nov. 13, 1872.

7-87. CHARLES FREDERICK MELOY, b. in Barker, N. Y., Dec. 17, 1843, m. in Arcade, N. Y., Sept. 22, 1869, *Caroline Antoinette Hitchcock*, who was b. in China, N. Y., Oct. 28, 1841, dau. of Orange and Mercy Hitchcock. They res. 1873, in Attica, N. Y., where he is editor and publisher of *The Attica Weekly News*. He was formerly editor and publisher of *The True Patriot*, newspaper, at Cuba, N. Y. They have one ch.:

8–92. Grace, b. in Wyoming, Wyoming Territory, June 30, 1871.

7-91. THEODORE RICHMOND, lawyer, b. in Jefferson, O., March 2, 1837; educated at the Baptist University, Lewisburg, Pa.; m. at Navarre, O., Jan. 21, 1862, *Harriet Burgert*,[2] who was b. at Massillon, Stark Co., O., Aug. 17, 1838. They removed from Columbus, O., to Athens, McMinn Co., Tennessee, 1865, and thence to Chattanooga, Tenn., 1871, where they now reside (1873). He is widely known as a lawyer of ability and influence, and is very successfully engaged in the practice of his profession. They have had four children:

8–93. Charles Burgert, b. in Ligonier, Ind., Dec. 3, 1862, d. in Cleveland, O., June 7, 1864.
8–94. Grace Chestnutwood, b. in Madison, O., Oct. 19, 1864.
8–95. Theodore Leaming, b. in Athens, Tenn., Sept. 17, 1868.
8–96. Sarah Bessie, b. in Athens, Tenn., Nov. 17, 1870.

7-92. *Amelia Richmond*, b. in Stockton, N. Y., June 5, 1840, m. in Ligonier, Ind., May 12, 1862, LOUIS DAVIES THOMAS,[3] dry goods merchant, who was b. in Elkhart Co.,

---

[1] Son of Milford Rider (b. in Cheshire, Mass., Aug. 10, 1809), and wife Christiana S. Card (b. at Petersburg, N. Y., March 21, 1821), m. in Trenton, N. Y., May 9, 1841; gr. son of Lloyd and *Elizabeth Alma* Rider.

[2] Dau. of Adam Burgert, merchant (b. in Bedford Co., Pa., March 15, 1809, d. in Chattanooga, Tenn., Aug. 22, 1872), and w. Sarah Chestnutwood (b. in Berks Co., Pa., Dec. 30, 1811, d. in Athens, Tenn., June 22, 1870), m. at Massillon, O., Nov. 16, 1837; gr. dau. of David Burgert (b. at Antietam, Md., 1763, d. in Paris, Stark Co., O., 1825), and w. Catherine Heffner (d. in Paris, O., Jan., 1854, aged 85, dau. of Benj. Heffner), m. in Franklin Co., Pa. David Burgert, last named, was son of David Burgert, a native of Berne, Switzerland, who settled in Maryland. Sarah Chestnutwood, above named, was dau. of Abraham and *Sarah Jones* Chestnutwood.

[3] He was the first white child b. in Elkhart county, son of Thomas Thomas, the first county clerk of that county, incumbent of the office for fourteen years, a soldier of the war of 1812. His father's name was also Thomas Thomas, a soldier of the Revolution; son of John Thomas, who came from Wales. The maiden name of Louis D. Thomas' mother was Mary Kelly. She was of Irish descent, but b. in Va.

Ind., May 12, 1830. He was elected, in the fall of 1871, recorder of his native county. They res. 1873, at Goshen, Ind., and have had three children:

8–97. Frank Warren, b. in Ligonier, March 13, 1863, d. in Goshen, Oct. 6, 1864.

8–98. Caroline Isabella, b. in Goshen, Aug. 21, 1865.

8–99. Katharine, b. in Goshen, Aug. 17, 1869.

7–93. CHARLES HENRY RICHMOND, merchant and dairy farmer, b. in Fredonia, N. Y., Dec. 14, 1842, m. in Collamer, O., April 2, 1865, *Mary Tracy*,[1] who was b. in Granger, Medina Co., O., Oct. 19, 1843. They res. 1873, in Brighton, Lorain Co., O. One child:

8–100. Harriet Tracy, b. in Cleveland, O., Dec. 27, 1867.

7–94. *Grace Adelia Richmond*, b. in Warsaw, N. Y., April 13, 1846, m. July 10, 1864, HARVEY BARTHOLOMEW,[2] druggist, who was b. in Watertown, N. Y., Feb. 13, 1841. They res. 1873, in Ai, Fulton county, O., and have three children:

8–101. Edith, b. in Lagrange, Fulton Co., O., April 8, 1867.

8–102. Herbert, b. in Lagrange, July 28, 1869.

8–103. Frederick, b. in Ai, Dec. 1, 1871.

7–96. *Katherine Richmond*, b. in Deposit, N. Y., Dec. 25, 1850, m. in Goshen, Ind., June 8, 1870, WILLIAM EDWARD POOLEY,[3] who was b. June 8, 1845, in Lenawee Co., Mich. They res. 1873, in Brighton, Lorain Co., Ohio. One child:

8–104. Frank Richmond, b. in Goshen, Jan. 7, 1872.

---

[1] Dau. of Rev. Abel Tracy, a Methodist minister, who d. in Jackson, Mich., about 1862.

[2] In the U. S. service, with three brothers, during the civil war. He was third son and seventh child of Daniel Bartholomew, an early settler of Watertown, N. Y., now of Fulton Co., O., (b. in Augusta, Oneida Co., N. Y., Jan. 19, 1796), and w. Sarah Garner Parker (b. in Middletown, Vt., March 21, 1807), m. Nov. 13, 1828; gr. son of Oliver Bartholomew, a soldier of the Revolution 4 years and 3 months, a resident of Watertown, N. Y., from 1800 (b. in Branford, Ct., Oct. 20, 1757, d. in Watertown, June 18, 1850, aged 93), and w. Hannah Lacy (b. June 23, 1758, d. at Watertown, Oct. 3, 1848, aged 90), m. July 6, 1780, lived together 68 years; gt. gr. son of Josiah Bartholomew, an early resident of Branford, Ct. Concerning his gr. father, Oliver Bartholomew, Mr. H. B. writes as follows: "There were but three men in or around Watertown when he went there. He was the first to propose having religious meetings, and the first of these was held at his house, where a Baptist church was organized in 1801." Sarah Garner Parker, above named, was dau. of Joseph Parker (b. in Chelsea, Vt., Aug. 1, 1762), and w. Lydia Watts, a native of Elsted, Vt. Hannah Lacy, above named, was fifth of eleven children of Ebenezer Lacy (b. in Old Milford, Ct., April 19, 1727), and w. Freelan Canfield (b. in Conn., Dec. 29, 1726).

[3] Son of Nathan Pooley, farmer and tradesman, (b. in Suffolk, England, Feb. 10, 1822, res. 1871, Goshen, Ind.), and w. Mary Jane Bilby (b. in Trenton, N. J.,

7-97. *Julia Anna Keeler*, b. in Union, N. Y., Jan. 12, 1833, m. in Union, Dec. 5, 1855, CHARLES BARTHOLOMEW MERCEREAU,[1] merchant, who was b. in Union, Feb. 27, 1827. They res. 1873, in Fulton, Ill., and have two children, both b. in that place:

8-105. Grace Edith, b. Feb. 27, 1863.
8-106. Catharine Belle, b. Dec. 8, 1869.

7-98. *Adelaide Amelia Keeler*, b. in Union, N. Y., Aug. 20, 1836, m. in Union, Jan. 10, 1858, Dr. LEONARD MELANCTHON JOHNSON, allopathic physician, who was b. in Le Raysville, Pa., Jan. 24, 1830, brother to Harriet N. Johnson, w. of Theodore S. Rogers (7-73). He served in the civil war as surgeon to the Third Regt. N. Y. Inf. Vols., being for some time stationed at Fortress Monroe. He was also one of the surgeons for the Confederate sick in the prison camp at Elmira, N. Y. They res. 1873, at Greene, N. Y., where he is engaged in the practice of his profession. Two children:

8-107. Stella Tracy, b. in Union, N. Y., Aug. 26, 1861.
8-107*b*. Harriette Narcissa, b. at Greene, N. Y., Oct. 3, 1871.

7-99. HARLAN CEPHAS DRESSER, engineer, b. in East Otto, Cattaraugus Co., N. Y., Sept. 2, 1843. He enlisted Oct. 23, 1861, as a private in company B., Ninth Regt. N. Y. Vols. The regiment completed its organization at Albany in November, and proceeded to Washington, near which city they were encamped until the following spring. A fruitless march to Manassas, which was found to be guarded only by a few pickets and "quaker guns" (wooden logs in the semblance

---

June 19, 1824), m. in Marion, Wayne Co., N. Y., Sept. 25, 1844; gr. son of Edward Pooley (b. in England, d. in Am., 1834), and w. Maria Smith (b. in Suffolk, England, d. Aug. 25, 1724).

[1] Son of Henry Mercereau (b. in Union, N. Y., Dec. 4, 1800), and w. Catharine Bartholomew (b. in Vestal, N. Y., Aug. 1, 1809), m. Nov. 2, 1825; gr. son of Joshua Mercereau, who was b. in Woodbridge, N. J., Oct. 27, 1762, and m. Dec. 12, 1784, Keziah Drake (b. May 6, 1769, d. 1842), dau. of Col. Drake, a Rev. officer. They removed to Broome Co., N. Y., between 1791 and 1795, where he d. 1805. He was a son of John Mercereau, who kept an inn at Woodbridge, N. J., famous in his day for his "flying machines" — a fast line of stages between Phila. and New York. These and the inn were conducted jointly by J. M. and his brother Joshua, a Rev. officer, afterwards one of the earliest judges of Tioga Co., N. Y. These were gr. sons of Joshua Mercereau, who, with other children of John Mercereau, a Huguenot who d. in France, removed to England 1685, and shortly after settled at Staten Island.—See *Annals of Binghamton*, pp 100-4, 106-8; Whitehead's *Contributions to East Jersey History*, 283-5; also letter of Miss Josephine Mercereau, Union, N. Y., to compiler hereof.

of cannon) was followed by their return to Washington, whence they were ordered to Fortress Monroe, and from thence successively to the ruins of Hampton, Yorktown, West Point, White House and again to Washington. After this the regiment joined Gen. Siegel at Sperryville, Va., moved to Culpepper, and participated in the battle of Cedar Mountain. They were under fire for three days during Gen. Pope's retreat and the second Bull Run battle, and later were quite heavily engaged at Berryville, in the Shenandoah valley, all in 1862. Soon after the latter battle, Mr. Dresser was taken sick and sent to Washington. When sufficiently recovered he was detailed for hospital duty until the last of October, 1863, and after a furlough of two weeks returned to his regiment, November, 1863; took part in Gen. Meade's Mine Run campaign, and went with his regiment into winter quarters near Culpepper. In 1864, he participated in the battles of the Wilderness, Todd's Tavern, and Spottsylvania, and while on a raid in the rear of Gen. Lee's army, went within the outer works of Richmond, and could hear the alarm bells of that city giving notice of the approach of the Union forces. The regiment then went to Malvern Hill, soon after which he was again taken sick, and spent the remainder of the three years for which he was enlisted in hospital at Washington.[1] He m. in Dunkirk, N. Y., March 5, 1867, *Margaret Anastasia O'Conner*, who was b. at Holland Landing, C. E., Aug. 25, 1849. They res. 1871, at Dunkirk. One child:

8–108. Ellen, b. in Tidioute, Pa., Sept. 11, 1868.

7-105. *Helena Dawson*, b. in Fair Haven, Ct., June 9, 1850, m. in Plymouth, Ct., Sept. 8, 1872, DANIEL ROSSITER, teacher. They res. 1873, in Plymouth.

7-109. CLIFFORD DAWSON PARSONS, b. at Broad Brook, East Windsor, Conn., Nov. 14, 1838, m. Jan. 2, 1864, *Elizabeth Lovlett*, who was b. in England, Sept. 16, 1837. He served in the civil war four years and eight months, as a member, successively, of the Third Conn. Vols. and Eighth Conn. Veteran Volunteers, participating in the following engagements: Bull Run, Roanoke Island, Newbern, siege at Fort Macon, South

---

[1] See *Prescott Memorial*, p. 562.

Mountain, Antietam, Fredericksburgh, siege of Suffolk, and the campaign of Gen. Grant in front of Petersburgh and Richmond, 1864–65. They res. 1873, in Bristol, Conn., and have one child:

8–109. [PARSONS.] Norton Clifford, b. at Broad Brook, Sept. 1, 1866.

7–110. ARTHUR PARSONS, b. at Broad Brook, East Windsor, Conn., Aug. 28, 1840, m. Sept., 1866, *Mary E. Spencer*, who was b. in Houlton, Me., Jan. 18, 1846. He served in the civil war, three months in the Third Conn. Vols., and three years in the Sixteenth Conn. Vols. They res. 1873, in Bristol, Conn. Two children:

8–110. Clara May, b. in East Windsor, May 20, 1867.
8–111. Eveline Sybil, b. in Windsorville, Aug. 1, 1871.

7–111. CHARLES RUSSELL PERKINS, b. in New Hartford, Ct., Jan. 25, 1844, m. Jan. 22, 1867, *Caira J. Deyo*, who was b. at Highland, N. Y., March 2, 1847. They res. 1873, in Meriden, Ct.

7–114. *Elizabeth E. Bissell*, b. in East Windsor, Ct., Aug. 8, 1841, m. Sept. 1, 1863, CHARLES W. DAVENPORT, who was b. at New Fane, Vt., Oct. 1, 1820. They res. 1873, at Broad Brook, East Windsor, Ct. Two children, both b. at Broad Brook:

8–112. Lilla, b. Nov. 23, 1864.
8–113. Ida May, b. July 23, 1867, d. July 30, 1868.

7–119. ALBERT MARSHALL SIGOURNEY, b. in Bristol, Ct., Aug. 1, 1850, m. Nov. 24, 1869, *M. Angie Manross*, b. Aug. 1, 1850. They res. 1873, at Bristol.

7–122. *Mary Esther Evans*, b. in Bristol, Ct., Dec. 15, 1854, m. in Troy, N. Y., Aug. 22, 1872, ORSON P. WOODRUFF, who was b. in Avon, Ct., July 13, 1847. They res. 1873, in Bristol.

7–131. *Frederica Grace Kinney*, b. in Erieville, N. Y., Dec. 5, 1835, m. in Bloomingdale, Ill., Feb. 26, 1856, CHARLES GOODWIN,[1] merchant and farmer, who was b. in Vernon, N.

[1] Son of Hiram Goodwin (b. in Litchfield, Ct., Oct., 11, 1801, d. in Aurora, Ill., Dec. 1, 1864) and M. Nancy Jones, (b. in Saratoga Co., N. Y., Feb. 15, 1804), m. Sept. 1828; gr. son of Russell Goodwin, (b. in Conn., 1767, d. in New York,

Y., Aug. 16, 1832. They res. 1873, in Grouse, Kane Co., Ill. Three children:

8–114. [Goodwin.] Lucia Newton, b. in Aurora, Ill., Jan. 18, 1863.
8–115. Lenore Denton, b. in Aurora, Aug. 21, 1864.
8–116. Newton Lee, b. in Sugar Grove, Kane Co., Ill., Jan. 2, 1870.

7–135. *Lucia Diane Dawson*, b. in Cazenovia, N. Y., July 9, 1839, m. in Windsor, N. Y., March 5, 1854, Isaac John Gray, who was b. in Chenango, N. Y., Jan. 10, 1832, and d. at Binghamton, N. Y., July 25, 1873, aged 41. She res. 1873, in Binghamton. Three children:

8–117. Jennie Augusta, b. in Fenton, N. Y., Dec. 18, 1854, res. Binghamton. Erskine.
8–118. Lucius De Forest, b. in Fenton, April 5, 1860.
8–119. Florence Bates, b. in Binghamton, Aug. 16, 1869.

7–136. *Frances Mary Dawson*, b. in Linklaen, N. Y., June 26, 1841, d. in Chenango, N. Y., Jan. 23, 1860, aged 19. She m. in Lisle, N. Y., July 2, 1856, George Wellington Parker, who was b. in Chenango, May 23, 1832, where he res. 1870; trackmaster of the Syracuse and Binghamton R. R. They had two children, both b. in Chenango:

8–120. Charles Lamont, b. June 11, 1857.
8–121. Frank, b. April 30, 1859.

7–137. Lee De Forest Dawson, b. in Linklaen, N. Y., Aug. 22, 1843. He enlisted during the first year of the civil war, 1861, as a private in the 27th Regt. N. Y. State Vols., but after a few months of hard service, principally in Virginia, broke down completely in health, and received an honorable discharge. He m. June 10, 1863, widow Caroline Stone — maiden name *Whitbeck*. No children. Res. 1873, Binghamton: clerk.

7–140. Edward Francis Bates, physician, b. in township of Cazenovia, Madison Co., N. Y., Dec. 30, 1840, d. in Washington, D. C., March 6, 1864, aged 23 years. At the commencement of the civil war he was a student in the Medical Department of the State University of Michigan, at Ann Arbor.

May 19, 1839), and w. Ruth Church, (b. in Conn., 1770, d. in N. Y., June 30, 1834), m. in New Lenox, Ct., July 4, 1789. The gt. gr. father said by correspondent to have been from England, but it is queried whether the English emigrant was not probably some generations more remote? The name formerly *Godwin*.

In the summer of 1862, in advance of an assuredly high and honorable graduation, he repaired to Washington, in company with a few other patriotic young men of his class, and entered the service of the United States as a Medical Cadet. He was assigned to duty in Carver Hospital in July of that year, where he manifested a degree of talent and a thoroughness of preparation which caused him to be speedily promoted, in December, 1862, to the rank of assistant surgeon, and a few months later to that of surgeon of volunteers. Not long after the latter advancement he received the notable distinction of an assignment to duty as a member of the Medical Board of examiners, in Washington, and he was still engaged in that service when he was attacked by the malady which terminated his life. He was a diligent and methodical as well as an enthusiastic student, and of untiring industry in his profession. Notwithstanding his youth, it is not too much to say, that as an officer he evinced the highest order of efficiency. He was the author of several graceful poetical compositions, and his talents were brilliant and varied.[1] He m. in Cleveland, O., Jan. 26, 1863, *Eusebia Fleming Moore*, niece of Hon. J. H. Wade, of that city, where she now resides (1873).

7-141. William Rufus Bates, lawyer and editor, was b. in Cazenovia township, Madison county, N. Y., June 28, 1845. He was educated at the Oneida Conference Seminary, in Cazenovia, and in the Law Department of the Michigan State University; and has been editorially connected with several newspapers, especially the Saginaw, Mich., *Daily Enterprise*, and the Chicago, Ill., *Republican*. He was elected, in the fall of 1870, from Bay county, Michigan, a representative in the state legislature, and, though the youngest member of that body, is already distinguished in his state for his ability as a legislator and as a political orator and leader. In the spring of 1871 he was appointed, by the President, register of the United States Land office at Saginaw, which office he now holds (1873). He is, of course, republican in politics. He m. in Flint, Mich.,

[1] His remains were removed to Cazenovia for burial. The following — in raised letters, within the American Shield — is the inscription upon the monument: "Major Edward F. Bates, Surgeon U. S. V., died at Washington, D. C., March 6, 1864, aged 23 years, 2 months, 11 days."

Jan. 11, 1866, *Gertrude Amelia Belcher*,[1] who was b. in Richford, N. Y., Dec. 10, 1843. They res. 1873, in Saginaw, and have two children, both b. in Flint, Mich.:

8–122. [BATES.] Irving Belcher, b. Feb. 3, 1867.
8–123. Eusebia Florence, b. May 11, 1871.

7–159. ALBERT EMILIUS COLMAN, bank clerk, b. in Ellicottville, Cattaraugus Co., N. Y., Feb. 8, 1835, m. 1st. Feb. 7, 1859, *Emma Melissa Chapman*, who was b. in New Market, N. H., Oct. 24, 1842, and d. in Dunkirk, N. Y., June 20, 1863, aged 21, dau. of Jeremiah Y. Chapman. They had two children, both b. in Dunkirk:

8–124. Sophia Jane, b. March 15, 1860.
8–125. Harry Truman, b. Jan. 23, 1862, d. March 24, 1862.

Mr. COLMAN, m. 2d. in Jeffersonville, Ind., April 6, 1865, *Eliza Russell*, b. May 13, 1843.[2] They res. 1873, in Dunkirk, and have had three children, all b. in that place:

8–126. Paul Russell, b. Nov. 13, 1865.
8–127. Emma Sophia, b. March 23, 1868.
8–128. Alice Russell, b. Oct. 28, 1870.

7–160. *Lydia Beecher Colman*, b. in Ellicottville, N. Y., June 8, 1837, d. in Dunkirk, N. Y., Oct. 8, 1872, aged 35. She m. in Dunkirk, Jan. 6, 1857, JAMES HENRY VAN BUREN,[3]

---

[1] Dau. of Major Horatio Belcher, of the 8th Regt. Mich. Inf. Vols., b. in Berkshire, Tioga Co., N. Y., Dec. 6, 1816, killed at the battle of Weldon Railroad, near Petersburg, Va., Aug. 19, 1864. He entered the army as Lieut. of a company from Flint, Mich., in 1861, and was in many engagements, and had been wounded in three battles before his last fatal hurt. In one of the previous engagements his right arm had been rendered useless, and on the day of his death he was thrice wounded. "Consistent and gentlemanly in his intercourse with all, pure and blameless in his life, he lived and died a Christian and a patriot." He m. Mary A. Hungerford, who was b. in Caroline, Tompkins Co., N. Y., Feb. 26, 1821, dau. of Spencer and *Electa Dunham* Hungerford (res. 1872, in Flint,) Maj. B. was the son of Joseph and *Wealthy Whiting* Belcher. His only son, Major Irving Belcher, also sacrificed his life for his country.

[2] Dau. of Norris Russell (b. in Elizabethtown, Ind., 1810, d. in New Albany, Ind., 1853), and w. Nancy Elizabeth Morris, who d. in New Albany, March 2, 1858; gr. dau. of John Russell, who res. 1870, in Elizabethtown.

[3] Son of Henry Brodhead Van Buren (b. in Pompey Centre, N. Y., Sept. 18, 1804, res. 1870, Dunkirk), and w. Caroline Eunice Kingsley (b. in Schagticoke, N. Y., Dec. 31, 1807), m. in Dunkirk, Feb. 22, 1830; gr. son of Peter Van Buren (b. at Kinderhook, N. Y., d. at Cassadaga, N. Y., Feb., 1860), and w. Elizabeth Upham. Caroline E. Kingsley was dau. of Jacob Kingsley, a native of Windham, Ct. The gr. father of Peter Van Buren, above named, was uncle to the President, Martin Van Buren.

merchant, who was b. in Dunkirk, Feb. 2, 1831, and res. 1873, in same place. They had six children, all b. in Dunkirk:

8–129. [VAN BUREN.] William Colman, b. Oct. 3, 1857, d. Apr. 25, 1858.
8–130. Ellen Colman, b. April 26, 1861.
8–131. Truman Colman, b. Jan. 1, 1865.
8–132. James Lyman, b. April 8, 1867.
8–133. Mary Colman, b. June, 25, 1869.
8–134. James Henry, b. Aug. 4, 1871.

7-161. *Ellen Sophia Colman*, b. in Ellicottville, N.Y., Aug. 25, 1840, m. in Dunkirk, N. Y., April 27, 1859, Capt. PATRICK BARRETT, who was b. at Ballyknock, in the parish of Downfeeney, Mayo county, Ireland, March 10, 1832. He was mortally wounded at the battle of Williamsburgh, Va., May 5, 1862, and d. at Yorktown the day following, aged 30.

Capt. Barrett came to this country in 1847, when about fifteen years of age, in company with his mother, sisters and brothers: his father, whose name was James Barrett, having died in Ireland about ten years previously. In the spring of 1849, he obtained employment on the Erie railway, and having, by his efficiency and diligence, attracted the favorable notice of the railway superintendent, he was soon placed by him in a line of promotion which led to his employment in various capacities of increasing trust and responsibility.

The following are extracts from an obituary published in the *Dunkirk Union*.[1] "In 1850, with his family, he made our village his home. Attentive and faithful in the performance of every duty, courteous and kind to all he met, thoughtful, studious, and of an active and enquiring mind, his leisure was employed with books, and in the society of the intelligent and cultivated; and as years passed on, the graceful, handsome, well mannered boy, ripened into the accomplished gentleman and active citizen......

"Capt. Barrett received the appointment of postmaster of our village from President Buchanan, and held the office during his administration. Happily connected by marriage, of commanding presence, with manly and shining qualities, uncommon

---

[1] From a pamphlet collection of obituary and other notices of Capt. Barrett, including extracts from the *Buffalo Sentinel*, *New York Tablet*, New York *Freeman's Journal*, reports of the meetings of the citizens of Dunkirk after receiving news of his death, order of arrangements for the funeral solemnities, etc. His remains were buried at Dunkirk.

energy and perseverance, a prosperous and successful career seemed open before him. He gratified his martial tastes and aptitudes by raising, mostly from among his countrymen, in our village, and for several years commanding, the Jackson Guards, an independent company ; and in drilling them and directing their movements he, in some measure, fitted himself for the service in which he has been distinguished.

"His patriotic ardor was aroused at the outbreak of the rebellion. On that memorable day when came flashing on the wires the startling news of the fall of Fort Sumter, Captain Barrett immediately repaired to our village armory, with his own hands raised the Stars and Stripes, and avowed his purpose of offering his services to the government. With much labor and sacrifice he gathered around him the brave men who followed him to the war. We recall, with melancholy pride, that bright summer day, almost a year gone by, when our noble contribution to the cause of the country, the two companies of Captains Barrett and Stevens, took up their march for the beleaguered Capital, and amid tears and benisons and prayers the youthful hero turned from his elegant home to go where duty called him. The summer months were profitably spent at Camp Scott, on Staten Island, in perfecting himself and his command in the service so soon to be their daily occupation. Ordered with the brigade last fall to Washington, they were soon assigned important duty in guarding the Maryland shore below the Capital, and delicate and responsible trusts were so well discharged by Captain Barrett as to meet the warm approbation of superiors in command. The captain and his company, and indeed the whole of the Third Regiment, mostly from this county, are said to have made great proficiency, and to have become accomplished soldiers. Connected with General Hooker's division, they formed a part of the pursuing force after the evacuation of Yorktown, and engaging the enemy's rear at Williamsburg, are represented in the records of that memorable engagement, as having 'fought with unprecedented bravery' ; and there, at the head of his company, bravely directing them against the foe, Captain Barrett received the wound that has robbed the service of a gallant officer, and plunged our community in grief."

Capt. B. was a member of the Catholic church. He was attended in his last hours, greatly to his comfort and consolation, by the Rev. Joseph O'Hagan, regimental chaplain, who was also his warm personal friend.

Mrs. B. res. 1873, in Dunkirk. They had one child:

8–135. [BARRETT.] Mary Colman, b. in Dunkirk, July 9, 1860.

7-162. *Mary Melissa Colman*, b. in Ellicottville, N. Y., Dec. 31, 1842, m. in Dunkirk, N. Y., Jan. 2, 1866, SAMUEL JAMES GIFFORD,[1] who was b. in Ashtabula, O., May 14, 1834; insurance agent. They res. 1873, in Dunkirk.

7-163. WILLIAM TRUMAN COLMAN, b. in Ellicottville, N. Y., Feb. 18, 1845, m. in Dunkirk, N. Y., June 15, 1870, *Grace Kennedy*, dau. of Charles Kennedy, sheriff of Chautauque county. They res. 1873, in Dunkirk. One child:

8–136. Agnes, b. July 30, 1872.

7-164. CHARLES DELOS SILL, b. in Ellicottville, N. Y., Aug. 28, 1843, m. in Ellicottville, Nov. 25, 1863, *Sophia L. Pettit*, who was b. in Fairview, Cattaraugus Co., N. Y., Jan. 4, 1848, dau. of Amos Pettit. Mr. Sill is a practical printer, and succeeded his father as proprietor and editor of the *Cattaraugus Freeman* (Ellicottville), but is now engaged in farming, having suspended the publication of the paper. He res. 1873, in Ellicottville, and has three children, all b. in that place:

8–137. Edith Pettit, b. May 8, 1865.
8–138. Jessie Beecher, b. Dec. 2, 1868.
8–139. Mary, b. May 17, 1872.

7-166. *Frances Emily Colman*, b. in Ellicottville, N. Y., March 22, 1839, m. in Dunkirk, N. Y., Dec. 12, 1861, THEODORE HINSDALE WHITTLESEY,[2] flour and grain merchant,

---

[1] Son of Samuel Gifford (b. in Belfast, Ireland, Aug. 1, 1799), and w. Rosanna Fraser, (b. in Belfast, Aug. 12, 1802, dau. of Robert Frazer and w. —— Duncan; Scotch), m. in Belfast, Oct. 16, 1823, came to this country about 1825; gr. son of Samuel Gifford (b. in Kilmore, county Down, Ireland), and w. Elizabeth Gibson, dau. of John Gibson.

[2] Son of Hon. Frederick Whittlesey (b. in New Preston, Conn., July 12, 1799, d. in Rochester, N. Y., Sept. 19, 1851), and w. Ann Hinsdale (b. in West Winsted, Conn., Oct. 16, 1802), m. 1826; gr. son of David Whittlesey (b. in New Preston, 1775, d. 1825), and w. Martha Pomeroy; m. Sept. 12, 1825. Hon. F. W. was vice chancellor of the eighth district of the state of New York, and during the famous Morgan excitement in that state wrote and spoke much in opposition to masonry.

who was b. in Rochester, N. Y., Dec. 17, 1833. They res. 1873, in Dunkirk, and have had six children, all b. in that place:

8–140. [WHITTLESEY.] Emily Colman, b. Sept. 12, 1862.
8–141. Frederic, b. Dec. 21, 1863.
8–142. Grace, b. Feb. 7, 1865, d. April 19, 1867.
8–143. Harlan Colman, b. Oct. 16, 1866, d. Jan. 28, 1867.
8–144. Frank Colman, b. Dec. 13, 1867.
8–145. Henry Tucker, b. Nov. 23, 1869.

7-167. *Juliette Clarissa Colman*, b. in Ellicottville, N. Y., Oct. 28, 1843, m. in Dunkirk, N. Y., May 4, 1869, Dr. DAVID GIBBS ALLING,[1] homeopathic physician, who was b. in Norwalk, O., Jan. 8, 1842. He was a surgeon in the U. S. army during the civil war. They res. 1873, in Dunkirk. One child:

8–146. Florence, b. Aug. 13, 1872.

7-168. *Grace Eunecia Colman*, b. in Ellicottville, N. Y., Aug. 1, 1845, m. in Dunkirk, N. Y., Oct. 14, 1867, WILLIAM EBER BUFF CANDEE,[2] hardware merchant, who was b. Oct. 4, 1844. Mr. C. served in the civil war two years and three months, having enlisted at New York, July 10, 1863; was appointed regimental quarter-master sergeant, and honorably discharged Oct. 5, 1865, with letters of highest approbation from his superior officers. They res. 1873, in Dunkirk, and have two children, both b. in that place:

8–147. Jean McGregor, b. Nov. 23, 1868.
8–148. Bertram Colman, b. March 12, 1870.

---

[1] Son of Prudden Alling (b. at Ballston Spa, N. Y., Nov. 8, 1808, res. 1871, at Norwalk, O.), and w. Eliza Lockwood Gibbs (b. at Norwalk, Ct., Feb. 16, 1811), m. at Norwalk, O., July 19, 1835; gr. son of Stephen Young Alling) b. at Newark, N. J., March 1, 1775, d. at Sodus, N. Y., Feb. 4, 1831), and w. Patty Cory (b. at Westfield, N. J., April 22, 1780, d. at Rochester, N. Y., July 7, 1840), m. March 10, 1798. Eliza Lockwood Gibbs, above named, was dau. of David Gibbs, a lawyer by profession, educated at Yale college. He served during most of the war of 1812, holding the office of first lieutenant, and was stationed at New London, Conn.

[2] Son of Fernando Cortes Candee (b. at Pompey, N. Y., Feb. 2, 1816) and w. Maria Wright O'Brien, (b. at Germantown, Pa., Dec. 4, 1818) m. at Collins, Erie Co., N. Y., Sept 21, 1842; gr. son of Eber Candee, (b. March 5, 1785, supposed in Oxford, Ct.) and w. Patience Potter, b. July 15, 1786, dau. of Nathaniel and Ruth Potter. Eber Candee was son of Nehemiah and Content Candee. Maria Wright O'Brien was dau. of William O'Brien (b. in Carlow, Ireland, Dec. 26, 1792) and w. Anne Greaves, b. at Bernah, county Tyrone, Ireland, Sept. 17, 1798; gr. dau. of Daniel and Mary O'Brien. Anne Greaves was of Scotch parentage — dau. of John and Mary Greaves.

7-172. *Sophie Skinner*, b. in Ellicottville, N. Y., July 22, 1851, m. in Ellicottville, Oct. 18, 1871, Dr. HARLAN S. SMITH, allopathic physician. They res. 1873, in Ellicottville.

8–149. Florence, b. Aug. 12, 1872.

7-195. *Amanda Dawson*, b. in Danby, N. Y., Aug. 6, 1828, m. in Danby, Nov. 1, 1851, AXFORD HART, who was b. in Danby, Feb. 13, 1826. Res. 1873, Wellsboro, Pa. Five children:

8–150. Judson, b. in Danby, N. Y., Aug. 15, 1852.
8–151. Sophia, b. in Charleston, Pa., July 7, 1854.
8–152. Aaron, b. in Charleston, Feb. 4, 1857.
8–153. Frances, b. in Charleston, May 16, 1859.
8–154. George, b. in Charleston, March 3, 1862.

7-196. HARMON JACKSON DAWSON, b. in Danby, N. Y., April 13, 1830, m. in Danby, Sept. 8, 1857, *Harriet Louisa Meacham*, who was b. in De Witt, Onondago Co., N. Y., Oct. 26, 1836. They res. 1873, in Wellsboro, Pa. Two children:

8–155. Anna Curtis, b. in Charleston, Pa., Jan. 16, 1861.
8–156. John James, b. in Delmar, Pa., Nov. 11, 1866.

7-197. CHARLES RYLE DAWSON, b. in Danby, N. Y., July 31, 1832, m. in Wellsboro, Pa., July, 1863, *Cordelia Wetherbee*, who was b. in Delmar, Tioga Co., Pa., May 14, 1836. They res. 1873, in Wellsboro. No children.

7-198. JOHN JAMES DAWSON, b. in Danby, N. Y., April 29, 1834. He was drafted for service in the army, Feb. 22, 1864, and assigned in April of that year to the 168th Regt. Pa. Cavalry, then stationed at Cumberland, Md. He performed his duties as a soldier faithfully and well, but being of a delicate constitution, and unacustomed to riding, the long and hard marches on horseback, which became necessary, overtaxed his powers of endurance, and cost him his life. He died in hospital, at Clarksburg, W. Va., of remittent fever, Aug. 14, 1865, after an illness of twenty-one days, twelve of which he spent in camp previous to admission to the hospital. He m. in Charleston, Pa., April 23, 1862, *Juliette Amelia Cooledge*, who was b. in Charleston, Oct. 25, 1837, and res. 1873, in that place. One child:

8–157. Robert Hopestill, b. Dec. 24, 1864.

7-199. *Wealthy Dawson*, b. in Danby, N. Y., June 21, 1836, d. in Charleston, Pa., Jan. 30, 1863; m. in Charleston, June 13, 1856, ABEL NICKERSON, who was b. in Salisbury, N. Y., July 22, 1806, and res. 1873, in Wellsboro, Pa. They had one child:

8–158. Louisa, b. in Richmond, Pa., Aug. 22, 1859.

7-201. GEORGE SMITH DAWSON, b. in Danby, N. Y., Sept. 15, 1845, m. in Charleston, Pa., Jan. 3, 1865, *Amanda Forsyth*, who was b. in Candor, Tioga Co., N. Y., March 22, 1845. They res. 1873, in Wellsboro, Pa. Two children:

8–159. Almira, b. in Charleston, Pa., March 2, 1866.
8–160. Wealthy, b. in Wellsboro, Aug. 8, 1871.

7-209. ASA WESLEY BUTTON, farmer, b. in Danby, N. Y., March 15, 1834, m. in Danby, Feb. 10, 1856, *Catharine Smith*, who was b. in Danby, Jan. 8, 1832. They res. 1873, in Danby, and have two children, both b. in that town:

8–161. Charles Fremont, b. April 6, 1860.
8–162. George Elmer Ellsworth, b. Feb. 1, 1865.

7-211. CHESTER LORENZO WERDON, moulder, b. in Newfield, Tompkins Co., N. Y., Oct. 20, 1840, m. in Ulysses, N. Y., Oct. 17, 1861, *Mary Frances Wiggins*, who was b. in Hector, Tompkins Co., N. Y., Oct. 6, 1844. They res. 1872, in Ulysses, Tompkins Co., N. Y. One child:

8–163. Ida Mary, b. in Ulysses, April 19, 1865.

7-212. *Ophelia A. Werdon*, b. in Newfield, Tompkins Co., N. Y., Oct. 11, 1844, m. Feb. 11, 1866, DANIEL D. SLOCUM, wagon maker, who was b. in Newfield, Feb. 1, 1844. They res. 1872, in Sullivanville, Chemung Co., N. Y. Two chn.:

8–164. Frank Daniel, b. in Sullivanville, March 18, 1868.
8–165. Wealthy Louisa, b. in Sullivanville, April 27, 1871.

7-213. *Emeline Adams Fox*, b. in Caroline, Tompkins Co., N. Y., Aug. 11, 1832, m. in Brighton, Livingston Co., Mich., March 18, 1849, RANSOM R. FULLER. Res. 1870, Owasso, Shiawassee Co., Mich.

7-214. WILLIAM JOHN FOX, b. in Addison, Steuben Co., N. Y., March 2, 1834, m. 1st. in Bennington, Shiawassee Co.,

Mich., Oct. 1, 1868, *Sarah Jane Pope*, who d. May, 1869. 2d. in Novi, Oakland Co., Mich., *Susan Taylor*. They res. 1870, in Venice, Shiawassee Co., Mich.

7-215. CHESTER DAWSON FOX, b. in town of Erwin, Steuben Co., N. Y., Dec. 18, 1835, m. in Rush township, Shiawassee Co., Mich., July 16, 1859, *Rachel Sophia Pope*. They res. 1870, in Fairfield township, Shiawassee Co., Mich.

7-216. *Angeline S. Fox*, b. in Southfield township, Oakland Co., Mich., Nov. 29, 1838, m. in Bennington, Shiawassee Co., Mich., Oct. 1, 1868, EARL STIMPSON HALL. They res. 1870, in Owasso, Mich.

7-219. MILTON DAWSON FOX, b, in Brighton, Livingston Co., Mich., Dec. 8, 1844, m. in Fairfield, Shiawassee Co., Mich., June 30, 1868, *Artemicia Brigham*, who was b. in Darke Co., Ohio, Aug. 15, 1848. They res. 1873, in Duplain, Clinton Co., Mich. Two children:

8–166. William C., b. April 25, 1869, d. July 17, 1870.
8–167. Lewis S., b. Aug. 2, 1871.

7-220. *Casandra A. Fox*, b. in Cahocta township, Livingston Co., Mich., Dec. 14, 1850, m. in Owasso, Shiawassee Co., Mich., Sept. 30, 1869, BARTON GAINER. Res. 1870, in Venice, Shiawassee Co., Mich.

7-221. MYRON HAVILLAH DAWSON, b. in Spencer, Tioga Co., N. Y., March 24, 1837, m. June 21, 1857, *Maryette Clark*, who was b. in Sharon, Litchfield Co., Conn., Dec. 11, 1839. He enlisted, Aug. 12, 1862, as a private in Co. I., 109th Regt. N. Y. S. Vols., and after a few months' service was taken sick in consequence of exposure and fatigue, and d. in military hospital at Beltsville, Md., Nov. 1, 1862, aged 25.[1] They had one child:

8–168. Sidney, b. in Spencer, N. Y., March 22, 1858.

7-223. JOHN DAWSON, b. in Spencer, Tioga Co., N. Y., Dec. 19, 1842, m. Nov. 1, 1868, *Mary Emma Bassett*, who was b. in Calais, Washington Co., Me., Aug. 17, 1847. He enlisted, Aug. 1, 1862, as a private in Co. I., 109th Regt. N.

[1] His. wid. m. Oct. 6, 1872, Samuel Miller, of Wolcott, Wayne Co., N. Y.

Y. S. Vols., and was in several engagements, in one of which he was severely wounded through the wrist. He was discharged for disability, occasioned by his wound, July 12, 1863. They res. 1873, Spencer, N. Y. One child:

8–169. Hattie, b. June 18, 1872.

7-224. *Ruth Diana Dawson*, b. in Spencer, N. Y., Feb. 23, 1847, m. Dec. 31, 1863, WILLIAM PERRIN, who was b. in Spencer, June 16, 1847. They res. 1873, in Spencer. One child:

8–170. Lavergne, b. in Spencer, July 29, 1871.

7-226. SETH WARREN DAWSON, b. in Spencer, N. Y., Dec. 16, 1841, m. in Spencer, Sept. 18, 1868, *Phebe Andrus*. They res. 1873, in Spencer. One child:

8–171. Lena, b. in Spencer, Feb. 11, 1870.

7-229. *Isabel German*, b. in Ithaca, N. Y., May 27, 1840, m. in Mansfield, O., Feb. 24, 1859, EMANUEL HERSHA KEYSER, who was b. in Richland Co., O., Aug. 28, 1835. They res. 1872, in Mansfield. Three children:

8–172. Ida May, b. June 20, 1859.
8–173. Milton, b. Sept. 22, 1862.
8–174. Mary, b. July 23, 1867.

7-231. *Lydia Ann German*, b. in Danby, N. Y., Oct. 22, 1845, m. in Mansfield, O., Feb. 16, 1865, MELVIN MONROE GATES, who was b. in Richland Co., O., Nov. 16, 1840. They res. 1872, in Mansfield. One child:

8–175. Scott Horace, b. in Richland Co., O., April 28, 1867.

7-236. WALLACE ADELBERT MORSE, b. in Spencer, N. Y., June 6, 1851, m. Res. 1873, in Chicago, Ill. One ch.:
8–176. Hattie Viola.

7-239. *Martha Maria Barnes*, b. in Paris, N. Y., Oct. 27, 1833, m. Dec. 6, 1863, HIRAM H. DAVIS. They res. 1870, in Mich. Three children:

8–177. Eva Jane, b. Sept. 7, 1864.
8–178. Lucinda, b. July 3, 1866.
8–179. Edwin Orlando, b. Dec. 12, 1867.

7-240. *Mary Jane Barnes*, b. in Paris, N. Y., March 2, 1835, m. Feb. 22, 1857, Elam Tuttle, b. in Oneida Co., N. Y., Feb. 10, 1832.[1] They res. 1870, at Rockford P. O., Kent Co., Mich. Two children:

8-180. Charles Morette, b. Nov. 12, 1857.
8-181. Willis Melvin, b. Dec. 10, 1860.

7-241. Horace Lamotte Barnes, b. in Sharon, Mich., March 27, 1836, m. July 26, 1860, *Martha Anderson.* They res. 1870, in Mich. Two children:

8-182. Mary Theresa, b. June 12, 1861.
8-183. Adelaide Estelle, b. May 26, 1865.

7-243. John Milton Barnes, b. in Cortland, Mich., March 27, 1839, m. Nov. 9, 1861, *Lucy Anderson.* They res. 1870, in Mich. Two children:

8-184. Ella, b. March 17, 1864.
8-185. Eliza, b. May 7, 1865.

7-247. Lucien Denison Barnes, b. in Cortland, Mich., April 11, 1847, m. Feb. 10, 1869, *Mary E. Spencer.* They res. 1870, in Mich. One child:

8-186. George Martin, b. March 1, 1870.

7-250. Edwin Woodbury Barnes, farmer, b. in Verona, Oneida Co., N. Y., Nov. 4, 1834, m. at Big Prairie, Newaygo Co., Mich., Nov. 20, 1862, *Alina Ermina French*, who was b. in Tecumseh, Mich., 1843. He served three years during the civil war as private and sergeant in the Fifth Regt. Mich. Cavalry Vols. They res. 1870, at Big Prairie. Five children:

8-187. Eddie Augustus, b. 1863.
8-188. Ida Estelle, b. 1864.
8-189. Alina Edith, b. 1866.
8-190. Inez Adelle, b. 1868.
8-191. Burton Eugene, b. 1869.

---

[1] Son of Charles Tuttle (b. in Oneida Co., N. Y., June 22, 1807) and w. Harriet Tuttle, m. April 10, 1831; gr. son of Elam Tuttle (b. in Woodbridge, Ct., June 29, 1777) and w. Mary Scofield, m. May 1, 1802; gt. gr. son of Uri Tuttle (b. in Hamden, Ct., 1738), and w. Thankful Ives, m. 1764. Uri Tuttle was son of Nathaniel and *Mary Todd* Tuttle, of North Haven, Ct.; gr. son of Nathaniel and Esther Tuttle; gt. gr. son of Jonathan and *Rebecca Bell* Tuttle. Jonathan was fourth child of Wm. and Elizabeth Tuttle of New Haven, the original emigrants. [Mem. Chauncey Tuttle (b. Sept. 19, 1771, son of Uri Tuttle, above named) m. Mrs. Elizabeth Peck, and had a son Mansfield Tuttle who m. Mary Dawson, *of what family?*]

7-251. AUGUSTUS MILTON BARNES, b. in Verona, Oneida Co., N. Y., Sept. 16, 1836, m. at Otisco, Ionia Co., Mich., Oct. 19, 1868, *Frances Cleora Andrews*, who was b. in Vergennes, Kent Co., Mich., 1846. He served three years in the civil war as a private in Co. F, Second Mich. Cavalry Vols., is a farmer, and carpenter and joiner. They res. 1870, in Gratton, Kent Co., Mich. No children.

7-253. IRAM CURTIS BARNES, farmer, b. in Verona, Oneida Co., N. Y., April 15, 1843, m. in Cortland, Kent Co., Mich., Jan. 2, 1864, *Charlotte Augusta Foote*, who was b. in Canastota, Madison Co., N. Y., May 20, 1845. They res. 1873, in Cortland, Mich. Three children:

8–192. Carey Amanzo, b. Nov. 10, 1864.
8–193. Alfred Adelbert, b. April 20, 1866.
8–194. Sheridan Foote, b. Oct. 10, 1868.

7-261. *Eunice Rebecca Homiston*, b. in Fond du Lac, Jan. 16, 1847, m. May 1, 1865, JOHN BROWNELL JOHNSON, who was b. in Watertown, Wis., Nov. 18, 1841. He is a locomotive engineer. They res. 1873, in Winona, Minn. One child:

8–195. Edward Dwight, b. in Milwaukee, Wis., April 9, 1867.

7-268. *Susan Delphine Doolittle*, b. in Bradford, Rock county, Wis., Aug. 24, 1847, m. in Candor, N. Y., Nov. 6, 1870, JAMES K. POLK HOLLY, who was b. in Candor, Feb. 15, 1845. They res. 1873, in Candor. One child:

8–196. Charles Atherton, b. March 8, 1872.

7-271. SYLVESTER LEGRAND DOOLITTLE, b. in Danby, N. Y., Jan. 21, 1845, m. in Eau Clair, Wis., Nov. 30, 1869, *Adelle Horrey*, who was b. in Sparta, Wis., March 23, 1852, dau. of George and Hattie Horrey. They res. 1873, in Oshkosh, Wis. Two children:

8–197. Myrtle Leona, b. in Eau Clair, Jan. 31, 1871.
8–198. Frank Rea, b. in Milwaukee, May 31, 1873.

7-278. *Mary Elizabeth Doolittle*, b. in Oswego, N. Y., Jan. 18, 1850, m. in Delavan, Wis., May 1, 1870, ALEXANDER HAMILTON ALLYN, b. in Hartford, Ct., Sept. 1, 1835, son of Timothy M. and Susan Ann Allyn, of Hartford. They res. 1873, Delavan, Wis.

7-279. *Florence Adelaide Doolittle*, b. in Oswego, N. Y., July 26, 1852, m. in Racine, Wis., May 4, 1869, RALPH McDOUGAL RECTOR, farmer, b. in Duanesburgh, N. Y., Oct. 25, 1835, son of Joseph and *Mary Ann McDougal* Rector. They res. 1873, Walworth, Wis. One child:

8–199. Frances Leonora, b. Aug. 25, 1872.

7-291. EDWIN GARRIT DOUD, farmer, b. in Freedom, O., Dec. 17, 1831, m. 1st. in Nelson, O., April 10, 1853, *Jane Sperry*,[1] who was b. in Nelson, June 10, 1833, and d. in Freedom, Feb. 28, 1854. They had one child:

8–200. Jane Sperry, b. in Freedom, O., Jan. 17, 1854, res. 1873, Freedom. CLARK.

Mr. D. m. 2d. in Edinburg, O., Aug. 20, 1854, *Sarah A. Foley*, who was b. Oct. 28, 1832. They res. 1873, in Vassar, Tuscola Co., Mich. Two children:

8–201. John Foley, b. in Vassar, June 6, 1856.
8–202. Frederick Samuel, b. in Denmark, Tuscola Co., June 6, 1861.

7-292. HENRY RHOADS DOUD, farmer, b. in Freedom, O., June 30, 1833, m. in Nelson, O., April 10, 1854, *Parena Knowlton*,[2] who was b. in Nelson, Feb. 8, 1833. They res. 1873, in Freedom; three children, all b. in that town:

8–203. Willard Knowlton, b. April 8, 1855.
8–204. Julia Esther, b. Sept. 10, 1856.
8–205. Jessie Arvilla, b. Dec. 21, 1862.

7-293. *Julia Maria Dawson*, b. in Vernon, O., Oct. 8, 1840, d. Feb. 7, 1860, m. May 26, 1859, HENRY WANENAKER. They had one child:

8–206. Eva, b. March 20, 1860, d. May 1, 1864.

7-294. ALBERT ADDISON DAWSON, b. in Fowler, O., Jan. 4, 1842, m. Dec. 27, 1866, *Cornelia Ryan*, who was b. in

---

[1] Dau. of Thaddeus Sperry, farmer, (d. in Hastings, Mich., March 3, 1869) and w. Sylvia Maria Landon (b. in State of N. Y., 1806, d. in Nelson, O., Sept. 30, 1866).

[2] Dau. of Willard Robin Knowlton, farmer and banker, pres. of the Garrettsville Savings Bank, (b. in Troy, N. Y., Dec. 6, 1800), and w. Hannah Ovilla Harrison (b. in Cornwall, Ct., Nov. 11, 1805), m. March 29, 1827, in Nelson, O., where they still reside (1871).

Chagrin Falls, Cuyahoga Co., O., June 28, 1849. They res. 1870, in Concord, DeKalb Co., Ind. No children.

7-295. *Ursula Amelia Dawson*, b. in Concord, Ind., Dec. 20, 1845, m. June 14, 1866, JOHN HAMILTON, who was b. in Concord, April 28, 1841. They res. 1870, in Concord. One child:

8-207. Corel Lorenzo, b. Jan. 28, 1869.

7-300. *Charlotte Jackson*, b. in Bazetta, O., Jan. 21, 1839, m. MOSES T. SCOTT, printer. They res. 1870, in Pittsburg, Pa. Four children:

8-208. Elmer, b. 1862.
8-209. Myra, b. 1866.
8-210. John, b. 1868.
8-211. A *son*, b. 1870.

8-36. *Sarah C. Williams*, b. in Geneva, O., April 25, 1847, m. in Jefferson, O., Feb. 18, 1868, FRANKLIN J. STONE, who was b. in Evans, Erie Co., N. Y., March 11, 1848. They have (1871) one child:

9-1. Jesse F., b. in Evans, N. Y., Nov. 26, 1868.

8-61. *Harriet Eliza Rogers*, b. in Chenango Forks, N. Y., May 9, 1843, m. May 13, 1868, Rev. ISAAC MILLS ELY. He was in 1869-71 pastor of the Presbyterian church at Chenango Forks, and previously pastor of the Presbyterian church at Ellicottville, N. Y. In 1872 Mr. and Mrs. Ely established at Chenango Forks a select family school for girls, which has now entered on its second year, with every promise of success and permanence. They have two children:

9-2. Emma Willard, b. in Ellicottville, Feb. 3, 1869.
9-3. William Rogers, b. in Chenango Forks, Feb. 3, 1871.

8-62. *Helen Mary Rogers*, b. in Chenango Forks, N. Y., Nov. 8, 1845, m. Sept. 19, 1866, Hon. JEROME B. LANDFIELD, who was b. in Harvard, Delaware Co., N. Y., Nov. 6, 1827. They res. 1873, in Newark Valley, Tioga Co., N. Y., where he is extensively engaged in business as a tanner. He was a member of the N. Y. state legislature, 1864, and was reëlected, 1872. They have had two children, both b. in Newark Valley:

9-4. [LANDFIELD.] Henry Clark, b. May 5, 1868, d. July 28, 1870.
9-5. Jerome Barker, b. May 7, 1871.

8-63. *Grace Meloy Rogers*, b. in Chenango Forks, N. Y., Jan. 28, 1848, m. Dec. 25, 1866, ROBERT D. JILLSON, railway ticket agent, who was b. in Cazenovia, N. Y., Oct. 6, 1828. They res. 1873, in Hornellsville, N. Y. Three children:

9-6. Willard Rogers, b. in Chenango Forks, Oct. 24, 1867.
9-7. Eliza Chittenden, b. in Hornellsville, April 21, 1870.
9-8.

8-117. *Jennie Augusta Gray*, b. in Fenton, N. Y., Dec. 18, 1854, m. July 19, 1871, ORRINGTON ELMER ERSKINE, who was b. in North Stoughton, Mass., Dec. 7, 1846, son of Robert and Joanna Erskine. They res. 1873, in Binghamton, N. Y. One child:

9-9. Robert Vernett, b. in Binghamton, July 22, 1873.

8-200. *Jane Sperry Doud*, b. in Freedom, O., Jan. 17, 1854, m. in Freedom, June 15, 1873, FRANK P. CLARK, miller, who was b. in Nelson, Portage county, Ohio, Oct. 12, 1852. They res. in Freedom.

NOTE. The foregoing record of the family of ROBERT DAWSON contains of the second generation, 2 names — first birth 1677, last death 1759; of the third generation, 13 names — first birth 1716, last death 1799; of the fourth generation, lineally descended from 6 of the third, 29 names — first birth 1742, last death 1840; of the fifth generation, lineally descended from 10 of the fourth, 54 names — first birth 1766, two living in 1873; of the sixth generation, lineally descended from 23 of the fifth, 142 names — first birth 1794, many living in 1873; of the seventh generation, lineally descended from 83 of the sixth, 332 names — first birth 1815; of the eighth generation, lineally descended from 92 of the seventh, 211 names — first birth 1841; of the ninth generation, 9 names — first birth 1867. The average number of children per family in the third generation was a fraction more than 6; in the fourth generation a fraction less than five; in the fifth generation a fraction more than 5; in the sixth generation a fraction more than 6. —

FAMILY OF THOMAS DAWSON,

OF NEW HAVEN, CONN., 1721–2.

Of this family but little is known. Nothing has been discovered to connect it with the family of ROBERT DAWSON, of East Haven.

1. March 5, 1721–2, John Hitchcock conveyed to "THOMAS DAWSON, formerly of Newport, on Road Island,[1] now of New Haven," 2½ acres in New Haven: consideration £100. (*New Haven Records*, vol. 6, p. 24).

April 14, 1722, THOMAS DAWSON, similarly described, in consideration of "love, good will and natural affection," conveyed to his "loving son,"

2–1. Job Dawson, of New Haven, a house, barn and home lot in New Haven,[2] and sundry household goods. (*N. H. Records*, vol. 6, p. 101. The same land bought of John Hitchcock).

2–1. JOB DAWSON and *Sarah Thomas*[3] were married at New

---

[1] *The R. I. Colonial Records*, 1636–1740, recently printed, have been examined without discovery of this name.

[2] This house was in West Lane. Adjoining it on either hand were the residences of the Nott and Beecher families, and next beyond the latter that of the Thomas family, with which Job D. became connected by marriage. See "A plan of the town of New Haven, as taken by Mr. Joseph Brown in the year 1724."— Barber's *Antiquities of New Haven*, p. 109.

[3] Records of conveyances by Job and Sarah Dawson are as follows:

July 20, 1724. To Jona. Atwater jun., of New Haven, 3½ acres "in said New Haven, lying in Plainfield, and in the first division of sequestered land."— *N. H. Records*, vol. 6, p. 466.

Dec. 24, 1733. To Samuel Brown, of New Haven, a certain quantity of meadow land lying in the "subhards" quarter in the town aforesaid, being half the meadow lying in Hill's cove, formerly belonging to Samuel Thomas, of the town aforesaid, deceased, and in the division of said Thomas's estate by the freeholders set to Sarah, the wife of Job Dawson.— *Records*, vol. 9, p. 392.

Feb. 24, 1734–5. To Jona. Atwater, a half division lot of land in township of New Haven, containing 21½ acres, "being a lot that was drawn and laid out in the name of our honored father, Samuel Thomas, deceased."— *Records*, vol. 10, p. 53.

Feb. 22, 1728–9, recorded May 7, 1735. To Joseph Thomas, of New Haven, "land lying in the subhards quarter in New Haven, being one acre which accrued to the said Sarah as part of her portion in the estates of her father, mother and sister, deceased."— *Records*, vol. 10, p. 93.

Haven, Feb. 12, 1718–19. He d. before Oct. 21, 1745.[1] She was the daughter of Samuel Thomas. They had five chn.:

3–1. Ann, b. June 28, 1720. WANTWOOD.
3–2. Sarah, b. March 27, 1724.[2]
3–3. Elizabeth, b. Feb. 4, 1727–8.
3–4. Rhoda, b. Aug. 5, 1731.
3–5. Job, b. March 6, 1734–5.

3–1. *Ann Dawson* and BENJAMIN WANTWOOD, both of New Haven, "were joyned in marriage" March 30, 1743. He was b. July 20, 1712, son of Benjamin Wantwood, of East Haven. They had:

4–1. Phebe, b. June 5, 1745. (The date of this birth is also recorded in same volume, March 30, 1744–5, and March 30, 1748, making the record abundantly confusing and wholly inexplicable. It would appear that the mother must have d. before 1747, and B. W. m. 2d, Sarah——. The birth of a son is recorded as follows: "Benjamin, son of Benj. and *Sarah* Wantwood, Nov. 5, 1747").—*N. H. Records of births, marriages,* &c., pp. 227, 267 and 504.

---

[1] On that date the Court of Probate at New Haven appointed Lt. Thomas Holt of New Haven, guardian of Rhoda Dawson, minor child of "Job Dawson, late of New Haven, deceased."

[2] She never married. Administration on her estate was granted to Joseph Peck of New Haven, Nov 5, 1787. It was divided between Rhoda and Elizabeth, her sisters, then also *unm.*

FAMILY OF JOHN DAWSON,

OF MONROE, CONN., ABOUT 1785–90.

1. JOHN DAWSON,[1] was b. in England, June 4, 1749. He graduated at Oxford, and was sent to America in the British army, a member of a regiment called the Legion, commanded by Major Cochran. He was at the taking of Philadelphia, in 1777, and at the battle of the Cowpens, 1781, "got whipped by Morgan." He was concerned in an engagement at Egg Harbor with a brig called the Middletown, which was taken by the British, although the crew escaped. The prize money gained by the capture of the brig was the subject of an altercation between him and the major of his regiment, in the course of which he struck the major with his fist, and knocked him down. According to the articles of war he would have been liable to be put to death for striking a superior officer, and he deserted to save his life. He went into the state of Connecticut, where he was joined by his w. whom he had m. in Philadelphia. Her maiden name was *Elizabeth Maria Hamilton Maxfield*, and she was b. in Ireland, May 1, 1754. Her mother, a Miss Hamilton, had m. a man named Knox, and he dying, she m. 2d. a protestant minister named Maxfield. Their dau. Elizabeth came to America for her health, and lived with an aunt in Philadelphia. The war broke out six months after her arrival, and when the British army was at Philadelphia, her half brother, who was a naval officer, and had been a classmate of Dawson, invited him to see her. A mutual attachment sprang up between them, and led to their marriage. They settled in Monroe, Fairfield Co., about sixteen miles north of Bridgeport. From this place they removed to New Haven county before 1792,

[1] The information in regard to this family chiefly communicated by Mr. William Dawson, Hotchkissville, Ct., but the history of JOHN DAWSON from his son, Mr. Richard Hawley Dawson, of Iowa.

and finally to Greene Co., N. Y., where they died — he, March 18, 1818; she, Feb. 2, 1834. They had nine children, all probably b. in Conn.:

2–1. John, d. in Greene Co., N. Y.; three sons, res. near Binghamton, N. Y.
2–2. Francis, d. in Greene Co., N. Y.; son Sheldon, res. 1870, Jacksonville, same county.
2–3. Betsey, b. in Monroe, Ct., Jan. 15, 1788, d. Feb. 11, 1869, a. 81. CARLEY.
2–4. Prudence, m. SPRING. (Of this family, Edmund Spring, Ansonia, Ct.)
2–5. Hugh F., b. in New Haven Co., Ct., April 26, 1792, d. in Greene Co., N. Y., June 10, 1862, a. 70; *m.*
2–6. Polly, m. WHITFORD. (Of this family, Joel Whitford, Sharon, Ct.)
2–7. Richard Hawley, res. 1870, Orange P. O., Clinton Co., Iowa; *m.* and said to have three sons and three daughters, all res. in Iowa.
2–8. Sally, m. WARD. (Of this family, John T. Ward, Woodbury, Ct.)
2–9. Catharine.

2–3. *Betsey Dawson*, b. in Monroe, Ct., Jan. 15, 1788, d. Feb. 11, 1869, m. July 6, 1806, JAMES CARLEY,[1] who was b. Dec. 25, 1778, d. March 17, 1858. They had:

3–1. John, b. May 31, 1807, d. in state of N. Y., Dec. 17, 1848; was m.; no records.
3–2. Eli A., b. April 12, 1809, d. Feb., 1867; *m.*
3–3. Hugh, b. Oct. 7, 1811, d. Aug. 18, 1873; *m.*

2–5. HUGH F. DAWSON, b. in New Haven county, Ct., April 26, 1792, d. in Greene Co., N. Y., June 10, 1862, aged 70, m. in Greene county, *Nancy Pearsall*, who was b. in that county, March 14, 1793, and d. in same place, March 24, 1850, aged 57. They had nine chn., all b. in Greenville, N. Y.:

3–4. Betsey Ann, b. Feb. 14, 1816, res. 1870, New Rutland, Ill. HALSTEAD.
3–5. Francis, b. Jan. 17, 1818, res. 1873, Hotchkissville, Ct.; *m.*
3–6. William, b. June 20, 1820, res. 1873, Hotchkissville, Ct.; *m.*
3–7. Henry, b. June 22, 1822, res. 1873, Hotchkissville, Ct.; *m.*
3–8. Maria, b. Sept. 11, 1824, d. March 18, 1865. AUSTIN; BAKER.
3–9. Polly, b. March 13, 1827, res. 1870, La Prairie Centre, Ill. LAMOREAUX; HALSTEAD.
3–10. Lewis, b. June 19, 1829, res. 1873, Metuchen, N. J.; *m.*
3–11. John, b. April 1, 1832, res. 1873, Hotchkissville, Ct.; *m.*
3–12. Hawley, b. July 11, 1835, d. Feb. 12, 1839.

---

[1] The record of the family of James Carley communicated by Mr. G. H. Carley, of Danbury, Ct.

3-2. ELI A. CARLEY, b. April 12, 1809, d. Feb., 1867, m. *Laura Hubbell.* They had eight children:

4-1. Lucia, m.——MUNSON.
4-2. James.
4-3. Ellen, m.——LAKE.
4-4. Horatio.
4-5. Eli.
4-6. John.
4-7. Emmitt.
4-8. Charles.

3-3. HUGH CARLEY, b. Oct. 7, 1811, d. Aug. 18, 1873, m.——*Fuller.* They had three children:

4-9. George H., res. 1873, Danbury, Ct.
4-10. Jennie E., m. W. A. BEDIENT.
4-11. Julia A., m. W. S. BAILEY.

3-4. *Betsey Ann Dawson*, b. in Greenville, N. Y., Feb. 14, 1816, m. JOHN HALSTEAD. They res. 1870, in New Rutland, La Salle Co., Ill. Three children:

4-12. Christina.
4-13. Adaline.
4-14. Elizabeth.

3-5. FRANCIS DAWSON, b. in Greenville, N. Y., Jan. 17, 1818, m. 1st., July 1, 1843, *Betsey Ann Halstead*, who d. June, 1858; 2d., Sept. 7, 1859, *Elizabeth Merriam*, who was b. in Watertown, Ct., May 6, 1836. He is a manufacturer of woolen goods, being engaged in that business with his brothers, William, Henry and John. Res. 1873, Hotchkissville, Litchfield Co., Conn. Children:

4-15. Sophronia, b. Jan. 30, 1845.
4-16. Caroline, b. Feb. 10, 1847.
4-17. Nancy, b. March 11, 1850.
4-18. Lewis, b. May, 19, 1856, d. 1857.
4-19. Louis Eugene, b. May 26, 1864.
4-20. Erwin Clinton, b. May 1, 1871.

3-6. WILLIAM DAWSON, b. in Greenville, N. Y., June 20, 1820, m. May 13, 1850, *Mary P. Thompson*, who was b. in South Britain, Ct., July 12, 1828. Res. 1873, Hotchkissville, Conn. Children:

4-21. Alice, b. in Medusa, N. Y., April 14, 1857.
4-22. Emma, b. in Stuyvesant, N. Y., June 28, 1861.

3-7. HENRY DAWSON, b. in Greenville, N. Y., June 22, 1822, m. *Sarah A. Ward.* Res. 1873, Hotchkissville, Conn. One child:

4-23. Catharine.

3-8. *Maria Dawson*, b. in Greenville, N. Y., Sept. 11, 1824, d. March 18, 1865. She m. 1st., ELIAKIM AUSTIN; 2d., LUMAN BAKER. Two children:

4-24. Emeline.
4-25. Lucius.

3-9. *Polly Dawson*, b. in Greenville, N. Y., March 13, 1827, m. 1st., ALVAH LAMOREAUX; 2d., SAMUEL HALSTEAD. Res. 1870, La Prairie Centre, Marshall Co., Ill. Five chn.:

4-26. Lorenzo.
4-27. Ida.
4-28. Emma.
4-29. Marcella.
4-30. Frank.

3-10. LEWIS DAWSON, b. in Greenville, N. Y., June 19, 1829, m. June 6, 1860, *Serina Thomas*, who was b. in Woodbury, Ct., June 17, 1838. Res. 1873, Metuchen, Middlesex Co., N. J. Two children:

4-31. Effie, b. Feb. 19, 1864.
4-32. May, b. May 20, 1866.

3-11. JOHN DAWSON, b. in Greenville, N. Y., April 1, 1832, m. 1st., March 2, 1857, *Mary Allen*, who was b. in Bethlehem, Ct., Aug. 2, 1835, d. in Hotchkissville, Dec. 28, 1858; 2d., June 6, 1860, *Clementine S. Thomas*, who was b. in Hotchkissville, Sept. 24, 1841. Res. 1873, Hotchkissville, Ct. Two children:

4-33. Rosetta, b. June 11, 1864, d. aged 15 months.
4-34. A *daughter*, b. and d. Jan. 30, 1866.

NOTE. WILLIAM DAWSON and w. *Emeline*, with children Sarah J., Ann E., Diantha, Martha and Anna, also one Josephine Dawson, were listed as residents of Woodbury, Conn., between 1st. Nov., 1852, and 1st. March, 1853. —See Cothren's *Woodbury*, p. 798. From Mr. William Dawson, of Hotchkissville, is learned the facts that his namesake of Woodbury removed thence to Norwalk, and, while employed there in a woolen mill, disappeared suddenly, and has never been heard from since. He had a brother, James Dawson, in Rockville, Ct., and one named Robson Dawson, who "went west and died." They were born in England.

FAMILY OF PETER DAWSON,

OF BARNET, VERMONT, ABOUT 1800.

From Mr. Adam Dawson, of New London, Ct., 1870–73, *and others, the following:*

1. PETER DAWSON, a cabinet maker, noted for the perfection of his workmanship, was b. about 1770, at Linlithgo, near Edinburgh, Scotland, where his father, James Dawson, lived and died.[1] His uncle, Abram Dawson, was a large and wealthy distiller of that place. His mother's maiden name was Jenny Drummond, and he had two brothers — William, who d. in Scotland, though he had resided for a short time in this country, and Adam, who d. young. He m. in Scotland, *Margaret Selkirk*, and emigrated shortly after to the city of New York, about the year 1800, where he had a married sister, who had preceded him — the wife of a merchant named Lang. Mr. Dawson and his wife remained in the city only a few months, and removed thence to Barnet, Caledonia Co., Vermont, where they resided for many years. They afterwards removed to Derry, N. H. He d. in Windham, near Derry, 4 Sept., 1829, aged 59, and she d. in Methuen, Mass., Feb., 1838, aged 57. They had nine children, all b. in Barnet, Vt.:

2–1. James, b. April, 1802, res. 1873, in Worcester, Mass.; *unm.*
2–2. Jane, b. Oct., 1803, d. in Harvard, Mass., 1861, aged 58. INGERSON.
2–3. Adam, b. Sept. 4, 1805, res. 1873, New London, Ct.; *m.*
2–4. Margaret Barr, b. July 9, 1807, res. 1873, Clinton, Mass. COULTER.
2–5. Janet Monteith, b. March 4, 1809, res. 1873, in Methuen, Mass. STICKNEY.
2–6. John Selkirk, b. Sept., 1811, res. 1873, Putnam, Ct.; *m.*

[1] Probably related to ADAM DAWSON, Esq., of Bonnytoun, Linlithgowshire, who m. *Frances Mac Kell*, dau. of Patrick Mac Kell, Esq., of Craigie, and had (his third son) Adam Dawson, Esq., of Bonnytoun, b. 1793, educated at the University of Edinburgh, a justice of the peace and deputy lieutenant for Linlithgowshire, proprietor of Bonnytoun, and formerly one of the sheriff's substitutes for Linlithgowshire. He m. 1824, Helen, dau. of John Ramage, Esq., of Edinburgh, and has, with other issue, Adam, a magistrate and sheriff's substitute for county Linlithgow, b. 1829.— Walford's *County Families of the United Kingdom.*

2–7. Hannah, b. abt. 1813, d. in Derry, N. H., Jan., 1830, aged 17.

2–8. Isabella, b. Aug. 22, 1817, d. in Springfield, Mass., March 28, 1857. MATTOON.

2–9. Sarah Gilson, b. abt. Jan. 1819, res. 1872, in Lancaster, Mass.; *unm.*

2–2. *Jane Dawson*, b. in Barnet, Vt., Oct., 1803, m. in Wilmington, Mass., DAVID H. INGERSON, of Vermont. She d. in Harvard, Mass., 1861, leaving five sons:

3–1. William Wallace, b. in Windham, Mass., res. 1873, in Worcester, Mass.; *unm.*

3–2. James, b. in Grafton, Mass., res. Worcester, Mass.; *unm.*

3–3. John S., b. in Orono, Me., d. abt. 1864, in Trenton, Mass.; *unm.*

3–4. Frederick A., b. in Lancashire, N. H., res. 1873, New London, Ct.; *m.*, no children.

3–5. David Harvey, b. in Lancashire, N. H., res. Worcester, Mass.; *m.*, no children.

2–3. ADAM DAWSON, b. in Barnet, Vt., Sept. 4, 1805, m. in Albany, N. Y., Jan. 24, 1843, *Louisa Jones*, of Westfield, Mass. He res. 1873, in New London, Ct.

Mr. Dawson has been engaged for the past forty years in the building of railroads and other public works. In 1831, he constructed, under contract, a portion of the Boston and Lowell R. R.—the first railroad in New England. In 1833–4 he built a section of the Boston and Worcester R. R., and in 1835 a part of the Bangor and Piscataquis R. R., of Maine. After this he had a contract on the Croton Water Works, at New York, which occupied him a year and a half. The Hartford and New Haven R. R., 1839, and the Western (Boston and Albany) R. R., 1840-41, were his next undertakings. In 1844-5 he built eleven miles of the Fall River and Myrick R. R., besides doing other railroad work in New England. In 1846 he built the foundation of the Bay State Mills, at Lawrence, Mass., and in the two following years, in connection with his brother-in-law, Mr. Mattoon, he built the Worcester and Nashua R. R., forty-five miles in length. Twelve miles of the Ohio and Mississippi R. R. were built by him in 1852, and the masonry of fifteen or twenty miles of the Wabash Valley R. R., besides a part of the grading of same, in 1853-55. In 1856-57 he constructed the masonry of the Suspension Bridge, at Cincinnati, O., and in 1858 he contracted for the building of the Brooklyn, N. Y.,

Water Works, to which he devoted the two following years. The extension of the Boston and Fall River R. R. to Newport was done by him in 1861-62, after which, during the civil war, he was engaged in various public works in the city of Worcester, Mass. In 1867, in company with two other gentlemen, he purchased the extensive and valuable granite quarries at East Lyme, Conn., and has since built a number of light houses on the New England coast, of which that at Sabin's Point, at the mouth of Providence river, built in 1872, is the largest and costliest — being one of the best of the government works of this character. It would be difficult to point to a life more industriously or usefully spent.[1] Mr. Dawson has had five children :

3–6. Mary Louisa, b. in Springfield, Mass., Nov., 1843, res. New London, Ct. ; *unm.*

3–7. Adam, b. in Worcester, Mass., May, 1845, d. April, 1846.

3–8. Margaret, b. in Worcester, Oct. 20, 1847, d. April, 1853.

3–9. Caroline Elizabeth, b. in Worcester, April 9, 1849, res. New London, Ct. ; *unm.*

3–10. Marion Augusta, b. in Worcester, June, 1850, d. Aug. 29, 1851.

2–4. *Margaret Barr Dawson*, b. in Barnet, Vt., July 9, 1807, m. Nov. 28, 1832, James W. Coulter, who was b. in Cambridge, Washington Co., N. Y., Aug. 31, 1806, and d. Feb. 4, 1871. He enlisted, 1861, in the 22d Regt. N. Y. Vols., for two years ; was discharged at expiration of term of service, June 6, 1863 ; reënlisted in the 2d N. Y. Veteran Cavalry, and after serving about one year was discharged on account of old age. She res. 1873, Clinton, Mass. They had eight children :

3–11. Peter, b. in Jackson, N. Y., Oct. 7, 1833, d. Oct. 27, 1833.

3–12. Henrietta, b. in Troy, N. Y., May 2, 1836, res. 1873, in Clinton, Mass. ; *unm.*

3–13. Clarence L., b. in Troy, N. Y., July 1, 1838, enlisted in the 123d Regt. N. Y. Vols., and d. in hospital at Alexandria, Va., Oct.

---

[1] Mr. D. wrote, May 29, 1870, as follows :

"I left Vermont at the age of 22, and have not resided there since. I did not know of any other family of our name in the state, and have seldom met any of the name since I left it. Although I have traveled through all the New England states and most of the western states, I have not seen more than three or four that I remember. In 1838, I looked over the *Directory* in New York city, and found but three or four of that name in it, and as the name has greatly multiplied since that time I think there must have been some fresh arrivals from over the water, of late years." [Mr. Dawson is quite right in regard to the new comers — they are very numerous — but he is in error in regard to the number of Dawsons named in the New York *City Directory* for 1838. It contained the addresses of fourteen persons and one business firm of our name.]

2, 1863, from wounds received at the battle of Chancellorsville. He was *unm.*

3–14. [COULTER]. William James, b. inTroy, Feb. 13, 1841, res. 1873, in Clinton, Mass.; *m.*

3–15. John T., b. in Troy, May 4, 1843, res. 1873, in New London, Ct.; *m.*

3–16. Fannie S., b. in Jackson, N. Y., Aug. 27, 1844, res. 1873, in Clinton, Mass. HUNT.

3–17. Sarah M., b. in Cambridge, Aug. 3, 1846, d. in Clinton, Mass., Nov. 25, 1866, *unm.*

3–18. Dawson, b. in Cambridge, March 13, 1849, res. 1873, in Clinton, Mass.; harness maker; *unm.*

2–5. *Janet Monteith Dawson*, b. in Barnet, Vt., March 4, 1809, m. April 5, 1831, JOHN STICKNEY, who was b. in Atkinson, N. H., June 12, 1806. Res. 1873, in Methuen, Mass. Three children, all b. in that town:[1]

3–19. Andrew Jackson, b. May 15, 1832, res. 1873, in New London, Ct.; *unm.*

3–20. William Hardy, b. Sept. 24, 1833, res. 1873, in Methuen; *m.*

3–21. Lafayette, b. Sept. 21, 1844; res. 1873, in Warren, Maine; *m.*

2–6. JOHN SELKIRK DAWSON, railroad contractor, b. in Barnet, Vt., Sept., 1811, res. 1873, Putnam, Ct. He m. about 1838, *Salome Emerson*, and had:

3–22. Fanny E., b. in Bangor, Me., May, 1839, res. 1873, Sacramento, Cal.; *unm.*

2–8. *Isabella Dawson*, b. in Barnet, Vt., Aug. 22, 1817, m. in Troy, N. Y., May 11, 1843, WILLIAM MATTOON, railroad contractor, who was b. in Vienna, N. Y., May 21, 1814. She d. in Springfield, Mass., March 28, 1857. Mr. Mattoon res. 1873, in Springfield. They had three children:

3–23. William Peter, b. in Springfield, April 9, 1844, res. 1873, Springfield; *m.*

3–24. Isabella Jane, b. in Avon, N. Y., Nov. 4, 1852, res. 1873, Springfield; *unm.*

3–25. Edmund Freeman, b. in Springfield, Feb. 6, 1856, res. 1873, Springfield; *unm.*

3–14. WILLIAM JAMES COULTER, b. in Troy, N. Y., Feb. 13, 1841, enlisted, July 12, 1861, as a private in the 15th Regt. Mass. Vols., served through the entire war, and was discharged with the rank of first lieutenant; was a brave and gallant soldier;

[1] See *Stickney Genealogy*.

a prisoner for some time in various Confederate prisons. He res. 1873, at Clinton, Mass.; is publisher of the Clinton *Courant*.

He m. Miss *Selina Craven*, who was b. in England, March 18, 1842. They have two children:

4–1. [COULTER.] Clarence C., b. in Clinton, Mass., June 1, 1868.
4–2. Annie May, b. in Philadelphia, Pa., May 31, 1870.

3–15. JOHN T. COULTER, b. in Troy, N. Y., March 4, 1843, enlisted, June 6, 1861, in the 22d Regt. N. Y. Vols., for two years; was discharged Nov. 25, 1861, for reason of physical disability; reënlisted, May 8, 1862, in 25th Regt. Mass. Vols., for three years; was wounded May 14, 1864, while near the outer works of Fort Darling, Va.; and was discharged May 8, 1865, at expiration of his term of service. He m. June 19, 1871, *Olive Loring*, who was b. in Sutton, Mass., Feb. 12, 1844. They res. 1873, in New London, Ct. One child:

4–3. Arthur M., b. June 20, 1872.

3–16. *Fannie S. Coulter*, b. in Jackson, N. Y., Aug. 27, 1844, m. in Clinton, Mass., April 6, 1863, GEORGE HUNT. They res. 1873, in Clinton. One child:

4–4. Frank D., b. March 11, 1864.

3–20. WILLIAM HARDY STICKNEY, b. in Methuen, Mass., Sept. 24, 1833, m. Feb. 17, 1859, *Sarah A. McNeil.* They res. 1873, in Methuen. Two children:

4–5. Frederick W., b. Aug., 1860.
4–6. Albert A., b. Oct., 1862.

3–21. LAFAYETTE STICKNEY, b. in Methuen, Mass., Sept. 21, 1844, enlisted, March 30, 1864, in Co. K., 57th Regt. Mass. Vols., was wounded in the battle of Fort Steadman, March, 1865, and discharged in June, 1865, the war being ended. He m. Dec. 25, 1871, *Elsie C. Coburn.* They res. 1873, in Warren, Me. One child:

4–7. Clarence Edson, b. April 6, 1873.

3–23. WILLIAM PETER MATTOON, b. in Springfield, Mass., April 9, 1844, m. Sept. 8, 1870, *Laura A. Goodnow.* They res. 1873, in Springfield. One child:

4–8. Laura Isabella, b. July 28, 1871.

NOTE. There may have been Dawsons in Vermont of earlier date than the family of Peter Dawson, of Barnet. At the time when jurisdiction over the territory of Vermont was claimed by the Province of New York, numerous tracts of land in Vermont were granted or sold to citizens of New York by the authorities of that Province.

The following memoranda are from the "Land Papers" of New York, preserved at Albany:

Vol. XIX, page 117, July 25, 1765. Return of Survey for John Dawson, and four others, "late corporals in the 80th Regt." for 1000 acres, in Shelburne, Vermont.

Vol. XXVII, page 8, April 3, 1770. Return of Survey of 600 acres of land in Danville, Caledonia Co., Vermont, to Frederick Dawson and others.

Whether either of these Dawsons removed to Vermont is not known.

In New Hampshire the name is as rarely met with as in Vermont. Peter Dawson, of the foregoing record, lived for a time in New Hampshire, and d. there. Benjamin Dawson, of Salem, in that state, a deaf mute, pupil at the Deaf and Dumb Asylum, Hartford, Ct., was killed at Hartford, Oct. 17, 1857, a train on the Hartford and New Haven R. R. passing over him.

FAMILY OF HENRY DAWSON,

Of Millbury, Mass., and Broad Brook, Conn., 1845-1868.[1]

From the Misses Dawson, of South Norwalk, Conn., 1873, and others, the following:

1. John Dawson,[2] grandfather of Henry Dawson, above named, was b. in Kendall, Westmoreland, England, probably between 1735 and 1740. He was by trade a wool comber, and is reputed to have been a person of fine appearance, and of more than ordinary address and education for a man in his station (being able to read and speak Latin), but of somewhat improvident habits. He lived to be 75 years of age, or upwards. He m., about 1765, *Margaret Calvert*, dau of Matthew Calvert, of Lancaster. Their eldest son was:

2–1. Matthew, named for his maternal gr. father, by whom he was "bound to the sea," at the age of twelve years. At the age of twenty-four he sailed from Liverpool for Africa, the second in command of a merchantman or trader. The captain d. of fever on the voyage, and he of the same disease after reaching the coast of Guinea, within a year after leaving England. The news of his death hastened that of his mother, who d. soon after.

2–2. Mark, second son of John Dawson, became a tailor, and lived and d. in Preston, Lancashire, where his children now reside.

2–3. John, a seaman, married, and when last heard of was living in Whitehaven, Cumberland.

There were six daughters, two of whom d. in infancy, and two more d. unmarried. The others were:

2–4. Agnes, m. John King, and had several children; lived in Blackburn, Lancashire; and

2–5. *Mary*, b. in Hawes, Yorkshire, Dec. 10, 1775, d. at Holcombe, Lancashire, Sept. 4, 1845; mother of

3–1. Henry Dawson, the emigrant above named, born in Preston, Lancashire, Oct. 13, 1799. She m. in Preston, Thomas Crompton, b. in Holcombe, Parish of Bury, Lancashire, May 13, 1768, d. Nov. 27, 1849, eldest son of Ralph Crompton. They had seven children, all b. in Lancashire:

---

[1] No. 3–1 of this Record.

[2] His father, Henry Dawson, was game keeper on a nobleman's estate, called *Leven's Park*, for forty years. The father of Henry Dawson, game keeper, was also a game keeper on the same estate for about the same length of time. His Christian name is not known.

3–2. [CROMPTON.] James, b in Preston, April 15, 1803, res. 1873, Windsor Locks, Ct.; *m.*
3–3. Rachel, b. in Preston, Dec. 21, 1804, d. Feb. 21, 1806.
3–4. William, b. in Preston, Sept. 10, 1806, res. 1873, Windsor, Ct.; *m.*
3–5. Ellen, b. in Holcombe, March 30, 1811, res. 1873, Hartford Co., Ct. CROMPTON.
3–6. Ralph, b. in Holcombe, Oct. 7, 1814, d. in Rochester, Wis., March 18, 1872; *m.*
3–7. Matthew, b. in Holcombe, Nov. 19, 1818, d. aged 7 mos.
3–8. Margaret, twin sister of Matthew, d. aged 3 mos.

3–1. HENRY DAWSON, b. in Preston, Lancashire, England, Oct. 13, 1799, m. 1821, *Alice Wostenholme*, dau. of John Wostenholme, of Holcombe, Lancashire. He came to America in 1845, and in the subsequent year his family followed him. They lived for two years in Millbury, Mass., whence they removed to Broad Brook, Hartford Co., Conn., which was his home the remainder of his life, and where he d. after a short illness, in February, 1868. He had an excellent memory, and great love for and success in gardening. His wid. res., 1873, at Broad Brook[1]. They had fifteen children, all b. in Lancashire, England, as follows:

4–1. John, b. in Nuttall Lane, Jan. 11, 1822, res. 1873, Worcester, Mass.; *m.*
4–2. Samuel, b. in Nuttall Lane, Aug. 1, 1823, d. Oct. 2, 1827.
4–3. Mary, b. in Nuttall Lane, March 12, 1825, d. Nov. 1, 1826.
4–4. George, b. in Nuttall Lane, Jan. 12, 1827, res. 1873, Blair, Neb.; *m.*
4–5. Mary, b. in Nuttall Lane, Oct. 22, 1828, res. 1873, Broad Brook, Ct. BENJAMIN; NICHOLS.
4–6. William A., b. in Nuttall Lane, July 15, 1830, res. 1873, Beloit, Wis.; *m.*
4–7. Charles, b. in Nuttall Lane, April 9, 1832, res. 1873, Holden, Mass.; *m.*
4–8. Robert W., b. in Nuttall Lane, Nov. 3, 1833, res. 1873, Blair, Neb.; *m.*
4–9. Alice L., b. in Nuttall Lane, March 12, 1835, res. 1873, So. Norwalk, Ct.; *unm.*
4–10. Elizabeth, b. in Belmont, Dec. 4, 1836, res. 1873, Canaan, Ct. ADAMS.
4–11. Rachel M., b. in Belmont, July 21, 1839, res. 1873, South Norwalk, Ct.; *unm.*
4–12. Henry, b. in Belmont, March 29, 1841, res. 1873, Worcester, Mass.; *m.*

---

[1] Mrs. Dawson, her son Robert, and daughters Mary, Elizabeth and Alice, were of the twenty original members of the Congregational Church at Broad Brook, organized May 4, 1851.

4–13. Jane, b. in Belmont, March 31, 1843, res. 1873, South Norwalk, Ct.; *unm.*
4–14. James E., b. at Whitefield, May 28, 1845, res. 1873, Worcester, Mass.; *m.*
4–15. Joshua B., twin brother of James E., d. at Millbury, Mass., Oct. 31, 1847.

3–2. James Crompton, b. in Preston, Lancashire, England, April 15, 1803, resides 1873, at Windsor Locks, Ct. Chn.:

4–16. Margaret Johnson, res. Amesbury, Mass.
4–17. Thomas, res. Hartford, Ct.; *m.*; no further records.
4–18. Ellen Johnson, res. Amesbury, Mass.
4–19. Ann, *unm.*
4–20. Rachel Tate, res. Illinois.
4–21. James, res. Windsor Locks; *m.*; no further records.
4–22. Alice.
4–23. Mary.

3–4. William Crompton, b. in Preston, Lancashire, England, Sept. 10, 1806, came to America in 1836, and in the following year invented the loom which bears his name.[1] He res. 1873, in Windsor, Ct. He m. in England, May 26, 1828, *Sallie* (or *Sarah*) *Law*, b. in Holcombe, Lancashire, May 22, 1807, d. in Millbury, Mass., Jan. 30, 1849, youngest dau. of George and *Kitty Buckley* Law. They had eight children:

4–24. George, b. in Holcombe, March 23, 1829, res. 1873, Worcester, Mass.; *m.*
4–25. Elizabeth, b. in Holcombe, Nov. 17, 1830, res. 1873, Windsor, Ct.; *unm.*
4–26. Mariana, b. in Manchester, Eng., Nov. 12, 1832, res. 1873, Hartford, Ct.; m. Thomas Crompton; no issue.
4–27. Catharine, b. in Haslingden, Eng., Nov. 2, 1834, res. 1873, Windsor, Ct.; *unm.*
4–28. Sarah Anne, b. in Holcombe, Sept. 10, 1836, res. 1873, Windsor, Ct. Tuttle.
4–29. William, b. in Holcombe, May, 1839, d. Oct., 1839.
4–30. William Henry, b. in Millbury, Mass., June 28, 1845.
4–31. Thomas Ralph, b. in Millbury, Dec. 12, 1848, d. Aug., 1849.

3–5. *Ellen Crompton*, b. in Holcombe, Lancashire, England, March 30, 1811, res. 1873, Hartford Co., Ct., m. in Ramsbotham, Lancashire, Feb. 23, 1852, James Crompton, who d. Sept. 21, 1861. They had one child:

[1] Samuel Lawrence deposed that the invention and introduction of the Crompton Loom had been "of incalculable benefit to the wool and woolen interests of the country." The spinning mule was invented by a relative, Samuel Crompton, of England.

4–32. [CROMPTON.] Mary Alice, b. in Ramsbotham, Dec. 4, 1853, d. in Pleasant Valley, Ct., Dec. 5, 1868.

3–6. RALPH CROMPTON, b. in Holcombe, Lancashire, England, Oct. 7, 1814, d. in Rochester, Wis., March 18, 1872; m. July 4, 1844, at Prestwich Church, near Bury, Lancashire, *Margaret Bradley*, who was b. in Marton, Yorkshire, England, Dec. 12, 1816, dau. of Thomas Bradley. Two children:

4–33. Mary Jane, b. in Millbury, Mass., Nov. 15, 1845, res. 1873, Rochester, Wis. JACKSON.
4–34. Elizabeth Ellen, b. in Springfield, Mass., Nov. 17, 1848.

4–1. JOHN DAWSON, b. at Nuttall Lane, Lancashire, Eng., Jan. 11, 1822, machinist, m. in Bolton, Lancashire, Feb. 28, 1842, *Jane Berry*, who was b. in Longworth, Eng., June 15, 1818, dau. of Henry and Sarah Berry. They res. 1873, in Worcester, Mass. Four children, all of whom res. 1873, in Worcester:

5–1. Sarah Ann, b. in Worcester, July 14, 1844.
5–2. William Henry, b. in Millbury, May 20, 1846; *m.*
5–3. Louisa Alice, b. in Millbury, April 6, 1848.
5–4. John Albert, b. in Worcester, Aug. 26, 1860.

4–4. GEORGE DAWSON, farmer, b. at Nuttall Lane, Lancashire, England, Jan. 12, 1827, m. in Chepachet, R. I., July 29, 1849, *Alice Ann Wolfenden*, who was born in Lancashire, June 13, 1824. They removed to Wisconsin in 1850, and thence in 1870 to Grant, Washington Co., Nebraska, where she d. Feb. 21, 1871, and where he now resides (1873). Five chn.:

5–5. Elizabeth Alice, b. in Wawatosa, Wis., May 12, 1852.
5–6. Jessie Theresa, b. in Wawatosa, Aug. 15, 1855.
5–7. Mary Jane, b. in Rochester, Wis., Oct. 19, 1857.
5–8. Agnes, b. in Waterford, Wis., Feb. 25, 1861.
5–9. Irwell Charles, b. in Waterford, Oct. 24, 1862.

4–5. *Mary Dawson*, b. at Nuttall Lane, Lancashire, Eng., Oct. 22, 1828, m. 1st., at Scantic, Conn., June 30, 1850, ISAAC BENJAMIN, b. in N. Y. and d. leaving one dau.:

5–10. Annie R., b. at Broad Brook, Ct., Nov. 10, 1856.

The mother m. 2d., at Broad Brook, May 31, 1868, SABIN S. NICHOLS. They res. 1873, at Broad Brook, and have one dau.:

5–11. Marian J., b. at Broad Brook, Aug. 27, 1870.

4-6. William A. Dawson, b. at Nuttall Lane, Lancashire, Eng., July 15, 1830, m. in Springfield, Mass., Aug. 1, 1853, *Caroline W. Blodgett*, who was b. in East Windsor, Conn. They res. in Beloit, Wis., having removed to that state in 1857. Mr. Dawson was in the Union service during the late war, having enlisted for three years, but during a part of the time was detailed for the repairing of guns, etc., for his company or regiment. He was at one time taken prisoner, and was confined in Libby Prison, Richmond, for twelve days. In his business of a machinist he is remarkably ingenious, and is much resorted to for the construction of models of new inventions, patterns, dies, etc. — all requiring in the artisan employed on them something of the inventive faculty. Eight children:

5-12. William B., b. at Meriden, Ct., Jan. 8, 1856.
5-13. George W., b. at Broad Brook, Ct., July 2, 1857.
5-14. Edwin R., b. at Spring Prairie, Wis., Nov. 13, 1858.
5-15. Henry A., b. at Beloit, Wis., June 25, 1861.
5-16. Alfred R. L., b. at Beloit, March 13, 1866, d. at Beloit, July 23, 1866.
5-17. Harriet A., b. at Beloit, Nov. 16, 1868.
5-18. Charles F., b. at Beloit, March 24, 1871.
5-19. Wallace J., b. at Beloit, Feb. 10, 1873.

4-7. Charles Dawson, b. at Nuttall Lane, Lancashire, Eng., April 9, 1832, manufacturer of flannels, m. in North Lee, Mass., July 2, 1852, *Jane E. Osborn*, who was b. in Mass. They res. 1873, in Holden, Mass. Four children:

5-20. Alida A, b. in Broad Brook, Ct., Feb. 16, 1854.
5-21. Carrie E., b. in Springfield, Vt., March 30, 1856.
5-22. Charles A., b. in Pittsfield, Mass., Sept. 6, 1860.
5-23. Freddie H., b. in Brattleboro, Vt., July 9, 1863, d. Sept., 1863.

4-8. Robert W. Dawson, photographer, b. in Nuttall Lane, Lancashire, Eng., Nov. 3, 1833, m. at Vienna, Wis., March 22, 1860, *Lucy M. Freeman*, who was b. at Milwaukee, Wis., Dec. 27, 1840. They res. 1873, at Blair, Washington county, Nebraska. Four children:

5-24. Clara Z., b. at Elgin, Ill., Nov. 14, 1860.
5-25. Elva E., b. at Elgin, Nov. 29, 1861.
5-26. Robert Nelson, b. at Elgin, March 1, 1865.
5-27. Charles Henry, b. at Woodstock, Ill., Jan. 27, 1866.

4-10. *Elizabeth Dawson*, b. at Belmont, Lancashire, England, Dec. 4, 1836, m. in Broad Brook, Ct., Jan. 17, 1860, HORATIO N. ADAMS, who was b. in Conn. They res. 1873, at Canaan, Ct. Five children :

5-28. James B., b. at Broad Brook, April 15, 1861.
5-29. Herbert M., b. at Canaan, June 27, 1862.
5-30. Elsie M., b. at Canaan, Aug. 29, 1864.
5-31. Mary E., b. at Canaan, Jan. 27, 1866.
5-32. Lester H., b. at Canaan, Jan. 24, 1867.

4-12. HENRY DAWSON, machinist, b. at Belmont, Lancashire, Eng., March 29, 1841, enlisted in the Union army early in the civil war, and was in active service upwards of four years, participating in more than twenty battles and skirmishes, but was never wounded or taken prisoner, and never sick. He m. at Keene, N. H., May 25, 1869, Mrs. Fostina M. Ballou, (maiden name *Whitcombe*) who was b. in New Hampshire. They res. 1873, in Worcester, Mass.

4-14. JAMES E. DAWSON, book keeper, b. at Whitefield, Lancashire, Eng., May 28, 1845, m. in Leominster, Mass., April 28, 1870, *Emma A. Howe*, who was b. in Vermont. They res. 1873, in Worcester, Mass.

4-24. GEORGE CROMPTON, b. in Holcombe, Lancashire, Eng., March 23, 1829, m. in Hartford, Ct., Jan. 9, 1853, *Mary Christina Pratt*, and res. 1873, in Worcester, Mass. He has made improvements from year to year on the invention of his father, the Crompton Loom, which he manufactures on an extensive scale, shipping his looms to all parts of the world. He has a family ; no records.

4-28. *Sarah Anne Crompton*, b. in Holcombe, Lancashire, Eng., Sept. 10, 1836, m. in Boston, Mass., May 10, 1853, Rev. REUEL HOTCHKISS TUTTLE, who was b. in Old Town, Me., July 16, 1824.[1] He is rector of the Episcopal church in Windsor, Conn., where they reside (1873). Five children :

5-33. Annie Elizabeth, b. in Hartford, Ct., March 13, 1854.
5-34. Mariana, b. in Salisbury, Ct., May 10, 1855.

---

[1] Tenth child of Samuel Tuttle (d. July 5, 1850, aged 77), and w. Betsey Hotchkiss, (b. May 2, 1779, d. Aug. 2, 1831), m.——— ; gr. son of Samuel Tuttle and w. Bethiah Miles ; gt. gr. son of Capt. Joseph Tuttle and w. Mercy Thompson. See p. 48, n. 1.

5-35. [TUTTLE.] Lorine Russell, b. in Salisbury, July 3, 1858, d. in Salisbury, Sept. 24, 1858.
5-36. Amy Crompton, twin sister of Lorine R., d. in Windsor, Ct., May 24, 1861.
5-37. Reuel Crompton, b. in Windsor, Sept. 24, 1863.

4-33. *Mary Jane Crompton*, b. in Millbury, Mass., Nov. 15, 1845, m. in Rochester, Wis., Dec. 20, 1871, GEORGE JACKSON, who was b. in Poughkeepsie, N. Y., Dec. 10, 1831. They res. 1873, in Rochester, Wis.

5-2. WILLIAM HENRY DAWSON, b. in Millbury, Mass., May 20, 1846, m. in Worcester, Mass., Sept. 14, 1870, *Susan Evelyn Forbes*, who was b. in Rutland, Mass., March 4, 1849, dau. of Lyman R., and Nancy B. Forbes. They res. 1873, in Worcester. One child:
6-1. Henry Lyman, b. July 2, 1873.

"JOHN DAWSON, of Monroe, Conn." Since the record beginning on page 131 was printed, additional information has been received by the compiler, which necessitates the following corrections and additions:

JOHN DAWSON came to America under command of General Clinton, 1775. He was at the battle of Bunker Hill, and afterwards joined a corps of cavalry and mounted infantry called the Legion, commanded by Major Tarleton (not *Cochran*). Himself and wife first settled in Connecticut, on the Shepaug river, in Litchfield county, where they lived several years. They afterwards lived in Fairfield and New Haven counties, and finally removed to Greene county, N. Y., as stated in the record referred to. Their children, all b. in Conn., are now named in the order of birth, as follows:
I. *Catharine*, who m. JOHN SHARP, and d. aged 36, without issue. II. JOHN CHARLES, b. in Litchfield county about 1785, d. in Greene county, N. Y., aged 46, m. *Betsey Benson*, and had children: George, David, Ebenezer, Polly, Harriet and Susan. III. *Sally*, m. WHEELER BEARDSLEY, and had dau. who m. Thomas Ward; their son, John T. Ward, of Woodbury, Ct. IV. FRANCIS MAXFIELD, had son Sheldon, res. Greenville, N. Y. V. *Betsey*, concerning whom see p. 132. VI. *Mary Hamilton*, m.—— WHITFORD, and had six children, who res. with their families, in Sharon, Ct., viz.: Joel, Hawley, Levi, William, Abby, Betsey. VII. HUGH F., concerning whom see p. 132. VIII. *Prudence*, b. April 3, 1794, m. REUBEN SPRING, and res. a widow near

Ansonia, Ct. Five children, all res. near that place, viz.: 1. Edmond, m.— Buel; two children. 2. George, m.— Austin; two children. 3. Antoinette, m. Harvey Bryant. 4. Sarah, m.— Farnham. 5. Mary, m. Fayette Fairchild. IX. Richard Hawley, b. in Monroe, Ct., April 10, 1797, removed to Greenville, N. Y., about 1817, and m. there, *Milly Pearsall,* April 12, 1818. In 1839 they removed to Clinton county, Iowa, where she d. June 19, 1872. He res. 1873, at DeWitt, in that county, and has six children, viz.: 1. Sally Ann, who m. John Miller. He d. 1845. She res. in Iowa, and has three sons. 2. James Knox, twice m., has eight children: George, Wilmot, Lewis, Joseph, Elmore, Ada, Ann, Bertie. 3. Caroline, m. Hiram Brown, and had six children: Francis Marion, William, Emma, Ella, Caroline, Hattie. 4. Catharine, m. Norman Evans, and has seven children: Lyman Hawley, Edgar, Madison, Charles, Caroline, Matilda, Ella. 5. Richard Hawley, m. Helen Quick, and had five children, all d. 6. Smith G., m. Esther Jane Hungerford, and has five children: Loretta, Ida, Emma, Hattie, William.

NEW YORK.

Notes relating to early settlers, and records of the families of HENRY DAWSON, of Long Island, ROPER DAWSON, of New York and Staten Island, GEORGE DAWSON, of New York and Michigan, ABRAHAM DAWSON, of New York city and Ithaca, HENRY DAWSON, of Brooklyn and Cohoes, N. Y., JAMES and THOMAS DAWSON, of New York city, JOHN and JAMES S. DAWSON, of Brooklyn, and others.

Unfortunately for his design, the compiler, although residing in or near the city of New York a number of years, has been able to devote but little time to the collection of the records of the families of his name in this locality. Some of the records which are herewith presented are, therefore, imperfect and fragmentary, but the insertion of them in their present state is rendered unavoidable from the fact that an attempt to perfect them now would unduly delay the publication of this work, and their omission would be inconsistent with the spirit in which the work has been undertaken. To the genealogical student the injunction, "Gather up the fragments that remain, that nothing be lost," is an ever present inspiration. He treasures up every name, fact and date which suggests the possibility of aiding him in his inquiries, of throwing any light upon the history of families or individuals within the line of his investigations.

The following specimen "treasure trove" may be of service to whomsoever shall attempt to do more thoroughly, what the compiler hereof reluctantly leaves to other hands in the field of family research:

One HANS DAWSON was a resident of Broad street, in the city of New York, when the Dutch ruled here. Whence and when came he?[1]

THOMAS DAWSON, who described himself as "of the parish of St. Paul, Shadwell, in the county of Middlesex" [England], "marriner, aged nine and thirty years, or thereabouts," made an affidavit dated Feb. 19, 1691, setting forth the condition of affairs in New York, at the time of his arrival, "on or about the eight and twentieth day of January, with Captain Richard Ingoldsby, in the ship Beaver."[2]

A marriage license was granted to THOMAS DAWSON and *Mary Thaxter*, by Lord Cornbury, governor of the province, June 9, 1705.[3]

THOMAS DAWSON was, in 1711, a contributor towards building the steeple of Trinity church.[4]

WILLIAM DAWSON and *Elizabeth Read* were, upon due filing of a marriage bond, licensed to marry, June 23, 1738.[5]

These were similarly licensed in 1756: April 12, *Rachel Cuyler* and DENNIS VAN DORSON[6]; April 23, *Susannah Dawson* and ELIAS ANDERSON; June 7, *Mary Dawson* and MYNDERT VAN EVERA.

---

[1] Letter of Henry B. Dawson, Esq., Sept. 9, 1854.

[2] See *N. Y. Historical Society's Collections*, 1868, p. 318, "Documents relating to the administration of Leisler."

[3] *N. Y. Gen. & Biog. Record*, vol. 2, p. 27.

[4] Berrien's *History of Trinity Church*, p. 322.

[5] Bonds were formerly required to be given in New York on obtaining license to marry. They were not required after 1783.— *New York Marriages*, printed by order of the secretary of state, 1860. All the licenses after mentioned from this source.

[6] This probably was Van Duursen or Van Dursen; but Dawson was often written Dorson.

In 1758 (June 3), BOSWELL DAWSON and *Phebe Pell*, were licensed to marry.[1]

In 1760, licenses were issued to *Eleanor Dawson* and JOHN SHERMAN, Nov. 3d; and to VOLKERT DAWSON and *Gertrey Denison*, Dec. 15th.[2]

In 1762, a part of the Brevoort Estate, lying north of 16th street, New York, and consisting of 23 acres, was sold to "Mr. DAWSON."[3]

Marriage licenses were issued to HENRY DAWSON and *Catharine Kemper*, June 15, 1763;[4] RICHARD DAWSON and *Elizabeth Van Norden*, Feb. 28, 1764,[5] *Elizabeth Dawson*, and JACOBUS VAN NORDEN, Oct. 14, 1766.

FREDERICK DAWSON was a soldier at Oswego in or before 1764, belonging to the Fourth Battalion of Royal Americans.[6]

JOHN DAWSON was one of several disbanded non-commissioned officers, who petitioned the government, June 13, 1766, praying that money paid to the surveyor general of the Province for their Patents might be refunded,[7] and JOHN DAWSON was a goldsmith in New York in 1767, having his shop in Old Slip.[8]

JOSEPH DAWSON was one of several who made assignment of their right to bounty lands about this date.[9]

One HENRY DAWSON, a Baptist preacher, arrived in New York "from Dr. Gifford's church, in London," in 1767. He "offered himself to our Association, but being under the censure of his church, was rejected again and again, so that he stands alone, railing at associations and regular ministry." He removed to Newport, R. I., and there reconstituted a church which had fallen to pieces, adding to it a few which he himself baptized. Of the church thus organized his unfriendly contemporary says they "are not likely to hold together long."—[10] He appears to have returned to England a few years later, and to have been no better liked there.[11]

These received license to marry: *Rachel Dawson* and JOHN REEVES, April 11, 1775; THOMAS DAWSON and *Lena Magee*, March 6, 1778.

DANIEL DAWSON was a fifer — enlisted for three years, in Col. Peter Gansevoort's company, Third New York Regiment — in winter quarters at Albany from Dec. 1, 1778 to March 15, 1779.[12]

MARY DAWSON of New York, widow, made a will 16 Jan., 1783, which was probated on the 17th of March following, naming a dau. Sarah, w. of David Man,

---

[1] Roseville Dawson and Phebe, his wife (probably the same persons, the discrepancy in names occasioned by clerical mistake) conveyed land in New York to John Ousterman, 1773.—*N. Y. Co. Records of Deeds*, vol. 40, p. 468.

[2] "1772, Dec. 22. Volkert Dawson, from New York, has arrived here [Albany] at 8 o'clock in the afternoon."—*Ten Eyck Family Records*, *N. Y. Gen. & Biog. Record*, No. 4, p. 30.

1785, Dec. 22. The city clerk of Albany was ordered to draw an order on the city chamberlain for £9 to pay account of Volkert Dawson.—Munsell's *Collections*, vol. 2, p. 261.

1786, Feb. 7. The same official, on same, order for 3 bushels of wheat, favor of Volkert Dawson.—*Ibid*, 263.

"Volkert Dawson [Daason] and w. Geertruy Hilton (?) had six children, Barent, b. Oct. 26, 1765; Ryckert, b. Oct. 25, 1765?: Maria, b. and bapt. Dec. 25, 1769; Ariaantze, b. Dec. 11, 1771; Willem, b. Aug. 2, 1778."—Pearson's *Contributions to the Genealogies of the first Settlers of Albany*.

[3] *Todd Genealogy*, p. 22.

[4] Henry Dawson sold land in New York to Walter Franklin, 1768.— *N. Y. Co. Records of Deeds*, vol. 38, p. 237.

[5] Richard Dawson had conveyance of land in New York from Cornelius Tiebont and w. 1765.—*Ibid*, 39, 483.

[6] *English Manuscripts*, at Albany, vol. 93, p. 7. (See p. 140).

[7] *Ibid*, vol. 94, p. 22. (See p. 140).

[8] *New York during the Revolution*, from papers in the Mercantile Library. John Dawson and Elizabeth, his wife, sold land in New York to George Gosman, 1794, and Andrew Hamersley, 1804. Conveyances were made to John Dawson by Barnet Mooney, 1789, and Ann, Jane and Luke Kiersted, 1796, 1799 and 1801.— *N. Y. Co. Records of Deeds*, vols. 54 and 142. John Dawson made will dated 25 Sept., 1807, probated 12 Jan., 1808, naming two children, David and John, both then minors.— *N. Y. Co. Surrogate's Records*.

[9] *Land Papers*, at Albany, vol. 53, p. 95.

[10] *Materials for a History of the Baptists in Rhode Island*.— By Rev. Morgan Edwards, in *R. I. His. Soc. Collections*, 6, 342.

[11] "Some froward men" [are already emboldened] "to set up for themselves, under the color of Protestant dissenters; and among the rest, lately, one Mr. Dawson, a Sabbatarian Baptist, not long since in New England." Letter of Rev. Benj. Wallin, of London, Aug. 30, 1777, to Rev. James Manning, first president of Brown University, R. I.—See *Life, Times and Correspondence of James Manning*, 249.

[12] Saffel's *Records of the Revolutionary War*, p. 168.

butcher; a dau. Mary, formerly w. of Minard Van Everen (above named Myndert Van Evera), now w. of Archard Getfield; a dau. Susannah, w. of Alias Anderson (*Elias* Anderson above), and their dau. Elizabeth; a gr. dau. Mary Weeks; a son Richard Dawson, and his sons, Charles and James; and a son Borevelt Dawson (Boswell or Roseville Dawson above named), who was then d. The connection of several of the before mentioned is thus indicated.[1]

In 1784 (27th of 10th month) the Friends worshipping in Queen (now Pearl) street, New York, "agreed with NATHAN DAWSON to take care of the meeting-house at £12 per annum."[2]

JOHN DAWSON, of Glenville, Schenectady Co., m. *Jacomyntje Groot*, about 1808.[3]

ABRAM DAWSON was a preacher in the Tioga Circuit, Susquehanna District, N. Y., (M. E. Church), and in Canaan Circuit, same district, 1819. "He was a good preacher, but his success was not marked."[4]

No one of the name is mentioned in the first *Directory* of New York, which was published in 1786.[5] The *Directory* of 1790 contains the names of JOHN DAWSON, who was a hair-dresser in Courtlandt st., and of JOSHUA DAWSON, 4 Magazine street. The latter is not afterwards mentioned, but the name of the former reappears until 1805. THOMAS DAWSON, a miner, came in 1791, and was here also the next year; WILLIAM DAWSON, jeweler, was here from 1795 to 1797; THOMAS, a mariner, was here in 1796, 1799, 1803, and 1805 — perhaps absent on voyages the intermediate years; ABRAHAM, also a mariner, appears once only, 1796;[6] FRANCIS, a boarding-house keeper and ship-broker, was here from 1797 till 1803; TUNIS, a cartman, 1801; JONATHAN, a painter, 1802 and 1806, and JONATHAN B., same occupation, 1808–11; THOMAS, a doctor, from 1802 until 1810;[7] another THOMAS, blacksmith, 1802 and 1804; ROBERT, a livery-stabler, came in 1804, and reappears annually, in same business, for 15 years after, and is still named, without occupation stated, for two years more; SAMUEL, trunkmaker, 1805–15; JOHN, ferry-man, 1805; WILLIAM, mariner, 1806 and 1814; JAMES, ropemaker, 1807; MICHAEL, a mason, 1809 and 1810; ROBERT, a ship-master, 1810–15 and 1818–21; JAMES, a mariner, here in 1815; JOSEPH, tinman, 1815–18, JAMES, same occupation, 1820, and JOSEPH again, 1824; SAMUEL, a mariner, 1815, 1820, and 1821; THOMAS, a marketman or "fruiter," 1815, 1818, and 1819, and THOMAS A., a fruiter, 1822; WILLIAM, a merchant, 1816, was of firm of William Dawson & Co., 1817; GEORGE, book-binder, 1816, was father of Hon. George Dawson, now of Albany, N. Y.;[8] CALEB, saddler, here in 1818 and 1820; JAMES, cartman, 1819–21; WILLIAM, tailor, 1819, merchant, 1820; ISABELLA, a school teacher, 1820–25; JACOB H., a cabinet-maker, 1822–25;[9] JOSEPH, tailor, 1822; JAMES, weaver, 1823–1826; JOHN, mariner, 1824, and THOMAS, grocer, 1824–26. It is doubtful if more than two or three of these were natives of this country; they were probably for the most part emigrants from England and Ireland, though Scotland was also represented. But few seem to have established families.

Since 1825, the names of Dawsons in the city *Directory*, which in that year were eight only, have increased five-fold, and are "too numerous for mention."[10] Among the more prominent have been the English firm of DAWSON Brothers (WILLIAM[11] and

---

[1] *N. Y. Co. Surrogate's Records.*

[2] *American Historical Record*, March, 1872.

[3] She was b. Dec. 2, 1788, dau. of Simon C. Groot jr., son of Cornelis Groot.— *Am. Gen. & Biog. Record*, Jan., 1873. Art.: Groot Family.

[4] Dr. Geo. Peck's *Early Methodism*, pp. 320, 326. One of this name res. at Pratt's Hollow, Onondaga Co., N. Y., 1850.

[5] The population of the city in this year was 23,614; the *Directory* contains only 926 names.

[6] His wid. lived at 2 Dover St., 1799.

[7] His wid., Catharine, here in 1811 and 1812.

[8] Both father and son were natives of Scotland; see record, following.

[9] Also in same business, 1828-1838, afterwards a lumber-dealer for many years; now resides in Newark, N. J.; see record following. (Family of Henry Dawson, of Long Island).

[10] The city *Directory* of 1872 contains the addresses of 40 Dawsons, and 2 Dawsans, the latter evidently misprinted.

[11] Mr. William Dawson became a member of the St. George's Society (English residents) of New York, in 1826, and a life member in 1831; he was a steward of the Society several years, assistant Secretary, 1829, and its Secretary, 1830-1833. Jan. 21, 1853, Mary Ann Dawson, and Robert L. Dawson (whose house was in England) gave notice by advertisement for claims "against the

Robert), established in 1825, a large mercantile house for twenty-five years after; George H., cabinet-maker, 1834–1848; William B., watchmaker and jeweller, 1837–1845; George W., clothier, 1838–1843, furniture, 1844–1853, said to have been b. in Scotland; his wid., Esther, milliner, afterwards photographs, 1854-1868; John, a well-known Scotch poulterer in Fulton Market, 1844–1872;[1] Benjamin F., 51 Bond St., 1833; Elizabeth, wid. of Benj. F., school, 41 Bond St., 1834; Benjamin F., clerk, merchant and banker, 1836–1866; his son, Benjamin F., physician and editor, 1867–1872;[2] Henry B., bookkeeper, printer and publisher, secretary and editor, 1844–1872;[3] John, druggist, 1849–1854; from Queens Co., Ireland, Ralph, brassfounder, 1849–1867; William H., fruit merchant, 1849-1854;[4] Peter, grate maker, 1847 1853, assemblyman, N. Y. Legislature, 1854-1856, clerk and inspector, custom house, 1855-1861, various occupations, 1862-1872; Abraham, butcher, 1850-1853-1862; Samuel, segars, 1853-1864; George, carpenter, 1853-1866; Rollin L., gold pens, 1854-1857;[5] Charles C., accountant, 1855, mineral waters, 1869-1872;[6] John H., druggist, 1856-1872;[7] John M.,[8] spices, 1854, broker, 1855, drugs, 1856-1862, hops and malt, 1863-1865, spices, etc., 1867-1872; Henry P., physician, 1857; James, manufacturer of britannia ware, etc., 1857-1872;[9] Thomas, "artist," 1857, painter, 1858-1872;[10] Albert F., clerk, 1862, copyist, 1865, commissioner, 1867, stenographer, 1868-1872;[11] Jacob H., express, 1863-1865, hardware, 1866, skates, 1867;[12] Henry, books, 1864-1866; Henry Jr., books and printer, 1867-70;[13] Henry, stationer, 1872;[14] Robert L., crockery, 1864, merchant, 1867, 1868; George H., lumber, 1865-1872;[15] Edwin H., hardware, 1866, skates, 1867, secretary, 1872;[16] Andrew H. H., lawyer, 1868-1871;[17] T. W. (Rev), 1868;[18] Richard, liquors, 1869-1872;[19] Charles, secretary, 1871-1872;[20] James B., elevator, 1871, 1872; and Oliver S., broker, 1872.

---

estate of William Dawson, late of New York, deceased," to be presented at the place of business of Robert Dawson, 160 Pearl St.—

"*Married*, on Sept. 22, 1870, at Walcot Church, Bath, England, by the Rev. D. Malcolm, clerk, cousin of the bride, Rector of Kingston Deverill, assisted by the Rev. H. Robinson, of the Octagon Chapel, Colville Frankland, Esq., Captain 103d Royal Fusiliers, younger son of Sir Frederick Frankland, Bart., to *Mary Jay*, only daughter of the late William Dawson, Esq., of New York."

[1] Mr. Dawson res. in Brooklyn; he has no children.

[2] See record following.

[3] See record following. (Family of Abraham Dawson).

[4] See page 64 (6-33).

[5] See page 86 (6-72).

[6] See page 78 (6-60).

[7] John Healey Dawson, b. in Waltham, Lincolnshire, England, one of eight children of William and Ann Dawson, both b. and d. in Lincolnshire. Mr. D. m. in N. Y., and has children living: 1. Carrie Lavina; 2. Harry; 3. John William; 4. Frank; 5. Charles Mark (1872).

[8] John M. Dawson, b. near Arno Park, Queens county, Ireland, 1815, (son and gr. son of John Dawson, both of whom d. in Queens Co.), emigrated to New York, April, 1850, and succeeded his cousin, John Dawson, above named, in business as a drug, spice and hop broker, 1854, and res. 1873, cor. 10th Av. and 21st St. New York. He m. in Ireland, *Jane M. Meredith*, and had, besides several children who d. young, Anna M., who m. Alfred Lewis, and d. in Newark, N. J., July, 1872, leaving son Alfred Meredith Lewis; and Lizzie M., res. New York, *unm.* Mr. Dawson had brother Henry, d. in Queens Co., Ireland, 1872, whose son, John M., came to America, May, 1868, and res., 1872, in Louisville, Ky., clerk in auditor's office, Louisville and Nashville, R. R., *unm.*

[9] See record following.

[10] See record following.

[11] See record following. (Family of John Dawson, of Brooklyn).

[12] See record following. (Family of Henry Dawson, of Long Island).

[13] See record following. (Family of Henry Dawson, of Brooklyn and Cohoes).

[14] Of Gresham and Dawson, 58 Broadway; res. Brooklyn; b. in Halifax, N. S., about 1845, youngest son of Benjamin Dawson, b. in Co. Cavan, Ireland, long in publishing and bookselling business in Montreal, and succeeded by his sons Samuel E., William Valentine, and Benjamin Jr., forming the firm of Dawson Brothers. Mr. John Thomas Dawson, of Middleton and Dawson, booksellers and publishers, Quebec, is eldest son of B. D., above named.

[15] *and* [16] See record following. (Family of Henry Dawson, of Long Island).

[17] See Maryland record. (Family of Wm. Dawson, of Caroline Co., Md.).

[18] Mr. D. was, in 1868, pastor of the Seventh Presbyterian church, New York city; res. 1873, Oakland, Cal.

[19] Born in N. of Ireland about 1834, emigrated to N. Y., about 1857, res. 1872, in N. J.

[20] Born in Erie Co., N. Y., July 29, 1835, d. in New York city Nov. 12, 1872, leaving one child, a dau.; only son of John Dawson, b. in Derbyshire, England, about 1800, emigrated to this country about 1825, res. 1872, in England: his father, also named John Dawson, b. in Wales.

In the Brooklyn *Directories* the first name found is that of DARBY DAWSON, stevedore and boatman, 1823 and 1829.[1] STATES or STAATS DAWSON is named in 1829, and in most of the years following until 1854, with the various occupations of butcher, inspector of weights and measures and of beef and pork, mayor's marshal, and policeman; ROBERT, musician and bell hanger, was here in 1829 and some years later; JOHN, a ropemaker, came in 1832, and one of same name was grocer in 1837, and butcher in 1843, and later; FRANCIS, a master's mate in the U. S. N., is named in 1843 and 1844, was a gunner, 1847-51, and mate, 1853 and 1854; EDWARD, a painter, is first named in 1845, and HENRY D., bookkeeper, in 1847; JOHN, a poulterer, first named in 1847, and RODMAN B., counselor, in 1848, are both still residents of Brooklyn; ABRAHAM was a coal merchant in 1848; JOHN L., butcher, 1848, has since been many years a policeman; SAMUEL B., stationer, THOMAS, carpenter, and HENRY, machinist, came in 1849; JAMES, printer, 1852; JOHN, machinist, BERNARD, carpenter, and HENRY, bookbinder, 1856; CHARLES, hatter, EDWARD, clerk, JAMES S., shipjoiner, SAMUEL, painter, and WILLIAM, cigarmaker, all came in 1857; DANIEL, painter, RALPH, brassfounder, and THOMAS M., cooper, were among the new comers of 1859; THOMAS W., came also in 1859, and is in 1873 a furniture dealer, in Myrtle avenue,[2] ROBERT, an engraver, THOMAS J., grocer, and WILLIAM, mason, came in 1860; NICHOLAS, painter, 1861; JOHN W., shirtmaker, 1861, shoe dealer, 1873;[3] THOMAS, straw goods, and WILLIAM H. JR., clerk, 1862; CHARLES H., cutter, JOHN P., cigarmaker, and WILLIAM S., seaman, appeared in 1863; ALBERT F., copyist and reporter, is first named in 1865; ALEXANDER, currier, and FRANCIS, lawyer, 1866; GILBERT E., broker, RICHARD, liquors, and ROBERT, iron founder, came in 1868; and THOMAS, tinsmith, in 1869.

Some of these names will be found in the records which follow.

---

1 One of the first trustees of the "St. James Roman Catholic church" of Brooklyn, incorporated Nov. 20, 1822, the first Roman Catholic church on Long Island.—Furman's *Notes relating to Brooklyn.*

2 Thomas Whitley Dawson, b. in Hertfordshire, England, has been in U. S. about 16 years.

3 John W. Dawson, who styles himself "the shu-may-kur" was b. in England; in U. S. about 18 years.

FAMILY OF HENRY DAWSON,

OF LONG ISLAND, about 1760–1803.

1. HENRY DAWSON, a native of Dublin, Ireland, came to America about 1760, and lived for a time at Jamaica, L. I., but afterwards removed to Brooklyn, where the greater part of his life was spent. He was of good family, and is said to have held a commission at one time in the British army, but to have emigrated because of dissatisfaction with the disposal of his father's estate, which, after the fashion of the country, went chiefly to the eldest son, named John Dawson, which is supposed to have been also the name of the father. In 1774 (Oct 20), his mother, Jane Dawson, then living at Chapel Izod, Dublin county, made a will, in which, having declared her belief that her son John had already had "three times as much" of his father's estate as he was entitled to, she left to him only a small nominal legacy, but provided that her property should go principally to her son Henry, then in the province of New York, and to her daughter, Elizabeth George, of Chapel Izod, "widow of Delancy George, Esq., late Lieutenant in the Royal Artillery." The will also mentioned her daughter's sons, Ramsey and Joshua George; and her own son, William, who had "been long abroad," and for whom she made provision "in case he should ever return."[1] Henry Dawson m. at Jamaica, Miss *Morton*, a sister of General Jacob Morton, who was for twenty-six years

[1] It is said that he was a lieutenant in the royal army, and went to Montreal. Was he afterwards on Long Island? "Capt. WILLIAM DAWSON m. about 1780 *Lydia Hallett*, dau. of Samuel Hallett, son of William Hallett, both of Newtown, L. I., and the last named b. in Dorsetshire, England, 1616, removed to Greenwich, Ct., thence to Hellgate, L. I."— Riker's *Annals of Newtown, L. I.*, Art.: Hallett Family, p. 463. The license for the marriage was issued Aug. 29, 1783.— See *N. Y. S. Record of Marriage Licenses*, vol. 40, p. 14.

the clerk of the common council of the city of New York.[1] His second w. was *Elizabeth Comes*, dau. of John and Heziah Comes, of Jamaica. They were an English family, in good circumstances.[2] By his second w. he had six children. One of his name, perhaps himself, was a captain of provincial troops in the king's service some years prior to the Revolution.[3] He kept a public house in Brooklyn, near the old ferry, in Doughty street; and in 1789 he was appointed one of the three ferry men of "Brookland Ferry" by the corporation of New York.[4] In connection with this appointment he is styled "Captain Henry Dawson," which title may have been acquired in the provincial service, as above suggested, or possibly indicated his rank in the British army.[5] He held the ferry until his death in 1803.[6] It is said of him, that, "retaining all the sportsmanlike tastes of his early life, he kept a pack of dogs, as well as hunting studs, with which he frequently took 'a brush' in the country around the village of Brooklyn."[7] He was a subscriber to a fund for building the Academy at Jamaica in 1792.[8] Some of the family appear to have returned to Jamaica, and to have resided there

---

[1] See Stiles' *History of Brooklyn*, vol. 2, pp. 48, 49. Stiles states that the first w. was Miss *Coombs*, of Jamaica, and the second, Miss *Morton*. The compiler's information is from Jacob H. Dawson, Esq., of Newark, N. J., gr. son of Henry Dawson, and is believed to be correct.

[2] Henry Dawson and the widow Heziah Comes, executors, offered for sale, March 8, 1773, the farm, at Jamaica, of John Comes (his father-in-law) deceased.— Onderdonk's *Queens County in Olden Times*, p. 45. John Comes is said to have been a magistrate at Hempstead.

[3] See petition, Dec. 30, 1765, of Capt. Henry Dawson and others, late belonging to the troops raised in the province of New York, for a grant of land to each, pursuant to royal proclamation.— *Land Papers* at Albany, vol. 20, p. 111. Also, Deposition concerning an attack on the jail of Dutchess county, at Poughkeepsie, and the release of a prisoner therefrom, by men belonging to Capt. *Dorson's* company. Poughkeepsie, March 13, 1764.—*English Manuscripts*, Albany, vol. 92, p. 94.

[4] See Stiles' *Brooklyn*. His house was called the "Corporation House."

[5] *Stiles* states that he was a major in the British army.

[6] The date of his death is incorrectly stated by *Stiles* to have been 1808. His will, in which he is described as "Henry Dawson, of Brooklyn, Long Island, gentleman," was dated 2 May, 1803, and probated 16 August, in the same year. It mentions his w. Elizabeth, and "youngest daughter, Jane," and refers to "the rest" of his children, but not by name. The w. and John I. Dawson (probably his son, but not so described), were named executrix and executor. George Hicks signed as witness. — (Kings county Surrogate records).

[7] *Stiles*......."1786. There will be a fox chase from Mr. Dawson's, Brooklyn ferry, Oct. 19th." .... "1787. The fourth of July was celebrated at Dawson's, Brooklyn, by a number of gentlemen. Toasts were drunk, and rockets fired."— Onderdonk's Collections for History of Kings county in olden times.— (L. I. Historical Society's Library.)

[8] Onderdonk's *Queens County in Olden Times*, p. 80.

after his death.[1] His wid. d. in New York abt. 1825. Their children were:

2–1. Henry, b. in Jamaica, March 6, 1773,[2] d. in Brooklyn abt. 1828, aged 57; *m.*
2–2. John I., d. abt. 1806, at sea; *m.*
2–3. Gilbert, d. in New York, abt. 1810, *unm.*
2–4. Betsey, d. in Brooklyn, abt. 1860, aged abt. 80. CONKLIN.
2–5. Ann, m. WM. BUCKLE; lived in Brooklyn, where both d. without issue.
2–6. Jane, d. abt. 1805 or '06; *unm.*

2–1. HENRY DAWSON jun., was b. in Jamaica, L. I., March 6, 1773, d. in Brooklyn, abt. 1828, aged 57, m. *Miriam Hicks*, who was b. Feb. 18, 1780, and d. in Brooklyn, 1841.[3] They lived in Doughty street, in Brooklyn, and he continued the ferry after his father's death, up to 1810 or '12. "He was more enthusiastic in sporting matters, even, than his father, and it was said of him that 'he had not a bone in his body that had not, at one time or another, been broken' by the falls and accidents he had experienced in his favorite diversion."[4] They had nine children:

3–1. Staats (or *States*[5]), b. Oct. 15, 1797, d. in Brooklyn, abt. 1856; *m.*
3–2. Jacob Henry, b. in Brooklyn, May 30, 1800, res. 1873, Newark, N. J.; *m.*
3–3. John I., b. Dec. 11, 1802, d. in Brooklyn, Oct. 18, 1829, aged 27; *m.*
3–4. Phebe Ann, b. May 9, 1805, res. 1873, Brooklyn. BAYLIS.
3–5. Mary Hewlette, b. Oct. 26, 1806, d. in Brooklyn, Sept. 23, 1872. BARRE.
3–6. George Hewlette, b. Aug. 26, 1808, d. in New York, 1851; *m.*
3–7. Henry, b. in Brooklyn, June 23, 1810, d. young.
3–8. Elizabeth, *twin sister of Henry*, res. 1873, Brooklyn. WEEKS.
3–9. Jannett, b. June 4, 1814, res. 1873, Brooklyn; *unm.*

2–2. JOHN I. DAWSON, m. *Mary Hicks*, dau. of John Hicks, and cousin to the w. of his brother Henry. They lived in New York and Brooklyn. He was a sea captain, and d. at sea, about

---

[1] Mrs. and Miss Dawson kept a school at Jamaica, 1819. And Miss Dawson was a pew holder in Grace Church, Jamaica, 1822-1825.— Onderdonk's *Queens County*, pp. 102, 107.

[2] Stiles (*History of Brooklyn*) says 1771, but the above from the family record.

[3] Dau. of Jacob and *Phebe Hewlette* Hicks, and a niece of Elias Hicks, the Quaker preacher.

[4] Stiles' *Brooklyn*, vol. 2, p. 49.

[5] So written in the family record.

1806.[1] They had no issue. His widow m. John Seaman, and d. at Saugerties, N. Y., about 1865.

2-4. *Betsey Dawson* m. HENRY CONKLIN, and d. a widow in Brooklyn, about 1860, aged about 80. They had two children:

3-10. Henry, sea captain, d. at Sailors' Home, Staten Island, m. but childless.
3-11. Elizabeth, m. MILES HOPSON, res. a widow in New York; no chn.

3-1. STAATS (or STATES) DAWSON, b. Oct. 15, 1797, lived in Brooklyn, where he filled for many years, acceptably, various minor public offices, and where he d. about 1856. He m. *Ellen Lozier*, of Pompton, New Jersey, who res. a widow in Brooklyn (1873). They had eleven children:

4-1. John Lozier, res. 1873, in Brooklyn, policeman; m. but no issue.
4-2. Ann Maria, d. in Brooklyn. SIMONSON.
4-3. Marian, d. young.
4-4. Thomas, m. and res. in Brooklyn.
4-5. Jefferson, m. and res. in Brooklyn; no issue.
4-6. Staats.
4-7. Ellen, m. JAMES SEAMAN, res. Brooklyn.
4-8. Caroline, d. in Brooklyn; m. GEORGE BRADFORD; two children.
4-9. Nicholas, d. *unm.*
4-10. Hicks, d. *unm.*
4-11. Marian, m. and res. in Brooklyn.

3-2. JACOB HENRY DAWSON, b. in Brooklyn, May 30, 1800, began business as a cabinet maker in New York, in 1822, in which he continued until about 1838, and was afterwards a lumber dealer for many years. In 1851 he joined his eldest son, in Newark, N. J., in manufacturing patent and enameled leather — a business which was then in its infancy, but has now become one of the chief industries of Newark. Mr. Dawson removed to Newark about 1855. He is a director of the Peoples' Insurance Company of that city, and is still actively engaged in the leather business. He m. 1st., in New York, Aug. 5, 1821, *Eliza Cornell*, who d. in New York, April 20, 1823, leaving one son:

4-12. Jacob Henry, b. Aug. 5, 1822, d. May 13, 1841.

---

[1] The will of "John I. Dawson, of the city of New York, mariner," was dated in New York, 1 Dec., 1801, and was probated in Brooklyn, 10 July, 1806. It directed that all his property should go to his w. for her use during life, and in case she should die without issue, then to his father and mother, or the survivor of them, neither named.

He m. 2d., Aug. 11, 1824, *Hannah Williams*, dau. of Ichabod and *Hannah Hetfield* Williams, of Elizabeth, N. J. They res. 1873, in Newark, and have had eight children, all b. in New York city:

4–13. Thomas Williams, b. Sept. 17, 1825, res. 1873, Newark, N. J.; *m.*
4–14. George Hewlette, b. March 1, 1827, res. 1873, New York; *m.*
4–15. William Craig, b. Dec 28, 1829, d. in Newark, March 10, 1859; *m.*
4–16. Ichabod Williams, b. Sept. 23, 1831, res. 1873, Newark; *m.*
4–17. Eliza Ann, b. April 8, 1835, res. 1873, Newark. MACKNET.
4–18. Edwin Hicks, b. Aug. 13, 1837, res. 1873, Newark; *m.*
4–19. Hannah Williams, b. Nov. 17, 1839, m. in Newark, May 27, 1873, GEORGE G. ANDREWS, of Brooklyn.
4–20. Jacob Henry, b. Nov. 5, 1842, res. 1873, in Newark; *m.*

3–3. JOHN I. DAWSON, b. in Brooklyn, Dec. 11, 1802, d. in Brooklyn, Oct. 18, 1829, aged 27. He m. *Rachel Bowne*, who was b. June 1, 1805, and d. a widow in Brooklyn, June 20, 1871.[1] They had two children, who d. young; also:

4–21. Rodman Bowne, b. Feb. 15, 1825, res. 1873, Brooklyn; *m.*
4–22. Samuel Bowne, b. Feb. 17, 1828, res. 1873, Brooklyn; *unm.*

3–4. *Phebe Ann Dawson*, b. May 9, 1805, m. in Brooklyn, April 17, 1830, THOMAS BAYLIS, who was b. in Springfield, L. I., Feb. 16, 1806. She res. a widow in Brooklyn, 1873, having four children, all b. in Brooklyn:

4–23. Mary Elizabeth, b. July 20, 1832, res. 1873, Brooklyn. NEARING.
4–24. Jannette, b. Oct. 3, 1835, res. 1873, Orange, N. J. MCCOY.
4–25. Thomas, b. Sept. 1, 1838, res. 1873, Brooklyn; *m.*
4–26. Anna, b. Jan. 23, 1848, res. 1873, Brooklyn. VAN DYCK.

3–5. *Mary Hewlette Dawson*, b. Oct. 26, 1806, m. 1825, WALTER BARRE, coal merchant, of Brooklyn. They lived many years in that city, and d. there. He d. June 18, 1871, and she, Sept. 23, 1872. They had six children, all b. in Brooklyn:

4–27. William, b. Nov. 19, 1826, res. 1873, Brooklyn; *m.*
4–28. Mary Elizabeth, b. about 1828, m. SMITH T. BAKER, res. 1873, Brooklyn.
4–29. Walter, d. in Brooklyn, Jan., 1872; *unm.*

---

[1] Dau. of Gilbert Bowne, Esq. of New York, and niece of Rodman and Samuel Bowne, of Brooklyn, for 30 years proprietors of the Catharine Ferry. (Natives of Westchester county, N. Y.).

4–30. [BARRE.] George Hewlette, b. Sept. 3, 1836, res. 1873, Brooklyn; *m.*
4–31. Kate, b. 1841, res. 1873, Brooklyn; *unm.*
4–32. Thomas Baylis, res. 1873, Brooklyn.

3–6. GEORGE HEWLETTE DAWSON, b. Aug. 26, 1808, m. *Emma Chatfield*, of Catskill, N. Y., and d. in New York, about 1851, leaving five children:

4–33. Jacob Henry, purser, 1873, White Star Line, Ocean Steamers, m. (no record).
4–34. Staats, res. 1873, New York; m. (no record).
4–35. Catharine Bedell, m.—— BURNS, res. New York.
4–36. Rachel Bowne, m.—— RENNEY, res. Australia.
4–37. Emma, res. in New York.

3–8. *Elizabeth Dawson*, b. June 23, 1810, m. Dec. 8, 1831, JOSEPH S. WEEKS, who was b. at Oyster Bay, L. I., 1807, son of Jacob and Phebe Weeks. They res. 1873, in Brooklyn. Six children:

4–38. Phebe Ann, b. in Brooklyn, Nov. 2, 1832, res. 1873, Brooklyn. HAWXHURST.
4–39. Jacob H., b. in Brooklyn, Aug. 24, 1834, d. in Brooklyn, April 16, 1871; *unm.*
4–40. Mary B., b. in Brooklyn, Aug. 20, 1838, res. 1873, in Brooklyn; *unm.*
4–41. James H., b. in Oyster Bay, Oct. 26, 1842, d. in Brooklyn, April 27, 1872; *unm.*
4–42. Elizabeth P., b. in Oyster Bay, Sept. 3, 1844, res. 1873, Brooklyn; *unm.*
4–43. Joseph S., b. in Oyster Bay, Aug. 9, 1846, res. 1873, Brooklyn; *unm.*

4–2. *Ann Maria Dawson* (dau. of Staats, 3-1), m. CHARLES SIMONSON. She d. in Brooklyn, leaving one son:

5–1. Henry.

4–13. THOMAS WILLIAMS DAWSON, b. in New York, Sept. 17, 1825, m. in that city, Oct. 7, 1847, *Eliza Jane De La Montagnie*, b. May 3, 1828, dau. of Edward De La Montagnie, Esq., who d. in Newark, March 19, 1872, in his 80th year. At the time of his marriage, Mr. Dawson was in the lumber and mahogany trade with his father in New York, but in November, 1848, he purchased the business of a relative who had commenced, in Newark, N. J., the manufacture of patent and enameled leather, to which place he removed in the following spring. He sold out this establishment shortly after, and in 1851 erected a new factory, for the manufacture of the same kind of goods, being at this time joined by his father, with whom, and a brother (I.' W. Dawson, Esq.), he is now associated in the firm of J. H. & T. W. Dawson & Co., leading manufacturers of that class of goods in Newark. Besides contributing largely to the active management of the very extensive business of this firm, Mr. Dawson is one of the managers and vice president of the Dime Savings Institution of Newark, a director of the City National Bank, one of the directors of the Firemen's Mutual Insurance Company, (of which he was the originator), and vice president of the Stevens and Condit Transportation Company. He is also sole owner of a steamer engaged in the Newark trade. He was for several years a member of the Newark city Board of Education, and was president of the board during the years 1861, '62 and '63. He was president of the city Board of Trade in 1869. Mr. and Mrs. Dawson have had twelve children, (all b. in Newark, except the eldest, who was b. in New York city):

5–2. Edward Thomas, b. Dec. 5, 1848, d. in Newark, July 29, 1850.
5–3. Ella Augusta, b. March 6, 1852.
5–4. Lewis Grover, b. Oct. 19, 1853.
5–5. Eliza De La Montagnie, b. June 15, 1856.
5–6. Jacob Henry, b. March 23, 1858.
5–7. Thomas Williams, b. Sept. 16, 1859.
5–8. Robert De La Montagnie, b. Dec. 19, 1860.
5–9. Anna, b. May 19, 1862, d. June 24, 1863.
5–10. Mary, b. Feb. 1, 1864.
5–11. Jennie, b. May 21, 1865.
5–12. Alice, b. Aug. 31, 1866, d. July 20, 1867.
5–13. Mabel, b. May 31, 1868.

4–14. George Hewlette Dawson, b. in New York, March 1, 1827, m. widow Laura Jenness of New York, and res. 1873, in that city. He is a lumber merchant. Two chn.:

5–14. Laura, m. 1873, William Stienkampf, res. New York.
5–15. Eliza, res. New York; *unm.*

4–15. William Craig Dawson, b. in New York, Dec. 28, 1829, d. in Newark, March 10, 1859, m. *Amanda Conover*, of Red Bank, N. J. They had three children, all b. in Newark:

5–16. Amanda, res. 1873, in Newark ; *unm.*
5–17. Hannah Williams, d. in Newark, July 23, 1872, aged 15.
5–18. Mary Louisa, res. 1873, Newark.

Mrs. Dawson m. 2d., Mr. Thomas Seeley, and res. 1873, in Newark.

4–16. Ichabod Williams Dawson, b. in New York, Sept. 23, 1831, manufacturer of patent and enameled leather, Newark, of firm of J. H. & T. W. Dawson & Co. ; m. 1st., Oct. 15, 1856, *Mary Louise Coger*, dau. of Daniel Coger, of New York, who d. in Newark, Sept., 1857, without issue. He. m. 2d., March 20, 1861, *Mary C. Linen*, dau. of George and Sarah Linen, of Newark. She d. in Newark, Sept. 7, 1866, aged 31, leaving two children :

5–19. Louise C., b. Jan. 21, 1862.
5–20. Elizabeth, b. Jan. 21, 1864.

Mr. Dawson m. 3d., May 28, 1873, *Mallie B. Baldwin*, dau. of Bethuel and Susan Baldwin, of Newark. They res. in Newark.

4–17. *Eliza Ann Dawson*, b. in New York, April 8, 1835, m. in Newark, N. J., May 13, 1858, Theodore Macknet, hardware merchant, who was b. in Newark, Dec. 15, 1831, son of Charles Shaffer and Hetty Macknet. They res. 1873, in Newark. Two children living :

5–21. Eliza Dawson, b. June 3, 1861.
5–22. Carrie Amanda, b. Nov. 16, 1866.

4–18. Edwin Hicks Dawson, b. in New York, Aug. 13, 1837, m. in Newark, N. J., Oct. 6, 1859, *Julia M. Hollister*, who was b. in Newark, May 1, 1837, dau. of Benjamin and Maria V. Hollister. They res. 1873, in Newark, and have had four children, all b. in that city :

5–23. Harry Hollister, b. Oct. 31, 1860.
5–24. Leonard F. H., b. Dec. 24, 1863.
5–25. Isabel, b. June, 1865, d. Aug. 7, 1865.
5–26. Grace, b. Nov. 19, 1868.

Mr. Dawson was a member of the Newark city Board of Education, 1868–70, and president of the same one year.

4-20. JACOB HENRY DAWSON jun., b. in New York, Nov. 5, 1842, m. Oct. 9, 1867, *Julia Christine Hay*, who was b. in New York, dau. of George and Julia Hay. They res. 1873, in Newark. One child:

5-27. William Charles, b. in Newark, April 1, 1869.

4-21. RODMAN BOWNE DAWSON, b. in Brooklyn, Feb. 15, 1825, m. June 12, 1848, *Sarah Parish Lyon*, who d. Oct. 22, 1854, aged 26. He is a lawyer, and was in 1855, '56, '57 and '58, surrogate of Kings county. He res. 1873, in Brooklyn. They had two children:

5-28. Rodman Bowne, b. March 22, 1849, d. May 24, 1867, aged 18.
5-29. Sarah P., d. 1853, aged 11 mos.

4-23. *Mary Elizabeth Baylis*, b. in Brooklyn, July 20, 1832, m. Nov. 2, 1858, WOODBRIDGE NEARING, coal merchant. They res. 1873, in Brooklyn, and have five children:

5-30. Thomas Baylis.
5-31. William Woodbridge.
5-32. Anna DeWitt.
5-33. Abraham Burtis Baylis.
5-34. Elizabeth Buddington.

4-24. *Jannette Baylis*, b. in Brooklyn, Oct. 3, 1835, m. Sept. 23, 1857, ADAM RAMSAY MCCOY, leather merchant. They res. 1873, in Orange, N. J. One child:

5-35. Anna Jane.

4-25. THOMAS BAYLIS, physician, a member of the Brooklyn Board of Health, b. in Brooklyn, Sept. 1, 1838, m. Oct. 24, 1866, *Alice Tillinghast Hoyt*. They res. 1873, in Brooklyn. Two children:

5-36. Anna Van Dyck, d. young.
5-37. William Spelman.

4-26. *Anna Baylis*, b. in Brooklyn, Jan. 23, 1848, m. Oct. 1, 1867, ANTHONY V. B. VAN DYCK, broker. They res. 1873, in Brooklyn. One child:

5-38. Annete.

4-27. WILLIAM BARRE, b. in Brooklyn, Nov. 19, 1826, m. 1st., March 4, 1847, *Emily Fielder*. They had three chn.:

5–39. [BARRE.] Mary, b. Oct. 3, 1848.
5–40. William, b. about 1850.
5–41. George, b. Jan. 1, 1853.

Mr. Barre m. 2d., Oct. 20, 1859, *Marie Antoinette Kline.* They res. 1873, in Brooklyn, and have three children:

5–42. Jennie, b. Sept. 4, 1860.
5–43. Marie Louise, b. April 22, 1862.
5–44. Lena, b. Dec. 25, 1863.

Mr. Barre was elected, November, 1873, register of Kings county: of which he has been many years assistant register.

4–30. GEORGE HEWLETTE BARRE, b. in Brooklyn, Sept. 3, 1836, m. Sept. 25, 1862, *Mary E. Miller.* They res. in Brooklyn. Four children:

5–45. Jennie E., b. Jan. 9, 1864.
5–46. Mattie M., *twin sister of Jennie E.*
5–47. George H., b. May 2, 1865.
5–48. Charles F., b. July 7, 1868.

4–38. *Phebe Ann Weeks*, b. in Brooklyn, Nov. 2, 1832, m. Nov. 5, 1857, SAMUEL W. HAWXHURST. They res. 1873, in Brooklyn. He is engineer in chief on Aspinwall line of steamers. Two children:

5–49. Isabel W., b. in Brooklyn, Sept. 7, 1858.
5–50. Harry Dawson, b. in Brooklyn, Dec. 17, 1872.

FAMILY OF ROPER DAWSON,

OF NEW YORK and STATEN ISLAND, 1758–1771.

1. ROPER DAWSON, son of Major George Dawson, (b. 1689, killed at Carthagena, 1741), was b. in England, bapt. 21 July, 1724, and was of Ferriby Grange, North Ferriby, Yorkshire. His family was of the landed gentry of that shire.[1] He removed from England to New York, and thence to Staten Island, where he d. 14 June, 1771.[2] It is believed that his w. resided there at the time of their marriage. She was *Rachel Burnett*, and was b. 17 March, 1739. He was a merchant in New York, as early as 1758.[3] They had three children, all minors at the time of their father's death :

2–1. George ; *m.*
2–2. Harriet. McDONOUGH.
2–3. Charlotte.

2–1. GEORGE DAWSON, m.————, and had :

3–1. Alexander, of whom nothing further is known.
3–2. A *daughter*, who m.——COLEMAN.
3–3. A *daughter*, who m. WASHINGTON JACKSON.

---

[1] See page 8, note 1. He had a sister Elizabeth, who m. Kingston Venner, of Boredon, county York; a sister Ann, who m. Col. Rion, and had son Edward Rion. captain royal navy, killed at Copenhagen, 1801; and a brother, George Dawson, of Osgodby, county York, b. 1739, d. 1811, m. Isabella, dau. of Edward Charlton, of Shropshire, through whom the family is perpetuated in England. Another account of the ancestry of Major George Dawson differs from that of Burke, in the note referred to. It makes him son of William, of Heworth, York, d. 1704; son of John, of Heworth, b. 1616, d. 1676; son of George, of Ripon, York, who m. Priscilla, dau. of Sir Stephen Proctor, of Kent; son of Robert, of Ripon; son of Gilbert Dawson, of Azerley, York, who m. Katharine Conyers.— Berry's *Visitations of Kent, Sussex, Berkshire, etc.*

[2] His will, dated 22 March, 1771, probated 15 Aug., 1771, mentions w. Rachel, son George, a minor, and daus. Harriet and Charlotte.

[3] See petition of Roper Dawson, of New York, merchant, and others, owners of ship *Thornton*, of 18 guns, (*privateer?*) for a commission for John Eagleson as her commander, Jan. 5, 1758.— *English Manuscripts*, at Albany, vol. 85, p. 64. See, also, petition of Roper Dawson, of New York, merchant, owner of Brigantine *Royal American*, 8 guns, for a commission for her commander, James Fairly, June 8, 1761.— *Eng. MSS.*, 89, p. 140. Roper Dawson received conveyance of land in New York, from William Bell, 1759, and sold land to John Gill, 1758.— *N. Y. Co. Records of Deeds*, vol. 35, pp. 22, 520.

2-2. *Harriet Dawson* m. THOMAS MCDONOUGH, who had been private secretary to Gov. John Wentworth, of New Hampshire. The marriage, for which license was issued July 23, 1778,[1] occurred after he had left Portsmouth. Some time prior to 1800, Mr. McDonough was appointed British Consul at Boston, which office he held until his death in 1805, aged about 65. He was buried at Milton, Mass., in the tomb of his son-in-law, the Hon. Peter O. Thatcher. They had twelve children, for an account of whom see *Wentworth Genealogy*, vol. 2, p. 380.

---

[1] See *N. Y. S. Record of Marriage Lieenses*, vol. 25, p. 139, referred to in "New York marriages," printed by order of the Secretary of State, 1860.

FAMILY OF GEORGE DAWSON,

OF NEW YORK AND MICHIGAN, 1816–1849.

1. GEORGE DAWSON (son of George Dawson, a gardener, who d. near Edinburgh, Scotland), was b. in Scotland, 1789. He served his time as an apprentice to the bookbinder's trade with the Constables of Edinburgh, and afterwards removed to Falkirk, where he lived several years. He removed thence to America, arriving in New York in 1816, in which city he remained about two years. In 1818, he removed to Toronto (then Little York) Canada, where he prosecuted his trade for six years, after which he lived, first in Niagara, Canada, and then in Rochester, N. Y., following the same occupation. From Rochester, in 1836, he emigrated to the state of Michigan, where he died (at Royal Oak) in 1849, aged 60 years.[1] He m. in Scotland, *Mary Chapman*, who d. at Royal Oak, Michigan, in 1841, aged 50. They had four children:

2–1. James, b. in Edinburgh, Scotland, 1811, d. in Clayton, Mich., 1864; *m.*
2–2. George, b. in Falkirk, Scotland, March 14, 1813, res. 1873, Albany, N. Y.; *m.*
2–3. Ellen, b. in Falkirk, Scotland, 1815, res. 1873, Warren, Mich. HOYT.
2–4. Jane, b. in Toronto, Canada, 1822, res. 1873, Flint, Mich. SMITH.

2–1. JAMES DAWSON, b. in Edinburgh, Scotland, 1811, d. in Clayton, Mich., 1864, aged 53, m.————. His widow res. 1873, in Mich., with her children:

3–1. James, farmer, Flint, Mich.
3–2. Edward, farmer, Royal Oak, Mich.

---

[1] He had a brother, named James Dawson, a mariner, from Greenock, who was in New York 1815, and d. in that city two or three years later, leaving children of whom nothing more is known.

Geo. Dawson.

3–3. Isaac, farmer, Royal Oak.
3–4. Sarah Jane, Royal Oak, *unm.*
3–5. Mary, Royal Oak, *m.*

2–2. George Dawson, b. in Falkirk, Scotland, March 14, 1813, came with his mother, brother and sister to New York, in 1817–18, the father having preceded them some eighteen months. In 1824 (his family having removed that year from Toronto to Niagara, Canada), he entered as an apprentice to the printing business in the Niagara *Gleaner* office. He was then but eleven years old, and had previously but scanty educational advantages. The family removing to Rochester in 1826, he entered there an apprentice in the office of the *Anti-Masonic Enquirer*, of which Hon. Thurlow Weed was the editor. In 1831, Mr. Weed having established in Albany the *Albany Evening Journal*, Mr. Dawson followed him to that city, and became foreman of the office, which position he held (occasionally writing, and regularly reporting in the legislature) until the spring of 1836, when he was called to the editorship of the Rochester *Daily Democrat.* In this service he continued until August, 1839, when he assumed the editorial charge of the Detroit, Mich., *Daily Advertiser.* His political friends, assuming that he was chiefly instrumental in securing that state to the whigs, made him State Printer, which office he held for three years, and until a fire (in 1842) destroyed the establishment. Returning to Rochester, he resumed his position of editor of the *Daily Democrat*, and continued therein until August, 1846, when he returned to Albany, upon the invitation of Mr. Weed, and became his associate in the editorial management of the *Evening Journal*, of which paper Mr. Dawson has been senior editor and proprietor since the retirement of Mr. Weed, in 1862. During his connection with it the *Journal* has been twice named the State Paper, and now holds that designation. In the politics of the state it wields an influence second to that of no paper outside of the city of New York. Indeed, the paper has a National reputation and influence, and Mr. Dawson, in his editorial chair, and as a political manager and adviser, is, like his predecessor and former associate, Mr. Weed, recognized as a "power behind the throne" often "greater than the throne."

Mr. Dawson was, against his protest, appointed postmaster of Albany by President Lincoln in 1861, and held the office for six years, when he resigned, being unwilling to continue under Mr. Johnson's administration, which he opposed.

He united with the Baptist church in Rochester in 1831, and still holds his connection with that denomination, finding great pleasure in Sabbath school and other work incidental to his church relationship.

Mr. Dawson is a disciple of Isaac Walton who should hold a place very near to the heart of the great master of the rod and line. In a knowledge of the habits and haunts of the finny tribes, and in a genuine love of nature, he is excelled by few in these utilitarian days. Of himself, in a letter to the compiler, he says: "What little leisure I have I employ in angling — a recreation of which I am very fond, and which I prosecute with an enthusiasm which my friends find it difficult to comprehend. But as I find in it both health and amusement, I am not sorry to know that the passion grows with my years. I can understand the feelings with which Christopher North lovingly scanned his fly-hook on his death bed." Before the war, Mr. Dawson published in the *Journal* a series of racy letters entitled "Wood Notes from the Adirondacks." A new series of these delightful sketches of forest life, full of vigorous and piquant description, appeared in 1873.

He m. in June, 1834, *Nancy M. Terrell*, who was b. in Connecticut. Their children who survived birth, were:

3–6. George S., b. Nov., 1838, d. at Albany, Dec. 6, 1864, from wounds received in battle at Petersburg, Va.; major Second N. Y. Vol. Artillery; *unm.*[1]

3–7. Burritt S., b. Aug. 31, 1844, res. 1873, Albany; *unm.*

2–3. *Ellen Dawson*, b. in Falkirk, Scotland, 1815, m. April 4, 1836, James Warren Hoyt, farmer, b. in Norwalk,

[1] "He was wounded in the leg in the assault on Petersburg, and sustained an amputation. He remained in the hospital at Washington for a long time in a most critical condition, but by the end of September was well enough to be brought home. About five weeks ago a large abscess was developed, soon after followed by two more. His system was too much exhausted to sustain the drain upon it, and death put an end to his sufferings. He was in full possession of his faculties until within a few minutes of his death, and expressed full faith and abiding confidence in a happy hereafter. Peace to the gallant young soldier."— Albany *Express.* (Munsell's *Collections of the History of Albany*, vol. 2, p. 216).

Ct., Dec. 8, 1815, son of Josiah Hoyt. They res. 1873, in Warren, Macomb county, Mich., and have had seven children, all b. in Norwalk, Ct. :[1]

3–8. George, b. Dec. 1, 1836, d. in Norwalk, April 12, 1837.
3–9. Harriet E., b. March 3, 1838, m. Feb. 5, 1856, NATHAN W. HALSEY, farmer, res. 1873, Warren, Mich.
3–10. George D., b. April 23, 1839, d. in Norwalk, March 23, 1840.
3–11. Mary J., b. April 29, 1842, m. Jan. 1, 1860, GEORGE WALKER, carpenter ; res. 1873, Warren, Mich.
3–12. Hannah E., b. Oct. 23, 1845, m. Sept. 24, 1866, WILLIAM KINGSCOTT ; res. Mich.
3–13. Helen D., b. April 11, 1850, res. Warren, Mich. ; *unm.*
3–14. William Wallace, b, June 17, 1852, res. Warren, Mich., farmer.

2–4. *Jane Dawson*, b. in Toronto, Canada, 1822, m. CARLTON SMITH. They res. 1873, Flint, Mich. Three children, all res. 1873, Flint :

3–15. George, farmer.
3–16. Levi, carpenter.
3–17. Darwin, horticulturist.

---

[1] See *The Hoyt Family*, p. 510.

FAMILY OF BENJAMIN F. DAWSON,

OF NEW YORK, about 1823–1866.

1. BENJAMIN FRANKLIN DAWSON, b. in England, about 1808, son of a clergyman of the established church, d. in New York city, June 24, 1866, aged 58. He came to New York while a mere lad, about the year 1823. An obituary thus speaks of him: "Left alone, at the age of fourteen, to battle with the world, his high moral and Christian character enabled him to resist the demoralizing influences of a large city. Industrious and upright in business, he won the respect and confidence of older men. At the age of twenty-four he became a partner in the house of Buchanan, Caulder & Co., one of the largest and most prosperous in the world. In this house he remained until the death of the chief partner dissolved the firm. Subsequently, when the English house of Dennistoun & Co. opened a branch in New York, Mr. Dawson was made one of the partners, and remained in that position until the troubles of 1857, soon after which he retired from business, and through his almost single handed exertions the present firm almost owes its existence. * * * * New York has lost a good and true man."

Mr. Dawson is said to have had three brothers lost at sea; also one who d. of cholera in New Orleans about 1832. He was related to Pudsey Dawson, Esq., of Hornby castle, England,[1] where he spent some months with a son, while on a visit to his native country a few years before his decease.[2] He had, besides several daughters, two sons, one of whom d. when 18 years of age. The other son is:

2–1. Dr. BENJAMIN FREDERICK DAWSON, b. in New York, 1844, res. 1873, at 8 East 15th street, New York city. Doctor Dawson is editor of the *American Journal of Obstetrics*, and a well known and highly esteemed lecturer in the medical schools of New York on subjects connected with his special studies.

---

[1] See page 10, note 4.

[2] His will, dated Dec. 24, 1859, probated July 24, 1866, mentions his brother-in-law, Laughton Osborn, wife Elizabeth, and sisters Elizabeth and Mansfield.

FAMILY OF ABRAHAM DAWSON,

OF NEW YORK CITY AND ITHACA, N. Y., 1834–1872.

1. ABRAHAM DAWSON was b. July 10, 1795, at Wisbech, Cambridgeshire, England. His father was a Lincolnshire man, who had emigrated to Wisbech in early life, and m. there Miss Hephzibah Culy, of the locally celebrated Huguenotic family of that name then living on a farm called Guyhirn, near Wisbech, which property they still occupy. The father d. in 1799, and at the age of twelve years Abraham Dawson was sent to Gosberton, in the vicinity of Spalding and Boston, Lincolnshire, to learn a trade. He m., May 15, 1820, Miss *Mary Barton*, b. Nov. 5, 1794, second daughter of John Barton, a respectable farmer of Bicker, of that shire, and settled at Gosberton, where he had born one son and four daughters. Two of the latter d. young, and with the other three children and their mother, he emigrated to the United States, landing in New York city, June 9, 1834. It is said that the chief reason which induced him to emigrate was his dissatisfaction with the government in his native land. Soon after his arrival in this country he removed to Manhattanville, on the upper end of New York island, and commenced the life of a gardener, which business became his permanent occupation. In 1836–37 he was gardener at the Bloomingdale Lunatic Asylum. He removed in the fall of 1837, with his family, to Ithaca, N. Y.,[1] where he resided until his death, which occurred Jan. 13, 1872, in the 77th year of his age. "No more sturdy champion of the truth, as he understood it, ever lived, and no one died more generally lamented by those who knew him. He was a faithful husband, affectionate father and honest man."[2] His wife d. in Danby, Tompkins Co., N. Y., Dec. 4, 1856. They had seven children :

2–1. Henry Barton, b. at Gosberton, June 8, 1821, res. 1873, Morrisania, N. Y. ; *m.*

---

[1] *Historical Magazine*, Dec., 1868.

[2] *New England Historical and Genealogical Register*, April, 1872.

2–2. Jane Barton, b, at Gosberton, April 14, 1824, d. at same place, March 21, 1826.

2–3. A *daughter*, d. unnamed.

2–4. Jane, b. at Gosberton, Dec. 25, 1827, d. at Ithaca, N. Y., Nov. 9, 1867. TURRILL.

2–5. Mary, b. at Gosberton, Aug. 11, 1831, res. 1873, Ithaca, N. Y. DUSENBURY.

2–6. Sarah Ann, b. at Manhattanville, New York city, Dec. 17, 1835, d. in Danby, N. Y., July 29, 1856; *unm.*

2–1. HENRY BARTON DAWSON, eldest child and only son of Abraham and *Mary Barton* Dawson, was b. in Gosberton, Lincolnshire, England, June 8, 1821, and emigrated thence with his parents in 1834 to New York city. He enjoyed good educational advantages in his native place, and after his arrival in New York attended the public schools of that city for some time. In March, 1836, he left school in order to assist his father in his business of gardening, and continued to work with him until the removal of the family to Ithaca, N. Y., in the fall of 1837. In Ithaca, after a short term in the service of Mr. Isaac Bower, wheelwright, he became a clerk in the bookselling and publishing house of Messrs Mack, Andrus and Woodruff. This engagement was succeeded by a clerkship to a resident of Ithaca, engaged in the lumber business, in whose service he returned to New York in April, 1839. In this business he remained under successive employers until May, 1844, after which, until the summer of 1847, he was bookkeeper and cashier to firms engaged in the sale of drugs and patent medicines.

Having loaned some money, in 1845, to the proprietor of *The Crystal Fount*, a temperance and literary newspaper, he was obliged to take the printing office and paper in payment of his claim. For more than a year, besides attending to his duties as bookkeeper for his employers, he edited and published this paper, being obliged to devote his evenings to the latter employment. Finding this double duty too burdensome, owing partly to failing health, he resigned his situation in 1847, and devoted his whole time to his newspaper. The literary enterprise thus undertaken finally failed, but no doubt had great influence in shaping his future career. While subsequently engaged as agent of the International Art Union and of the American Art Union, and as an officer of the Wall street Ferry Company, the Emigrant Aid

Henry B. Dawson

Company, and of three different insurance companies, his pen was not idle. He early developed a taste for historical studies, particularly those connected with the annals of the city of his adoption. The failure, in 1855, of an insurance company with which he was connected, left him without regular employment, and he accepted an offer from Messrs Johnson, Fry & Co., publishers, to write a work for them on the military and naval history of this country. This was his first book, although he had before become known by *The Park and its Vicinity*, written for and published in the *Manual* of the common council of New York city, for 1855; the *Life and Times of Anne Hutchinson*, written for the Baptist Historical Society; and *The Retreats through Westchester, in* 1776, written for the New York Historical Society. In accordance with his arrangement with Messrs Johnson, Fry & Co., *The Battles of the United States by Sea and Land* was published as a serial in forty elegantly printed and illustrated numbers, beginning in the autumn of 1858, and proved very successful. In the progress of this work he was led into a controversy concerning the merits of Major General Israel Putnam, with two literary gentlemen of Hartford. The letters on both sides were afterwards collected in a sumptuous volume which has commanded prices as high as fifty dollars per copy. In 1863-4 he published an edition of *The Fœderalist*, with much original illustrative matter from his own pen, being the first of a projected series of historical works relating to the constitution of the United States. This enterprise also elicited a heated controversy, in which he was assailed by Hon. John Jay, grandson of one of the authors of the original work, and by James A. Hamilton, son of another of its authors. Mr. Dawson replied to each successively in a manner that showed a ready command of facts which satisfied his friends if not his opponents. Since this time his historical papers have been so numerous as to render impracticable even a mention of their titles in this connection. Several of them, having been printed in limited editions, now command extremely high prices from collectors of works relating to American history and for public libraries.

For every literary undertaking he has prepared himself by the most laborious, conscientious and exhaustive study. He has no sympathy for the current fictions of history, no respect for paper-made heroes and statesmen. The extent, minuteness and variety of his information in regard to the history of our country, and the enthusiasm and perseverance which he carries into new fields of historical research, render him formidable both as a controversialist and critic. For this kind of literature his talents admirably fit him. He wields a vigorous pen, is ingenious and skillful in the use of arguments, and shows himself a remorseless iconoclast, dealing his blows with reckless directness, not heeding the consequences to himself or others.

In 1866 he bought *The Historical Magazine*, of which he became the editor and publisher. Ten volumes of this magazine having already been completed, he commenced with the first number issued by him, a new and enlarged series, to which he has since contributed many valuable papers. Under his management, which is still (1873) continued, it has attained a very high reputation.

He has been employed by the state authorities of New York to examine and report on the boundaries of that state on the lines of New Jersey, Massachusetts and Connecticut, and the Vestry of Trinity Church, New York, has manifested its sense of his ability by inviting him to become the historian of that venerable and celebrated parish.

Mr. Dawson's correspondents include most of the historians, and many of the prominent public men — military and civil — in the country. He has been elected a member of numerous historical and statistical societies, and he is the fortunate possessor of one of the largest and best working libraries on American history to be found in the state in private hands.

He was brought up a Baptist of the old school, and is a resolute and uncompromising Calvanist in his religious views. In politics he was originally a Democrat, as he is still according to his own declaration, but he has by no means uniformly adhered to the party claiming to represent Democratic principles in the United States. He is a rigid opponent of a centralized power either at Albany or Washington.

In 1869, having sought to apprentice one of his sons, William M. Dawson, to the bricklayers' trade in Morrisania, he took a bold stand in resisting the unreasonable terms prescribed by the Bricklayers' Union of that place. The son's discharge having been effected through the compulsory action of that association, Mr. Dawson brought civil and criminal suits against certain members of the Union, and succeeded, not only in obtaining judgment against them for the loss of his son's services, but in convicting them criminally, and having them sentenced as conspirators to interrupt trade. His son was already apprenticed and at work in New York, and in these proceedings he was actuated merely by a desire to sustain what he considered to be his right as a citizen to enter into and fulfill, without mischievous interference, a lawful contract with one of his neighbors.[1]

In his private relations Mr. Dawson is eminently happy. His manifold engagements do not prevent a due regard to the social amenities of life, and he is apt to take his friends into the inner sanctuary of his affections.

The compiler is indebted to him for many kindnesses during the preparation of this work.

Mr. Dawson m. May 28, 1845, *Catharine Martling*, b. in Tarrytown, N. Y., Dec. 8, 1821, dau. of Abraham D. and *Esther Whelpley* Martling — one of the most ancient families of Westchester county. They have had nine children:

3-1. Spencer H. Cone, b. May 11, 1846, d. at West Farms, N. Y., July 9, 1871; *unm.*
3-2. Henry Barton, b. Dec. 19, 1847; printer.
3-3. William Martling, b. Aug. 29, 1849; bricklayer.
3-4. Stephen Van Rensselaer, b. Sept. 21, 1851.
3-5. George Cooley, b. Sept. 25, 1853.
3-6. Mary Dawson, b. June 17, 1855.
3-7. Catharine Martling, b. April 9, 1859.
3-8. Esther Martling, b. July 17, 1861, d. March 16, 1865.
3-9. Caroline Dutcher, b. Aug. 31, 1863.

They have also an adopted daughter:
Anna Augusta, b. Oct. 30, 1851.

2-4. *Jane Dawson*, b. at Gosberton, England, Dec. 25, 1827, d. at Ithaca, N. Y., Nov. 9, 1867, aged 40. She m. in

[1] The above sketch is in part condensed from "A memoir of Henry B. Dawson, Esquire, by John Ward Dean," published in *The Historical Magazine* for December, 1868, which number of the magazine was entirely edited by Mr. Dean, its original editor. Accompanying the article referred to is a fine steel portrait of Mr. Dawson, a copy of which, from the same plate, is presented herewith. See also, Duyckinck's *Cyclopedia of American Literature.*

Ithaca, June 11, 1858, WILLIAM O. TURRILL. They had three children, all b. in Ithaca:

3–10. Henry William, b. Feb. 3, 1859.
3–11. Adele Virginia, b. Sept. 28, 1861.
3–12. Annette Louisa, b. May 21, 1864.

2–5. *Mary Dawson*, b. at Gosberton, England, Aug. 11, 1831, m. in Ithaca, N. Y., Feb. 15, 1871, Rev. FRANCISCO DUSENBURY, a Baptist minister. They res. 1873, in Ithaca.

FAMILY OF HENRY DAWSON,

OF BROOKLYN and COHOES, N. Y., 1848–1873.

1. HENRY DAWSON, b. in Nottingham, England, 1815, emigrated from Nottinghamshire to America in 1848. He lived in Brooklyn in 1849, where he followed his trade as a machinist, but removed soon after to Cohoes, Albany county, where he has been for some years engaged in business as a manufacturer of needles. (H. Dawson & Son, 1869; Dawson & Knott, 1872). He m. in Radford, Nottinghamshire, 1833, *Ann Radford*, who was b. in Nottingham, 1817, dau. of John and Elizabeth Radford. They res. 1873, in Cohoes, and have had seven children:

2–1. Henry, b. in Nottingham, Eng., Oct., 1834, res. 1873, Brooklyn; *m.*
2–2. Ann SHANNON, b. in Radford, Eng., July, 1836, res. 1873, Cohoes; 2 children.
2–3. John, b. in Radford, June, 1839, res. 1873, in Cohoes; *m.*
2–4. Lucy, b. in Radford, Feb., 1843, res. 1873, in Brooklyn. HERON.
2–5. Eliza, b. in Radford, Feb., 1846, m. WILLIAM DAVIS, res. 1873, in Troy, N. Y.
2–6. William, b. in Brooklyn, N. Y., June, 1849, res. 1873, in Cohoes.
2–7. James Radford, b. in Cohoes, May, 1852, res. 1873, in Cohoes; *unm.*

2–1. HENRY DAWSON Jun., b. in Nottingham, England, Oct., 1834, m. in Brooklyn, N. Y., Nov., 1853, *Sarah Green.* He was a bookbinder and manufacturer of blank books, in Brooklyn and New York, 1856–1870; president of the Woodman and Kaufman Republican club, Brooklyn, 1870; alderman of the eighteenth ward, 1871-72; and assistant U. S. assessor, 1870-72. They res. 1873, in Brooklyn, E. D., and have five children, all b. in Brooklyn:

3–1. James Henry, b. 1855.
3–2. Frances Ann, b. 1857.
3–3. Lucy Elizabeth, b. 1860.
3–4. Frederick William, b. 1866.
3–5. Harry Radford, b. 1870.

2-3. John Dawson, b. in New Radford, England, June 21, 1839, emigrated with his parents from Nottinghamshire to America about 1848. He m. in Cohoes, N. Y., Jan. 15, 1862, *Mary Long*, who was b. in Hathorn, England, Jan. 17, 1842, dau. of John and Maria Long. He is a needle maker. They res. 1873, in Cohoes, and have four children, all b. in that place:

3-6. William, b. Dec. 28, 1862.
3-7. Lincoln, b. May 22, 1865.
3-8. Lizzie, b. Aug. 17, 1868.
3-9. Maria, b. March 5, 1872.

2-4. *Lucy Dawson*, b. in Radford, England, Feb., 1843, m. William Heron. They res. 1873, in Brooklyn. Two chn.:

3-10. Harry.
3-11. Gertrude.

FAMILIES OF JAMES AND THOMAS DAWSON,

Of New York City, 1849-1871.

1. Mr. James Dawson states that he was b. in Corlea, county Donegal, Ireland, March 17, 1833, and came to America in June, 1849. His father, Michael Dawson, d. in Corlea, Aug. 15, 1842, aged 31 years; his mother was Catharine Dawson, dau. of Daniel Dawson, of Kildoney, county Donegal.[1] He m. in New York, Feb. 19, 1857, *Ann Killien*, who d. at their

[1] His father's ancestors were originally Dowsons, and were Scotch, but changed the name to Dawson after coming into Ireland. His mother's family claimed to have sprung from the name MacDevitt. "Thus," he says, "I am a double Dawson, or rather a Dowson-MacDevitt-Dawson; but how or why the name of my mother's family became changed from MacDevitt to Dawson I cannot say. This I do know, we are not of English stock. If we were, we might be land owners; but we were all tenants, and haters of English rule." (See remarks on the origin of the name Dowson, page 4, and for explanation of the change of MacDevitt to Dawson — a change in form, merely, for in signification they are the same — see note 1 of same page). His father was son of James Dawson, who d. in Ireland, Aug. 16, 1832, aged 54; son of James Dawson, d. July 10, 1811, aged 56; son of Bernard Dowson or Dawson, b. in town of Athlone, county West Meath, d. in Corlea, May 11, 1768. The last named said to be descended from David Dowson who emigrated from Scotland into county Donegal some time in the seventeenth century.

residence, 38 Ridge street, July 10, 1871, aged 36 years. He is a manufacturer of britannia and silver plated ware. They had five children, as follows:

2–1. John, b. in New York, Feb. 2, 1858, d. April 28, 1859.
2–2. Mary Emily, b. in New York, Aug. 29, 1859.
2–3. Rebecca Jane, b. in Beverly, Mass., Feb. 20, 1862.
2–4. Frank O'Malley, b. in Brooklyn, N. Y., Dec. 10, 1864, d. Jan. 15, 1865.
2–5. Katie, b. in New York, July 8, 1870, d. March 27, 1871.

1. Mr. THOMAS DAWSON, (brother of Michael Dawson, the father of James Dawson, above named), was b. in Corlea, Ireland, Sept. 9, 1823, and resides, 1871, at 688 Second avenue, New York city, being by trade a painter. He m. in New York, May 22, 1849, *Mary Killien*, who d. Dec. 24, 1860. They had five children, all b. in New York:

2–1. James Henry, b. Jan. 24, 1851, d. May 24, 1855.
2–2. Thomas Francis, b. Feb. 15, 1852, d. Feb. 22, 1871.
2–3. Mary Emily, b. March 5, 1854.
2–4. James Henry, b. Feb. 28, 1856; printer.
2–5. Ambrose, b. Nov. 20, 1860, d. May 19, 1865.

FAMILIES OF JOHN AND JAMES S. DAWSON,

OF BROOKLYN, E. D., N. Y., 1870.

The following from Mr. James S. Dawson, of 215 Kent St., Brooklyn, E. D., Dec., 1870.

1. JOHN DAWSON was b. in England, near the Scottish line, and m. there *Margaret Seaton*. They emigrated to St. Johns, Province of New Brunswick, and had three sons:

2–1. John, who is believed to be now living in N. B., where he has a family.
2–2. Thomas, of whom nothing more is known.
2–3. James S., b. in St. Johns, 1794, d. in Kingston, Jamaica, W. I., before 1830.

2–3. JAMES S. DAWSON, b. in St. Johns, 1794, d. in Kingston, Jamaica, was a ship carpenter. He m. *Catharine T.*

Cochran, who survived him, and removed to New York city, about 1830, with her family, consisting of:

3–1. John, b. in New Brunswick, res. 1870, in Brooklyn, E. D.
3–2. Margaret Ann, b. in Eastport, Me.
3–3. James S., b. in New Brunswick, 1825, res. 1870, in Brooklyn, E. D.
3–4. William, b. in New Brunswick, d. in California, from drowning; *unm.*

3-1. John Dawson, b. in New Brunswick, res. 1870, in Brooklyn, E. D., is a ship caulker. He m. in New York, *Sarah Kirk*, and has living, two sons and two daughters:

4–1. Albert F., shorthand legal reporter, res. 1870, in Brooklyn, E. D.; has a family.
4–2. Caroline.
4–3. William Augustus.
4–4. Jane.

3-3. James S. Dawson, was b. at Mason's Bay, N. B., March 11, 1825, res. 1870, at 215 Kent St., Brooklyn, E. D., is a ship carpenter. He m. *Amelia Osborn*, of New York city, and has had two sons, both deceased, and one daughter.

"George Dawson, of New York and Michigan." Since the record beginning on page 166 was printed, additional information has been received by the compiler, as follows:

2–1. James Dawson, farmer, b. in Edinburgh, Scotland, 1810, d. in Clayton, Mich., 1865, aged 55. He m. in Mich., March 18, 1836, *Almira Cotton*, who was b. in Cayuga county, N. Y., 1814, dau. of Alpheus Cotton. She res. a widow 1873, at Royal Oak. Their children, all b. in Mich., are now named in the order of birth, as follows: I. Sarah Jane, b. at Royal Oak, June 7, 1837, res. 1873, Royal Oak, *unm.* II. James W., b. at Troy, July 7, 1839, res. 1873, Flint, Mich., m. Jan. 1, 1862, *Hattie A. Williams;* three children: Ida E., b. Oct. 3, 1863, Ada A., b. Jan. 12, 1866, d. July 7, 1868, Matilda E., b. Jan. 10, 1868. III. Isaac, b. at Royal Oak, April 2, 1841, res. 1873, Royal Oak, m. July 7, 1868, *Amelia Schonhit*; one son, George William, b. Aug. 30, 1869. IV. Edward, b. in Troy, March 8, 1843, m. April 2, 1871, *Matilda Norris*, and res. 1873, at Royal Oak. V. *Mary A.*, b. at Royal Oak, Aug. 23, 1847, m. 1st., Oct. 17, 1864, C. L. Hitchcock, who d. Nov. 16, 1866, leaving dau., Nettie D., b. Nov. 20, 1865, d. Nov. 21,

1869. Mary A., m. 2d., Feb. 20, 1867, HENRY RUSSELL, and res. 1873, at Royal Oak; one dau., Julia E., b. June 3, 1868.

2–4. *Jane Dawson*, b. in Toronto, Canada, Oct. 5, 1822, m. March 20, 1826, CARLTON SMITH, who was b. in Orwell, Rutland, Vermont, 1818, son of Nathaniel and Sarah Smith. They res. 1873, in Flint, Mich., and have three children: I. GEORGE D., b. in Richfield, Mich., Feb. 5, 1837, m. Dec. 12, 1859, *Julia McCoy*, res. Flint; one son, Edgar B., b. May 4, 1860. II. LEVI R., b. in Richfield, Sept. 27, 1839, m. May 17, 1872, *Alice Brewer*, res. Flint. III. Darwin P., b. in Warren, Mich., Oct. 17, 1851, res. Flint.

3–7. BURRET S. DAWSON, m. Nov. 21, 1873, *Annie I. Thompson*, of Albany, N. Y.

FAMILY OF HENRY HODGESON DAWSON,

OF SYRACUSE, N. Y., 1873.

1. WILLIAM DAWSON, of Hackneywick, London, England, m. *Amelia Fevouz*, who was of French descent. They had five children, all b. in London:

2–1. Walter, b. 1828.
2–2. Sidney R., b. 1830, d. 1872.
2–3. Amelia, b. 1833.
2–4. Mary Ann, b. 1835.
2–5. Henry Hodgeson, b. 1837, res. 1873, Syracuse, N. Y.; *m.*

2–5. HENRY HODGESON DAWSON, b. in London, 1837, m. *Abigail Shaw*, of Concord, N. H. He is a master mechanic of the Syracuse and Binghamton R. R. Res. Syracuse, N. Y. They have one child:

3–1. Amelia H., b. in New York city, March, 1861.

NEW JERSEY.

For records of several families now of this state see the preceding pages.

Southern New Jersey contained residents of the name at an early day. The following record comprises such information as the compiler has been able to obtain in reference to these families.

FAMILY OF FRANCIS DAWSON,

Of Burlington County, N. J., 17—.[1]

1. Francis Dawson, a Quaker, was a resident of Northampton township, Burlington county, N. J., 1729, and probably some years earlier. Whence he came is not known, but it is surmised that he may have been of the family of Frances Dawson, who was of Talbot county, Md., 1688; perhaps a son of her son Richard Dawson, who m. Susanna Foster, 1698. (See *Maryland* records). He m. 9 mo. 19, 1729, Rachel Jess, widow of Zachariah Jess, and dau. of Restore and Rachel Lippincott. Nothing is known as to issue of this marriage, if any; but by a former wife Francis Dawson had children as follows:

2–1. Rachel, m. 1737, James Southwick.
2–2. Richard, of whom presently.
2–3. Francis, m. 1758, *Sarah Southwick*.

2–2. Richard Dawson m. *Lydia Silver*, 1743. They lived at or near Salem, N. J., and had:

3–1. Francis, b. 12 mo. 28, 1754, d. April 2, 1824; *m.*

The following, all of Salem, are supposed to have been also

---

[1] For extracts from Quaker records relating to this family, the compiler is indebted to W. F. Corbit, Esq., of Philadelphia.

children of Richard and Lydia Dawson, probably b. before Francis. All of them were disowned by the Salem monthly meeting of Friends, at the dates below given, for "outgoing in marriage"— marrying out of the Society. For this reason their further history is not traceable in the records of the Society. They may have been related to the families of our name at Falls meeting, Bucks county, Pa. (See *Pennsylvania* records). Lydia, one of the supposed daughters of Richard and Lydia Dawson, received a certificate from the Salem meeting, to go to the Falls meeting, 10 mo. 31, 1768, but appears not to have removed, as she was a few years later disowned by the Salem meeting. Richard Dawson and family were granted a certificate by the Salem meeting, 6 mo. 29, 1772, to move to Haddonfield, but it would seem remained in Salem, for the next year (1 mo. 25, 1773) they also were disowned by that meeting, doubtless on account of having been present at the marriage of one of their children where the ceremony was performed by a "priest," as the Friends denominated any minister of the Gospel not of their Society. Disownment was then, among Friends, a common penalty for marrying a non-member, or for being present at any marriage consummated otherwise than by Friends' ceremony. The following are the disownments above referred to of supposed children of Richard and Lydia Dawson:

3–2. Ann, disowned as Ann Pedrick, late Dawson, 6 mo. 24, 1767.
3–3. Aaron, 4 mo. 27, 1772.
3–4. Moses, 4 mo. 4, 1774.
3–5. Lydia, as Lydia Cowgill, late Dawson, 7 mo. 25, 1774.
3–6. Zedediah, 12 mo. 31, 1787.

3–1. Francis Dawson, b. 12 mo. 28, 1754, a birth-right member of the Society of Friends, was disowned by the Salem, N. J., meeting, on his twenty-fourth birth-day, 12 mo. 28, 1778, probably on account of his marriage, a few months before (April 12, 1778), to *Hannah Beetle.* She was his first wife, b. 1757, d. June 21, 1780.[1] They had one child:

4–1. Sarah, b. June 14, 1779.

[1] "Hannah Dawson, wife to Francis Dawson, was drowned out of a shallop in the eir of our Lord 1780. It happened the 21st day of Jeun that she was drowned, and was found the 25th day, and was beurred 26 day of Jeun."— Extract from a record, made by Francis Dawson, on the fly leaves of an old volume, published by Joseph

He m. 2d. ("minister North" performing the ceremony), April 2, 1781, *Lucy Long*, b. Sept. 2, 1761, d. Feb. 20, 1796,[1] dau. of Jonas and Ann Long. They had six children :

4–2. Hannah.
4–3. Lucy.
4–4. Richard, b. 1785, d. 1788.
4–5. Mary.
4–6. Elizabeth, b. 1793, d. 1795.
4–7. Ann, b. Dec. 8, 1795, d. Dec. 21, 1795.

Francis Dawson m. 3d., Dec. 18, 1798, *Deborah Macgomery*. They lived in Pedricktown, Salem county, N. J., where he d. April 2, 1824, aged 70 years, and she d. Sept., 1824. They had six children, all b. in Pedricktown :

4–8. Francis, b. Nov. 14, 1799, d. near Salem, N. J., about 1861 ; *m.*
4–9. Richard, b. April 24, 1803, d. in Centre Square, N. J., about 1858 ; *m.*
4–10. Deborah, b. May 9, 1806, res. Gloucester Co., N. J. DAWSON.
4–11. Amy, b. Feb. 18, 1809, d. near Centre Square, N. J., about 1862. COOKER.
4–12. Dorcas, b. Jan. 24, 1812, res. 1873, Philadelphia, Pa. APPLEGATE.
4–13. Rebecca, b. Oct. 11, 1817, res. 1873, Auburn, Salem Co., N. J. STRING ; CASTLE.

4–8. FRANCIS DAWSON, b. in Pedricktown, N. J., Nov. 14, 1799, d. near Salem, N. J., about 1861, m. *Elizabeth Beetle*. They had seven children, who res. in Salem Co., N. J., and have families :

5–1. Samuel.
5–2. Jonathan, res. Bridgeton, N. J. ; a son in Methodist ministry.
5–3. George.
5–4. John.
5–5. Francis.
5–6. Mary Ann.
5–7. Elizabeth.

4–9. RICHARD DAWSON, b. in Pedricktown, N. J., April 24, 1803, d. in Centre Square, N. J., about 1858, m. *Martha Atkinson*. They had seven chn., who res. in Gloucester Co., N. J. :

5–8. Edmund J., m. *Zebiah Corson*, res. Bridgeport, N. J. ; several chn.

Cruikshank, in Philadelphia, 1781, entitled *The Plainness and Innocent Simplicity of the Christian Religion*, now in possession of Rev. Thomas M. Dawson, Oakland, California.

1 "February, 20th day, in the eir of our Lord, 1796, then the Lord saw fit to take my deir and beloved wife from me. Her age was 34 years, 4 mos. and 20 days."— *Ibid.*

5–9. Francis, m.——.
5–10. James, m.——.
5–11. Charles, m.——.
5–12. Richard, m.——.
5–13. Deborah, m. Joseph Roberts.
5–14. Susannah, *unm.*

4–10. *Deborah Dawson*, b. May 9, 1806, m. Thomas Dawson, a distant relative. They resided near Centre Square, Gloucester county, N. J., and had two children:

5–15. Caroline, b. 1830, d. Sept., 1866. Tozer.
5–16. Thomas M., b. April 10, 1840, res. 1873, Oakland, Cal.; *m.*

4–11. *Amy Dawson*, b. in Pedricktown, N. J., Feb. 18, 1809, d. near Centre Square, N. J., about 1862, m. William Cooker. They had three children:

5–17. Lewis.
5–18. Henry.
5–19. Emeline.

4–12. *Dorcas Dawson*, b. in Pedricktown, N. J., Jan. 12, 1812, m. Israel Applegate, carpenter, and res. 1873, 1927 Callowhill St., Philadelphia, Pa. They had three children:

5–20. Mary.
5–21. Hannah.
5–22. Emma, *unm.*

4–13. *Rebecca Dawson*, b. in Pedricktown, N. J., Oct. 11, 1817, m. 1st., William String. They had four children:

5–23. Adeline.
5–24. Sarah Jane.
5–25. William.
5–26. Robert.

She m. 2d., Mahlon Castle, and res. 1873, Auburn, Salem Co., N. J. Two children:

5–27. Abigail.
5–28. Mahlon.

5–15. *Caroline Dawson*, b. in Gloucester Co., N. J., 1830, m. about 1851, John E. Tozer, and d. Sept., 1866, leaving seven children:

6–1. Caleb B.
6–2. Anna Eliza.
6–3. Rachel.
6–4. Thomas Stephen.

6–5. [TOZER.] Martha.
6–6. John.
6–7. Charles Joseph.

5–16. Rev. THOMAS M. DAWSON, was b. near Centre Square, Gloucester Co., N. J., April 10, 1840. After the usual preliminary education he graduated at Auburn Theological Seminary, N. Y., May 10, 1866. In June, 1866, he received the degree of A.M. from the Wabash College, Indiana, and in the same month was ordained and installed pastor of the First Presbyterian church in Lewisburg, Pa. He remained there one year, and accepted a unanimous call to the Seventh Presbyterian church, in New York city. The summer of 1870 he spent in company with his wife in Europe, traveling through England, France, Switzerland and Scotland. After a pastorate of three and a half years in New York city, he removed to Monticello, N. Y., where he remained two years as pastor of the First Presbyterian church of that place. In November, 1872, he accepted a unanimous call to the First Presbyterian church, in Brooklyn (now Oakland), near San Francisco, California. In May, 1873, he was a delegate from the Presbytery of San Francisco to the General Assembly in Baltimore, Md. While in New York he was moderator of the Third Presbytery of N. Y., and published a semicentennial discourse on the *History of the Seventh Church.* Many of his sermons, on various topics, have been published, and he has published several stories, as *Ralph Donaldson*, *Mrs. Thornesdale*, etc., also a *History of the Ancient Aztecs*, and uncounted newspaper articles. He m. Feb. 23, 1869, *Mamie E. Brush*, of Brooklyn, N. Y. They res. in Oakland, and have one child:
6–8. Mamie B., b. May 17, 1871.

JOHN DAWSON was a private in New Jersey state militia during Rev. war.—See *Officers and Men of N. J. in Rev. war*, p. 568.

PENNSYLVANIA.

For an account of one of the principal families of the name in this state, originally established in Maryland, reference must be had to the *Maryland* records ; while one of the records which are here inserted concerns families now almost wholly of Maryland, emigration having, in these cases, reversed the relationship to the original (American) ancestors.

A record of the descendants of John and Dorothy Dawson, of Abington, Pa., which should, by reason of priority of settlement, be the first inserted of the Pennsylvania records, is postponed to the close of this work, time being required for further additions and corrections.

Records of several other families, distinct, so far as known, from each other and from those above mentioned, are here added. Altogether, they constitute but a very imperfect record of the families of our name in Pennsylvania, which have been numerous from an early date.[1]

The following are various notices of names, as yet unclassified, preserved by way of memoranda for future reference. It is hoped that others more immediately interested may undertake to supply the deficiencies of this work.

The will of EMANUEL DAWSON, mason, of Philadelphia, dated March 31, 1708, proved May 26, 1708, mentions w. Hannah, and children William, Rebecca, Thomas, Charles and Susannah. The wid. sold part of the estate same year. John Dawson, son of Emanuel, d. 3 mo. 29, 1698.

WILLIAM DAWSON, schoolmaster, of Philadelphia,[2] died about middle of last century ; the widow, Mary, m. Robert Moore, joiner. William

---

[1] The *Directory* of the city of Philadelphia for 1870–71 contains the names of upwards of seventy Dawsons — double the number contained in the New York *Directory* of that year, and about equal to those found in the *Directories* of New York and Brooklyn combined, in which cities, next to Philadelphia, the representatives of the name are, relatively to the population, more numerous than in any other of the large cities of the country. The Pittsburgh city *Directory* contains seventeen names of Dawsons ; that of Buffalo, two only ; that of Rochester, four — which facts illustrate the greater frequency of the name in western Pennsylvania as compared with western New York.

[2] Perhaps author of " The Youth's Entertaining Amusement, or a Plain Guide to Psalmody, being a choice collection of tunes sung in the English Protestant Congre-

and Mary Dawson had dau. Ann. Ann Dawson d. in Philadelphia, intestate, 1758.

ABRAHAM DAWSON, Philadelphia, d. intestate, 1774. Edward Dawson appointed administrator.

MATTHEW DAWSON, of Philadelphia, by will dated Oct. 2, 1849, proved Aug 15, 1755, left all his estate to his brother James Dawson.

MICHAEL DAWSON, pilot, and w. Sarah, lived in Philadelphia about 1780–88, and afterwards removed to Delaware.

THOMAS DAWSON, Philadelphia, d. intestate, March 4, 1798; widow Elizabeth, administratrix; three children.

GEORGE H. DAWSON, d. intestate, 1798; Margaret Dawson, administratrix, Philadelphia. In Bucks county, Pa., about 1800, *Sarah Stapler*, dau. of Thomas and *Margaret Allen* Stapler, m.——DAWSON, and had Thomas, b. about 1801, Margaret, b. about 1803.

Rachel Dawson m. ROBERT DRAKE, at Falls meeting (Society of Friends) in Bucks Co., Pa., 1798.

Mary Dawson m. WILLIAM MALICE, at Christ Church, Philadelphia, 1752. Mary Ann Dawson buried at Christ Church, July 27, 1717.

The following marriages are from the records of the old Swedes church (*Gloria Dei*) at Philadelphia: JAMES DAWSON and *Sarah Engle*, Dec. 10, 1751; *Elizabeth Dawson* and JOHN FENBYE, April 21, 1751; DANIEL DAWSON and *Hannah Hurst*, Jan. 20, 1771; JOHN DAWSON and *Margaret Carroll*, Oct. 12, 1773; JAMES DAWSON and *Elizabeth Neil*, April 3, 1774; *Sarah Dawson* and JAMES BOWCHER, Oct. 18, 1786; *Elizabeth Dawson* and GEORGE STREATON, April 24, 1788; *Mary Dawson* and GEORGE BLINFORD, Feb. 28, 1774. No births or deaths recorded.[1]

ISAAC DAWSON and JEREMIAH DAWSON were privates in Capt. Thomas Robinson's Co. of Col. Anthony Wayne's Penn. Battalion, at Ticonderoga, Jan. 5, to Nov. 26, 1776.[2]

ANTHONY DAWSON, was a private in Co. 4, Capt. Rippey, Col. Jerome's Pa. Regt., at Mt. Independence, Nov. 28, 1776.[3]

SAMUEL DAWSON was appointed captain in the Eleventh Pa. Regt., by the Council of Safety at Philadelphia, Nov. 13, 1776;[4] was allowed £1760 for "recruiting service, 1779";[5] died Sept. 25, 1779.[6] He served under Col. Brodhead, at Pittsburgh.[7]

---

gation in Philadelphia, with rules for learning, By W. DAWSON," which was advertised in 1754 as just published.—Watson's *Annals of Philadelphia*, 651. The annalist remarks on the title of the work as "a curious inadvertency," because it suggests the idea of combining "entertainment" with "psalmody."

[1] Many marriages at the Swedes church and also at Christ church (Episcopal) were of those belonging to other religious sects, as Quakers, Presbyterians and Baptists; consequently no account of the *issue* of such marriages appears on the records of these churches. The compiler is indebted to W. F. Corbit, Esq., of Philadelphia, for the above extracts.

[2] Saffel's *Records of the Revolutionary War*, 195.

[3] *Ibid*, 209.

[4] *Colonial Records*, XI, 2.

[5] Saffel's *Records*, 227.

[6] *Colonial Records*, XII, 435, 436.

[7] *Penn. Archives*, 1790, appendix, 145.

Henry Dawson was ensign and quartermaster and lieutenant and quartermaster, from Feb. 22, 1778 to Dec. 6, 1781, in Col. John Gibson's Detachment, western Department of the army; received a land warrant for his services.[1]

William Dawson, a corporal in the continental army, from Bensalem, Bucks Co., Pa., was among soldiers captured by the British, at Fort Washington, New York, Nov., 1776.[2]

FAMILY OF ROBERT DAWSON,

Of Philadelphia, 1738-1746.

From letters of the late Mordecai L. Dawson, of Philadelphia, 1872, *and other sources, the following:*

1. Robert Dawson emigrated to this country from Ireland before 1738. He was a merchant, and m. at Christ Church, in Philadelphia, March 5, 1738, *Mary Warner.* He afterwards united with the Society of Friends, and d. 6 mo. 2, 1746. They had two sons, both b. in Philadelphia:[3]

2–1. William, b. 1738, d. in Philadelphia, 5 mo. 12, 1816; *m.*

2–2. Robert, b. about, 1739, d. in Philadelphia, 1818; *m.*

The widow of Robert Dawson m. at Swedes church, in Philadelphia, Aug. 6, 1751, George Morrison. She had no issue of 2d. marriage.

2–1. William Dawson, a cutler by trade, b. about 1738, d. in Philadelphia, 1816, having been engaged in the business of a brewer in that city for many years. He m. 12 mo. 8,

---

[1] Saffel's *Records*, 280, 501.

[2] *American Historical Record*, Nov., 1873, p. 505.

[3] Possibly also two daughters, viz.: *Sydney*, who m. John Morrison, and *Mary*, who m. J. L. Coates, and had J. R. Coates. The relationship is suggested by Mr. W. F. Corbit, of Philadelphia, 1873, to whom the compiler is indebted for information respecting this family. In 1746 administration was granted in Philadelphia on the estate of one Robert Dawson (b. probably about 1700). The widow, name not given, declined to administer, and others were appointed. This R. D. appears to have been wealthy, and had apparently just arrived with a ship load of goods, or died on the voyage, as the administrators' accounts show that some goods were still on the vessel at his death. Was this the Robert, above named? M. L. D. stated that his ancestor, of this name, "came early in the last century, bringing little with him, save a good character and the regrets of his honest neighbors."

1763, *Elizabeth Sugar*, b. 1739, d. June 15, 1821, dau. of Thomas Sugar. They had eight children:

3–1. Robert, b. 10 mo. 4, 1764.
3–2. Mary, b. 7 mo. 25, 1766.
3–3. Anne, b. 2 mo. 29, 1768, m. 6 mo. 17, 1790, THOMAS ROGERS, son of Thomas and Elizabeth Rogers.
3–4. Thomas, b. 12 mo. 10, 1769, d. 11 mo. 3, 1772.
3–5. George, b. 9 mo. 5, 1771.
3–6. William, b. 10 mo. 16, 1773, d. in Philadelphia, 3 mo. 3, 1800; *m.*
3–7. Thomas, b. 7 mo. 26, 1775, d. 3 mo. 3, 1800.
3–8. Warner, b. 12 mo. 12, 1783.

2–2. ROBERT DAWSON, stay maker, b. about 1739, d. in Philadelphia, 1818, m. 6 mo. 25, 1765, *Esther Elfreth*, only dau. of Jeremiah and Elizabeth Elfreth. They had, besides probably other children who d. young:

3–9. Rebecca, b. 1770, d. 1 mo. 25, 1855, *unm.*
3–10. Josiah, b. 9 mo. 1, 1772, d. 8 mo. 29, 1858, aged nearly 86. He never married. See sketch below.

JOSIAH DAWSON (3-10 of this record) was educated a Friend, and went to Jeremiah Paul's school, quite celebrated in those early days. He served an apprenticeship with John and Elliston Perot, well known tradesmen of Philadelphia, but, being of a very timid and retiring disposition, never went into business. He inherited wealth, which by frugality and judicious management, he largely increased. His maternal grandmother was a descendant of Elves Berendtz,[1] a German who emigrated to this country in 1700. She took 20,000 pounds to her husband, which at that time was considered a great fortune. But the fortune of Josiah Dawson was not derived from this source. It partly arose from the great increase in the value of real estate, some of it having been kept for more than one hundred years, the possession of two long lived generations, combining the simplicity of Quakerism with the thrift and saving of the German character. He encouraged the accumulation of property through frugality, by precept and example, but devoted his life and fortune to works of beneficence and charity. By his will, after various private bequests, he gave about $3,000 to the Friend's Asylum for the Insane, $25,000 to the West-

[1] This name, *Anglicized*, became BARNES, which is the family name in this country

town Boarding School, $11,000 to the Contributors of the Pennsylvania Hospital, for the benefit of that institution, and the residue of his estate, amounting to some $225,000, or $250,000, he left to his executors, the proceeds and clear income of the same to be disposed of according to their discretion for the benefit of the charitable and benevolent institutions of Philadelphia, and to alleviate the sufferings and promote the improvement and comfort of individuals and families of the industrious and deserving poor of that city.[1]

3–6. WILLIAM DAWSON, brewer, b. 10 mo. 16, 1773, d. in Philadelphia, 3 mo. 3, 1800, m. 6 mo. 15, 1796, *Rachel Lewis*, dau. of Mordecai and Rachel Lewis, of Philadelphia. They had three children, all b. in Philadelphia :

4–1. William Lewis, b. 4 mo. 17, 1797, d. young.[2]
4–2. Ann, b. 3 mo. 25, 1798, m. 11 mo. 29, 1822, WILLIAM MORRISON, son of John and Sydney Morrison.[3]
4–3. Mordecai Lewis, b. 4 mo. 3, 1799, d. in Phila., 12 mo. 8, 1872 ; *m.*

4–3. MORDECAI LEWIS DAWSON, b. in Philadelphia, 4 mo. 3, 1799, entered Westtown school, 1812, d. at his residence in Philadelphia, 12 mo. 8, 1872, aged 73. He was a member of the monthly meeting of Friends, of Philadelphia, and one of the executors of the will of the above named Josiah Dawson (3–10). In 1821 he succeeded his grandfather, William Dawson, in his business of a brewer, in which he continued until 1849. He was conspicuous in many charitable and benevolent objects. He was a manager of the Pennsylvania Hospital nearly twenty-eight years, and president of the board of managers sixteen years. He was a director of the Pennsylvania Institution for the Deaf and Dumb for thirty years, of which he was also vice-president ; a manager for twenty years and vice-president of the Magdalen Society of Philadelphia, and a director of Girard College for fourteen years, being active also in many other benevolent institutions. He m. 11 mo. 10, 1820, *Elizabeth Poultney*. They had eleven children. :[4]

---

[1] *Friends' Intelligencer*, ninth month, 1858.
[2] William L. Dawson entered, a student, at Westtown school, 1809, and Ann, 1811.
[3] See p. 189, n. 3.
[4] M. L. D. wrote the compiler, in 1872, "I know of no relatives in this city of our name."

5–1. William, b. 7 mo. 3, 1821, d. 7 mo. 19, 1827.
5–2. Letitia Poultney, b. 7 mo. 25, 1824, res. Philadelphia. COLLINS.
5–3. Rachel, b. 9 mo. 3, 1827, res. Philadelphia. MORRIS.
5–4. Elizabeth W., b. 12 mo. 1, 1828.
5–5. James Poultney, b. 3 mo. 18, 1830, d. 10 mo. 18, 1830.
5–6. Anna Morrison, b. 7 mo. 28, 1831.
5–7. Sarah W., b. 10 mo. 1, 1833, d. 7 mo. 24, 1834.
5–8. Mordecai Lewis, b. 8 mo. 15, 1835, d. 8 mo. 16, 1836.
5–9. William Morrison, b. 5 mo. 2, 1838, lost on steamer Evening Star, wrecked, about 1867, off Charleston harbor.
5–10. Charles Poultney, b. 5 mo. 18, 1842, res. 1872, Philadelphia ; *m.*
5–11. Mary Poultney, b. 11 mo. 4, 1843.

5–2. *Letitia Poultney Dawson*, b. in Philadelphia, 7 mo. 25, 1824, m. 8 mo. 28, 1844, FREDERICK COLLINS, son of Isaac and Margaret Collins. They res. Philadelphia. Two children:

6–1. Elizabeth D., b. 1 mo. 23, 1847.
6–2. Anna Morrison, b. 4 mo. 26, 1849.

5–3. *Rachel Dawson*, b. 9 mo. 3, 1827, m. STEPHEN P. MORRIS, who d. in Philadelphia, son of Henry Morris. She res. in Philadelphia. One child:

6–3. Elizabeth D.

5–10. CHARLES POULTNEY DAWSON, b. in Philadelphia, 5 mo. 18, 1842, m. 10 mo. 28, 1863, *Emily C. Pearsall*, dau. of Robert and Emily Pearsall. They res. 1872, at 1114 Pine St., Philadelphia. Two children:

6–4. Helen G., b. 8 mo. 3, 1864.
6–5. Emily F., b. 6 mo. 25, 1866.

FAMILY OF ELIAS DAWSON,

Of Philadelphia, Pa., 1765–1805.

From Dr. Mordecai M. Dawson, of Easton, Md., Edward M. Dawson, Esq., of Washington, D. C., and others, the following:

1. Elias Dawson and *Elizabeth Morton*, dau. of James Morton, were m. at Grange meeting, near Charlemont, county Armagh, Ireland, 5 mo. 25, 1763. They were members of the Society of Friends, and emigrated to Philadelphia about the year 1765, where she d. 9 mo. 19, 1768, aged 24 years. They had three children:

2–1. Mary, b. in Ireland, 3 mo. 11, 1764, d. 10 mo. 31, 1841, m. 12 mo. 9, 1784, Jacob Sinton, son of Thomas and Mary Sinton, of Ireland; said to have lived in Wilkesbarre, Pa.
2–2. William, b. in Philadelphia, 3 mo. 26, 1766, d. 12 mo. 23, 1782.
2–3. Sarah, b. in Philadelphia, 3 mo. 26, 1768, d. 11 mo., 1768.

Elias Dawson m. 2d., at Pine street meeting, Philadelphia, 6 mo. 30, 1773, *Elizabeth Offley*, dau. of Daniel Offley, of that city. Mr. Dawson was a merchant, and d. in Philadelphia, 5 mo. 14, 1805, and his widow Elizabeth, d. in Maryland, 10 mo. 1, 1842, in her 92d year. They had nine children, all b. in Philadelphia, as follows:

2–4. Rachel, b. 2 mo. 5, 1774, d. 12 mo. 1, 1774.[1]
2–5. Elizabeth, b. 9 mo. 1, 1775, d. 6 mo. 15, 1777.
2–6. Sarah, b. 8 mo. 16, 1778.
2–7. Elizabeth, b. 4 mo. 24, 1780, d. 7 mo. 1, 1783.
2–8. Thomas Hammersley, b. 8 mo. 5, 1782, d. 11 mo. 14, 1841; *m.*
2–9. Daniel, b. 4 mo. 11, 1784.
2–10. Rachel, b. 2 mo. 1786, d. 9 mo. 1786.
2–11. Ann P., b. 1 mo. 23, 1789.
2–12. Ruth, b. 5 mo. 25, 1791.

2–8. Thomas Hammersley Dawson, b. in Philadelphia, 8 mo. 5, 1782, was educated a physician, and graduated at the University of Pennsylvania. He entered into business as a

[1] From W. F. Corbit, Esq., Philadelphia, dates from Friends' records, as follows: *Rachel*, d. 12 mo. 6, 1774, aged 10 mos.; *Elizabeth*, d. 7 mo. 7, 1777, aged 18 mos.

druggist in Philadelphia in 1805, and about the year 1808 he removed to Easton, Md., where he followed the same business for many years. Later in life, his elder son being associated with him in trade, he found leisure for other affairs, and accepted the position of teller in the branch at Easton, of the Farmers' Bank of Maryland. This position he held until his death, which occurred in Easton, 11 mo. 14, 1841. He m. in Baltimore county, Md., 10 mo. 3, 1810, *Edith Matthews*, dau. of Mordecai and Ruth Matthews, of Gunpowder, in that county.[1] They had eight children:

3–1. Thomas Scott, b. 10 mo. 7, 1811, d. in Easton, Md., 8 mo. 11, 1842; *m.*
3–2. Ruth Ann, b. 12 mo. 21, 1813, res. 1873, Baltimore. BALDERSTON.
3–3. Edward Matthews, b. 2 mo. 12, 1816, d. in Easton, 12 mo. 31, 1870; *m.*
3–4. Mordecai Matthews, b. 9 mo. 10, 1818, res. 1873, Easton; *m.*
3–5. Elizabeth, b. 6 mo. 8, 1822, res. 1873, Easton. JENKINS.
3–6. Elias Offley, b. 11 mo. 28, 1826, res. 1873, Easton; *m.*
3–7. William Powell, b. 5 mo. 14, 1828, res. 1873, Baltimore; *m.*
3–8. Edith, b. 12 mo. 2, 1832, res. 1873, Baltimore. CARTER.

3–1. THOMAS SCOTT DAWSON, b. in Easton, Md., 10 mo. 7, 1811, educated at Westtown Friends' School, Chester Co., Pa., (entered 1825), d. at Easton, 8 mo. 11, 1842. He m. 11 mo. 5, 1839, *Maria E. Groome*, dau. of Peregrine and Maria Groome, of Easton. They had two children:

4–1. Ella Groome, b. 8 mo. 3, 1840, m. PHILEMON T. KENNER, and res. a widow, 1873, at Easton.
4–2. Thomas Scott, b. 12 mo. 20, 1841, d. 1 mo. 1845.

3–2. *Ruth Ann Dawson*, b. in Easton, Md., 12 mo. 21, 1813, a pupil at Westtown school, 1829, m. 5 mo. 13, 1834, JACOB BALDERSTON, son of Hugh and Margaret Balderston. They res. 1873, in Baltimore. One child:

4–3. Margaret, b. 6 mo. 23, 1836.

---

[1] This lady, with her two elder children, returning from a visit to her parents in 1814, had taken passage with others by sloop across the Chesapeake, when the vessel was captured by the British, and all on board taken prisoners to the flag ship of the British squadron then lying off Tangier's islands. The passengers, among whom were a newly married couple, were detained about two weeks, and in compliment to the bridal pair had several large parties given to them on board the admiral's ship. Dr. Dawson and other gentlemen chartered another vessel, went with it under a flag of truce, and procured the release of all the party, with their effects — the sloop excepted. The lady who was then an infant prisoner still preserves, as a memento of the occasion, a silver spoon presented to her by the admiral.

3-3. EDWARD MATTHEWS DAWSON, b. in Easton, Md., Feb. 12, 1816, d. in same place, Dec. 31, 1870, in his 55th year, was for over twenty years bookkeeper in the bank at Easton now known as the Easton National Bank. He was also a farmer. He m. in Easton, Dec. 13, 1838, *Susan Hambleton Parrott*, dau. of James and *Susan Hambleton* Parrott, and sister to the wife of his brother, Dr. M. M. Dawson. She was b. in Talbot Co., Md., Nov. 3, 1816, and res. 1873, in Easton. They had ten children, all b. in Easton:

4-4. Gustavus Parrott, b. Oct. 3, 1839, d. June 29, 1850, aged 11.
4-5. Edward, b. Aug. 3, 1841, d. May 10, 1842.
4-6. Edward Matthews, b. May 21, 1843, res. 1873, in Washington, D. C.; *m.*
4-7. Charles Scott, b. July 23, 1845, res. 1873, in Easton; *m.*
4-8. Alfred Hunt, b. Sept. 5, 1847, res. 1873, in Easton; *m.*
5-9. Samuel Hambleton, b. Nov. 3, 1849, res. 1873, in Easton; druggist.
4-10. Franklin, b. Jan. 25, 1852, res. 1873, Easton; farmer.
4-11. Susan Parrott, b. Jan. 2, 1854, d. young.
4-12. Thomas Hambleton, b. June 22, 1856, res. 1873, Easton.
4-13. Gustavus Parrott, b. April 19, 1861, res. 1873, Easton.

3-4. MORDECAI M. DAWSON, physician and druggist, b. in Easton, Md., 9 mo. 10, 1818, entered Westtown Friends' School, Chester Co., Pa., 1847, m. 11 mo. 3, 1846, *Deborah Cornelia Parrott*, dau. of James and *Susan Hambleton* Parrott, above named. They res. 1873, in Easton, and have had six children:

4-14. Cornelia Parrott, b. 7 mo. 24, 1847.
4-15. Thomas H., b. 7 mo. 17, 1849, d. 3 mo. 21, 1854.
4-16. James Parrott, b. 7 mo. 22, 1852.
4-17. Josephine Parrott, b. 7 mo. 15, 1855.
4-18. Henry Carter, b. 3 mo. 8, 1859, d. 1 mo. 21, 1863.
4-19. Mary Hand, b. 11 mo. 26, 1861.

3-5. *Elizabeth Dawson*, b. in Easton, Md., 6 mo. 8, 1822, res. 1873, in same place. She m. 3 mo. 25, 1845, Dr. EDWARD JENKINS, son of William and Elizabeth Jenkins. Dr. Jenkins d. 1 mo. 5, 1865. They had five children:

4-20. Edith, b. 3 mo. 25, 1849.
4-21. Edward, b. 9 mo. 9, 1854.
4-22. Elizabeth, b. 1 mo. 25, 1857.
4-23. Thomas H., b. 5 mo. 9, 1859.
4-24. Mary, b. 1 mo. 2, 1861.

3-6. Elias Offley Dawson, druggist, b. in Easton, Md., 11 mo. 28, 1826, entered Westtown Friends' school, 1840, m. 2 mo. 6, 1862, *Anna Kennard Groome*, dau. of William H. and Elizabeth Groome. They res. 1873, in Easton. Six children:

4–25. Elizabeth Groome, b. 11 mo. 21, 1862.
4–26. William Groome, b. 3 mo. 30, 1864.
3–27. Edith, b. 11 mo. 15, 1867, d. 9 mo. 17, 1868.
4–28. Anna Kennard, b. 7 mo. 26, 1869.
4–29. Edith Offley, b. 9 mo. 19, 1871.
4–30. Elias Offley, b. 2 mo. 6, 1873.

3-7. William Powell Dawson, b. in Easton, Md., 5 mo. 14, 1828, entered Westtown Friends' school, 1843, m. 11 mo. 25, 1856, *Mary Jones Matthews*, dau. of Thomas R. and Mary J. Matthews, of Baltimore. They res. 1873, in Baltimore. Mr. Dawson is of the firm of Thomas R. Matthews & Sons, ship and commission merchants, of that city. Two children:

4–31. Edith M., b. 10 mo. 13, 1858.
4–32. Thomas Matthews, b. 9 mo. 23, 1864.

3-8. *Edith Dawson*, b. in Easton, Md., 12 mo. 2, 1832, entered Westtown Friends' school, 1847, m. 5 mo. 12, 1859, Henry Clay Carter, of Baltimore, where they res. 1873. Two children:

4–33. Ruth, b. 11 mo. 8, 1861.
4–34. Florence, b. 9 mo. 18, 1868.

4-6. Edward Matthews Dawson, b. in Easton, Md., May 21, 1843, m. in Baltimore, Dec. 18, 1866, *Clara Amanda Cox*, who was b. in Easton, Dec. 2, 1846, dau. of Hon. Christopher Christian Cox, M. D., LL.D.,[1] and wife Amanda Northrup, who was of New Haven, Conn.

Mr. Dawson, a lawyer by profession, holds a responsible clerkship in the office of the U. S. commissioner of Pensions, Washington, where he resides, 1873. Three children:

5–1. Susan Hambleton, b. Oct. 4, 1867.
5–2. Clarence Edward, b. July 31, 1869.
5–3. Christine Amanda, b. July 31, 1871, d. July 7, 1872.

4-7. Charles Scott Dawson, b. in Easton, Md., July 23, 1845, res. 1873, in same place, bookkeeper in the Easton

[1] Then lieut. governor of Maryland, since U. S. commissioner of Pensions, and now, 1873, president of the Board of Health of the District of Columbia.

National Bank. He m. in Baltimore, Oct. 10, 1871, *Effie Cook Seegar.* They have one child:

5–4. Lillian, b. in Easton, Aug. 5, 1872.

4–8. ALFRED HUNT DAWSON, b. in Easton, Md., Sept. 5, 1847, res. 1873, in same place, dry goods merchant, of the firm of J. W. Cheezum & Co. He m. in Easton, Oct. 3, 1871, *Ella North Cheezum*, dau. of John W. and *Sarah Emory* Cheezum. They have one child:

5–5. Charles Emory, b. 10 mo. 5, 1872.

FAMILY OF JAMES DAWSON,

OF CUMBERLAND and WASHINGTON COUNTIES, PA., before 1776.

From Mr. Robert Dawson, Effingham, Ill., 1872, and others, the following:

1. JAMES DAWSON, and his brother Robert,[1] emigrated to America from the north of Ireland before the Revolution. The future wife of James, named *Catharine Morrow*, and her father came in the same vessel with him. They were married shortly after landing, and settled in Carlisle, Cumberland county, Pa., whence they removed, after a few years, to Washington county, in the same state, where they spent the remainder of their lives on a farm. He died at the age of about one hundred years. They had daughters named Catharine, Sarah, Margaret, Jane and Elizabeth, besides five sons, namely:

2–1. Matthew, lived in 1853, near New Wilmington, Lawrence Co., Pa.; was known as *Capt.* Matthew Dawson; had 18 children.
2–2. John, b. in Carlisle, 1769, d. in Illinois, Feb. 27, 1866, aged 97; *m.*
2–3. Thomas, lived in Harrison Co., Ohio; no family.
2–4. James, d. in Washington Co., Pa.; had a family.
2–5. William,[2] lived in Washington Co., Pa., on his father's farm; had a family.

2–2. JOHN DAWSON, b. in Carlisle, Pa., 1769, m. 1804, in Washington Co., Pa., *Jane Van Emman*, dau. of Geo. Van Emman. They removed to Wayne Co., Ohio, April, 1816, thence, about 1832, to Cuyahoga county, in the same state, where they resided until 1846, when they removed to Illinois.

---

[1] For an account of family of ROBERT DAWSON see next record following. In 1767, William Dawson, of Cumberland county, Pa., sold lands on the Juniata river, patented to him by John and Richard Penn in 1766 — 300 acres. The deed is recorded in Philadelphia. Was not this the father of the brothers, James and Robert, above named?

[2] Of Matthew, Thomas, James and William, and their sisters, above named, his uncles and aunts, Mr. R. D. says: "All of these I think are now dead, and I don't know where their families are. They were all farmers."

He died in Brown Co., Ill., Feb. 27, 1866,[1] aged 97. He served as a soldier in the war of 1812–14. They had twelve chn.:

3–1. Rebecca, the eldest dau., m. in Wayne Co., O., SAMUEL FERGUSON; d. some years ago.
3–2. Jane, d. Sept., 1845, in Mt. Sterling, Ill.
3–3. Catharine, m. JOHNSON LEEPER; res. 1873, at Mt. Sterling, Ill.; five children.
3–4. George, m. in Wayne Co., O., *Isabel Dunlavy*, and res. 1872, on a farm near Versailles, Brown Co., Ill.; two children.
3–5. Robert, b. in Washington Co., Pa., May 15, 1806, res. 1872, Effingham, Ill.; *m.*
3–6. Scott, d. at age of 18, *unm.*
3–7. Matthew, res. 1870, in Wood Co., Ohio.
3–8. John, res. 1870, in De Witt Co., Ill., d. before Oct., 1872, leaving a family.
3–9. James, res. 1870, near Hillsdale, Michigan; has a family.
3–10. Joseph, d. before Oct., 1872, in Brown Co., Ill.; left a family.
3–11. William, res. 1870, in Michigan; has a family.
3–12. Thomas, b. in Wayne Co., Ohio, March 8, 1821, res. 1873, Mt. Sterling, Ill.; *m.*

3–5. ROBERT DAWSON, b. in Washington county, Pa., May 15, 1806, res. 1873, in Effingham, Ill. He removed to Ohio with his father in 1816, and thence to Illinois, 1839.[2] He m. in Wayne, Co., Ohio, Oct. 16, 1828, *Nancy Baker*, who d. Jan. 25, 1853. They had seven children:

4–1. Franklin W., b. March 17, 1830, res. 1872, Effingham, Ill.; *m.*
4–2. Joseph, b. March 27, 1832, d. April, 1835.
4–3. Louisa, b. June 4, 1835, d. in Marshall Co., Ill., July 26, 1871. POTTER.
4–4. Arthur M., b. Dec. 22, 1837, res. 1872, in Effingham Co., Ill.; *m.*
4–5. Elbridge, b. Jan. 8, 1841, d. April 27, 1868.
4–6. Sarah Jane, b. Dec., 1845, res. 1872, Jasper Co., Ill. HESS.
4–7. Robert, b. Jan., 1848, d. June, 1849.

3–12. THOMAS DAWSON, b. in Wayne Co., O., March 8, 1821, removed from Cuyahoga Co., O., 1844, to La Grange,

---

[1] Another account says he d. Feb. 4, 1866; also locates William (3–11) in Canada, 1872.

[2] "The whole family, from my grandfather down, have generally followed the avocation of farming. My ancestors were all, or nearly all, strict members of the old Presbyterian church; but, with a few exceptions, the younger members, like myself, do not belong to any church. As to politics, nearly all are and have been, 'Jeffersonian Jackson Democrats,' opposed to the late war. I have been in business for about forty years, about thirty years in the dry goods trade, and the last six years in the lumber business." R. D., 1870.

Ill., and m. there Feb. 22, 1848, Miss *L. A. Brook.* She d. Dec. 31, 1848, aged 21. He went to California in April, 1849, and returned to Illinois in 1851, and was m. May 17, 1851, to Miss *E. M. Brook*, sister to his former wife. They res. 1873, at Mt. Sterling, Ill., and have seven children:

4–8. Estella Jane, b. June 28, 1852.
4–9. James B., b. June 7, 1858.
4–10. Elizabeth B., b. Feb. 11, 1859.
4–11. Ida M., b. Aug. 27, 1861.
4–12. John B., b. June 2, 1862.
4–13. Thomas O., b. Oct. 1, 1863.
4–14. Anna Lula, b. Feb., 1869.

4–1. FRANKLIN W. DAWSON, lumber dealer, b. in Ohio, March 17, 1830, res. 1872, Effingham, Ill. Two children:

5–1. Cora, b. 1854.
5–2. Ella, b. 1863.

4–3. *Louisa Dawson*, b. in Ohio, June 4, 1835, d. in Marshall county, Ill., July 26, 1871, m.—— POTTER. Three children:

5–3. Ellsworth, b. 1862.
5–4. Lulu, b. 1865.
5–5. Ida, b. 1868.

4–4. ARTHUR M. DAWSON, b. in Ohio, 1837, res. 1873, Effingham, Ill. Three children:

5–6. Robert S., b. 1863.
5–7. Nellie, b. 1866.
5–8. Franklin E., b. 1868.

4–6. *Sarah Jane Dawson*, b. in Illinois, Dec., 1845, res. 1872, Effingham, Ill., m.—— HESS. Three children:

5–9. David, b. 1864.
5–10. Anna, b. 1867.
5–11. Robert, b. 1870.

FAMILY OF ROBERT DAWSON,

OF WESTMORELAND and WASHINGTON COUNTIES, PA., about 1776–1800.

The following from the Rev. John B. Dawson, Ovid, Mich., 1873:

1. ROBERT DAWSON emigrated to America from the North of Ireland before the Revolution.[1] He d. before the birth of Mr. Robert Dawson, his grand nephew, named for him, born May 15, 1806, now of Effingham, Ill. Robert and his brother James emigrated together. They lived in Ligonier Valley, Westmoreland county, removing thence to Pigeon Creek, in Washington county, both counties being in southwestern Pennsylvania.[2] Robert m. about 1775, a Miss *Pinkerton*, and had five sons and four daughters. The order of their births is not known. Their names were as follows:

2–1. Thomas, lived in Guernsey Co., Ohio; *m.*
2–2. Joseph, d. in Washington, Iowa, 1850; *m.*
2–3. James, settled in Ky., about 1812; had a large family; sons said to be now in Ill. (1873).
2–4. Robert, went down the Ohio and Miss. rivers from Pittsburg, about 1812, with a load of flour and spirits destined for New Orleans; was never heard from after; supposed to have been murdered.
2–5. John, b. at Pigeon Creek, Pa., April 22, 1783, d. in Knox Co., Ohio, June 25, 1855; *m.*
2–6. Mary STRINGER.
2–7. Jane SHEARER.
2–8. Margaret GAILEY.
2–9. Elizabeth WELSH.

---

[1] According to one account he came in 1773, with *two* brothers, James and Thomas; James settled in Washington county, Pa., and Robert near Carlisle, in that state; while Thomas "went south, probably to Va. or Georgia." As to the date, see preceding record. James had a son born in Carlisle in 1769. As to Thomas *query?* The same account that says there was a brother Thomas, gives Robert only four sons, *not naming Thomas.*

[2] See preceding record for an account of the family of James Dawson, brother of Robert Dawson, the emigrant above named.

2–1. Thomas Dawson, farmer, b. in Pa., m. ———, and removed to Cumberland, Guernsey Co., Ohio, where he d. in 1852. He had seven children:

3–1. Jane.
3–2. Nancy.
3–3. Elizabeth.
3–4. Ann.
3–5. Mary.
3–6. John.
3–7. Robert.

2–2. Joseph Dawson, b. in Pennsylvania, m. 1801, *Barbara Gailey*.[1] They lived in Pa. until 1816, when they removed to Richland county, Ohio. He lived in Ohio until 1848, then moved to Iowa, and d. at Washington, in that state, in 1850. They had nine children:

3–8. Sarah, res. 1873, near Mansfield, O. Finney.
3–9. Jane, res. Washington county, Iowa. Fulton.
3–10. Robert, b. in Mercer Co., Pa., Nov. 14, 1806, d. in Washington, Iowa, Aug. 10, 1871; *m.*
3–11. James, res. Washington county, Iowa; *m.*
3–12. Mary, res. Iowa. Nelson.
3–13. Joseph, b. in Mercer Co., Pa., July 30, 1813, d. in Washington Co., Iowa, July 8, 1854; *m.*
3–14. John, res. Iowa; *m.*
3–15. Matthew, d. in Iowa, 1846; *m.*
3–16. Alexander, res. Iowa; *m.*

2–5. John Dawson, b. at Pigeon Creek, Washington Co., Pa., April 22, 1783, m. May 11, 1802, *Jane Welsh*, b. July 31, 1781, d. Aug. 2, 1843, aged 62. He was a physician; resided in his native county until 1836, when he removed to Danville, Knox Co., O., where he d. June 25, 1855, aged 72. He had five sons and four daughters, all b. in Washington Co., Pennsylvania:

3–17. Robert, b. March 11, 1803, d. in Martinsburg, Knox Co., O., July 17, 1865; *m.*
3–18. George W., b. April 26, 1805, m. *Margaret Batliff*, July 1, 1831, and d. childless, in New Orleans, of cholera, Jan. 20, 1849.
3–19. Louisa, b. Aug. 26, 1807, res. 1872, near Millwood, O.; *unm.*
3–20. Eleanor, b. Nov. 11, 1811, res. near Danville, O. McFarland.

---

[1] The account of descendants of Joseph Dawson, from a letter of his gr. son, Gen. A. R. Z. Dawson, of Washington, Iowa, to the Rev. John B. Dawson, of Ovid, Mich. (1873).

3–21. Mary Jane, b. June 23, 1814, res. near Millwood, O. CRITCHFIELD.
3–22. John Pinkerton, b. Aug. 22, 1817, d. in Knox Co., O., July 1, 1855; *m.*
3–23. James, b. Dec. 24, 1819, d. in Columbus, O., Feb. 17, 1852; *m.*
3–24. Joseph, b. Dec. 14, 1821, res. in Knox Co., O.; *m.*
3–25. Elizabeth, b. Sept. 22, 1824, res. 1872, at Osage Mission, Kansas. TRACY.

3–8. *Sarah Dawson*, m. 1836, JAMES FINNEY, of Richland county, Ohio, and res. 1873, near Mansfield, in that state. Three children:

4–1. Joseph C.
4–2. Jane.
4–3. Elizabeth.

3–9. *Jane Dawson*, m. 1838, JAMES FULTON, of Ashland county, Ohio, and removed to Washington county, Iowa, in 1842, where she now resides. One son:

4–4. Joseph.

3–10. ROBERT DAWSON, b. in Mercer county, Pa., Nov. 14, 1806, m. in Washington county, Pa., Dec. 3, 1830, *Sarah Rea*, who was b. in Lancaster county, Pa., Aug. 12, 1805, dau. of Andrew and Elizabeth Rea. They removed to Ohio, where they lived until 1857, then moved to Washington, Iowa, where he d. Aug. 10, 1871. Six chn., all b. in Ashland county, Ohio:

4–5. Elizabeth B., b. Jan. 15, 1832, res. 1873, Washington, Iowa. GIBSON.
4–6. Joseph H. C., b. Aug. 3, 1833, was a member of Company H., Second Regt. Iowa Inf. Vols., and d. at Cairo, Ill., Sept. 28, 1861; *unm.*
4–7. Andrew R. Z., b. May 10, 1835, res. 1873, at Washington, Iowa; *unm.*[1]
4–8. Luther G., b. April 15, 1837, res. 1873, in Washington, D. C.; *m.*
4–9. John P., b. March 5, 1839, res. 1873, St. Louis, Mo.; *m.*
4–10. Mary A., b. Feb. 20, 1841, res. 1873, Washington, Iowa. BENNETT.

3–11. JAMES DAWSON m. 1st., 1830, *Elizabeth Shannon*, of Pa. They moved to Iowa, 1839, where she d. They had five children:

---

[1] A. R. Z. Dawson enlisted at Mansfield, Ohio, April 17, 1861, as a private in the 15th Ohio Vol. Infantry, and was promoted through all grades to brigadier general. He participated in every battle fought by General Thomas in the army of the Cumberland, was twice wounded, and twice brevetted for gallant services. He was mustered out of service, Jan. 20, 1866.

4–11. Sarah J., d. about 1861. ANDERSON.
4–12. Josiah B., d. 1863 ; *m.*
4–13. Mary, d. 1854, w. of JAMES ANDERSON.
4–14. Martha S., res. 1873, Washington, Iowa.
4–15. George S., d. in New Mexico, 1863.

Mr. Dawson m. 2d., 1853, *Jannett French*, of Iowa. They had three children:

4–16. Helen F., res. 1873, Washington, Iowa.
4–17. Marietta F., res. 1873, Washington, Iowa.
4–18. William, d. May 5, 1872.

Mr. Dawson m. 3d., 1860, Mrs. Nancy Clark, of Ohio. Three children, all res. 1873, in Washington, Iowa:

4–19. Harlan H.
4–20. Robert L.
4–21. Llewellyn John.

3–12. *Mary Dawson* m. 1830, MATTHEW NELSON, of Ashland county, Ohio. They removed to Iowa, 1841. Six sons:

4–22. Calvin, res. 1873, Nebraska.
4–23. Joseph, res. Washington, Iowa.
4–24. William, res. Washington, Iowa.
4–25. Alexander, res. Washington, Iowa.
4–26. Hugh, res. Washington, Iowa.
4–27. Robert, killed in U. S. army, 1864.

3–13. JOSEPH DAWSON, b. in Mercer county, Pa., July 30, 1813, d. in Washington, Iowa, July 8, 1854, m. in Ashland county, Ohio, May 2, 1843, *Ann Nelson*, who was b. in Wayne county, Ohio, May 9, 1824, dau. of William and Elizabeth Nelson. They removed to Washington, Iowa, 1844, where she res. 1873. Three children, all b. in Washington, Iowa:

4–28. James, b. March 28, 1848, d. May 29, 1873.
4–29. William, b. Feb. 11, 1850, res. 1873, Burlington, Iowa.
4–30. Joseph, b. Aug. 22, 1854, res. 1873, Washington, Iowa.

3–14. JOHN DAWSON, m. 1st., 1838, *Jane Marshall*, of Ohio, and removed to Iowa, 1842. They had five children:

4–31. William, killed in U. S. army, 1863.
4–32. Samuel, m. and res. 1873, at San Diego, Cal.
4–33. James, d. 1858.
4–34. George, m. and res. in Iowa.
4–35. Sarah Jennett, m. and res. in Kansas.

Mr. Dawson m. 2d., Miss *McColough*, of Iowa. Eight children, names not communicated.

3–15. MATTHEW DAWSON, m. 1842, *Annie Adair*, of New York: removed to Iowa, 1844, d. 1846. Two children:

4–36. Alexander, res. 1873, Kansas.
4–37. Matilda, m. ALEXANDER STEVENS, res. Washington, Iowa.

3–16. ALEXANDER DAWSON moved to Iowa, 1842, and m. 1844, *Martha Anderson*. She d. 1844, leaving one son:

4–38. Joseph Alexander, m. and res. 1873, Washington, Iowa.

3–17. ROBERT DAWSON, b. in Washington Co., Pa., March 11, 1803, m. *Phebe Ross*, Oct. 26, 1826, and remained in his native county until 1846, when he removed to Martinsburg, Knox Co., Ohio, where he settled on a farm, which he occupied until his death, July 17, 1865. He had seven children, all b. in Mt. Pleasant, Washington Co., Pa.:

4–39. John B., b. July 27, 1827, res. 1873, Ovid, Mich.; *m.*
4–40. Mary Ann, b. Jan. 12, 1830, res. 1873, with her mother in Martinsburg, O.; *unm.*
4–41. James Ross, b. Oct. 16, 1831, d. in Illinois, 1868; *m.*
4–42. Robert Welsh, b. May 28, 1834, d. in Knox Co., O., Aug. 22, 1855.
4–43. Emma Jane, b. Sept. 6, 1839, res, 1873, Mt. Vernon, O. RALSTON.
4–44. Hannah Louisa, b. Aug. 28, 1843, res. 1873, Cadiz, Harrison Co., O. EDGELL.
4–45. Joseph Mitchell, b. May 19, 1845, d. in Knox Co., O., Sept. 17, 1855.

3–20. *Eleanor Dawson*, b. in Washington Co., Pa., Nov. 11, 1811, m. GEORGE McFARLAND, tailor. After remaining a short time at Hickory, in that county, they removed near Danville, Knox Co., O., and have had three children:

4–46. John.
4–47. Jane.
4–48. Nancy Ann.

3–21. *Mary Jane Dawson*, b. in Washington Co., Pa., June 23, 1814, m. March 27, 1838, LEWIS CRITCHFIELD, farmer, b. in Howard township, Knox Co., O., Aug. 11, 1812, son of Joseph and Ellen Critchfield. They settled near Millwood, Knox Co., O., and have had six children:

4–49. Joseph, b. about 1839.
4–50. George W., d. in infancy, 1840.
4–51. John Dawson, b. about 1842; an attorney at law, res. 1873, Mt. Vernon, Ohio.

4–52. [CRITCHFIELD.] Eleanor, b. about 1844.
4–53. Jane, d. in infancy, 1846.
4–54. Mary Jane, b. about 1847.

3–22. JOHN PINKERTON DAWSON, b. in Washington Co., Pa., Aug. 22, 1817, m. in Knox Co., O., April 1, 1847, *Rachel McFarland*, and settled near Danville, Knox Co., where he d. July 1, 1855. She was b. in Washington Co., Pa., June 16, 1823, dau. of Neil and Nancy McFarland. They had two children, both b. in Howard township, Knox Co., O., and res. in same township, 1873:

4–55. James Lycurgus, b. Nov. 1, 1849; farmer.
4–56. Louisa Ann, b. Dec. 18, 1853.

3–23. JAMES DAWSON, b. in Washington Co., Pa., Dec. 24, 1819, d. in Columbus, O., Feb. 17, 1852. He m. *Margaret Walker*, and had:

4–57. Ruth, b. Oct. 17, 1860.

3–24. JOSEPH DAWSON, b. in Washington Co., Pa., Dec. 14, 1821, removed to near Danville, Knox Co., O., and m. *Mary Osborn*, June 1, 1843. They res. 1872, on a farm at Mt. Vernon, Knox Co. He is foreman of the Mt. Vernon and Delaware R. R. machine shops at that place. Six children, all b. in Knox Co.:

4–58. George W., b. Oct. 10, 1844; *m.*
4–59. Clara Jane, b. Sept. 16, 1847, m. ALBERT T. MARTIN, carpenter; res. 1872, Mt. Vernon, O.
4–60. Lewis James, b. Aug. 14, 1849, d. 1851.
4–61. Ella Louisa, b. Dec. 7, 1852; *unm.*
4–62. John Louis, b. May 14, 1857, d. July 20, 1863.
4–63. Frank Chase, b. July 15, 1864.

3–25. *Elizabeth Dawson*, b. in Washington Co., Pa., Sept. 22, 1824, m. CHESTER P. TRACY, April 9, 1846, and settled near Gambier, Knox Co., O. They removed to Iowa, and thence to Osage Mission, Neosha county, Kansas, where she now resides. They had six children:

4–64. Marvin.
4–65. Benton.
4–66. John Dawson.
4–67. Paulina.
4–68. Carr H.
4–69. Charles.

4-5. *Elizabeth B. Dawson*, b. in Ashland county, Ohio, Jan. 15, 1832, m. 1865, Rev. JOHN GIBSON, of Vermont. They res. 1873, in Washington, Iowa. One child:

5-1. Sarabell.

4-8. LUTHER G. DAWSON, b. in Ashland county, Ohio, April 15, 1837, m. in Washington, Iowa, May 7, 1867, *Helen M. Chipman*, who was b. in Union county, Ohio, July 3, 1839, dau. of Norman and *Sarah Parker* Chipman. They res. 1873, in Washington, D. C. He is clerk of the Police court of that city. One child:

5-2. Belle Chipman, b. in Mankato, Minn., Feb. 23, 1868.

4-9. JOHN P. DAWSON, b. in Ashland county, Ohio, March 5, 1839, m. 1865, *Belle S. Stafford*, of Alabama. They res. 1873, in St. Louis, Mo. Two children:

5-3. Rowland S.
5-4. Alice Belle.

4-10. *Mary A. Dawson*, b. in Ashland county, Ohio, Feb. 20, 1841, m. in Washington, Iowa, Oct. 11, 1860, Hon. GRANVILLE G. BENNETT, who was b. in Butler county, Ohio, Oct. 9, 1833, son of Peter and *Mary Pinkerton* Bennett. Two children:

5-5. Estelline Rea, b. in Washington, Iowa, Jan. 9, 1868.
5-6. Helen Marie, b. in Washington, Iowa, Sept. 17, 1872.

4-11. *Sarah J. Dawson*, m. GEORGE ANDERSON. She d. about 1861, leaving one child:

5-7. Clara.

4-12. JOSIAH B. DAWSON m. *Rosa Hamil.* He d. 1863, leaving one child:

5-8. Annie Belle.

4-39. JOHN B. DAWSON, b. in Mt. Pleasant township, Washington Co., Pa., July 27, 1827, received a liberal education, and studied Theology under the instruction of Rev. George Gordon, of Iberia College, Ohio. He was licensed to preach the Gospel in the Free Presbyterian church, in the Central Presbytery of Ohio, May 5, 1860, and ordained Oct. 19, in that year. He first preached at West Alexander, Washington

Co., Pa., and moved thence to Martinsburg, Knox Co., O., where he resided five years, during which time he was chiefly engaged in teaching. He removed, in 1868, to Hartford, in Licking Co., O., where he had charge of the Union schools for three years, preaching also for a church at Olive Green, in the adjoining county of Delaware, during the years 1868 and 1869, for which church he preached also in 1872. In 1871, he preached for the churches at Hartford and Lock, Ohio. He was originally a member of the old school Presbyterian church, with which he united in 1847, but in consequence of the position of that church on the slavery question, he transferred his membership in 1853 to the Free Presbyterian church. In 1869 he united with the Congregational conference of central Ohio, and in the same year became a member of the Ohio state conference. He removed to Ovid, Clinton county, Mich., in May, 1863, having accepted a call from the First Congregational church of that place. He m. 1st., June 30, 1857, *Mary E. Hervey*, dau. of Rev. Henry Hervey, D.D., of Martinsburg, Ohio. She d. Aug. 29, 1858. He m. 2d., Aug. 28, 1861, in West Alexander, Washington Co., Pa., *Mary Elizabeth Sutherland*, who d. Oct. 28, 1870. They had four children :

5–9. John Lewis, b. in West Alexander, Pa., June 27, 1862.
5–10. Robert Lorian, b. in Martinsburg, O., Feb. 12, 1864.
5–11. William Chester, b. in Martinsburg, O., Oct. 11, 1866.
5–12. Mary Blanche, b. in Hartford, Licking Co., O., Aug. 8, 1870.

Mr. Dawson m. 3d., Aug. 24, 1871, *Mattie Louisa Moores*. They res. 1873, at Ovid, Mich. It is to his kindness that the compiler hereof is indebted for the foregoing records.

4–41. JAMES ROSS DAWSON, b. in Mt. Pleasant township, Washington county, Pa., Oct. 16, 1831, m. *Flora Pearson*, 1860, and settled in Illinois. Both d. 1868. One child :

5–13. Lewis.

4–43. *Emma Jane Dawson*, b. in Mt. Pleasant township, Washington county, Pa., Sept. 6, 1839, m. in Martinsburg, Ohio, Oct. 3, 1867, EPHRAIM P. RALSTON, miller, b. in Wayne township, Jefferson county, O., Dec. 21, 1840. They res. 1873, at Mt. Vernon, Ohio. Two children :

5–14. Chester Fairman, b. in Fairview, Harrison Co., O., May 21, 1870.
5–15. Mary Estella, b. at Lock 17, Tuscarawas Co., O., Oct. 20, 1871.

4–44. *Hannah Louisa Dawson*, b. in Mt. Pleasant township, Washington county, Pa., Aug. 28, 1843, m. in Martinsburg, Knox county, Ohio, Dec 18, 1867, Rev. BENJ. E. EDGELL, a minister of the Methodist church, b. in Newport, Washington county, O., Nov. 8, 1839. They resided at Cadiz, Harrison county, Ohio, until October, 1873, in which month, having been appointed missionaries of the M. E. church to China, they sailed from San Francisco, to reside at Pekin or Fou Chou.

4–58. GEORGE W. DAWSON, b. in Knox county, Ohio, Oct. 10, 1844, m. March 8, 1866, *Ellie R. Baker.* He is proprietor of the "Low Mills" at Howard, Knox Co., O., where they res. 1873. One child:

5–16. Linna Evaline.

FAMILY OF WILLIAM DAWSON,

OF WESTMORELAND CO., PA., 1809–1844.

From letters of Robert M. and James B. Dawson, Mendota, Ill., 1871, and others, the following:

1. WILLIAM DAWSON, b. abt. 1776, was a native of Dromore, county Down, Ireland,[1] where he m. 1801, *Jane McBride*, b. 1779. They emigrated to America, in 1802, and after brief periods of residence in Philadelphia, Pa., and Wilmington, Del., removed, in 1809, to Westmoreland county, Pennsylvania, where they spent the remainder of their lives. They were farmers, and d. at their homestead, he in 1844, aged 68 years, and she in 1842, aged 63. He had been a soldier in the Black Hawk war. They had seven children:

2–1. Elizabeth, b. in Dromore, Ireland, 1802, d. in New Castle, Pa., Feb., 1854. CAMPBELL.
2–2. William, b. in Wilmington, Del., Nov., 1805, res. 1873, Shadyside, Pittsburg, Pa.; *m.*
2–3. Robert Madison, b. in Wilmington, Del., Nov. 21, 1807, res. 1871, Mendota, Ill.; *m.*
2–4. John, b. in Westmoreland Co., Pa., 1809, res. 1871, Culmerville, Alleghany, Co., Pa.; *m.*
2–5. Margaret, b. in Westmoreland Co., 1811, res. 1871, Kingston, Linn Co., Iowa. THOMPSON.
2–6. Jane, b. in Westmoreland Co., 1813, res. 1871, Culmerville, Pa. DAWSON.
2–7. Mary, b. in Westmoreland Co., 1815, d. 1826.

2–1. *Elizabeth Dawson*, b. in Dromore, Ireland, 1802, m. THOMAS CAMPBELL, of Westmoreland county, Pa., and removed shortly after to New Castle, Lawrence county, in that state, where she d. Feb., 1854, and he d. before 1871. They had seven children, all residing 1871, at New Castle, as follows:

3–1. John.
3–2. William.
3–3. James.

([1]) His father, named John Dawson, is said to have been b. in England, and to have returned there to live after a residence of many years in Ireland. Two other sons, named John and Ralph, are said to have emigrated to America. They came before William, but it is not known where they settled.

3–4. [CAMPBELL.] Robert.
3–5. David J.
3–6. Sarah Jane.
3–7. Mary Ann.

2–2. WILLIAM DAWSON, formerly steamboat-captain, b. in Wilmington, Del., Nov., 1805, m. Aug., 1832, *Susannah Scott*, who was b. in Pittsburg, Pa., April, 1810, dau. of George and Elizabeth Scott. They res. 1873, at Shadyside, Pittsburg, and have had six children:

3–8. Mary Elizabeth.
3–9. Harriet Jane.
3–10. William Albert.
3–11. Edwin Alexander.
3–12. Caroline.
3–13. Annie Lee.

2–3. ROBERT MADISON DAWSON, b. in Wilmington, Del., Nov. 21, 1807, m. May 14, 1833, in Pittsburg, Pa., *Catharine Brown*,[1] who was b. in Sherman Valley, Perry Co., Pa., Aug. 20, 1811. He learned the trade of a tinsmith in Pittsburg, and carried on the business in that city until 1844, when he was burned out, and removed to Bridgewater, Beaver Co., Pa., where he remained in business until 1855, in which year he removed to Mendota, Ill., where he resides (1871). They have had eight children:

3–14. James Brown, b. in Pittsburg, April 11, 1834, hardware merchant, res. 1871, Mendota, Ill.; *unm.*
3–15. William J., b. in Alleghany city, Pa., April 7, 1836, res. 1873, Brookfield, Mo.; *m.*
3–16. Charles R., b. in Pittsburg, March 30, 1838, d. March 8, 1839.
3–17. Mary Jane, b. in Pittsburg, March 28, 1840, res. 1871, Mendota, Ill. COOK.
3–18. Anna Elizabeth, b. in Pittsburg, July 5, 1842, res. 1871, Alleghany city, Pa. TAYLOR.
3–19. Henderson Madison, b. in Bridgewater, Oct. 3, 1844, d. Nov. 23, 1847.
3–20. Robert Madison, b. in Bridgewater, Oct. 23, 1846, d. Nov. 24, 1847.
3–21. Catharine Elizabeth, b. in Bridgewater, Aug. 26, 1852, res. 1871, Mendota, Ill.

2–4. JOHN DAWSON, farmer, b. in Westmoreland Co., Pa., 1809, m.———, res. 1871, at Culmerville, Alleghany Co., Pa. Eight children, names not communicated.

---

[1] Dau of Rev. James Brown, a descendant of Rev. John Brown, of Haddington, Scotland.

2-5. *Margaret Dawson*, b. in Westmoreland Co., Pa., 1811, m. JOHNSTON THOMPSON, res. 1871, Kingston, Linn Co., Iowa. Six children:

3–22. William D.
3–23. Robert John.
3–24. James.
3–25. Alfred.
3–26. Jane.
3–27. Sarah Ann.

2-6. *Jane Dawson*, b. in Westmoreland Co., Pa., 1813, m. RALPH DAWSON, farmer. They res. 1871, at Culmerville, Alleghany Co., Pa., and have one son:

3–28. William.

3-15. WILLIAM J. DAWSON, b. in Alleghany city, Pa., April 7, 1836, blacksmith and wagon maker, m. in Brooklyn, Lee Co., Ill., 1858, *Ellen Hyde*, who was b. in Lexington, Ohio, 1838, dau. of Benjamin and Mary Hyde. At the beginning of the civil war he was engaged in farming near Mendota, Ill. He enlisted March, 1864, in the 15th Ill. Inf. Vols., and followed the fortunes of that regiment at Beaufort, Goldsborough, Raleigh, Richmond and Washington, and thence went westward with it nearly across the continent. He was mustered out of service at Springfield, Ill., in Nov., 1865. They res. 1873, at Brookfield, Linn Co., Mo. Five children:

4–1. Ida Fidelia, b. in Brooklyn, Lee Co., Ill., Feb. 16, 1860.
4–2. Lelia Ada, b. in Brooklyn, Lee Co., Ill., Oct. 19, 1861.
4–3. Mary Ellen, b. in Dixon, Lee Co., Ill., March 16, 1863.
4–4. James Brown, b. in Brooklyn, Lee Co., Ill., Jan. 31, 1864.
4–5. Kitty Bell, b. in Brookfield, Mo., June 27, 1872.

3-17. *Mary Jane Dawson*, b. in Pittsburg, Pa., March 28, 1840, m. WILLIAM F. COOK, of Mendota, Ill. They res. 1871, in Mendota. Two children:

4–6. Mary L., b. July 6, 1861.
4–7. Katie D., b. Oct. 21, 1863.

3-18. *Anna Elizabeth Dawson*, b. in Pittsburg, Pa., July 5, 1842, m. at Mendota, Ill., Sept. 4, 1867, JAMES I. TAILOR. They res. 1871, at Alleghany city, Pa., and have two children, both b. in that city:

4–8. Catharine B., b. Aug. 1, 1868.
4–9. Anna Mary, b. July 3, 1870.

MARYLAND.

The records which follow, relating to the Dawsons of Maryland and their descendants, have been compiled principally from the letters of several correspondents who have kindly communicated such information as they possessed.

The accounts given by these correspondents of the supposed original families, while affording evidence of the common original of large numbers of the name now widely scattered, differ very materially in many particulars, and are not, without more investigation, capable of being wholly reconciled. An almost entire reliance upon tradition for a knowledge of their early ancestry in this country has led many into error in regard to their family history. A careful examination of the records of Maryland deeds and wills — especially in the counties of Talbot, Caroline, Queen Anne, Prince George, Alleghany and Montgomery — would doubtless be fruitful of most valuable information for the genealogist, and supply many links now wanting in the chain of family history herewith imperfectly presented. It is to be hoped that some competent hand will ere long attempt the task.

The question, Who was the first of the name in Maryland? has not been satisfactorily determined. It appears to be pretty certainly established that there were two families of Dawsons in the then province of Maryland at a very early date — one on the east shore of the Chesapeake, in Talbot county — and one on the western side, probably in Prince George county — both probably some time before 1700.

John Dawson, of Talbot county, is said by one of his descendants (probably on the authority of *tradition*, which is always open to question, but entitled to consideration until disproved by better evidence) to have emigrated from England to America about the year 1685. He made a will in 1710, being then "very sick and weak in body," wherein he refers to his wife, their family of five minor children, to his brothers

James, Richard and Robert, their sister Rachel, and his "loving father, Ralph Dawson, deceased." It would seem almost certain that his father died in this country. If his family were nearly related to the one which settled on the opposite side of the Chesapeake, the relationship does not as yet appear.

According to the best information as yet obtained the founder of the Prince George county family of Dawsons was also named JOHN DAWSON. He doubtless came from England, but whether from Whitehaven, in Cumberland county (as one says is the traditional story), or from Yorkshire (as says another), is not known. He is reputed to have come with two brothers, named (as one believes, but it is not certain), Nicholas and William, who are said to have gone South — "to Georgia and the Carolinas" — while John, the eldest, remained in Maryland. The two brothers who "went South" are supposed by some to be the ancestors of the Dawsons in that part of the country; but those of the name there, best informed in matters of family history, trace their descent from other originals. Another account names Nicholas and John only as the original emigrants, bringing them into Maryland by way of Philadelphia, supposes them companions of Penn, and retains Nicholas in Maryland, while John is sent South; his descendants being supposed to be "now in nearly all the Southern States." By another account, another John, of another group of brothers, is the ancestor of the southern branch of the family, especially of the Georgia Dawsons, prominent among whom was the late Hon. William C. Dawson, United States senator from that state. But this account also is incorrect,[1] and it is indeed highly improbable that there was in this country of the generation of the original settler — John Dawson, ancestor of the Montgomery county families — any other than himself.

---

[1] Equally erroneous is another account which supposes the late senator was descended from William Dawson (said to have emigrated to Georgia) son of William, son of John, son of Ralph Dawson of Talbot county. (This account states that William m. *Sarah Russell*; also that their son William m. a Miss *Carrideane*, of Queen Anne Co., and emigrated to Georgia, and supposes him the senator's ancestor).

FAMILY OF RALPH DAWSON,

OF TALBOT CO., MD. (deceased before 31 July, 1710).

The records of this family are gathered from the two wills below printed, and from letters of Dr. James Dawson, of St. Michaels, Talbot Co., Philip T. Dawson, Esq., of Baltimore, Md., and others.

I. *Copy of the will of John Dawson, of Talbot Co.*, 1710.

"In the Name of God, Amen. I, John Dawson, of Talbot county, in the Province of Maryland, Gentleman, being very sick and weak in body, but of perfect mind and memory, thanks be to God therefor, calling unto mind the mortality of the body, and knowing that it is appointed for all men once to dye, do make and ordain this my last Will and Testament, that is to say, principally and first of all, I give and recommend my soul into the hands of God who gave it, and for my body I recommend it to the earth, to be buried in a Christianlike and decent manner, at the discretion of my Executors, nothing doubting but at the general Resurrection I shall receive the same again by the mighty power of God, and touching such worldly estate wherewith it hath pleased God to bless me in this Life, I give, devise and dispose the same in the following manner and form:

"Imprimis: I give and bequeath to my son John and to the heirs of his body lawfully begotten the upward or eastward moiety of all the Lands I am now possessed with lying on St. Michaels River, and I will and bequeath to my loving wife Mary Dawson the other moiety of the said Land [with the use of the house to[1]] dwell in during her life, and my will is y^{t}. my said wife shall keep the dwelling house in good order and repair and give such security for so doing as Mr. Matthew Tilghman Ward and Robert Ungle shall think fitt, within twelve months after the *date hereof.*[2] And after the decease of my said wife my will is

[1] Indistinct in Ms. from which this is copied, the same being a verified copy of original.

[2] The date of the probating of this instrument is not known. It was evidently made in the expectation that the testator would not long survive.

that all the above mentioned Lands and Tenements given to her during her natural life shall go to my said son John and to the heirs of his body lawfully begotten forever."

[Clause providing that in case John should die without issue the lands and tenements above specified should go to the testator's son William, and in default of issue to him then to the testator's son Ralph, and in case he should die without issue then to the testator's daughter Susannah, and she dying without issue then to his daughter Elizabeth, &c.— nothing however to prejudice the testator's wife in the possession of her moiety during life.]

"Item. If it should so happen that when my son John arrives arrives at the age of twenty-one years he should marry or that my wife and he should not agree,[1] then my desire is that my said wife shall cause to be built finisht for my said son (on his moiety of the above said lands) one dwelling house with two rooms on a floor, which shall be such a house as Mr. Matthew Tilghman Ward and Robert Ungle (who if then living I desire to take the trouble on them) shall appoint.

"Item. I give and bequeath to my son William all the Land due to me in Gallaway Neck, part of Gallaway, part of Batchelour's Range, part of Batchelour's Range addition and Halton's Hope, to him the said William and the heirs of his body lawfully begotten," [and in case of death without issue the land to go to Ralph, Susannah, Elizabeth and John, and next heirs, successively.]

"I give to my son Ralph Dawson all the Land on the other side Gallaway where Charles Sinclair now dwells, to him and heirs forever; but if it should happen that my son Ralph should die before he arrives at twenty-one years of age, then my will is that the aforesaid Land shall go to my daughters Susannah and Elizabeth and their heirs, to be equally divided betwixt them when they come of age, or at the day of their marriage, and if either of them die without heirs, then to the survivor and her heirs forever.

"Item. I give to my loving brother, James Dawson, all the right, title interest and claim which I have or ought to have of

[1] *Quere:* Was she "second wife"— step-mother to the eldest son?

in or to a certain tract of land lying on St. Michaels Creek, called by the name of Frith Land, to him and his heirs forever.

"Item. I give to my son John and my daughter Susannah one negro man named Tom, one negro woman called Judith, two negro children called Mingo and Grace, and all the increase of the said negroes, to be equally divided betwixt my said son and daughter when they come at due age, and if my said daughter should be disposed of in marriage before my said son is at age, then a division may be made for her part, and the residue with their increase kept in hands of my executors till my said son arrives at age (provided nevertheless that the first child which shall be born of the above named negro Judith I do hereby give and bequeath to my son Ralph, notwithstanding my general bequest of the whole increase of the said negroes) and further my will and order is, that if my son John should die before he arrives at the age of twenty-one years or my said daughter Susannah before she arrives at due age or marries, then only the four first named negroes shall go to the survivor, and all the increase except the negro given to Ralph (if any such there be) shall be equally divided amongst all my children, the said Ralph coming in for an equal share over and above the said negro (if any such there be).

"Item. I give to my son William and my daughter Elizabeth two negro children called Peter and Ann, with all their increase, to be equally divided betwixt them when my said son shall arrive at the age of twenty-one years, or when my said daughter shall be disposed of in marriage, but if my said son William should die before he arrives at the said age, or my said daughter Elizabeth before she arrives at due age or is married, then my will is that the said negroes and their increase shall go to the survivor and his or her heirs forever.

"Item. All the rest of my estate whether real or personal or of what nature soever, I do hereby give and bequeath to my loving wife Mary Dawson, under such restrictions and limitations as is hereafter mentioned. First, I order that my said wife pay to each of my children before named, when the boys arrive at twenty-one years of age and the girls at due age or be married (which shall first happen), forty pounds in current money of this province or in such commodities as this country affords, and I do further order my said wife to give to my son John and daughter Susannah each a bed and furniture of about six pounds price. Secondly, I do further order my said wife and my other executors hereafter named to pay to my two brothers Richard and Robert Dawson five thousand five hundred pounds of tobacco, in such manner as to my said executors shall seem meet, provided the said payment be made within twelve months after the date of this my last will and testament, the said tobacco being to be equally divided betwixt my said two brothers, as was desired by my loving father Ralph Dawson deceased.

"Item. And whereas the Land called Batchelour's Range addition is supposed to be foul of some elder surveys, whenever the bounds of the said land shall be ascertained, so that the said tract of land shall have its due meets and bounds, according to Patent, then I do hereby empower and authorize my executors hereafter named to make over and convey to Rachel the daughter of my father Ralph and her heirs or assigns, about one hundred acres of the said tract of land, so to be laid out as may least prejudice the land given to my children William and Ralph.

"Item. I do moreover desire and request my executors hereafter named that if any difficulty should arise in the executing any part of this my last Will and Testament, that they will apply themselves to my loving friends Mr. Mathew Tilghman Ward and Robert Ungle, who I doubt not will aid assist and advise them to the best advantage of my loving wife and children, and I do hereby request my said two friends to give all the help and assistance to my said executors that they are capable of.

"Lastly. I do hereby appoint my loving wife Mary Dawson and my loving brother James Dawson, to be my executors of this my last Will and Testament, and I do hereby utterly disallow, revoke and make null and void all and every other former Testament, Will, Legacy or Codicil whatever by me made willed or bequeathed, ratifying and confirming this and no other to be my last Will and Testament.

"In witness whereof I have hereunto set my hand and affixed my seal the Thirty-first day of July in the ninth [year of the reign of our Sovereign Lady Anne, by the Grace] of God of Great Britain France [and Ireland] Queen, Defender of the Faith, Anno Domini, 1710.

(signed) JOHN DAWSON. [L.S.]

"Signed, sealed, delivered, published, pronounced and declared per John Dawson to be his last Will and Testament in presence of us:

(signed) SAMUEL WADE,
ABIGAIL WISE,
JAIRUS WRIGHT."

II. *Copy of the will of William Dawson, of Queen Anne's Co., Md.*, 1759.

"In the Name of God, Amen. I, William Dawson, of Queen Anne's county, Planter, doth give dispose of and in the following manner and form.

"Imprimis. I give and bequeath to my son William Dawson all the land called Huntington that I hold, and seventy-eight ½ acres of the Neglect and to the heirs of his body lawfully begotten forever.

"Item. I give and bequeath to my son John Dawson all the Land called Sprigley's Fortune and to the heirs of his body lawfully begotten forever.

"Item. I give and bequeath to my son Thomas Dawson two hundred acres of land where William Ostin now dwells, one hundred out of Batchellor's Range and the other hundred out of Batchellor's Range addition,[1] to him and the heirs of his body lawfully begotten forever.

"Item. I give and bequeath to my son James Dawson one hundred and fifty acres of land in Batchellor's Range on the North East side of Gallaway Branch where Joseph Duling now lives called Grub[d] Neck, and the heirs of his body lawfully begotten forever.

"Item. I give and bequeath to my son Parry Dawson one hundred and fifty acres of land on the south west side of Gallaway Branch, part of Gallaway and part of Batchellor's Range addition, to him and the heirs of his body lawfully begotten forever

"Item. My Will is that my wife shall have the Plantation where I now dwell for her thirds of all my lands during her life;

---

[1] These tracts of land were derived from the testator's father's estate, under the preceding will.

and then my Will is that it shall go to my son Robert Dawson and the heirs of his body lawfully begotten forever. I also give to my son Robert the negro boy called Tim.

"Item. I give and bequeath to my daughter Mary Thomas one negro boy named Matt.

"Item. I give and bequeath to my daughter Rebecca Dawson one negro girl named Mary.

"Item. I give and bequeath to my daughter Sarah Dawson one negro girl named Fanny.

"Lastly. I do hereby appoint my loving wife Sarah Dawson and my son William Dawson to be my Executors of this my last Will and Testament, and I do hereby utterly disallow revoke and make null and void all and every other former Testament, Will, Legacy or Codicil whatsoever by me made willed or bequeathed, ratifying this and no other to be my last Will and Testament.

"In Witness whereof I have hereunto set my hand and affixed my seal the 24th day of December in the year of our Lord God one thousand seven hundred and fifty-nine.

(signed) W. DAWSON. [L.S.]

"In y[e] Presents of:
THOS. CLAYLAND,
EDMUND THOMAS junr.,
ARTHUR EMORY,
her
SARAH × YOUNG."
mark

"Queen Ann's County,
The first day of February, 1760.

"Thomas Clayland, Edmund Thomas, jr., Arthur Emory, and Sarah Young, the subscribing witnesses to the foregoing Will, being duly and 'solomly' sworn on the Holy Evangelists of Almighty God, do depose and say That they saw the Testator, William Dawson, sign the foregoing Will, and heard him publish and declare the same to be his last Will and Testament, that at the time of his so doing he was, to the best of their apprehension, of sound and disposing Mind and Memory, and that they subscribed their respective names as witnesses to the said Will in the Presence of the Testator and at his Request. Which oath was taken by the said witnesses in the presence of

William Dawson, heir at law of the Testator, which same William Dawson did not object to the Probate of said Will.

"Sworn to before

THOMAS WRIGHT, Dept. Comis'y.
of Queen Ann's County."

Letters of Administration, as to the Estate of the deceased not disposed of by will, were issued to Sarah Dawson and William Dawson, March 9, 1760.

III. *Record.*

1. RALPH DAWSON, deceased before 31 July, 1710, mentioned in the will of his son John of that date (see foregoing copy.) He had children:

2–1. John, the testator in the will of 1710.
2–2. James, executor, with the wife of John, of the latter's will.
2–3. Richard, }
2–4. Robert, } legatees, named in their brother's will.
2–5. Rachel. }

2–1. JOHN DAWSON, of Talbot county, son of Ralph, made will 1710, probably then under 50 years of age, his five children being then all minors. He is said to have emigrated from England to America about 1685. If so, probably came with or was accompanied by his father. His lands, situated on the eastern shore of the Chesapeake, are said to have been a grant, taken up under the proprietary government of Lord Calvert. He was of the class termed *Gentlemen* in England — being of those holding a middle rank between the nobility and yeomanry — and was of considerable estate. He m. *Mary* ——, and had five children, all of whom were minors at the date of their father's will, in 1710:

3–1. John.
3–2. William.
3–3. Ralph.
3–4. Susannah.
3–5. Elizabeth.

3–2. WILLIAM DAWSON, of Queen Anne's county, son of John, was under age 1710, made will December, 1759, and died before Feb. 1, 1760, at which date the will was probated. He was probably 60 years of age, or more, at his death. It is probable that his children were all then of age. One of his daughters was married, and he appointed his son William one of his executors. A portion of the estate left by him was inherited from his father. He m. *Sarah* ———, and had nine children:

4–5. [1]William, executor, with his mother, of his father's will.
4–6. John.
4–7. Thomas.
4–8. James.
4–9. Parry.
4–10. Robert.
4–11. Mary THOMAS.
4–12. Rebecca.
4–13. Sarah.

[Note. Dr. James Dawson, of Talbot county, writing under date of March 8, 1871, refers to John Dawson (2–1) son of Ralph (1) as his *great grandfather*, and says: "I am the son of John, who was the son of John, who was the son of John, who was the son of Ralph." He also says that his father "had uncles named William, George and Robert [Dawson] of Queen Anne county." In another letter he states that his father, John Dawson, *died in* 1854, *aged* 84; he consequently was born in 1770. Now, the children of John Dawson, the son of Ralph, were all born before 1710, and of these the eldest was named John, and was probably 15 years of age or more at that date. This could hardly have been the grandfather of Dr. Dawson, as he supposes, as it is not probable he would have had a child born as late as 1770 (he being then, if indeed living, about 85 years of age). A link therefore seems to be lacking, which being supplied would make Dr. D. one generation further removed from the original emigrant. The record of the family of his grandfather, John Dawson, will be given presently. The *great grandfather's* children were, of course, John (the Dr.'s grandfather), and William, George and Robert (the Dr.'s father's uncles). Now, who was the father of these four? It is probable that he was John (3–1 of the foregoing record) the *grandson* of Ralph; being the son of Ralph's son John, (2–1 of record) and brother to William of Queen Anne county (3–2 of record). Assuming this to have been the case, the record will proceed as follows [2]:]

3–1. JOHN DAWSON, of Queen Anne county, son of John, *supposed* father of:

4–1. John, lived and d. in Talbot Co.; *m.*
4–2. William, lived and d. in Talbot Co.; *m.*
4–3. George, d. young; *unm.*
4–4. Robert, lived and d. in Queen Anne's Co.; *m.*

4–1. JOHN DAWSON, farmer, m. *Mary Russell*, and had:

5–1. John, b. 1770, d. 1854—so writes his son Dr. James Dawson, who says his father had six brothers, viz.:
5–2. Michael, d. about 1810; *unm.*

---

[1] For 4–1 to 4–4, inclusive, see forward.

[2] "The link you speak of as being broken can only be filled up as you suggest in your letter of June 17th." Dr. James Dawson, Sept. 19, 1873.

5–3. William, d. young.
5–4. Thomas Russell, b. in Talbot Co., July 15, 1780, d. in Baltimore, Aug. 20, 1862 ; *m.*
5–5. James, d. young.
5–6. Joseph, m. in Baltimore, and d. about 1840, leaving one dau. who m. but d. childless about 1840.
5–7. Richard, d. about 1831 ; *m.*

4–2. William Dawson, resided in Talbot county, on Miles or St. Michael's river, and d. leaving children, all of whom d. without issue. Two daus. lived to an advanced age, but never m., namely :

5–8. Nancy.
5–9. Betsey.

4–4. Robert Dawson, of Queen Anne's county, m. late in life, and had one child :

5–10. William Russell, b. about 1804, lived in Queen Anne's county.

5–1. Maj. John Dawson, b. in Talbot county, April, 1770, d. at the old Dawson homestead in that county, May, 1854, aged 84. He assisted in the suppression of the Whiskey Insurrection in Pennsylvania, 1794 ; also served as a captain in the war of 1812. He m. 1st., *Fanny Caulk*, who d. early, childless. 2d., 1797, *Mary Darden*, who d. 1827. They had eight children :

6–1. Robert, b. 1798, d. in Talbot Co., 1827, aged 29 ; *unm.*
6–2. Mary, b. about 1801, d. in Talbot Co., 1855, aged 53 ; *unm.*
6–3. Louisa, b. about 1802, res. 1872, in Talbot Co. ; *unm.*
6–4. Ann Matilda, b. 1803, m. Morris O. Colston, both d. She d. about 1859, aged 56; no issue.
6–5. John, b. about 1804, d. in Talbot Co., 1858, aged 53 ; *m.*
6–6. James, b. Nov. 8, 1805, res. 1873, St. Michaels, Talbot Co. ; *m.*
6–7. Caroline, b. 1813, res. 1873, in California. Neilson.
6–8. Alexander, d. 1827.

Maj. Dawson m. 3d., Feb., 1828, *Mary Robson*, b. in Talbot county, Sept., 1794, dau. of Thomas and *Eve Spry* Robson. She res. 1873, in Talbot Co., aged 79. They had five children, all b. in Talbot Co. :

6–9. Eliza Jane, b. Nov. 23, 1828, res. 1873, Lawrenceville, Ill. Gold.
6–10. Frances Selina, b. Jan., 1831, res. 1873, Talbot county ; *unm.*
6–11. Sarah Lavinia, b. Dec., 1833, res. 1873, Talbot county ; *unm.*
6–12. Emma Lucretia, b. March, 1835, res. 1873, Talbot county ; *unm.*
6–13. Robert Morris, b. March, 1839, res. 1873, with his mother and sisters at the old homestead, Royal Oak, Talbot county, Md. He is a physician ; *unm.*

5-4. THOMAS RUSSELL DAWSON, was b. in Talbot county, Md., July 15, 1780. He conducted for many years a very successful business in Baltimore as a merchant tailor, from which he retired in 1834. The two following years were passed upon a farm in Talbot county, and the remainder of a very peaceful, but useful and most exemplary life, was spent in Baltimore, where he d. Aug. 20, 1862, aged 82.

"Mr. Dawson was small in stature, with a well knit frame, capable of enduring fatigue. He was a great walker, having been known to go on foot seventeen miles in one day, after he attained his sixtieth year. His features were rather prominent, and the expression was one of firmness and benevolence. He delighted in the company of friends, and was unusually talkative. In his earlier life he was an ardent whig, and a great admirer of Henry Clay. Although he never sought office he was devotedly attached to his political party, and made strenuous efforts, as an individual, to promote its success. Just and upright in all his dealings, he passed a long life without a stain. Litigation was abhorrent to his feelings, and he was always ready to compromise, or suffer loss, rather than resort to law. 'Seek peace and pursue it' was the law of his life. Pure in his principles, simple in his tastes, quiet in his manners, and a great lover of truthfulness, he enjoyed the confidence of those who knew him. In his younger days he was strongly inclined to the tenets of the Society of Friends, but after his children grew up and most of them attached themselves to the Methodist church, he generally worshipped with them, uniting with the church, however, only quite late in life."[1] He m. in Baltimore, 1861, *Catharine Sumwalt*, who was b. in Baltimore, Feb. 23, 1787,

[1] "Among my earliest recollections is that of seeing him bowed daily in prayer. He was doubtless a servant of God, but always timid, and fearful of making a profession of godliness. He never thought himself good enough to belong to the church. Toward the end of his pilgrimage, however, he became more trustful, and finally, when near eighty, united with the M. E. church, and enjoyed the ordinances of the sanctuary. His last days were his best, and his end was peace. For some years before his death the powers of nature gradually failed, and without any special form of disease, he quietly passed from earth, we trust to a better home, a few weeks after he entered on his eighty-third year. His wife, Catharine, was a meet partner for such a husband. Her days were spent in faithful attention to home duties. 'A good wife, and a good mother' might well be her epitaph. She was an humble Christian for many years, and like her dear husband gradually faded out of life in a good old age. Their tombstones, side by side in the cemetery, proclaim the remarkable coincidence that they were both of one age at the time of their decease, each being eighty-two years, one month and five days old." JOSEPH H. DAWSON, Norfolk, Va., 1873.

4–17. [ALLEN.] James R., b. Feb. 24, 1868.
4–18. Elizabeth, b. March 23, 1870.

3–14. *Sarah E. Dawson*, b. in Cocke Co., Tenn., Feb. 26, 1843, m. HENRY C. LEFTWICH, of that county, where they reside (1871). They have one child:

4–19. Mary L., b. in Cocke Co., Tenn., Nov. 15, 1869.

late Paymaster Samuel Hambleton, U. S. N. He has seven children living, as follows:

7–4. William Hambleton, b. Sept. 15, 1836, res. 1873, at Bay Hundred, Talbot county; physician.
7–5. Helen, b. Sept. 1, 1838, res. 1873, California. TILDEN.
7–6. Lydia Rolle, b. 1840, res. Talbot Co.
7–7. Rowena, b. 1845, res. Talbot Co.
7–8. John Alvan, b. 1852, res. Talbot Co.
7–9. Douglass Hambleton, b. 1856, res. Talbot Co.
7–10. Emma Louisa, b. 1858, res. Talbot Co.

6–7. *Caroline Dawson*, b. in Talbot county, Md., 1813, res. 1873, in California. She m. about 1838, THOMAS NEILSON, of Baltimore. Two children living:

7–11. Charles Frederick Mayer, b. in Baltimore, res. 1873, Omaha, Neb.; physician.
7–12. Ella, m. JOHN PARKER GAILLARD, of S. C., and res. 1873, San Francisco, Cal.

6–9. *Eliza Jane Dawson*, b. in Talbot county, Md., Nov. 23, 1828, m. in same county, Dec., 1861, DANIEL L. GOLD, who was b. in Washington, Va., 1824, son of Daniel and Floyd Gold. They res. 1873, in Lawrenceville, Ill. One child:

7–13. Annie Roberta, b. in Springfield, Ill., Aug., 1863.

6–14. *Elizabeth Ann Dawson*, b. in Baltimore, Md., Jan. 14, 1817, d. in same city, Jan. 15, 1861, m. April 19, 1838, CYRILLUS JOHN ROSAN, who d. in Baltimore, Dec. 5, 1864, son of Alonzo and Mary Rosan. They had six children:

7–14. Alonzo Thomas, b. in Baltimore, May 21, 1839, d.
7–15. Charles William, b. in Balto., Aug. 25, 1841, res. 1873, Brooklyn, N. Y.
7–16. Joseph Henry Dawson, b. in Balto., Oct. 10, 1843, res. Brooklyn.
7–17. Sterling, b. in Balto., Oct. 9, 1845, res. Bel Air, Md.; *m.*
7–18. Serena Heard, b. in Balto., July 31, 1849, m. Oct. 4, 1870, J. WARD SCOTT, M.D., res. Baltimore.
7–19. Philip Dawson, b. at Westminster, Md., Feb. 13, 1852, d.

6–15. PHILIP THOMAS DAWSON, b. in Baltimore, Oct. 6, 1818, m. 1st, in Baltimore, Oct. 31, 1844, *Mary Wilson*, who d. without issue, March, 1851, dau. of Robert and Maria Wilson. He m. 2d, in Baltimore, Oct. 19, 1852, *Sarah Bell*

stronger than ever." *Jan.* 1871. "I have practiced medicine for more than forty years in the same locality, St. Michael's; am sixty-seven years of age, and near my journey's end, with hope and faith sure of a happy immortality, which I pray you and I may both inherit." *Jan.* 1873.

Trotton, b. in Baltimore, Jan. 22, 1831, d. May 22, 1856, dau. of Thomas and Eliza Trotton. Mr. Dawson res. in Baltimore. One son living:

7–20. Thomas Trotton, b. in Baltimore, April 27, 1854.

6–16. *Maria Sumwalt Dawson*, b. in Baltimore, May 29, 1820, m. Dr. JOSIAH G. SANBOURN, of Illinois. They had two children:

7–21. Josiah.
7–22. Eunice.

She m. 2d, GEORGE LOCKWOOD, of Illinois. Three chn.:

7–23. George.
7–24. Daniel.
7–25. Philip D.

After her death, Mr. LOCKWOOD m. 2d, her sister *Catharine Dawson* (6–18) who was b. in Baltimore, Aug. 15, 1826. They res. near Salina, Kansas. No issue.

6–17. JOSEPH H. DAWSON, b. in Baltimore, March 12, 1823, m. in Richmond, Va., March 15, 1848, *G. Louisa Drake*, b. in Norfolk, dau. of Rev. Ethelbert Drake and w. *Mary Godwin Green.*[1] They res. 1873, in Norfolk. Five children, all b. in Va.:

7–26. Mary Catharine, b. in Norfolk.
7–27. Russell Soule, b. in Norfolk.
7–28. Virginia Croel, b. in Richmond.
7–29. Laura Louisa, b. in Norfolk.
7–30. Martha Sumwalt, b. in Norfolk.

6–19. *Caroline Dawson*, b. in Baltimore, Sept. 3, 1829, m. in Baltimore, Nov. 14, 1854, MILTON D. METTEE, who was b. in Baltimore, June 24, 1831, son of Martin and Elizabeth Mettee. Three children, all b. in Baltimore:

7–31. Anna Sumwalt, b. Aug. 14, 1855.
7–32. Milton Howard, b. March 23, 1857.
7–33. Jennie Barron, b. April 11, 1859, d. June 30, 1859.

6–20. THOMAS RUSSELL DAWSON, b. in Talbot Co., Md., June 29, 1828, m. in Yonkers, N. Y., June 15, 1870, *Annie*

---

[1] Rev. Ethelbert Drake, of the Va. Conference M. E. church, b. in Chatham county, N. C., 1787, son of Richard and *Louisa Drake* Drake. Mary Godwin Green, b. in Norfolk, Va., 1797, dau. of Rev. Richard Lee Green, of Lancaster county, and w. Grizzie Cowper, of Nansemond county, Va.

A. Anstice. He is a wholesale dry goods merchant, and res. 1873, in Philadelphia. They have one child:

7–34. Henry Anstice, b. in Philadelphia, March 23, 1871.

6–21. JOSEPH COLUMBUS DAWSON, b. in Talbot county, Md., April 11, 1829, m. in Norfolk, Va., April 5, 1859, *Mary C. Ghieslin*, dau. of William and Mary Ghieslin. They res. 1873, in Philadelphia. Five children:

7–35. Harry Hamilton, d. in infancy.
7–36. Ellen Blanche, b. in Petersburg, Va., April 28, 1861.
7–37. Joseph Columbus, b. in Norfolk, Va., Oct. 29, 1865.
7–38. Horace Nimmo, b. in Philadelphia, Dec. 26, 1868.
7–39. William Edgar, b. in Philadelphia, April 10, 1873.

6–22. *Susan Dawson* (dau. of Richard, 5-7), m. Nov. 5, 1853, LEWIS METTEE, who d. Aug. 8, 1861. She res. at St. Michael's, Talbot Co., Md. Three children:

7–40. Martin Russell, b. March 6, 1855.
7–41. Frank Kennedy, b. May 14, 1859.
7–42. Lurellen Virginia, b. Feb. 17, 1862.

6–23. *Ellen Dawson* (dau. of Richard, 5-7), m. Nov. 13, 1867, DANIEL HOPE. They res. 1873, at Sharp's Island, Chesapeake bay. Three children:

7–43. Thomas Summerfield, b. Sept. 27, 1868.
7–44. Joseph Dawson, b. March 27, 1871.
7–45. Mary, b. Aug. 30, 1872.

7–5. *Helen Dawson*, b. in Talbot county, Sept. 1, 1838, m. in Baltimore, Nov. 12, 1859, Dr. THOMAS W. TILDEN, who was b. in Caroline county, Md., Feb. 1, 1825, son of Dr. Charles and *Sarah Townsend* Tilden. They emigrated to California in 1860, returned to Maryland in 1861, removed again to California, and now, 1873, reside at Chico, Butte county, in that state. Four children:

8–1. Mary Ridgeley, b. in Chico, Cal., Oct. 7, 1860.
8–2. James D., b. in Talbot Co., Md., June 30, 1862.
8–3. Edwin Marmaduke, b. in Talbot Co., July 2, 1865.
8–4. Louisa Hambleton, b. in Marin county, Cal., July 19, 1867.

7–17. Col. STERLING ROSAN, attorney at law, b. in Baltimore, Md., Oct. 9, 1845, m. May 11, 1871, *Helen Georgie Heald*, of Harford county, Md. They res. 1873, at Bel Air, in Harford county. One child:

8–5. Maggie, b. Feb. 25, 1872.

FAMILY OF JOHN DAWSON,

OF PRINCE GEORGE COUNTY, MD., about 1700.

From Geo. W. Dawson, Esq., of Dawsonville, Md.; Hon. John Dawson, of Uniontown, Pa.; Mrs. Louisa Dawson Patterson, of Pittsburg, Pa.; Mr. John B. Dawson, of Calcutta, Ohio, and others, the following:

1. JOHN DAWSON is said to have emigrated from the north of England sometime before 1700. Whether he came from Whitehaven, in Cumberland,[1] or from Yorkshire,[2] is uncertain. By some he is said to have gone into Maryland by way of Philadelphia, where he tarried for a while; others understand that he emigrated directly to Maryland. It is a tradition, not, however, sustained by any facts which have come to the knowledge of the compiler hereof, that he was accompanied by two brothers named Nicholas and William.[3] Possibly two *sons* thus named were the traditional brothers. He is said to have emigrated when a young man, and to have been quite advanced in years when he died. His death is supposed to have occurred before 1720, from the fact that his son Thomas, who died in 1800, aged 92, and was, consequently, born in 1708, barely remembered the event as one which happened in his childhood.

He married *Rebecca Doyne*, daughter of John Doyne, an Irish gentleman, who had a grant of land on Chickamoxon creek, in Charles county, about thirty miles below the place where the city of Washington now is. They settled on Broad creek, near the Potomac river, about twelve miles below the site of Washington, in Prince George county, where he died. Mr. G. W.

---

[1] "Whitehaven, in Cumberland," a small town on the Irish sea, north of Liverpool. G. W. D.

[2] Hon. J. D., 1854.

[3] Mr. G. W. D. says, 1854, these "went south, to Virginia and the Carolinas, and from them the Dawsons of those states, Georgia, and the other southern states, are descended. One of the brothers, Nicholas, I suppose, left a son named Nicholas, in Maryland, whose descendants still live near the Point of Rocks (Loudon Co., Va.)." The supposition in regard to the Georgia and Carolina families, is, as has been already stated, erroneous. The Nicholas Dawson referred to was probably *son*, not *brother*, of John Dawson, the emigrant.

D. says there were, of the issue of this marriage, besides a daughter named Eleanor, four sons named John, George, *William*, and Thomas; and he adds: "There may have been, and I think it likely there were, other children of John and *Rebecca Doyne* Dawson, but of this I am not certain." Hon. J. D. mentions, of this family, John, George, Thomas and *Nicholas*, thus omitting William, named in the list first quoted, and adding Nicholas. Probably both names should be retained, and thus we have issue of John and *Rebecca Doyne* Dawson as follows:

2–1. John, who, according to Mr. G. W. D.'s information, "died in early life, unmarried."[1]
2–2. George, resided in Montgomery Co., ancestor of Pennsylvania families.
2–3. William, d. in early life, unmarried.[2]
2–4. Thomas, b. in Prince George Co., 1708, d. Aug., 1800, aged 92, ancestor of Montgomery Co. families.
2–5. Nicholas, ancestor of Loudon Co., Va., families.
2–6. Eleanor, who m. a gentleman named BAYNE.[3]

2–2. GEORGE DAWSON resided in Montgomery county, near where the city of Washington now stands. He m. *Ann Lowe*, sister of the w. of his brother Thomas.

---

[1] Hon. J. D. erroneously supposed that the above named John Dawson "emigrated to Georgia, and was grandfather of Senator Dawson."

[2] This from G. W. D., who supposed one of this name went South. Did he not move, with his brother George, into Pennsylvania? *William Dawson* is named in a list of settlers in Fayette county, then called Springhill township, forming a part of Bedford county, 1772.—Veech's *The Monongahela of Old*, p. 200.

[3] "A grandson of hers, named John Dawson Harrison, died at an advanced age some time last year in Alexandria, Va., leaving a numerous family."—G. W. D., 1854. "She has descendants now living in Maryland, Virginia, and perhaps elsewhere."—G. W. D., 1871.

Since this record was arranged a different account of the original of the family has reached the compiler, communicated by Mr. Augustine M. Dawson, Calcutta, Ohio, 1873. He states that the founder of the family in Maryland was THOMAS DAWSON, who, between 1630 and 1640, "came to Maryland clothed with the second office in the state," Lord Baltimore being governor. Dawson "had a grant of two manors of land, to be selected in any place where the land was unoccupied, and he located one near Port Tobacco, on the Potomac, below Washington, and the other in Montgomery county, each manor consisting of some thousands of acres. Title to the first described tract long since passed out of the family, but of the second a portion yet remains in the Dawson name. Thomas Dawson, 2d, laid out a town on this tract called Dawsonville; he lived to be 103 years old; and *his* son Thomas" (presumed to be 2-4 of the above record) "died there, being 93 years old."— But the Thomas last named appears to have given a different account of the family, and that his father's name was *John*, not Thomas, was clearly a fact derived from him. It may be noted that the second Lord Baltimore received his grant from King Charles in 1682, but never resided in Maryland. His brother Leonard was his lieutenant, and arrived in 1634.

Mr. G. W. D. wrote, 1854, as follows: "George had a large family. He lived in this county [Montgomery] not far from the present city of Washington, and *died there*. One of his sons, named Benjamin, married and died in early manhood, leaving an only son named Abraham, now quite an old man, widower and childless, living in this county. A daughter of George also married in Maryland, and some of her descendants, of almost every name, still reside in this state. After his death, his widow, with the rest of his children, removed to western Pennsylvania, and settled at what was then called Red Stone, now Brownsville. If I am correctly informed, the Hon. John L. Dawson, now member of Congress from that district of Pennsylvania, is a descendant of the Dawsons then so emigrating from Maryland. This emigration took place, as near as I can learn, some time about the date of the Revolution — say 1775 — a few years earlier or later." In the same year (1854) Hon. J. D., uncle to Hon. J. L. D., above named, wrote as follows: "My father was a native of the state of Maryland, but died while I was an infant. He migrated *with his father*, George Dawson, to the southwestern part of Pennsylvania, *then* supposed to be within the limits of Virginia. This was about 1770. My father's name was Nicholas Dawson, and his mother's maiden name was Lowe. He was born in Montgomery county, near Washington." No doubt the latter account is correct. George Dawson was named as a resident of Tyrone township in 1772, which then embraced a part of what is now Fayette county, Pa.[1] When he accompanied his family on their migration westward he must have been upward of sixty years of age. His life was therefore mainly spent in Maryland, where his

---

[1] See *The Monongahela of Old*, p. 203. George Dawson was named one of the executors of Thomas Gist, of Fayette county (then Westmoreland) son of the locally celebrated Christopher Gist, who "was among the earliest adventurers into this region of country," having gone thither "as agent of the old Ohio company, and settled on the Mount Braddock lands in 1753," in which year he accompanied Washington as a guide in an expedition to the French posts on the Alleghany. Thomas Gist d. on the Mount Braddock estate in 1786, and George Dawson *being already dead*, his son Nicholas, who was *his* executor, was supposed to be thereby entitled to become executor of Gist. Nicholas had, however, in 1783, removed into the Virginia "pan handle" on the Ohio, just below the state line of Pa., and on account of non-residence could not serve. "The Dawsons owned and resided on the lands in North Union township, recently the home of Col. William Swearingen."— *The Monongahela of Old*, p. 116, and note 2.

children probably all grew to maturity. He may have had others besides the following:

3–1. Benjamin, father of Abraham, both above named.
3–2. Nicholas, removed with his father to Pa., d. in Va.; *m.*
3–3. Henry, said to have "emigrated to the west." (Western Pa. or Ohio).
3–4. John, removed with his father to Pa.; *m.*
3–5. Verlinda, d. in Washington Co., Pa. MOORE.
3–6. Eleanor, m. JOHN SWEARINGEN.
3–7. Rebecca, m. DANIEL SWEARINGEN.
3–8. Elizabeth, m. WM. SWEARINGEN, lived in Fayette Co., Pa.[1]
3–9. Nancy, m. THOMAS DAWSON, son of Benoni (3–11).
3–10. *A daughter* remained in Maryland and "intermarried with a Mr. GARRETT; some of her descendants live in Frederick county." (J. D., 1854). "One son and *two daughters* remained in Maryland." (G. W. D., 1871).

2–4. THOMAS DAWSON, b. at Broad Creek, in Prince George county, Md., 1708, m. *Elizabeth Lowe*, dau. of John Lowe, of that county, ancestor of the late Governor Lowe, of Maryland. He d. in Montgomery county, Md., August, 1800, aged 92. They had ten children, named in the order of birth, as follows:

3–11. Benoni, b. 1742, d. in Beaver Co., Pa., May 6, 1806; *m.*
3–12. Mary, m. BENJAMIN MACKALL, whose sisters m. Benoni and Nicholas L.
3–13. Sarah, m. WILLIAM BLACKMORE.
3–14. Eleanor, m. LAWRENCE ALLNUTT.
3–15. Nicholas L., b. 1751, d. in Montgomery Co., Md., 1831; *m.*
3–16. Verlinda H., m. JAMES ALLNUTT, brother to Lawrence.
3–17. Robert Doyne, b. 1758, d. in Montgomery Co., Aug., 1824; *m.*
3–18. Elizabeth, d. *unm.*
3–19. Rebecca, m. BENJAMIN MACKALL, nephew to the above named. (See forward).
3–20. Jane, m. WEAVER JOHNS.

2–5. NICHOLAS DAWSON, of Prince George county, brother of George and Thomas, above named, appears to have been the ancestor of the Dawsons of Loudon county, Va., and other families. His w. was *Martha Ann* ——, who d. Jan. 28, 1795, in her 80th year. They had:

3–21. Nicholas, b. in Prince George county, June 14, 1750, d. in Frederick Co., Md., March 18, 1806; *m.*
3–22. Charles, d. in Dearborn Co., Indiana; *m.*[2]

---

[1] See p. 231, *note*.

[2] Nicholas Dawson had, it is supposed, several children. There is some doubt as to whether Charles (3-22) was his son, but he was of Loudon county, Va., b. in Maryland, and *probably* of this connection.

3-1. Benjamin Dawson, lived in Montgomery Co., Md., m. and d. in early manhood, leaving an only son:

4-1. Abraham, who was living in same county, 1854, at an advanced age, a widower, and childless.

3-2. Nicholas Dawson (son of George, 2-2), b. in Montgomery county, Md., near the city of Washington, removed with his father's family to the southwestern part of Pennsylvania, then supposed to be within the limits of Virginia, about the year 1770. He must have been then of age or nearly so, and he was in 1772 the owner of 300 acres of "uncultivated lands" in Tyrone township, forming a part of what is now Fayette county, Pa.[1] A few years later he was a volunteer in Crawford's expedition against Sandusky.[2] He m. *Violet Littleton*, dau. of John and Violet Littleton, of Westmoreland, England, and had in 1783 taken up his residence on what was acknowledged Virginia soil—now known as the "pan-handle"[3]—where he d. about 1800. They had two sons:

4-2. George, b. March 17, 1783, d. at Brownsville, Pa., June 19, 1871; *m.*

4-3. John, b. July 13, 1788, res. 1873, at Uniontown, Pa.; *m.*

3-4. John Dawson, (son of George, 2-2) m.—— and removed west. He settled in Champaign county, O., some time before the war of 1812, and d. at Urbanna, in that county, about 1860, aged nearly 100 years. He had, besides four daus., four sons, named as follows:

4-4. Harry.

4-5. William, b. July 20, 1778, d. in Pa., Sept. 10, 1853; *m.*

4-6. Thomas, removed to Natchez, Miss., and d. there leaving one child—a dau.

4-7. John, d. in Champaign Co., about 1830; *m.*

---

[1] *The Monongahela of Old*, p. 204.

[2] Butterfield's *Crawford's Campaign*, p. 253. It is there stated he was of Westmoreland, and lived near Beesontown, 1778.

[3] See p. 231, *note*. "Nicholas d. at what was called Muchmore's Bottom, on the Va. shore, more than seventy years ago."—A. M. D., 1873.

"Nicholas [Dawson] having married Violet Littleton in Maryland (?) followed the course and shared the fortunes of his father. They were stern partisans of Virginia in the boundary controversy, and removed several times to secure a residence within the limits of that commonwealth, although they never relinquished their possessions in Fayette county."—From a *Sketch* by Chauncey F. Black, Esq., intended to be introductory to a collection of Speeches of Hon. John L. Dawson. (Unless Nicholas Dawson went back to Maryland for his bride, it seems doubtful whether he m. there. Their eldest child was b. in 1783, some 13 years after the date of his emigration to Pa).

3-5. *Verlinda Dawson* (eldest dau. of George, 2–2), m. AUGUSTINE MOORE, of Kent Co., Md. They lived at Briceland's Cross Roads, Washington county, Pa., where both d. at an advanced age. They had nine children:

4–8. Rachel, b. Aug. 31, 1777, d. near Calcutta, O., July 19, 1846, aged 68, w. of NICHOLAS DAWSON, son of Benoni (3–11).

4–9. William, m. *Susan Maxwell,* lived in Wellsville, Columbiana Co., O., where both d., he aged about 83; they had six sons and four daus., all m. but one dau.

4–10. John, never m.; was a river man, and d. in La.

4–11. Elizabeth, m. DANIEL McCONNELL, blacksmith; both d., children live in Tuscarawas Co., O.

4–12. Asenath, m. JOHN JACKSON, both d. in Knoxville, Knox Co., Ill.; several children.

4–13. Verlinda, d. at Briceland's Cross Roads, aged 25; *unm.*

4–14. Eleanor, m. JOHN McCONNELL; they res. 1873, near Briceland's Cross Roads, Washington Co., Pa.; several children.

4–15. Mary, m. CHARLES HAY, and removed to Ashland Co., O., where he d., and she res. 1873; one son, Joseph J., res. New Orleans, La.

4–16. Rebecca, m. GILBERT COOL; they res. 1873, near Clinton, Alleghany Co., Pa.

3-11. BENONI DAWSON, b. 1742, m. in Md., *Rebecca Mackall,* and about the year 1782 [1] emigrated to western Pennsylvania (now Fayette county) where he joined the family of his uncle George Dawson (2–2), who had gone before him. After a brief halt in that neighborhood he went further west, (Sept., 1790[2]) and settled in the lower corner of what is now called Beaver county, Pa., the village of Georgetown being on his land. He took with him from Maryland his family, cattle and slaves,[3] and while tarrying in Fayette county sent men on to Beaver county to clear land for a homestead. A cabin was built on Mill creek bottom, near the Ohio river, and about ten acres planted with corn. He moved by water, but his sons and slaves went by land, and drove the stock. He was a member of the Episcopal church, "a good man to the poor," and one of those strong, wise, just men whose influence is widely felt for good, especially in a new community, as a counselor

[1] "My father came with his father to Fayette county, Pa., when he was ten years old; he was b. in 1772."— A. M. Dawson, of Calcutta, O., son of Nicholas, son of Benoni (311).

[2] A. M. Dawson, 1873.

[3] "Among the largest slave owners, as shown by the Registers, were Robert Beale, 18........, Benoni Dawson, 7........, Augustine Moore, 4," etc.—*The Monongahela of Old,* p. 99, *note.*

and peace maker, whose judgment and advice were generally respected.[1] He built a mill on Mill creek, and d. at his homestead, May 6, 1806, aged 64.[2] He had fourteen children, the order of their births not known as to all:[3]

4–17. Thomas, b. about 1765, d. at Georgetown, Pa., aged about 52; *m.*
4–18. Benoni, b. in Md., Aug. 20, 1769, d. near Georgetown, Nov. 14, 1844; *m.*
4–19. George, lived at Mill creek, d. at about 50; *m.*
4–20. Mackall, lived and d. near Georgetown; *m.*
4–21. Nicholas, b. 1772, d. near Calcutta, O., 1855; *m.*
4–22. Henry.
4–23. Mary, m. JAMES BLACKMORE. (See forward).
4–24. Elizabeth, m. CHARLES BLACKMORE. (See forward).
4–25. Rebecca Mackall, m. WILLIAM WHITE; left 9 children.
4–26. Nancy Brooks, m. JOHN BEVER. (See forward).
4–27. John L., d. near Wooster, O.; *m.*
4–28. Benjamin, d. at about 50; *m.*
4–29. Robert D., d. aged 21; *unm.*
4–30. James M., d. without issue.

3–15. NICHOLAS L. DAWSON, b. in Montgomery Co., Md., 1751, d. near Dawsonville, in that county, in 1831, aged 80. He m. early, *Mary Mackall*, sister to the w. of his brother Benoni, and to his sister Mary's husband. They had several children, of whom was:[4]

4–31. James M., b. 1774, d. near Dawsonville, 1866, in his 92d year; *m.*

3–17. ROBERT DOYNE DAWSON, b. in Montgomery county, Md., 1758, d. at or near Dawsonville, in that county, August, 1824, aged 66. He was twice m. By his 2d wife he had three daus., two of whom d. young. His first wife was *Sarah N. Chiswell*, dau. of an English gentleman, from Lancashire. They had seven sons and four daughters, all b. in Montgomery county, as follows:

---

[1] "People used to say, 'Did Benoni Dawson say so? Then it is right.'" A. M. D.

[2] "The first man buried in Georgetown graveyard was Jacob Clark, a white man, shot by hostile Indians, in Sept., 1773. Since then great numbers of grandfather Benoni Dawson's family, including himself, wife, children, grandchildren and great grandchildren, have been buried there."—A. M. D.

[3] "I suppose that all his immediate children are d., but their descendants, almost as numerous as Pharaoh's frogs, have spread themselves all over the western and northwestern states." — G. W. D., 1854. "Thomas was the eldest; I give the names of the others as remembered; I cannot give the order of their births." — G. W. D., 1871. "Thomas was the eldest son, Benoni was second son, Nicholas the middle child." — A. M. D., 1873.

[4] G. W. D., 1854.

4–32. William C., b. 1784, d. at Russellville, Ky., about 1848 or 49 ; *m.*
4–33. Mary D., d. young.[1]
4–34. Verlinda H., d. in Missouri about 1864. ALLNUTT.
4–35. Thomas, d. in 1832, a childless widower.
4–36. Stephen N., b. Aug. 10, 1788, d. in Montgomery Co., Tenn., Dec. 23, 1855 ; *m.*
4–37. Robert D., b. 1790, d. in New Madrid, Mo., about 1842 ; *m.*
4–38. Sarah N., d. young.
4–39. Elizabeth, d. 1852 ; *unm.*
4–40. Joseph N., d. at the homestead, in Montgomery county, Md., July, 1869, in his 74th year. He never married.
4–41. Benoni, physician, d. in 1851, in Md., leaving a widow (still living, 1871), and two sons and six daus. ; three of the daus. *m.*, the other three and the sons, *unm.*
4–42. George W., b. Nov. 28, 1799, res. 1873, at Dawsonville, Md. ; *unm.* *See below.*

GEORGE W. DAWSON, Esq. (4–42 of this record), was educated to the legal profession, and in early life was somewhat engaged in the practice ; but having no fondness for it he soon relinquished it, keeping up, however, a nominal connection with the bar, and sometimes, though not often, taking part in the trial of causes in which his personal friends were interested. He has devoted no small part of his life to public matters, having been frequently honored by his neighbors with public trusts. He has repeatedly represented his county of Montgomery in the state legislature, has been presiding justice of the court of Probate, trustee of public schools, trustee of the poor, poormaster, justice of the peace, etc. ; also a collector of Internal Revenue of the United States for the Fifth District of Maryland, and state assessor of Montgomery county.

Writing under date of Feb. 13, 1871, Mr. Dawson says : "For the last two years I have held no public trust — shall never, I hope, hold another. For nearly forty years before the death of my brother Joseph we lived together, jointly engaged in farming and milling. His death terminated our partnership, and unwilling at three score years and ten to commence, as it were, the world anew, I sold my farm to my nephew, and make my home with him. I have never married. I live at the family homestead, and am less than four miles from the Virginia line." (Dawsonville, Md.). To this gentleman the compiler hereof

[1] "Mary and Sarah d. young, before I was born."— G. W. D., 1871.

is indebted for much of the information contained in the foregoing pages.

3-19. *Rebecca Dawson* (dau. of Thomas, 2-4), m. BENJAMIN MACKALL, nephew to Benjamin Mackall, husband of her sister Mary. They lived in Frederick Co., Md. Of their children only the names of the following are known:

4-43. Thomas; *m.*
4-44. Eleanor, b. Jan. 10, 1796, m. BENONI BLACKMORE, son of Charles and *Elizabeth Dawson* Blackmore (4-24).
4-45. Benjamin; *m.*

3-21. NICHOLAS DAWSON (son of Nicholas, 2-5), was b. in Prince George county, Md., June 14, 1750, and removed thence to near Frederick city, Md., sometime, as is supposed, prior to the war of the Revolution. He was a magistrate of the county of Frederick for many years. He d. March 18, 1806, aged 55 years 9 months 4 days. He m. 1st, widow Lydia Mackall, Feb. 14, 1778. She d. Oct. 14, 1780, without issue. He m. 2d, Sept. 4, 1781, *Elizabeth Bayne*. It is said that "they loved mutually before his first marriage, and were only prevented from consummating their affection by the positive opposition of her family, who did not like her lover's wild and dissipated habits. He reformed after marriage, and became a good and exemplary husband."[1] They had four children:

4-46. Polly, b. Feb. 9, 1784, m. THOMAS CROMWELL, and lived at Pittsburg, Pa. She d. without issue, while on a visit to her native county. She is reputed to have been a woman of great beauty, both of person and character.
4-47. Philip, b. Feb. 4, 1786, d. Jan. 20, 1806, aged 20. He was a promising youth, and had just completed the study of medicine in Philadelphia.
4-48. Samuel, b. Sept. 9, 1787, d. in Va., Dec. 11, 1845; *m.*
4-49. Henrietta, b. Sept. 13, 1789, m. THOMAS GASSAWAY, and d. in Leesburg, Va., without issue. She was many years a widow, a very amiable lady, and beautiful even in her old age.

3-22. CHARLES DAWSON (supposed son of Nicholas, 2-5), b. in Md., lived in Loudon Co., Va., and d. in Dearborn county, Indiana. It is said that he owned slaves, on account

(1) So writes his grandson, Nicholas Dawson, Esq., of Baltimore, 1871. It may be surmised that *Elizabeth Bayne* was her husband's cousin, dau. of his father's sister Eleanor who m. a Bayne. See record of family of John and *Rebecca Doyne* Dawson, p. 230.

of which he with his family removed to Indiana before it was admitted to the Union as a state, where he set his slaves free. He had six children : [1]

4–50. Thomas.
4–51. John Charles.
4–52. Elijah.
4–53. William.
4–54. Mary TALOCH.
4–55. *A dau.* m. —— CHEEK.

4–2. GEORGE DAWSON (son of Nicholas, 3–2), b. March 17, 1783, d. at Brownsville, Pa., June 19, 1871, m. *Mary Kennedy*, whom he survived some years. She "was an intellectual, as well as an excellent woman." He "was remarkable, not less for his natural parts, than for the nature and extent of his acquirements. His historical researches extended over a wide field; his memory was astonishing; he was a brilliant and instructive talker." [2] They had ten children:

5–1. Sarah, d. at Connellsville, Pa. ASHMAN.
5–2. John Littleton, b. Feb. 7, 1813, d. at Friendship Hill, Fayette Co., Pa., Sept. 18, 1870 ; *m.*
5–3. Mary Kennedy, d. *unm.*
5–4. Louisa, d. CASS.
5–5. Elizabeth, d. at Uniontown, Pa., 1868. HOWELL.
5–6. Catharine Harrison, d. at Uniontown about 1864. WILLSON.
5–7. George Nicholas, thrown from a horse, and killed instantly, when 10 years old.
5–8. Ellen, res. 1873, New York city. CASS.
5–9. Samuel Kennedy, res. 1873, Eastport, Me. ; *m.*
5–10. George Fielding, res. 1873, Connellsville, Pa. ; *m.*

4–3. Hon. JOHN DAWSON (son of Nicholas, 3–2), b. in Virginia, July 13, 1788, m. Jan. 4, 1820, *Ann Bailey*, who was b. in Uniontown, Sept. 8, 1799, and d. in Uniontown, May 6, 1859, aged 60 years. Mr. Dawson, a lawyer of distinction, presided for some years as associate judge of the Common Pleas for Fayette county, and res. 1873, at Uniontown. They have had nine children, all b. at Uniontown :

---

[1] His grandson, John W. Dawson, son of John C., was editor of the Fort Wayne, Ind., *Times*, 1854. His father had lived in Ky., near Bordentown, and removed thence into Indiana. Another grandson, Elijah Dawson, son *as supposed* of Elijah (4–52), res. at Independence, Ind., 1873.

[2] From a *Sketch*, by Chauncey F. Black, Esq., intended to be introductory to a collection of Speeches of Hon. John L. Dawson.

5–11. Ellis Bailey, b. Oct. 29, 1820, res. 1873, Uniontown; attorney, *unm.*
5–12. Ellen Moore, b. April 13, 1826, m. Jan. 4, 1848, ADDISON RUBY, and res. 1873, a widow at Uniontown.
5–13. Emily Violet, b. Jan. 24, 1828, m. Oct. 4, 1853, Dr. WILLIAM STURGEON, and res. 1873, Uniontown.
5–14. Maria, b. Jan. 21, 1832, m. Sept., 1856, HENRY BALDWIN, res. 1873, Springfield, O.
5–15. Henry Clay, b. Feb. 1, 1834, m. May, 1867, *Mary McCloskey*, res. near Hillsboro, O.[1]
5–16. Ruth Elizabeth, b. Jan. 26, 1835, m. April, 1867, A. K. JOHNSON, res. near Hillsboro, O.
5–17. Louisa Cass, b. March 8, 1836, m. Feb. 11, 1858, JOHN M. BERRY, res. near Lexington, Ky.
5–18. John Nicholas, b. Dec. 6, 1839, m. Sept. 9, 1863, *Lucy Strother Evans*, res. Uniontown, Pa.[2]
5–19. Richard W., b. Feb. 25, 1841, d. at Fortress Monroe, Va., Feb. 1, 1865.[3]

4–5. WILLIAM DAWSON (son of John, 3–4), b. July 20, 1778, d. near Pittsburg, Pa., Sept. 10, 1853, m. June 15, 1808, *Ellen Dawson*, b. April 12, 1782, d. Sept. 3, 1853 (dau. of Thomas, 4–17). They had eleven children:

5–20. John, b. May 8, 1809, d. July 10, 1810.
5–21. Thomas, b. June 11, 1811, res. Indiana; *m.*
5–22. Harrison, b. Oct. 14, 1813, d. at Little Rock, Ark., Sept. 8, 1844, leaving family.
5–23. Nancy A., b. Dec. 9, 1815, m. March 12, 1836, SAMUEL STEVENSON; both d.
5–24. Benoni, b. Aug. 4, 1817, res. Georgetown, Beaver Co., Pa.; *m.*
5–25. Cyrus, b. Dec. 15, 1819, m. July 25, 1849, *Mary A. Bruce*, d. March 20, 1851, leaving one child.
5–26. Elizabeth, b. Sept. 5, 1821, m. Oct. 8, 1849, —— TOWNSEND.
5–27. Catharine, b. June 14, 1823, m. May 7, 1846, THOMAS MACKALL (4–43).
5–28. Ellen, b. Dec. 25, 1827, m. April 8, 1865, JOHN MACKALL, son of Thomas, son of Benjamin (4–45).
5–29. William, b. Feb. 23, 1830, res. 1873, Little Rock, Ark.
5–30. Rebecca J., b. July 9, 1832, d. April 15, 1836.

---

[1] Capt. Henry C. Dawson served with the 8th Regiment Pa. Reserves during the war; was wounded at Fredericksburg, Md.

[2] Mr. John N. Dawson (5–18) forwarding the above record, states that John and Ann Dawson (4–3) have had 35 gr. chn., of whom 25 are living, 1873. Names of the gr. chn. not communicated.

[3] Capt. Richard W. Dawson served during the war, until his death in 1865. He was on the staff of Gen. Ames at the time of the assault on Fort Fisher, at which he was wounded, Jan. 15, 1865, dying at Fortress Monroe on the first of the month following.

4–7. JOHN DAWSON (son of John, 3–4), d. in Champaign Co., Ohio, about 1830. He had three children:

5–31. William C., b. in Champaign Co., 1816, res. 1873, Petersburg, Ill.; m.
5–32. Mary.
5–33. Thomas.

4–17. THOMAS DAWSON (son of Benoni, 3–11), b. in Md., about 1765, emigrated with his parents to Pennsylvania in 1782, and settled in Beaver county, about five miles from Georgetown, where he d. about 1817.[1] He was an elder in the Presbyterian church. He m. *Nancy Dawson* (3–9 of this record), and had nine children:

5–34. Benoni, d. *unm.*
5–35. George, d. in Glasgow, Beaver Co., Pa.; *m.*
5–36. Nicholas, d. *unm.*
5–37. Mackall, d. *unm.*
5–38. Thomas, m. —— *Cameron*, d. leaving family in Indiana.
4–39. Henry. m. *Verlinda Patterson*, d. leaving family in Beaver Co., Pa.
5–40. Ellen, b. April 12, 1782, m. WILLIAM DAWSON (4–5 of this record).
5–41. Rebecca, lived in Beaver Co., Pa. REED.
5–42. Nancy, m. SAMUEL STEVENS, and had six children.

4–18. BENONI DAWSON (son of Benoni, 3–11), b. in Frederick, Md.. Aug. 20, 1769, d. in Beaver, Co., Pa., Nov. 14, 1844, m. Nov. 15, 1792, *Katherine P. D. McKennon*, b. in Annapolis, Md., Oct. 20, 1775, d. in Beaver Co., Pa., Dec. 18, 1848. They lived near Georgetown. He served two terms, of six months each, as a frontier guard against hostile Indians. The service was called "standing on the station." They had nine children:

5–43. Elizabeth, b. April 22, 1794, res. 1873, Beaver Co., Pa., *unm.*
5–44. Benjamin, b. June 20, 1796, d. Oct. 4, 1838, m. Oct. 22, 1817, *Sarah Bayne.*
5–45. Rebecca, b. Oct. 11, 1798, d. Feb. 5, 1844, m. April 5, 1838, JOHN CRISTLER.
5–46. Robert, b. July 30, 1801, living 1873, m. Feb. 9, 1826, *Elizabeth Reed.*
5–47. JAMES M., b. Jan. 25, 1804, d. Aug. 21, 1846, m. March 1, 1832, *Matilda B. White.*
5–48. Sarah, b. Dec. 20, 1806, living 1873, *unm.*
5–49. Ruthy, b. July 30, 1809, living 1873, m. Nov. 3, 1837, ISAAC EVANS.

[1] "Thomas, the eldest of Benoni's sons, has been dead over 50 years." G. W. D., 1871.

5–50. Mary A., b. Nov. 1, 1811, living 1873, m. March 28, 1839, JAMES JOHNSON.
5–51. Daniel, b. May 20, 1814, res. 1873, Ohioville, Beaver Co., Pa., *m.* (See forward).

4–19. GEORGE DAWSON (son of Benoni, 3–11), m. *Jane Mackall*, and lived at the mill built by his father on Mill creek, Beaver Co., Pa. "He d. at about 50, leaving eleven children all now d. but one son, George, and one dau., Elizabeth."[1] The names of only five children communicated:

5–52. Robert.
5–53. Benjamin.
5–54. George, res. 1873, Georgetown, Beaver Co., Pa.
5–55. Benoni.
5–56. Elizabeth, b. April 25, 1820, m. BENONI DAWSON (5–24).

4–20. MACKALL DAWSON (son of Benoni, 3–11), lived and d. in Beaver Co., Pa., near Georgetown. He had:

5–57. Nicholas, *m.*
5–58. Thomas, *m.*
5–59. Benoni, *m.*
5–60. Abrilla, res. Steubenville, O. HILL.
5–61. Rebecca, m. AMOS DAWSON, son of Benjamin (4–28).
5–62. Susan. CROFT.
5–63. Nancy, d. *unm.*

4–21. NICHOLAS DAWSON, farmer (son of Benoni, 3–11), b. in Md., 1772, d. near Calcutta, O., 1855, aged 83 years. In 1793 and '94, he "stood on the station" six months in each year, as a part of the frontier guard of southwestern Pennsylvania against hostile Indians. At an early day he joined the Presbyterian church, of which he was an elder. He was a life-member of the American Bible Society, a man of liberal charities, and earnest practical Christianity. He m. *Rachel Moore*, b. Aug. 31, 1777 (4–8 of this record). She d. near Calcutta, July 19, 1846, aged 68 years. They had six sons and six daus., of whom only two or three survive:

5–64. Mackall, d. in Adams Co., O.; *m.*
5–65. Augustine M., b. Feb. 19, 1800, res. 1873, Calcutta, O.; *m.*
5–66. Benoni, d. near Calcutta, O., aged 71; *m.*
5–67. William, d. in Pittsburg, Pa., Dec., 1872; *m.*
5–68. George A., b. Nov. 3, 1817, res. 1873, near Belair, Ill.; *m.*
5–69. Nicholas, d. aged about 35; *unm.*

---

[1] A. M. Dawson, Calcutta, O., 1873.

5–70. Verlinda, m. THOMAS CREIGHTON, lived in Jackson Co., Ohio, where both d.; no account of family.

5–71. Narcissa Bever, b. Feb. 11, 1806, m. GEORGE DAWSON, son of Benjamin (4–28).

5–72. Barbara Jones, d. in Medina Co., O., w. of JAMES ARMSTRONG. (See forward).

5–73. Rebecca, b. Feb. 7, 1810, m. THOMAS CREIGHTON, *not* the above named. (See forward).

5–74. Rachel, res. near Calcutta, O., w. of JOHN ARMSTRONG. (See forward).

5–75. Elizabeth, d. in infancy.

4–23. *Mary Dawson* (dau. of Benoni, 3–11), m. JAMES BLACKMORE; lived and d. near Smith's Ferry, Beaver Co., Pa. Four children:

5–76. Samuel; *m.*

5–77. Thomas; *m.*

5–78. Betsey, m. SAMUEL MACKALL.

5–79. Rebecca, m. JAMES FITZ SIMMONS. (See forward).

4–24. *Elizabeth Dawson* (dau. of Benoni, 3–11), m. CHARLES BLACKMORE; lived in Brooke Co., Va., now Hancock Co., W. Va., buried at Georgetown, Pa. Three children:

5–80. Thomas, m. *Nancy Dawson*, dau. of Benjamin (4–28). Both d., no issue.

5–81. Mary, m. GEORGE DAWSON (5–35, of this record). See forward, 5–35.

5–82. Benoni, b. June 29, 1793, m. *Eleanor Mackall* (4–44 of this record). See forward, 5–82.

4–26. *Nancy Brooks Dawson* (dau. of Benoni, 3–11), m. JOHN BEVER, of Beaver Co., Pa.; a man of prominence in that part of the state. They had one child:

5–83. Myrtilla, m. JAMES L. BOWMAN, of Brownsville, Pa., several children, all of whom, with parents, are dead.

4–27. JOHN L. DAWSON (son of Benoni, 3–11), early moved to central Ohio, and d. on his farm near Wooster, in that state. He m. *Mary Cotton*, who is also dead. They had:

5–84. Benoni, m. and res. Holmes Co., O.

5–85. John L., m. and res. Holmes Co., O. (Millersburg).

5–86. Nicholas, m. and res. Holmes Co., O.

5–87. James, m. and d.

5–88. Betsey, m.—— VULGAMOT, res. Holmes Co., O.

5–89. Rebecca, m.——.

5–90. Millie, m.——.

5–91. Rachel, m. THOMAS EWING, res. Holmes Co., O.

4-28. BENJAMIN DAWSON (son of Benoni, 3–11), was a ferry master on the Ohio river, and lived in Beaver Co., Pa., where he d. aged about 50. He m. *Elizabeth Wilkinson*, who lived to see her grand daughter's grand children. (Children of John and Mary E. Blackmore, 7–40 of this record). They had eleven children:

5–92. Amos, res. Beaver Co., Pa.; *m.*
5–93. Joshua Wilkinson, d. in Greene Co., Ind.; *m.*
5–94. George, b. July 12, 1804, d. near Calcutta, O., Aug. 9, 1866; *m.*
5–95. John Low, m. *Phebe Dix;* lives in Steuben Co., Ind.
5–96. Nancy, m. THOMAS BLACKMORE (5–80, of this record). Both d., no issue.
5–97. Catharine, m. Dr. JOHN DIXON, res. Athens Co., O., two daus., *unm.*
5–98. Olivia, d. in Wellsburg, W. Va. HARVEY.
5–99. Rebecca, m. PETER FISHER, res. Cameron, Mo. (See forward).
5–100. Eliza, m. MICHAEL FISHER, res. near Calcutta, O. (See forward).
5–101. Amassa, m. HENRY FISHER, d. She res. near Calcutta. (See forward).
5–102. Myrtilla, res. Ohioville, Pa. SCROGGS.

4-31. JAMES M. DAWSON (son of Nicholas L., 3–15), b. 1774, d. near Dawsonville, 1866, in his 92d year. He lived with his gr. father (Thomas Dawson, 2–4) at the time of the latter's death in 1800, and derived from him the information chiefly relied on as the true account of the early history of this family. He had:

5–103. Lawrence A., res. 1854, Rockville, Md.; lawyer.

4-32. WILLIAM C. DAWSON (son of Robert D., 3–17), b. in Montgomery Co., Md., 1784, removed to Logan county, Ky., 1810, and d. at Russellville, in that county, about 1848 or 1849, farmer. He m. in Maryland, 1809, Miss *Vorse* (or *Virse*) of Montgomery county. She d. in Logan Co., Ky., 1864, aged 76. They had six children:

5–104. Caleb, m. 1830,—— res. near Russellville, Ky.
5–105. Benoni, m. 1843, Miss *Hogan*, d. 1862.
5–106. George, *twin brother of Benoni*, m. 1854, Miss *Sherwood*, res. near Russellville.
5–107. William, m. 1849, Miss *Price*, res. near Russellville.
5–108. Robert, m. 1840, Miss *Darby*, d. 1871, near Russellville.
5–109. John, m. 1856, Miss *Milligan*, res. near Russellville.

4-34. *Verlinda H. Dawson* (dau. of Robert D., 3–17), m. DANIEL ALLNUTT, removed to Ky., in 1816, thence to Mo.

about 1861, where she d. a few years later. She had three children, who res. 1871, at Chillicothe, Livingston Co., Mo.

5–110. Robert.
5–111. John.
5–112. Sarah.

4–36. Stephen N. Dawson, b. in Montgomery Co., Md., Aug. 10, 1788 (son of Robert D., 3–17), served in the war of 1812, and was in the battle of Bladensburg. He removed to Logan county, Ky., 1816, and thence in 1843, to Montgomery county, Tenn., where he d. Dec. 23, 1855, aged about 67; was a large farmer, and a man of wealth and influence. He m. in Maryland, 1815, *Ann N. White*, who was b. Nov. 20, 1791, and d. Feb. 10, 1864, dau. of Stephen and Ann White, of Montgomery Co., Md. They had nine children, all b. in Logan county, Ky.:

5–113. Mary, b. April 1, 1819, res. 1873, near Russellville, Ky. McCuddy.
5–114. Thomas J., b. Jan. 14, 1821, res. near Russellville; *m.*
5–115. Stephen William, b. Sept. 5, 1822, res. 1873, Clarksville, Tenn.; *m.*
5–116. Amanda, b. Aug. 11, 1825, d. 1857, Clarksville; *unm.*
5–117. Julia, b. May 5, 1827, res. 1873, Clarksville. Rice.
5–118. Margaret, b. Jan. 3, 1830, res. Clarksville; *unm.*
5–119. Henry Clay, b. Nov. 22, 1833, res. Clarksville; *unm.*
5–120. Myrtilla, b. July 29, 1835, d. in Montgomery Co., Tenn., 1854; *unm.*
5–121. Sally, b. Feb. 1, 1837, res. Graves Co., Ky. Hester.

4–37. Robert D. Dawson, b. in Montgomery Co., Md., 1790 (son of Robert D., 3–17), removed to Logan Co., Ky., 1812, and thence to New Madrid, Mo., 1814, where he d. about 1842, aged 52 years. He was a physician, and became a prominent politican; was a member of the convention that formed the first state constitution of Missouri, and subsequently served as a state senator for many years. He m. in Missouri, Miss *Walker*, dau. of John Walker, Esq., of New Madrid, where she d. 1854, aged 50 years. They had six children, all b. at New Madrid:

5–122. Mary, m. —— Augustin.
5–123. Thomas, m. Miss *Laforge*, res. New Madrid.
5–124. Parmelia, m. Dr. Watson, res. New Madrid.
5–125. Sarah, m. —— Watson, res. New Madrid.
5–126. Laura, m. —— Laforge, res. New Madrid.
5–127. Washington, m. Miss *Lavalle*, and d. at New Madrid, 1863.

4–43. THOMAS MACKALL (son of Benjamin and *Rebecca Dawson* Mackall 3–19), m. May 7, 1846, *Catharine Dawson* (5–27 of this record), b. June 14, 1823, in Beaver Co., Pa. They had:

5–128. Myrtilla, m. SAMUEL BLACKMORE (son of Benoni, 5–81 of this record).

4–45. BENJAMIN MACKALL (son of Benjamin and *Rebecca Dawson* Mackall, 3–19), had sons:

5–129. Samuel; *m.*
5–130. James; *m.*
5–131. Thomas; *m.*

4–48. SAMUEL DAWSON (son of Nicholas, 3-21), the only child of his father who had issue, was b. in Frederick county, Md., Sept. 9, 1787. He was, like his father, a magistrate of that county, but shortly after the war of 1812-15, in which he took part as captain of militia, participating in the battles of North Point and Bladensburg, he moved to Virginia. It is said of him that he possessed an exceedingly pleasing manner, being affable, kind and charitable in a remarkable degree.[1] He lived on a farm in Loudon county, Va., not far from Point of Rocks, Md., and twelve miles below Harper's Ferry. He d. Dec. 11, 1845, his first two children being then grown, and his other six young. He m. 1st, about 1819, *Ann Mason* (dau. of Thompson Mason, and grand dau. of George Mason, author of the Va. Bill of Rights). They had two children:

5–132. Eugenie.[2]
5–133. Mason.[3]

Mr. Dawson m. 2d, March 20, 1834, *Sarah A. Bayne*, his first cousin (dau. of Colman Bayne, Esq., of Accomac county, Va.). They had six children:

---

[1] "He was the best man of the name I have ever known or heard of. It is grateful to the feelings of his children, to hear his name, even at this distance of time, by the lowly, as well as well as by those in high station, mentioned in terms of commendation." N. D. (5-134), 1871.

[2] She m. a Mr. HOUGH, and resided in Morehouse Parish, La. She lost her husband and property during the civil war, and returned, directly after the close of hostilities, to Leesburg, Va., with her three minor children — two sons and a dau.

[3] He moved, after his father's death, to Morehouse Parish, La., and was a prosperous planter there until the commencement of the civil war, in which he took part as a private, and d. in the service of his state from fever, leaving a widow, and one child, a dau.

5–134. Nicholas.[1]
5–135. Charles G., m. and res. 1871, in Atlantic City, Cass Co., Iowa, a merchant.
5–136. Arthur, merchant, res. 1871, Leesburg, Loudon Co., Va ; *unm.*
5–137. Elizabeth H., m. RICHARD H. AYRES, Accomac Co., Va. ; one child, a daughter.
5–138. M. Henrietta, res. 1871, Leesburg, Va. ; *unm.*
5–139. Roger T., m. 1870, *Mattie Chamblin,* of Leesburg, Va., res. 1872, Point of Rocks, Md. ; merchant.

5–1. *Sarah Dawson* (dau. of George, 4–2), m. GEORGE ASHMAN. They resided at Connellsville, Fayette Co., Pa., where both d. They had three children:

6–1. Kate F., res. 1873, Connellsville; *unm.*
6–2. Louisa, m. D. H. VEECH, res. Pittsburg, Pa.
6–3. George Dawson, res. Connellsville.

5–2. Hon. JOHN LITTLETON DAWSON[2] (son of George 4–2), was b. at Uniontown, Fayette county, Pa., Feb. 7, 1813. His father removed to Brownsville during his infancy. He received a liberal education, pursuing his studies successively at Jefferson College, Pa., Kenyon College, Ohio, and Washington College, Pa., receiving his degree at the latter. While at these institutions he applied himself with special care to the studies and arts which have relation to public speaking. At Kenyon he was the contemporary of Judge David Davis, now of the Supreme Court of the United States, and of the late Edwin M. Stanton, with both of whom, though divided from them in political sentiment, he ever maintained relations of personal friendship. Endowed by nature with abilities of a high order, with wit, humor and geniality in large degree, with an imposing person, graceful and dignified manners, a voice of great power and melody, an energy of character which never flagged, and a flow of spirits which never ebbed, Mr. Dawson seemed born for public life, and destined to a distinguished career.

He read law in Uniontown, under the direction of his uncle, the Hon. John Dawson, and was admitted to the bar in 1836. In 1838 he was appointed by Governor Porter, Deputy Attorney

---

[1] He entered the army of Virginia, and served that state during the war against the Union. He removed to Baltimore in 1869, where he is a merchant, and *unm.*

[2] For this sketch the compiler has drawn from several newspaper notices of Mr. Dawson, published within a few days after his death, using the same language when convenient. He is especially indebted to the Pittsburg *Daily Post,* the Uniontown *Genius of Liberty,* the Omaha *Daily Herald* and the Philadelphia *Daily Press.*

John L. Dawson

General for Fayette county, and in 1845, by appointment of President Polk, he became United States Attorney for the Western District of Pennsylvania. This position he filled with marked ability until 1849. In 1848 he was the candidate of the democratic party for Congress in the district then composed of Fayette, Green and Somerset counties, but was defeated. He was renominated in 1850, and after a spirited canvass, elected on the same ticket a representative from this district to the thirty-second Congress. He was instantly recognized as a powerful accession to the democratic side of the house, and took a high place among the leaders of that party. In 1852 he was again nominated and elected by a district composed of Fayette, Washington and Greene counties. During the latter term he served as chairman of the Committee on Agriculture, which then had charge of a variety of business now divided between the committees on Agriculture, Public Lands, and Pacific Railroads. After a few years of voluntary retirement from public life, he was elected to Congress for a third term, from Fayette, Westmoreland and Indiana counties, in 1862, and reëlected from the same district in 1864. At the expiration of this term he declined another nomination. He was a frequent member of the state and national conventions of his party; a delegate to the conventions which nominated Mr. Polk for the presidency in 1844, Mr. Cass in 1848, Mr. Pierce in 1852, and of the Cincinnati convention of 1856, at which latter he made the speech, acknowledging, on behalf of Pennsylvania, the nomination of Mr. Buchanan for the presidency. He was also a member of the Charleston convention of 1860, and the New York convention of 1868. He was appointed governor of Kansas, by President Pierce, in 1855, but his strong local and home attachments induced him to decline the office, though it was urgently pressed upon him in the belief that he might be instrumental of great good in tranquilizing that disturbed territory. In 1868 his name was sent to the senate by President Johnson for confirmation as minister to Russia, and although it was well known that he had not sought the place and did not desire it, with such general respect and favor was he regarded that he failed of confirmation by only two votes in a senate composed almost entirely of political opponents.

During the administration of President Pierce, and soon after his entrance into Congress, Mr. Dawson was distinguished for bringing forward the Homestead bill, which had been previously defeated; and with the addition of a number of important provisions prepared by himself, pressing it, with rare force, eloquence and parliamentary tact, almost to a successful result. Though it failed for the time, he had the gratification of seeing it subsequently revived and enacted into a law. By this law it was sought to preserve the public domain for the use of actual settlers, and to furnish homes for all who desired them in the fertile plains and valleys of the Great West. Its wisdom is daily exemplified in the growing wealth and influence of the populous trans-Mississippi states that contribute so lavishly to the material wealth and prosperity of the country.[1]

Mr. Dawson was equally conspicuous for his faithful and persistent opposition to every scheme whereby it was sought to give the control of large bodies of the public lands to monopolists and speculators. He was, indeed, the stern and unyielding opponent of every form and grade of corruption and legislative extravagance, and to his efforts the country is indebted for many of the best laws that mark the national legislation of his time.

As a public man he left an unsullied record, which will always stand as a memorial of his unbending fidelity and incorruptible integrity, and as a private citizen his character was without a blemish.[2] In the family circle it shone especially bright. He

---

[1] "To the original Homestead bill Mr. Dawson drafted some important amendments, and by his intense zeal and unwearied efforts it was twice passed through the House of Representatives in the form in which it came from his committee. It was at length returned by the Senate with amendments which practically defeated the whole object of the bill, and left Mr. Dawson no alternative but to report his original bill to the House as the only one he could ever approve. He did so, and finding his term of public service drawing to a close, left this great measure to the care of his friends and associates, with a vindication of its goodness and wisdom which no man ventured to answer, and which time has converted into prophecy. But his interest in the success of his policy did not terminate with his official trust. On the contrary, his influence in its favor, although exerted from a private station, was sensibly felt throughout the whole struggle which preceded its final establishment. The revolution of a few years brought him that sort of triumph which statesmen prize above all others. He saw his favorite measure grow steadily in public esteem until, substantially as drafted by his own hand, it was enacted by a Congress controlled by his political opponents, signed by a President for whom he had not voted, and incorporated among the laws of his country almost as sacred and as highly cherished as the Constitution itself." From a *Sketch* by Chauncey F. Black, Esq., intended to be introductory to a collection of Mr. Dawson's Speeches.

[2] "The sagacity of his judgment upon men, and his own social fidelity, were proved by the surest of all tests. With him time and trials deepened every attachment of his

was devotedly attached to his home, and beloved by his family. He was familiar with all the history and traditions of the Monongahela valley, and felt a pleasure in recounting the local incidents of by-gone years. He was also warmly attached to his personal and political friends, and nothing gave him more gratification than seeing them at his own house. His hospitality was unbounded, and it was dispensed in a manner so entirely void of ostentation as to render all in his presence as free from restraint as if they were sitting down around their own firesides.

---

own heart, and intensified the admiration of those who possessed his confidence. If any man ever lived a life of scrupulous integrity, it was he. No temptation could move him one hair's breadth from his steadfast purpose to do justice and execute faithfully the trusts confided to him. He was not without that 'last infirmity of noble minds,' the ambition which seeks to deserve the confidence of his fellow men, and to do them all the good in his power. But he never sought place for his own sake, nor used office for his personal pleasure or profit. He served the people of his district for eight years in Congress, because he believed it his duty to do so; but he declined to be Secretary of the Commonwealth when the office was pressed upon him by the Governor, and refused the Governorship of Kansas when the President solicited him to take it. His character, as a public man, was formed upon the models which he found in the history of other times than these. We do not liken him to Cato, for he was a far better man than Cato, without one particle of his pretentious austerity. Indeed it was not the doubtful morality of Plutarch's heroes which excited his admiration: he drew the inspiration of his public life from the great statesmen of the Virginia school, who led the councils of the nation in the golden age of this republic. In the general cast of his mind, in his ardent love for the pure pleasures of country life and agricultural employment, in his keen sense of justice, his lofty scorn of wrong and his unmitigated contempt of whatever was base or false or hypocritical, in his profuse hospitality, in his devoted attachment to his friends, of the humblest as well as the highest classes, in his constant fidelity to his political convictions, in the immovable steadfastness of his honesty which made him set his face like a flint against all schemes of corruption in Congress, in all these respects, he bore a striking resemblance to Alexander Macon and John Taylor of Carolina.

"This is not the place to dilate upon Mr. Dawson's public services. The ardor, energy, and ability with which he pressed and carried the measures which he believed to be necessary for the general good, are seen in his speeches, and the other memorials of his work. But it is due to his memory that we should mention one or two facts which are not yet on any record. When Mr. Dawson was a private citizen (in 1857 or 1858) a matter in which he was largely interested, involving, indeed, a considerable part of his fortune, was referred to a cabinet officer who was his devoted personal as well as political friend, and with whom he was in habits of daily intercourse. He never once alluded to the subject, or made known the fact of his interest, for the reason, that, as it was a question of justice and law, the decision ought not to be influenced by personal considerations of any kind. Afterwards, when a measure in which he was very remotely and indirectly interested came before the Congress of which he was a member, he neither spoke nor voted for it, but quietly absented himself without making the slightest demonstration, or giving any reason for his conduct, or claiming any merit whatever. These incidents show his scrupulous and delicate sense of official propriety, and are given, because they illustrate the principles upon which he habitually acted, and because they happen to be within the special knowledge of the writer." * * * *

Hon. Jeremiah S. Black, in the Pittsburg *Daily Gazette*, Sept. 27, 1870.

He was a man of liberal public spirit, and was among the foremost in the promotion of measures for the development of the material resources of the country. He held the position of director of the Pittsburg, Fort Wayne and Chicago Rail Road, and was actively engaged in the development of the mineral interests of the Lake Superior region. In business affairs he was equally remarkable as in public life for careful preparation and far seeing wisdom, and his efforts were crowned with abundant success. And in business, as in politics, his honor and integrity were never called in question, in the hottest controversies, with the bitterest foes.[1]

---

[1] At the risk of occupying undue space (for a work of this character), the compiler cannot refrain from quoting the following admirable description, by Chauncey F. Black, Esq., of one Mr. Dawson's political speeches. It is from a *Sketch* (before noticed) prepared to accompany a volume of Mr. Dawson's speeches, about to be published. The compiler's acknowledgments are due to Mr. Black for his courtesy in permitting such use to be made of his MS.:

"It was shortly after the close of the civil war, and toward the termination of Mr. Dawson's life, that the writer saw him stand in the midst of a little assemblage of his country neighbors, and deliver an address of most singular and fascinating eloquence. The times were full of peril to the free institutions of the country; the evil passions excited by war had not yet subsided, and the various limits of Federal power were still in debate. Under these circumstances the people of Mr. Dawson's neighborhood had assembled to the number of a hundred and fifty or two hundred, in the open street of a little village on the banks of the Monongahela. The chairman of this rustic gathering had taken his seat on a porch elevated a foot or two above the roadway, deposited his hat, with a red handcherchief visible above the rim, conspicuously near his feet, and was proceeding with the business of the day much as if he was presiding at his own fireside. Opposite him, and at the farther side of the road, lay a log sheltered from the meridian sun by the ample foliage of an apple tree. On this log, amidst a group of the elder farmers, sat Mr. Dawson, in a posture of courteous attention, but seeing little, for he was then almost blind, and in the following year was obliged to suffer an operation for cataract. He had not come to speak, and, refusing to be persuaded, had taken this retired position, by way of intimation that importunities would be of no avail. The several addresses were — with one exception — excellent after their kind — indeed, far above the average of political harangues — but at each concluding sentence an agitating murmur ran through the little assembly, accompanied by earnest but respectful appeals to Mr. Dawson to break his unaccustomed silence. At length he arose, slowly, but with a kind of grace in singular harmony with the occasion, and leaning heavily with one hand upon a rude cane, uttered a few simple but impressive words, which seemed less like the exordium of a regular address, than the solemn admonition of one neighbor to another upon a subject of deep and mutual concern.

"Then came a momentary and appropriate pause, while the more aged and sedate secured places beneath the tree, and all drawing as near as possible leaned forward in attitudes of fixed attention. It was then that, to the eye of at least one of his auditors, he presented a figure inexpressibly majestic and venerable.

"The simplicity and dignity of his manner; the stateliness of his form, erect and firm as one of the oaks that grew in his own forest; his serene and noble countenance; his superb head, covered with an abundance of iron-grey locks; his dark eye, imperial even in its infirmity, but betraying its weakness by a slight wandering as if in search of the familiar light; made the whole spectacle at once affecting and sublime. The tones of his voice, which at first had been low and sweet, became gradually high and

He was one of the sufferers from the mysterious sickness which followed the public dinner at the National Hotel in Washington at the time of the inauguration of President Buchanan. Mr. Dawson's life was for a long time despaired of, but his powerful physical organization finally triumphed, although it is probable he never wholly recovered from the effects of the subtle poison to which was attributed the death of so many well known men, or the melancholy impairment of their powers which left them only a "lingering life."

He died at his elegant estate called Friendship Hill (the former home of Albert Gallatin), on the Monongahela river, near Geneva, on the 18th September, 1870, and on the 21st his remains were buried, as he had requested, in the grounds of the Episcopal church at Brownsville, a few miles distant.

"At the dawn of light a concourse of friends and neighbors gathered in the halls of the old mansion to participate in the simple but impressive ceremonies that attended the removal of the body from the home of the family to the steamer which lay

---

sonorous. He passed rapidly over some of the features of the late war, the melancholy strife of brethren in which victory was only less disastrous than defeat, the waste of treasure, the flow of blood, the desolation of homes, the torn bosoms and broken hearts, which marked the passage of that sad and needless carnage. With a few rapid touches he displayed in bold outlines the natural bonds of union between the states, the mutual dependence of interests, and the matchless power and glory which might be anticipated from their harmonious development.

"These were material considerations which reasonable men might not overlook. But it was when he spoke of the divine origin of mercy, and depicted the broken fortunes, the stricken hearts, the humbled pride, and the pure anguish of the vanquished, that he produced the strongest and most sensible effects.

"Then, availing himself of the better feelings of men awakened by this pathetic appeal, he told them how, in all times, the Almighty had punished the diabolical passion of revenge when indulged by one community against another. Those states which armed against the liberties of another, were in danger of losing their own: that people, which, tempted by the love of conquest or power, sought to trample down constitutional freedom in one section of the country, must be content to see it sacrificed in all. With startling force and precision, he traced this retributive process in the recent history of the United States, whereby a government which but lately was popular had now become imperial, and rights which had ever been held sacred were surrendered in rapid and fatal succession, the freedom of elections, the writ of habeas corpus, trial by jury, the sanctity of home and correspondence, with many others essential to the existence of a free state. And here, the tones of his voice, while even more distinct and penetrating than before, were low and solemn, as of one who delivers a message of strange and awful import. Concluding with an animated, but kindly appeal to the generation before him to preserve unimpaired the heritage which their fathers had kept for them, Mr. Dawson, in silence profound and almost oppressive, resumed his seat on the log near which he had stood. And if in all that stream of marvellous elocution there had been nothing else to be remembered, every listener would have carried away in his heart the lingering echoes of that voice, of which the compass and melody were surpassing among men."

in waiting to carry it to its last resting place. Between Geneva and Brownsville the funeral steamer was met by another which transferred to it sympathizing friends from many distant parts. At Brownsville, after a brief interval, during which many that knew and honored him in life looked for the last time on the features of the dead, the remains were carried to the church, and there, in presence of a numerous and deeply affected throng, were committed to the earth, according to the awful and beautiful solemnities appointed by the Church. Mr. Dawson sleeps among the nearest of his kindred, close to his mother, and closer to his child."[1]

Mr. Dawson m. Oct. 20, 1836, *Mary Clarke*, dau. of Robert and *Sarah Whaley* Clarke, of Brownsville. She survives him. They had four children, all b. at Brownsville:

6–4. Sarah Kennedy, b. Sept., 1838, res. 1873, Pittsburg, Pa. SPEER.
6–5. Louisa Cass, b. Oct. 4, 1839, res. 1873, Pittsburg. PATTERSON.
6–6. Mary Clarke, b. June 13, 1842, res. 1873, York, Pa. BLACK.
6–7. George Littleton, b. March 29, 1846, d. at Morgantown, Va., while attending school, Oct. 17, 1860.

5–4. *Louisa Dawson* (dau. of George, 4-2), m. Gen. GEO. W. CASS,[2] of Pittsburg, Pa. She d. leaving one dau.:

6–8. Sophia Lord, m. FRANK N. HUTCHINSON, and res. 1873, at Sewickly, Beaver Co., Pa.

Gen. Cass m. 2d:

5–8. *Ellen Dawson* (youngest daughter of George, 4-2). They res. 1873, in New York city.

5–5. *Elizabeth Dawson* (daughter of George, 4-2), d. 1868, w. of ALFRED HOWELL, Esq., a lawyer of distinction, residing, 1873, at Uniontown, Pa. Six children:

6–9. Mary Kennedy.
6–10. Frances.
6–11. Ellen Cass.
6–12. George Dawson.
6–13. Benjamin Betterton.
6–14. Catharine Wilson.

5–6. *Catharine Harrison Dawson* (daughter of George, 4-2),

---

[1] From a memorial volume, privately printed.

[2] Son of George W. Cass, who d. at Dresden, Ohio, Aug. 6, 1873, in his 83d year; for 73 years a resident of Ohio; brother of Gen. Lewis Cass, of Michigan, and son of Major Jonathan Cass, of whose family he was the last survivor.

d. at Uniontown, about 1864, m. Hon. A. EVANS WILLSON. He res. 1873, at Uniontown, judge of the district court of Fayette county. Three children:

6–15. Eliza Evans.
6–16. Catharine Dawson.
6–17. Mary Kennedy.

5–9. Gen. SAMUEL KENNEDY DAWSON (son of George, 4-2),[1] m. *Jeannette Weston*, and res. 1873, at Eastport, Me. Two children:

6–18. Jeannette.
6–19. Mary Kennedy.

5–10. GEORGE FIELDING DAWSON (son of George, 4–2), m. *Mary Patterson*, dau. of Alfred Patterson (Pres. of the Bank of Commerce, Pittsburg) and w. *Caroline Whiteley*. They res. 1873, at Connellsville, Fayette Co., Pa. He is of the firm of Dawson & Bailey, proprietors of the locomotive works at that place. Four children:

6–20. Alfred Russell, b. Oct., 1860.
6–21. Caroline Whiteley.
6–22. Mary Kennedy.
6–23. Elsie Patterson.

5–21. THOMAS DAWSON, b. June 11, 1811 (son of William, 4-5), m. *Rebecca Mackall*, dau. of Samuel (5-129). They reside in Indiana. Children:

6–24. Harrison, m.—— *Mackall.*
6–25. Benjamin, *unm.*
6–26. William, *unm.*
6–27. Thomas, d.
6–28. Catharine, m. SAMUEL PUGH.

5–24. BENONI DAWSON, b. Aug. 4, 1817 (son of William, 4-5), m. Sept. 4, 1842, *Elizabeth Dawson*, b. April 25, 1820 (dau. of George, 4-19). They res. 1873, at Georgetown, Beaver Co., Pa. Five children, all b. at Georgetown:

---

[1] "Cadet, 1835; second lieut. 1st artillery, July 1, 1839; first lieut., June, 1846; brevetted captain, for gallant and meritorious conduct in battle of Cerro Gordo (April 18, 1847), July, 1848; regimental quartermaster, April, 1848; captain, March, 1853; distinguished in conflict with large force of Seminoles, in Big Cypress, Fla., April, 1856; major, May 14, 1861; lieut. col., July 1, 1863; colonel, July 28, 1866."—Gardner's *Army Dictionary.* He retired from the army in 1873, holding at the time the rank of brigadier general.

6–29. Ellen, b. June 9, 1843, m. JAMES KINSEY, Jan. 10, 1867, and res. 1873, at Georgetown.
6–30. George, b. Sept. 22, 1844, res. Georgetown ; *m.*
6–31. Harrison, b. May 11, 1846, res. Georgetown ; *m.*
6–32. Myrtilla J., b. Aug. 27, 1848, m. March 7, 1868, CLIFFORD CROSS: res. Georgetown.
6–33. William H., b. April 24, 1852, d. March 26, 1853.

5-31. WILLIAM C. DAWSON (son of John, 4-7), b. in Champaign Co., Ohio, 1816, m. in same county, 1853, harness maker, res. 1873, in Petersburg, Ill. Two children:[1]

6–34. Mary Alice.
6–35. George D. Prentice.

5-35. GEORGE DAWSON (son of Thomas, 4-17), m. *Mary Blackmore* (5-81 of this record). They lived at Glasgow, Beaver Co., Pa., where he d. She is still living, 1873 ; seven children :

6–36. Benoni, m. 1st, *Cynthia Dawson*, dau. of Amos (5–92 of this record). 2d, *Ann E. Johnson.* Lived near Glasgow, Pa. No issue of either marriage.
6–37. James, lived at Glasgow ; *m.*
6–38. Nicholas, m. *Margaret Wright* ; res. near Austin, Texas.
6–39. George, *unm.*
6–40. William, res. Glasgow ; *m.*
6–41. Hawkins, d. in Glasgow ; *m.*
6–42. Nancy, m. THOMAS DAWSON (5–58 of this record).

5-41. *Rebecca Dawson* (dau. of Thomas, 4-17), m. ROBERT REED. Two children:

6–43. John, drowned.
6–44. Benoni, m.——, res. Beaver Co., Pa.

5-51. Capt. DANIEL DAWSON (son of Benoni, 4-18), m. *Mary Ann Blackmore*, dau. of Samuel (5-76 of this record). She d. leaving four children:

6–45. Samuel, m. *Hattie Anderson.*
6–46. John, *unm.*
6–47. Kate, m. HARRY BOYD.
6–48. Ida, *unm.*

5-57. NICHOLAS DAWSON (son of Mackall, 4-20), m. *Eliza Harvey.* Seven children :

[1] To Mr. Dawson the compiler is indebted for some account of the descendants of John Dawson, 3–4 of this record, in the line of his son John, 4-7. Information from other sources has enabled the compiler to determine the place belonging to these families in this record.

6–49. Harvey, m. *Eliza Elliott;* res. near Alleghany city, Pa.; one ch.
6–50. George W., m. Miss *Reed;* res. Beaver, Pa.; several children.
6–51. Amos, *unm.*
6–52. Myrtilla, m. LAUGHLIN ELLIOTT; 5 children.
6–53. Mary, m. W. B. Allen; res. Cleveland, O.; one child.
6–54. Louisa, m. Dr. LANGFITT, res. Alleghany city, Pa.; one child.
6–55. Abrilla, *unm.*

5–58. THOMAS DAWSON (son of Mackall, 4-20), m. 1st, *Nancy Dawson*, dau. of George (5-35 of this record). She d. leaving three children:

6–56. George, m. *Eliza Duncan;* res. Ohioville, Pa.; 2 children.
6–57. Nicholas, *unm.*
6–58. Elizabeth, m. BENJAMIN LITTELL, res. Glasgow, Pa.; one child.

Mr. Dawson m. 2d, *Eliza Eggleson* Dawson, widow of Hawkins Dawson (6-41 of this record). Res. Beaver Co., Pa.

5–59. BENONI DAWSON (son of Mackall, 4-20), m. *Sarah Ann Harvey*. Nine children:

6–59. J. H., m. *Mary McKean*, res. Steubenville, O.; 4 children.
6–60. Homer C., m. *Jenny Pennybacker;* one child.
6–61. Job H., *unm.*
6–62. Mackall, m.——.
6–63. Eliza, m. MARTIN SIMMS, res. Steubenville, O.; one child.
6–64. Rachel, *unm.*
6–65. Elma, *unm.*
6–66. Rebecca, *unm.*
6–67. Benjamin, *unm.*

5–60. *Abrilla Dawson* (dau. of Mackall, 4-20), m. PHILIP HILL. Res. Steubenville, Ohio. Twelve children, of whom only the following are now living:

6–68. Mackall Dawson, m. *Rachel Moore*, res. Steubenville; physician; several children.
6–69. Rachel, m. JOHN FISHER, killed in the battle of the Wilderness; six children.
6–70. Myrtilla, m. SAMUEL BLACKMORE, son of Thomas (5-77 of this record).
6–71. Nathaniel P., *unm.*
6–72. Eliza, m. J. B. SMITH, d. leaving one child.

5–62. *Susan Dawson* (dau. of Mackall, 4-20), m. JOHN CROFT. Four children:

6–73. West, m. Miss *Henderson.*
6–74. Chalkley, m.——.
6–75. Sarah Ann, d.
6–76. Hannah, *unm.*

5-64. MACKALL DAWSON (son of Nicholas, 4-21), tanner, m. *Elizabeth Reeder*; both d. in Adams Co., Ohio. They had four children:

6–77. William, lived at Alleghany City, Pa.; killed in the war, his w. also d.
6–78. Samuel K., b. April, 1826, m. June, 1847, *Mary Simpson*, b. in Dundee, Scotland, Dec., 1826. They res. Alleghany City. He is a machinist in the Fort Wayne shops, at that place.
6–79. Rachel.
6–80. Elizabeth, m. LORENZO F. FLETCHER, res. Van Wert Co., O.; several children.

5-65. AUGUSTINE M. DAWSON, merchant, b. at Smith's Ferry, Beaver Co., Pa., Feb. 19, 1800 (son of Nicholas, 4-21), res. 1873, Calcutta, O. He m. 1st, Nov. 16, 1826, *Maria Bever*, b. at Smith's Ferry, Nov. 23, 1801, d. Dec. 25, 1846. They had eight children:

6–81. Lavinia Bever, b. Aug. 29, 1827, res. 1873, Georgetown, Pa. HAMILTON.
6–82. Nicholas, b. May 27, 1829, d. Oct. 18, 1836.
6–83. William Bever, b. June 6, 1831, res. 1873, Canfield, O.; *m.*
6–84. Maria Jane Bever, b. Aug. 20, 1833, res. 1873, Calcutta, O. THOMPSON.
6–85. John Bever, b. Sept. 5, 1836, res. Calcutta, O.; *unm.*
6–86. Rachel Moore, b. Nov. 29, 1838, m. BENJAMIN PATTERSON DAWSON, son of Joshua W. (5–93 of this record). See forward, 6–146.
6–87. Augustine Moore, b. March 1, 1842, res. Haysville, Clay Co., N. C.; *m.*
6–88. Myrtilla Bowman, b. Jan. 15, 1845, d. Aug. 17, 1847.

Mr. Dawson m. 2d, July 24, 1849, *Mary Mendell*, who d. Jan. 14, 1851. They had one child:

6–89. Sarah Elizabeth, b. May 22, 1850, d. Sept. 29, 1850.

Mr. Dawson m. 3d, April 18, 1859, *Sarah C. Selby*, of Washington Co., Ohio. To him and to his son, Mr. John Bever Dawson, the compiler acknowledges his obligations for valuable assistance in the compilation of these records. Without the information obtained from them, an account of the descendants of Benoni Dawson (3-11 of this record), would have been almost entirely wanting.

5-66. BENONI DAWSON, farmer (son of Nicholas, 4-21), m. *Margaret Pollock*. They lived near Calcutta, O., where he

d. aged 71, and she d. Jan. 25, 1867, aged 58. Six children living:

6-90. Rachel m. THOMAS MARSHALL, res. near Alliance, O.
6-91. Jane, m. JAMES ORR.
6-92. Verlinda, m. JOHN M. KENNEY, merchant, res. Ohioville, Beaver Co., Pa.; three children.
6-93. Augustine, m.—— *Mackall*, res. Kansas.
6-94. Nancy, m. DAVID DUNCAN, livery stable proprietor, res. Alleghany City, Pa.; two children.
6-95. Benoni, *unm.*

5-67. WILLIAM DAWSON, tailor (son of Nicholas, 4-21), m. *Ann Irwin*, and lived at Alleghany City, Pa., where he d. Dec., 1872. Four children living:

6-96. Nicholas, m.——, res. Evansville, Ind.
6-97. Barbara Maria, m. JOHN HURFORD, clerk, res. Alleghany City, Pa.; three children.
6-98. William H., *unm.*
6-99. John, *unm.*

5-68. GEORGE A. DAWSON, farmer (son of Nicholas, 4-21), b. Nov. 3, 1817, m. Sept. 8, 1846, *Lucinda Swearingen*, b. Sept. 1, 1819, dau. of Benoni and Ruth Swearingen. She res. 1873, near Belair, Crawford Co., Ill. Six children, all *unm.*:

6-100. Sarah Ellen, b. May 29, 1847.
6-101. Lavinia Bever, b. Sept. 6, 1849, d. Feb. 27, 1858.
6-102. John Mayhew, b. July 11, 1851.
6-103. Barbara Maria, b. Aug. 24, 1853.
6-104. Augustine Moore, b. April 9, 1856.
6-105. George A., b. Oct. 17, 1858.

5-72. *Barbara Jones Dawson* (dau. of Nicholas, 4-21), d. in Medina Co., O., m. JAMES ARMSTRONG, and had four children:

6-106. William, m.——.
6-107. Elizabeth, *unm.*
6-108. Caroline, m. —— DADE, civil engineer, res. Ky.
6-109. Adelia, m.—— LORING, res. Iowa.

Mr. Armstrong m. again, and res. 1873, Belpre, Washington Co., O.

5-73. *Rebecca Dawson*, b. Feb. 7, 1810 (dau. of Nicholas, 4-21), m. THOMAS CREIGHTON. They lived near Calcutta,

O., where she d. Dec. 11, 1869, aged 59. They had one child:

6–110. [CREIGHTON.] Verlinda, m.—— MACKALL, farmer, res. near Calcutta; two children.

5-74. *Rachel Dawson* (dau. of Nicholas, 4-21), m. JOHN ARMSTRONG (bro. of James, 5-72). They res. 1873, near Calcutta, O., and have had ten children:

6–111. Jared M., b. March 2, 1834, d. Jan. 30, 1861, m. *Josephine A. Wise*, of Catlettsburg, Ky.; one dau.
6–112. James P., b. June 15, 1838, d. June 13, 1861, aged 22.
6–113. Rachel N., b. Nov. 19, 1840, d. May 18, 1861, aged 20.
6–114. Helena, b. Feb. 2, 1844, d. Oct. 16, 1851, aged 7.
6–115. Mary E., b. March 14, 1846, d. Oct. 2, 1851, aged 5.
6–116. John Z., b. Aug. 25, 1848, d. May 28, 1861, aged 12.
6–117. Lizzie C., b. Nov. 16, 1853, d. May 20, 1861, aged 7.
6–118. Zena, b. March 27, 1856, d. May 17, 1861, aged 5.
6–119. Ermina, res. Calcutta, O., *unm.*
6–120. Minerva, res. Calcutta, *unm.*

5-76. SAMUEL BLACKMORE (son of James, 4-23), m. 1st, Miss *Poe*, who d. without issue. 2d, *Jane Bane.* Two chn.:

6–121. John, m. *Mary E. Richeson*, gr. dau. of Michael and *Eliza Dawson* Fisher (5-100 of this record).
6–122. Mary Ann, m. Capt. DANIEL DAWSON (5-51 of this record).

5-77. THOMAS BLACKMORE (son of James, 4-23), m. *Sarah Laughlin.* They had four children:

6–123. Samuel, m. *Myrtilla Hill* (6-70 of this record).
6–124. James, d. young.
6–125. Nancy, m.——.
6–126. Mary, m.—— MERRICK. No issue.

5-79. *Rebecca Blackmore* (dau. of James, 4-23), m. JAMES FITZSIMMONS. Five children, and many gr. children. The names of the latter not communicated. Children:

6–127. James, m. *Rachel Todd.*
6–128. Thomas, m. *Mary Fisher.*
6–129. Rebecca, m. ABNER LENARD.
6–130. Betsey, m. THOMAS MANSFIELD.
6–131. Nancy, m. SAMUEL TODD.

5-82. BENONI BLACKMORE, b. in Brooke Co., Va., now Hancock Co., W. Va., June 29, 1793 (son of Charles, 4-24), m. Sept 18, 1817, *Eleanor Mackall*, who was b. in Frederick

Co., Md., Jan. 10, 1796 (dau. of Benjamin, 3–19 of this record). They removed to Columbiana county, Ohio, and settled upon a farm there early in the year 1818, where they remained until March, 1853, at which time they removed, with their family, to Greene county, Indiana. They purchased a homestead at Scotland, in this county, where he d. Oct. 3, 1870, and where she still res. 1873. They had ten children, all b. in Columbiana Co., Ohio:

6–132. George W., b. Sept. 24, 1818, res. 1873, Scotland, Ind., farmer and merchant; *unm.*
6–133. Benjamin M., b. June 19, 1820, d. Jan., 1822.
6–134. Elizabeth, b. April 20, 1822, d. Jan., 1826.
6–135. Charles, b. Oct. 25, 1824, res. Scotland, Ind., farmer and merchant; *unm.*
6–136. Thomas D., b. Nov. 20, 1826, d. Jan., 1834.
6–137. Samuel, b. March 17, 1828, res. Scotland, Ind.; *m.*
6–138. Dawson, b. June 23, 1831, res. Washington, Ind.; *m.*
6–139. Benoni, b. Feb. 28, 1834, res. California; *unm.*
6–140. James B., b. June 16, 1836, res. Scotland, Ind.; *m.*
6–141. Rebecca Jane, b. Sept. 9, 1838, res. Scotland, Ind. OGDEN.

5–92. AMOS DAWSON (son of Benjamin, 4-28), m. *Rebecca Dawson* (5-61 of this record). Res. Beaver Co., Pa. Nine children:

6–142. Benjamin, m. Miss *Hughes*, res. near Smith's Ferry, Beaver Co., Pa.
6–143. Mackall, m. *Susan Fisher*, dau. of Michael and *Eliza Dawson* Fisher (5-100 of this record). Res. near Smith's Ferry, Pa.
6–144. Joshua, m. Miss *Camp*, res. near Smith's Ferry.
6–145. James L. B., m. *Mary Ann Smith*, res. Beaver Falls, Pa.
6–146. Thomas, m. but w. d. childless; he was a Capt. in the late war; res. 1873, Chicago, Ill.
6–147. Scroggs, m. Miss *Calhoun*, res. near Smith's Ferry, Pa.
6–148. Amos, m. Miss *Hamilton*, res. near Smith's Ferry.
6–149. Cynthia, m. BENONI DAWSON (6-36 of this record).

5–93. JOSHUA WILKINSON DAWSON (son of Benjamin, 4-28), m. *Mary McLaughlin*, and d. in Greene Co., Indiana. Nine children, all res. in that county:

6–150. Benjamin Patterson, m. *Rachel Moore Dawson* (6–86 of this record). See forward, 6–150.
6–151. Amos Marion, m. *Mary Ann Leply.*
6–152. Joseph Henry, *unm.*
6–153. Franklin, m.——.
6–154. Charles, *unm.*

6–155. Ann Louisa, m. SAMUEL RECORD.
6–156. Helen C., m. JOHN FERGUSON.
6–157. Isabella Carpenter, m.—— WINTERS.
6–158. Mary Josephine, m.—— COBB.

5-94. GEORGE DAWSON, farmer, b. July 12, 1804 (son of Benjamin, 4-28), m. *Narcissa Bever Dawson*, b. Feb. 11, 1806 (dau. of Nicholas, 4-21). They lived near Calcutta, O., where she d. March 14, 1853, aged 47. Eleven children:

6–159. Elizabeth, b. April 9, 1826, d. in Ohio, Oct. 3, 1852, aged 26.
6–160. Rachel, b. Oct. 31, 1827, m. ELIJAH MOORE, and d. in Ohio, July 3, 1864, aged 36.
6–161. Benjamin, m.——.
6–162. William, m. *Ermina Calvin*, of Calcutta, O.; res. near Chenoa, McLean Co., Ill.; farmer.
6–163. Verlinda, m.——.
6–164. Nancy Ann, m.——.
6–165. *Infant*, b. Feb. 28, 1840, d. next day.
6–166. Mary, *unm.*
6–167. Thomas, *unm.*
6–168. Narcissa V., b. Aug. 18, 1847, d. Feb. 19, 1848.
6–169. Franklin, b. July 11, 1849, d. Feb. 22, 1851.

Mr. Dawson m. 2d, *Ellen Souder*, and d. Aug. 9, 1866, aged 62.

5-98. *Olivia Dawson* (dau. of Benjamin, 4-28), m. HARRISON HARVEY, of Wellsburgh, W. Va., where she d. leaving children:

6–170. Benjamin, m.——.
6–171. Amos, m.——.
6–172. Mary, unm., res. with her father, in Wellsburgh.

5-99. *Rebecca Dawson* (dau. of Benjamin, 4-28), m. PETER FISHER. Res. Cameron, Clinton Co., Mo. Children:

6–173. Catharine, m. Dr. GEO. McCOOK, of Pittsburg, Pa.; d. leaving one son.
6–174. Caroline, m. WILSON SMITH, Calcutta, O.
6–175. Elizabeth, m.——, res. St. Joseph, Mo.
6–176. Benjamin, m. *Mary Orr*, res. Calcutta, O.
6–177. Harry, m. Miss *Ruby*, res. Clinton Co., Mo.
6–178. George, d. of disease contracted in the army.
6–179. M. Van Buren, d. in the army.
6–180. Homer, m.——, res. Clinton Co., Mo.

5-100. *Eliza Dawson* (dau. of Benjamin, 4-28), m. MICHAEL FISHER, brother of Peter (5-99). Res. near Calcutta, O. Children:

6-181. Elizabeth. RICHESON.
6-182. Rebecca. GEORGE.
6-183. *A dau.* m.—— WILKINSON.
6-184. Susan, m. MACKALL DAWSON (6-143 of this record).
6-185. Nancy, *unm.*
6-186. Myrtilla, *unm.*
6-187. Laura C., *unm.*
6-188. George, m. Miss *George.*
6-189. John, m.——, res. Athens Co., O.
6-190. Benjamin, *unm.*, lives with his sisters on the old home farm, near Calcutta, O.

5-101. *Amassa Dawson* (dau. of Benjamin, 4-28) m. HENRY FISHER, who d. near Calcutta, O., where she res. 1873. He was brother of Peter and Michael Fisher (5-99 and 5-100 of this record). They had, besides children who d. unm.:

6-191. Olivia, m. JAMES SCROGGS, son of Dr. James and *Myrtilla Dawson* Scroggs (5-102).
6-192. Susan, m. GEORGE MORTON.
6-193. Eliza, m. SAMUEL EWING.
6-194. Samuel, m.—— *Crawford.*
6-195. Peter, m.—— *Reed.*
6-196. Harvey, m.—— *Laughlin.*

5-102. *Myrtilla Dawson* (dau. of Benjamin, 4-28), m. Dr. JAMES SCROGGS, of Ohioville, Beaver Co., Pa. He d. leaving children, of whom two only are now living:

6-197. James, m. *Olivia Fisher* (6-191 of this record).
6-198. Patterson.

5-110. ROBERT D. ALLNUTT,[1] b. in Md., Nov. 1, 1811 (son of Daniel, 4-34), m. in Ky., *Matilda Claridal,* and d. in or near Chillicothe, Mo., Dec. 23, 1860. They had ten children:

6-199. Stephen W., b. in Ky., Oct. 3, 1835.
6-200. Rachel V., b. in Ky., Jan. 20, 1837.

---

[1] Substitute for 4-34, pp. 243 and 244, the following:

4-34. *Verlinda H. Dawson,* b. in Md., Aug. 17, 1785 (dau. of Robert D., 3-17), m. Dec. 23, 1810, DANIEL ALLNUTT, b. in Md., Jan. 8, 1776. They removed to Ky., in 1816, where he d. May 4, 1851. She removed with her family to Mo., Nov., 1855, and d. in that state, Oct. 1, 1856. They had three children:
5-110. Robert D., b. in Md., Nov. 1, 1811, d. in Mo., Dec. 23, 1860; *m.*
5-111. Sarah J., b. in Md., June 6, 1814, res. Chillicothe, Mo. ALLNUTT.
5-112. John W., b. in Ky., Nov. 11, 1817, res. Chillicothe, Mo.; *m.*

6–201. [ALLNUTT.] Polly D., b. in Ky., Nov. 19, 1838, d. in Mo., Sept. 27, 1859.
6–202. Priscilla J., b. in Ky., Nov. 20, 1840.
6–203. Julia A., b. in Mo., Feb. 2, 1843.
6–204. Matilda M., b. in Mo., May 29, 1845.
6–205. Robert D., b. in Mo., Aug. 18, 1847.
6–206. King D., b. in Mo., Dec. 8, 1850.
6–207. Almeda E., b. in Mo., May 21, 1853.
6–208. Sarah J. F., b. in Mo., Oct. 3, 1855, d. June 28, 1869.

5–111. *Sarah J. Allnutt*, b. in Md., June 6, 1814 (dau. of Daniel, 4-34), m. in Ky., THOMAS H. ALLNUTT. Three children, all b. in Ky., res. in or near Chillicothe, Mo.:

6–209. James L., b. Aug. 15, 1835.
6–210. Thomas B., b. Oct. 23, 1836.
6–211. Joseph N., b. Sept. 29, 1838.

5–112. JOHN W. ALLNUTT, b. in Ky., Nov. 11, 1817 (son of Daniel, 4-34), m. in Ky., *Amanda Coghill*. Res. in or near Chillicothe, Mo. Eight children:

6–212. John T., b. in Ky., May 22, 1841.
6–213. Robert D., b. in Ky., Sept. 3, 1843.
6–214. James W., b. in Ky., June 7, 1847.
6–215. Nancy K., b. in Ky., June 20, 1848.
6–216. Verlinda W., b. in Ky., Dec. 1, 1850.
6–217. Wilhelmina, b. in Ky., Sept. 7, 1852.
6–218. Patsey C., b. in Mo., July 8, 1856.
6–219. Ambrose O., b. in Mo., Dec. 16, 1860.

5–113. *Mary Dawson*, b. in Logan Co., Ky., April 1, 1819 (dau. of Stephen N. Dawson, 4-36), m. May 12, 1836, NAPOLEON McCUDDY, farmer, b. in Woodford Co., Ky., March 13, 1807, son of Capt. Isaac B. and *Mildred Bahannan* McCuddy. They res. near Russellville, Logan Co., Ky. Nine children, all b. in Logan county:

6–220. Mildred A., b. April 7, 1837, m. Oct. 16, 1859, EDWARD W. VAUGHN; d. in Louisville, Ky., July 9, 1869.
6–221. Isaac Newton, b. Feb. 5, 1839, res. Russellville, Ky.
6–222. Lucy Jane, b. Dec. 15, 1841, m. Oct. 16, 1859, JAMES B. GRUBBS; res. Logan Co., Ky.
6–223. William Bowling, b. Jan. 8, 1843, m. May 1, 1871, *Mattie Morrison*; res. Earlington, Hopkins Co., Ky.
6–224. Laura, b. March 20, 1845, d. Sept. 12, 1848.
6–225. Mary Golden, b. Aug. 6, 1848.
6–226. James E., b. Oct. 19, 1849, d. Feb. 23, 1857.
6–227. Margaret A., b. March 9, 1852.
6–228. Henry White, b. July 16, 1854, d. March 17, 1873.

5-114. Thomas J. Dawson, b. in Logan Co., Ky., Jan. 14, 1821, d. May 3, 1869 (son of Stephen N., 4-36) m. 1840, Miss *America Drane*, b. in same county, dau. of John and *Martha Clark* Drane, gr. dau. of Thomas Drane, of Montgomery Co., Md. She res. near Russellville, Ky. Six children, all b. in Logan county:

6-229. Annie White, b. Jan. 3, 1848, m. 1869, Dr. B. F. Marshall, res. McCracken, Ky.
6-230. Stephen Newton, b. Feb. 14, 1851, m. 1871, *Fannie Colman*, res. Logan county.
6-231. Martha Clark, b. May 15, 1853.
6-232. John William, b. Dec. 30, 1858.
6-233. Julia, b. Dec. 9, 1860.
6-234. Mary Thomas, b. Sept. 11, 1869.

5-115. Dr. Stephen William Dawson, b. in Logan Co., Ky., Sept. 5, 1822 (son of Stephen N., 4-36), brought up as a farmer, removed to Montgomery county, Tenn., in 1843, studied medicine and graduated at Philadelphia, in 1849. He m. in Baltimore, Md., March 27, 1857, *Martha Lucretia Willson*, b. April 12, 1825, dau. of Charles and *Sarah Clark* Willson. They res. 1873, in Clarksville, Tenn., where he is engaged in his profession, also in farming, etc. They have two children:

6-235. Jennie, b. in Montgomery Co., Tenn., June 3, 1859.
6-236. Mattie Clark, b. in Montgomery Co., Oct. 24, 1860.

5-117. *Julia Dawson*, b. in Logan Co., Ky., May 5, 1827 (dau. of Stephen N., 4-36), m. 1840, Hon. Jos. E. Rice. They res. at Clarksville, Tenn. He is judge of the Tenth Judicial District of that state. Three children:

6-237. Alice Beatrice, b. March 21, 1845.
6-238. James William, b. April 28, 1851.
6-239. Wirt Zollicoffer, b. July 28, 1855.

5-121. *Sally Dawson*, b. in Logan Co., Ky., Feb. 1, 1837 (dau. of Stephen F., 4-36), m. Dec. 9, 1858, James C. Hester, planter and tobacco speculator, b. in Montgomery Co., Tenn., Dec. 20, 1831, son of Capt. Robert and Minerva Hester, of Va. They res. 1873, at Mayfield P. O., Graves Co., Ky. Six children:

6-240. Robert Oswald, b. in Montgomery Co., Tenn., Nov. 19, 1859.
6-241. Carrie, b. in Graves Co., Ky., Sept. 1, 1861.

6–242. [HESTER]. William Henry, b. in Graves Co., Feb. 12, 1863.
6–243. Annie Minerva, b. in Graves Co., Feb. 6, 1867.
6–244. James Raymond, b. in Graves Co., Sept. 26, 1869.
6–245. Helen Antonia, b. in Graves Co., Feb. 24, 1872.

5-129. SAMUEL MACKALL (son of Benjamin, 4-45), had:

6–246. Rebecca, m. THOMAS DAWSON (5–21 of this record). Res. Indiana. See p. 253.

5-130. JAMES MACKALL (son of Benjamin, 4-45), had:

6–247. A *daughter*, m. HARRISON DAWSON (5–22 of this record). Res. Arkansas. See p. 239.

5-131. THOMAS MACKALL (son of Benjamin, 4-45), had:

6–248. John, m. April 8, 1865, *Ellen Dawson*, b. Dec. 25, 1827 (5–28 of this record). See p. 239.

6-4. *Sarah Kennedy Dawson*, b. at Brownsville, Pa., Sept., 1838 (dau. of Hon. John L., 5-2), m. June 13, 1861, CHARLES E. SPEER. Res. near Pittsburg, Pa. He is assistant cashier of the First National Bank of that city. They have four children:

7–1. Mary Clarke, b. Oct., 1863.
7–2. Hetty Morrow, b. Nov., 1864.
7–3. John Littleton Dawson, b. June, 1866.
7–4. Louisa Dawson, b. Nov. 5, 1870.

6-6. *Louisa Cass Dawson*, b. at Brownsville, Pa., Oct. 4, 1839 (dau. of Hon. John L., 5-2), m. Oct. 25, 1866, Capt. HENRY WHITELEY PATTERSON, of the U. S. army,[1] son of Alfred and *Caroline Whiteley* Patterson (see 5-10 of this record). Capt. Patterson, having recently resigned his commission in the army, res. 1873, in Alleghany City, Pa. They have had three children:

7–5. Littleton Dawson, b. at Friendship Hill, Fayette Co., Pa., Nov. 12, 1867, d. at Pittsburg, Pa., April 13, 1871.

[1] Second lieut. 4th Inf., Oct. 24, 1861; first lieut. Dec. 28, 1862; reg. Q. M. Jan. 3, 1863; bvt. capt July 2, 1863; captain, April 21, 1866; discharged, Nov. 1, 1870. This regiment participated in the battles of Gaines' Mills, Va., 27 June, Malvern Hill, 1 July, Cedar Mountain, 9 Aug., Bull Run, 30 Aug., Antietam, 17 Sept., Fredericksburg, 13 Dec., 1862; Chancellorsville, 8 and 13 May, Gettysburg, 2 and 3 July, 1863; Wilderness, 5 and 6 May, Laurel Hill, 8 and 13 May, Spottsylvania, 16 May, North Anna River, 24 May, Bethesda Church, 1 and 3 June, Po. Potomail Creek, 2 and 3 June, Petersburg, 17, 20 and 21 June, and 30 July, Weldon Railroad, 19 and 21 Aug., and Chapel House, Va., 1 Oct., 1864.—*Army Register.*

7–6. [Patterson.] Alfred, b. at Fort Fetterman, Wyoming Territory, June 10, 1869, d. at Friendship Hill, Feb. 8, 1870.
7–7. Henry Whiteley, b. at Friendship Hill, Oct. 3, 1871.

6–6. *Mary Clarke Dawson*, b. at Brownsville, Pa., June 13, 1842 (dau. of Hon. John L., 5–2), m. April 16, 1863, Chauncey Forward Black, lawyer, b. at Somerset, Pa., Nov. 14, 1839.[1] They res. 1873, at York, Pa., and have three children:

7–8. Louisa Dawson, b. at Friendship Hill, Fayette Co., Pa., May 9, 1866.
7–9. Jeremiah Sullivan, b. at Friendship Hill, Oct. 20, 1869.
7–10. John Littleton Dawson, b. at York, Pa., Jan. 5, 1871.

6–30. George Dawson, b. at Georgetown, Pa., Sept. 22, 1844 (son of Benoni, 5–24), m. July 4, 1870, *Isadore Winch*. Res. Georgetown. One child:

7–11. Harry C.

6–31. Harrison Dawson, b. at Georgetown, Pa., May 11, 1846 (son of Benoni, 5-24), m. May 13, 1872, *Eliza McHaffie*. Res. Georgetown. One child:

7–12. William M.

6–37. James Dawson (son of George, 5–35), m. *Sarah McCulloch*. They lived at Glasgow, Beaver Co., Pa., where he d. leaving one child:

7–13. William H.

6–40. William Dawson (son of George, 5-35), m. *Maria Potter*. They res. at Glasgow, Pa. Three children:

7–14. James.
7–15. Annie Mary.
7–16. Evangeline.

6–41. Hawkins Dawson (son of George, 5-35), m. *Eliza Eggleson*. They lived in Glasgow, Pa., where he d. leaving one child:

7–17. George, d. in Glasgow.

---

[1] Son of Hon. Jeremiah Sullivan Black, and wife Mary Forward, dau. of Chauncey Forward, lawyer, of Somerset Co., Pa. Hon. Jeremiah S. Black, b. in Somerset Co., 1810 (son of Henry Black, associate judge of that county), was elected a judge of the Supreme Court of Penn., 1851, and again in 1854. He was attorney-general in the cabinet of President Buchanan, from March, 1857, to December, 1860, and secretary of state from Dec., 1860, to March, 1861.

The widow of HAWKINS DAWSON (6-41), became 2d wife of THOMAS DAWSON (5-58, of this record).

6-81. *Lavinia Bever Dawson*, b. Aug. 29, 1827 (dau. of Augustine M., 5-65), m. Nov. 7, 1850, Dr. SAMUEL T. HAMILTON, of Georgetown, Beaver Co., Pa., where they res. 1873. They have had eleven children:

7-18. Augustine Moore, b. Aug. 8, 1851, d. Jan. 31, 1852.
7-19. Samuel Quigley, b. Oct. 19, 1852.
7-20. Courtney Wood, b. Aug. 18, 1854, d. Aug. 9, 1864.
7-21. Maria Amelia, b. Feb. 18, 1856, d. Aug. 2, 1864.
7-22. Laura Wellman, b. Jan. 12, 1858, d. Feb. 27, 1860.
7-23. Meigs Steel, b. Aug. 18, 1860, d. Oct. 31, 1861.
7-24. Clyne Ackley, b. Aug. 12, 1862.
7-25. William Harvey, b. Oct. 30, 1864, d. Aug. 29, 1865.
7-26. Harriet Blythe, b. July 28, 1866, d. Feb. 22, 1869.
7-27. Clara Horton, b. Aug. 30, 1868.
7-28. Lavinia Bever, b. Aug. 8, 1870.

6-83. WILLIAM BEVER DAWSON, b. June 6, 1831 (son of Augustine M., 5-65), m. about 1852, *Maria Cornelia Wadsworth*, of Canfield, Mahoning Co., O., granddaughter of Gen. Wadsworth, of Revolutionary fame. They res. 1873, at Canfield. One child:

7-29. George Wadsworth.

6-84. *Maria Jane Bever Dawson*, b. Aug. 20, 1833 (dau. of Augustine M., 5-65), m. Aug. 8, 1854, JOHN THOMPSON, b. April 1, 1820, son of William and Eleanor Thompson. They res. 1873, at Calcutta, O., where they have had b. seven chn.:

7-30. William Augustine, b. Oct. 27, 1854.
7-31. Charles Fremont, b. Nov. 2, 1856.
7-32. George Cummins, b. Nov. 29, 1858.
7-33. Minnie B., b. Oct. 4, 1861, d. Dec. 11, 1864.
7-34. John McD., b. Sept. 25, 1863.
7-35. Ellen Maria, b. Feb. 7, 1866.
7-36. Luna Jane, b. Aug. 13, 1869.

6-87. AUGUSTINE MOORE DAWSON, teacher, b. in Calcutta, O., March 1, 1842 (son of Augustine M., 5-65), m. *Josephine Wise* Armstrong, widow of Jared Armstrong, and eldest dau. of Dr. James Wise, of Lewisburg, Va. Mr. Dawson is teacher of mathematics in the Hiwassee College, an institution under the patronage of the M. E. Church, South, near Sweetwater, Tenn. P. O. address and res., Hayesville, Clay Co., N. C. Three children:

7–37. Maria Bever.
7–38. Edwin Holly.
7–39. Virginia, d.

6–137. SAMUEL BLACKMORE, b. in Columbiana Co., O., March 14, 1828 (son of Benoni, 5-82), m. March 16, 1852, *Matilda Mackall*, who was b. in same county, Oct. 20, 1829, dau. of Thomas and *Sarah Foster* Mackall. They res. 1873, at Scotland, Greene county, Indiana, where he is engaged in farming, stock-raising and merchandising. Nine children, living:

7–40. Thomas D., b. Jan. 25, 1853.
7–41. Benoni W., b. Aug. 10, 1855.
7–42. Caroline V., b. March 10, 1857.
7–43. George F., b. April 3, 1859.
7–44. John M., b. Sept. 9, 1861.
7–45. Charles C., b. March 19, 1863.
7–46. Napoleon B., b. Nov. 18, 1865.
7–47. Samuel T., b. March 9, 1868.
7–48. Cora E., b. Feb. 4, 1873.

6–138. DAWSON BLACKMORE, b. in Columbiana Co., O., June 23, 1831 (son of Benoni, 5-82), m. May 29, 1872, *Mary Josephine Jones*, b. in Bloomfield, Greene Co., Indiana, May 29, 1844, dau. of John and *Sarah Glover* Jones. They reside temporarily, 1873, at Washington, Ind. Mr. Blackmore is of the firm of Laidley and Blackmore, commission merchants, 85 West 2d street, Cincinnati, Ohio. One child:

7–49. Dawson Jones, b. July 13, 1873.

6–140. JAMES B. BLACKMORE, farmer, stock-raiser and merchant, b. in Columbiana Co., O., June 16, 1836 (son of Benoni, 5–82), m. in Greene Co., Ind., Feb. 14, 1861, *Margaret Geddes*, b. in Columbiana Co., June 1, 1840, daughter of Samuel and *Margaret Herbert* Geddes. They res. at Scotland, Indiana, and have five children:

7–50. Charles A., b. Feb. 5, 1862.
7–51. Lizzie J., b. March 15, 1864.
7–52. George D., b. Jan. 30, 1866.
7–53. Samuel L., b. July 31, 1868.
7–54. Ellie J., b. March 20, 1871.

6-141. *Rebecca Jane Blackmore*, b. in Columbiana Co., O., Sept. 9, 1838 (dau. of Benoni, 5-82), m. Nov. 14, 1866, JOSHUA M. OGDEN, son of Dr. J. M. Ogden. They res. at Scotland, Ind. Two children:

7-55. George B., b. Dec. 9, 1867.
7-56. Dawson B., b. Aug. 28, 1869.

6-150. BENJAMIN PATTERSON DAWSON (son of Joshua W., 5-93), m. July 7, 1857, *Rachel Moore Dawson*, who was b. Nov. 29, 1838 (dau. of Augustine M., 5-65). They res. 1873, in Georgetown, Beaver Co., Pa., and have had seven children, all now living:

7-57. George Augustine, b. June 8, 1858.
7-58. Mary Maria, b. Oct. 29, 1860.
7-59. Clement L. Vallandingham, b. March 3, 1863.
7-60. Lavinia Hamilton, b. April 11, 1865.
7-61. Joshua Wilkinson, b. Feb. 19, 1867.
7-62. Ford, b. Feb. 27, 1869.
7-63. Benjamin Forest, b. Dec. 10, 1869.

6-181. *Elizabeth Fisher* (dau. of Michael and *Eliza Dawson* Fisher, 5-100), m. SAMUEL RICHESON. They had several children:

7-64. Mary E., m. John Blackmore (6-121 of this record).

6-182. *Rebecca Fisher* (dau. of Michael and *Eliza Dawson* Fisher, 5-100), m. Dr. EMANUEL GEORGE. They had one son:

7-65. Benjamin.

FAMILY OF JAMES DAWSON,

ALLEGHANY CO., MD., 1754.

From the Rev. John K. Dawson, of Martinsburg, Keokuk Co., Iowa, and others, the following:

1. JAMES DAWSON was b. in Maryland, about 1754. His son, the Rev. John K. Dawson, above named, says that he was *probably* a native of Alleghany Co.[1] He was a soldier in the Revolutionary war, also in the war of 1812-14; being, during his last term of service, a private in the Tenth Regiment of Infantry, from which he was honorably discharged, May 27, 1814. He was at this time sixty years of age.[2] He died in Knox Co., Tenn., aged 83, hence about the year 1837. He was a farmer, and a member of the Methodist church. He married, some time after the close of the Revolutionary war, *Jane Kitchen*, of New Jersey, who died in Wilkes county, North Carolina, August, 1807, to which state they removed before 1789, and where they resided until the time of her death. Their children were:

2–1. Ailsaba, b. in Caswell Co., N. C., 1789, now deceased.
2–2. Edmond, b. in Caswell Co., N. C., 1792. } [3]
2–3. David, b. in Caswell Co., N. C., 1795. }

---

[1] Rev. J. K. D. writes as follows: "James Dawson, my father, was b. in the state of Maryland, probably Alleghany county, about 1754. His father d. when he was young. I never saw him, and have forgotten his name. I remember seeing, when I was a small boy, a brother of my father, whose name was Thomas."

[2] The following is a copy of a certificate in the possession of his son:

"District Pay-Master's Office, Washington, June 1, 1814.

"I certify that JAMES DAWSON, born in Maryland, aged sixty years, five feet 7½ inches high, fair complexion, blue eyes, light hair, and by profession a farmer, late a soldier in the 10th Regiment of Infantry was discharged on the 27th day of May, 1814, by Lieut. Col. D. L. Clinch, and that his discharge is on file in my office.

(signed) "SAT. CLARK, D. P. M."

The above endorsed as follows:

"The discharge delivered Mr. Stephens of the Section of Bounty Lands, the 25th March, 1820.

(signed) "M. LATIMER, Clerk."

[3] These were both soldiers in the war of 1812; discharged 1814, but re-enlisted, and d. the same year from sickness, at Fort Strather, in the Creek Indian Nation. Both unmarried.

2–4. John Kitchen, b. in Caswell Co., N. C., Oct. 12, 1797, res. 1873, Martinsburg, Iowa ; *m.*

2–5. Margaret, b. in Wilkes Co., N. C., 1799, d. in same Co., Oct., 1807.

2–6. James, b. in Wilkes Co., N. C., Feb., 1802, d. in Cocke Co., Tenn., Oct. 2, 1858 ; *m.*

2–7. Esther, b. in Wilkes Co., N. C., Aug., 1805, d. in Tenn.

By a second marriage James Dawson had other children, whose names have not been communicated.

2–4. Rev. JOHN KITCHEN DAWSON was b. in Caswell Co., N. C., Oct. 12, 1797. His early educational advantages were small. In 1812, his father and two elder brothers being in the army, he lived in Wilkes county, N. C., where he joined the Baptist church in that year. In 1813 he went to Wythe Co., Va., and worked in the lead mines there. He returned to North Carolina in 1814, and removed from that state to Greene county, Tenn., in 1818, where, after a short time spent at school, he apprenticed himself to the cabinet making business, which, as well as the trade of a carpenter and joiner, farming, and other branches of business, he has since followed. In 1826 he became a licensed preacher in the Methodist Episcopal church, but on account of objections to the Episcopal form of government, left that connection, and united with the Methodist Protestant church in 1842, in the ministry of which he has since labored. He m. in Sevier Co., Tenn., Sept. 1, 1822, *Sarah Bitner*, who was b. in Greene Co., Tenn., May 3, 1802. They removed to Indiana in 1829, and thence to Iowa, in 1848. They have had eleven children, as follows :

3–1. William Riley, b. in Sevier Co., Tenn., May 26, 1823, res. 1873, Bainbridge, Indiana ; *m.*

3–2. Minerva Jane, b. in Sevier Co., Tenn., April 5, 1825, d. May 3, 1825.

3–3. Elizabeth, b. in Sevier Co., Tenn., Oct. 18, 1826, d. in Putnam Co., Ind., July 20, 1847, *unm.*

3–4. James Beckley, lawyer, b. in Sevier Co., Tenn., March 11, 1829, d. in Union Co., Iowa, June 16, 1856, *unm.*

3–5. Violet, teacher, b. in Rush Co., Ind., Aug. 16, 1831, d. in Keokuk Co., Iowa, Oct. 25, 1848, *unm.*

3–6. Mary Jane, b. in Rush Co., Ind., Aug. 7, 1834, res. 1871, Kansas. WILLIAMS.

3–7. Louisa Catharine, b. in Rush Co., Ind., Sept. 4, 1836, res. 1873, Newton, Jasper Co., Iowa. CHAPMAN.

3–8. Rachel Eddy, b. in Putnam Co., Ind., June 17, 1839, res. 1873, Martinsburg, Keokuk Co., Iowa. COLEMAN.
3–9. John Marion, b. in Putnam Co., Ind., Feb. 18, 1842, res. 1873, Bainbridge, Ind.; *m.*
3–10. Sarah Ellen, b. in Putnam Co., Ind., June 7, 1845, res. 1871, Iowa.
3–11. Benjamin Franklin, silversmith, b. in Putnam Co., Ind., June 4, 1848, d. in Keokuk Co., Iowa, Aug. 22, 1869, *unm.*

2–6. JAMES DAWSON, a painter by trade, but for twenty-seven years a dry goods merchant in Newport, Tenn., was b. in Wilkes county, N. C., Feb., 1802, and d. in Cocke Co., Tenn., Oct. 2, 1858. He m. in 1836, *Lucinda Clark*, of Newport. They had eight children, all b. in Newport:

3–12. James C., b. July 20, 1838.
3–13. Mary C., b. Jan. 17, 1841, res. 1871, Cocke Co., Tenn. ALLEN.
3–14. Sarah E., b. Feb. 26, 1843, res. 1871, Cocke Co., Tenn. LEFTWICH.
3–15. Rebecca J., b. Sept. 9, 1846.
3–16. Laura A., b. Aug. 23, 1849.
3–17. Ellen A., b. Aug. 30, 1850.
3–18. Florida E., b Feb. 20, 1852.
3–19. John K., b. May 21, 1855.

3–1. WILLIAM RILEY DAWSON, son of John K. Dawson (2-4), was b. in Sevier Co., Tenn., May 26, 1823. He was for four years principal of the Ashland, Iowa, Seminary, and has been also principal of the Bainbridge, Ind., Academy, and of the Sturgeon, Mo., Seminary. He m. in Putnam Co., Ind., July 30, 1854, *Elizabeth R. Taylor*, who was b. in Montgomery Co., Ky., Dec. 20, 1838, and d. in Montgomery Co., Ind., March 27, 1872. He res. 1873, in Bainbridge, Ind., and is still engaged in teaching, and is also a minister of the Christian Union congregation or church. Two children, both b. in Putnam Co., Ind.:

4–1. Mary Alice, b. June 19, 1855.
4–2. John William, b. Nov. 19, 1861.

3–6. *Mary Jane Dawson*, b. in Rush Co., Ind., Aug. 7, 1834, m. in Keokuk Co., Iowa, Feb., 1851, WILLIAM W. WILLIAMS, who was b. in Indiana. They res. 1871, in Kansas. Four children, all b. in Keokuk Co., Iowa:

4–3. Sarah C.
4–4. James F.
4–5. Martha J.
4–6. Eva A.

3-7. *Louisa Catharine Dawson*, b. in Rush Co., Ind., Sept. 4, 1836, m. in Mahaska Co., Iowa, July 30, 1854, JAMES H. CHAPMAN, who was b. in Putnam Co., Ohio, Nov. 18, 1828. They res. 1873, at Newton, Jasper Co., Iowa. Three children :

4-7. Eva E., b. in Washington Co., Iowa, Dec. 9, 1855.
4-8. Lula E., b. in Washington Co., Iowa, March 6, 1859.
4-9. Arthur B., b. in Jasper Co., Iowa, March 1, 1864.

3-8. *Rachel Eddy Dawson*, was b. in Putnam Co., Ind., June 17, 1839, m. in Keokuk Co., Iowa, April 8, 1860, JAMES A. COLEMAN, who was b. in Knox Co., Ohio, Dec. 10, 1833. They res. 1873, at Martinsburg, Keokuk Co., Iowa, and have had three children, all b. in that county :

4-10. Arthur E., b. Jan. 2, 1861.
4-11. Charles B., b. April 3, 1864, d. Sept. 26, 1865.
4-12. Martha L., b. Jan. 18, 1867.

3-9. JOHN MARION DAWSON was b. in Putnam Co., Indiana, Feb. 18, 1842. He enlisted, Oct., 1861, as a private in company D., 13th Regt. Iowa Infantry Vols., and participated in the battles of Pittsburg Landing and Corinth, in the siege of Vicksburg, and in General Sherman's Georgia campaign. In July, 1864, his company fell into the hands of the confederates. He was taken a prisoner of war to Andersonville prison, was thence removed to Charleston, S. C., and finally to the prison at Florence, where he was paroled, in December, of that year. As a paroled prisoner he was sent to the camp at Annapolis, Md. He was discharged in June, 1865, at Davenport, Iowa. He m. in Wapello Co., Iowa, May 4, 1870, *Sarah J. Taylor*, who was b. in Putnam Co., Ind., Oct. 4, 1853. He is a silversmith and jeweler. They res. 1873, at Bainbridge, Putnam Co., Ind., and have one child :

4-13. Carleton E., b. in Keokuk Co., Iowa, July 9, 1872.

3-13. *Mary C. Dawson*, b. in Cocke Co., Tenn., Jan. 17, 1841, m. WILLIAM E. ALLEN, of that county, where they reside (1871). They have had five children, all b. in Cocke Co. :

4-14. Lula Ann, b. Jan. 4, 1859, d. Oct. 18, 1861.
4-15. Louella, b. May 11, 1863.
4-16. Ida Ann, b. Jan. 13, 1867.

4–17. [Allen.] James R., b. Feb. 24, 1868.
4–18. Elizabeth, b. March 23, 1870.

3–14. *Sarah E. Dawson*, b. in Cocke Co., Tenn., Feb. 26, 1843, m. Henry C. Leftwich, of that county, where they reside (1871). They have one child:

4–19. Mary L., b. in Cocke Co., Tenn., Nov. 15, 1869.

FAMILY OF WILLIAM DAWSON,

OF CAROLINE CO., MD., 1760.

From Dr. Ezekiel Dawson, of Woodside Mills, Del., Dr. Thomas G. Dawson, of Cambridge, Md., Mr. William Meredith, Marydell, Md., Mr. John Beitler Dawson, Washington, D. C., Mrs. Rhoda A. Morris, of Milton, Ind., and others, the following :

1. WILLIAM DAWSON, according to a tradition in the family, was a Friend or Quaker, in England (county not certainly known), and with his wife, Isabella, fled thence to America, in order to escape the persecutions to which such as were of his faith were subjected at home. They settled in Caroline county, Maryland, about the year 1760,[1] and, being isolated from Friends, united themselves to a new religious society called Nicholites, a sect which originated in Kent county, Del., and spread into Eastern Maryland about the middle of the last century, taking the name of its founder and projector, Joseph Nichols, a native of Kent county.[2] This sect became merged into the Society of Friends about the year 1800. The Nicholites practiced extreme plainness of dress and manner of life, wearing only home-made materials in their natural shades, using no dyes whatever, and even abstaining from the cultivation of natural objects of beauty, as of flowers, which, considered in a spirit of severe self-denial, they did not regard as strictly necessary or useful. They

[1] On land then within the limits of Dorchester county, but now, by change of county lines, in Caroline. Under date of May 13, 1762, Lord Baltimore (by Horatio Sharpe, then governor general of the province) patented to "William Dawson, of Dorchester county," 261 acres of land called "Dawson's Hazard," and, March 25, 1765, confirmed to him an additional tract of 171 acres of vacant land adjoining that first granted, all resurveyed in one tract still called "Dawson's Hazard," and "lying in said county of Dorchester." Under date of Jan. 2, 1873, Dr. E. Dawson wrote as follows : "I learn that William Dawson had two brothers, Frederick and Joseph, but have some doubt of the authority."

[2] "Joseph Nichols died young, even before the society was fully organized......... The Nicholites reached about eight hundred in number, and owing to the want of extended organization, and to their close similarity and unity with the Friends, who had the advantage in extent of numbers, etc., they united almost in a body, and almost without a jar, with the Third Haven quarterly meeting of Friends, of the eastern shore of Maryland. Most of them were acceptable and honored members."—Dr. E. Dawson.

bore a strict and conscientious testimony against oaths, war and slavery, and were proverbial for their honesty and unostentatious piety. The legislature of Maryland, in an act passed for their benefit, styled them New Quakers. William Dawson was prominent among these people, and it appears from the archives of the society (still preserved in MS.), that he presided over the assemblage of delegates that perfected their organization and adopted rules and regulations for their government and discipline, Dec. 5, 1774. His name was first signed to the minutes of this meeting, and is followed by the names of sixteen others, " many of them of precious memory," the ancestors of some of the most solid and honored families of that section of the country. William Dawson and William Harris (whose children intermarried), and James Harris, were the first among the Nicholites who liberated their slaves, though all finally did so. Believing that any support, direct or indirect, given to war, would " defile his hands with blood," he went so far, in obedience to what he felt to be right, as to refuse to accept or make use of the paper currency that was issued for war purposes ; and although censured and reproached for this singularity of conduct, it is said that " he maintained the ground of his testimony with dignity and consistency." Such, indeed, was the confidence reposed in his honesty, sincerity and integrity, that in his trade of making carts and spinning wheels, his custom extended to a great distance. For his " testimony " against a " hireling ministry," which must have led him in some way to contravene the laws of the province, he suffered imprisonment, being confined in jail for some time at Cambridge, near thirty miles from his place of residence. He also suffered the loss of property by distraint, for conscience' sake. His situation in prison becoming known, great crowds of people were attracted, to whom he explained his principles and delivered his exhortations, " insomuch that on account of his influence with the people his persecutors thought best to set him at liberty." [1]

It is not known whether or not William and Isabella Dawson lived to unite with the Society of Friends. They were both dead at the date of their son Elisha's second marriage (1821) and had probably been dead many years. They had eleven chn. :

---

[1] See *Friends' Miscellany*, vol. 4, p. 244 ; Janney's *History of Friends*, vol. 3, Ch. 18 ; Michener's *Retrospect of Early Quakerism*, p. 415.

2–1. John, b. 5 mo. 24, 1754, d. in Caroline Co., Md., 1826 ; *m.*
2–2. Elizabeth, b. 7 mo. 17, 1755, m.—— Wilson.
2–3. William, b. 4 mo. 13, 1757, d. in Ky., about 1815 ; *m.*
2–4. Margaret, b. 6 mo. 13, 1758, m.—— Perry.
2–5. Jonas, b. 5 mo. 31, 1760, removed to Philadelphia, and thence to interior of Pa. ; it is said that he was a silversmith, and the inventor of suspender buckles ; no account of his family.
2–6. Edward, b. 12 mo. 9, 1761, of whom no further record.
2–7. Elijah, b. 3 mo. 9, 1764, lived in Kent Co., Del ; *m.*
2–8. Elisha, b. 1 mo. 20, 1766, d. near Camden, N. J., 5 mo. 1, 1837 ; *m.*
2–9. Shadrach H., b. 4 mo. 23, 1768, d. in Lancaster, Pa., May 24, 1838 ; *m.*
2–10. Frederick, b. 7 mo. 29, 1770, was a soldier in the war of 1812 (10th Regiment Infantry), shortly after which he went west ; had bounty land in Missouri ; trace of him lost.[1]
2–11. Joseph, b. 1 mo. 26, 1773, d. in Kent Co., Del., 1 mo. 29, 1824 ; *m.*

2–1. John Dawson, b. 5 mo. 24, 1754, m. *Anna Harris*, dau. of William and Anna Harris. They lived in Caroline Co., Md., where he d. 1826, leaving three daughters :

3–1. ——, m. Dr. Jefferson.
3–2. ——, m. William Griffith.
3–3. ——, m. William Harris, of Andersontown, Md.

2-3. William Dawson, b. in Caroline county, Md., 4 mo. 13, 1757, moved thence to Virginia, where he married, and shortly after removed to Kentucky, and settled on a farm in Anderson county, which is still occupied by some of his descendants. He d. there about the year 1815.[2] His children, all now dead, were :

3–4. Joseph, who d. in Anderson Co., Ky., 1848, aged about 60 ; *m.*
3–5. Peter, d. in Harrison Co., Ky. ; *m.*
3–6. John, d in Anderson Co., Ky. ; *m.*
3–7. Charles, d. in Tippecanoe Co., Indiana, 1830 ; *m.*
3–8. Elizabeth.
3–9. Mary.
3–10. Henrietta, m.—— Higgins ; d. in Ky.
3–11. Charlotte, m. William Miller ; res. Iowa.

---

[1] He received letters patent, founded on warrant 489, giving him as bounty land in Mo., a tract described as the S. E. qr. of Sec. 30, in tp. 58 N., and Range 20 W., of the principal Meridian.

[2] This account of William Dawson (2-3), and what follows in relation to his descendants, was communicated by his grandson, Andrew H. H. Dawson, Esq., formerly of Georgia, now (1873), of New York city. Mr. Dawson wrote the compiler in 1854, that his grand father was "a brother of the great Quaker preacher, Elisha Dawson, though not himself a Quaker."

2–7. Elijah Dawson, b. in Caroline county, Md., 3 mo. 9, 1764, m. *Catharine Broadaway*, dau. of Robert and *Sarah Russum* Broadaway.[1] They lived near Sandtown, in Kent Co., Delaware, where he d. in middle life, leaving two children :

3–12. Greenbury, b. 1785, d. in Kent Co., Del., April 6, 1847; *m.*
3–13. Sarah, d. in Camden, Del., Feb. 8, 1868. Dunn.

2–8. Elisha Dawson, b. in Caroline Co., Md., 1 mo. 20, 1766, was originally, like his father, in Christian faith a Nicholite, but about 1798, he, with many others of similar faith, united with the Society of Friends. It is said of him that about this time he was "brought into a close exercise" and "became very low in body and mind": and that he "became concerned that others might come to understand and enjoy the blessing pronounced by the Divine Master on the 'pure in heart.' Under this concern he first appeared as a minister among Friends about the year 1800." He gradually rose to eminence in the Society, and was much respected, as well for his abilities as a preacher, as for his personal piety, sincerity, and faithfulness in the discharge of whatever he conceived to be his duty. When the Society of Friends divided, in 1828, into what have since been known as the Orthodox and Hicksite parties, he went with the latter, and a few years later (1835), being provided with certificates of the unity and concurrence of his brethren, he went on a religious visit to Great Britain. "He traveled through many parts of England and Ireland, and visited the Island of Guernsey, discharging his duty as an Embassador of Peace and Salvation as way opened for religious labor."[2] Besides, he made many extended religious journeys through and into various states, and d. while on a visit of this character, near Camden, in New Jersey, after a brief illness, on the first of 5

[1] Sister to the wife of Joseph Dawson (2-11). Robert Broadaway was a man of influence, and highly esteemed in the church and by his fellow citizens generally. His widow m. Rev. Edward Callahan, a man of prominence and education, at one time state surveyor of Delaware. Their daughter Ann m. Shadrach H. Dawson (2-9).

[2] "He deserves the name of an *Evangelist*. His life was given up, 'to labor' (using his language), 'in the love of the Gospel' wherever the Spirit seemed to direct him. He went forth preaching the Gospel almost daily over the breadth of his own country, and found time to cross the ocean, bearing the message and spirit of the Gospel to England, Ireland and the Island of Guernsey. Some idea of his labors may be obtained by accounts in his journal of his visiting tours, occupying most of the time in the years mentioned. A portion of his journal is lost. From 1800 until his death his life was one of activity and labor. In 1827-28, at the time of the Separa-

mo., 1837, being then upwards of 71 years of age.[1] He belonged to Philadelphia yearly meeting. Voluminous journals of his travels and religious experiences are now in the possession of a relative, Dr. E. Dawson, of Woodside Mills, near Camden, Delaware, and it is hoped will ultimately be published. He m. 1st, 11 mo. 5, 1785, *Lydia Harris*, b. Jan. 4, 1771, daughter of William and Anna Harris, prominent members of the society called Nicholites.[2] They had six children, all b. in Caroline county, Md.:

3–14. Daniel, b. 11mo. 9, 1786, d. in Brooklyn, O., 9 mo. 6, 1838 ; *m*.
3–15. Deborah H., b. 9 mo. 22, 1789, d. in Wayne Co, Ind., 1 mo. 11, 1856. FRAMPTON.
3–16. Mary, b. 4 mo. 18, 1792, d. aged about 5 years.
3–17. William, b. 3 mo. 29, 1796, d. in Ind., 7 mo. 26, 1851 ; *m*.
3–18. James, b. 3 mo. 25, 1799, d. in Hancock Co., Ind., 10 mo. 20, 1850 ; *m*.
3–19. Elisha, b. 5 mo. 27, 1802, d. aged about 5 years.

Shortly after the birth of their youngest child, Elisha and Lydia Dawson removed to Sussex county, Delaware, where she d. 12 mo. 4, 1815.[3] He m. 2d, at North meeting, Philadelphia, 2 mo. 27, 1821, Mary Laws,[4] of Philadelphia, widow, who d. in Bristol, Pa., 1 mo, 31, 1866, aged 86. She had children, the issue of a former marriage, but none of this marriage.

tion, he traveled through Ohio, Indiana, Pa., and N. J.; in 1829, through Delaware, Va., and Md.; in 1830, through Pa. and N. J.; 1831, Delaware, Md., and Va.; 1832, N. Y. and Canada; 1833, New England; 1834, Ohio; 1835-37, England, Ireland, etc. Returning home, he ended his ministry by attending meeting in Camden, N. J., April 23, 1857. He went home with Joseph Kaign, of Kaign's Point, Gloucester Co., N. J., was taken suddenly ill, and d. May 1, 1837, in the faith of the Gospel." "His writings abound in the spirit of toleration."— Dr. E. Dawson.

[1] An interesting and valuable *Testimonial concerning Elisha Dawson*, prepared by the Camden, Del., monthly meeting of Friends, from which some portions of the above account are quoted, was published in *A Memorial of Deceased Friends*, by direction of the yearly meeting, 1841; S. B. Chapman & Co., Philadelphia.

[2] These names and dates from the Nicholite MS. records. In the *Memorial* of Camden meeting concerning Elisha Dawson, the names of his wife's parents are erroneously stated to have been *James* and *Mary* Harris. At the date of their marriage, Elisha and Lydia Dawson were respectively less than 20 and 15 years of age. Early marriages were very common in those days.

[3] She appears to have been a most amiable, meek and gentle Christian woman. Her "advices" to her children, a copy of which was kindly furnished the compiler by one of the family, give evidence of a wise and pure mind, and of a tender solicitude for the best welfare of her offspring. They were written about 1813; two years before her decease.

[4] Dau. of Elijah and Elizabeth Milson, of Sussex Co., Del., both d. at the time of her marriage to Elisha Dawson. She was a member of the monthly meeting of Philadelphia.

2–9. SHADRACH H. DAWSON, b. in Caroline county, Md., April 23, 1768, m. Dec. 13, 1787, *Ann Callahan*, b. April 14, 1770.[1] They lived for a time in Delaware, and removed thence to Lancaster, Pa., where she d. Aug. 26, 1818. He d. May 24, 1838, and was buried in Philadelphia.[2] They had ten chn.:

3–20. William, b. in Delaware, Oct. 10, 1788, d. Aug. 3, 1789.
3–21. Sarah, b. in Delaware, Feb. 14, 1790, d. in Phil., Feb. 11, 1870. TOLAND.
3–22. Isabella, b. May 12, 1791, m. JOSHUA H. NICHOLSON. No account of family.
3–23. Mary, b. Feb. 21, 1793, d. Sept. 20, 1796.
3–24. Margaret, b. April 9, 1795, m. about 1848, MARTIN FORD, of Kent Co., Del.; both d., no children.
3–25. Clementina, b. Jan. 18, 1797, d. Sept. 29, 1798.
3–26. Catharine, b. in York, Pa., March 13, 1799, d. in Philadelphia, May, 1847. MOORE.
3–27. Edward C. W., b. Dec. 17, 1800, d. in Lancaster, Pa., May 20, 1843; *m.*
3–28. Elizabeth, b. May 22, 1802, d. in Phil., m. PERRY PINDER, d. west; no issue.
3–29. John, b. Dec. 21, 1805, d. Dec. 23, 1805.

2–11. JOSEPH DAWSON, b. in Caroline county, Md., 1 mo. 26, 1773, d. near Mt. Moriah, in Kent county, Delaware, after a useful and honored life, 1 mo. 29, 1824.[3] He m. Mary Carter, widow of Edward Carter, and dau. of Robert and *Sarah Russum* Broadaway.[4] She was b. 3 mo. 4, 1762, and d. 7 mo. 5, 1833. They had five children:

3–30 William, d. aged 8 years.
3–31. Sarah, b. Dec. 14, 1795, d. infant.
3–32. Mary, b. Dec. 14, 1797, d. young.
3–33. Robert, b. Aug. 30, 1799, d. in his 28th year, m. *Maria Cooper*; no issue.[5]
3–34. Mary, b. 6 mo. 19, 1801, res. 1873, near Mt. Moriah, Del. GRUWELL.

3–4. JOSEPH DAWSON (son of William, 2-3), b. in Kentucky, about 1786, d. in Anderson county, in that state, 1846,

---

[1] Dau. of Rev. Edward Callahan and w. Sarah, formerly w. of Robert Broadaway. See p. 277, note 1.

[2] His will, recorded in Philadelphia, mentions w. Hannah. Hannah Dawson, widow, d. in Philadelphia, 1850.

[3] Or, Nov. 29, 1824.

[4] She had by her first husband three children. Sister to wife of Elijah Dawson (2–7), and half sister to wife of Shadrach H. Dawson (2-9).

[5] Dau. of John Cooper, and niece of Rev. Ezekiel Cooper. She m. 2d, a Mr. Fisher, and d. without issue by either husband.

aged about 60.[1] He had been an officer in the U. S. army,[2] and while stationed at Carlisle, Pa., met with *Wilhelmina Creswell*, youngest daughter of Samuel Creswell, Esq., then of Carlisle, formerly of Cecil county, Md. They were m. shortly after the close of the war. She was a gifted and lovely woman, and d. at Cynthiana, Ky., Dec., 4, 1819, after submitting to what is known as the Cæsarian operation for the delivery of her only child :[3]

4–1. Andrew Hunter Holmes, who was thus brought into the world, Nov. 26, 1819, res. 1873, New York city ; *m.*

3-5. Peter Dawson (son of William, 2-3), d. in Cynthiana, Harrison county, Ky., m. *Jane Rankin*, and had eight children, all b. in Ky. :

4–2. Jared S., m. *Catharine L. Armstrong*, res. Bellefontaine, O. ; 8 chn.
4–3. James, res. Missouri.
4–4. John, d. in Ohio ; had family.
4–5. Newton, *twin to John*, res. Missouri.
4–6. Sarah, m.—— Barrett, res. Ky.
4–7. Elizabeth.
4–8. Anna.
4–9. Wilhelmina.

---

[1] During his religious labors in the west in 1828, Elisha Dawson took occasion to visit some of his relatives who had emigrated to that country. He mentions in his journal, among others, Isaac and Deborah Frampton (3-15), and *his brother William's son Joseph.* His journal, being an account of his religious labors mainly, whatever else may be gleaned from it is merely incidental. On the 27th of 9 mo., 1828, he was at Richmond, Wayne county, Indiana. The following is his record of his next journeyings : "We went down to Milton, sixteen miles, and from thence seventy-five miles or near to it to my eldest son's, also to my brother William's son Joseph Dawson's, into a settlement of professing people of those four different societies called Presbyterians, Methodists, Baptists and Covenanters." The compiler is indebted to Dr. E. Dawson for the above extract, and for a careful, but unavailing, perusal of the journal, in the hope of adding to the information so obtained. Joseph Dawson's residence at that time was in Pleasant township, Switzerland county, Indiana, one of the southern counties of that state, bordering on the Ohio. He had m. a second wife, but never had any children by her. He was engaged in merchandising in Indiana, but after a residence of two or three years only in that state, he returned to Ky., in 1830. His son, Andrew H. H. Dawson, Esq., of New York city, well remembers Elisha Dawson's visit, and the fact that he was sent about the country on horse back to inform people of the neighborhood that Elisha Dawson would hold an "appointed meeting" at that place. The venerable preacher was listened to with great interest, a large audience of the country people having gathered to hear him. "The cordiality with which he was received," says Mr. D., "the affection with which he was treated, impressed my mind at the time as much as did the statement of the fact that he was a kinsman."

[2] "Dawson, Joseph, Kentucky, ensign 28th Inf., 20 May, and third lieut., August, 1813; second lieut. 4th Regt., April, 1814; disbanded, June, 1815."—Gardner's *Army Dictionary.*

[3] "My mother survived the event of my advent only nine days. She submitted to the Cæsarian section operation at the hands of Dr. Benjamin Dudley, of Lexington, Ky., and Dr. Israel Frazier, of Cynthiana, Nov. 26, 1819, and d. Dec. 4, 1819." —A. H. H. D.

3-6. John Dawson (son of William, 2-3), m. Miss *Mothershead*, and d. in Ky., leaving children:

4-10. William Henry, d. in Missouri.
4-11. John, planter, res. Forest City, Arkansas.
4-12. Wade, res. at the old homestead, Anderson Co., Ky.
4-13. Charles, res. at the homestead.
4-14. Charlotte, m. Cornelius Bogess, res. Anderson Co., Ky.
4-15. Mary Ann, m. John McGinness, res. Anderson Co., Ky.

3-7. Charles Dawson (son of William, 2-3), d. about 1830, in Tippecanoe Co., Indiana, leaving children:

4-16. William Henry.
4-17. Eliza.
4-18. Mary Ann.
4-19. Sarah.

3-12. Greenbury Dawson, farmer, b. 1785, d. in Kent Co., Del., April 6, 1847, aged 62, m. *Mary Smith*, who d. March 12, 1846, aged 54, dau. of Major Thomas Smith. They lived near Camden, Kent Co., Del., where from a small beginning they attained a competence, while they "established a character for the graces that make life respected." They had six children:

4-20. Catharine, b. Nov. 5, 1815, res. 1873, Kent Co., Del. Caulk.
4-21. William, b. June 24, 1817, d. near Smyrna, Del., Sept. 30, 1854; *m.*
4-22. Thomas, b. Jan. 4, 1820, d. in Kent Co., Del., Nov. 23, 1858; *m.*
4-23. Willard Hall, b. Oct. 23, 1822, d. near Smyrna, Del., July 26, 1862; *m.*
4-24. Mary Smith, b. Oct. 21, 1824, d. in Kent Co., Del., Sept. 4, 1859. Bonwill.
4-25. Ezekiel, b. Feb. 3, 1830, res. 1873, at Woodside Mills, Kent Co., Del.; *m.*

3-13. *Sarah Dawson* (dau. of Elijah, 2-7), m. Robert Dunn, of Little York, Pa., who was killed by accident in the prime of life by the hands of his friend and partner in business.[1] She d. in Camden, Del., Feb. 8, 1868, after a life of long widowhood and much affliction. They had three children:

4-26. Thomas, b. in York, Pa., Dec. 7, 1811, d. near Smyrna, Del., Dec. 1, 1849; *m.*
4-27. Robert, b. July 10, 1813, d. young.
4-28. Daniel Doudle, b. April 4, 1815, res. 1873, near Fort Wayne, Ind.; *m.*

---

[1] His grandmother, Wilhelmina Margaretta Doudle, who d. Oct. 28, 1810, was the sister of Gov. Snyder, of Pa.

3-14. DANIEL DAWSON, b. in Caroline county, Md., 11 mo. 9, 1786, m. 1st, 4 mo. 15, 1812, *Sarah Stapler*, daughter of Thomas and Margaret Stapler, of Stanton, Delaware. She d. 9 mo. 10, 1819, in her 37th year. They resided near Stanton, and had three children:

4-29. Margaret S., b. 10 mo. 31, 1813, res. 1873, Wilmington, Del.; *unm.*
4-30. Elisha, b. 5 mo. 15, 1816, d. aged 13 mos.
4-31. Thomas S., b. 8 mo. 27, 1819, res. 1873, Waterloo, N. Y., watchmaker, *unm.*

DANIEL DAWSON, m. 2d, *Martha Mitchell*, daughter of Henry and Martha Mitchell, and soon after removed to Ohio, where both d. He d. in Brooklyn, near Cincinnati, 9 mo. 6, 1838, aged 52. They had two children:

4-32. William Henry, d. young.
4-33. Mary Ann, d. in her 21st year.

3-15. *Deborah H. Dawson*, b. in Caroline Co., Md., 9 mo. 22, 1789, d. in Wayne county, Ind., 1 mo. 11, 1856, m. 1 mo. 22, 1806, ISAAC FRAMPTON, b. 7 mo. 28, 1782, d. 11 mo. 28, 1847, son of William and Margaret Frampton, of Caroline Co., Md. They lived in Talbot and Caroline counties until 1827, when, owing to their dissatisfaction with the institution of slavery, they removed to Wayne county, Indiana, near Milton. They afterwards settled in Milton, within the limits of Milford monthly meeting of Friends, of which meeting she was many years an elder, and both were consistent members. They had four children:

4-34. Lydia D., b. 1 mo. 31, 1807, d. young.
4-35. Margaret, b. 12 mo. 27, 1808, d. in Wayne county, Ind., 3 mo. 26, 1841. PRATT.
4-36. William D., b. 10 mo. 26, 1811, res. 1873, Pendleton, Ind.; *m.*
4-37. Rhoda A., b. 6 mo. 3, 1814, res. 1873, Milton, Ind. MORRIS.

3-17. WILLIAM DAWSON, b. in Caroline county, Md., 3 mo. 29, 1796, removed to Indiana, and had by first wife *Elizabeth*, one son:

4-38. James, b. in Md., d. in Ind., leaving a family.

By second wife, *Sarah* ——, W. D. had also one son:

4-39. George, b. in Ind., d. leaving a family.

W. D. d. 7 mo. 26, 1851, and was buried at Milton, Ind.

3-18. James Dawson, b. in Caroline county, Md., 3 mo. 25, 1799, m. in Wayne county, Indiana, 1830, *Anna Wright*, dau. of William and Olama Wright, who was b. in same county 1808, and d. at Fall Creek in Hancock county, 12 mo. 18, 1842. He d. at same place, 10 mo. 20, 1850. They had four children:

4-40. Lydia, b. at Fall Creek, Ind., 1831, d. at Richmond, Ind., 8 mo. 5, 1868. Stratton.
4-41. Sarah Ann, b. at Fall Creek, 1833, res. 1873, Lawrence, Kansas. Thomas.
4-42. Celia Anna, b. in Milton, Ind., 1839, res. 1873, Lawrence, Kansas. Geary.
4-43. Rhoda, b. at Fall Creek, 1842, res. 1873, Little Sandusky, Ohio. Orr.

3-21. *Sarah Dawson* (dau. of Shadrach, 2-9), b. in Delaware, Feb. 14, 1790, d. in Philadelphia, Feb. 11, 1870, m. July 28, 1814, William Toland, who was b. in Maryland, Jan. 28, 1783, son of James and Elizabeth Toland. They had seven children:

4-44. Margaret, b. in Lancaster, Pa., Aug. 26, 1815, res. 1873, in Philadelphia. Rhoads.
4-45. Ann, b. Sept. 23, 1817, d. Dec. 25, 1821.
4-46. William Shadrach, b. Nov. 5, 1819, res. 1873, Philadelphia; *m.*
4-47. Edward, b. July 19, 1822, d. June 11, 1823.
4-48. Emanuel H., b. Nov. 5, 1824, res. 1873, Philadelphia; *m.*
4-49. Catharine, b. Aug. 25, 1826, d. Sept. 4, 1842.
4-50. Hannah, b. Sept. 7, 1831, d. May 4, 1837.

3-26. *Catharine Dawson* (dau. of Shadrach, 2-9), b. in York, Pa., March 13, 1799, d. in Philadelphia, Pa., May, 1847, m. May 2, 1820, James Moore, who was b. in Kent county, Delaware, Jan. 23, 1791, and d. in Philadelphia, April, 1839. They had nine children:

4-51. Ann, b. Feb. 20, 1821, d. Oct. 13, 1825.
4-52. Isaac, b. July 29, 1822, res. Philadelphia; *m.*
4-53. William Edward, b. Dec. 21, 1823, res. Philadelphia; *m.*
4-54. Shadrach Dawson, b. Nov. 4, 1825, d. in Philadelphia, 1851; *m.*
4-55. Hannah, b. June 15, 1827, m. George Angood.
4-56. Catharine, b. May 20, 1829. Barber.
4-57. Perry, b. March 28, 1831, d. July 3, 1833.
4-58. James, b. Nov. 16, 1832, d. in Cuba, 1854.
4-59. Elizabeth Davis, b. April 23, 1834, d. Feb. 26, 1838.

3-27. Edward C. W. Dawson, b. Dec. 17, 1800. He was a hardware merchant in Lancaster, Pa., where he d. May

20, 1843. He m. Feb., 1824, *Catharine Raisner*, who d. in Philadelphia, March 27, 1847. (The remains of both interred in Monument Cemetery, Philadelphia). Their only child was :

4–60. John Beitler, b. in Lancaster, Dec. 9, 1824, res. 1873, Washington, D. C., coal and wood merchant, *unm.*

3–34. *Mary Dawson* (dau. of Joseph Dawson, 2-11), b. in Kent Co., Del., 6 mo. 19, 1801, resides, 1873, on her father's homestead, near Mt. Moriah, in Kent county. She m. June 21, 1822, ISAAC GRUWELL, who was b. 6 mo. 12, 1792, and d. 4 mo. 8, 1849, son of John and Rachel Gruwell. They had six children, all b. in Kent county :

4–61. Elizabeth, b. Oct. 7, 1824, d. aged 2 mos.
4–62. Joseph D., b. March 19, 1828, res. in Kent Co. ; *m.*
4–63. Eliza Ann, b. Oct. 7, 1831, m. Dec. 31, 1861, WM. MEREDITH, b. Jan. 18, 1809, res. 1873, at Marydell, Caroline Co., Md. ; no issue.[1]
4–64. John, b. Aug. 8, 1833, res. in Kent Co., Del. ; *m.*
4–65. Isaac, b. May 8, 1836, res. in Caroline Co., Md. ; *m.*
4–66. William, b. Sept. 28, 1839.

4–1. ANDREW HUNTER HOLMES DAWSON (son of Joseph, 3-4), commenced the study of law at Versailles, Ky., in 1838, under Thomas F. Marshall, and continued the study under Judge Stephen C. Stevens, at Madison, Indiana. He was admitted to the bar in Louisville, Ky., in April, 1841, and after practicing his profession a few months in that city, removed to St. Louis, Mo., in January, 1842. Considerations of health induced him to abandon a profitable practice there, in Feb., 1846, when he removed to Warrenton, Ga. Thence he removed in 1848 to Augusta, Ga., and thence in 1854 to Savannah, where he remained until 1860, having been, during his entire term of residence in Georgia, chiefly engaged in his professional business, wherein he had gained not only fame, but fortune. As a criminal lawyer, Mr. Dawson is said to have had few, if any, equals in the South. He is a brilliant and forcible, though an impetuous and somewhat erratic, speaker and writer. His oratory flashes with wit and humor, melts with pathos, and scathes and burns with satire and denunciation, by

[1] His 2d wife. By his 1st wife, *Sally Ann Knotts*, he had nine children. He was son of Job Meredith and his 2d wife Elizabeth Hatfield ; gr. son of Job (d. 1762), and *Rebecca Davis* Meredith ; gt. gr. son of Robert Meredith, who came from Wales, and settled in Kent county, Delaware, thirteen miles south of Dover.

Andrew H H Dawson

turns, as suits the subject, or the purpose he may have to accomplish. He possesses a remarkably retentive memory, and his facility of illustration, by apt quotations from a wide range of classical literature, and by the most varied and original anecdotes, is one of his most striking characteristics.

In 1860 he removed to Mobile, Ala., and having been appointed, shortly after, chairman of the state executive committee of the Constitutional Union party, and nominated a candidate for presidential elector on the Bell & Everett ticket, he stumped the state in its behalf, using all his influence to stay the tide which had already set in for secession, and which finally proved irresistible and overwhelming. Abandoning hope of a "constitutional union," he allied himself, on the outbreak of the civil war, to the fortunes of the South, and became an ardent supporter of the southern cause, although not in arms. During the first two years of the war he resided chiefly at Richmond, in order to be near his son who was in the Confederate army; after that, until the close of the struggle, he sojourned as a refugee in various southern towns and states. He was elected colonel of a Ky. Reg't. in the Confederate service, but was not commissioned. At the close of the war, the National Government having triumphed, he acquiesced, as a matter of principle, in the new order of things, and has since labored effectively, with tongue and pen, to promote harmony between the North and South, and for the best welfare, as judged from his stand point, of the whole country. He has been for many years the political and intimate personal friend of Hon. Alexander H. Stephens, of Georgia, with whom he maintains a frequent and confidential correspondence.[1]

In July, 1865, Mr. Dawson removed to New York city, where, in the midst of active and successful practice, he finds time for occasional addresses and lectures on literary, social and political topics.[2]

---

[1] L. J. Bigelow, in his *Bench and Bar; its Wit, Humor, Asperities, &c.*, relates an anecdote of Mr. Dawson and Mr. Stephens, in which Mr. D. is referred to as "formerly a member of Congress from Georgia." This is an error. Mr. Dawson was offered and declined a nomination for Congress while a resident of Georgia, but was never a candidate for that office.

[2] Mr. Dawson has taken an active interest in measures looking to the introduction and general use of steam power for canal navigation. He was largely instrumental in procuring the passage of an act by the New York state legislature in 1871, providing for a competitive trial of all inventions by which steam or any motor, other than animal power, could be practically and profitably applied to the propulsion of

He m. in Louisville, Ky., July 4, 1841, *Lucy Ann Wickersham*, dau. of Ambrose and *Catharine George* Wickersham, of that city. They have one son:

5–1. Joseph Story, b. in St. Louis, Mo., Sept. 8, 1842, res 1873, Arkansas; [1] *unm.*

4–20. *Catharine Dawson*, b. in Kent Co., Del., Nov. 5, 1815 (dau. of Greenbury, 3-12), m. Feb. 11, 1836, William S. Caulk, who was b. in Kent county, Del., Feb. 29, 1812. They res. 1873, in Camden, Kent county, Del., and have had nine children:

5–2. Deborah Ann, b. Dec. 10, 1836, res. 1873, Wilmington, Del., m. Sept. 17, 1863, A. Pitner Osmond: no issue.
5–3. Mary Catharine, b. July, 29, 1839, d. Dec. 28, 1864. Gooden.
5–4. Levin Dawson, b. July 14, 1841, res. 1873, Collinsville, Ill.; *m.*
5–5. William John, b. July 12, 1843, d. Jan. 24, 1865, while at school in Wilmington, Del.; *unm.*
5–6. Robert Kemp, b. Aug. 1, 1845, res. 1873, Collinsville, Ill.; *m.*
5–7. Sarah Lucretia, b. Jan. 21, 1848, d. Nov. 15, 1857.
5–8. Nathan Henry, b. Jan. 20, 1851, res. 1873, Camden, Del.; *unm.*
5–9. Susan Coburn, b. June 23, 1853, d. July 13, 1853.
5–10. Elizabeth Horsey, b. June 3, 1856, res. 1873, Camden, Del.

4–21. William Dawson, b. near Camden, Kent Co., Del., June 24, 1817, d. near Smyrna, Del., Sept. 30, 1854, aged 37. He was a man of more than ordinary force of character, a hard worker, amassing a good property, and one of the most successful farmers of Kent county. "His motto was, 'I must work to day as if I were to live forever here, and live and pray as if I were to die to morrow.'" He m. Dec. 29, 1840, *Elizabeth G. Brittingham.*[2] They had eight children:

5–11. Anna Mary, b. near Barrett's Chapel, Del., Oct. 17, 1841, d. Aug. 10, 1842.
5–12. Sarah Isabella, b. near Barrett's Chapel, Jan. 28, 1844, d. near Smyrna, Del., July 27, 1849.

---

boats on the canals; offering a reward of $100,000, for the introduction of any plan which should prove to be better and more economical than the existing method of towage. One of the competing inventors, Mr. Thomas Main, exhibited a boat named in Mr. Dawson's honor, the steamer "Dawson." The award of the commissioners is not yet made (Dec., 1873).

[1] Entered the Confederate army, as a private in the Third Ala. Regt., and was transferred to the Fourth La. Battalion, and after the expiration of his term of enlistment he re-entered the service in the Twelfth Ga. Battalion. He was promoted to the rank of captain, and though in forty-six regular battles and many skirmishes, was never wounded.

[2] She m. 2d, William P. Smithers, Esq., uncle to Hon. N. B. Smithers, lately a representative in Congress from Delaware. They reside in Smyrna.

5–13. Thomas Greenbury, b. near Barrett's Chapel, Dec. 12, 1845, served as private in the 6th and 7th Delaware Regts. in late war, and is now a practicing dentist at Cambridge, Md.; *unm.*
5–14. Mary J., b. near Barrett's Chapel, Dec. 1, 1847, res. 1873, Moorton Station, Del. SMITH.
5–15. Margaretta, b. near Smyrna, Del., Dec. 10, 1849, res. 1873, Bishop's Corner, Kent Co., Del. BISHOP.
5–16. William H., b. near Smyrna, March 12, 1851, res. near Kirkwood, New Castle county, Del.; *m.*
5–17. Ezekiel Warner, teacher, b. near Smyrna, July 25, 1853, res. 1873, New Castle, Del.; *unm.*
5–18. John George, b. in Camden, Del., May 12, 1855, student, 1873, at State Normal School, Millersville, Pa.

4–22. THOMAS DAWSON, b. in Kent county, Del., Jan. 4, 1820, d. in same county, Nov. 23, 1858, m. *Hester Green*, b. July 9, 1818, d. in Kent county, Feb. 8, 1865. They had five children:

5–19. Mary Emma, b. Jan. 21, 1845, d. Aug. 25, 1863; *unm.*
5–20. Edward, b. May 8, 1846, d. Nov. 3, 1856.
5–21. Theodore, b. Feb. 4, 1849, d. Aug. 9, 1859.
5–22. Eugene, b. Feb. 23, 1851, res. 1873, Wilmington, Del., watchmaker; *unm.*
5–23. Louisa S., b. Nov. 27, 1855, res. 1873, Philadelphia; *unm.*

4–23. WILLARD HALL DAWSON, b. in Kent county, Del., Oct. 23, 1822, resided at Raymond's Neck near Smyrna, Del. He d. suddenly, July 26, 1862, from being thrown from a horse before the knives of a reaping machine. He m. *Sarah Ann Herring*, who res. a widow, 1873, in Philadelphia. They had five children:

5–24. Elma, d. young.
5–25. Laura, m. NEHEMIAH DRAPER, res. 1873, Milford, Del.; one ch.
5–26. Olley, res. Philadelphia.
5–27. Jennie, res. Philadelphia.
5–28. Mary, res. Philadelphia.

4–24. *Mary Smith Dawson*, b. in Kent county, Del., Oct. 21, 1824 (dau. of Greenbury, 3-12), d. in same county, Sept. 4, 1859. She m. PETER L. BONWILL, who res. 1873, in Kent county. One child:

5–29. Emile Volney, b. Sept. 12, 1850, now at school in Philadelphia, *unm.*

4–25. Dr. EZEKIEL DAWSON, b. near Camden, Kent county, Del., Feb. 3, 1830, graduated in Medical Department of the

University of Pennsylvania, 1853. He first engaged in practice at Vernon, in Kent county, at which place, while hunting with a party of friends, he was accidentally shot by one of them, thus losing the sight of his left eye. Being disabled for some time by this accident, he relinquished his practice at Vernon, and while convalescing removed to Camden, in the same county, where he has since devoted many years to his profession, achieving a good reputation in medicine and surgery, and being especially successful in the treatment of the diseases of children. He became a licensed preacher in the Methodist Episcopal church in 1857. He entered the United States service in March, 1862, as assistant surgeon in the 3d Regt. of Delaware Infantry; was soon after commissioned as surgeon of the 2d Regt., and detailed for Post duty, being appointed medical director of the Post at Harper's Ferry. Failing health compelled him to resign his commission, but soon after, his health improving, he reëntered the service as volunteer surgeon, and served in Tilton Hospital, Wilmington, and afterwards at Annapolis Junction. Dr. Dawson m. in Camden, May 10, 1854, *Sallie Clark*, b. Aug. 31, 1830, d. in Camden, May 28, 1867, dau. of Frisby Bewley and *Maria Sharp* Clark.[1] They had six chn.:

5–30. Kate, b. Sept. 4, 1855, d. March 18, 1859.
5–31. Edgar Smith, b. Dec. 22, 1857, d. Dec. 27, 1860.
5–32. Maria Clark, b. May 8, 1860, d. Jan. 16, 1861.
5–33. Mary, b. March 18, 1862.
5–34. Anna Coburn, b. Aug. 9, 1864.
5–35. William, b. May 18, 1867.

Dr. Dawson m. 2d, Nov. 30, 1869, *Ruth Anna Coursey*, dau. of Thomas B. Coursey, Esq.,[2] of Spring Mills, Kent county, Delaware, and w. *Sally Ann Wilson*, dau. of William and *Ruth Cardeen* Wilson. Mrs. D. is an indefatigable sabbath

1 "Mrs. Dawson was more than usually respected and beloved, being so careful for the good and comfort of others she practiced much self denial. She was a Christian of the strongest faith. Dying fully concious, she gave up, without a murmur, children, husband and mortal life, for that she esteemed far better, Jesus and eternal life. She was a grand niece of Rev. Solomon Sharp, one of the old pioneer Methodist preachers of the county, and a man of great eloquence and strong character."—Dr. E. Dawson.

2 Mr. Coursey was nominated on the republican ticket for governor of Delaware in 1870, and although leading his ticket, was defeated. He is a writer of good ability, contributing regularly to local journals and magazines articles on temperance, agriculure, and sometimes purely literary subjects.

school worker, and greatly esteemed. They res. 1873, at Woodside Mills, near Camden, in Kent county, where he has recently erected and is conducting a factory for the manufacture of materials for the upholsterers' trade. Dr. Dawson is understood to be engaged in collecting materials for a history of the Nicholites, and an account of their descendants. The compiler is largely indebted to him for information in regard to the family of William Dawson.[1]

4-26. THOMAS DUNN, b. in York, Pa., Dec. 7, 1811, d. near Smyrna, Del., Dec. 1, 1849, m. 1831, *Ann Clements*, b. May 4, 1813, d. Dec. 1, 1849, dau. of Thomas and Mary Clements. They lived near Camden, Del. Seven children:

5-36. Robert G., b. 1832, res. near Camden, Del.; *m.*
5-37. Edwin, b. Dec. 22, 1834, res. 1873, Philadelphia; *m.*
5-38. Mary Hester, b. March 7, 1837, d. in Philadelphia, May 16, 1872, *unm.*
5-39. Sarah Isabel, b. Sept. 5, 1839, res. 1873, Camden, Del. TINLEY.
5-40. Francis Marion, b. Jan. 26, 1842, res. 1873, Marydell, Md.; *m.*
5-41. Thomas C., b. April 26, 1845, res. 1873, Philadelphia; *m.*
5-42. William, b. Aug. 14, 1847, d. 1849.

4-28. DANIEL D. DUNN, b. April 4, 1815, served in the war with Mexico, resides, 1873, near Fort Wayne, Indiana, m. 1st, *Harriet Marvel*, daughter of David Marvel, of Willow Grove, Del. She d. leaving one child:

5-43. Margaretta. CARTER; COPPEE.

Mr. DUNN, m. 2d, *Sarah Gooden*, daughter of John Gooden. She d. leaving one child:

5-44. John Wesley, d. suddenly, a young man, *unm.*

Mr. DUNN, m. 3d, *Caroline Wiggins*, of Indiana. They have three children, names not communicated.

4-35. *Margaret Frampton*, b. in Md., 12 mo. 27, 1808, m. in Md., 1827, HENRY PRATT. They removed to Indiana in

[1] Under a recent date, Dr. Dawson wrote as follows: "This I can say with deep gratitude: I know of no case of intemperance very closely allied to the family, nor have I any knowledge of any great scandal tarnishing its character. It has preserved the religious integrity of its parent stock. Nearly all the Dawsons have been and are professing Christians. They have been practical working people, but few of them ever attained wealth. Their connections by marriage have always been with families of equal or superior standing, save one or two exceptions. A mechanical genius is hereditary in the family; yet few of them have pursued trades, but have used the gift in a general practical way. A friendly feeling strengthening the relational tie has always seemed to pervade the family."

1828, and settled in Wayne Co., where she d. 3 mo. 26, 1841, leaving seven children :

5–45. Robert H., b. 7 mo. 16, 1828, d. in Ind. ; *m.*
5–46. William T., b. 5 mo. 15, 1830, d. young.
5–47. Caroline E., b. 1 mo. 4, 1832, d. 12 mo. 7, 1854. GRAY.
5–48. Philip, b. 10 mo. 10, 1833, res. near Indianapolis, Ind. ; has family.
5–49. Margaret A., b. 7 mo. 18, 1835, d. young.
5–50. Isaac F., b. 5 mo. 28, 1839, killed by rail road accident near Indianapolis, *unm.*
5–51. James, b. 2 mo. 12, 1841, res. near Indianapolis ; has family.

4–36. WILLIAM D. FRAMPTON, b. in Md., 10 mo. 26, 1811, m. in Milton, Ind., 1 mo. 25, 1838, *Sarah Bell.* They removed to Madison county, Ind., in 1860, within the limits of Fall Creek Monthly Meeting of Friends, of which they are members. They res. at Pendleton, and have had eleven chn. :

5–52. Henry Justice, b. 12 mo. 24, 1838, d. 6 mo. 26, 1843.
5–53. Isaac Bell, b. 8 mo. 20, 1840, d. 3 mo. 24, 1841.
5–54. William Calvin, b. 10 mo. 16, 1842, res. Pendleton, Ind. ; *m.*
5–55. Elisha Dawson, b. 4 mo. 22, 1844, d. 9 mo. 26, 1864 ; *unm.*
5–56. Arthur Elwood, b 6 mo. 12, 1847.
5–57. George Morris, b. 4 mo. 11, 1849.
5–58. Charles Launcelot, b. 12 mo. 26, 1851.
5–59. Mary Deborah, b. 1 mo. 10, 1854.
5–60. Anna Margaret, b. 4 mo. 15, 1856.
5–61. Joseph Justice, b. 4 mo. 7, 1858.
5–62. John Edgar, b. 1 mo. 14, 1861.

4–37. *Rhoda A. Frampton*, b. in Md., 6 mo. 3, 1814, m. in Milton, Ind., 12 mo. 22, 1831, GEORGE D. MORRIS, son of Aaron and Lydia Morris, of Wayne county, Indiana. He d. in Milton, 9 mo. 23, 1843, where she still resides. Five chn. :

5–63. William F., b. 12 mo. 9, 1832, res. Pendleton, Ind. ; *m.*
5–64. Aaron, b. 11 mo. 23, 1834, res. Milton, Ind. ; *m.*
5–65. Mary E., b. 7 mo. 20, 1837, res. Connersville, Ind. TATMAN.
5–66. Ruth Anna, b. 8 mo. 13, 1840, res. Richmond, Ind. HUSTON.
5–67. Elmira Jane, b. 4 mo. 8, 1843, res. Milton, Ind., *unm.*

4–40. *Lydia Dawson*, b. at Fall Creek, Hancock Co., Ind., 1831 (dau. of James, 3–18), m. in Richmond, Ind., JOSEPH STRATTON, who was b. in Richmond, 1837, son of Benjamin and Emily Stratton. She d. in Richmond, Aug. 5, 1868. He res. 1873, in Texas. Three children, all b. in Richmond :

5–68. [Stratton], Josie, b. 1862.
5–69. Russell, b. 1863.
5–70. Walter, b. 1866.

4–41. *Sarah Ann Dawson*, b. at Fall Creek, Ind., 1833 (dau. of James, 3-18), m. in Richmond, Ind., 1858, David Thomas, who was b. in Fayette county, Ky., 1827, son of Nathan and Martha Thomas. They res. in Lawrence, Kansas. Two children, both b. in Richmond:

5–71. Clara, b. 1858.
5–72. Emma, b. 1862.

4–42. *Celia Anna Dawson*, b. in Milton, Ind., 1839 (dau. of James, 3-18), m. in Richmond, Ind., Jan. 1, 1862, Solomon Geary, who was b. in Montgomery county, Pa., 1832, son of Peter and Lydia Geary. They res. in Lawrence, Kansas. Four children:

5–73. Viola E., b. in Richmond, Ind., Sept. 29, 1863.
5–74. Emma M., b. in Gallia Co., O., Oct. 6, 1866.
5–75. William T., b. in Richmond, Ind., Sept. 10, 1869.
5–76. Charles O., b. in Lawrence, Kansas, July 27, 1872.

4–43. *Rhoda Dawson*, b. at Fall Creek, Ind., 1842 (dau. of James, 3-18), m. in Muncie, Ind., 1868, Charles Orr, who was b. in Sandusky, O., son of James Orr. They res. 1873, Little Sandusky, O. One child:

5–77. Ada Bell, b. in Little Sandusky, 1872.

4–44. *Margaret Toland*, b. in Lancaster, Pa., Aug. 26, 1815 (dau. of William, 3–21), m. in Philadelphia, Dec. 10, 1839, Jeremiah Rhoads, who was b. in Berks Co., Pa., Sept. 5, 1817. They res. 1873, in Philadelphia. Seven children:

5–78. Catharine Ann, b. March 29, 1841, m. Edwin Dunn (5–37 of this record).
5–79. William Henry, b. July 14, 1842, d. Aug. 6, 1842.
5–80. Sarah Elizabeth, b. Dec. 10, 1844, res. Philadelphia. Ferrill.
5–81. William H., b. Sept. 29, 1847, d. March 27, 1848.
5–82. Joseph, b. Sept. 30, 1850, d. Oct. 4, 1850.
5–83. William, b. May 2, 1852, res. Philadelphia; *m.*
5–84. Edward Turner, b. Feb. 10, 1857, d. Feb. 26, 1857.

4–46. William Shadrach Toland, b. Nov. 5, 1819, m. in Philadelphia, Feb. 18, 1845, *Matilda Perkins*, who was b. in Phil., March 13, 1822, dau. of Henry and Cyrus Perkins.

They res. 1873, in Philadelphia, of which city Mr. T. is an alderman. They have four children:

5–85. Kate, b. Dec. 2, 1845, res. 1873, Mansfield, O. CUSTER.
5–86. Alice, b. Aug. 22, 1847, res. Philadelphia; *unm.*
5–87. Mary, b. Nov, 27, 1849, res. Philadelphia; *unm.*
5–88. William Perkins, b. Aug. 24, 1857, res. Philadelphia.

4–48. EMANUEL H. TOLAND, b. in Lancaster, Pa., Nov. 5, 1824, m. in Philadelphia, January, 1848, *Martha T. Matlack*, who was b. in New Jersey, 1822. They res. 1873, in Philadelphia. Mr. Toland is General Agent for the Methodist Episcopal Home Missionary Society of Philadelphia, and is a local preacher in his denomination. He has spent much of his life in Sabbath School Missionary work, and in the interests of the reformatory institutions of Philadelphia. Five children:

5–89. Emma Dawson, b. Nov. 2, 1848, res. 1873, Paulsboro, N. J. MCNIELL.
5–90. Sarah Louisa, b. Sept., 1851, res. Philadelphia; *unm.*
5–91. William Bartine, b. Aug. 8, 1854, res. Philadelphia.
5–92. Mary, b. April 20, 1857, d. 1861.
5–93. Laura V., b. Dec., 1861, d. Dec., 1868.

4–52. ISAAC MOORE, b. July 29, 1822, m. *Catharine Bassett Urch*, b. in Md., March 12, 1826. They res. 1873, in Philadelphia. Five children:

5–94. William, b. July 20, 1846, res. Philadelphia; *m.*
5–95. Isaac Albert, b. Sept. 26, 1848, res. Philadelphia.
5–96. George Evans, b. Jan. 27, 1851, res. Philadelphia.
5–97. Charlotte Elizabeth, b. Sept. 13, 1853, d. July 10, 1859.
5–98. Henry Clay, b. Nov. 30, 1855.

4–53. WILLIAM EDWARD MOORE, b. Dec. 21, 1823, m. *Sarah E. Tarbutton*. Res. Sutlersville, Queen Anne Co., Md. Five children:

5–99. James, m. res. Baltimore.
5–100. Charles.
5–101. William.
5–102. Emma.
5–103. Mary.

4–54. SHADRACH DAWSON MOORE, b. Nov. 4, 1825, d. in Philadelphia, 1851, m. *Sarah Painter*. One child:

5–104. Mary Shadrach, d. 1855.

4–56. *Catharine Moore*, b. May 20, 1829 (dau. of James, 3-26), m. DAVID L. BARBER. Four children:

5–105. [BARBER], Anna.
5–106. William.
5–107. Margaret.
5–108. Charlotte.

4–62. JOSEPH D. GRUWELL, farmer, b. in Kent county, Delaware, March 19, 1828, m. Jan., 1852, *Caroline Lewis*, dau. of John and *Susan Cooper* Lewis.[1] They res. 1873, in Kent county, at the former homestead of his grandfather, Joseph Dawson (2-11). Eight children:

5–109. Isaac L.
5–110. Eliza Jane.
5–111. Malinda.
5–112. Robert.
5–113. Joseph.
5–114. Hermon.
5–115. John Marley.
5–116. Susan Elva.

4–64. JOHN GRUWELL, farmer, b. in Kent county, Delaware, Aug. 8, 1833, m. Dec. 25, 1855, *Elizabeth A. Lewis*, sister to wife of Joseph D. Gruwell (4–62). They res. 1873, in Kent county. Six children:

5–117. William Walter.
5–118. Joseph Edward.
5–119. Mary Emily.
5–120. Watson.
5–121. Henry.
5–122.

4–65. ISAAC GRUWELL, farmer, b. in Kent county, Delaware, May 8, 1836, m. 1861, *Mary Ann Burt*. They res. 1873, in Caroline Co., Md. Four children:

5–123. Francis.
5–124. William.
5–125. Frederick.
5–126. Mary.

5–3. *Mary Catharine Caulk*, b. July 29, 1839 (dau. of William S., 4–20), d. Dec. 28, 1864, m. Feb. 13, 1861, GEORGE HENRY GOODEN, who d. Dec. 2, 1864, son of Thomas and Ellen Gooden, of Willow Grove, Del. Two children; res. 1873, Kent Co., Del.:

6–1. Edgar.
6–2. George.

---

[1] Susan Cooper was sister to wife of Robert Dawson (3-33), John Lewis was her second husband. She m. 1st, Edward Upton; 3d, Samuel S. Cooper; now a widow.

5-4. Levin Dawson Caulk, b. in Kent county, Del., July 14, 1841, m. *Mary Osmond*, dau. of Aaron P. Osmond. They res. 1873, Collinsville, Madison Co., Ill. One child living:

6-3. Florence.

5-6. Robert Kemp Caulk, b. in Kent county, Del., Aug. 1, 1845, m. *Anna Jones*. Res. 1813, near Collinsville, Ill. One child living:

6-4. Clarence.

5-14. *Mary J. Dawson*, b. near Barrett's Chapel, Del., Dec. 1, 1847 (dau. of William, 4-21), m. March 21, 1871, John M. Smith, M. D., who was b. near Smyrna, Del., March 19, 1839, son of William F. and Annie Smith. Residence, 1873, Moorton Station, Kent county, Del.

5-15. *Margaretta Dawson*, b. near Smyrna, Del., Dec. 10, 1849 (dau. of William, 4-21), m. Jan. 4, 1867, John H. Bishop. They res. 1873, at Bishop's Corner, Kent county, Del.

5-16. William H. Dawson, b. near Smyrna, Del., March 12, 1851, m. Feb. 12, 1873, *Carrie E. Stewart*. They res. near Kirkwood, New Castle county, Del.

5-36. Robert G. Dunn, b. 1832, m. April 12, 1858, *Rebecca Reynolds*, dau. of John and Margaret Reynolds. They res. 1873, near Camden, Del. Four children:

6-5. Lara, b. March 28, 1859, d. July 9, 1859.
6-6. William Francis, b. June 5, 1860.
6-7. Alfred Clifton, b. June 21, 1862.
6-8. George H., b. June 21, 1870.

5-37. Edwin Dunn, b. Dec. 22, 1834, m. Sept. 16, 1859, *Catharine Rhoads* (5-78 of this record). They res. 1873, in Philadelphia. Seven children:

6-9. William R., b. Sept. 10, 1860.
6-10. Thomas, b. Sept. 16, 1862, d. young.
6-11. Henry R., b. Nov. 27, 1863.
6-12. John W., b. Feb. 16, 1866.
6-13. Margaret, b. March 5, 1868.
6-14. Anna C., b. March 17, 1870.
6-15. Lillie M., b. May 12, 1872.

5-39. *Sarah Isabel Dunn*, b. Sept. 5, 1839 (dau. of Thomas, 4-26), m. Jan. 11, 1859, JOHN TINLEY, who d. Dec. 26, 1869, leaving one child:

6-16. Wilbur D., b. Jan. 25, 1864, res. Camden, Del.

5-40. FRANCIS MARION DUNN, b. in Kent Co., Del., Jan. 26, 1842, m. Jan. 3, 1867, *Josephine McIlvaine*, who was b. in Kent county, Del., Feb. 15, 1848, dau. of Thomas H. and *Jane Conwell* McIlvaine. They res. 1873, at Marydell, Del. Two children:

6-17. Thomas Francis, b. Feb. 3, 1868.
6-18. Frederick Conwell, b. Aug. 30, 1870.

5-41. THOMAS C. DUNN, b. April 26, 1845, m. 1869, *Mary Elizabeth McGuinness*. Res. 1873, Philadelphia, Pa. Two children:

6-19. Pierce Y., b. 1870.
6-20. Elmer, b. 1872.

5-43. *Margaretta Dunn* (dau. of Daniel D., 4-28), m. 1st, JOHN CARTER, who died early, leaving one child:

6-21. Emma Dawson.

Margaretta m. 2d, Mr. COPPEE, of Chestertown, Md.

5-45. ROBERT H. PRATT, b. 7 mo. 16, 1828, d. in Indiana from wounds received in late war, leaving one child:

6-22. Katie, res. 1873, Indianapolis.

5-47. *Caroline E. Pratt*, b. 1 mo. 4, 1832, d. 12 mo. 7, 1854 (dau. of Henry, 4-35), m. JOSEPH GRAY. One child:

6-23. Margaret, res. Dublin, Wayne Co., Ind.

5-54. WILLIAM CALVIN FRAMPTON, b. 10 mo. 16, 1842, m. 2 mo. 18, 1869, *Anna S. Cockayne*. They res. 1873, Pendleton, Indiana. Two children:

6-24. Martha Cockayne, b. 2 mo. 3, 1871.
6-25. Walter Henry, b. 1 mo. 1, 1873.

5-63. WILLIAM F. MORRIS, b. in Ind., 12 mo. 9, 1832, m. 12 mo. 25, 1856, *Mary Ellen Swain*, b. in Bucks county, Pa., 5 mo. 29, 1837, dau. of Charles and Sarah Ann Swain, since of Fall Creek, Ind. They res. in Pendleton, Ind. Six children:

6–26. Lizzie E., b. 7 mo. 12, 1858, d. young.
6–27. Emma Caroline, b. 9 mo. 20, 1860.
6–28. George D., b. 5 mo. 25, 1864.
6–29. Anna P., b. 9 mo. 5, 1866.
6–30. Willie, b. 1 mo., 1871, d. an infant.
6–31. Sarah Ella, b. 9 mo., 1872.

5-64. AARON MORRIS, b. in Ind., 11 mo. 23, 1834, m. 12 mo. 21, 1865, *Martha M. Thomas*, b. near Pendleton, Ind., 2 mo. 3, 1839, dau. of Lewis and Priscilla Thomas. They res. in Milton, Wayne Co., Ind. Two children:

6–32. Luella T., b. 7 mo. 30, 1867.
6–33. Willie, b. 4 mo. 18, 1871.

5-65. *Mary E. Morris*, b. in Milton, Ind., 7 mo. 20, 1837, m. in Milton, 1 mo. 11, 1872, JOSHUA DURBIN TATMAN, b. in Fleming county, Ky., July 7, 1827, son of Stephen and Nancy Tatman. They res. 1873, in Connersville, Fayette county, Indiana.

5-66. *Ruth Anna Morris*, b. in Ind., 8 mo. 13, 1840, m. 11 mo. 14, 1868, PAUL HUSTON, b. near Mt. Holly, N. J., 8 mo. 9, 1819. They res. near Richmond, Ind. One child:

6–34. Mary Jane, b. 8 mo. 22, 1869.

5-80. *Sarah Elizabeth Rhoads*, b. Dec. 10, 1844, m. March 22, 1866, JOHN FERRILL. They res. in Philadelphia. Two children:

6–35. Wilbur.
6–36. John Dawson.

5-83. WILLIAM RHOADS, b. May 2, 1852, m. 1871, *Kate Ottenger*. Res. 1873, Philadelphia. One child:

6–37. Margaretta.

5-85. *Kate Toland*, b. in Philadelphia, Dec. 2, 1845 (dau. of William S., 4-46), m. in Philadelphia, March 18, 1869, JOSEPH N. CUSTER, son of Nathan and Maria Custer. They res. 1873, Mansfield, Ohio. Two children:

6–38. William Nathan, b. in La Crosse, Wis., Jan. 19, 1870.
6–39. Emma Lloyd, b. in Mansfield, O., Oct. 19, 1872.

5-89. *Emma Dawson Toland*, b. Nov. 2, 1848 (dau. of Emanuel H., 4-48), m. 1868, THOMAS MCNIELL. Res. 1873, Paulsboro, N. J. Two children:

6–40. Florence.
6–41. Mattie.

5-94. WILLIAM MOORE, b. July 20, 1846, m. Dec. 24, 1869, *Martha Hickman*. They res. 1873, Philadelphia. One child:

6–42. Charlotte.

The following received too late for insertion in proper order in above record:

Andrew H. H. and Lucy A. Dawson (4–1) had six children, of whom one only, Joseph Story (5–1) is mentioned above. The others, all of whom d. young, were: Walter Warrick, b. in St. Louis, Mo., and William Crosby, Julian Randolph, Kate and Lucy Wilhelmina, b. in Georgia.

Jared S. and Catharine L. Dawson (4–2) had eight children, of whom five are living: Wilhelmina C. E., m.—— COOK, now a widow, two children; Robert A.; Jordena H., m. T. J. WEAKLY, Dayton, O.; Kate Florence and Oilla C., *unm.*

FAMILY OF PHILEMON DAWSON,

OF DORCHESTER CO., MD., about 1770-1815.

The following from Capt. James L. Dawson, Westminster, Md., and Maj. Lucien L. Dawson, Philadelphia, Pa., 1872.

1. PHILEMON DAWSON, b. in Dorchester Co., Md., about 1770, is said to have been an only child. His father's name is not known. His mother was a Miss *Le Compte*, sister to Charles Le Compte, of Dorchester, a descendant of John Le Compte a French Huguenot, who settled in Maryland about 1670.[1] He m. about 1796, in Whitehaven, Cumberland county, England, *Jane Lowes*, daughter of James and Ann Lowes, of that county. When in England at this time "he had his pedigree traced, and his coat of arms painted, which shows him to have been of the Lincolnshire branch."[2] He d. in 1815. He had seven children :

2–1. Jane Lowes, b. about 1797, resided in Baltimore, Md. PHENIX.
2–2. James Lowes, b. about 1799, res. 1872, Westminster, Md. ; *m.*
2–3. Mary Ann, res. in Washington, D. C. Cox.
2–4. Martha, res. in Baltimore, Md. PHENIX.
2–5. William Le Compte, d. 1843 ; *unm.*
2–6. Charles Le Compte, d. about 1838 ; *unm.*
2–7. Emily.

2–1. *Jane Lowes Dawson*, b. about 1797, m. about 1817, THOMAS PHENIX, of Baltimore, and d. before 1820. She had one child :

3–1. Eliza Jane, res. Washington, D. C. ORME.

2–4. Mr. PHENIX, m. 2d, 1820, his former wife's sister, *Martha Dawson*, who had six children :

3–2. Thomas, m. dau. of John E. Smith, Washington, D. C.
3–3. Dawson, commander U. S. N., m. in Valparaiso, S. A., d. abt. 1863.

---

[1] In memory of John Le Compte, the Huguenot, a fine monument has been erected in Greenmount cemetery, Baltimore, reciting his pedigree, etc.

[2] "His coat of arms, a battle axe in the dexter hand, and the motto, 'Deeds no words.'"—Letters of Maj. L. L. D., Oct. 12, 1872.

3–4. [Phenix.] Benjamin Howard, m. dau. of James Legare, Charleston, S. C., d. 1864.
3–5. Annie, m. Joseph Sprigg, of Baltimore, Md.
3–6. Emily, *unm.*
3–7. Isabella, *unm.*

2–2. James Lowes Dawson, b. about 1799, "now 73 years of age" (1872), residesat Westminster, Carroll Co., Md. He was in the U. S. army from 1819 to 1835, reaching the rank of captain of three years' standing, and, in 1824, serving as aid to the commander in chief, Gen. Jacob Brown.[1] Of the term of his service Capt. D., remarks: "It was a time of profound peace. The army in that period was something in the Shakspeare vein, 'The cankers of a calm world and long peace'; for there was no war, except the petty Black Hawk war in the North, and being at the extreme South, my regiment took no part." He m. in 1829, Miss *S. E. Baylor*, of Kentucky, dau. of Col. Walker Baylor, of that state.[2] They had six children:

3–8. James Lowes, b. 1829, res. 1872, San Antonio, Texas; *m.*, no children.
3–9. Eugene Wythe, b. 1833; *unm.*
3–10. Lucien Le Compte, b. at Natchez, Miss., 1836, res. 1872, U. S. Navy yard, Phila., Pa.; *m.*
3–11. Sophia M., b. 1838, m. Gen. J. G. Walker, formerly of U. S. Mounted Rifle Corps; four daus. living; two sons d.
3–12. John Baylor, b. 1840, d. in New Orleans, 1867; *unm.*
3–13. Fanny C., b. 1844; *unm.*

2–3. *Mary Ann Dawson*, m. 1817, William Cox, of Washington, D. C. They had four children:

3–14. William, now d.
3–15. George G., res. Washington.
3–16. J. D., res. Washington.
3–17. Jane, res. Washington.

3–1. *Eliza Jane Phenix*, m. D. Orme, Washington, D. C. They had:

4–1. Thomas.

---

[1] "Dawson, James L., Maryland, third lieut. Ordnance Department, Aug., 1819; second lieut. 7th Inf., May, 1821; adjt., 1821; first lieut. May, 1824; aid de camp to Maj. Gen. Brown, 1824; assistant quartermaster, with rank of captain, May, 1826, to Oct., 1830; captain, April, 1838; resigned, 31 Dec., 1835.—Gardner's *Army Dictionary*.

[2] Col. Baylor was of Virginia descent, his father having early emigrated from that state. He was Capt. of Lady Washington's Life Guards, and was wounded at Trenton in 1777. He m. a Miss Bledsoe, of Ky., relative of Hon. Jesse Bledsoe, U. S. S. and Justice of the Supreme Court of Ky.

3-10. Lucien Le Compte Dawson, captain and brevet major U. S. Marine Corps, was born at Natchez, Miss., 1836. His naval history is as follows: "Appointed from Texas; commissioned as second lieutenant, Jan. 13, 1859; steam sloop Hartford, East India Squadron, 1859-1861; commissioned as first lieutenant, 1861; San Jacinto, East Gulf Squadron, 1862; recruiting rendezvous, Philadelphia, 1863; steam frigate Colorado, North Atlantic Blockading Squadron, 1864-5; bombardment of and land assault on Fort Fisher, brevetted major for gallant and meritorious services, Marine Barracks, Pensacola, Fla., 1865-6; Marine Barracks, Philadelphia, 1867-8; steam frigate Franklin, flag ship European squadron, 1868-9;"[1] U. S. navy yard, Philadelphia, 1872. He m. in Philadelphia, Miss *Mary Barnes Tyson*. They have had three children:

4-2. Charles Lucien, b. Jan. 8, 1864.
4-3. Pauline, b. Dec. 18, 1864.
4-4. George Baylor, b. 1868.

[1] Hamersley's *Records of Living Officers of the U. S. Navy and Marine Corps*, 1870.

FAMILY OF ROBERT DAWSON,

Of Talbot County, Md., 1770-1823.

From Mr. John W. Dawson, of Skipton, Talbot Co., Md., the following:

1. Robert Dawson, who lived "at Deep Neck, near the Royal Oak" (now Royal Oak P. O., Talbot county, Md.), was b. about 1770, and d. about 1823.[1] He m. about 1810, a widow lady named Collinson, whose maiden name was *Walker*. Their children, all b. at Deep Neck, were:

2–1. Mary W., m. James Brinsfeld, res. near Royal Oak.
2–2. Robert S., res. 1873, Trappe, Talbot Co., Md.
2–3. Rebecca A., m. —— Shanahan. *See below.*
2–4. John W., b. Jan. 15, 1820, res. 1873, Skipton, Talbot Co., Md.; *m.*

2-2. Robert S. Dawson, res. 1873, at Trappe, Md.; has two sons:

3–1. John H. E.
3–2. Robert J.

2-3. *Rebecca A. Dawson*, now d., m. —— Shanahan. Two children:

3–3. John H. R., res. 1873, Easton, Md.
3–4. Susan, m. John J. Jump; res. Easton.

2-4. John W. Dawson, merchant, res. 1873, Skipton, Md., b. Jan. 15, 1820, m. 1845, *Mary E. Newton*, dau. of Major William Newton, an officer of the war of 1812. She d. leaving one child:

3–5. Mary E., d. aged 18 months.

Mr. Dawson m. 2d, 1852, ——. Three children:

3–6. Robert, d. young.
3–7. Elbert Williams, d. young.
3–8. Mary E., b. Jan. 11, 1857.

---

[1] He was doubtless of the family of Ralph Dawson, of Talbot Co. (see p. 215), but how related to him has not been ascertained. The date of his birth indicates him of the generation of Maj. John Dawson (see 5-1, of the Ralph Dawson Family record, p. 223), and Mr. J. W. D. states that they were cousins. Maj. John Dawson had an uncle Robert who may have had a son of the same name.

FAMILY OF NICHOLAS DAWSON,

OF TALBOT COUNTY, MD., about 1754-1838.

1. NICHOLAS DAWSON, b. about 1754, lived in Talbot county, where he d. about 1838, aged about 84. He had children:

2–1. Thomas Cook, d. in Dorchester Co., Md., March 12, 1840; *m.*
2–2. *A daughter*, only sister of Thomas C., and only surviving child of her father, res. 1871, Cornersville, Dorchester Co., Md.

2–1. THOMAS COOK DAWSON m. 1st, Miss *Linchicum*, of Dorchester county, Md. She d. about 1829, leaving one son:

3–1. James Nicholas, b. in Centreville, Md., Oct., 1828, res. 1873, Castle Haven, Md.; *m.*

Mr. Dawson m. 2d, *Ann Maria Coursey*, of Caroline Co., Md., who d. March, 1867. He d. in Dorchester Co., March 12, 1840. They had one son:

3–2. John Francis, b. in Centreville, Oct., 1833, res. 1873, near Greensboro, Md.; *m.*

3–1. JAMES NICHOLAS DAWSON, b. in Centreville, Queen Anne Co., Md., Oct., 1828, res. 1873, in Castle Haven, Dorchester Co., Md., on the Great Choptank river, is a farmer, and a gentleman of intelligence and fortune. He m. in 1848, *Catharine S. Muir*, dau. of John Muir, of Dorchester county. They have two children:

4–1. John T., physician, m. and res. in Dorchester Co.
4–2. Kate Muir, res. Dorchester Co.; *unm.*

3–2. Hon. JOHN FRANCIS DAWSON, farmer, b. in Centreville, Queen Anne Co., Md., Oct., 1833, removed, at an early age, with his mother, to Caroline county, Md., where he has since resided. He was nominated by the Democratic party of his county as candidate for Delegate to the General Assembly of Maryland, in the fall of 1864, and defeated; and in the fall of 1866 was again nominated, and was elected to the House of Delegates, serving in the session of 1867. In the fall of 1866 he was elected a school commissioner for Caroline county, and served in said capacity until a short time after his reëlection, in November, 1873, to the House of Delegates, of which he is now a member for the second time. He m. 1st, June, 1857, *Sarah Josephine Delahay*, daughter of William Delahay, of Greensboro, Md. She d. July, 1864, leaving one child:

4–3. William, d. Nov., 1867.

Mr. Dawson m. 2d, March, 1868, *Mary Emma Augusta Delahay*, sister of his former wife. They res. 1873, on their farm, "Oakland," near Greensboro, and have had one child:

4–4. A *son*, d. aged 1 mo.

FAMILY OF SOVRAN DAWSON,

Of Caroline County, Md., about 1773–1838.

1. Col. Sovran Dawson, b. near Federalsburg, Caroline county, Md., about 1773, d. 1838. He was a large land owner. He m. a Miss *Turpin*, and had sons:

2–1. M.——,physician, res. Lancaster, O.; *m.*
2–2. Jasper, farmer, res. Ocean View, Del.; *m.*

2–1. Dr. M. Dawson, res. 1873, Lancaster, Ohio, has son:

3–1. F. J., dentist, res. 1873, Somerset, Ohio.

2–2. Jasper Dawson, farmer, res. 1873, Ocean View, Sussex Co., Del., has son:

3–2. Jasper Turpin, b. April 24, 1873.

FAMILY OF JOHN DAWSON,

Of Charles County, Md., 1796–18—.

1. John Dawson, is understood, by his grand-sons now residing in Washington, D. C., to have been b. in Virginia, and to have removed into Charles Co., after his marriage. He m. Miss *Garrow*. Both d. in Charles county some years before 1829. Their children all b. in Charles county, were:

2–1. William, b. March 6, 1796, d. in Washington, D. C., June 16, 1862; *m.*
2–2. Thomas, d. in Belleville, Ill., about 1838; *m.*
2–3. Robert, lived in Springfield, Ill.; *m.*
2–4. John, d. in Charles Co., Md.; *unm.*
2–5. Sarah, m. ——— Murdock.
2–6. Ann, m ——— Posey.
2–7. Mary, d. *unm.*

2–1. William Dawson, b. in Charles county, Md., March 6, 1796, d. in Washington, D. C., June 16, 1862, m. Feb. 26, 1829, *Susanna Ridgeway*, who was b. April 6, 1809, and res. a wid. 1873, in Washington. They had eight children:

3–1. Thomas Henson, b. Jan. 24, 1830, res. 1873, Washington, painter.
3–2. Frances Anna, b. May 8, 1832, d. April 9, 1834.
3–3. Jane Roberta, b. April 11, 1834, d. Sept. 10, 1836.
3–4. John William, b. Feb. 18, 1836, d in Memphis, Tenn., April 29, 1872.[1]
3–5. James Francis, b. Oct. 6, 1838, res. Washington; druggist.
3–6. Robert Joseph, b. July 17, 1840, res. 1873, East Washington; carpenter.
3–7. Mary Susanna, b. Oct. 5, 1842, res. Washington, *unm.*
3–8. William Garrow, b. Jan. 30, 1848, res. Washington; druggist.

2–2. Thomas Dawson, d. in Belleville, Ill., about 1838, several of his children also dying at that time, all from cholera, then epidemic. One son:

3–9. William Edward, lives in Ill.

2–3. Robert Dawson, blacksmith, m. in Georgetown, D. C., ——— *Wallace*, and was living about 1865, in Springfield, Ill. Several children, one of whom was:

3–10. John, saddler, res. Ill.

---

[1] Col. John W. Dawson was of the 46th Tenn. Confederate Regiment, and a prominent citizen and merchant of Memphis, where he d. He was several times severely wounded while in the army, and his health had been in consequence much impaired for some years before his death. He was m. but d. without issue.

FAMILY OF FRANCES DAWSON,

OF TALBOT COUNTY, MD., 1688.

The following are extracts from the records of the Third Haven Monthly Meeting of Friends, of Talbot county, Md., for which the compiler is indebted to Mr. Wm. F. Corbit, of Philadelphia. From this family of Friends may have sprung one or more of the families of Eastern Maryland mentioned in the foregoing pages, but the compiler is unable to state what connection, if any such, existed. The Third Haven Monthly Meeting was composed of a number of English emigrants and their families, and is said to have been the first Monthly Meeting of Friends established in America.

"FRANCES WILLIS' children by her first husband:[1]

1. Obadyar Dawson, b. 13th of 4th mo., 1672.
2. Richard Dawson, b. 13th of 9th mo., 1674.
3. Elizabeth Dawson, b. 19th of 11th mo., 1677.
4. Sarah Dawson, b. 15th of 9th mo., 1678.
5. John Dawson, b. 7th of 6th mo., 1681.
6. Anthony Dawson, b. 13th of 4th mo., 1683."

---

[1] The name of the *first* husband is not given. Her children by her *second* husband, Richard Willis, were Richard, 1684, John, 1686, Francis, 1688. She was probably a widow, *after the death of her second husband*, when the above record of births was made. She married, 3d, Edward Fisher, 1699. Her former husbands may not have been Friends. Was she from Berkshire, in Old England? *Frances Dawson*, with other Quakers, was committed to prison in Berkshire, July 27, 1662.—Besse's *Sufferings of the People called Quakers*. Other victims of the spirit of persecution which prevailed in those days may be noted here for want of a better opportunity. The accounts are taken from *Besse*.

"July 31, 1670. Charles Dawson, of Lancashire, was, with other Quakers, arrested, and next day sent to House of Correction.

"Feb. 10, 1660. Edward Dawson, of Lancashire, taken out of a religious meeting, and for refusing to swear, sent to Lancaster jail.

"June 16, 1661. Edward Dawson, arrested on coming out of meeting, and refusing an oath, was sent to Lancaster jail.

"Jan. 20, 1660. Robert Dawson, of Hartfordshire, taken out of a meeting at Ware, and committed to prison for refusing an oath.

"1683. William Dawson, glover, of Bristol, was fined £60 for absence from the National Worship.

"1660. William Dawson, of Monmouth, haberdasher, for refusal to swear committed to prison at Usk (Wales) and put into the dungeon.

"1668. William Dawson, of Monmouth, for contempt of magistrates, again committed to prison.

1. "Obadyar Dawson died 21st of 10th mo., 1694."

2. "Richard Dawson, planter, and Susannah Foster, spinster, both of Dorchester county, in ye province of Maryland, were married 23d 8 mo., 1698, in ye meeting house near the head of Transquaking river, in ye county of Dorchester." *See p.* 182.

Richard Dawson was a subscribing witness to the marriage of Joseph Adkinson and Naomi Wright, 1699, to the marriage of Nehemiah Beckwith and Frances Taylor, 1712; and to the

---

"1675. Matthew Dawson, of Hilton, Westmoreland, distressed for absence from National Worship.

"1660. Elizabeth Dawson, of Yorkshire, sent to Beverly jail for attending religious meeting at house of Thomas Hutchinson.

"1663. Elizabeth Dawson committed to prison, by the mayor of York, for attending religious meeting.

"1660. John Dawson, of the West Riding of Yorkshire, sent to prison for refusing an oath.

"1671. John Dawson, of Sedbridge meeting, Yorkshire, distressed.

"1690. Jonathan Dawson, of Yeadon, Yorkshire, distressed.

"1683. Joshua Dawson committed to York jail for attending religious meeting.

"1660. William Dawson, of Key, Yorkshire, taken to prison for attending meeting."

MEMORANDA. For an important family of Maryland, the descendants of Elias Dawson, an early emigrant to Philadelphia, but now mostly found in Talbot and Baltimore counties, Md., See *Pennsylvania Records*, "Family of Elias Dawson."

Frederick Dawson, a merchant of great respectability in Baltimore, 1854, was the son of William Dawson, an Englishman, who established himself as a merchant in that city about 1820 or 1825, perhaps earlier, using the business name of William Dawson & Sons. The father d. several years prior to 1854, probably as early as 1838 or before.

In 1838, Frederick Dawson, of Baltimore, contracted to furnish the Texan Government, then an independent power, with several armed vessels.— Yoakum's *History of Texas.*

W. Dawson was British Consul at Baltimore about the time of the Revolution.— See General Index of Dodsley's *Annnal English Register*, vol. 58, p. 207.

Joseph Dawson, probably of Md. or Va., was a comptroller at Washington, 1791. See copy of a letter from him, dated "Register's Office, Nov. 16, 1791."— Saffel's *Records of the Rev. War*, p. 138.

William Dawson, an Englishman, came to America about the time of the Rev. War, and m. in Delaware; had two children, a son and dau. The son, also named William, had two sons, one of whom is James B. Dawson, b. 1819, now, 1873, of 825 Orange St., Wilmington, a machinist, whose only child, Washington H. Dawson, baker, also res. in Wilmington. Mr. J. B. D.'s brother res. in Linwood, Delaware Co., Pa.; has a family.

Asa Dawson, farmer, lived in southern part of Kent county, Delaware. He had brothers, Thomas and Zebulon or Zebdiel, who lived near him. He m. *Sarah Meredith*, who survived him, and now lives, at quite an advanced age, in Kent county. (1873). They had, besides a dau. who d. young: I. Rhoda Ann, m. Henry M. Hill, res. Wyoming, children: Anna, Elma, Cooper. II. Asa, wheelwright, m. *Miriam Walton* Sharp, widow of Eccleson Sharp. They lived at Bridgeville, Sussex Co., Del., where she still res. He was accidentally killed in the summer of 1873, being thrown from a wagon. Two children: 1. William, *unm.* 2. Anna, m. Richard W. Cannon, druggist, nephew of the late Gov. Wm. Cannon, of Delaware, res. Bridgeville, children: Elizabeth, Estella, Walton.

marriage of his half brother, John Willis, and Margaret Cox, 1712. His wife, Susannah Dawson, was a subscribing witness to the marriage of William Foulks, of Accomac and Mary Foster (probably her sister) of Dorchester, 1704.

5. John Dawson was a subscribing witness to the marriage of William Parratt and Susannah Silvester, 1704; of Nehemiah Beckwith and Frances Taylor, 1712; of his halfbrother, John Willis, and Margaret Cox, 1712; and of Peter Harwood and Susannah Stewart, both of Talbot county, 1744.

FAMILY OF GEORGE FRANCIS DAWSON,

OF WASHINGTON, D.C., 1873.

1. FRANCIS DAWSON, Esq., grandfather of the above named, was b. in Yorkshire, England, about 1760, where he inherited a large estate, and had a famous racing stable. His devotion to the turf induced him to reside principally at Fordham Abbey, a newly purchased estate near New Market, where he d. in middle life. He m. a sister of Col. Thomas Thoroton, of "The Guards," and of Sir John Thoroton, a chaplain to the Duke of Rutland.[1] They had nine chn., of whom the sons were:

2–1. Francis, chaplain to the House of Commons, and subsequently canon and sub-dean of Canterbury.

2–2. William Francis, captain R. E., and military secretary to the late Sir Edward Barnes, governor of Ceylon.[2]

2–3. John Francis, commander R. N., killed in command of the heavy division of the British flotilla during the Burmese war, Dec. 2, 1825.[3]

2–4. Thomas Francis, d. on board the *San Josef.*

2–5. George Francis, d. Oct. 11, 1850, vicar of Orpington, and incumbent of St. Mary's Cray, Kent.[4]

2–6. Gilbert Francis, commander R. N., retired 1832; lieutenants' reserved list, 1864; res. 1873, England. *See forward.*

---

[1] Another sister m. Rev. Dr. Manners Sutton, afterwards Archbishop of Canterbury, a younger son of the Duke of Rutland, who acquired large estates on the demise of the Earl of Lexington, by adding "Sutton" to his family name The issue of this union was the Rt. Hon. Manners Sutton, who for seventeen years was speaker of the House of Commons, and who was afterwards elected to the peerage, with the titles of Viscount Canterbury and Baron Bokkesford.

[2] Capt. Dawson became a distinguished officer of engineers, and is still remembered in Ceylon as having planned the public roads which have done so much for the prosperity of the island. He d. in his prime, from excessive mental exertion, after constructing the remarkable road from Candy to Columbo, where a monument to his memory has been erected by a grateful people.

[3] Described by Sir James Brisbane, in his dispatches, as an officer who owed his promotion "to high professional character," "whose gallantry was conspicuous on all occasions," and "who fell at the moment when success had crowned his efforts."

[4] Rev. Geo. Francis Dawson entered the army in his youth, under the patronage of the Duke of York. He was employed in Canada towards the close of the war of 1812–14, and served in the army of occupation in France after the battle of Waterloo. His next service was in Ireland, whence his company was dispatched to Malta, where occurred events which entirely changed his course of life. He had become, within a comparatively recent period, a religious man — not in name, merely, but in

2-6. Gilbert Francis Dawson, ninth child and youngest son of Francis Dawson, Esq., is, in 1873, the only surviving child of this family. He was b. April 14, 1800, and entered the R. N. March 18, 1813, as first class volunteer on board the 74 gun ship *Waspite*. He distinguished himself by gallant service in several engagements, and received high encomiums for qualities of personal courage, enterprise and endurance displayed in difficult and perilous undertakings.[1] He was promoted to the rank of lieutenant in June, 1824, and after service on several vessels, the last of which was the *Hyacinth*, of 18 guns, he was invalided in 1832, since which time he has not been officially

that earnest and devout sense which was unfortunately not then common in the army, and which exposed him, with others similarly conscientious and guarded in conduct, to ridicule as infected with what was sneeringly nicknamed *Methodism*. At Malta it had been the custom of the army (by firing salutes, etc.), to take part in the religious ceremonies of the people, held in honor of their tutelar saints, etc., but Lt. Dawson, regarding such an act as idolatrous, refused the customary homage, and was with a brother officer, similarly conscientious, placed under arrest by Sir Thomas Maitland, tried by court martial, and dismissed the service. His influential relatives and his patrons at home joined for the time with his military superiors in condemning him; and finding himself shut out from his intended career, he accepted the aid of friends, through whose liberality he was enabled to go to Trinity College, Dublin, where he took his degree in due time. In 1828 he was ordained deacon, and shortly after admitted to priest's orders and licensed as incumbent of a chapel at Guernsey, where he served five years. After several transfers, he, in 1848, accepted at the hands of his brother, as canon of Canterbury, the living of Orpington, and the curacy of St. Mary's Cray. Here he labored with great zeal, ability, and fidelity until his death, which occurred suddenly, from disease of the heart, Oct. 11, 1850. "He was a man of clear and penetrating intellect, marked originality and humor, indomitable perseverance, unflinching courage, and unbending integrity. Nothing revolted him more than any approach to cant or insincerity." A biography of this remarkable man was published shortly after his death in the *Church Record*, and has since had a wide circulation in Great Britain, India, etc., having passed through several editions in book or pamphlet form.

[1] As a passed midshipman, "On 31 March, 1823," says O'Byrne's *Naval Biography*, "he commanded one of the boats of the *Thracian*, 18 guns, when, in conjunction with those of the *Tyne*, 26 guns, — the whole carrying 47 men, under command of the present Admiral Walcott — they boarded and captured, after an engagement of 45 minutes, the *Zaragozana*, a notorious piratical schooner of 13 guns, and upwards of 70 men. On this occasion, Mr. Dawson with his own hands took prisoner the pirate-chief, the celebrated Marquis Cayotano Arogonez, as the latter, having with others jumped overboard, was wading through the water to the shore. For his conduct he received the thanks of the commander-in-chief." Subsequently, in command of Vice-Admiral Halstead's own barge, he joined an expedition, headed by Lieutenant Commander Cawley, to hunt out and destroy the pirates in the Isle of Pines and other places. "In the execution of this service, Mr. Dawson, who piloted, and who sketched and drew plans of the enemy's lurking places, displayed zeal which was gratefully acknowledged" by the commander of the expedition and by the admiral. "As an instance of the hard service Mr. Dawson went through," says *O'Byrne*, "we may mention that on one occasion he was for a fortnight absent in a five oared gig in pursuit of pirates, on short allowance, and exposed to a scorching sun in the day, and to heavy dews at night. At another time he nearly lost his life from yellow fever."

afloat. He was placed on the retired list of lieutenants in 1851, and was promoted to the rank of commander July, 1, 1864. After he left the *Hyacinth* Capt. Dawson commanded various merchant ships and steamships. He was for over three years chief police magistrate at Manganui, New Zealand; has been superintending civil engineer of an important railway in England; and has also had charge of the new coal docks at Llanelly, in South Wales. He m. 1st, *Marguerite Jane Paddock*, dau. of John Paddock, Esq., staff surgeon in the royal army. They had two sons:

3–1. William, b. abt. July, 1832, d. in command of an East India vessel, in the Arabian gulf, abt. 1869; no issue.

3–2. George Francis, b. at St. Heliers, Island of Jersey, Oct. 27, 1834, res. 1873, Washington, D. C.; *m.*

Capt. DAWSON m. 2d, *Harriet Heywood Styles*, dau. of William Hancock Styles, Esq., of New House Farm, Northfleet, county Kent. Their sons are:

3–3. Augustine Rawlins, educated at Cambridge, now govt. agt. at Kajalla, Ceylon.

3–4. Llewellyn Styles, b. at Llanelly, South Wales, April, 1847, lieutenant R. N., now at new Guinea.[1]

3–5. Harry Percy, sub-lieutenant R. N., now at Bermuda, W. Indies.

3–6. Edward Harrison, clerk in the London and County Bank, Croydon, England.

3–7. Sidney Pace, *twin bro. of Edward H.*, clerk in the Oriental Bank Corporation, Haldumulla, Ceylon.

3–2. GEORGE FRANCIS DAWSON, b. at St. Heliers, Island of Jersey, Oct. 27, 1834, passed several years of his childhood in New Zealand, but returned to England as soon as old enough to enter the Royal Naval School at Greenwich, where he spent three years, completing the course of study, but choosing not to remain the regulation term of four years, without which a certificate of graduation is not granted. After leaving the Naval

---

[1] Lt. Llewellyn Styles Dawson entered the royal navy, 1861, and has since become distinguished as a scientific officer, conducting scientific surveys in China, South America, etc. For explorations on the Upper Yangtse river in 1870 he received the thanks of the Chamber of Commerce of Shanghai and of Admiral Keppel, and was promoted to his present rank of lieutenant. In 1872 he was selected by the Royal Geographical Society, out of one hundred competitors, to command the expedition equipped by the society for the search for and relief of Dr. Livingstone, and in February of that year sailed on the *Abydos* from London for Zanzibar. The circumstances which partially defeated the objects of this expedition are well known. Lt. Dawson is now engaged in a survey of the Island of New Guinea.

Geo. Frs. Dawson.

School, Mr. Dawson spent a few years at sea in the merchant service, and has been, in the course of his life, three times around the world. He came to the United States from China in March, 1852, landing at San Francisco, California, a youth of 17, eager for adventure, whereof he had a large experience in the few years following, during which he engaged in a great variety of occupations, including mining. In 1856, while in Nevada City, California, he entered the office of Hon. A. A. Sargent, now United States Senator from California, as a student of law, and in the following year became connected with the press of San Francisco, first as law reporter for the *Evening Argus*, and afterwards, editorially and otherwise, with the *Bulletin*, *Call* and *Alta Californian*. He has also been connected with the Sacramento *Union* and *Record*, of which latter he is now the regular Washington correspondent.[1] About 1864, Mr. Dawson was engaged as superintendent of some American mining operations in Sinaloa, Mexico, in which he was employed about eighteen months, suffering finally the loss of his property there through the spoilations of the French army. Shortly after returning from Mexico he went to the state of Nevada, where, as conductor of the Virginia City *Enterprise*, then and now its leading paper, he was successfully engaged in the great struggle for the admission, under the enabling act, of that state into the Union. He went to New York city in January, 1865, and March 3, 1866, established there the *Journal of Mining*, and while editor of that paper was, in 1869, elected a member and manager of the American Institute. The unprecedented financial success of the Industrial Exhibition of 1867, was largely due to Mr. Dawson's management. After this, beginning with the first inauguration of President Grant, Mr. D. held a clerkship in the House of Representatives at Washington, until Nov. 1870, when he resigned the position to accept an appointment as superintendent of the American Institute National Industrial Ex-

---

[1] Mr. Dawson possesses a remarkably fertile pen and retentive memory, gifts which have enabled him to perform, as a newspaper man, tasks which are rarely equalled: as, in the conduct of one of the San Francisco daily papers for some weeks at one time *without assistance from any other pen*, yet producing the usual variety and amount of literary work in each issue, and in the reporting, *entirely from memory*, at the length of two columns of solid minion, of a lecture to which he had listened, the report being afterwards complimented by the lecturer as one of singular fidelity.

hibition of 1871.[1] He has since devoted much time in efforts to secure the establishment of a permanent Free Exhibition of the Industries of the Nation, on an immense scale, at New York, advocating the project with rare eloquence and ability, by means of pamphlets and otherwise. He res. 1873, in Washington, having in 1872, been reäppointed assistant clerk of the House of Representatives. Mr, Dawson m. in New York city, Dec. 28, 1870, *Rosalie Anne Richardson*, dau. of Thomas Richardson, Esq., of New York. They have one ch:

4–1. Gilbert Francis, b. in Washington, Nov. 11, 1872.

---

[1] "The American Institute Industrial Exhibition of 1871, was considered the best that had ever been held in the United States, and fiancially, the results during the forty days of its existence have never yet been equalled, although previous and subsequent exhibitions have had the benefit of from ten to over one hundred per cent., more days of exhibition." Mr. Dawson's scheme, projected by him, but fully endorsed by the managers of the institute, of a vast permanent exhibition of the world's industries and industrial processes in New York, formed, as MR. WALT WHITMAN stated, "the spinal part" of the poem, *After All not to Create Only*, read by him at the opening of the exhibition of 1871.

VIRGINIA.

Besides the Dawsons emigrating into Virginia from Maryland, of whom some account has been given in the foregoing records, other families of the name were very early planted in that state. Bishop Meade mentions the name among those prominent in the records of some of the oldest districts in the state in "the times long since gone by."[1]

Three clergymen of the name — all of the church of England, are known to have been in the colony more than one hundred years ago. Two of these, the Reverends WILLIAM and THOMAS DAWSON, were brothers; the third, the Rev. MUSGRAVE DAWSON, was cotemporary with them, and may have been of the same family.

The Rev. WILLIAM DAWSON, one of the brothers above named, was the second president of William and Mary College,[2] succeeding the Rev. William Blair, who had held the office from the foundation of the institution until his death, April 18, 1743, a period of fifty years. The second president was sent over from England. He was graduated at Oxford, and was accounted an able scholar.[3] His predecessor in the presidency had also held, by appointment from the bishop of London, the office of commissary in the colonies of Virginia and Maryland, by virtue of which he had a seat in the Council of State, and received £100 per annum as councillor. To this office President Dawson also succeeded. His brother Thomas, who had been chiefly educated at Williamsburg, under his direction, and had been master of the Indian school, was called to the rectorship of the church of Breeton parish, in 1750.[4] The latter succeeded

[1] Especially of Warwick county and parish, which composed one of the eight original shires of Va.— *Old Churches and Families of Virginia*, vol. 1, p. 240.

[2] At Williamsburg. The college was chartered in 1692, and named after the Royal Grantors.

[3] "Mr. William Dawson, M. A., brought up at Queen's, where he lived nine years........by the unanimous consent of the Visitors elected President."— Perry's *Papers relating to the History of the Church in Virginia.*

[4] Duyckinck's *Cyclopedia of American Literature;* Meade's *Old Churches and Families of Va.*, vol. 1, p. 167. Breeton parish was in Williamsburg, the college town. See also, Perry's *Papers.*

the Rev. William Dawson as commissary, in 1752, while the presidency passed at the same time to William Stith, the historian of Virginia, who held the office until 1755, when the Rev. THOMAS DAWSON became president, being thus the fourth incumbent of the office, which, with the commissaryship, he retained until his death in 1761. Commissary Dawson married a sister of Stith, the historian and president.[1] Bishop Meade intimates that the usefulness of the second Dawson was somewhat impaired by indulgence in drink, a fault at that time not uncommon with the clergy who came over from England, and that his unfortunate habit led at one time to his arraignment by the visitors of the College. The offence was, however, passed over, on the plea that the excesses complained of had been occasioned by his poor health, and the burdens and vexations of his official duties.[2] The third clergyman of this name was the Rev. Musgrave Dawson, who was minister of Raleigh parish, Amelia county, Va., in 1754,[3] and of the parish of St. Mary's, in Essex county, in 1758.[4] Whether either of these left issue is not known, though Bishop Meade mentions "the Dawsons" in a list of the early clergy of Virginia, ancestors, as he thinks, of large bodies of Virginians.[5] The widow of one of the presidents was probably living in Williamsburg, in 1777,[6] and it is surmised that JOHN DAWSON, who was a Representative in Congress from Virginia, 1797, was a descendant of one of the clergymen above named. He graduated at Harvard University in 1782; was chosen presidential elector from the seventh district of Virginia, 1793, Washington's second term; was a member of Congress, 1797 to 1814; served in one of the State Conventions of Virginia, and in the General Assembly; was a member of the Executive Council of Virginia; rendered service in the war with Great Britain, in 1813, as aid to the commanding

[1] Duyckinck's *Cyclopedia*, vol. 1, p. 138.

[2] *Meade*, vol. 1, p. 168. He was badly treated by the professors of the college, and shamefully maligned by Rev. William Robinson, who was appointed his successor.— Perry's *Papers*.

[3] *Ibid*, vol. 2, p. 20.

[4] *Ibid*, vol. 1, p. 409.

[5] *Ibid*, p. 192.

[6] In August, 1777, "Lady Washington, the amiable consort of his Excellency General Washington," arrived at Williamsburg. She was "saluted with the fire of cannon and small arms," and was entertained at the house of Mrs. DAWSON. — Frank Moore's *Diary of the Revolution*, vol. 1, p. 477.

general on the lakes; and was appointed bearer of dispatches to France, in 1801, by President Adams. He died in Washington city, March 30, 1814, aged 52 years.[1] The frequent notices of his speeches and other acts in Congress contained in Benton's *Abridgement of Debates of Congress*, prove that he was an active and influential member and a successful legislator.

Other early representatives of the name, supposed to be Virginians, were as follows:

JAMES DAWSON, a private in Co. No. 4 (Captain Thomas Tibbs), in Col. Morgan's Riflemen, as they stood April 30, 1777; ROBERT DAWSON, a sergeant, and BENJAMIN DAWSON, a private, in Co. No. 8 (Captain Francis Taylor), in Col. Morgan's Riflemen, as they stood April 1, 1777; BENJAMIN DAWSON, a private in Co. No. 6 (Captain Alexander Breckenridge), Col. Nathan Gibbs' Virginia regiment, 1777, and another BENJAMIN DAWSON, a private in the 8th or major's company of same regiment, 1777; WILLIAM DAWSON, an ensign, commissioned Feb. 26, 1776.[2]

The Rev. MARTIN DAWSON was extensively known towards the close of the last century as a Baptist minister in the Albemarle District, Virginia, where he commenced preaching about the year 1774, being then in his thirtieth year. He was not ordained in the ministry until some years later, his first pastoral charge being the church at Ballinger's Creek. It is said of him that for many years he presided over the Albemarle Association with much dignity. "Besides the church called Ballenger's Creek, he served at different times several other churches. His talents, though not showy, were of the useful kind. He did much good. . . . . . . He married early in life, and was the father of a numerous offspring, for whose support, by his industry, he made ample provision."[3] The date and place of his death, and the names of his children, are not known. The

[1] Lanman's *Dictionary of Congress.* There have been five of the name in the U. S. Congress, viz.: John Dawson, of Va.; John B. Dawson, of La.; John L. Dawson of Pa.; William C. Dawson, of Geo.; William J. Dawson, of N. C.

[2] Saffel's *Records of the Revolutionary War*, pp. 272, 273, 287, 288, 289. The three first named may have been Pennsylvania or Maryland men. "Ensign Dawson" is frequently mentioned in the "Orderly Book of that portion of the Am. Army stationed at Williamsburg, Va., March to August, 1776, under command of Gen. Andrew Lewis."

[3] Taylor's *Virginia Baptist Ministers*, vol. 1, p. 261.

work from which the above account is extracted is provokingly deficient in the facts which would especially interest the genealogist, and they have not been learned elsewhere; but from coincidences of names, locality (central Virginia) and religious profession, it is supposed that he was of, or nearly related to, the family whose records herewith follow:

From Rev. John Dabney Dawson, Superintendent of the Kentucky Female Orphan School, Midway, Woodford Co., Ky. (quoting letters of his uncle Elisha Dawson, of Lincoln Co., Ky.), 1855, *and from Rev. Wm. C. Dawson, New York City,* 1873, *the following:*

1. Rev. J. D. Dawson states that the parents of his grandfather Dawson emigrated to Virginia, the father from England, the mother from Wales. Their names are not known. Their sons were:

2–1. Martin, of whom presently.
2–2. Robert, perhaps the sergeant above mentioned; no information concerning his family, if any.
2–3. Joseph, of whom presently.
2–4. John, of whom presently.

And perhaps others. These are named in the order given by Mr. Elijah Dawson, son of the last named, on whose authority it is also stated that Martin and Joseph, who lived and died, as he states, in Amherst county, Virginia, within a mile of each other, each lived to the extraordinary age of 115 years.[1]

2–1. Martin Dawson was described by Mr. Elijah Dawson, as follows: "He was a spare, thin visaged man, and had black hair and eyes. It was said of him that he had been a great hunter, but he was a farmer when I knew him. He had married the second time. The name of his last wife was *Carter.* He had a good many children by each wife. The names of some of his children were" as follows:

3–1. Martin, a Baptist preacher.
3–2. William, a Methodist preacher.
3–3. Nelson, a farmer.
3–4. Jesse, a farmer.
3–5. Zechariah, a farmer.

[1] The longevity of an English namesake appears to have far exceeded anything mentioned in these records: "Nov. 28, 1818. Ann Dawson d. at Harrowgate, England, aged 161."—Munsell's *Every Day Book of History and Chronology*, p. 452.

Of these Mr. E. D. says: "I knew all but William and Martin. They were preachers, and had left the neighborhood before my recollection. One was a Baptist, the other a Methodist preacher. Martin was a Baptist preacher, if I recollect aright. Zechariah was high sheriff, and at an early day emigrated to North Carolina.

2-3. JOSEPH DAWSON, a "large and fleshy man," was a farmer. He had two sons:

3-6. Lewis, a Methodist preacher, said to be very able.
3-7. Pleasant.

2-4. JOHN DAWSON died in Virginia before 1796, when his widow emigrated with her sons John and Elijah—the latter then only twelve years old—to Lincoln county, Kentucky, whither her daughter Mary had preceded her in 1795. He was "a large man, with blue eyes and fair complexion." His wife's family, resided in Prince Edward county, Virginia. Her maiden name was *Watkins*. Their children were:

3-8. Mary, b. Feb. 27, 1774, d. before 1855. STEELE.
3-9. Susan, d. before 1855. CALLISON.
3-10. John, b. 1779, went to Ky. 1796, returned to Va. 1797, and was drowned the same year in James river.
3-11. James, b. Oct. 11, 1781, d. Oct. 25, 1836; *m.*
3-12. Elijah, b. April 12, 1784, d. in Lincoln Co., Ky., abt. 1857; *m.*

3-8. *Mary Dawson*, b. in Va., Feb. 27, 1774 (d. before 1855), m. WILLIAM STEELE, and emigrated to Lincoln Co., Ky., 1795. Their children were:

4-1. John D., "a man extensively known as a preacher of the gospel, and as extensively loved and admired."
4-2. Betsey.
4-3. Susan.

3-9. *Susan Dawson*, sister of Mary, above named, b. in Va., about 1777, d. in Ky., before 1855.[1] She m. JOSEPH CALLISON. Their children were:

4-4. William.
4-5. Charity.
4-6. Dawson.
4-7. Gilmore.

---

[1] Concerning this lady and her sister, Rev. John D. Dawson, their nephew, writes: "They were the meekest of women; they possessed in an eminent degree 'the ornament of a meek and quiet spirit,' which in the sight of God is of great price."

4–8. [CALLISON.] Josiah.
4–9. Susan.
4–10. Polly.
4–11. Nancy.
4–12. Robert.

"Several of the sons are useful members of the church as local preachers." (J. D. D., 1855).

3–11. JAMES DAWSON, b. in Va., Oct. 11, 1781, learned the saddlery business in Lynchburg, Va., and removed to Ky. about 1797. He resided at Danville, in that state, where he d. Oct. 25, 1836. He was one of seven members of the Baptist church at that place who were tried for alleged heresy and excommunicated, they having embraced the doctrines of the church of the Disciples or Christian church, of which church, when organized at Danville, they became the original members. As to stature, etc., the same description applies to Mr. Dawson as to his father (2-4). He m. *Phebe Walker*, dau. of David Walker, a native of Buckingham county, Va., and an early emigrant to Ky. Their children were:

4–13. Walker Murrell, d. young.
4–14. Lucretia, m. ——WEBB, and res. in Ky.
4–15. John Dabney, res. 1855, Medway, Ky.; 1873, Louisiana, Mo.; *m.*
4–16. Josephine, m. ——STRONG, res. 1872, in Ill.
4–17. Joel Watkins.
4–18. James Wade, d. in Lexington, Ky.; *m.*
4–19. Susan, m. ROY STEWART, Stanford, Lincoln Co., Ky.; no chn.
4–20. Phœbe.
4–21. Rhoda, m. —— RHODES, res. 1873, St. Joseph, Mo.
4–22. Mary Eliza, m. —— CARNES, Jacksonville, Ill., d. about 1855, leaving one child.

3–12. ELIJAH DAWSON, b. in Va., April 12, 1784, removed with his mother to Lincoln Co., Ky., when in his twelfth year, where he d. about 1856. He m. 1805, *Sarah Logan*, and was thus connected with one of the old and noted families of Kentucky. He served in the war of 1812, under General Harrison; was an elder in the church for many years, and was greatly beloved by his neighbors and fellow citizens. His children, "scattered through Ky. and Mo.," were as follows:

4–23. John Logan, farmer, res. 1873, on his father's estate in Lincoln Co., Ky.
4–24. Sarah.

4–25. Patsy.
4–26. Susan.
4–27. James Franklin.
4–28. Robert Beatty.
4–29. Elijah Wade.
4–30. Matthew Evermont.

4–15. Rev. John Dabney Dawson, b. at Danville, Ky., about 1813, a contributor to these records, was educated at Center College, in Danville, and at Transylvania University, Lexington, Ky. At the latter institution, where he graduated, he was a room mate of the Hon. Montgomery Blair. At about the time of his graduation he was ordained to the ministry in the church of the Disciples, and he has been a teacher and local preacher all his life. He was the first superintendent of the Kentucky Female Orphan School, at Midway, filling that office from 1849 until 1857, a period of eight years. In 1858 he became a professor in the Christian College, at Columbia, Mo. (a denominational school of a high order, for young ladies), but resigned the position in 1861. He now (1873) resides on his farm near Louisiana, Mo. He m. in Ky., Mrs. Mary Jane Bell. Their children, besides some who d. young, were:

5–1. Theodore Bell, b. at Lexington, Ky., 1838, res. 1873, Warsaw, Ill.; *unm.*
5–2. William Chipley, b. in Scott Co., Ky., 1841, res. 1873, New York city; *m.*
5–3. Mary Eloise, b. in Hannibal, Mo., 1846, res. 1873, Louisiana, Mo.; *unm.*
5–4. James Parrish, b. in Midway, Ky., 1851, res. 1873, Louisiana, Mo.; *unm.*

4–18. James Wade Dawson, m. Miss *Van Pelt*, and resided at Lexington, Ky., where he d. leaving one child:

5–5. Joseph K., dentist, res. 1873, Little Rock, Ark.

5–2. Rev. William Chipley Dawson, b. in Scott Co., Ky., 1841, was educated at the University of Missouri, and at Bethany College, Virginia, graduating at the latter institution in 1865, in the last class graduated by the Rev. Dr. Alexander Campbell, the eminent founder of the college, and its president for twenty-five years. While a student, Mr. Dawson served as adjunct professor of languages in the University of Missouri, and has since received the degree of Master of Arts from that institution. Soon after leaving college he entered the ministry of the Christian church, and has been in pastoral charge of churches of that denomination at Decatur, Ill., Lexington, Mo., Louisville, Ky., and New York city. His removal to New York took place in the fall of 1872, since which time he has been pastor of the Christian church, in Twenty-eighth street.

He m. at Bethany, W. Va., 1866, *Jane C. Campbell*, niece of Dr. Alex. Campbell. They have three children:

6–1. Campbell, b. in Lexington, Mo., 1868.
6–2. William Chipley, b. in Louisville, Ky., 1871.
6–3. Theodore Bell, b. in New York city, 1873.

[Note. An abstract of the records immediately preceding having been sent, in 1871, to the Rev. Samuel G. Dawson, Toledo, O., he wrote, referring to the family described, as follows: "I have no doubt of their being of my father's family stock, but have no means of ascertaining the fact." He stated, however, that according to the tradition in his family, the original emigrant in Virginia came from Scotland. This was Mr. D.'s great grandfather. He was named MARTIN DAWSON, and settled in Amherst county. His wife's maiden name was *Gaines.* They had, besides several daughters, an only son named Nelson. May not this have been the Martin Dawson, of Amherst county, numbered 2–1 of the foregoing record, according to which account he was *twice* married, and had, besides other sons,.one named Nelson? As to the place of his nativity the accounts disagree, but these being in each case merely traditional, the discrepancy is not important. The compiler inclines to the belief that the above suggests the true explanation of this somewhat puzzling genealogical enigma, but deems it unsafe to assume the truth of the explanation suggested without further investigation. If it should prove to be correct, the record of Martin Dawson's family, as given above (2–1) and as given below (1) should be consolidated, as follows: "MARTIN DAWSON, of Amherst county, Virginia, married, 1st,—— *Gaines.* They had, besides several daughters, one son named Nelson. He married 2d,—— *Carter.* They had sons named Martin, William, Jesse and Zechariah."]

From Rev. Samuel Gaines Dawson, Toledo, Ohio, the following:

1. MARTIN DAWSON came from Scotland, and settled in Amherst county, Virginia. His wife's maiden name was *Gaines.* They had, besides several daughters, one only son named:

2–1. NELSON C. DAWSON,[1] whose first wife was *Lucy Goode*, of Charlotte Co., Va. They lived in Amherst county, and had one son and four daughters, as follows:

---

[1] Nelson C. Dawson was a corporal, and Benjamin R. and Martin N. Dawson (brothers?) were privates in Capt Cornelius Sales' company, 8th Regt., 4th Brigade, Va. Militia, under Gen. John H. Cooke, 1814-15, each serving 5 mos. and 20 days.

3–1. Samuel Gaines, b. about 1796, d. near Zanesville, O., 1835; *m.*
3–2. Lucy, m.— Wingfield.
3–3. Betsey, m.— Ware.
3–4. Nancy, m.— Lambkin.
3–5. Matilda, m. in Lynchburg.

Name of Nelson C. Dawson's second w., and whether any issue of that marriage, not stated.

3–1. Samuel Gaines Dawson, b. in Amherst county, Va., about 1796, went from his native county as surgeon's assistant under Dr. Austin, in Leftwich's Brigade, which went from Bedford county, Va., in the war of 1812. On the death of Dr. Austin he was promoted surgeon, served till the end of the war, and was discharged on its close, at Ellicott's Mills, in Maryland. After the war he settled in Salem, Roanoke county, Va., as a practicing physician, and was there married, in 1816, to *Maria Burwell*, dau. of Major Lewis Burwell, and w. —— *Digges*, daughter of Dudley Digges, Esq. After a residence of two years in Salem, he removed to Lynchburg, Va., where, in partnership with Jacob Haas, he published the *Lynchburg Press*. He remained in Lynchburg about four years. Having sold his shares in his *Press* to Pleasants (who afterwards fell in a duel) he returned to Salem, and resumed the practice of medicine. Thence he removed, in 1831, to Putnam, one of the suburbs of Zanesville, Ohio, where he died in 1835, aged 39. His widow still survives, and resides, 1873, in Davenport, Iowa. Their children were:

4–1. Fanny, d. in infancy.
4–2. Martha, m. in Putnam, David Munch; res. 1873, near Lima, Allen Co., O.
4–3. Nelson Burwell, d. Davenport, Iowa, 1856; no family.
4–4. Lucy Ann, m. near Columbus, O., —— Armstrong; res. Iowa.
4–5. Mary Jane, m. in Crawford Co., Gilbert Erwin; res. 1873, Cleveland, Henry Co., Ill.
4–6. Fanny D., m. —— Swan; res. 1873, Davenport, Iowa.
4–7. Rosalie, res. 1873, Davenport, Iowa.
4–8. Edwin, res. 1873, Laramie, Wyoming.
4–9. Samuel Gaines, b. in Salem, Va., March 17, 1831, res. 1873, Toledo, O.; *m.*
4–10. Thomas Lewis, res. 1873, Laramie, Wyoming.
4–11. Edmonia, m. Capt. H. C. Hamilton; res. 1873, Richwood, Union Co., Ohio.

4-9. Rev. SAMUEL GAINES DAWSON, was b. in Salem, Roanoke county, Va., March 17th, 1831. In his twenty-seventh year, he left the mercantile life in which he had been engaged from his fifteenth year, and after a brief course of study, was ordained a minister of the Baptist denomination, beginning his ministerial life near Marietta, Ohio. He preached in Virginia and Ohio until 1861, when he became pastor of the Baptist church at Lancaster, Ohio. In 1863, he assumed the charge of a Mission church in East Toledo, Ohio, where he is still located as pastor of the Second Baptist church of that city.[1] He m. in McConnellsville, O., Sept. 4, 1854,

"[1] It will be remembered that this evening, at 7½ o'clock, Rev. S. G. Dawson will deliver a discourse concerning his ten years' pastorate in East Toledo, in the Baptist church, East Side, at 7½ o'clock. After the service in the church, the friends will gather at his house, on Fourth and Oak streets, for a social reunion and entertainment.

"The experience of any man who stands by a great city, and watches its development for a period of ten years, is replete with interest. How much more so must be the experience and recollections of a clergyman, who for an unbroken decade has marked not only the physical and material, but the spiritual growth of such a field as that which the returning years have ripened under his ministration. We trust the Rev. gentleman will pardon us if on the eve of his anniversary service we take occasion to allude somewhat personally to the labors whose history the Baptist church of East Toledo can regard only with pleasure and satisfaction. His ministry, like his field, was comparatively a new one. Three years in the building of a church and the organizing of a congregation on the Ohio river, near Marietta, and two years at Lancaster, in this state, had filled the short interval between an active business life in Davenport, Iowa, and his undertaking what was then the mission work of East Toledo. One of the most influential of those through whose counsel Mr. DAWSON entered this field was the late HORACE L. SARGENT, the fruit of whose labors is still abundant, notwithstanding his earthly work is ended. We may well imagine, though we cannot fully comprehend, with what anxiety and solicitude this field was entered. The possibilities were great, but the obstacles, from a human stand point, were even greater, and after all his toil another might come to gather in his harvest. And so we say, that standing in the present with the vague possibilities of those bygone years crystallized into clear cut facts, the past seems but a story of some other and well nigh forgotten generation.

MR. DAWSON came into East Toledo on the 26th day of November, 1863, the day before Thanksgiving. At that time Toledo's boastful friends claimed 16,000 people. In the bounds of his parish on the east side, there were supposed to be about 800. But that parish extended from Grassy creek to the bay, and from the east bank of the Maumee to Clay Junction, about seven miles by ten. In these boundaries he has labored just ten years. * * * *

* * * The Baptist church was formed with nine members, aside from the pastor and his wife. The church has had in all, 154 members, and to-day numbers 114. There are two Sunday schools, enrolling over one hundred each.

The reader may gather a faint idea of the work of these ten years when we give the following figures:

MR. DAWSON has preached 1,750 sermons; attended over 1,000 prayer meetings; has superintended two Sunday schools most of these ten years, while teaching a class in each school; and has been Sunday school chorister all of this time. He has made visits innumerable, has attended over 200 funerals, and more than 50 weddings. He has seen the city grow from fifteen to forty thousand; his own parish from eight

Anna Maria Barker, dau. of Luther D. and *Maria Devol* Barker. They have had three children, all of whom d. young:

5–1. Frank Henry.
5–2. Maria B.
5–3. Mary B.

The compiler is indebted to Mr. Dawson for valued assistance in the compilation of these records.

The records of what is supposed to be another branch of this family were contributed by the Rev. James Madison Dawson, of Owensboro, Ky., 1872, as follows:

1. John Dawson lived in Stafford county, Va. He was an officer in the Revolutionary service, and was six feet six inches in height. He m. in Va., and, taking with him his family (except a son who had previously emigrated to Louisiana, and perhaps a married daughter), he removed, in 1817, to Shelby county, Ky. Thence he removed to Jacksonville, Ill., where he d. at the age of 89, and was buried with the honors of war. He had nine children:

2–1. Samuel, b. in Stafford Co., Va., abt. 1780, d. in Ohio Co., Ky., 1844; *m.*
2–2. Bailey.
2–3. John, removed to Louisiana before 1817.
2–4. Barnett or Bernard, d. in Ill.; *m.*
2–5. Elijah.
2–6. Lemuel, *m.*
2–7. Barton.
2–8. Lydia.
2–9. Hannah.

2–1. Samuel Dawson, b. in Stafford Co., Va., about 1780, m. 1st, in Va., about 1807, *Susan Hardin*, and about 1817, emigrated to Shelby county, Ky., removing thence about 1829, to Davies Co., in the same state. He d. at his son Jackson's, in Ohio Co., 1844. By his first wife, above named, he had nine children, all of whom settled in Ky., and are named in the order of their ages, as follows:

---

hundred to twenty-five hundred; church members on the east side increased from a dozen to three hundred; one church building to six; and Sunday school scholars from thirty to four hundred.

But while figures will not lie, they cannot tell all of the truth. This is simply the skeleton of ten years of toil and anxieties in the Black swamp of Ohio. It may be good as a skeleton, but this is all; for the hopes and fears, the burdens and joys of such a life cannot be measured or expressed." — *Toledo Blade*, Nov. 26, 1873.

3–1. Harrison, b. in Va., 1807, d. at Owensboro, Ky., 1855 ; *m.*
3–2. Nelson, d. in Shelby Co., Ky.
3–3. Gipson, b. in Va., 1809, res. 1872, in Davies Co., Ky. ; *m.*
3–4. Madison, d. in Shelby Co., Ky.
3–5. Samuel, d. in Shelby Co., Ky.
3–6. Jackson (or John), b. 1817, res. in Ohio Co., Ky. ; *m.*
3–7. Martha, m. 1st, OSBORNE KING, 4 children ; 2d, —— HARPER, 3 children ; res. 1872, Ohio Co., Ky.
3–8. Linia, d. in Ohio Co., Ky., m. 1st, —— WESTERFIELD, 2 daus. ; 2d, —— POOL, 1 son.
3–9. Jane, m. GEO. W. RHODES ; 7 children, all res. Ohio Co., Ky.

Mr. Dawson's second wife was a widow whose maiden name was *Myers*. She d. in 1833. They had one son :

3–10. Jacob M., b. in Ky., July 30, 1828, res. 1872, Decatur, Ill.

2–4. BARNETT (or BERNARD) DAWSON m. ——— ; d. in Illinois. One son :

3–11. Bailey, b. about 1832, res. 1872, Jacksonville, Ill. ; *unm.*

2–6. LEMUEL DAWSON, m. *Mary* ——, had son :

3–12. Benjamin, who res. 1872, in Missouri.

3–1. HARRISON DAWSON, farmer, b. in Prince William Co., Va., 1807, removed with his parents to Kentucky, 1817, and d. at Owensboro, in that state, 1855. He m. *Susan Bassett.* They had twelve children, of whom some d. young. The wid. and six children res. in Illinois.

3–3. GIPSON DAWSON, carpenter, b. in Prince William Co., Va., 1809, removed with his parents and gr. father into Shelby Co., Ky., in 1817, and res. 1872, in Davies Co., in that state. He m. Nov. 1, 1832, *Catharine Griffin*, who d. in Ky., of palsy, in 1870. They had three sons, all b. in Davies Co. :

4–1. James Madison, b. Jan. 17, 1836, d. at Owensboro, Ky., 1873 ; *m.*
4–2. William Harrison, b. Nov. 30, 1841, res. 1872, Hawesville, Ky. ; *m.*
4–3. John Coleman, b. Jan. 18, 1846, d. in Owensboro, Jan. 30, 1857, aged 11.

3–6. JACKSON (sometimes called JOHN) DAWSON, was b. in the wilderness, at the foot of the Alleghany mountains, during the journey of his parents into Kentucky, in 1817. He m. *Bethany Bishop*. They had four children, all of whom are m. and res. in Ohio Co., Ky. :

4–4. William.
4–5. Byron.
4–6. Fanny.
4–7. Sally.

4–1. Rev. JAMES MADISON DAWSON, b. in Davies Co., Ky., Jan. 17, 1836, resided 1872, at Owensboro, in same county. He entered the ministry of the Baptist denomination, July, 1855, and had, in 1872, the pastoral care of four churches. He m. at Litchfield, Grayson Co., Ky., March 26, 1862, *Ruth Ann Dowden*, dau. of Rev. D. and Sarah N. Dowden, of Brandenburg, Ky. They had seven children, all b. in Davies Co.: [1]

5–1. Theodosia, b. Jan. 15, 1863.
5–2. Pendleton, b. Feb. 23, 1865.
5–3. Sally Kate, b. Oct. 16, 1866.
5–4. James Robert, b. March 8, 1868.
5–5. Maple, b. Nov. 12, 1869.
5–6. Herbert, b. Aug. 29, 1871, d. Sept. 9, 1871.
5–7. Mary Lutitia, b. Aug. 28, 1872.

4–2. Rev. WILLIAM HARRISON DAWSON, b. in Davies Co., Ky., Nov. 30, 1841, entered the Baptist ministry in that county in June, 1846, and removed, March, 1869, to Hawesville, Hancock Co., in same state. He is now pastor of the Baptist church at that place, and serves other village churches along the river. He m. in Davies Co., Nov. 12, 1865, *Martha W. Howard.* They have two children:

5–8. John Coleman, b. July 6, 1869.
5–9. George Walter, b. May 14, 1871.

From Mr. Benj. Dawson, Leonardstown, Md., and Mr. David Dawson, Heathsville, Va., 1873, the following:

1. JOHN DAWSON, of Northumberland county, Va., gave, in 1754, a deed of 50 acres of land to his son

2–1. JOHN DAWSON, whose will was recorded in 1805. Probably his death occurred near that time. He was twice m. and had by 1st wife eight children, all now dead, as follows:

[1] A notice of Mr. Dawson's death was received from Rev. Mr. Dowden, September, 1873. A request was immediately forwarded to Mr. Dowden for the date of Mr. Dawson's death, and a sketch of his life. The compiler regrets that these have not been communicated for insertion in this work.

3–1. George.
3–2. John, has a son Richard, now living in Richmond Co., Va.
3–3. Christopher ; *m.*
3–4. Samuel, d. *unm.*
3–5. Thomas, m. *Hannah Hall.*
3–6. Jane, d. *unm.*
3–7. William, m. ; no issue.
3–8. Mary. VANLANDINGHAM ; BEACHUM.

The 2d wife of JOHN DAWSON was *Polly Hall.* They had one son :

3–9. Benjamin, b. Dec. 12, 1791, d. Feb. 16, 1863.

3–3. CHRISTOPHER DAWSON m. *Susan Headley.* He was taken prisoner by the British in last war with England ; was carried off, and never returned. One son :

4–1. Christopher, res. 1873, in Northumberland county, Va.

3–8. *Mary Dawson* m. 1st,—— VANLANDINGHAM. They had :

4–2. William.
4–3. George.

She m. 2d, —— BEACHUM. They had :

4–4. Linzey.

3–9. BENJAMIN DAWSON, farmer, b. in Northumberland Co., Va., Dec. 12, 1791, d. Feb. 16, 1863, m. *Frances Headley.* They had ten children, all b. in Northumberland county, and nearly all members of the Baptist church :

4–5. Polly H., b. 1815, res. Lottsburgh, Northumberland Co. WINSTED ; DODSON.
4–6. William, b. 1816, res. Union village, Northumberland Co. ; *m.*
4–7. Nancy, b. 1818, d. young.
4–8. Daniel, b. 1821, m. *Roberta Holliday ;* res. Union village ; no issue.
4–9. Benjamin, b. 1823, res. Leonardstown, Md. ; *m.*
4–10. Richard, b. 1826, res. Union village ; *m.*
4–11. Lewis L., b. 1828, d. 1868 ; *m.*
4–12. David, b. 1831, m. *Emma J. Hall,* res. Heathsville, Northumberland Co. ; no issue.
4–13. Joseph W., b. 1833, res. Union village ; *m.*
4–14. Frances J., b. 1835, res. Kinsale, Westmoreland Co., Va. ALLEN.

4–5. *Polly H. Dawson*, b. in Northumberland county, Va., 1815, m. 1st,—— WINSTED. They had four children :

5–1. [WINSTED.] Joseph.
5–2. Dandridge.
5–3. Isabel.
5–4. Fannie.

She m. 2d,—— DODSON, and res. 1873, at Lottsburgh, Va.

4–6. WILLIAM DAWSON, b. in Northumberland Co., Va., 1816, m. *Elizabeth Cookman*, and res. 1873, at Union village, same county. Four children:

5–5. Zernah.
5–6. Tecumseh.
5–7. John W.
5–8. Alonzo.

4–9. BENJAMIN DAWSON, b. in Northumberland Co., Va., 1823, m. *Mary E. Raley*, and res. 1873, in Leonardstown, St. Mary's Co., Md. They have had ten children:

5–9. Sarah F.
5–10. Olie.
5–11. Martha.
5–12. William H.
5–13. Nanie.
5–14. John.
5–15. Mary.
5–16. Alice.
5–17. David L.
5–18.

4–10. RICHARD DAWSON, b. in Northumberland Co., Va., 1826, m. 1st, *Elizabeth Cookman*, who d. without issue; 2d, *Elizabeth Jackson*, who also d. without issue; 3d, *Lucy Damron*. They have six children, and res. 1873, at Union village, in Northumberland county:

5–19. Braxton.
5–20. Ferdinand.
5–21. Laura.
5–22. Robert L.
5–23. Elizabeth.
5–24. Lucy M.

4–11. LEWIS L. DAWSON, b. in Northumberland Co., Va., 1828, m. *Juliet A. Sandy*, and d. 1868. They had three children, who res. 1873, at Union village, in that county:

5–25. William C.
5–26. Emma J.
5–27. Edward E.

4-13. JOSEPH W. DAWSON, b. in Northumberland county, Va., 1833, m. *Zartanie Lewis.* They res. 1873, at Union village, same county. Three children:

5-28. Henrietta S.
5-29. Benjamin F.
5-30. Lloyd M.

4-14. *Frances J. Dawson*, b. in Northumbland Co., Va., 1835, m. WILLIAM ALLEN. They res. 1873, at Kinsale P. O., Westmoreland Co., Va. Eight children:

5-31. John P.
5-32. Mary J.
5-33. William B.
5-34. Daniel W.
5-35. Fannie P.
5-36. Elizabeth S.
5-37. Eugene H.
5-38. Arthur G.

From Mr. Benjamin T. Dawson, of Masonville, Daviess Co., Ky., 1873, *the following:*

1. BENJAMIN DAWSON, a farmer, b. about 1785, was a native of Virginia, and d. in Henry Co., Ky., 1848. He was a deacon in the Baptist church. His father, who d. in Va., was twice m., and is said to have raised a family of twenty-two children. Benjamin had brothers Gabriel, Armstrong, James and Thomas, and several sisters, who lived in Ky., several having made their homes in the same county, Fayette, where he first located. His first wife was a Miss *McCann.* She dying, he m., about 1810, her sister, widow Lyon. They had six children:

2-1. Joseph M., b. in Fayette Co., Jan. 4, 1811, d. in Daviess Co., Ky., Feb., 1868; *m.*
2-2. James S., b. in Fayette Co., about 1816, d. in Daviess Co., Ky., 1858; *m.*
2-3. Ellis, d. in Henry Co., 1847, aged about 25 years; *unm.*
2-4. Betsey, d. in Indiana, about 1844, m. LAWRENCE OWEN.
2-5. Lucy, d. in Henry Co., Ky., about 1838, m. JERRY CRABB.
2-6. Mildred, d. in Henry Co., 1870, m. MARTIN DUVALL.

2-1. JOSEPH M. DAWSON, b. in Fayette Co., Ky., Jan. 4, 1811, d. of consumption, in Daviess Co., Ky., Feb., 1868, aged 57. He was a farmer; a deacon in the Baptist church; m. *Elizabeth Miller*, who res. 1872, in Daviess county. They had eleven children:

3–1. Benjamin T., b. Aug. 25, 1836, res. 1873, Masonville, Ky.; *m.*
3–2. James Ellis, b. Aug. 26, 1838, res. Daviess Co.; *m.*
3–3. William Henry, b. Jan. 26, 1841, res. Daviess Co.; *m.*
3–4. Joseph Peyton, b. Aug. 12, 1843, res. Daviess Co.; *m.*
3–5. Sarah J., b. April 2, 1846, d. May 17, 1862.
3–6. Mary K., b. Sept. 12, 1848, res. Daviess Co. COTTRELL.
3–7. Martha P., *twin sister of Mary K.*, res. Daviess Co. YEWELL.
3–8. Emma J., b. April 22, 1851, res. Daviess Co.; *unm.*
3–9. Ira W., b. Oct. 8, 1853, res. Daviess Co.; *unm.*
3–10. Bettie A., b. Oct. 1, 1857, res. Daviess Co.; *unm.*
3–11. Louella, b. June 15, 1861, d. July 3, 1864.

2–2. JAMES S. DAWSON, b. in Fayette Co., Ky., about 1816, d. in Daviess Co., Ky., 1858, of consumption. He was a Baptist preacher, and in the ministry in Henry Co. about twelve or fifteen years. He m. about 1837, *Mary J. Moore*, who is still living (1872). They had eleven children, all d. except two, both young, residing with their mother in Masonville, Ky.:

3–12. William H.
3–13. Joseph T.

3–1. BENJAMIN T. DAWSON, b. in Ky., Aug. 25, 1836, m. *Nancy J. Conyers*, and res. 1873, at Masonville, in that state. He is a deacon in the Baptist church. They have five children:

4–1. Charles Ellis, b. 1859.
4–2. Minnie Kate, b. 1860.
4–3. Joseph Coleman, b. 1866.
4–4. William Peay, b. 1868.
4–5. Ada Clyde, b. 1872.

3–2. JAMES ELLIS DAWSON, b. in Ky., Aug. 26, 1838, m. *Kate Ford*, and res. 1873, in Daviess Co., Ky. They have three children:

4–6. Alverda Jasper, b. 1866.
4–7. Eben Ford, b. 1868.
4–8. Arthur Hathaway, b. 1873.

3–3. WILLIAM HENRY DAWSON, b. in Ky., Jan 26, 1841, m. *Virginia B. Ford.* They res. 1873, in Daviess Co. Two children:

4–9. Buelah, b. 1866.
4–10. Herbert, b. 1869.

3-4. Joseph Peyton Dawson, b. in Ky., Aug. 12, 1843, m. *Mary Bell Staple.* They res. 1873, in Daviess Co. Two children:

4-11. Nettie Belle, b. 1870.
4-12. Bertha Alice, b. 1872.

3-6. *Mary K. Dawson*, b. in Ky., Sept. 12, 1848, m. James H. Cottrell, res. 1873, Daviess Co., Ky. One child:

4-13. Estelle, d.

3-7. *Martha P. Dawson*, b. in Ky., Sept. 12, 1848, m. Benjamin F. Yewell, res. 1873, Daviess Co. Three chn.:

4-14. Emma Kate, b. 1868.
4-15. Dora Alice, b. 1870.
4-16. Lulie Belle, b. 1872.

From William D. Dawson, Esq., Elizabethtown, Colfax Co., New Mexico, 1871, the following:

1. William R. Dawson (son of a Baptist minister, name not stated, whose ancestors came to Virginia in the colonial times) emigrated from Richmond in 1830, and settled in St. Louis Co., Mo., as a practicing lawyer, where he m. *Ann Eliza Paynter*, dau. of Julius Paynter, a cabinet maker, who had emigrated from Lynchburg, Va., a year or two previously. From St. Louis, W. R. D. moved to Franklin and Washington counties, Mo., where he engaged in school-teaching, farming, and the law, until about 1839. In this year he again moved to St. Louis, where he occupied himself in the newspaper business until 1847, when he again left the city. He shortly after settled in Cape Girardeau, Mo., and purchased there the *South Missourian* printing office and newspaper, which latter he converted into the *Western Eagle*, and continued to publish the same until his death in 1853. (His wid. m. Mr. John J. Sterne, of Jefferson city, Mo., and res. 1871, at Monticello, in that state). Two children:

2-1. William D., above named.
2-2. Clay D., b. 1842.

Mr. William D. Dawson, the elder son, continued the publication of the *Eagle*, at Cape Girardeau, until 1856, when he sold out, and removed to Jefferson city, Mo., where he was also engaged in the printing business, and continued in the same until 1859. In this year, he emigrated to Colorado, where he engaged in printing, mining, farming and milling, until 1865, when he again went to Missouri. From this state, after a residence of two years, he removed to Colfax county, New Mexico (1867), where he has since been engaged in mining and publishing. He is now editor and publisher of the *Railway, Press and Telegraph*, at Elizabethtown, in that county.

Mr. CLAY D. DAWSON has also followed the business of his father, and is now (1871) one of the publishers and proprietors of the *Maysville Daily and Weekly Appeal*, one of the leading newspaper publications in California.

The following from Gen. James A. Dawson, Louisville, Ky., 1873:

1. JOHN DAWSON, b. either in Md. or Va., probably abt. 1720 to 1730, lived in Bedford county, Va. He m. *Susan Wood*, who was of English descent. They had four sons and several daughters:

2–1. Jeremiah, b. in Bedford Co., May 30, 1763, d. in Hart Co., Ky., Feb. 10, 1846; *m.*
2–2. John, removed to the Kanawha valley, W. Va.; had a family.
2–3. Thomas, } said to have removed to Georgia, with their father,
2–4. William, } after his two elder sons "moved West."
2–5. Nancy, eldest dau., m. PETER FITZHUGH. The names of other daus. not communicated.

2–1. JEREMIAH DAWSON was b. in Bedford county, Va., May 30, 1763. He was old enough to take part in the Revolutionary struggle before its close; enlisted at the age of 17 as a private in the company of Capt. Watkins' Va. Vols., and participated in at least one fight, the battle of Guilford Court-House, N. C. (March, 1781). Some years after peace was declared, he m. in Bedford Co., Va., *Nancy Dollard*, who was b. in that county, Oct. 6, 1766, and was of Scotch and Welsh descent. They remained a few years in Virginia, but removed before the beginning of the present century to Kentucky, and settled for a short time in Madison county; then removed to Hardin (now Hart) county, on the banks of Green river, about a mile and a half from Munfordsville, where he d. Feb. 10, 1846, aged 83, and she d. Dec. 9, 1852, aged 87. He was a man of sober, excellent habits, simple tastes and high moral character. He received an ordinary English education, possessed strong natural sense, was six feet two inches in height, large, "raw boned" and muscular, a man of great physical power. He cared little for the acquisition of wealth, devoting his early years to the manly sports of bear and deer hunting, only giving that attention to his farm required for the maintenance of his family, and the education of his children. They had five sons and six daughters:

3–1. John, b. in Bedford Co., Va., abt. 1791, d. in Ky., abt. 1864, aged abt. 73; *m.*

3–2. Thomas, b. in Bedford Co., abt. 1792, res. 1873, in Hart Co., Ky.; *m.*

3–3. Mary, b. in Bedford county.

3–4. Susan, b. in Hart Co., Ky., m. CHARLES RADER; d. leaving several children.

3–5. Jeremiah, b. in Hart Co., d. young.

3–6. Nancy, b. in Hart Co., m. RICHARD BOSTICK, and res. a wid. in Hart Co.: several children.

3–7. William, b. in Hart Co., d. young.

3–8. Mildred, b. in Hart Co., m. HIRAM KELLEY; d. leaving several children.

3–9. Elizabeth, b. in Hart Co., m. 1st, JAMES ORCHARD; 2d, — MCCOMBS; d. in Mo.

3–10. Ransom A., b. in Hart Co., res. 1873, at the homestead, near Munfordsville; *m.*

3–11. Boice, m. MOSES STEWART; d. in Mo., leaving one or two children.

3–1. JOHN DAWSON, b. in Bedford Co., Va., about 1791, d. in Hart Co., Ky., 1864, aged abt. 73. He m. *Mary Reynolds*, and had eleven children. The sons were:

4–1. James, d. in Hart Co., Ky., 1872, leaving several children, still in Hart Co.

4–2. Miles, res. Kansas; has family.

4–3. Fielding, res. Rowlett's Station P. O., Hart Co., Ky.; *unm.*

4–4. John Will, m. ——, res. Missouri.

3–2. THOMAS DAWSON, b. in Bedford Co., Va., abt. 1792, res. 1873, in Hart Co., Ky., aged 81. He has all his life been a farmer. He m. *Nancy Fitzhugh*. Eight children:

4–5. Robert B., farmer, res. near Newton, Jasper Co., Iowa, of which county he has been Probate judge; has a family.

4–6. Jeremiah, farmer, res. near Munfordsville, Hart Co., Ky.; has family.

4–7. Peter F., physician, d. in Hart Co., 1857, aged 35; *m.*

4–8. Thomas T., farmer, res. near Newton, Iowa ; has family.
4–9. Elizabeth, res. Hart Co., Ky. FUQUA.
4–10. Mary, m. JONATHAN GARDNER, res. Powder Mills P. O., Hart Co., Ky.
4–11. Nancy, m. A. H. SHRYGLEY, res. Bacon Creek P. O., Ky.
4–12. Melinda, m. HAYDEN LOYSDEN, res. Munfordsville, Ky.

3–10. RANSOM A. DAWSON, b. in Hart Co., Ky., near Munfordsville, 1808, res. 1873, on the paternal farm. He m. in Hart county, 1833, *Elizabeth L. Wright*, who was b. in Hart Co., and d. Feb. 2, 1845, dau. of Allen Wright. They had five children :

4–13. James A., b. April 2, 1834, res. 1873, Louisville, Ky. ; *m.*
4–14. William W., d. young.
4–15. Thomas C., d. young.
4–16. Jeremiah J., b. 1840, res. 1873, Winfield, Kansas ; farmer.
4–17. Nannie A., b. 1842.

Mr. DAWSON m. 2d, Nov. 4, 1846, Martha A. S. Hodges, wid. of William Hodges, b. in Pittsylvania Co., Va. Her maiden name was *Price.* They had five children :

4–18. Sarah Elizabeth, b. 1847, m. W. A. WILSON, farmer ; res. 1873, Bacon Creek P. O., Hart Co., Ky.
4–19. Drury T., b. 1849, res. Hart Co., Ky.
4–20. Miles H., b. 1851, res. Hart Co.
4–21. Mattie M., b. 1853, res. Hart Co.
4–22. Ransom A., b. 1855, res. Hart Co.

4–7. PETER F. DAWSON, physician, d. in Hart Co., Ky., June 24, 1857, aged abt. 35, m. in Hart Co., 1852, *Rebecca Norton*, dau. of William Norton. Three children :

5–1. Thomas F., b. June 23, 1853, reporter, 1873, Louisville *Daily Ledger.*
5–2. Ellen F., b. Aug. 23, 1854.
5–3. Maria L., b. Sept. 18, 1856.

4–9. *Elizabeth Dawson* m. JESSE FUQUA. Res. Hart Co., Ky. Seven children :

5–4. Thomas D., farmer, res. Munfordsville, Ky.
5–5. Robert, farmer, res. Newton P. O., Jasper Co., Iowa.
5–6. Charles, farmer, res. Kansas.
5–7. Nancy, m. ALBERT LOYSDEN, res. Munfordsville, Ky.
5–8. Martha, m. JOSEPH LOYSDEN, res. Kansas.
5–9. Elizabeth, m. FIELDING KINNEY, res. Munfordsville, Ky.
5–10. Laura, m. FRANCIS BUTLER, res. Bacon Creek P. O., Hart Co., Ky.

4–13. Gen. JAMES A. DAWSON was b. in Hart county, Ky., April 2, 1834. At abt. the age of 18 he began to write for the press. He studied law before his majority, was elected clerk of Hart county in 1858, and reëlected in 1862. He was a democrat, but opposed to secession, voting for Mr. Douglass in 1860, and entering the Federal army in 1862, but resigning the next year, on receiving the nomination of the "Union Democracy" for register of the state land office. He was elected in August, and in the following month removed to Frankfort, the state capital. In 1867 he was reëlected register, and before the second term expired, he organized and took editorial charge of the Louisville *Daily Ledger*, the first number of which was issued Feb. 16, 1871. On the inauguration of Gov. Leslie, in Sept., 1871, Mr. Dawson was tendered by him, and accepted, the position of adjutant-general of the state, which office he still holds. He has for the past two years resided in Louisville. [1] He m. Aug. 23, 1859, *Margaret H. Connelly*, b. in Columbiana Co., O., Aug. 18, 1840, dau. of Dr. P. J. Connelly (b. in Ireland, now of Des Moines, Iowa) and w. *Ann Weimer* (of German descent, b. in Penn.). They have had four children:

5–11. Henry S., b. in Hart Co., Ky., Aug. 14, 1860, d. July 24, 1868.
5–12. Anna Wilder, b. in Hart Co., Sept. 7, 1862.
5–13. Elizabeth L., b. in Frankfort, Ky., June 22, 1864.
5–14. Howard Henderson, b. in Frankfort, Aug. 18, 1867.

William Henry Dawson, Blacksburg, Va., 1871:

1. The father (name not communicated) of Wm. Henry Dawson, above named, came from England, and m. at Carlisle, Pa., about 1812, *Sarah Preston*, a native of that state. After his marriage he was sent as a soldier in the United States service to Detroit, Michigan, where he died shortly after, of a fever. His wife was with him at the time of his decease, and about one

[1] The *Daily Ledger*, which Mr. Dawson still edits, is now a well-established, prosperous and influential journal. "Gen. Dawson is a terse, clear writer; a marked political economist, and a man of severe moral courage. As an orator he has few equals, being ever ready in debate, strong in argument, and sure in all details of facts. He has several times canvassed the state of Ky., and has attained great popularity as a speaker. The *Daily Ledger* was established under great pecuniary difficulties, and its present firm existence is due to the untiring energy and perseverance of Gen. Dawson. It is now regarded as the official organ of the Democratic party in Kentucky." — Maj. H. T. Stanton, Frankfort, Ky., 1873.

Jas. A. Dawson.

month after that event gave birth to their only child. She still (1871) survives, at the age of nearly 90 years. Her son

2-1. William Henry Dawson, was raised and educated in Carlisle, and is by profession a teacher, which occupation he has followed nearly forty years. He m. Jan., 1840, *Anna Croy*, who was b. in Va., and is of German descent. They have nine children, all b. in Blacksburg, and all living in 1871, as follows:

3-1. Robert Marion, b. April 24, 1841, res. 1871, Knoxville, Tenn.; *m.*
3-2. William Thomas, b. Feb. 2, 1843, res. 1871, Edinburg, Ind., m. *Mattie Mayhew*; 2 children.
3-3. Melissa Jane, b. 1845, res. Blacksburg, *unm.*
3-4. Wesley McDonald, b. 1847, res. Lewisburg, W. Va., m. *Ellen Foster*; 2 children.
3-5. Martha Virginia, b. 1849, m. Rev. Wm. B. Beamer, Methodist minister, res. Lexington, Va.; one child.
3-6. Sarah Elizabeth, b. 1851; *unm.*
3-7. Mary Matilda, b. 1853; *unm.*
3-8. Maggie Ribble, b. 1857.
3-9. Ellen Pauline, b. 1863.

3-1. Robert Marion Dawson, contributor to these records, was b. in Blacksburg, Va., April 24, 1841, m. in Lynchburg, Dec., 1864, *Ruberta C. Minton*, a native of that city. He is a portrait painter by profession; a talented and industrious artist, who after much patient study, mostly self directed, and years of labor, ill requited, begins, in more prosperous days, to realize that he is also a successful one. The pencil, palette and brush have been his companions almost constantly from boyhood, though laid aside for a time during the civil war, in which he took up arms on behalf of his native state. A short time after the close of the war he removed to Knoxville, Tenn., where he now resides (1872). He has had four children:

4-1. Carrie Bell, b. in Blacksburg, April 24, 1866.
4-2. Minton West, b. in Blacksburg, May 19, 1867, d. Sept. 20, 1867.
4-3. Willie Anna, b. in Knoxville, July 17, 1868.
4-4. Herbert Marion, b. in Knoxville, May 11, 1870, d. June 29, 1870.

Notes. I. *Virginians in war of* 1812-14. *From Pay-rolls.* Joseph and Gabriel Dawson, privates, Capt. Wilson's company, 2d Regt. Va. Militia, 1814, served each 2 mos. and five days; Henry Dawson, lieut.

Capt. Scott's Co. 28th Reg. Va. Mil., from Nelson county, 6 mos. ; THOMAS DAWSON, private, 2 mos. 13 days, Capt. Jarvis, Northampton county, 27th Va. Mil., 1813-14 ; JOHN DAWSON, private, 17 days, Capt. Groyn, Gloucester county, 21st Va. Mil., 1814 ; HENRY DAWSON, 6 mos. and HIRAM A. DAWSON, 5 mos. 10 days, privates, Capt. Timberlake, 17th Va. Mil., 1814-15 ; BENJAMIN DAWSON, sergeant, 4 mos. 2 days, and GEORGE and HENRY DAWSON, privates, each 3 mos. 13 days, Capt. Henderson, Northumberland county, 37th Va. Mil., 1813-14 ; JEREMIAH and SAMUEL DAWSON, each 2 mos. 18 days, and JOHN DAWSON jun., 1 month, privates, Capt. Stranghan, Northumberland county, 37th Va. Mil., 1814 ; JOHN DAWSON, private, 2 mos. 4 days, Capt. Way, 37th Regt. Va. Mil., 1813-14 ; EPPA DAWSON, drummer, 1 mo. 23 days, Capt. Deshield, 4th Va. Mil., attached to 37th Regt., 1813-14 ; ROBERT DAWSON, private, 25 days, Capt. Shield, Va. Mil., 1813 ; and see p. 320, *note*.

II. *Confederate Dead, Hollywood Cemetery, Richmond.* W. H. DAWSON, Co. H., 19th Geo. Regt., d. May 19, 1864 ; W. R. DAWSON, Co. C., 44th Ala. Regt., d. Sept. 2, 1864; T. DAWSON, Co. A., 23 So. Carolina Regt., d. Sept. 2, 1864 ; R. H. DAWSON, Co. E., 2d Md. Regt., d. April 24, 1865.

NORTH CAROLINA.

The name of DAWSON is an old and honored one in North Carolina. Its earliest representative in the colony, so far as known, was JOHN DAWSON, who was one of the governor's council during the administration of Arthur Dobbs, chief-magistrate of the colony from 1754 to 1765. The governor was from Ireland. Whether or not the members of his council were of the same nativity is not stated.[1]

FAMILY OF JOHN DAWSON,

1754-1765.

1. It is not certainly known that the above named JOHN DAWSON had a family; but there is little reason to doubt, and strong reason to believe, that he had three sons, all of whom became prominent in the country, and were members, nearly at the same time, of the North Carolina House of Commons, as follows:

2-1. Levi, member from Craven county, 1790-1791; *m.*
2-2. John, member from Northumberland and Halifax counties, 1780-1790; *m.*
2-3. William J., member from Bertie county, 1791. *See forward.*

2-1. Major LEVI DAWSON early espoused the cause of the country against Great Britain, and was appointed major of the Fifth North Carolina Regiment, by the Provincial Congress, which met at Halifax, in that state, April 4, 1776. He represented Craven county in the state legislature, then styled the House of Commons, during the years 1790 and 1791. It is understood to have been his son who was afterwards a member of the House from the same county, namely:

3-1. John B., member from Craven county, 1833. *See forward.*

[1] Wheeler's *History of North Carolina*, which see for lists of members of the House of Commons, etc. It is a family tradition, however, that the ancestor was from England.

2-2. John Dawson was a member of the North Carolina House of Commons from Northumberland county during the years 1780, 1781 and 1782, and from Halifax county in 1787 and 1790. He settled on the Roanoke river in that county, and m. a Miss *Atherton.*[1] They d. leaving four young children, all sons, as follows:

3-2. Jesse Atherton, several years a member of the House of Commons from Halifax Co.; *m.*
3-3. Henry, m. a Miss *Alston,* and d. without issue.
3-4. John, d. in Maury Co., Tenn., 1843; *m.*
3-5. William, m. but d. without issue.

2-3. William Johnson Dawson was a member of the House of Commons of North Carolina from Bertie county, 1791, and a representative in the United States Congress from that state from 1793 to 1795. He resided at Edenton, now in Chowan county. Very little more is known concerning him.[2]

2-1. John B. Dawson, a member of the House of Commons from Craven county, in 1833, afterwards removed to Louisiana, and represented that state in Congress from 1841 up to the time of his death, which occurred at St Francisville, La., June 26, 1845. It is said that he was born at Nashville, Tenn., in 1800.[3] His parents were probably among the early emigrants to that state, but seem to have retained an interest in their former home, as the son is found there in 1833. At all events, there is no doubt of the connection of the congressman of La., with this family.[4]

3-2. Jesse Atherton Dawson, a wealthy planter of Halifax county, N. C., represented that county in the House of

---

[1] For information in regard to their descendants the compiler is indebted to Mrs. Ala F. Dawson, Canton, Miss., 1873. According to Mrs. Dawson's information John Dawson (2-2) had been a member of Congress. If so he must have gone from Virginia. See p. 315.

[2] Lanman's *Dictionary of Congress.* In 1795, a deed of "William Johnson Dawson of Edenton, N. C., gentleman," manumitting a slave named Primus, was recorded in Philadelphia.

[3] Lanman's *Dictionary of Congress.*

[4] Mrs. A. F. Dawson, Canton, Miss., states, 1873, that in 1843 she paid a visit to Mr. John Dawson of Maury county, Tenn. (3-4 of this record), and was told by him that Gen. John B. Dawson, then in Congress from Louisiana, was his "own" or "first" cousin.

Commons during the years 1816, 1817, 1818, 1820 and 1821. He left one son:

4–1. John Henry, m. a Miss *Taylor*, and d. early, leaving two daus., who are still living.

3–4. John Dawson, b. in North Carolina, m. *Martha Green Hunter*. They emigrated to Shelby county, Tenn., abt. 1822, and in 1824 removed to Maury county, in the same state, where he d. in the fall of 1843. His wid. is still living at Mt. Pleasant, in that county. He was a large farmer. They had eleven children, as follows:

4–2. John, res. 1873, in Maury county, Tenn.; *unm.*
4–3. Henry A., physician, res. Maury county; *unm.*
4–4. William Leon, b. in Warren county, N. C., Oct., 1820, d. in Maury Co., Tenn., Oct., 1844; *m.*
4–5. Martha Green, m. ——— Frierson, res. Columbia, Maury Co., Tenn.
4–6. Jesse Atherton, m. ———, res. Oakalona, Miss.[1]
4–7. Temperance Alston, m. ——— Barrow, res. Mt. Pleasant, Maury Co., Tenn.
4–8. Jacob Hunter, res. Forest city, Arkansas; has a family.
4–9. Mary P., m. ——— Dobbin, res. Mt. Pleasant, Tenn.
4–10. Elizabeth T., m ——— Long, res. Mt. Pleasant.
4–11. Charity Alston, m. ——— Kitrell, res. Mt. Pleasant.
4–12. Mann, res. Mt. Pleasant; *unm.*

4–4. William Leon Dawson was b. in Warren county, N. C., Oct., 1840. His parents removed to Shelby county, Tenn., about 1822, and in 1824 to Maury county, in the same state. He was educated at La Grange College, Franklin county, Ala., and m. Jan., 1841, *Ala F. Winter*, b. at Tuscumbia, Ala., 1825.[2] They removed to Madison county, Miss., in 1843, where he engaged in business as a cotton planter. He d. in Oct., 1844, while on a visit to his parents in Maury county, Tenn. Mrs. Dawson res. 1873, at Canton, Miss. They had two sons:

5–1. John, b. in Maury Co., Tenn., Dec., 1841, d. in Canton, Miss., Oct., 1872; *unm.* *See forward.*
5–2. William Leon, b. at Tuscumbia, Ala., Oct., 1842, d. in Yazoo Co., Miss., June, 1871; *unm.* *See forward.*

---

[1] A promising son, William L., was drowned in the Mississippi river a few years since. Mr. D. has other children.

[2] Youngest daughter of William Hooe Winter and *Catharine Starke Washington*; the former from Charles county, Md., the latter dau. of Col. Harry Washington, Prince William Co., Va.

JOHN DAWSON (5-1 of this record) was b. in Maury Co., Tenn., Dec., 1841. He entered the state University of Miss., at 14, and after a year spent there, went to the Jesuit College at Georgetown, D. C., where he also remained a year. In Sept., 1859, he entered the Junior class at Princeton, N. J., where he was graduated in June, 1861, but left to join the Confederate army before his diploma was awarded. He entered what was called the Army of Tennessee as a private, and gradually rose in position to a captaincy, and, though in many battles, passed unhurt through the war, until near its close. In August, 1864, while sitting in the trenches near Atlanta, he was struck by a fragment of shell, and received injuries which were supposed to be mortal, the lower part of his face being torn away, and the chin and chest bones fractured. He, however, recovered sufficiently to return to Miss., in 1865, and for a time he edited a county newspaper, until elected clerk of the Circuit court. After serving one term in this office, he was reëlected without an opposing vote. He was afterwards displaced, to make room for an appointee of the military authority, and became associated with Oliver S. Luckett, Esq., in the practice of law. Failing health, however, constrained a cessation of all labor, and after an unavailing visit to the medicinal springs of northern Alabama he returned to Canton, where he d. in Oct., 1872, *unm.* He was talented and highly accomplished, brave, modest and refined in character. He d. in the faith of the Protestant Episcopal church, to which he belonged.[1]

WILLIAM LEON DAWSON (5-2 of this record), b. at Tuscumbia, Ala., Oct., 1842, entered the Jesuit College at Georgetown, D. C., in 1858, and in 1860 removed to Princeton, to re-

[1] "He was truly a gallant soldier, and bore his honors with the modesty of a maiden. Always present where danger led, in the front rank he received the fatal shell which so mangled and disfigured him. I saw him daily in his sufferings, and no one can truly appreciate John Dawson that did not see him then. To be brave in the fight was his nature; but stricken down, mangled, disfigured, his future and bright hopes gone, to witness in his sufferings his patience, gentleness and filial affection to his dear and devoted mother, was to see John Dawson in his greatness of heart and loving nature. The honors of the battle field he wore meekly, the sufferings of wounds he bore patiently. Of more than ordinary culture, he delighted in the classics, and amidst the beauties of poesy his nature revelled. He was gentle but firm, and I believe that no circumstances could be arranged, however difficult or trying, but what John Dawson would be the gentleman. As a son he was loving, kind and tenderly affectionate; as a soldier he was the bravest among the brave."—*Memorial Address*, by Major B. J. Semmes, delivered on the occasion of decorating the graves of the Confederate dead at Canton, April 26, 1873.

ceive private lessons and be near his brother, then a student at the University. After the commencement of the civil war he returned to Miss., and after the passage of the Confederate conscript law, compelling all youths of his age to enlist in the army, he chose the cavalry service, and during the siege of Vicksburg acted as the private secretary of Gen. Pemberton, for whom he entertained great affection. After the surrender of that city, and his exchange, he was attached to the Brigade of Gen. Wirt Adams. In consequence of exposure during the war he contracted rheumatism, from which, after a lingering illness, he d. in Yazoo Co., Miss., in June, 1871, *unm.*

FAMILY OF ROBERT DAWSON,

OF ONSLOW COUNTY, N. C.

From Mr. Robert W. Dawson, of Onslow C. H., N. C., 1873, *the following :*

1. ROBERT DAWSON, an English emigrant, lived on New river, at a place called Town Point, in Onslow county. He had a bro. Zephaniah who went back to England. Also a son:

2–1. Robert, b. abt. 1767, d. in Onslow county, Oct. 25, 1827 ; *m.*

2–1. ROBERT DAWSON, b. abt. 1767, d. in Onslow county, N. C., Oct. 25, 1827, aged abt. 60, m. *Sabra Kiff*, who d. abt. 1851, at a very advanced age. They had eight children:

3–1. John, b. March 22, 1793, d. in Onslow Co. ; *m.*
3–2. Ann, m. WASHINGTON N. CARR ; d. without issue.
3–3. Lucretia, m. ABRAHAM KOONCE ; d. without issue.
3–4. Robert, d. in Onslow Co., 1849 ; *m.*
3–5. Mary, d.
3–6. Briton, res. Onslow county ; *m.*
3–7. Hosea, d. aged abt. 35 ; *unm.*
3–8. William, d.

3–1. JOHN DAWSON, b. March 22, 1793 (son of Robert, 2–1), d. in Onslow Co., m. 1st, *Nancy Webb.* They had three children:

4–1. Elizabeth, b. April 25, 1818, d.
4–2. Hannah, b. Feb. 18, 1821, res. Onslow Co.
4–3. James, b. Feb. 8, 1823, d.

He m. 2d, *Hannah* ——, who had four children:

4–4. William R., b. Feb. 5, 1827.
4–5. Amos, b. Oct. 9, 1830.
4–6. Nancy, b. Dec. 12, 1834.
4–7. Julia, b. Oct. 13, 1840.

He m. 3d, *Nancy Pettaway.* They had five children:

4–8. Louisa.
4–9. Mary A., b. Jan. 20, 1852.
4–10. Ruthy E., b. Aug. 23, 1854.
4–11. Penny, b. Feb. 24, 1857.
4–12. Micajah, b. Sept. 1, 1860.

3-4. ROBERT DAWSON (son of Robert, 2–1), d. in Onslow county, N. C., Sept., 1849, aged abt. 52. He m. 1821, *Rebecca Wilder*, who d. Oct., 1853, aged 53. They had nine children:

4–13. Sarah Ann, b. Feb. 4, 1822, res. Wilmington, N. C.
4–14. Hester, b. April 5, 1824, res. Knoxville, Tenn.
4–15. Lucretia, b. Aug. 1, 1827, res. Wilmington, N. C.
4–16. Robert W., b. Dec. 18, 1829, res. Onslow C. H., N. C.; *m.*
4–17. Rebecca, b. Feb. 11, 1821, res. Onslow C. H.
4–18. Mary S., b. June 28, 1834, res. Onslow C. H.
4–19. John W., b. Aug. 28, 1836, res. Onslow C. H.; *m.*
4–20. Catharine, b. May 8, 1839, res. Wilmington, N. C.
4–21. Caroline M., b. Jan. 28, 1845, res. Onslow C. H.

3-6. BRITON DAWSON (son of Robert, 2–1), res. at Onslow C. H., N. C., m. Martha Bryant, formerly *Martha Williams*. They had five children:

4–22. Leonard.
4–23. Sarah.
4–24. Martha.
4–25. James.
4–26. Robert.

4-16. ROBERT W. DAWSON (son of Robert, 3-4), b. Dec. 18, 1829, res. 1873, at Onslow C. H., N. C. He m. 1st, May 17, 1854, *Margaret Jane Shivan*, who d. March 9, 1865. They had five children:

5–1. Sarah E., b. June 18, 1855.
5–2. Margaret M., b. March 1, 1857.
5–3. Rebecca R., b. March 11, 1859.
5–4. Alice A., b. Nov. 25, 1861.
5–5. Adah Jane, b. Nov. 5, 1864.

He m. 2d, Feb. 25, 1866, *Susannah Wooten*. They have had four children:

5–6. Naomi Caroline, b. Jan. 14, 1867.
5–7. James B., b. Oct. 17, 1868.
5–8. John Robert, b. Oct. 5, 1870.
5–9. Lucretia, b. Dec. 12, 1872.

4-19. JOHN W. DAWSON (son of Robert, 3-4), b. Aug. 28, 1836, m. *Hester A. Shivan*, sister to first w. of Robert W. Dawson (4-16). They res. at Onslow C. H., N. C. One child:

5–10. Laura, b. Nov. 20, 1872.

Mr. JAMES T. DAWSON, a planter, residing at Enfield, Halifax Co., N. C., stated (1870) that his father, JAMES DAWSON, was b. in that county in 1792, and was son of JOHN DAWSON, said to have emigrated from England in 1769. The latter is reputed to have had brothers in this country, but the history of them and their descendants, if any, is not known.

Mr. JOHN DAWSON, merchant, and Mr. JAMES DAWSON, banker, wealthy and influential citizens of Wilmington, N. C., are brothers, b. near Castle Dawson, county Derry, Ireland, the former about 1802, the latter about 1817.

Mr. JOHN DAWSON emigrated to this country about 1818, and some five years later settled in Wilmington. He was for several years mayor of that city. He has been twice m. His children, issue of the first marriage, were a son, Richard, who d. young, and a dau., Mrs. Hall, also now deceased, leaving children.

Mr. JAMES DAWSON emigrated to Wilmington about 1838, entering the service of his brother as a clerk. He has been for many years engaged in banking, and is the founder and president of The Dawson Bank, of Wilmington, an institution chartered by the state. He has several children.

GEORGE DAWSON, an Englishman, father of the late senator, Wm. C. Dawson, of Georgia, lived for a short time in this state and m. here widow Ruth Skidmore. See *Georgia* records.

SOUTH CAROLINA.

The oldest family of Dawsons in South Carolina appears to have been that of JOHN DAWSON, a native of Rowell, Westmoreland, England. A portion of the information which follows in regard to him and his descendants, was communicated in 1854-55, by his then only surviving son Charles Postell Dawson, Esq., of Charleston; by Arnoldus V. Dawson, Esq., of Charleston, a grandson; and by N. H. R. Dawson, Esq., then of Cahaba, now of Selma, Alabama, a great-grandson of the founder of the family in Charleston. For more recent information (1871-73) the compiler is indebted to Mrs. Caroline H. Dawson, of Aiken, S. C., to N. H. R. Dawson, Esq., above named, and to others, whose kindness is hereby gratefully acknowledged.

FAMILY OF JOHN DAWSON,

OF CHARLESTON, 1759-1812.

This family has been and is distinguished at the South for its wealth and culture, numbering among its members and connected by intermarriage with many of the leading merchants, planters and professional men of the country, and retaining much of the old-time spirit which esteems with just pride the memory of a virtuous and honorable ancestry. Its founder,

1. JOHN DAWSON, b. April 14, 1735 (N. S.), emigrated to the colony of South Carolina previous to 1759, and settled in Charleston, where he was an enterprising and successful merchant.[1] He was also the proprietor of extensive plantations. He was a member of the South Carolina convention of May,

[1] "I have seen in one of his old letter books, in the possession of a relative, copies of letters to his correspondents in London, during the war, and among them an account of the battle of Fort Moultrie." — N. H. R. D.

1788, which adopted the Federal constitution of the United States.[1] He m. in South Carolina, Oct. 9, 1760, *Joanna Broughton Monck*, dau. of Col. Thomas Monck, and gr. dau. of Col. Thomas Broughton, of South Carolina.[2] She was b. at Milton plantation, in the parish of St. John, Berkeley, S. C., Oct. 7, 1743 (N. S.). They lived together fifty-two years, and d. in Charleston, he on the 7th May, 1812, and she July 5, 1859. He left a large estate. They had eleven children, as follows :

2–1. Mabel, b. at Dorchester, S. C., Aug. 5, 1761, d. June 14, 1762.
2–2. Joanna Monck, b. in Charleston, Oct. 29, 1762, m. Col. JOHN GLAZE, March 8, 1781, d. at "The Ponds," S. C., July 19, 1781.
2–3. John, b. in Charleston, July 8, 1765, d. in Charleston, June 3, 1823 ; *m.*
2–4. Mary, b. in Charleston, March 25, 1768, d. in Charleston. POSTELL.
2–5. Thomas, b. in Charleston, March 23, 1771, d. in Charleston ; *unm.*
2–6. Elizabeth, b. in Charleston, Sept. 18, 1772, d. in Charleston ; *unm.*
2–7. Anna, b. in Charleston, April 25, 1774, d. in Pendleton, S. C., June 3, 1843. HALL.
2–8. William, b. in Charleston, Jan. 1, 1777, d. in Charleston, March 27, 1822 ; *m.*
2–9. Martha, b. in Charleston, Dec. 24, 1778, d. Aug. 25, 1783.
2–10. Lawrence Monck, b. in Charleston, Dec. 29, 1783, d. at Pineville, S. C., Oct. 3, 1823 ; *m.*
2–11. Charles Postell, b. in Charleston, Nov. 7, 1785, d. in Charleston, about 1864 ; *m.*

2–3. JOHN DAWSON, b. in Charleston, July 8, 1765, became a large merchant, and filled several public offices in his native city with honor. He was elected intendant of Charleston for three years successively, filling the office from Sept., 1806, until Sept., 1809. He was also one of the trustees of the Orphan Asylum, and was called, from his benevolence to the poor, "the Howard of Charleston." In 1811 he became cashier of the Bank of Charleston, which position he held until

[1] His sons-in-law, Col. John Glaze and William Postell, were delegates to the same convention, and all were delegates from St. George's parish, Dorchester. — See Elliot's *Debates*, *South Carolina*, vote on the adoption of the constitution. One THOMAS DAWSON was one of 210 persons, styling themselves "principal inhabitants" of Charleston, who, soon after the fall of that city, in 1780, signed an address to Sir Henry Clinton, praying to be re-admitted to the character and condition of British subjects. Was he related to JOHN DAWSON, above named ? — See Sabine's *Loyalists*, pp. 80, 243.

[2] A somewhat extended genealogical chart of the Monck family, originally LeMoyne, is in possession of the compiler, the contribution of Mr. C. P. D., who also furnished a similar chart of the Dawsons claiming descent from the Norman D'Ossone, and showing another early intermarriage with the Monck family.

his death, June 3, 1823.[1] He m. *Mary Huger*, who was of Huguenot descent, a daughter of Col. John Huger,[2] of Charleston, where she d. Nov. 11, 1823. They had twelve children, as follows:

3–1. Charlotte Motte, b. in Charleston, Nov. 13, 1789, d. in Charleston, Jan. 29, 1856; *unm.*
3–2. Joanna Monck, b. at Field Wateree, S. C., Nov. 18, 1790, d. in Charleston, Sept. 15, 1794.
3–3. Emma Monck, b. in Charleston, July 11, 1795, d. in Charleston, Dec. 6, 1863; *unm.*
3–4. Mary Anne, b. in Charleston, Nov. 1, 1796, d. in Charleston, June 28, 1860; *unm.*
3–5. John Huger, b. in Charleston, Dec. 9, 1798, res. 1873, near Brenham, Washington Co., Texas; *m.*
3–6. Lawrence Edwin, b. in Charleston, Dec. 9, 1799, d. at Carlowville, Ala., Feb. 8, 1848; *m.*
3–7. Joanna Septima, b. in Charleston, May 15, 1801, d. in Charleston, June 21, 1837; *unm.*
3–8. Octavius Huger, b. in Charleston, Oct. 2, 1802, d. in Aiken, S. C., July 2, 1856; *m.*
3–9. Anna Cecelia, b. in Charleston, Oct. 21, 1803, res. 1873, in Charleston; *unm.*
3–10. Adelaide Decima, b. in Charleston, Feb. 11, 1805, d. in Charleston, Oct. 2, 1823; *unm.*
3–11. Jacob Drayton, b. in Charleston, Dec. 31, 1806, d. in Charleston, Dec. 17, 1839; *m.*
3–12. William Henry, b. in Charleston, March 27, 1808, d, in Charleston, March 7, 1857; *m.*

2–4. *Mary Dawson*, b. in Charleston, March 25, 1768, d. in same city, m. Jan. 21, 1786, WILLIAM POSTELL, who d. in Charleston, Aug. 21, 1822. They had one child:

3–13. Joanna, b. in Charleston, d. in Charleston. INGRAHAM.

2–7. *Anna Dawson*, b. in Charleston, April 25, 1774, d. at Pendleton, S. C., Jan. 3, 1843, m. Feb. 27, 1806, Dr. GEORGE HALL, who d. at Pendleton, Jan. 9, 1829. They had four children, all b. in Charleston:

---

[1] It is said that when a boy of fifteen he ran away from his father, and joined the Continental army, under Gen. Greene, shortly before the battle of Eutaw Springs, in which he took part. His father wrote to Gen. Greene, who sought him out, and caused him to be sent home.—N. H. R. D.

[2] He was a man of large wealth, and filled many positions of honor in society. He was one of the members of the Council of Safety for the Province of South Carolina (composed of twelve of the most prominent gentlemen of the province) nominated and appointed by the Provincial Congress in 1775.—See *Journal of Council of Safety, Collections of Historical Society of South Carolina*, vol. 2.

3–14. [HALL.] George Ann, b. May 26, 1807. BURT.
3–15. John Dawson, b. Aug. 3, 1806, d.——; *m.*
3–16. Joanna Louise, b. Sept. 14, 1811, res. 1873, Greenville, S. C. TOWNES.
3–17. George Abbott, b. Oct. 28, 1813, d. at Cherry Hill plantation, S. C., May 25, 1814.

2–8. WILLIAM DAWSON, b. in Charleston, Jan. 1, 1777, d. in Charleston, March 27, 1822, m. Dec. 29, 1802, *Caroline Prioleau*, of Charleston, who d. in that city, 1872.[1] They had five children, all b. in Charleston:

3–18. Joanna, b. July 28, 1804, res. 1873, Charleston. GAILLARD.
3–19. William Alfred, b. July 15, 1806, res. 1873, at Spring Hill, near Mobile, Ala.; *m.*
3–20. Samuel Prioleau, b. Sept. 30, 1808, d. in Charleston, 1855; *unm.*
3–21. Catharine Cordes, b. May 4, 1811, d. at Sullivan's Island, near Charleston, Aug. 1832. BALL.
3–22. John Cordes, b. Oct. 6, 1813, res. 1873, at Spring Hill, near Mobile, Ala.; *m.*

2–10. LAWRENCE MONCK DAWSON, b. in Charleston, Dec. 29, 1783, d. at Pineville, S. C., Oct. 3, 1823, m. April 1, 1812, *Jane Vanderhorst*, of that city, where she d. Dec. 5, 1823. They had five children:

3–23. Harriet Honey, b. in Charleston, Sept., 1813. ANCRUM.
3–24. John Lawrence, b. at Milton plantation, March 28, 1815, res. 1873, Charleston; *m.*
3–25. Lawrence Monck, b. in Charleston, 1816, d. Oct., 1820.
3–26. Arnoldus Vanderhorst, b. in Charleston, Sept. 11, 1818, d. in Charleston, Feb. 26, 1871; *m.*
3–27. Theodore Dehon, b. in Charleston, 1820; was a student at South Carolina College, 1836-7; became a physician, and d. in New Orleans, about 1842; *unm.*

2–11. CHARLES POSTELL DAWSON, b. in Charleston, Nov. 7, 1785, d. in Charleston about 1864, m. Dec. 1, 1812, *Harriet Osborne*, who d. in Charleston, Dec. 10, 1824. He was a

---

[1] "The richest and most populous Huguenot settlement in South Carolina was that of Charleston. Here Elias Prioleau became the first pastor, a descendant of Antoine Prioli, the Doge of Venice in 1618."— Disosway's *Huguenots in America*, appended to Smiles' *Huguenots*, p. 436. Other Huguenot names will be noticed in this record, as Huger, Gaillard, Cordes, Ravenel, etc. Rev. Elias Prioleau, the founder of the distinguished family of that name in South Carolina, emigrated to the province in 1685, soon after the revocation of the Edict of Nantes, and brought with him a considerable part of his Protestant congregation. "He was *grandson* of Anthoine Prioli, who was elected Doge of Venice in 1618."— Ramsay's *History of South Carolina*, vol. 1, p. 6, *note*.

lawyer, of good abilities; admitted to the bar of South Carolina in 1807. They had six children:

3–28. Thomas Osborne, b. Nov. 9, 1813, res. 1873, in Charleston; *m.*
3–29. Charles Postell, b. Sept. 10, 1815, d. Dec. 6, 1818.
3–30. Harriet Ann, b. May 10, 1817, d. Dec. 15, 1818.
3–31. John Edward, b. May 28, 1818, physician, res. 1873, Mt. Pleasant, near Charleston.
3–32. Catharine Joanna, b. July 4, 1820, res. 1873, Charleston, w. of Dr. John L. Dawson (3-24).
3–33. Elizabeth Harriet, b. Feb. 8, 1823.

3-5. John Huger Dawson, formerly a prominent merchant in Charleston, afterwards a planter at St. John's parish, Berkeley, which parish he represented a number of years in the senate of South Carolina, was b. in Charleston, Dec. 9, 1798, where he m. 1st, Feb. 26, 1824, *Frances Lavinia Ford*, who d. without issue, March 27, 1829, fourth dau. of Jacob Ford, Esq., of Charleston. He m. 2d, April 7, 1830, *Ann Cornelia Ford*, who also d. without issue, Jan. 10, 1831, second dau. of Jacob Ford, Esq. In 1843, Mr. Dawson removed to Texas, and now res. (1873) near Brenham, Washington county, in that state. He m. there, 3d, Feb. 11, 1852, Mrs. Mary Ann Armstrong, widow, dau. of the late Mr. William Mann. She was b. in Montgomery county, Tenn., Sept. 19, 1826, and d. in Washington county, Texas, Oct. 3, 1865. They had two children:

4–1. Mary Huger, b. Nov. 16, 1853, d. Sept. 21, 1857.
4–2. Mabel, b. Dec. 5, 1861, res. 1873, with her father, near Brenham.

3-6. Lawrence Edwin Dawson, b. in Charleston, Dec. 9, 1799, d. at Carlowville, Dallas county, Ala., Feb. 8, 1848, in his 49th year. He m. 1826, *Mary Wilkinson Rhodes*, of Beaufort, S. C., eldest dau. of Dr. Nathaniel H. Rhodes, and gr. dau. of Paul Hamilton, governor of South Carolina, and secretary of the U. S. navy, under President Madison. He studied law with his relative, Col. William Drayton, of Charleston, and was admitted to the bar, Jan. 12, 1821. He was a graduate of Judge Gould's Law School, of Litchfield, Conn. He practiced in Charleston until 1829, when he removed to Beaufort District, near Coosawhatchie, and practiced there until he was forced from ill health to abandon a very heavy and lucrative professional business in the year 1834. He then removed to the parish of St John's, Berkeley, where he occupied himself in planting and in literary pursuits, until 1842, when he emigrated to the state of Alabama, and settled near Carlowville, in the county of Dallas. He resumed the law in Alabama, and at the time of his death was getting into a large and very litigated practice. He was several times a member of the South Carolina legislature, but, preferring the profession in which he had been reared, and the ease and happiness of domestic life, he declined the nomination of his party for Congress in that state, in the year 1833–34, and was thereafter little in political life. He was a states' rights man, and in the exciting contests which resulted in nullification, gave the weight of his influence and talents to what he conscientiously believed to be the true doctrine of the constitution.[1]

He was a communicant of the Episcopal church, from his 17th year, and died as he had lived, a devoted member of that communion. His w. was b. in South Carolina, Jan. 8, 1808, and d. at Carlowville, Ala., June 6, 1851. They had six children:

4–3. John, b. in Charleston, 1828, d. 1829.
4–4. Nathaniel Henry Rhodes, b. in Charleston, Feb. 14, 1829, res. 1873, Selma, Ala.; *m.*
4–5. Mary Huger, b. in Charleston, Feb. 17, 1830, res. 1873, near Fayetteville, Ala. LIDE.
4–6. Lawrence Edwin, b. in Beaufort District, S. C., June 20, 1831, res. 1873, near Camden, Ark.; *m.*
4–7. John Rhodes, b. at Spring Grove plantation, St John's, Berkeley, 1836, d. 1837.
4–8. Reginald Heber, b. at Spring Grove, March 19, 1838, res. 1873, at Camden, Ala.; *m.*

---

[1] "He was gifted with a fine manly person. He was tall and well formed, and possessed of features exceedingly striking and attractive. His manners were at once so graceful, and his general appearance so dignified, that no one could see him without feeling that he was in the presence of a finished gentleman, in the true sense of the term. When he first appeared before the Supreme Court of Alabama, the Bench and Bar were struck forcibly by his person and address, and the remark was general: 'There stands a perfect model of the hightoned, elevated, and accomplished advocate of South Carolina, upon whom seems to have fallen the mantle of Hale and Mansfield.' The language of Mr. Dawson at the Bar was energetic and lofty, his voice sonorous and manly, his action appropriate and full of authority. He had the rare gift of combining eloquence of diction and a flow of melodious and well considered periods, the ornaments of speech, with convincing, clear and perspicuous reasoning." — From an extended notice of Mr. Dawson in O'Neal's *Bench and Bar of South Carolina*, contributed to that work by the Hon. Benj. F. Porter. (II. 518).

3-8. OCTAVIUS HUGER DAWSON was b. in Charleston, Oct. 2, 1802. He entered his father's counting room while a mere lad, intending in time to become a partner, but his father dying while he was yet too young to conduct the business, he sought other occupation, and became connected with the State Bank of Charleston, as discounting clerk. He held this office until 1846, when, his health failing, he was induced to remove to Aiken, in the neighborhood of which place he purchased a farm, where he was gradually restored to health, and where he remained until his death, July 2, 1856. He was a man of the strictest integrity in all the relations of life. He m. *Caroline H. Deas*, dau. of Thomas H. Deas, Esq., of Charleston, where she now resides (1873). They had seven children:

4-9. Caroline Deas, b. in Charleston, Sept. 14, 1831, res. 1873, Charleston; *unm.*
4-10. Mary Huger, b. in Charleston, Sept. 16, 1832, res. 1873, Aiken, S. C. RAVENEL.
4-11. John Huger, b. Aug. 27, 1834, res. 1873, Charleston; *m.*
4-12. Thomas Deas, b. June 11, 1837, d. July 11, 1838.
4-13. Emma, b. in Charleston, 1841, res. 1873, Charleston. HALL.
4-14. Margaret, b. in Charleston, Feb., 1844, res. 1873, Barnwell C. H., S. C. WILLIAMS.
4-15. Harriet, b. in Aiken, S. C., Sept., 1848, res. 1873, Charleston. HALL.

3-11. JACOB DRAYTON DAWSON, b. in Charleston, Dec. 31, 1806, d. in Charleston, Dec. 17, 1839, m. Jan. 7, 1834, *Cecelia J.* ——, who also d. in Charleston, Dec., 1839. He was a lawyer, admitted to the bar of South Carolina, 1828. They had three children, all born in Charleston:

4-16. Mary Fraser, b. April 23, 1835, m. and d. without issue.
4-17. Joanna Adelaide, b. Feb., 1838, d. June, 1838.
4-18. Emma Monck, b. July 31, 1839, m. and d. without issue.

3-12. WILLIAM HENRY DAWSON, b. in Charleston, March 27, 1808, d. in Charleston, March 7, 1857, m. March 12, 1829, *Margaret Ann Stock*, of Charleston, where she now resides (1873). They had ten children:

4-19. William Henry, b. Dec. 28, 1829, res. 1873, Charleston; *m.*
4-20. Margaret Ann, b. July 19, 1831.
4-21. Anne Alice, b. July 20, 1833, d. Aug. 6, 1835.
4-22. John Stock, b. March 4, 1835, d. Aug. 10, 1835.
4-23. Alfred Huger, b. July 4, 1836, d. young.

4–24. Elizabeth, d. young.
4–25. Charlotte.
4–26. Rebeeca, d. *infant.*
4–27. Rebecca L.
4–28. Thomas Corbett, d. young.

3–13. *Joanna Postell*, b. and d. in Charleston, m. *Henry Ingraham*, d. They had three children:

4–29. William Postell, b. July 28, 1809.
4–30. Mary, b. in Charleston, m. GEORGE ROBINSON, d. without issue.
4–31. John Henry, b. in Charleston, d. 1849.

3–14. *George Ann Hall*, b. in Charleston, May 26, 1807, res. 1873, Marietta, Ga., m. April 26, 1831, Hon. FRANCIS BURT, a lawyer of distinction, of Pendleton, S. C. He was admitted to the bar of South Carolina, 1828, held the office of third auditor in Washington, for several years, and was appointed by President Pierce, governor of Nebraska. He d. in Oct., 1854, soon after assuming the office. They had eight children:

4–32. Francis St. Julien, b. at Pendleton, March 17, 1832, d. ; *unm.*
4–33. George Ann Catharine, b. at Pendleton, Oct. 2, 1833, res. 1873, Charleston, S. C., w. of WM. H. DAWSON (4–19).
4–34. Harriet, b. Jan. 13, 1836, m. D. L. YOUNG, res. Marietta, Ga.
4–35. Joanna, res. Marietta.
4–36. Kate, res. Marietta.
4–37. Armistead, res. Marietta.
4–38. Frank, res. Marietta.
4–39. Mary, m. WILLIAM E. JOHNSTONE, res. Charleston, S. C.

3–15. JOHN DAWSON HALL, b. in Charleston, Aug. 3, 1809, d.——, a skillful physician, educated at the medical schools of Paris, m. 1st, March 21, 1837, *Septima Thayer*, who d. near Benton, Ala., 1841. He m. 2d, Miss *Bryan*, of St. John's, Berkeley, S. C., d.

3–16. *Joanna Louise Hall*, b. in Charleston, Sept. 14, 1811, d. in Greenville, S. C., June 19, 1856, m. in Pickens, S. C., Jan. 23, 1834, Major SAMUEL A. TOWNES, a lawyer of distinction, b. in Greenville, Dec. 23, 1806, d. in Edgefield Co., S. C., June 20, 1873.[1]

Major Townes was educated at the academies of Pendleton

[1] Second son of Samuel A., and Rachel Townes. Samuel A. Townes sen., was one of the first settlers of Edgefield county.

and Greenville, S. C., and at the Virginia University. After leaving the university he read law, was admitted to the bar of S. C., and commenced practice at Abbeville. While at Abbeville he edited a newspaper devoted to the cause of nullification, which exercised a controlling influence on the politics of that county. He removed to Perry county, Ala., where he practiced law and edited a newspaper, and after residing there some years returned to his native state, and was elected by the Legislature, Commissioner in Equity for the Greenville district. This office he filled for several years, and he also edited for some years the Greenville *Mountaineer*. While in Alabama he became the author of a biographical history of the prominent men of Perry county, and he essayed a similar work relating to the distinguished men of South Carolina, but never completed it. He was generous, cordial, of great wit and humor, had fine literary tastes, and was a writer of marked force and ability. They had seven children:

4–40. Byron, b. in Marion, Ala., Jan. 11, 1836, d. in Marion, Sept. 26, 1836.
4–41. Fanny Joanna, b. in Marion, April 4, 1838, d. in Edgefield, S. C., Dec. 21, 1868. BULLER.
4–42. Samuel A., b. in Marion, May 27, 1840, res. 1873, Greenville, S. C.; *m.*
4–43. George Anna, b. in Marion, Oct. 30, 1842, res. 1873, Edgefield Co., S. C. HARRIS.
4–44. Henry Howard, b. in Marion, Aug. 15, 1845, res. Edgefield Co., S. C.; *m.*
4–45. George Franklin, b. in Greenville, S. C., Feb. 11, 1849, res. Edgefield, S. C.; *unm.*
4–46. John Allen, b. in Greenville, Dec. 18, 1850, d. in Texas, Dec. 26, 1869.

3–18. *Joanna Dawson*, b. in Charleston, July 28, 1804, res. 1873, Charleston, m. Sept. 29, 1824, AUGUSTUS T. GAILLARD, who d. in New York, Sept. 19, 1837. They had six children, all b. in Charleston:

4–47. Joanna Caroline, b. Dec., 1825, d. Oct. 3, 1848; *unm.*
4–48. Ellen Martha, b. Dec., 1828, d. at Aiken, S. C., 1862. CANNON.
4–49. Augusta Catharine.
4–50. Theodoré, m. WILLIAM GOURDIN YOUNG, of Charleston.
4–51. Augustus Theodore.
4–52. William Dawson, m. *Elizabeth Moultrie Lee*, of Charleston.

3-19. WILLIAM ALFRED DAWSON, b. in Charleston, July 15, 1806, res. 1873, at Spring Hill, near Mobile, Ala.; m. in Scotland, *Jane Ogilvie*, who was b. in Scotland, Aug. 1, 1820, and d. at Spring Hill, May 12, 1859. Mr. D. has retired from business, after a very successful mercantile career, during which he resided much abroad. Eight children:

4–53. William Ogilvie, b. at Spring Hill, July 24, 1843, res. 1873, Mobile, Ala.; *unm.*
4–54. John Abercrombie, b. at Mobile, March 14, 1845, res. Mobile; *m.*
4–55. Catharine Cordes, b. at Spring Hill, Sept. 27, 1846, m. 1872—— WILKINSON; res. Mobile.
4–56. Helen Ogilvie, b. at Spring Hill, Aug. 21, 1848.
4–57. Samuel Prioleau, b. in Charleston, April 1, 1850.
4–58. Charles Postell, b. at Spring Hill, Sept. 18, 1852.
4–59. Philip Gendron, b. at Spring Hill, 1853.
4–60. Isabella Maclean, b. at Spring Hill, April 13, 1855.

3-21. *Catharine Cordes Dawson*, b. in Charleston, May 4, 1811, d. on Sullivan's Island, near Charleston, Aug., 1832, m. Nov. 26, 1829, Dr. ELIAS BALL, a prominent physician of Charleston, who d. in that city, 1834. One child:

4–61. Elizabeth Catharine Carolina, b. in Charleston, 1830. SHUBRICK.

3-22. JOHN CORDES DAWSON, merchant, b. in Charleston, Oct. 6, 1813, res. 1873, at Spring Hill, near Mobile, Ala. He m. 1st, in Mobile, April 29, 1846, *Rose Earle Harrison*, who was b. in Pendleton, S. C., April 9, 1823, d. at Spring Hill, Dec. 7, 1857, dau. of Thomas and Hannah Harrison. They had five children:

4–62. Carolina Prioleau, b. in Mobile, Aug. 13, 1847.
4–63. Rose Earle, b. at Spring Hill, Dec. 21, 1849.
4–64. Samuel Ferguson, b. at Spring Hill, July 29, 1851, d. Oct. 8, 1862.
4–65. Cordes, b. at Spring Hill, Sept. 5, 1853.
4–66. Hannah Harrison, b. at Spring Hill, Nov. 18, 1857.

Mr. DAWSON m. 2d, in Mobile, July 26, 1859, *Louise Townsend Spencer*, who was b. in Evansville, Ind., Feb. 10, 1831, dau. of John and Rhoda Spencer. They have two children:

4–67. Jessie Cordes, b. at Spring Hill, June 11, 1862.
4–68. Pauline Buell, b. at Spring Hill, Feb. 25, 1864.

3-23. *Harriet Honey Dawson*, b. in Charleston, Sept., 1813, m. WILLIAM WASHINGTON ANCRUM, Esq., gr. son of Col.

N. H. R. Dawson

William Washington, a distinguished officer in the Revolutionary service. Their eldest dau.:

4–69. [ANCRUM.] Annie S., m. Col. THOMAS Y. SIMONS, lawyer, res. 1873, Charleston, one of the editors of Charleston *Courier*.

3-24. DR. JOHN LAWRENCE DAWSON, b. at Milton plantation, near Charleston, March 28, 1815, res. 1873, in Charleston, is a prominent physician of that city. He was city register of Charleston in 1852. He m. 1st, Nov. 3, 1836, *Jane Simons*, sister of Col. Thomas Y. Simons, above named (4-69). 2d, *Catharine Joanna Dawson*, b. July 4, 1820, dau. of Charles Postell Dawson (2-11 of this record). Children:

4–70. Jane, m. —— PINKNEY.
4–71. Hester, m. —— WARING.
4–72. John Lawrence.
4–73. Eliza.
4–74. Harriet.

3-26. ARNOLDUS VANDERHORST DAWSON, b. in Charleston Sept. 11, 1818, d. in Charleston, Feb. 26, 1871, a lawyer, graduate of Yale College, 1837, admitted to the bar of South Carolina in 1840, m. Jan. 16, 1844, *Esther B. Simons*, who was b. in Charleston, Jan. 20, 1819, and d. in Columbia, S. C., July 7, 1856, dau. of Dr. Benjamin B. and *Maria Vanderhorst* Simons. They had four children:

4–75. Lawrence Monck, b. April 20, 1846, res. Acworth, Ga.; *m.*
4–76. Louisa Blake, b. Dec. 18, 1848, res. Charleston, S. C.
4–77. Arnoldus Vanderhorst, b. June 9, 1850, res. Charleston.
4–78. John Bryan, b. July 1, 1852, d. July 22, 1862.

3-28. THOMAS OSBORNE DAWSON, b. Nov. 9, 1813, res. 1873, in Charleston, m. March 10, 1839, *Jane Elizabeth Trenholm*, who d. abt. 1860. They had:

4–79. Charles.

4-4. NATHANIEL HENRY RHODES DAWSON, b. in Charleston, Feb. 14, 1829, was educated at St. Joseph's College, Mobile, read law under his father and the Hon. George R. Evans, was admitted to the bar in 1850, and began the practice of his profession in Cahaba, Ala., in 1851. In 1855 he was nominated for the legislature, but, although he ran ahead of his ticket, he was defeated, his party being at that time largely in a minority in the county. He was a delegate to the National Democratic Convention of 1860, at Charleston and Baltimore, and the next year, after the outbreak of the civil war, he entered the service of his state, as captain of a volunteer company, the Selma cadets, forming part of the Fourth Alabama Infantry, whose fortunes and dangers he shared during twelve months in Virginia. In 1863 and 1864 he represented his county of Dallas in the state legislature. Towards the close of the wâr he commanded a battalion of mounted men which operated on the coast. Since 1858 he has resided in Selma, where he is now in the midst of an extensive practice, associated with Gen. E. W. Pettus, a distinguished officer of the Confederate service, and one of the ablest lawyers of the state. Col. Dawson is also a large and successful planter. "He has an imposing personal appearance, polished and agreeable manners, and stainless moral character. He has talents of a substantial order, combined with a cultivated mind and varied information."[1] He has a strong hereditary, as well as personal attachment to the Episcopal church, and in its parish and diocesan councils has taken an active part. He has also served as a lay deputy from Alabama in two successive General Conventions. In the fall of 1872, he was a candidate for presidential elector on the democratic state ticket. He had not been consulted as to the choice of his name, but he accepted the nomination, and participated actively in the canvass. His talents as a writer, and his ability, fluency and eloquence as a speaker, are well attested. In fortune, dignity, culture, the strength of his convictions and the courage and fidelity with which they are maintained, and his unfailing courtesy and politeness, he appears a truly representative man of the highest type of American character. He is yet in the prime of life, and though, out of aversion to that indescribable mixture of things called politics in Alabama, standing rather aloof from public life, seems peculiarly fitted for public trusts, and destined to a career of the highest honor and usefulness.

The compiler is indebted to Col. Dawson for much assistance in the compilation of these records. He m. 1st, Jan. 22, 1852,

[1] Brewer's *Alabama; her History, Resources, War Records and Public Men*, p. 223. See, also Garrett's *Public Men of Alabama*, p. 729.

Ann Eliza Mathews, dau. of Col. Joel Early Mathews [1] and w. *Elizabeth Woods Poage*, of Dallas county. She d. at Cahaba, Oct. 7, 1854, leaving one child:

5–1. Elizabeth Mathews, b. at Cahaba, Jan. 7, 1853.

He m. 2d, June 17, 1857, *Mary E. Tarver*, dau. of Benjamin J. and Caroline M. Tarver, of Dallas county. She d. at Selma, May 8, 1860, leaving one child:

5–2. Mary Tarver, b. at Selma, Feb. 11, 1860.

He m. 3d, May 15, 1862, *Elodie Breck Todd*, b. April 1, 1840, dau. of Hon. Robert S. Todd, and w. *Elizabeth S. Humphreys*, of Lexington, Ky. They res. 1873, at Selma, and have had three children, all b. in that city:

5–3. Alexander Todd, b. Jan. 9, 1863, d. Jan. 13, 1863.
5–4. Nathaniel H. R., b. April 15, 1864.
5–5. Lawrence Percy, b. Jan. 9, 1869.

4–5. *Mary Huger Dawson*, b. in Charleston, Feb. 17, 1830, m. Jan. 30, 1850, CORNELIUS MANDEVILLE LIDE, planter.[2] They res. 1873, near Fayetteville, Talladega county, Ala., and have had thirteen children, all b. in Carlowville, Ala., except the last below named:

5–6. Mary Lawrence, b. March 8, 1851.
5–7. Frances Jane, b. Sept. 1, 1852.
5–8. Ann Rhodes, b. Sept. 6, 1853, d. Dec. 4, 1853.
5–9. Cornelius M., b. Feb. 9, 1855.
5–10. Lawrence E., b. April 25, 1856, d. Aug. 16, 1857.
5–11. Ellen Smith, b. Nov. 20, 1857.
5–12. Henry Dawson, b. March 24, 1859.
5–13. Morton Waring, b. Nov. 16, 1860.
5–14. Elizabeth Dawson, b. April 16, 1864.
5–15. Reginald Dawson, b. March 28, 1866.
5–16. Mary Dawson, b. Oct. 22, 1867.
5–17. Florence Lee, b. April 30, 1869.
5–18. Julia Edith, b. in Talladega county, Ala., April 9, 1871.

4–6. LAWRENCE EDWIN DAWSON, b. in Beaufort District, S. C., June 20, 1831, planter, m. Jan. 1853, *Caroline E. Lide*, dau. of Eli H. Lide, Esq., of Dallas county, Ala. He was

---

[1] Grandson of Gen. Mathews, of the Virginia line, afterwards governor of Georgia.

[2] For an account of the Lide family, see a history of the upper part of South Carolina, by Rt. Rev. Alexander Gregg, Bishop of Texas, entitled *History of the Old Cheraws.*

captain of a company in an Arkansas Regiment, Gen. Price's Division, Confederate service, during the war. They res. 1873, near Camden, Ouachita county, Arkansas, and have had seven children, all b. in that county:

5–19. Nathaniel H. R., b. Nov. 15, 1853, d. Sept. 22, 1859.
5–20. Mary Wilkinson, b. March 23, 1858, d. Sept., 1859.
5–21. Eli Lide, b. June 3, 1859.
5–22. John Huger, b. Oct. 5, 1860.
5–23. Hannah M., b. Sept. 12, 1864.
5–24. William Drayton, b. Jan. 31, 1868.
5–25. Martha Blackwell, b. April 25, 1870.
5–26. Edward Hamilton, b. May 6, 1873.

4–8. REGINALD HEBER DAWSON, b. at Spring Grove plantation, St. John's, Berkeley, S. C., March 19, 1838, was educated at the University of Alabama, and has been for many years a prominent lawyer of that state. He was lieutenant-colonel of the 13th Alabama Regiment in the Confederate service, and had special mention in General Orders for gallantry in the battle of Seven Pines, receiving also other marks of distinction. In 1860 and 1864 he was elected solicitor of the eleventh circuit of his state. He m. March 9, 1858, *Georgia Anne Craig*, dau. of Thomas L. and *Alabama Rutherford* Craig, of Cahaba.[1] They res. 1873, at Camden, Wilcox Co., Ala., and have had three children:

5–27. Lawrence Edwin, b. at Cahaba, Feb. 28, 1859.
5–28. Thomas Craig, b. at Cahaba, Dec. 15, 1861.
5–29. Anne Matthews, b. at Camden, Oct. 11, 1863.

4–10. *Mary Huger Dawson*, b. in Charleston, Sept. 16, 1832, m. in Aiken, S. C., Aug. 1858, HENRY W. RAVENEL, who was b. in St. John's parish, Berkeley, S. C., May, 1814, son of Dr. Henry and *Catharine Stevens* Ravenel.[2] He is a dis-

---

[1] Col. Dawson was proposed for nomination as a candidate for Congress in 1872. A local paper thus spoke of him: "He is now in the very prime of life, possessing a high order of intellect. In debate he is witty, eloquent and logical. His private character does him honor wherever he is known, standing preëminent for integrity as well as ability. A lawyer by profession and practice, educated, refined and sociable, he is every way fitted to do the state service and honor."— *Wilcox Vindicator*, June 7, 1872.

[2] Dr. Henry Ravenel d. recently in Charleston. The Ravenel family are one of the oldest in the state, and of the Huguenot stock. Writing to the compiler, 1873, Mr. R. says: "I myself have had somewhat of the same antiquarian fondness for old family records, and have been able to fill out charts of the families of seven of my Huguenot ancestors, going back to the original immigrants, at the close of the seventeenth century.

tinguished botanist and scientific writer. He graduated at the South Carolina College, in Columbia, but studied no profession : devoted some eighteen years of his life, after leaving college, to cotton planting, but, his health failing, he removed to Aiken, near which place he owns and conducts a fruit and vegetable farm, devoting his leisure to botanical studies. They res. 1873, at Aiken, and have five daughters :

5–30. [RAVENEL.] Caroline Deas, b. July 4, 1859.
5–31. Susan Stevens, b. July 20, 1861.
5–32. Elizabeth Gaillard, b. July 4, 1864.
5–33. Mary Huger, b. Jan. 4, 1867.
5–34. Tiphaine, b. Feb. 17, 1870.

4–11. *John Huger Dawson*, b. in Charleston, Aug. 27, 1834, real estate agent and collector, m. Oct. 1858, *Juliana Hazlehurst.* They res. 1873, in Charleston, and have two daughters :

5–35. Martha Hazlehurst, b. Oct. 1859.
5–36. Susan Linning, b. Jan. 1864.

4–13. *Emma Dawson*, b. in Charleston, 1841, m. in Aiken, Nov. 1870, HENRY H. HALL, son of Henry Hall. They res. 1873, in Charleston. One child :

5–37. Henry Harrison, b. 1871.

4–14. *Margaret Dawson*, b. in Charleston, Feb. 1844, m. in Aiken, Oct. 1866, B. T. WILLIAMS, b. 1844. They res. 1873, Barnwell C. H., S. C. Two children :

5–38. Caroline Hall.
5–39. Benjamin Wyley.

4–15. *Harriet Dawson*, b. in Aiken, S. C., Sept. 1848, m. in Aiken, Dec. 1870, TUDOR T. HALL, bro. of Henry H. Hall (4-13). They res. 1873, in Charleston.

4–19. WILLIAM HENRY DAWSON, b. in Charleston, Dec. 28, 1829, real estate agent and collector, m. Oct. 29, 1854, *George Ann Catharine Burt*, b. in Pendleton, S. C., Oct. 2, 1833, dau. of Hon. Francis and *George Ann Hall* Burt (3-14 of this record). They res. 1873, in Charleston. Six children, all b. in that city :

5–40. Frances Burt, b. Nov. 29, 1855.
5–41. Charles Postell, b. Jan. 4, 1858.
5–42. William Henry, b. Aug. 30, 1859, d. Dec. 24, 1864.
5–43. Ann Hall, b. March 22, 1862, d. Aug. 24, 1864.
5–44. Joanna Martha, b. Jan. 15, 1864.
5–45. John Lawrence, b. Aug. 3, 1866.

4–41. *Fanny Joanna Townes*, b. in Marion, Ala., April 4, 1838, d. in Edgefield, S. C., Dec. 21, 1868, m. in Greenville, S. C., May 27, 1862, GEORGE BULLER, who d. ——. They had three children:

5–46. Fanny Townes, b. July 22, 1863, d. Aug. 3, 1864.
5–47. Jane Tweedy, b. Sept. 9, 1865, d. Sept. 16, 1873.
5–48. George, b. March 5, 1868, d. Aug. 14, 1868.

4–42. SAMUEL A. TOWNES, b. in Marion, Ala., May 27, 1840, m. in Greenville, S. C., Nov. 9, 1871, *Mary Thompson.* They res. in Greenville. One child:

5–49. Mary, b. Jan. 14, 1873.

4–43. *George Anna Townes*, b. in Marion, Ala., Oct. 30, 1842, m. in Greenville, S. C., June 5, 1861, Col. WILLIS G. HARRIS. They res. 1873, at Hamburg P. O., Edgefield Co., S. C., and have had three children:

5–50. Irvine Townes, b. June 3, 1862, d. June 1, 1863.
5–51. Willis Glover, b. June 30, 1866.
5–52. Irene, b. Dec. 21, 1872, d. June 12, 1873.

4–44. HENRY HOWARD TOWNES, b. in Marion, Ala., Aug. 15, 1845, m. in Edgefield Co., S. C., Oct. 15, 1868, *Sally V. Harris.* They res. in Edgefield Co., and have had three children:

5–53. Joanna Lois, b. Jan. 14, 1870, d. Oct. 15, 1872.
5–54. Willis Glover, b. April 2, 1871.
5–55. Henry Howard, b. Sept. 2, 1872.

4–48. *Ellen Martha Gaillard*, b. in Charleston, S. C., Dec., 1828, d. at Aiken, S. C., 1862, m. July, 1850, DAVID CANNON, of Liverpool, England, who was lost at sea, Sept., 1858. They had one child:

5–56. Joanna Carolina, b. in Charleston, July, 1851.

4-54. John Abercrombie Dawson, b. in Mobile, Ala., March 14, 1845, m. Feb. 27, 1872, *Florence Acre Tucker*, dau. of Dr. Joseph Tucker, of Mobile. They res. in Mobile.

4-61. *Elizabeth Catharine Carolina Ball*, b. in Charleston, S. C., 1830, m. Jan. 9, 1850, Edmund T. Shubrick, of Charleston, who d. at Pendleton, S. C., 1860. They had five children:

5-57. Caroline Prioleau, b. in Charleston, 1851.
5-58. John Templer, b. in Charleston, 1853.
5-59. Edmund Templer, b. in Charleston, 1854.
5-60. Earnest, b. in Pendleton, 1856.
5-61. Catharine Cordes, b. in Pendleton, 1858.

4-75. Lawrence Monck Dawson, b. in Charleston, S. C., April 20, 1846, m. Dec. 31, 1868, Mrs. Eliza A. Walraven. They res. 1873, Acworth, Ga. Two children:

5-62. John.
5-63. William Ancrum.

FAMILY OF REV. THOMAS DAWSON,

Of Pendleton, S. C., 1872-3.

1. Isaac Dawson, grandfather of the above named Rev. Thomas Dawson,[1] was born at Maidstone, in Kent, England, 1719, and d. at Maidstone about 1817, being then in his 99th year. He, with his father, suffered persecution on account of belonging to the then despised sect of Baptists. He left but few descendants, several of his children, among whom were Samuel, Thomas, and one or two daughters, having d. without issue. His wife, Jane Dawson, d. at Maidstone about 1814, aged 90. Their only children who had families were:

2–1. Joseph, b. at Maidstone, abt. 1760, a Baptist minister at Lyme Regis, Dorsetshire, England, d. at London, abt. 1822 or 1823; and

2–2. Mary, who m. John Beeching, of Maidstone, and left three children, (John and two daughters), still living in Kent, England (1871).

2–1. Joseph Dawson, b. at Maidstone about 1760, d. in London, about 1822 or 1823, was, as above stated, a Baptist minister at Lyme Regis, Dorsetshire, England, and m. Miss *Eliza Clark*, of that place. They had nine children, only four of whom lived to be of age:

3–1. Thomas, b. at Lyme Regis, March 4, 1790, res. 1872, at Pendleton, S. C.; *m.*

3–2. Samuel, was controller of customs on Prince Edward's Island, N. S., and d. there *unm.*

3–3. Joseph, b. at Lyme Regis, April, 1797, d. near Atlanta, Geo., March, 1871; *m.*

3–4. John Clark, was captain of an English East India ship, and d. at Sumatra or Java, of yellow fever, about 1821; *unm.*

---

[1] "I have heard my grandfather say there were three branches of the Dawsons, the Yorkshire, Kentish and Irish branches. I am a descendant of the Kentish. . . . . . My great grandfather was also a native of Kent (Maidstone), and when a widower, of upwards of 60 years of age, stepped in between his eldest son and the intended wife of the latter and married her, of which union my grandfather was the third child, his father being at that time 68 years old. [Born, therefore, about 1651.] My grand uncle was so displeased that he emigrated to America, I think to Virginia, I have no certain knowledge of him, but think I have found some of his descendants in Georgia."—Rev. T. D., 1871. See record of the Baptist Dawsons of Virginia, who were, like this family, remarkable for instances of longevity.

3-1. Rev. THOMAS DAWSON, b. at Lyme Regis, Dorsetshire, England, March 4, 1790, emigrated to this country in 1816 or '17, and m. Aug. 10, 1822, at Valleytown Mission, Cherokee Nation, *Mary Randal Lewis*, whose parents were from Wales. She was b. in Burlington, N. J., Nov. 28, 1802, d. at Pendleton, S. C., April 22, 1872. At the venerable age of more than four score years he is still, in 1873, performing the duties of a Baptist minister at Pendleton, S. C. They had nine children:[1]

4-1. Eliza Clark, b. in the Cherokee Nation, Sept. 11, 1823, res. 1873, near Perryville, S. C. HUNNICUTT.
4-2. Joseph Lewis C., b. in Pendleton Dist., S. C., Dec. 4, 1825, d. at Anderson C. H., S. C., April 23, 1873; *m.*
4-3. Edwin J. E., b. in Pendleton Dist., April 10, 1828, res. 1873, Walhalla, S. C.; *m.*
4-4. Maria Earle, b. in Pendleton Dist., Sept. 3, 1830, res. 1873, near Perryville, S. C. ABBOTT.
4-5. Elias S. Earle, b. in Pendleton, Feb. 10, 1833, res. 1872, Edisto Island, S. C.; *m.*
4-6. Thomas William, b. in Pendleton Dist., Sept. 6, 1835, res. 1873, near Gadsden, S. C.; *m.*
4-7. Sarah Harrison, b. in Pendleton Dist., Oct. 12, 1838, res. 1872, Pendleton, S. C.; *unm.*
4-8. James Harrison, b. in Pendleton Dist., Dec. 4, 1840, res. 1872, near Jacksonville, Fla.; *m.*
4-9. Edward Franklin, b. in Pendleton Dist., July 29, 1845, res. 1872, near Port Orange, Fla.; farmer; *unm.*

3-3. JOSEPH DAWSON, b. at Lyme Regis, Dorsetshire, England, April, 1797, d. near Atlanta, Ga., March, 1871, aged 74 years. He m. 1st, in England, Sept. 3, 1818, *Fanny Baker*, of Staines, Middlesex, dau. of James Baker. She d. in England. They had six children:

4-10. Samuel B., b. at Maidstone, Kent, Sept. 1, 1819, res. 1873, at New Prospect, Winston Co., Miss.; *m.*
4-11. John Clark, b. in Stepney parish, Middlesex, Jan. 26, 1824, res. 1873, Liqua, Chili, S. A.; *m.*
4-12. Jane Elizabeth, b. in Stepney parish, Oct. 20, 1825, res. 1873, London, Eng. LOVELOCK.
4-13. James Baker, b. in Stepney parish, May 30, 1827, res. 1873, at New Prospect, Miss.; *m.*
4-14. Maria Fanny, b. at St. Leonards, London, m. JOHN LANCASTER, res. 1873, Blackville, Barnwell Co., S. C.
4-15. Joseph, d. in infancy.

---

[1] Of his sons, Mr. D. says (Oct., 1872): "Five were in active service all the war, and the sixth the last twenty-one months, and by the goodness of God, all came home to me safe."—

Mr. Dawson m. 2d, *Caroline Prigmore*, of London. They had three children:

4–16. Elizabeth, b. in St. Olave's parish, Surrey, Eng., abt. Dec. 1839, res. 1873, Atlanta, Ga.
4–17. Frank, b. in Shore Ditch parish, Middlesex, May 2, 1845, d. at Raleigh, N. C., April 4, 1865 (killed in battle).
4–18. Washington Taylor, b. in Pickens Dist., S. C., abt. Aug. 1847, res. 1872, Birmingham, Ala.

4–1. *Eliza Clark Dawson*, b. in the Cherokee Reservation, Sept. 11, 1823 (dau. of Rev. Thomas, 3-1), m. Dec. 13, 1838, MILTON REESE HUNNICUTT, who was b. in Pendleton, S. C., July 2, 1813, son of William and Elizabeth Hunnicutt. They res. 1873, at Perryville, Oconee Co., S. C. Fourteen children:

5–1. Thomas William, b. March 14, 1840, res. 1873, Perryville, S. C.; *m.*
5–2. Mary Elizabeth, b. March 25, 1842.
5–3. Nancy Sloan, b. June 28, 1843, res. 1873, Seneca city, S. C. HARBIN.
5–4. Milton Reese, b. March 20, 1845, d. July 21, 1861.
5–5. Lewis Young, b. Dec. 12, 1846, d. Feb. 8, 1849.
5–6. Alice Eliza, b. Oct. 30, 1848.
5–7. Sarah Kate, b. Oct. 6, 1850, res. 1873, Seneca city. LOWERY.
5–8. Miles Norton, b. July 25, 1852, d. Oct. 12, 1867.
5–9. James Clarke, b. Aug. 26, 1854.
5–10. John Sloan, b. Aug. 22, 1856.
5–11. Ezekiel Young, b. May 9, 1859.
5–12. Jefferson Davis, b. May 31, 1861.
5–13. Milledge Reese, b. Aug. 31, 1863.
5–14. Clarence Eugene, b. Sept. 7, 1865.

4–2. JOSEPH LEWIS C. DAWSON, b. in Pendleton District, S. C., Dec. 4, 1825, d. at Anderson C. H., S. C., April 23, 1873, m. Aug. 18, 1857, *Martha M. Gassaway*, who was b. in Anderson Co., S. C., Dec. 29, 1834, dau. of Benjamin and *Margaret Hall* Gassaway. She res. 1873, at Anderson C. H. Two children:

5–15. Anna V., b. Feb. 4, 1859.
5–16. Emma M., b. Jan. 12, 1861.

4–3. EDWIN J. E. DAWSON, farmer, b. in Pendleton District, S. C., April 10, 1828, m. 1st, Nov. 5, 1850, *Martha Lancaster*, who d. Oct. 31, 1869, aged 44 years and 6 mos., dau. of Jesse and Mary Lancaster. He m. 2d, June 12, 1872,

Adaline Dodd, b. July 10, 1850, dau. of G. W. and E. A. Dodd. Res. 1873, Walhalla, Pickens Co., S. C. Children:

5–17. Mary E., b. Nov. 17, 1858.
5–18. Sarah Ida, b. Jan. 21, 1860.
5–19. George T., b. March 18, 1873.

4–4. *Maria Earle Dawson*, b. in Pendleton Dist., Sept. 3, 1830 (dau. of Rev. Thomas, 3-1), m. Dec. 23, 1847, Rev. WILLIS ABBOTT, who was b. in Pendleton, June 16, 1822, son of William and Judith Abbott. They res. 1873, Perryville, Oconee, S. C., and have eleven children, all res. at Perryville:

5–20. H. S., b. Dec. 1, 1848, m. JOSEPH HAYS. (See forward).
5–21. Mary E., b. Oct. 21, 1850.
5–22. Martha J., b. Oct. 17, 1852.
5–23. S. C., b. Dec. 10, 1853, m. May 8, 1872, M. Hopkins; one child; C. C. Hopkins.
5–24. William Thomas, b. June 23, 1856.
5–25. G. A., b. Aug. 29, 1857.
5–26. John B., b. April 11, 1860.
5–27. R. H., b. Aug. 20, 1862.
5–28. James B., b. May 2, 1865.
5–29. J. M., b. Nov. 16, 1867.
5–30. D. M., b. Feb. 2, 1870.

4–5. ELIAS S. EARLE DAWSON, farmer, b. in Pendleton, S. C., Feb. 10, 1833, m. *Mary Blanch Westcott.* Res. 1872, Edisto Island, S. C. Five children, of whom three only were then living. Names not communicated.

4–6. THOMAS WILLIAM DAWSON, railroad agent, b. in Pendleton Dist., S. C., Sept. 6, 1835, m. Dec. 11, 1856, *Martha A. Hornsby*, who was b. in Coba, S. C., Oct. 1, 1833, dau. of James S. and Mary A. Hornsby. Res. 1873, near Gadsden, Richland Co., S. C. Seven children:

5–31. Mary Alice, b. in Coba, S. C., Dec. 18, 1857.
5–32. E. Spurgeon, b. in Anderson, S. C., May 25, 1859.
5–33. Isadore, b. in Anderson, June 5, 1861.
5–34. Willie Thomas, b. in Gadsden, S. C., July 19, 1866.
5–35. James Katon, b. in Gadsden, Oct. 12, 1867.
5–36. Lee Hornsby, b. in Gadsden, Nov. 11, 1869.
5–37. Annabel, b. in Gadsden, June 7, 1872.

4–8. JAMES HARRISON DAWSON, railroad agent, b. in Pendleton Dist., S. C., Dec. 4, 1840, m. *Mary Mingas.* Res. 1872, near Jacksonville, Fla. One child, name not stated.

4–10. Samuel B. Dawson, farmer, b. at Maidstone, Kent, England, Sept. 1, 1819, m. Dec. 8, 1852, *Frances Tucker*, b. in Anderson Dist., S. C., May 24, 1825, dau. of Thomas and Abigail Tucker. Res. 1873, near Louisville, Winston Co., Miss. Six children, all b. in Winston Co.:

5–38. Abigail Eugenie, b. Jan. 12, 1855.
5–39. Joseph Clark, b. Feb. 3, 1858.
5–40. James Franklin, b. March 31, 1862.
5–41. Sarah Elizabeth, b. June 1, 1864.
5–42. Frances Emma, b. Sept. 19, 1866.
5–43. Martha Angeline, b. Nov. 8, 1869.

4–11. John Clark Dawson, b. in Stepney parish, Middlesex, England, Jan. 26, 1824, res. 1873, Liqua, Chili, S. A. He is a civil engineer. Seven children:

5–44. Eliza.
5–45. Placido.
5–46. Fanny.
5–47. Caroline Elizabeth.
5–48. Orlando Washington.
5–49. John Clark.
5–50. Elfrosina.

4–12. *Jane Elizabeth Dawson*, b. in Stepney parish, Middlesex, England, Oct. 20, 1825, m. William Lovelock, and res. 1873, Bride St., Liverpool road, London. Five children, all b. in Islington parish, Middlesex:

3–51. William.
5–52. George.
5–53. Thomas.
5–54. John.
5–55. Emily.

4–13. James Baker Dawson, farmer, b. in Stepney parish, Middlesex, England, May 30, 1827, m. *Elizabeth Boon*, of Stonemarket, Suffolk, dau. of William Boon. Res. 1873, New Prospect, Winston county, Miss. Five children:

5–56. Emma, b, May 11, 1848.
5–57. Fanny Elizabeth, b. Sept. 22, 1850.
5–58. Sarah Jane, b. Jan. 2, 1853.
5–59. James William, b. March 5, 1856.
5–60. Maria Emily, b. June 5, 1858.

NOTES. I. A clergyman of the church of England, named Dawson, was in South Carolina in the colonial times. He arrived in the colony in 1766.—Ramsay's *History of South Carolina*, vol. 2, p. 7, *note*.

II. JOSEPH DAWSON, a native of the south of Ireland (county Kerry or Cork), emigrated to Charleston in 1832, with family of four sons and four daughters. The sons were: 1. John, who d. in California. His sons, Francis J., accountant, and Richard, clerk, res. 1873, in Charleston. 2. Job, grocer, res. 1873, in Charleston, has son, Job, jun., stencil cutter, also of Charleston. 3. Francis, res. 1873, New York. 4. Joseph, druggist, res. 1873, Charleston; has family.

III. "FRANCIS W. DAWSON, of *The News* (Riordon, Dawson & Co., 1867), was born in London, England, in 1840. At the time of the breaking out of the war between the Confederate States and the Federal Union, he was engaged on the editorial staff of a London newspaper. In December, 1861, he enlisted at Southampton, England, as a sailor on the Confederate steamship *Nashville*. On the arrival of the steamer at Beaufort, North Carolina, early in 1862, he was appointed a master's mate in the navy of the new Confederacy. This position he resigned in June, 1862, and joined the "Purcell Battery," Hill's division, army of Northern Virginia, as a private. In August, 1862, he was commissioned first lieutenant of artillery, and assigned to duty as ordnance officer on the staff of General Longstreet. In the spring of 1864 he was promoted to a captaincy of artillery, and in the fall of the same year was transferred to the staff of Gen. Fitz Hugh Lee, where he served until the end of the war. When the Richmond *Examiner* was revived, in 1865, Mr. DAWSON became one of its local reporters. After the *Examiner* had been suppressed by the United States' military authorities, Mr. DAWSON accepted a position among the corps of editors of the Richmond *Dispatch*, and held it until the fall of 1866, when he became assistant editor of the Charleston *Mercury*, Nov. 19, 1866. This position he held until October, 1867, when he became one of the proprietors and editors of the Charleston *Daily News*."—From *The Newspaper Press of Charleston*, p. 181. Mr. D. is still, in 1873, a resident of Charleston, and editor of the *News*.

GEORGIA.

In regard to the family history of the late U. S. Senator, William C. Dawson, of Georgia, there has been much misapprehension. It has been generally supposed by the Maryland Dawsons, and those of Maryland descent, that he was descended from a family originally settled in that state. As will be seen below, his father came from England, and planted in Georgia a distinct and original family. As to the traditional southern offshoot of the Maryland stock, see some curious information accompanying the records of the families of that state.

FAMILY OF GEORGE DAWSON,

Of Greene Co., Georgia, 1784.

Under date of March 3, 1871, the late Dr. Thomas H. Dawson, of Glenville, Ala., nephew of Senator Dawson, wrote as follows: [1]

"My grandfather's name was George Dawson. He came to the United States a British soldier during the war between England and the colonies, and believing England wrong in her course towards our people, he deserted as soon as he came in reach of Washington's lines, and remained a soldier under him to the end of the war. After peace was declared he stopped a year or two in North Carolina,[2] and there married a young widow, Mrs. Ruth Skidmore, then the mother of one child,

[1] The letter was addressed to A. H. H. Dawson, Esq., of New York city, to whose kindness the compiler is indebted for the use of it.

[2] Peace was not formally "declared" until after the signing of the definitive treaty of peace in Paris, 3d Sept., 1783; but the war was considered as practically ended by the surrender of Lord Cornwalls at Yorktown, 19 Oct., 1781. In consequence of a general persuasion that peace was at hand, large numbers of soldiers were immediately paroled, went home, and were never recalled. Probably it was while paroled, pending the conclusion of the treaty, that George Dawson "stopped a year or two in North Carolina." Otherwise the term of his residence in that state must have been brief, as he was living in Georgia in January, 1784, in which month the eldest child was born.

Samuel Skidmore. Shortly after their marriage they moved to Georgia, and settled on the head waters of the Ogeechee river, in Greene county,[1] the Indians having but recently left that part of the state to occupy the lands on the west of the river Oconee. Here my father, Gen. THOMAS DAWSON, was born, under a shelter covered with bark, on the 25th of January, 1784. He was the first white child born in the county of Greene. Here he grew to manhood, and filled most of the offices of trust and honor in the gift of the people. He died 26 Feb., 1846, near Greensboro, the county seat. My grandfather had five sons, Thomas, Reuben, John, George and William C. Dawson. The character and services of the latter are doubtless well known to you.

"My father, Thomas Dawson, had six sons, George Ashley, Thomas Henry, John Rogers, James Crosby, Reuben Josiah and William Curran, all of whom are dead, except Reuben, William and myself. Add to these Edgar G. Dawson, the only surviving son of my uncle, William C. Dawson, and you have all the living male representatives of my grandfather, except our sons, of whom there are some eight or ten.

"Our great grandfather's name was JOHN DAWSON, of Sutterby, in the county of Lincoln, England. His arms were granted in 1640. George, our grandfather, was born in Lincoln county, England. This is the best account we have been able to get of the early history of the family. Our grandfather never corresponded with any of his relatives after the Revolutionary war, but a letter received as late as 1866 from Richard Dawson, of Hertfordshire, England, furnishes these statements in regard to John Dawson, from whom, doubtless, we have descended. He states that all the men of the family were tall, with ruddy complexions, and blue or hazel eyes, were great sportsmen, keeping first rate horses of every class, and the best stock of all kinds."[2]

---

[1] Greene county was laid out in 1786, having previously formed a part of Washington county, which was established in 1784, and included "all the territory from the Cherokee corner, north, extending from the Ogeechee to the Oconee, south to Liberty county."—*Historical Collections of Georgia*, pp. 476 and 676.

[2] The original of the letter of Richard Dawson, Esq., of Hertfordshire, above referred to, having been forwarded to the compiler by a member of Dr. Dawson's family, it is copied in full below. The letter alone *gives no substantial ground* for the statement that Dr. Dawson's gt. gr. father was the John Dawson, of Sutterby, whose arms

From the foregoing, and letters of Reuben J. Dawson, Esq., of Greensboro, Ga., Edgar E. Dawson, Esq., of Baltimore, Md., and others, with the use of sketches of Senator Dawson and family in various published works, the following record has been compiled.

1. George Dawson, said to have been a native of Lincoln county, England, came to America a British soldier during the revolutionary war, and deserted the British service to espouse the American cause. He m. in North Carolina, widow Ruth Skidmore, and with her removed to Greene county, Georgia, where they, in common with others, encountered the hardships and perils incident to all early settlements in our western and south western states. The Indians had not yet been removed from their neighborhood, and privations, self-denial, self reliance

---

are said to have been granted in 1640. Perhaps Dr. Dawson may have followed up the clue given in the letter, and obtained satisfactory evidence as to the ancestry of his grandfather, George Dawson, founder of the family in Georgia. *If an ancestor*, John Dawson of Sutterby, 1640, must have been some generations removed from the Georgia settler of 1784. The letter is as follows :

"Albury Hall, Ware, Hertfordshire, May 7, 1866.

"Sir,

Your letter has been forwarded to me from Withcall, where my father resided, and after his death I remained there ten years, when I bought my present property. I will tell you what I can of my family. If you belong to us you are descended from my ancestor, Jno. Dawson, Esq., of Sutterby, in the county of Lincoln, whose arms were granted in 1640.* The Dawson family were all tall, fine men, ruddy complexions, with blue or hazel eyes, have always been great sportsmen, keeping first rate horses of every class, and the best stock of all kinds. It strikes me very forcibly that I have heard my father mention that one of the family belonging either to his uncle or great uncle was lost. The whole of my father's family are dead. Several of the names you state are our family names, John, Thomas, William and Sarah. I recollect a cousin of my father's, William, who had only one child, a son, George, who married the only child of Captain Stephens. They both died without issue, so *that* branch is extinct. I am the only son of Richard Dawson, and have two sisters ; am married, and have one child ; am a magistrate for the county of Hertford. I will seal this with our arms. We have few relations.

"If Jno. Wood, whom you mention, be the son of Wm. Wood, the cattle dealer, I have bought beasts of him, and fancy he and his brother, who were partners, were Yorkshire men. They were large jobbers. I have not seen either of them for 16 or 18 years.

"Several of our family are buried in St. Botolph's, Lincoln, and the monuments of the earlier branches are in the church at Sutterby, near Spilsby. It strikes me very forcibly that your grandfather was the brother of Wm. Dawson, who would now be about 110 years old, were he living. William had only one brother, and he himself standing about six feet high, a fine man, he is buried in St. Botolph's.

"Sincerely yours,

"Richard Dawson."

"Mr. Reuben J. Dawson."

* According to Burke, the arms of the Dawsons of Sutterby were granted to James Dawson in 1664.— *See p. 5 of this work.*

and courage, were among their virtues aud their experiences. They had nine children, all b. in Greene county:[1]

2–1. Thomas, b. Jan. 25, 1784, d. in Greene county, Feb. 26, 1846; *m.*
2–2. Mary, b. May 17, 1785. McIntosh.
2–3. Sarah, b. July 4, 1786. Furlow.
2–4. Elizabeth, b. March 25, 1789. Mulkey.
2–5. John, b. May 10, 1792, known as Major John Dawson, served in war of 1812–14, m. *Elizabeth Cessna;* no male descendants living, 1871.[2]
2–6. Reuben, b. Dec. 10, 1793; *m.*
2–7. George, b. March 28, 1795; *m.*
2–8. William Crosby, b. Jan. 4, 1798, d. in Greensboro, Ga., May 6, 1856; *m.*
2–9. Rutha C., b. May 15, 1803, m. Furnifold H. Greene, of North Carolina, a relative of Gen. Nathaniel Greene, for whom Greene county was named.

2–1. Thomas Dawson, b. in Greene county, Ga., Jan. 25, 1784, remained all his life a resident of that county, which he represented frequently in the state legislature, and of which he was also sheriff. He served as captain of a volunteer company in the war with England (1812-14) and as major under Gen. Adams in the war with the Creek Indians. At the time of his death, which occurred near Greensboro, Feb. 26, 1846, he was engaged in business as a commission merchant and factor at Augusta, Ga. He m. Dec. 1, 1803, *Susanna H. Rogers*, who d. Oct. 1, 1864, dau. of John Rogers, of North Carolina. She was a woman of cultivated mind and exemplary Christian character. They had eight children, all b. in Greene county:

3–1. Leonore Boykin, b. Oct. 7, 1805, m. Dec. 1, 1824, John D. Turner, of Va., and d. near Madison, Ga., Sept. 23, 1825; one child.

---

[1] "I may be prolix and prosaic, but I love to remember the mothers of fifty years ago, those who gave birth to Lucius Q. C. and Mirabeau B. Lamar, to William C. Dawson, Bishop George Pierce, Alexander Stuart and Joseph Lumpkin. I knew them all, and, with affectionate delight, remember their virtues, and recall the social hours we have enjoyed together, when they were matrons, and I the companion of their sons. And now, when all are gone, and time is crowding me to the grave, the nobleness of their characters, the simplicity of their bearing in the discharge of their household duties, and the ingenuousness of their manners in social intercourse, is a cherished, venerated memory. . . . . . . They were sensible, modest and moral women, and their virtues live after them in the exalted character of their illustrious sons."— Sparks' *The Memories of Fifty Years*, p. 100.

[2] John Dawson is mentioned as among the early settlers of Cass county, Ga.— *Historical Collections of Georgia*, p. 298.

3–2. George Ashley, b. Aug. 12, 1807, admitted to the Bar, 1828, m. June 27, 1828, *Martha K. Butt*,[1] and d. at Warrenton, Ga., Sept. 12, 1829, without issue.
3–3. Thomas Henry, b. April 8, 1809, d. in Glenville, Ala., June 19, 1873; *m.*
3–4. John Rogers, b. Dec. 20, 1810, d. in Columbus, Ga., Oct. 29, 1852; *m.*
3–5. James Crosby, b. Oct. 27, 1812, many years in importing dry goods trade, d. May, 1866.
3–6. Ann Winefried, b. April 19, 1814, m. April 21, 1831, THOMAS P. F. THREEWITS: res. 1873, Columbus, Ga.; 5 children.
3–7. Reuben Josiah, b. April 21, 1816, res. 1873, Greensboro, Ga.; *m.*
3–8. William Curran, b. Sept. 17, 1818, res. 1873, Glenville, Ala.; *m.*

2–2. *Mary Dawson*, b. in Greene county, Ga., May 17, 1785, m. in Greene county, Col. DAVID McINTOSH. Two children:

3–9. Crosby.
3–10. Parazade.

2–3. *Sarah Dawson*, b. in Greene county, Ga., July 4, 1786, m. DAVID FURLOW. They had seven children:

3–11. Osborn, m. *Sarah Ann Bunkley*, of Greene county.
3–12. Rutha.
3–13. James Thomas, m. *Sarah Ann Hutchinson*, of Greene county.
3–14. Mary.
3–15. Ann.
3–16. George, m. *Lucy Dickens*, of Clarke county, Ga.
3–17. Albert, m. *Jane Shuptrine*, of Upson county, Ga.

2–4. *Elizabeth Dawson*, b. in Greene county, Ga., March 25, 1789, m. Dr. —— MULKEY. They had one son:

3–18. George.

2–6. REUBEN DAWSON, b. in Greene Co., Ga., Dec. 10, 1793, m. Sept. 13, 1814, *Hannah Walton Mathews*.[2] They had six children:

3–19. Malvina, m. Gen. CHARLES NELSON.
3–20. Sarah, m. BENJAMIN GOODE.
3–21. Antoinette, m. EDWIN J. MAPP.
3–22. Upzier, m. Dr. E. H. METCALF, of Texas.
3–23. Carrie, m. GEORGE DOWNING.
3–24. Richard, went west, d.

---

[1] She m. 2d, Dr. RICHARD BANKS, of Elbert county, and res. a wid. at Gainesville, Ga. (1873).

[2] Reuben Dawson was a member of the first grand jury of Campbell county, Georgia.— See *Historical Collections of Georgia*, p. 293.

Engraved by J. C. Buttre from a Daguerreotype.

Wm. C. Dawson

SENATOR FROM GEORGIA

2-7. Col. George Dawson, b. in Greene county, Ga., March 28, 1795, m. June 17, 1818, *Sarah Branch*, of North Carolina; was many years sheriff of Greene county; d. leaving one son:

3-25. George Malcomb, d.

2-8. Hon. William Crosby Dawson was b. in Greene county, Ga., Jan. 4, 1798. After an academic course, taken under the direction, first, of the Rev. Dr. Cumming, a Scotch-Irish divine of great learning and piety, and afterwards at the county academy in Greensboro, he entered the Franklin College, of Athens, at an early age, and was graduated from that Institution in 1816. He devoted the following year to the study of the law in the office of the Hon. Thomas W. Cobb, at Lexington, and then entered the famous law school of Judges Reeve and Gould, at Litchfield, Conn., where he took a full course of lectures. On his return to Greensboro, in 1818, he was admitted to the bar, and at once entered upon the labors of his profession in his native county. He had a buoyant temperament, a vigorous constitution, and studious, industrious habits, and he soon acquired a large practice, which was also a lucrative one for those times. Although in the course of his life often in public service, he was, up to the time of his death, except when on the bench, a laborious practitioner, and even when a member of the United States Senate the recesses of Congress were occupied with professional labors.

In 1821 he was elected clerk of the House of Representatives of the state legislature, which office he continued to fill through frequent changes of party supremacy, for ten or twelve consecutive years. In 1828 he compiled and published, by legislative appointment, the statutes of Georgia, and in 1834-5, he represented his native county in the state senate. He was captain of a volunteer company in the Creek and Seminole war of 1836, and was entrusted by General Scott with a separate command, and detailed for a special service, in the performance of which he distinguished himself for his gallantry and courage. From that year until 1841 he was a representative in the National Congress. In 1840 he was nominated by the Whig party for governor, but was defeated. His defeat was attributed to a vote he had given in Congress in favor of including tea and coffee in the tariff for revenue; and construing his defeat into a disapproval of his congressional course, he resigned his office of representative, and gave himself up to his profession. He was a very effective advocate, and where important interests had to be litigated he was generally retained as leading counsel.

In 1845 he was appointed, by Governor Crawford, a judge of the Supreme Court of the Ocmulgee district, to fill a vacancy. He accepted the office until an election could be had by the legislature, but declined being a candidate for the bench, although assured of an election had he been willing to continue in the office.[1] Two years later he was elected to the senate of the United States, in which body he held an honored place and commanded a wide influence until the expiration of his term of office in 1855. His failure of a reëlection was no doubt a serious disappointment to him, but he declared that he should leave the senate without any personal regrets. Probably no one of the many offices of trust and honor which he held through the partiality of his fellow citizens was more esteemed by him than that of grand master of the Grand Lodge (masonic) of Georgia, which high position he held from 1843 until his death.[2] This event occurred suddenly, with only a few hours' warning, at his home in Greensboro, May 6, 1856. The announcement took the country by surprise, and the press everywhere noticed it in terms of the highest respect for his character, and sorrow for his death.

In the performance of his public duties he was remarkable for his patience, urbanity and frankness, and his habits were always

---

[1] "Although the most affable of men, open to the approaches of every honest class of the people at appropriate times, relishing keenly the flash of forensic wit and the play of popular humor, and despising the false dignity which so often covers shallow minds and cold hearts, yet few of our judges maintained with better effect the grave earnestness, the quiet order, and the solemn authority so necessary to the administration of justice. With steady hand he balanced the scales; and the best commentary upon his brief administration is found in the uncomplaining acquiescence of bar and people in the soundness, independence and impartiality of his judgments."— Hon. E. A. Nesbit, in Miller's *Bench and Bar of Georgia*, vol. 1, p. 310.

[2] His portrait was published, in a handsome lithograph, by the proprietors of the *Masonic Signet and Journal*, at Atlanta, about the time of his death; and masonic bodies throughout the country testified by resolutions and otherwise their deep sense of his loss. The following is a list of masonic lodges supposed to have been named in his honor: *Dawson Lodge*, No. 16, Washington, D. C.; *ditto*, 183, Winchester, Wayne Co., Miss.; *ditto*, 129, Scottville, Claiborne Parish, La.; *ditto*, 69, Crawfordsville, Taliaferro Co., Ga.; *ditto*, 68, Social Circle, Walton Co., Ga.; *ditto*, 244, Oakey Street, Butler Co., Ala.— *Universal Masonic Record and Directory*, 1860.

those of a vigilant, industrious man of business. He was characterized by good sense and a manly independence. In Congress his capacity for affairs secured for him the chairmanship of two important committees, one of which, that on claims, is considered one of the most laborious and useful positions appertaining to the national legislature. He spoke rarely, and when he did take the floor it was upon a question requiring action. His constituents were served with the utmost fidelity, and, if not a great statesman, he was a conscientious, intelligent, liberal minded legislator, whose public acts were never influenced by a corrupt or unworthy motive.[1]

The testimony of those who knew him well is that he was ever, in his private life, one of the purest and most blameless of men. He delighted in the sports of the turf and the field, always keeping a fine pack of fox-hounds, the fleetest in the country, which he spared no expense in procuring.[2] Though highly refined and courtly in his manners, he was eminently social in his nature and habits. He had a keen wit, was skillful in repartee,

---

[1] "Will you, who yet live, and were children when I was a child, turn back with me in memory to those days, and to those who were your school fellows and playmates then? Do you remember who were the brave and generous, kind and truthful among them? and do you recall their after lives? Answer me; were not these the true men in that day? Do you remember William C. Dawson, Joseph H. Lumpkin, Lucius Q. C. Lamar, and his brother Mirabeau B. Lamar, Eugenius Nesbit, Walter T. Colquitt and Eli S. Shorter? How varied in temperament, in character, in talents, and yet how like in the great leading features of the soul! Love for their country, love for their kind, love for the good was common to them all; unselfish beyond what was necessary to the wants of their families, generous in the outpourings of the soul, philanthropic and full of charity. They hoarded no wealth, nor sought it as a means of power or promotion. Intent upon the general good, and content with an approving conscience and the general approbation, their lives were correct and their services useful, and they live in the memory of a grateful people as public benefactors."— Sparks' *The Memories of Fifty Years*, p. 168, see also pp. 174, 180, 485.

[2] "His hounds and blooded steeds were his subordinate pets. He loved the echo of the mellow horn, the dashing ride, the incoming at the death, and the festive glee that crowned the chase. Upon such occasions the dignity of the senator gave place to the harmless *abandon* of the boy."—Judge Nesbit, in *Bench and Bar of Georgia*. The ollowing is from a letter to the author of that work from Edgar G. Dawson, Esq., son of the senator: "My father . . . . . was the best horseman I ever saw, and surpassed all his companions in his exploits upon the field with his horse and hounds. I have frequently seen him from daybreak until nightfall in the chase (of the red fox, the fleetest and most enduring of the species), and then return home and work until twelve or one o'clock in his office. I think he was one of the most industrious men I ever knew, and at the same time the most social. He made companions of his children, ... upon the circuit, at Washington, in his travels, upon the plantation,— and seemed delighted, in the chase, to see his sons well mounted, contesting with him the palm of horsemanship in leaping fences and ditches, and in keeping nearest the hounds in full pursuit through woods and fields."

and for harmless fun and innocent frolic he had a peculiar relish. The recollection of his anecdotes, his pleasantries, and his practical jokes, is still fondly cherished by his former associates.[1]

"In the courts and in tavern-halls, on the wayside and in grave assemblies, his sympathies with the people found means of expression. Without effort on his part, he was always the centre of a listening crowd, eager to know his opinions, and to catch the playful humor of his conversation. He knew more men personally than any man of his day; and those he did not know he seemed to know. A cordial grasp of the hand, a word of recognition, a bow, a pleasant inquiry, or a bantering salutation, as well as good offices, were the price which he was wont to pay for golden opinions. But let it not be understood that for selfish ends he thus bought the favor of the people. That a man of his sagacity should not know that such means would result in available popularity is not a possible conclusion; yet those who knew him well are convinced that, irrespective of availability to such an end, his mode of intercourse would have been the same. As a proof of his attractiveness as a man, and in memory of the kindliness of his nature, let it be recorded that many of his clients, whilst opposed to him in opinion, sustained him as a politician. Rarely, indeed, do party ties yield to the claims of private friendship. The former are usually stronger than even those of nature. The personal qualities referred to, with his firm mind, and strong, pure character, made him for many years the most popular man in Georgia.

"His knowledge of men was very remarkable, as well as his tact in their management. If required to name the quality of mind which, more than any other, contributed to a career as a lawyer and statesman which cannot be designated otherwise than as brilliant, I should point to his power of insight into character. No man knew better how to control the conduct of others by touching those springs of action which are hid from the ordinary observer. This faculty was native; yet it derived efficiency from a large experience. He studied men as some people study books, and made a better use of them than philosophers often make of the facts of science. In the extracting of testimony from an unwilling witness, in its elucidation before the jury, in

[1] See *Historical Collections of Georgia*, pp. 260—317.

the selection of jurymen, in fencing and foining with an adversary, in detecting the idiosyncrasies of the judge, and more especially in exposing fraud lurking in the details of complicated transactions, it availed him as an instrument of tremendous power. Shrewd and quick of eye, he was prompt to seize a vantage-ground, to recover from a false move, or to discover and storm the weak points in a cause. He knew when to beat a retreat, or how to capitulate with the honors of war, to break the force of an argument by a timely jest, or to overwhelm his antagonist with the clear, outstanding equity of his case. And if, perchance, there was anything ludicrous in the claims or conduct of the adverse litigant, he was wont to ignore gravity, and 'laugh the case out of court.' Without disparaging his learning, it must be conceded that he was most powerful in the management of a cause and as an advocate.

"In legal decisions he relied more upon elementary principles than adjudicated cases, and was greatly indebted to the native suggestions of a vigorous mind. His was not the error of crushing a case under accumulated authority, or the folly of stifling it in a cloud of remote analogies. It was not his habit (like his great contemporary, John Macpherson Berrien) to reduce an argument to mathematical exactness whilst he clothed it in the drapery of the most exquisite rhetoric, yet it was his good fortune to see the strong points of a cause, and to present them with a sturdy logic.

"Judge Dawson was noted among his brethren for his skill in settling cases out of court, more especially such as he foresaw would scarcely be settled favorably in the court-house. He knew the value of compromising. Nor is it otherwise than true that his out-door settlements were characterized by liberality and forbearance. At all events, the loser not unfrequently came out of his hands believing that he was, after all, the favored party.

"It was his thorough knowledge of human nature that enabled him to adapt himself with such peculiar facility to the company he might chance to be in. He was not a learned man, yet he was at home more than most men in a circle of savans. And he was equally at his ease on the streets of Greensboro and at the dinings of Count Bodisco at Washington. He was all things to all men, not in the sense of hypocritical adaptation, but of amiable accommodation.

"The person is to be considered in acquiring correct views of a man. Especially is it an element of strength or of weakness in oratory. In this regard he was favored. He was above medium height, but well knit, combining strength with activity. His face would attract the observation of a stranger, not because of its intellectuality, but through its benevolent and various expression. His voice was strong, his walk elastic, and his attitude erect. And pleasant, indeed, it was to observe the movements of his small, quick, vigilant and hilarous gray eyes. He was a free and ready speaker, rather vehement in manner, handling facts with adroitness and arguments with force. He owed little to the schools or the classics. He was not wanting in sensibility (the soul of true eloquence) nor in a just appreciation of great themes or great occasions. Hence his most successful efforts were made when some great question of popular right had stirred the masses, or the life or estate of a client hung upon the verdict of a jury. At such times he was eloquent. Sensible himself to every generous or noble or compassionate emotion, and detesting every form of meanness, I have seen the listening jury melt beneath his appeals or glow beneath the fire of his denunciations."[1]

Mr. Dawson m. 1st, in 1819, *Henrietta M. Wingfield*, dau. of Dr. Thomas and Sidney Wingfield, of Greensboro. Her father was an eminent physician, whose family had emigrated to Georgia from the state of Virginia. She was b. 1802, and d. in Washington city, D. C., April 7, 1850. To use her husband's own language, she was "the chief source of his happiness and success;" and in the language of another, "She was a lady of great beauty, of refined tastes, easy yet dignified manners, remarkable for good sense, and distinguished for her intense yet unostentatious piety. She possessed in a remarkable degree the almost indescribable quality which is indicated by the word 'sensible,' a word which, in its application to women, means an almost intuitive perception of what is proper under all circumstances. Without bringing down upon herself the unpleasant observation of the world, or violating the delicacies

[1] Judge Nesbit, in *Bench and Bar of Georgia*, vol. 1, pp. 311, 312.

peculiar to her sex and station, she, with consummate address, became his strongest auxiliary in every honorable aspiration of his life. With him she ascended gracefully to the highest level of social life at Washington. She adapted herself to his circumstances, gave to practical things the aid of her sound judgment, to the hospitalities of his house the elegancies of a cultivated taste, to her children the unwearied assiduities of a mother, to the poor profuse charity, and to God the devotion of a meek and quiet spirit. Judge Dawson appreciated the character of his wife, and repaid her love with the most marked respect and most unremitting tenderness."[1] They had eight children:

3–26. William Reid, d. 1838, while a student in the University of Ga.; *unm.*
3–27. Henry Mounger, d. aged 3 years.
3–28. George Oscar, a lawyer, several times a representative in the Georgia legislature from Greene county; captain Co. I, 8th Georgia Confederate Regiment, d. June, 1865.[2]
3–29. Henrietta Wingfield, res. 1873, Columbus, Ga. HILL.
3–30. Edgar Gilmer, lawyer, res. 1873, Baltimore, Md.; *m.*
3–31. Emma Caledonia, res. 1873, South Carolina. SEABROOK.
3–32. Lucien Wingfield, Passed Midshipman, U. S. N., d. 1865; *m.*
3–33. Thomas Wingfield, M. D., m. *Anna Cody*, of Columbus, Ga.; d. 1859, without issue.

In November, 1854, Senator Dawson m. 2d, Mrs. Eliza M. Williams, an accomplished lady of Tenn. She survived him, and res. 1873, in Memphis.

3–3. Dr. THOMAS HENRY DAWSON was b. in Greensboro, Greene county, Georgia, April 8, 1809. After the usual academic course, he studied medicine, and practiced extensively, becoming eminent in his profession. He united, while very young, with the Methodist Episcopal church, and was remarkable from his earliest years for the purity and probity of his life. He lived in various places in Georgia and Alabama, and every where, by the force of his character, the light of his virtues, and the power of his intellect, he was prominent, influential and useful. He was, for some time, a representative and senator in the state legislature, and was tendered, but declined, a nomination to Congress. In later years he became noted in his part

[1] Judge Nesbit, in *Bench and Bar of Georgia*, vol. 1, p. 317.

[2] Capt. Dawson commanded the 8th Regt., in the battle of Garrett's Landing, July 28, 1862. See his report of that battle, in *Rebellion Record*, vol. 9, p. 519.

of the state as a preacher, having been licensed in 1833. He always remained, however, what is known in the peculiar economy of the Methodist church as a "local" preacher, not devoting himself exclusively to the ministerial work, but combining with it the labors of a doctor, planter and legislator, thus "serving the church and his fellow men in the use of all his gifts." He was ordained a deacon in 1837, and an elder in 1843. He is described by Bishop Pierce, of Alabama, as having possessed "a striking presence, a glowing countenance, a soft, ringing voice, a quick, fertile, ready intellect, a heart of tender sensibility and powerful enthusiasm, all sanctified by simple, fervent piety." As a minister he was popular, able and effective, and the common opinion of those best fitted to judge of his qualifications for the ministry, his endowments of heart and intellect, is, that if he had given himself entirely to this work he would have ranked foremost among preachers. A great part of his life was spent in labor among the poor and obscure in works of simple, unostentatious charity, wherein, as minister and physician, and as freely in one character as the other, he devoted himself to the humblest of the numerous very poor of his neighborhood. He had in a rare degree the faculty of adapting himself to any company in which he might be thrown, and hence was a great favorite in social life. Families vied with each other in their efforts to secure his company, and cherished the recollection of his visits as among the most pleasant episodes of their home life. He was truthful, candid, unbiassed, a safe counsellor, and a frequent arbitrator in cases of difficulty between neighbors. Before the outbreak of the civil war Dr. Dawson had become a man of large wealth. The war cost him the loss of the greater part of his estate, and financial misfortunes followed which for a time embarrassed and depressed him. But he speedily rallied, and at the time of his decease had, to a considerable extent, repaired his wasted fortunes. At all times his house was the home of his friends, and it was rarely without a visitor. He d. at Glenville, Ala., from apoplexy, June 19, 1873. On the previous day he had, in apparent health, been about his usual avocations, visiting among others an indigent patient whom he had attended gratuitously for more than a year, and while informing her that she must shortly die, so directing her thoughts and his own that both passed a very happy hour together. That evening he led a prayer meeting, and so closed an exemplary and eminently useful life, for his death occurred suddenly in the night a few hours after, and almost at the same moment, it is said, his patient died also. The language of a resolution passed by the Eufaula District Conference, July 30, 1873, "That in the death of Dr. Thomas H. Dawson the church has lost one of her ablest and most beloved ministers, the state a wise and true Christian patriot, his companion and children an affectionate husband and father, and the community in which he lived its *most useful* citizen," expresses sentiments which were repeated in substance in numerous newspaper notices of his decease, and by the various societies and associations with which he was connected.[1]

Dr. Dawson m. 1st, in Columbia Co., Ga., Feb. 23, 1830, *Ann Blair*, who was b. June 11, 1811, and d. June 23, 1842, leaving two children:

4–1. Mary E., b. in Columbia Co., Ga., Sept. 8, 1831, res. 1873, Glenville, Ala. McGough.

4–2. George William, b. in Columbia Co., Nov. 12, 1835, res. 1873, Bullock Co., Ala.; *m.*

Dr. Dawson m. 2d, July 26, 1843, *M. Hardwick*, who was b. Sept. 11, 1821, and d. Dec. 20, 1847, leaving one child:

4–3. Henry H., b. in Columbia Co., Ga., April 27, 1844, res. 1873, Glenville, Ala.; *m.*

Dr. Dawson m. 3d, Sept. 26, 1849, *Annie Snider*, who was b. Sept. 18, 1827, dau. of Hon. Benj. and Margaret T. Snider, of Savannah. She res. 1873, at Glenville. Two children:

4–4. Annie Tommie, b. in Ala., July 21, 1850, res. 1873, Glenville. Mitchell.

4–5. Susie Snider, b. in Ala., April 28, 1852, res. 1873, Glenville. Mitchell.

3–4. John Rogers Dawson, b. in Greensboro, Ga., Dec. 20, 1810, became a prominent merchant of Columbus, and one

[1] "In all the social relations of life, Dr. Dawson was a model gentleman. So kind, considerate and tender, so patient, forbearing and magnanimous, a peace maker in society, an active leader in the church. In his family his presence was sunshine. His household worship morning and evening incense. His piety grew with his years, ripened, mellowed. The last day of his life was bright, beautiful and blest. Diligent in his business, fervent in spirit, happy in the love of God and the hope of heaven, he ministered to the sick and dying, led a prayer meeting, returned home, lay down to rest and sleep, and woke in heaven."— Bishop Pierce.

of its most wealthy and influential citizens. He m. in Columbus, March 24, 1836, *Jane Amoret Towns*, and d. in same place, Oct. 29, 1852. They had five children:

4–6. Henry Rogers, b. July 26, 1837, m. Jan. 7, 1867, *Mary Ellen Cowan*, res. 1873, Union Springs, Ala.
4–7. D. Towns, b. July 14, 1839.
4–8. Mary Ella, b. July 8, 1841, m. June 15, 1867, J. C. CLAPP, d. Nov. 22, 1871, leaving two children.
4–9. John Fountaine, b. July 22, 1843, m. Nov. 13, 1866, *Maldenetta Cowan*, res. 1873, Union Springs, Ala.
4–10. Amoret Towns, b. April 15, 1849, m. June 21, 1870, WM. C. GRAY.

3–7. REUBEN JOSIAH DAWSON, b. in Greene Co., Ga., April 21, 1816, became early a student of law, but abandoned the profession on account of ill health. He was a soldier in the Creek war of 1836, and has been somewhat prominent in political life in his locality, having held various minor public offices. Prior to the late war he was engaged in business as a cotton commission merchant at Augusta, Ga., and as a planter both in Alabama and Georgia. By the war he lost the principal part of his estate. He res. 1873, at Greensboro, in his native county. He m. Feb. 18, 1841, Mrs. Elizabeth Janes who was b. in Wilkes county, Ga., 1815, dau. of John H. and Mary Gresham. They have had seven children:

4–11. John Thomas, b. in Taliaferro Co., Ga., Dec. 10, 1841, res. 1873, Greensboro; *m.*
4–12. Susan Lurena, b. in Greene Co., Ga., Nov. 23, 1843, d. in Greensboro, Feb. 13, 1861.
4–13. Emma Hazeltine, b. in Greene Co., June 11, 1845, d. at Glenville, Ala., 1870. HENDERSON.
4–14. James Henry Threewits, b. in Greene Co., Oct. 22, 1848, res. 1873, Atlanta, Ga.
4–15. Henrietta Wingfield, b. in Greene Co., Nov. 30, 1850, d. Oct. 16, 1851.
4–16. William Crosby, b. in Greensboro, May 6, 1855, res. 1873, Atlanta.
4–17. Elizabeth Gresham, b. in Greensboro, March 21, 1857, res. Atlanta.

3–8. WILLIAM CURRAN DAWSON, b. in Greene county, Ga., Sept. 17, 1818, served in the Creek war of 1836, represented Russell county in the Alabama state legislature, 1855, merchant and planter, at Glenville, Ala., 1873, m. *Martha M.*

Colbert, dau. of Capt. John Colbert, of Morgan Co., and has four children:

4–18. Anna, m. JOHN TYLER HOWARD, of Ala.
4–19. Susan, m. CRAWFORD GRIFFITHS, of Ala.
4–20. Florence.
4–21. Colbert.

3-29. *Henrietta Wingfield Dawson* (dau. of Hon. Wm. C., 2-8), m. 1849, JOSEPH B. HILL, and res. 1873, Columbus, Ga. Four children living:

4–22. William Dawson.
4–23. Joseph B.
4–24. Emma S.
4–25. Lucy T.

3-30. EDGAR GILMER DAWSON (son of Hon. Wm. C., 2-8), lawyer, served as major of the Terrell Light Artillery, Confederate army, m. 1856, *Lucy F. Terrell*, only dau. of Dr. William Terrell, of Sparta, Ga.[1] They res. 1873, in Baltimore, Md., and have had four children:

4–26. William Terrell.
4–27. Louise.
4–28. Joseph Hill.
4–29. Edgar Rhodes.

3-31. *Emma Caledonia Dawson* (dau. of Hon. Wm. C., 2-8), m. 1854, EDWARD W. SEABROOK, of .S C., nephew of Gov. Seabrook, of that state. Res. 1873, in South Carolina. Four children:

4–30. Henrietta Hill.
4–31. Edgar Dawson.
4–32. Marion.
4–33. Henry.

3-32. LUCIEN WINGFIELD DAWSON (son of Hon. Wm. C., 2-8), Passed Midshipman U. S. N., m. 1856, *Eliza Carey Dent*, dau. of George Dent, Esq., of Athens, Ga. He d. 1865, leaving two daughters:

4–34. Frances Henrietta.
4–35. Emma.

4-1. *Mary E. Dawson*, b. in Columbia Co., Ga., Sept. 8, 1831 (dau. of Dr. Thomas H., 3-3), m. July 27, 1852, JOHN

[1] A distinguished agricultural writer, and formerly member of the U. S. Congress.

McGough, who was b. in Monroe Co., Ga., Sept. 15, 1812, son of Robert and S. C. McGough. They res. 1873, in Glenville, Ala. Eight children:

5–1. Annie Blair, b. in Columbus, Ga., Dec. 19, 1854, m. May 8, 1873, Wm. C. Hart, b. Feb. 23, 1850, son of John and E. Hart. Res. Eufaula, Ala.
5–2. Robert, b. in Columbus, Jan. 10, 1857.
5–3. Thomas Dawson, b. in Columbus, July 1, 1859.
5–4. Hugh Blair, b. in Columbus, Sept. 8, 1861.
5–5. George Lafayette, *twin with Hugh Blair.*
5–6. John L., b. in Barbour Co., Ala., Jan. 21, 1864.
5–7. Mamie Elizabeth, b. in Barbour Co., Aug. 16, 1866.
5–8. Susie Snider, b. in Glenville, Ala., July 20, 1869.

4–2. George William Dawson, b. in Columbia Co., Ga., Nov. 12, 1835, m. in Columbus, Jan. 13, 1858, *Annie Sankey*, who was b. in Montgomery county, Ala., Nov. 19, 1835, dau. of John T. and Margaret Sankey. They res. 1873, at Perote P. O., Bullock Co., Ala. Five children:

5–9. Elvie A., b. in Columbus, Ga., Jan. 27, 1856.
5–10. Amoret, b. in Columbus, Nov. 9, 1858.
5–11. George William, b. in Columbus, June 20, 1861.
5–12. Annie Sankey, b. in Bullock Co., Ala., Feb. 14, 1864.
5–13. Mattie Holt, b. in Bullock Co., Dec. 14, 1870.

4–3. Henry H. Dawson, b. in Columbia Co., Ga., April 27, 1844, m. Dec. 6, 1867, Miss *Montieg Griffith.* Res. 1873, Glenville, Ala.

4–4. *Annie Tommie Dawson*, b. in Ala., July 21, 1850 (dau. of Dr. Thomas H., 3-3), m. April 28, 1868, Dr. William A. Mitchell, who was b. in Glenville, Ala., April 4, 1848, son of Col. A. C. and Mary E. Mitchell. They res. 1873, at Glenville. One child:

5–14 Willie Annie, b. in Glenville, March 4, 1869.

4–5. *Susie Snider Dawson*, b. in Alabama, April 28, 1852 (dau of Dr. Thomas H., 3-3), m. Oct 23, 1873, A. C. Mitchell jun., youngest son of Col. A. C. and Mary E. Mitchell. Res. Glenville, Ala.

4–11. JOHN THOMAS DAWSON, b. in Taliaferro Co., Ga., Dec. 10, 1841, m. Sept. 20, 1865, *Bessie Park*, and res. 1873, Greensboro, Ga. Two children:

5–15. John Park.
5–16. Nannie Louise.

4–13. *Emma Hazeltine Dawson*, b. in Greene Co., Ga., June 11, 1845 (dau. of Reuben J., 3-7), m. JOSEPH HENDERSON, and d. at Glenville, Ala., 1870, leaving one child:

5–17. Annie.

FAMILY OF JOHN EDMONDS DAWSON,

OF WASHINGTON and MORGAN COUNTIES, GA., 1802-11.

From Mrs. A. P. Hill, of Atlanta, Ga., 1873, and others, the following:

1. Major JOHN EDMONDS DAWSON, b. in Virginia, 1775, m. near Petersburg, in that state, *Annabella Burwell*, a native of Dinwiddie county, daughter of John Burwell. They removed from Virginia to Georgia about 1802, and settled in Washington county, near Oconee river. After a residence of some years in that county, during which he was its representative in the state legislature, they removed to a plantation on Little Indian creek, four miles from Madison, in Morgan county, Georgia, where he d. in 1811, aged 36.[1] He was elected to the legislature in Morgan county two weeks before his death. He was the intimate friend of Governors Milledge and Irwin, a man of great popularity, a successful planter, wealthy and talented. His wife survived him. They had five children:

2–1. Ann Burwell, d. in Wetumpka, Ala. COOK.
2–2. John Edmonds, b. in Washington Co., Ga., March 7, 1805, d. in Tuskegee, Ala., Nov. 18, 1860; *m.*
2–3. Mary Frances, d. in La Grange, Ala. COOK.
2–4. Armistead Burwell, d. in Mississippi, 1855; *m.*
2–5. Annabella Powell, b. 1810, res. 1873, Atlanta, Ga. HILL.

2–1. *Anna Burwell Dawson* (dau. of Major John E.), m. SIDNEY COOK. She d. in Wetumpka, Ala., leaving six children:

3–1. Algernon Marcus, physician, res. 1873, Butler Co., Ala.; *unm.*
3–2. Anna S., m.—— ELLSWORTH.[2]
3–3. Mary F., m. B. F. NOBLE, res. 1873, Montgomery, Ala.[3]

---

[1] It is said that he was the eldest child and only son of his parents, and it is a tradition, for the fact is not stated positively, that his father was Henry Dawson son of an English emigrant. Major John E. Dawson had sisters, Mary and Rebecca. Mary m. Col. Richard Blount, of Va., and d. in Milledgeville, Ga., leaving one child, Mary Ann, who res. 1873, at Milledgeville, widow of the late Gen. John W. A. Sandford. Rebecca m. a Mr. Turner of Northampton county, Va., and d. there, leaving several children.

[2] A daughter m.—— RANDLE. There were also two sons young and *unm.* 1873.

[3] A daughter m. Col. TATE, of London, England. There were also two daughters and two sons, *unm.* 1873.

3-4. [COOK.] Monimia, d.——, m. Dr. J. T. TICHENOR.[1]
3-5. Barclay, m. *Patty Blivins*, of Selma, Ala., d. soon after marriage.
3-6. John, killed in battle of Chancellorsville, Va., May, 1863; *unm.*

2-2. Rev. JOHN EDMONDS DAWSON was b. in Washington county, Ga., March 7, 1805, and spent several years of school life at the academy at Madison, in that state. He m. before attaining his majority, and shortly after, in 1827, himself and wife united "by experience" with the Indian Creek Baptist church, of the Ocmulgee district, Georgia. In his whole subsequent life he was active and earnest in whatever he deemed calculated "to promote the glory of God and the interests of the church." Following the business of a planter for some years after his union with the church, he was yet early engaged as its trusted and honored agent in various capacities, and was largely influential in shaping the affairs of the denomination in that new country. In 1834 he was licensed by a unanimous vote of his church "to exercise his gifts in preaching and exhortation," and in 1835 was formally "ordained and set apart to the work of the gospel ministry." He preached that year at Eatonton, and in the following January became pastor of the Baptist church at Columbus. The next year, 1837, he spent near his former residence in middle Georgia, as pastor of the churches at Indian Creek and Eatonton, with occasional service at Monroe, Monticello and Forsyth. He resided at Eatonton from 1838 until 1841, and had, in addition to the pastoral care of the church at that place, charge, during most of the time, of the church at Forsyth. In 1841 he removed to Madison, and opened a female school, the management of which he resigned the year following, upon his removal to La Grange, where he became principal of the Female Academy and pastor of the Baptist church. The work of teaching was irksome to him, "his whole heart being in the ministry," and after a short time arrangements were made that enabled him to devote his time entirely to his favorite work. In 1847 he resigned the ministry of the church at La Grange, and commenced his second pastorate in Columbus, in November of that year. In 1853, while still pastor of the Columbus church, he went on a mission to New Orleans, under

[1] President of the Agricultural College, Auburn, Ala. Two daughters, Mamie Bell and Kate, *unm.*

an appointment from the Domestic Board of Missions, and during a residence of some months there organized the First Baptist church of New Orleans, and secured funds and matured plans for the erection of a fine house of worship. In 1856 want of health compelled his resignation of his pastoral care at Columbus, and thereafter, except by an occasional sermon, he did not engage in the work of the ministry. When, subsequently, health seemed partially restored, he accepted an agency to raise money for the endowment of a professorship in Mercer University, an institution in whose welfare he always felt a deep interest. In 1858 the degree of D.D. was conferred upon him by the University, and in 1859 he was tendered and accepted the editorial chair of the *South Western Baptist*, and, though then in confirmed consumption, he conducted that periodical with marked ability, writing "with great vigor, and versatility, showing a logical acumen above his ordinary pulpit efforts, and a power of analysis and discrimination quite remarkable, with a style luminous, tasteful and spirited." His brave and hopeful, but unavailing struggle with disease terminated in his death, which occurred at the house of his friend, Dr. Cullen Battle, in Tuskegee, Ala., Nov. 18, 1860. His remains were removed to Columbus, for interment, where the church erected an elegant monument to his memory.

"Dr. Dawson was long one of the most influential of the Baptists of Georgia. He was possessed of talents of uncommon order, of an eloquence that carried all before it, of a zeal that consumed his own life, of a piety that was undoubted." . . . . "He had a delicate sense of honor, keen sensibilities, and quick, impetuous temper, combined with generous impulses, and a warm, sympathetic nature. He was a very fearless man, and was the embodiment of courage, both mental and physical. . . . . Grace subdued him, and modified all his character. . . . . He never studied oratory, he never tried to be an orator, he was an orator because he could not help it; his eloquence was inborn; he had only to rise in an assembly, and every eye was fixed on him; he had only to speak, and that in the most artless and effortless manner, and every ear was attentive." [1]

[1] Extracts from estimates of his character and services, quoted in *The Life and Services of Rev. John E. Dawson, D.D.*, by his sister, Mrs. A. P. Hill, Atlanta, Ga., 1872; an admirable biography of a great and good man.

Dr. Dawson m. 1st, Dec. 15, 1825, *Eliza Walker*, only daughter of Mr. John M. Walker, of Morgan county, Ga. She d. April 12, 1834, leaving four children:

3–7. John W.[1]
3–8. Georgia, m.—— WILLIAM FANNIN, and d. a widow, Dec. 3, 1860.[2]
3–9. Annabella, m. HENRY HOLCOMB BACON.[3]
3–10. Alexander A., res. 1873, at Atlanta, Ga.[4]

Dr. Dawson m. 2d, about 1835, *Mary Sanford* who survived him less than a year. She d. at Columbus, Ga.; had no issue.

2–3. *Mary Frances Dawson* (daughter of Major John E.), m. Col. HENRY H. COOK, and d. at La Grange, Troup county, Ga., leaving two children:

3–11. Cordelia, m. Col. AUGUSTUS FANNIN, of Tuskegee, Ala.[5]
3–12. Mary McKennie, m.—— HARGROVE, of Montgomery, Ala.[6]

2–4. Hon. ARMISTEAD BURWELL DAWSON (son of Major John E.), a lawyer, was president, in 1850, of the Harper county, Georgia, Bible Society, auxiliary to the American Bible Society. He removed to the state of Mississippi, and became a judge of the Superior Court of that state, where he d. 1855. He m. *Mary Ann Jordan*. Two *unm.* daughters survive:

3–13. Sarah.
3–14. Adelaide.

2–5. *Annabella Powell Dawson*, b. in Georgia, 1810 (dau. of Major John E.), m. 1827, Hon. EDWARD YOUNG HILL, who was b. in Abbeville district, S. C., Jan. 10, 1805. He graduated at Franklin College, Georgia, in 1824, studied law and was admitted to the bar in Monticello, Ga., became solicitor general of the Ocmulgee circuit, was at different times representative and senator from the county of Jasper in the state legislature, and was afterwards judge of the circuit of which he had previously been solicitor. While still residing at Monticello, he was elected judge of the Coweta circuit, and removed at once

[1] Twice married; no account of his family received.
[2] A son and daughter survive, both *unm.*
[3] Now a widow. Her eldest daughter m. Charles Collins, of Albany, Ga. She has, also, four daughters and one son, *unm.*
[4] Provision merchant. Six children, all young and *unm.*
[5] Three sons and two daughters living.
[6] Eldest daughter, Cordelia, m.——GIBSON. Three other children, *unm.*

to La Grange, where he was twice reëlected to the same office, which he filled with signal ability until the autumn of 1853, when he voluntarily retired from the bench, and resumed the practice of his profession. He was candidate of the Whig party for governor of Georgia in 1869, and, although defeated, bore himself gallantly in the contest and received all the support which the state of politics in Georgia at that time would enable the most popular leader of his party to command. As a judge he was eminently distinguished for a prompt and clear perception of all the points in a case, and for the ease, grace and vigor with which he separated, arranged and combined them. In the moral attributes of a good magistrate he was no less eminent than in the intellectual. Scrupulously honest, he guarded incessantly against the inroads of passion and prejudice, and held the scales of justice with an even hand. *To do right* was his constant aim. In private life he was noted for his kindness of heart, amiability of temper, urbanity of manner, and generous hospitality. While addressing a meeting of his fellow citizens at La Grange, he was stricken with paralysis, and from that time he declined rapidly until his death, a few days later, Nov. 20, 1860.[1] Mrs. Hill res. 1873, at Atlanta, where she is principal of the Orphan School. She is the author of an admirable "Life" of her brother, the Rev. Dr. John E. Dawson, and of other works. They had eleven children:

3–15. Elizabeth Scott, d. in infancy.
3–16. Catharine, d. in infancy.
3–17. Indiana, d. aged 4 years.
3–18. Jarrett Jordan, d. in infancy.
3–19. Mary Louisa, d. in infancy.
3–20. Edward Young, b. in Monticello, Ga., March 31, 1833, killed at the battle of Gaines' Mills, Va., June 27, 1862. *See forward.*
3–21. John Dawson, b. in Monticello, 1839, killed at the battle of Sharpsburg (Antietam), Sept. 17, 1862. *See forward.*
3–22. Beatrice H., m. 1st, HUNTER CHAPMAN POPE, who d. 1864; 2d, 1871, Col. ALEXANDER POPE, of Marshall, Texas, a prominent lawyer, who d. July 18, 1872; res. 1873, a widow at Atlanta, Ga.; one dau. *unm.*
3–23. Mary R., m.—— WALKER; d. in Birmingham, Ala., July 26, 1873, leaving five children.
3–24. Charles Montgomery, physician, res. 1873, Atlanta; *unm.*
3–25. Annabella Martha, d. *unm.*

---

[1] From a report and resolution adopted by the Bar of Troup Superior Court, Nov. 21, 1860.

3-20. Capt. EDWARD YOUNG HILL, b. in Monticello, Ga., March 31, 1833, at the age of twelve removed with his parents to La Grange, where he received a liberal education, and developed, early in life, fine literary tastes, and a strong inclination towards literary pursuits. He undertook the editorship of the La Grange *Reporter*, in which capacity he displayed excellent talent. Relinquishing his editorial connection for the purpose of devoting himself to the law, he removed to Marengo county, Ala., and while there contributed to the *Reporter* in prose and verse.[1] At the outbreak of the civil war he espoused the cause of the South, entered the Confederate army, and was killed in the battle of Gaines' Mills (Coal Harbor), June 27, 1862, at the time being a captain in the 9th Ala. Regt. He lost his life at the head of his company. He m. in Alabama, *Maggie Baptist*, formerly of Virginia, who survived him but a short time. They had no issue.

3-21. JOHN DAWSON HILL, was b. in Monticello, Ga., in 1839. His parents removed to La Grange in 1845, where he received the ground work of his education. In 1855 he entered the military school at Marietta, where he remained three years, maintaining a very high grade of scholarship. At the inauguration of the civil war he was pursuing his chosen profession, civil engineering, but a short time after, he joined the Evans Guards, just organized in Troup county, and was elected second lieutenant. In the formation of the Regiment he was appointed adjutant of the 13th Georgia, with which he served through the winter of 1861-2 in Western Virginia. In the spring he was

[1] One of his best poems is entitled GEORGIA. It was first published in the *Reporter*, but has been extensively reproduced by the press of the country. It is a fitting tribute to a noble state:

I. "Fair Georgia! how my full heart swells
As that proud name salutes mine ears:
What scenes it wakes in memory's cells,
How proud thy destiny appears!
Although no more among thy hills,
Thy wandering son a home may claim,
My lyre in boldest measure thrills,
Whene'er I breathe thy glorious name.

VIII. "Great Empire of the sunny South,
Thy wanderer greets thee from afar,
Thy praise is ever in my mouth,
Upon our flag thou brightest star!
May thy June rays beam ever bright,
Thus will I pray where'er I roam,
May no fell discord quench thy light,
Land of my birth — my youth's loved home!"

recalled to Georgia (Savannah) for state defense, and in June, 1862, was again ordered to Virginia, where he participated in the battle of Gaines' Mills (in which his brother, captain E. Y. Hill, lost his life), and in the second battle of Manassas. At Sharpsburg (Antietam) the command, by the death of Colonel Douglass, devolved on him, acting as adjutant general of the Brigade. Here he also fell, and was left breathing his last in the hands of the Union soldiery. His life had been a pure and upright one, and his death was that of a Christian. In his last communication to his friends at home, the concluding sentence, after referring to the prospect of hard fighting, was as follows: "I do not know that I shall again escape, but if I fall, I have a good hope of a blessed immortality through the shed blood of our Redeemer." In gentleness, refinement, and social and Christian virtues, there were indeed few to rival him.[1] He never married.

NOTES. I. THOMAS H. DAWSON, Esq., a lawyer, residing at Vienna, Dooly county, Ga., communicated in Sept., 1854, the following account of his family, since which time no communication has been had from him, nor has other trace of the particular branch of the family which he mentions been found. The material parts of his letter are here quoted:

"Your favor would have been sooner answered, but for professional engagements, and want of time to think over the matter. I fear, however, I shall be able to enlighten you but little on the subject enquired about. I have been away from my family for a long time, and all I know with regard to it I received from my grandfather when I was quite a boy. Such, however, as it is, I cheerfully give it.

"My grandfather, RICHARD DAWSON, was a native of South Carolina. He informed me that *his* grandfather, Joseph Dawson — I think that was the name — was born in Ireland, married an English lady, and had two sons who emigrated to America. One of them, I think named THOMAS DAWSON [see note II. below], settled in South Carolina, and was my great-grandfather. He is said to have come to this country while quite young, about the year 1750, or later. His brother, whose name I have forgotten, settled in North Carolina or Virginia. The elder Dawson was said to be a near relative of Lord Percy."

II. THOMAS DAWSON was granted a lot of land in Savannah, June 2, 1742, and another, Dec. 28, 1742, by the Court of President and Assist-

[1] Condensed from a sketch of his life and character, by Mrs. Sarah Ferrel.

ants. — See *Historical Collections of Georgia*, pp. 32, 33. He was one of many residents of Georgia, who, in 1741, signed a complaint in regard to the Colonial government. — *Georgia Historical Society's Collections*, vol. 2, p. 186. Soon after the fall of Charleston, in 1780, and when disaffection to the Whig cause was general, two hundred and ten persons, who styled themselves "principal inhabitants" of the city, signed an address to Sir Henry Clinton in which they stated that they had every inducement to return to their allegiance, and ardently hoped to be reädmitted to the character and condition of British subjects. Thomas Dawson of Charleston, was one of the signers of this address.— Sabine's *Loyalists*, pp. 80, 243.

III. A Mrs. Dawson had died in Richmond county, Ga. (in or near Augusta), prior to 1855, aged over 91. See "instances of longevity" mentioned in *Historical Collections of Georgia*, p. 597.

LOUISIANA.

1. John Dawson, b. Feb. 14, 1769, son of a merchant of Horncastle, Lincolnshire, Eng., emigrated to America about 1798, living first in New York. He visited New Orleans for purposes of trade and returned to New York in 1799, and in the fall of the same year to England. He had previously shipped goods to America (woolens, calicoes, etc.), sending home the products of the country. While in London (1799), he forwarded small consignments to New York and Charleston, and in the spring of 1800 he sailed to Nassau, W. Indies, taking with him goods to the value of £16,000 sterling, the joint venture of a friend in London and himself. He went thence the same year to New Orleans, where he settled permanently as a merchant, and d. in 1816. He m. abt. 1810, *Mary Beaulieu*, a native of New Orleans, of French descent. She is still living (1873). They had two children:

2–1. John, b. Aug., 1811, res. 1873, in New Orleans; *m.*
2–2. Matilda, b. 1813, d. abt. 1826; *unm.*

2–1. John Dawson, b. in New Orleans, Aug., 1811, many years a respected merchant of that city, m. 1835, *Mary Elizabeth Martin*, a native of New Orleans, where they reside, 1873. They have eight children living, all *unm*:

3–1. Louisa Matilda, res. New Orleans.
3–2. John, merchant, res. New Orleans.
3–3. Joseph Alfred, a well known musical artist.
3–4. Laura.
3–5. Alice.
3–6. Amelia.
3–7. Eliza.
3–8. Edward.

Gen. John B. Dawson, b. at Nashville, Tenn., 1800, was a representative in Congress from Louisiana from 1841, to the time of his death, which occurred at St. Francisville, La., June 26, 1845. — Lanman's *Dictionary of Congress*. See *North Carolina Records*, p. 338.

JOHN DAWSON, Alexandria, Rapides parish, THOMAS DAWSON, Jackson, East Feliciana parish, and TOUMES DAWSON, Lisbon, Claiborne parish, were planters in La., 1870.

For a branch of the family, now of Louisiana, see *South Carolina Records*, family of Rev. Thomas Dawson, of Pendleton, p. 362.

OHIO.

FAMILY OF JOHN DAWSON,

Of Greene County, O., 1830–1870.

From Dr. W. W. Dawson, and Mrs. John F. Follett, of Cincinnati, Ohio, and others, the following :

1. John Dawson, was b. in Pittsburg, Pa., in 1782. The names of his parents are not known, but he is believed to have been a descendant of George Dawson, who emigrated from Maryland to Pennsylvania about 1770 — if so, probably a son of his son Henry.[1] He m. at Hagerstown, Md., *Nancy Hays*, whose father was of Irish birth. They removed early to Virginia, and settled at Darkesville (now in Berkeley county, W. Va.), where he engaged in the tanning business, which was his trade. He is said to have been a man of high moral character, "strong in sense, integrity and determination." About 1830 he removed with his family to Greene county, Ohio, and settled at Jamestown, where he d. in April, 1870, aged 88.[2] His wife was born in Maryland, and d. in Ohio, 1866, aged 83. They had eleven children, most of whom were b. in Virginia :

2–1. Henry, d. young.
2–2. Samuel, d. young.
2–3. Salanie, res. a wid. in Boone Co., Iowa. Evans.

---

[1] See pp. 231 and 232. One correspondent believes, but is not sure, that the father of John Dawson, above named, was named Harry. Henry, son of George, above referred to, may have been familiarly so called. The following is an extract from a letter from Capt. Henry C. Dawson, of Lynchburg, Ohio (see p. 239, 5-15), received with the printers' proofs of the foregoing lines of this note and of the above record. "Nicholas Dawson, my gr. father, was an Indian fighter. He was with Crawford, and I think with Harmer and Wayne, and was in the Revolutionary army *with his brother Henry, gr. father of Dr. W. W. Dawson*" (of Cincinnati, 2-11 above). For Nicholas Dawson's record in this work, see p. 233, 3-2.

[2] He had a brother James, a stone cutter by trade, who lived in Pittsburg, Pa., and d. some years ago at an advanced age.

Jno. Dawson M.D.

2–4. John, b. in Hagerstown, Md., 1810, d. at Columbus, O., Sept. 5, 1866; *m.*
2–5. Elizabeth, res. 1873, Marietta, Iowa. Hixson.
2–6. Ann, d. in Jamestown, Ohio. Jenkins.
2–7. James R., res. Bellbrook, Ohio; *m.*
2–8. Mary Payne, d. in Jamestown, Ohio. Syfers.
2–9. George Keller, farmer, Rondo, Polk Co., Mo.; fourteen years of his life were spent on the Pacific coast, in California, Oregon and British Columbia; *unm.*
2–10. Harriet, res Jamestown, Ohio. Adams.
2–11. William W., res. 1873, Cincinnati, Ohio; *m.*

2–3. *Salanie Dawson* (daughter of John, 1), m. in Virginia, Isaac Evans. They removed to Ohio with her father about 1830, and for a number of years lived in Greene county. About 1851 they moved to Marshall county, Iowa. She now res. a widow, in Boone Co., Iowa. Eleven children:

3–1. John D., res. New Westminster, British Columbia; *unm.*
3–2. Henry W., m. Miss *Torbit*, res. Salt Lake, Utah; 3 children.
3–3. Isaac U., m. Miss *Glass*, res. Jamestown, O.; 4 children.
3–4. Samuel, m. Miss *Ingledue*, res. Marshalltown, Iowa; 5 children.
3–5. Dr. Edward H., m. Miss *Hanley*, res. Jamestown, O.; one child.
3–6. Mary A., m. Isaac Ringland, res. Malvern, Mills Co., Iowa; 3 children.
3–7. James D., m. Miss *Shewalter*, res. San Francisco, Cal.; 2 children.
3–8. Noah H., m. Miss *Anson*, res. Boone Co., Iowa.
3–9. Oliver H., res. New Westminster, British Columbia; *unm.*
3–10. Wesley T., res. Boone Co., Iowa; *unm.*
3–11. Rufus H., res. New Westminster, British Columbia; *unm.*

2–4. Dr. John Dawson was b. in Hagerstown, Md., 1810, but removed early with his parents to Darkesville, Va., (now in Berkeley Co., W. Va.), where he grew to manhood. About 1830 he removed with his father to Greene county, Ohio, and located at Jamestown, where he commenced the study of medicine, having for his preceptor, Dr. M. Winans, one of the leading physicians of the county, a good scholar, of large medical experience, and peculiarly qualified to be the guide and counselor of a young student.

Before entering upon the practice of his profession, Dr. Dawson attended a course of lectures at the Cincinnati Medical College, but his degree of Doctor of Medicine was conferred by the Medical Department of the University of Louisville, Ky., in consequence of contributions from his pen to the *Western Journal of Medicine, and Surgery*, published in Louisville. He commenced practice as the associate of his former preceptor, Dr. Winans (his father-in-law), at Jamestown, and pursued his profession through life with a devotion which insured success, and was rewarded by public confidence and private attachments. He was peculiarly a self-made man. Though absorbed in a large and laborious country practice he found time to contribute many valuable papers to the medical journals of his day, and was soon recognized as a writer of decided force and ability.

In 1851 he removed with his family to Columbus, Ohio, where he took high rank in his profession. At the solicitation of the trustees of the Starling Medical College (Columbus), he accepted the professorship of Anatomy and Physiology in that institution, which he continued to hold to the time of his death. As a lecturer he was exceedingly instructive and popular. For many years Dr. Dawson was sole editor and proprietor of the *Ohio Medical and Surgical Journal*, in connection with which he acquired an extended reputation as a perspicuous and able writer on professional topics. As a reviewer he was brought into correspondence with many of the most distinguished medical writers of England and America, by whom, it is said, he was regarded as one of the finest medical critics of his age. He wrote, also, on questions of scientific and political interest, evincing a remarkable fertility of mind and breadth of observation. An article from his pen, entitled "The Commingling of the Races," in which he argued, from a scientific standpoint, that the negro race was incapable of a spontaneous civilization, was essentially inferior to the white race and incapable of equal elevation, attracted much attention and made him favorably known to a large circle of readers outside of his profession. At the time of his death, which occurred Sept. 5, 1866, Dr. Dawson had in contemplation a work on anatomy, which he intended should be the crowning labor of his busy life, but his mind and body had been taxed to the utmost, and he passed away while yet in the strength of manhood, after a brilliant career of professional and literary reputation and personal honor. He m. *Adelia Winans*, dau. of Dr. M. Winans, above named. They had eight children :

3–12. Samuel, d. young.
3–13. Frances Mary, res. 1873, Cincinnati, Ohio. FOLLETT.

3–14. Clementine, m. LUCAS SULLIVANT, res. Kanzas city, Mo.
3–15. Anna, d. aged 16.
3–16. James William, physician, d. in Texas, aged 23.
3–17. Joshua Martin, a student, 1873, in Washington and Lee College, Lexington Va.
3–18. Minnie, } twins, now in Europe, under the care of their mother,
3–19. Nellie, } attending school.

2–5. *Elizabeth Dawson* (daughter of John, 1), m. in Jamestown, Ohio, Dr. O. F. HIXSON, and about 1851 removed to Marietta, Marshall Co., Iowa, where they now reside (1873). They have nine children:

3–20. Newton L., m. Miss *Nichols*, res. Albion, Marshall Co., Iowa; 4 children.
3–21. John S., m. Miss *Rosseau*, res. Albion; 3 children.
3–22. Ann Maria, m. JAMES L. INGLEDUE, res. Marshalltown, Marshall Co., Iowa; 2 children.
3–23. Mary, m. BROOKS CALDWELL, res. Marshalltown; 3 children.
3–24. Erasmus C., m. Miss *Ivans*, res. Marshalltown; no children.
3–25. Harriet A., m. ALVERT A. THOMAS, res. Lyons, Burt Co,, Neb.; one child.
3–26. Salanie Evans, m. SAMUEL J. COPE, res. Missouri Valley, Iowa; one child.
3–27. George J., m. Miss *Allison*, res. Marietta, Iowa; one child.
3–28. Alice C., res. Missouri Valley, Iowa; *unm.*

2–6. *Ann Dawson* (dau. of John, 1), m. J. H. JENKINS, a merchant of Jamestown, Ohio, where she d. a few years after marriage, leaving four children:

3–29. Mary, d.
3–30. Harriet, d.
3–31. William, d.
3–32. George K., merchant, m. Miss *Power*, res. Kinmundy, Ill.: 2 chn.

2–7. Dr. JAMES R. DAWSON, studied medicine in Jamestown, Ohio, and received his degree in Cincinnati, Ohio. He m. *Ellen Barnett.* They res. 1873, in Bellbrook, Ohio, and have two children:

3–33. Kate, *unm.*
3–34. Samuel, *unm.*

2–8. *Mary Payne Dawson* (dau. of John, 1), m. L. L. SYFERS, a merchant of Jamestown, Ohio, where she d. a few years after marriage. They had two children:

3–35. A dau. d. young.
3–36. Rufus K., res. Terre Haute, Ind.; *m.*

2-10. *Harriet Dawson* (dau. of John, 1), m. in 1840, John Adams. They res. 1873, in Jamestown, Ohio, and have two children:

3-37. Sarah Amanda.
3-38. Anna. Stewart.

2-11. Dr. William W. Dawson, studied medicine in Jamestown, Ohio, and received his degree from the medical college of Ohio, in which he soon after became Professor of Anatomy. Resigning this position, he lectured for a time upon clinical surgery in the Cincinnati Hospital. In 1871 he was elected Professor of Surgery in the Medical College of Ohio, and surgeon to the Good Samaritan Hospital at Cincinnati. In 1869 he was elected President of the Cincinnati Academy of Medicine, and in 1871, President of the Ohio Medical Society. He has been a large contributor to medical journals, and is an industrious collector of medical and surgical statistics, frequently giving to the profession in pamphlet form, or otherwise, the valuable results of his labors. In the midst of an extensive practice he is an unwearied student. As a surgeon, Dr. Dawson is reputed among the most eminent of the profession in this country. He m. in Ohio, *Margaret Yates Hand*, dau. of Dr. James Hand, of Hillsboro, and grand dau. of Gen. Edward Hand, a distinguished officer of the Revolutionary army.[1] They have no children. Res. 1873, Cincinnati, Ohio.

3-13. *Frances Mary Dawson* (daughter of John, 2-4), m. Hon. John F. Follett, a distinguished lawyer of Cincinnati, where they reside, 1873. Mr. Follett was in 1868 speaker of the Ohio House of Representatives. They have two children:

4-1. John Dawson.
4-2. W. W. Dawson (*a dau.*).

3-36 Rufus King Syfers, wholesale grocer, m. *Adelia Harper*. They res. in Terre Haute, Ind., and have one child:

4-3. Mary.

[1] Gen. Hand, born 1744, was a native of Leicester province, Ireland. He was Col. of a Pa. Reg't of riflemen, and participated in the battles of Long Island and Trenton, 1776, was commissioned brigadier general in 1777, and was a member of the court of inquiry concerning Andre, at Tappan, Sept., 1780. After the war he was much engaged in civil affairs of trust, and his name is attached to the Pennsylvania constitution, of 1790. He d. in 1803, greatly esteemed.

Engd by H.B. Hall & Sons 62 Fulton St N.Y.

W. W. Dawson M.D.

FAMILY OF MOSES DAWSON,

OF CINCINNATI, O., 1819-1844.

1. MOSES DAWSON was b. June 9, 1768, in or near the city of Belfast, county Antrim, Ireland. According to one account he was a native of Carrickfergus, a small port on Belfast Lough, which is in the same county. He received his education, which appears to have been liberal, in Belfast, and spent his boyhood in that city. His ancestors were English, or of English descent; his great grandfather, whose name was William Dawson, a native of Lancashire, England, having removed into county Antrim about the close of the seventeenth century.[1] Moses Dawson served an apprenticeship to the business of his father, also named Moses Dawson, who was a linen draper; and he subsequently followed the same trade, in partnership with a brother, until the destruction of their establishment by fire. In his boyhood and youth, an intense feeling of hatred of British domination pervading Ireland, was organized and widely extended the society of United Irishmen, a secret social and political organization, having for its central object the independence of Ireland. Of this society he was an active and zealous member, and for his participation in it he was twice (in 1793 and 1795), arrested on the charge of seditious conduct, and imprisoned, barely escaping the fate of associates who were convicted and hanged as traitors and rebels. After his acquittal Mr. Dawson remained twenty years in Ireland, and resumed in part his old business, but he remained a warm Irish politician. He opposed

[1] He m. at Lisburn, in county Antrim, a lady named Carson, and had sons named Robert, Samuel, William and Moses. Moses m. at Belfast a lady named Taylor, daughter of Andrew Taylor, of Belfast, and sister of Jesse Taylor, who came to America in 1799, and settled in Alexandria, Va. These were the parents of Moses Dawson, the emigrant, who is said to have had three brothers who also came to America. One of these was Washington Dawson, who emigrated to Philadelphia, where he d. and where his daughter, Mrs. Matilda Ward, yet lives. The names of the other two are not known. One is said to have come in 1792 to Philadelphia, and afterwards removed to Va.; the other in 1797 to New York, where he d. in 1816. One of his sons was in the United States service in the war of 1812.

the measures which resulted in the union of the Irish and British Parliaments, and in his old age strongly avowed his faith in the cause of the United Irishmen, and gloried in having been a "Rebel." When the political currents had become especially unsatisfactory to him, he took up the cause of the rising generation, and during the years 1810, 1811 and 1812, he was active in Belfast in the organization and administration of schools founded upon new methods of teaching, then recently introduced by Joseph Lancaster, a Quaker, and Andrew Bell, an English clergyman. In 1816-17 Mr. Dawson was concerned in the publication of a periodical at Glasgow, Scotland, wherein political subjects were discussed in a manner not at all, in the estimation of the authorities, edifying or agreeable. When his opponents were prepared for summary measures, he eluded an arraignment by crossing to America. The provost marshall of Glasgow offered a reward for his apprehension, but all efforts to get possession of his person failed. His family remained in Ireland up to 1822. They held the property from confiscation, but were not allowed to dispose of it, until 1821. In May, 1817, he arrived in Philadelphia, where he remained some time, but lost all his books and papers by fire. Thence he went to Lexington, Ky., where he remained, however, only a few months, and then removed to Cincinnati, Ohio, about 1818 or 1819, where he settled permanently. Here, soon after his arrival, he opened and taught a school on his favorite system (the Lancasterian), one of whose chief excellencies, in his view, was its freedom from religious proselytism. The school is said to have been conducted with great ability, but it was not well supported, and he abandoned it. He nevertheless remained a teacher, for he became an editor, and continued in Cincinnati, his familiar and congenial habit of writing for the public, begun in Ireland. He became in 1821, an associate editor, and in 1823 sole editor and proprietor of the Cincinnati *Advertiser*, and thus commenced a career in which he filled a very prominent position in the public eye, and was, for nearly twenty-five years, one of the most influential laborers of his time in disseminating intelligence, and molding public opinion. An extended series of articles, entitled "Reminiscences of Moses Dawson," were written for the Cincinnati *Commercial* by his friend C. Reemelin, Esq., of

Cincinnati, and appeared in that paper, in November and December, 1869, and the early months of 1870. That writer, from whose Reminiscences most of the above facts have been obtained, says: "It is proper to state that the prominent trait of Mr. Dawson's life was his conduct as a partisan editor (using the term in its best sense), during the heated contests preceding General Jackson's election, and the warm discussions during Jackson's and Van Buren's administrations. Mr. Dawson did more to elect Jackson, and to make Van Buren his successor, than any other of their contemporaries, and he did it with the purest motives. His earlier life in Ireland, and his manifold editorials on numerous subjects, as well as his biographies of General Harrison,[1] and Van Buren,[2] are also interesting mementoes of his labors; but his relation to General Jackson, his defense of Mrs. Jackson,[3] and his action as the leader in the cause in which Jackson, Van Buren, Calhoun, Benton, Woodbury, Felix Grundy and Polk, were the great men on one side, and Clay, Clinton, Harrison, Hammond and others, were on the other, constitute altogether, the most important part of Mr. Dawson's life."

Mr. Dawson was *the* Democratic editor "out west" in his time.[4] He d. at Cincinnati, Dec. 4, 1844, a short time after making a trip to the Hermitage, the home of Jackson. The latter survived him but a short time. He wrote a letter, dated "Hermitage, Jan. 2, 1845," saying he was so sick as hardly to be able to hold a pen. Mourning the death of his friend, he said: "Peace to his memory, and consolation to his family."

Mr. Dawson m. at Carrickfergus, Aug. 21, 1796, Mrs. Jane Phillips (maiden name, *Jane Blair*), who was b. at Carrickfergus, Feb. 28, 1765, and d. in Cincinnati, O., Oct. 27, 1834. They had seven children, all b. in Ireland, as follows:

---

[1] *A Memoir of the Life and Services of Major General Wm. H. Harrison*, by Moses Dawson, editor of the Cincinnati Advertiser, Cincinnati, 1824: 8vo, pp. 464.

[2] *Sketches of the Life of Mr. Van Buren*, by Moses Dawson, Cincinnati, 1840: 12mo.

[3] Mrs. Jackson testified her sense of obligation to him by presenting him with a suit of clothes of her own manufacture. These, with many papers and other mementoes of President Jackson, were long preserved by Mrs. Dawson, and probably still remain in her family.

[4] "In 1825, the *Gazette*, under Hammond, was whig, and the *Advertiser*, under Dawson, was democratic. These journals became bitter foes, and the warfare between Hammond and Dawson was a relentless one. Oceans of ink were wasted in the conflict."— Hudson's *Journalism in America*, p. 199.

2–1. Jane, b. at Carrickfergus, May 21, 1797, d. in Cincinnati, Oct., 1832 ; *unm.*
2–2. Thomas, b. at Carrickfergus, May 24, 1799, d. in Cincinnati, Oct. 4, 1851 ; *m.*
2–3. Washington, b. at Carrickfergus, Jan. 8, 1803, d. in Cincinnati, Sept. 15, 1835 ; *unm.*
2–4. George Washington, b. at Carrickfergus, June 19, 1804, d. in Cincinnati, June 23, 1837 ; *unm.*
2–5. Franklin, b. at Carrickfergus, Nov. 26, 1805, d. in Cincinnati, Aug. 25, 1838 ; *unm.*
2–6. William Vesey, b. at Belfast, Jan. 8, 1809, res. 1873, in Cincinnati ; is a printer ; *unm.*
2–7. Ellinor Mary, b. at Belfast, Feb. 8, 1811, d. in Cincinnati, Aug. 3, 1870. BELLOWS.

2–2. THOMAS DAWSON, b. at Carrickfergus, Ireland, May 24, 1799, d. in Cincinnati, O., Oct. 4, 1851, was a miniature painter, and commenced the practice of his art in Cincinnati, in 1825. He married in that city, Dec. 22, 1830, Miss *Eliza Oliver*, who resides 1873, in the same place. Two children :

3–1. Edward A., bookkeeper, res. 1873, Cincinnati ; *unm.*
3–2. Ellen E., m. Sept. 15, 1873, JOSEPH DEBAR, res. Cincinnati.[1]

2–7. *Ellinor Mary Dawson*, b. in Belfast, Ireland, Feb. 8, 1811, m. in Cincinnati, O., WILLIAM BELLOWS, and d. in that city, Aug. 3, 1870. Three daus., all res. (1873), in Cincinnati :

3–3. Mary E.
3–4. Annette.
3–5. Jane M.

---

[1] Cincinnati *Catholic Telegraph*, Sep. 28, 1873.

FAMILY OF ROBERT DAWSON,

OF CUYAHOGA COUNTY, O., abt. 1831-1871.

From Dr. Thomas K. Dawson, of Cleveland, O., 1872, the following:

1. ROBERT DAWSON, b. in England, 1794, son of Francis (or Frank) Dawson, of the neighborhood of Whitby, Yorkshire, m. in England *Jane Ward*, b. 1801, and emigrated abt. 1825, to New Market, Ontario county, Canada (now York, Province of Ontario). They had born there three children, and removed thence abt. 1831 to Bedford, Cuyahoga county, Ohio, near which place he purchased a farm which he occupied abt. forty years, and on which he d. March 19, 1871. They had eight children:

2–1. James William, b. in Canada, April 30, 1828, res. 1872, Bedford, O.; *m.*
2–2. John, b. in Canada, d. in Bedford, O., 1862, leaving a widow, but no children.
2–3. Amelia, b. in Canada, res. 1872, Bedford, O. MIGHTON.
2–4. Robert F., b. in Ohio, res. 1872, Bedford, O.; *m.*
2–5. Mary Jane, b. in Ohio, d. in Bedford, 1867, aged 31; *unm.*
2–6. Martin B., b. in Ohio, res. 1872, Bedford, O.; *m.*
2–7. George F., b. in Ohio, d. 1861, aged 22; *unm.*
2–8. Thomas K., b. in Ohio, res. 1872, Cleveland, O., physician; *unm.*

2–1. WILLIAM DAWSON, farmer and nurseryman, b. in Canada, April 30, 1828, m. Dec. 11, 1862, *Helen Frances Bosworth*, of Solon, O., b. Sept. 11, 1841, res. 1872, Bedford, O.; four children:

3–1. William, b. March 7, 1864.
3–2. Caroline Blanche, d. March 5, 1866.
3–3. Emma Grace, b. Feb. 2, 1868.
3–4.

2–3. *Amelia Dawson*, b. in Canada, m. THOMAS MIGHTON, farmer, res. 1872, Bedford, Ohio; six children:

3–5. Jane.
3–6. Septa.
3–7. Charles.
3–8. Mariot.
3–9. Patia.
3–10.

2-4. Robert F. Dawson, farmer, b. in Cuyahoga county, Ohio, m. in Cleveland, O., Miss *L. N. Clapp*, of Painesville, O., res. 1872, in Bedford, O.; two children:

3-11. Nellie.
3-12. Nettie.

2-6. Martin B. Dawson, merchant, b. in Cuyahoga county, Ohio, m. Miss *Lotta Button*, of Bedford, O., res. 1872, Bedford; two children:

3-13. Frank.
3-14.

Notes. I. Nathaniel Dawson, Esq., of Wells, Jefferson county, Ohio, d. May 4, 1857, aged 67.

"Mr. D. was b. in Maryland, Aug. 12, 1789, and moved with his parents, when a boy, to Western Virginia (the Pan-Handle,) near the close of the last century. About 1802, his father and family settled in Jefferson, Ohio, where he resided from that time up to his death. He was a man of punctuality, and upright and honest in all his dealings; and from small beginnings, by industry and economy, in less than half a century, he accumulated a large estate, left to be distributed among his numerous offspring. He was a man of some talent, which he employed, not only for his own benefit, but also for the benefit of the community in which he lived. For more than twenty years he acted as a justice of the peace in and for Wells township. His judgments, rendered in cases of law suit which came before him, were generally correct, and gave satisfaction, so that but few appeals were taken; and if at any time he erred in judgment in a law case, it was an error of the head, and not of the heart. In early youth he made a profession of religion, and joined the Methodist Episcopal church, to which his parents belonged." — Crosby's *Annual Obituary Notices*, 1857.

II. George Dawson, a soldier of 1812, d. near New Burlington, Clinton Co., Ohio, abt. Dec. 1, 1872, in the 86th year of his age.

III. Benjamin Dawson, for some years past a resident of Cincinnati, a dealer in tin, copper and sheet iron ware, is a native of Brandon, county Cork, Ireland. He has two sons engaged in business with him (1873), Robert and William.

PENNSYLVANIA.

The following records were postponed, out of their regular order, for insertion at the close of this work, in order that time might be gained for additions and corrections. (See p. 187). The labor expended upon them, during the brief time thus secured, has resulted in largely extending and improving them, and has given opportunities for their revision and correction, to a considerable extent, by correspondents and friends interested. The compiler desires to acknowledge his obligations especially to W. F. CORBIT, Esq., of Philadelphia, for a large part of the information embodied in these records.[1]

The following facts, not clearly understood at the time of printing the former portion of "Pennsylvania" records, should be noted.

There were at an early day, in Philadelphia and its immediate vicinity (Bucks and Chester counties, Pa.), no less than five heads of families bearing the name of JOHN DAWSON.[2] These were:

I. JOHN DAWSON, hatter, of Moreland township, in Bucks county, and Philadelphia, said to have come to this country with his wife Dorothy, from London, in 1710. He joined the Quakers at Abington, 1730, and d. in Philadelphia, 11 mo. 27, 1742.

II. JOHN DAWSON, wheelwright, son of above, d. in Philadelphia, 1740. The father administered on his estate.

III. JOHN DAWSON, farmer, of Solesbury township, Bucks Co., whose will, dated May 31, 1753, was proved May 26, 1759. He was a Quaker of prominence, and a resident of Bucks Co., 1719, and probably earlier.

IV. JOHN DAWSON, of West Nottingham, Chester county, whose will, dated Feb. 24, 1756, was probated in 1757. His will mentions a son

---

[1] Mr. Corbit has been engaged for several years in preparing for publication an account of the descendants of all those persons who came to America with William Penn in the ship "Welcome," in 1682 — a work which is expected to include over 50,000 names. His familiarity with the sources of original information for a record of this character has greatly facilitated the progress of this work.

[2] John Dawson, son of Emanuel, who d. 3 mo. 29, 1698, was probably an infant. Jane Dawson, w. of Emanuel, d. in Philadelphia, 1 mo. 30, 1698. Compare this with p. 187. She was probably *first* wife of the Emanuel Dawson there mentioned.

Joseph, and his w. Anne ; sons Samuel, Isaac and Nathan, each of whom m. and had children ; also a son John who was m. and had a son William.[1]

V. JOHN DAWSON, son of John, of West Nottingham, above named. It is not supposed that John of Nottingham was related to those of his name in Bucks county, nor does it appear that those two were related to each other. One, or perhaps two of these, may have come up from Eastern Maryland, but probably each of them had emigrated from the old country.

Of the descendants of John Dawson, of West Nottingham, nothing more is known than the will reveals.[2]

But a meagre account has been obtained of the descendants of John Dawson, of Solesbury. Probably a more careful examination of the deeds, wills, etc., of Bucks county than is at present possible, may throw further light on the history of his family. Such information as has been obtained is embodied in the first of the following records.

The records of the descendants of John and Dorothy Dawson, which follows that of the family of John Dawson of Solesbury, embraces nearly two thousand names. But few of all the numerous living descendants of this couple now bear the name of Dawson. It seems, indeed, almost a misnomer to designate this as a Dawson family, when page after page is occupied wholly with other names. The record should be further extended and separately published under a title more expressive of its real character.

[1] Isaac entered a caveat against the probating of any will of his father which had been executed subsequent to 1749, but soon withdrew the caveat, and allowed his brother John to act as executor.

[2] It may have been an unworthy scion of this family, David Dawson, of *Chester Co.*, who was attainted of treason, and executed at Philadelphia, in 1780. James Dawson joined the British at Philadelphia, was captured at sea, and came near suffering a similar fate.—Sabine's *American Loyalists; Pennsylvania Archives*, 1783–1786, p. 609.

FAMILY OF JOHN DAWSON,

Of Solesbury, Bucks Co., Pa., 1719–1759.

1. John Dawson, a member of the Society of Friends, residing in Solesbury township, Bucks Co., Pa., was at Falls meeting as early as 1719,[1] and was elected an assessor in that county in 1725, 1730 and 1734. He was appointed an overseer of Buckingham meeting, 2 mo. 4, 1730, and was released from the office 4 mo. 5, 1733. He seems to have been an active and useful member of the Society. His name appears in the records of the proceedings of nearly every meeting held for several years. His will, dated May 31, 1753, was proved May 26, 1759, and is recorded at Doylestown, in Bucks county. Children:

2–1. Thomas, sole executor of his father's will; his daughter, name not given, a legatee.

2–2. Elizabeth, m. 1720, Thomas Browne, had probably d. before date of her father's will, not being named therein. *See below.*

2–3. Ann, m. 1729, Joseph Browne, received legacy under her father's will. *See below.*

2–2. *Elizabeth Dawson*, m. at Falls meeting, Bucks county, Pa., 1 mo. 20, 1720, Thomas Browne. They removed to Abington in 1739. A son:

3–1. Moses, b. 10 mo. 26, 1727, d. 2 mo. 26, 1758; *m.*

2–3. *Ann Dawson*, m. at Falls meeting, Bucks county, Pa., 1 mo. 29, 1729, Joseph Browne, brother of Thomas (2-2). Four children:

3–2. Abraham, b. 4 mo. 23, 1730.
3–3. Isaac, b. 6 mo. 18, 1731.
3–4. Ann, b. 2 mo. 10, 1733.
3–5. Joseph, b. 7 mo. 8, 1737; *m.*

---

[1] "A.— P.—'s condition is such that he is reduced to poverty, and doth stand in need of assistance, particularly a cow; therefore this meeting doth appoint John Dawson to procure one."—Falls meeting records, 1719; quoted in Michenor's *Retrospect of Early Quakerism*, p. 214.

3-1. Moses Browne, b. 10 mo. 26, 1727, m. in Abington, then in Bucks county, now Montgomery, 12 mo. 31, 1753, *Sarah Oldsworth.* He d. 2 mo. 26, 1758, leaving two children:

4-1. Elizabeth, b. 6 mo. 1, 1754.
4-2. Thomas, b. 7 mo. 16, 1757.

3-5. Joseph Browne, b. 7 mo. 8, 1737, m. *Mary Preston*, dau. of Jonas and Jane Preston. She d. 11 mo. 23, 1764, leaving two children:

4-3. Ann, b. 12 mo. 11, 1760.
4-4. Sarah, b. 10 mo. 3, 1762.

Note. On the 7th of Feb., 1733-4, "John Dawson, of Solebury, in the county of Bucks, yeoman," mortgaged 120 acres of land to the Trustees of the General Loan-Office of the Province of Pennsylvania. The land was situated in Solebury, adjoining lands of Thomas Head, Henry Paxton, Randal Spakman and Joseph Pike. The amount of the mortgage debt was £96. in the provincial bills of credit.

FAMILY OF JOHN DAWSON,

OF BUCKS CO., PA., AND PHILADELPHIA, 1710-1742.

1. JOHN DAWSON and w. Dorothy are said to have come from London, England, to America, in 1710. Their dau. Ann was then five years old. It is probable that their sons John and Daniel also came with them. His trade was that of a hatter. They appear to have been connected with the Society of Friends in England, but it is certain that he, at least, did not ask to be received in membership among Friends here for some years after their arrival. The family tradition is that he had been unfortunate in business in London. That he had left behind him debts there, appears from the following extracts from the Abington meeting records:

"1 mo. 3, 1729. Friends of Horsham requested on the account of John Dawson that he might be united to Friends, but being come from Old England without a certificate, by reason of some debts left unpaid, therefore the meeting do appoint John Cadwallader, Sampson Davis, and Thomas Lloyd to draw a letter to some of Dawson's creditors that are Friends in England to see if they are willing to forgive ye debt, and bring the letter to the next monthly meeting."

"2 mo., 28, 1729. A letter was brought, subscribed [addressed] to Friends in London in behalf of John Dawson, which was signed by several Friends."

The result of these friendly offices is seen in the following, extracted from the records of the same meeting:

"4 mo. 29, 1730. John Dawson produced a certificate from Friends of Horsleydown monthly meeting in London, which was read and accepted."

He was a resident of Moreland township (Bucks county, now Montgomery[1]), and kept at Hatborough,[2] in that township, a

[1] John and Daniel Dawson were both returned as having land taxable in Moreland township in 1734. Bucks Co. was one of the original counties formed by William Penn in 1682. Montgomery county was organized in 1784.

[2] [MORELAND.] "The largest village was Hatborough, better known as the "Crooked Billet," containing about 18 houses (half of which were built of logs), a store, tavern, etc. This place derived its name from one of the first stone houses built here, which not long after became a tavern, and had for its sign, a *Crooked Billet*, which name was originally derived from a popular inn then in Water St.,

tavern called the "Crooked Billet," carrying on also the hat-making business. He removed to Philadelphia in 1740,[1] or earlier, and d. in that city 11 mo. 27, 1742.[2]

His widow, who is said to have been a member of Abington meeting many years before her husband united with it, seems to have retained her connection with that meeting, and to have returned, soon after her husband's death, to her former home or neighborhood. Later in life she made her home with her daughter, Ann Tomkins, near Phenixville, in Chester Co., and

---

Philadelphia. John Dawson subsequently kept this house, and in connection followed his occupation of making hats, from which its more recent name of Hatborough. This house, it is reported was built about 1705, and has since been altered into a two story dwelling, now occupied by Jesse Walton, coach maker".—W. J. Buck's *History of Moreland*, in *Collections* of *Historical Society of Pa.*, vol. 6, p. 189.

Other accounts are as follows: "John Dawson was the original settler of the 'Crooked Billet,' afterwards called Hatborough, where he carried on the hatting business. He there built a stone house, with the assistance of his daughter Ann, who afterwards married Bartholomew Longstreth. Here he kept a house of private entertainment, and had for a sign a hewn crooked billet of wood; hence the name, the "Crooked Billet." His hatters' tools were brought up to Abington in a lime wagon. Thence he set out into the woods, and for several miles had to open a road with axe and spade for his horse and cart to pass along." — *Longstreth MSS.*

"The Crooked Billet near Hatboro, was first settled by John Dawson, hatter, who having been unfortunate in trade in London, emigrated with his family to Philadelphia."— *Letter of Daniel Longstreth to Watson, the Annalist.*

"It would appear from some of my inquiries respecting the early settlement of Hatborough, that our ancestor, John Dawson, had lived in three different houses [there] on as many sites. The first was built of logs, in the rear of a house now standing nearly opposite to the end of the new road at the Upper Tavern on the west side of York road...........The second house......was of stone.........its site opposite to Mordecai Thomas' hip-roofed house. It was on the east side of York road, and was the original 'Crooked Billet' tavern. My great grandmother, Ann Dawson, was mason-tender, and carried the mortar on a board, and the stones in her apron, whilst her father executed the masonry.........His last and third residence was in the east end of the old stone house on the west side of York road, between the old tavern and the creek.........Like the others it was originally but one story high, and now exhibits on the front, on the south side of the door, the initials I. D. D.— 1745." *Daniel Longstreth*, 1831. (If the initials were intended for *John and Dorothy Dawson*, as suggested by a correspondent, the date, as given, could not have been a part of the original inscription.— *See notes as to his removal and death, below.*

[1] He was appointed administrator of the estate of his son John in 1740, and was then described as *of Philadelphia.*

[2] Philadelphia meeting records. "Cousin Susanna Smedley, who resides with her son-in-law, Jonathan Hood, at Radnor, told me that our ancestor, John Dawson, a free mason, and founder of Hatborough (he was a hatter by trade), removed to Philadelphia, and d at the corner of Church alley and Second St. in the house which John F. Watson, in his "Annals of Phila." says was the first brick house built in the city. The city regulation mark was always on this house." — *Daniel Longstreth to Susanna Longstreth*, 12 mo. 17, 1831. "The house continued to be occupied by some of his descendants until some time after the Revolution." — D. L. 1832. "John Dawson d. in Philadelphia, corner Second St., and Church alley, in the *fifth* brick house built in the city." — W. F. C. "No record of administration on his estate in Philadelphia: probably to be found at Doylestown, Bucks Co." (as he owned property in that county). — W. F. C.

her remains are said to have been the first interred in the Friends' burying ground, belonging to Pikeland monthly meeting, near Kimberton, in that county.[1] Their children were:

2–1. John, wheelwright, d. in Philadelphia, his father appointed administrator of his estate, 1740.[2]
2–2. Ann, b. in London, 1705, d. 3 mo. 18, 1783. LONGSTRETH; TOMKINS.
2–3. Daniel, d. in Philadelphia, 1 mo. 1, 1746; *m.*
2–4. Sarah. HANCOCK.
2–5. Isaac, d. in Philadelphia, 9 mo. 12, 1748; *m.*
2–6. Benjamin, b. about 1718, d. at Smyrna, Del., 12 mo. 5, 1793; *m.*
2–7. James.[3]

2-2. *Ann Dawson*, b. in London about 1705, came to America with her parents in 1710.[4] She m. 1st, at Horsham, Pa., 11 mo. 29, 1727, BARTHOLOMEW LONGSTRETH,[5] who was

---

[1] "Widow Dorothy Dawson lived with her daughter, Ann Tomkins, in Charlestown, Chester county, in the house which she, A. T., built on the hill by Mason's tavern. Whilst on her death bed, hearing that water frequently rose in the graves at Providence, she requested that they 'would not drown her after she was dead,' but take her corpse to Pikeland, which was just established. She was the first one interred in that grave yard, and her gr. dau. Elizabeth Starr, w. of Joseph Starr, planted an apple tree at the head of her grave, which blew down a few years since, and the place is now supplied by a Lombardy Poplar." — D. Longstreth, 1831.

[2] John is named first in the list of children, on the supposition that he was the eldest child, and the names of the other children follow in the order of birth *as conjectured.* What family John left, if any, is not known. The administration bond was dated Aug. 30, 1740, and the intended signers were, John Dawson, hatter, of Philadelphia city, Bartholomew Longstreth, of Bucks Co., yeoman, and Daniel Dawson, of Philadelphia county. The bond was signed only by the two latter. A blank left for the signature of John Dawson, was not filled, and no inventory of the estate was filed.

[3] Signed marriage certificate of Benjamin Dawson and Elizabeth Fussell as witness, 1744. Supposed to have been a brother of the groom.

[4] So she informed Isaac Longstreth, her grandson. He related the facts to his nephew, Daniel Longstreth, who made record of them.

[5] The name was variously written Longstreth, Longstroth, Langstreth, Langsteroth, etc. Longstreth is now the generally accepted orthography, and is therefore used uniformly in these records. For notices of the name and family, see Whitaker's *History and Antiquities of the Deanery of Craven*; Fuller's *Worthies of England* (Yorkshire), etc. According to a tradition, the father of Bartholomew was named Christopher. At the christening of the son, it is said that the father and godfather not agreeing as to a name, the officiating priest christened him in honor of the saint (Bartholomew) on whose day he was born. "He was five feet 8½ inches high," and "his person was heavy, thick set;" but his brother Martin, who also emigrated to America, and d. about 1727, "is said to have been seven feet 2½ inches in height. He was by trade a brazier, and occasionally travelled about the country seeking employment. He was familiarly called 'the long tinker.'" He had a daughter Elizabeth, who m. Francis Littlejohn, and d. near Philadelphia, in 1753, leaving eight children; and a son Bartholomew (sometimes called Bartholomew, junior), who in 1769 lived 150 miles west of Philadelphia, and had five children. Some of his descendants are said to have removed to Va. Daniel Longstreth, late of Warminster, Bucks county, Pa., from whose copious family memoranda much has been drawn for these records, noted the fact that he had "often heard that Bartholomew Longstreth had a brother Philip."

b. in Longstroth Dale, Deanery of Craven, Yorkshire, England, 8 mo. 24, 1679, and was therefore at his marriage 48 years of age, while she was only 22. He had emigrated from Yorkshire, England, in 1698, taking with him a letter from the Friends of Settle meeting in that shire, certifying, according to a practice still in use in the Society on the removal of deserving members, to such facts as were calculated to commend him to the confidence and fellowship of the brethren among whom he expected to live.[1] This commendation and confidence his subsequent life fully justified. He was one of the petitioners, among whom were nearly all the leading men of Pennsylvania, who, about the year 1700, when he could scarcely have more than attained his majority, joined in a petition to the king of England praying that William Penn might not be deprived of his government in the province. This early act shows that even then Bartholomew Longstreth was recognized as a man of some substance and character.[2]

Prior to his emigration he had been for some years in the employ of a grazier or cattle drover, in whose service he had proved discreet and trustworthy. After his arrival in Pennsylvania he worked as a laborer until, by his frugal and industrious

---

1 "Whereas, Bartholomew Langsteroth having acquainted us how he doth intend to remove himself into Pennsylvania in America, if the Lord give him ability, there to live among Friends, and we, having taken care to inquire, do certify you, our friends and brethren, whom it may concern, how that he hath obtained and discharged his business and affairs so that he doth thereby give no just occasion to any person to reflect upon him, and further that the said Bartholomew Langsteroth is clear from any engagements or entanglements with any person on the account of marriage, so that so far as we know if he hereafter be concerned in order to marry, this may certifie our friends that may be therein concerned accordingly that as he hath been of a pretty good behavior since the time that he hath frequented our meetings, so his removing is with ours as also with his father's consent and approbation, and if the Lord lengthen out his days that he get to the end of his intended journey, you may receive him as one whom the Lord in his love has visited and reached unto in mercy, and it is our fervent desire and prayer to God for him that he may proceed in faithfulness that those blessings may be continued to him to the end of his days. So, with the salutation of love in Jesus Christ our Lord and Savior, we rest and remain your brethren in the fellowship of the Gospel of Grace.

"From our monthly meeting at Settle, in Yorkshire, in old England, the first day of the first month, 1698-9.

[*Signed by twenty Friends.*]

2 Penn's second visit to America was made in 1699. Not long after his arrival he learned that there was a measure before the House of Lords for bringing all the proprietary governments under the Crown, and he returned to England, in 1701, probably taking with him the petition above referred to. It was never presented to the king, as, happily, before its arrival all danger of Penn's removal had passed. The original petition is now in possession of the Historical Society of Pennsylvania.

Rockwood Process, N. Y.

THE LONGSTRETH HOMESTEAD.

habits, he had laid up about £400. One half of this he ventured on a trading voyage to Tortola, one of the Virgin group of the West India islands, then as now noted for its exports of sugar, molasses, rum, etc., and for its unhealthy climate. He sailed for the island in another vessel from that to which he intrusted his property, which was supposed to have foundered at sea, as it was never after heard of; and on arriving at the island he was taken sick, and narrowly escaped with his life. Returning to Pennsylvania, he resumed work as a laborer, and after a time bought a tract of 300 acres of land on Edge Hill, in Moreland township, then in Bucks county, now Montgomery.[1] On this he settled and commenced its improvement, but becoming dissatisfied, he sold the land, with the determination of returning to England.[2] While waiting in Philadelphia for a passage home he met with Thomas Fairman, surveyor to William Penn, who induced him to abandon his intention of leaving the country, and from whom he purchased 500 acres of unimproved land in Warminster township, in the county of Bucks.[3] He afterwards purchased other tracts of land in that neighborhood, and at the time of his death left a large and valuable estate, including more than one thousand acres of land and monies at interest.[4] When he

---

[1] "B. L. first settled on the county line, between Bucks and Montgomery counties...... It was on Edge Hill. The house was a long, stone building."— *Letter of Anna T. Raab*, 1873.

[2] At Middletown, Bucks county, meeting, 3 mo. 2, 1706, Bartholomew Longstreth was granted a certificate "to whatever meeting he is likely to belong to." This was probably when he was about returning to England, as traditionally related by the family.— W. F. C.

[3] The same tract of 500 acres that was deeded by Wm. Penn, in 1685, to John Dwight, and by John Dwight's heirs, in 1707, to John Talbot, and by John Talbot, in 1709, to Thomas Fairman. The deed from Thomas Fairman to Bartholomew Longstreth is dated Dec. 23, 1710."— S. T. L. "For this tract B. L. paid £175 Pennsylvania currency, or seven shillings per acre. In 1713 he purchased from the proprietary agents [Richard Hill, Isaac Norris and James Logan], twenty-six acres adjoining, for £6.10, or five shillings per acre."— D. L.

[4] The old homestead he willed to his son Daniel, who d. in 1803, and he bequeathed the same to his son Joseph, who d. in 1840. He left the property to his only son Daniel, who d. in 1846, and under his will the homestead, which then included the dwelling house and out buildings, and fifty-six acres of land, was sold. His eldest son, John Lancaster Longstreth, now of Philadelphia, became the purchaser, and in 1850 Mr. L. sold the premises to Isaac Rush Kirk, who d. in 1859, leaving the property in possession of his widow and children, who now reside there (1873). The old homestead, as it appeared when photographed in 1872, had been built at three separate dates. The central part was built by B. L. in 1713; the east end by D L. in 1750, and the west end, which was much larger than either of the other parts, was built by D. L. in 1766. At the time of the completion of the final addition (by workmen from Philadelphia), it was considered the finest house in that part of the country. The dates were ascertained from date stones found in different

first went into Warminster the country there was a wilderness, without roads, and with only a cattle path through the woods. His first house was of logs. When he was better accommodated he opened a store in a part of his dwelling, which he continued to keep for the accommodation of the neighborhood for some years after his marriage, being assisted in his business by his wife. Indeed, it may be supposed that his habit of frequenting the markets in old England had given him an inclination to trade. It may have prompted him to modest ventures which resulted successfully, helping him in the accumulation of the snug capital which he had at command within a few years after his arrival in America, and a part of which he lost in the unfortunate expedition to Tortola; and it may, also, have had an influence in leading him to engage in this later enterprise in which he undertook the business of a storekeeper.[1]

He was held in good esteem by members of the religious Society to which he belonged,[2] and he was frequently called on to settle estates, and to transact a variety of public affairs. As supervisor of Warminster he opened a portion of what is known as the York road. He was charitable to the poor, who never, it is said, left his door empty-handed; and he was, withal, a man of great firmness of purpose, strength of mind and energy of character. He d. very suddenly in the road, without previous illness, Aug. 8, 1749, and was buried in Horsham grave yard.[3]

parts of the building. After April, 1872, Mrs. Kirk took down those parts which were built in 1713 and 1750, and erected a new building on their site. While the wall of the east end was being torn down a copper medal was found which was struck in commemoration of the taking of Porto Bella, by Admiral Vernon "with six ships only," Nov. 22, 1739.

[1] It is said, however, that this was rather his wife's enterprise than his own: that she borrowed a small sum of money from her husband, as her original capital, with which to buy goods in Philadelphia, and gradually increased her stock and extended her business, attracting customers from Wrightstown and other distant places; and that the business continued to prosper until the increasing cares of her family obliged her to relinquish it. "On closing her accounts and refunding the original loan with interest, there was a balance of £600. in her favor." — D. L., 1831.

[2] "B. L. appears to have been an active man among the early Friends in Pennsylvania. On the 30th of 5 mo., 1733, he was appointed by Abington meeting to attend the quarterly meeting as a representative." — W. F. C.

[3] "I now think proper to give a short relation of my father's death. The eighth day of August, 1749, he went into the field to set the negroes to plowing, and stay with them till about eight o'clock, and finding himself much out of order he left them and went to a school-house which was built in our field, and sent my sister home for me to take a horse for him to ride on. Accordingly I did, and he went to a stump, got upon it with help, and so upon the horse, and I got on behind him. When we rode about thirty perches he fell back into my arms. There being two

It is a tradition that his marriage with Ann Dawson was the result of "love at first sight," under circumstances which, if not quite romantic, were altogether befitting the times, and the good, substantial men and women who founded Pennsylvania. While her father was building his house at the Billet she acted as mason tender, carrying the mortar on a board, and the stones in an apron of stout cloth, whilst her father executed the masonry. While she was so engaged it is said that Bartholomew passed by, "was smitten with her glowing charms and filial piety, and then and there chose his wife."[1] They were married at Horsham meeting house, to which she rode on a pillion behind her father, departing from it with her husband on his horse in a similar manner. Tradition says that while she was busy talking with her young friends Bartholomew became somewhat impatient to take his prize away, and summoned her in the broad speech of Yorkshire with the inquiry: "Ann, art thou gooing, or art thou noot."

According to the custom of the times, but few even of Friends excepting, they employed slave labor, both in the field and in their domestic affairs; and some of their descendants remember to have seen in the old homestead a mark on the wall between the sitting room and kitchen where (though closed for many years) had been a small window at which Ann was wont to sit

men riding a distance before us, I called to them, and they rode back quickly. One of them took him down from me in the road, and he took about four or five breaths, and died away, being sensible to the very last." — *Daniel Longstreth to friends in England*, 1752.

"A clouded marble slab was placed at his head by his son Daniel, with '1749 — Bartholomew Longstreth, aged 69 years 11mo. 15 days' on it. Some years after, an uneasiness being expressed by some of the members of the meeting with this stone, an attempt was made to remove it, but Daniel Longstreth replied, 'not while I live shall any one disturb it.' It remains there to this day." — Daniel Longstreth (gr. son of Daniel above named), 1831. It is still there (1873).

[1] The tradition may be true as to him, but if another story concerning the pair has any foundation in verity it is evident she was not similarly inspired. The difference in their ages is to be remembered. "Previous to their marriage she, when having her fortune alphabetically tried, said: 'I care not who knows the initials that turned up for me, for they were B. L. That would stand for old Bartholomew Longstreth, and I am sure I never will have him!'" From an account of B. L., accompanying a Family Tree in possession of Alfred Longstreth, of Philadelphia. The following is an extract from Abington Meeting Records: "At our monthly meeting held ye 29th of ye 11th mo., 1727. Whereas Bartholomew Longstreth and Ann Dawson having declared their intentions of marriage with each other before two monthly meetings, enquiry being made by persons appointed, and found clear of all others on account of marriage, are left to accomplish ye same orderly." On the 26th of 12 mo., 1727, the marriage of B. and A. was reported to have been "orderly performed."

to watch her slave women at work in the kitchen. Almost the last act of Bartholomew Longstreth's life was to go into the fields to direct his negroes about their work. Many of Bartholomew and Ann's descendants, however, have been conspicuous for their opposition to slavery, and the Society to which they belonged, at a very early day made the holding of slaves a subject of discipline, and, where persisted in, a ground of disownment.

Ann had been a thrifty housekeeper and good manager. An inventory of her estate taken 2 mo. 1, 1753, shows that it amounted, after deducting all claims against it, to nearly £2000, and included *servants* valued at £100. Her husband had left her the entire income of all his landed property, until his sons, who were to inherit it, should respectively come of age, except her son Daniel, whose estate was to remain in her hands until he should arrive at the age of 25 years, after which he was to pay her annually £6 during her life or widowhood.[1] They had eleven children:

3–1. Sarah, b. 11 mo. 8, 1728-9,[2] d. 9 mo. 21, 1800. FUSSELL.
3–2. John, b. 4 mo. 10, 1730, d. 1737.
3–3. Daniel, b. 2 mo. 28, 1732, d. 11 mo. 19, 1803; *m.*
3–4. Jane, b. 1 mo. 18, 1733-4, d. aged 20 mos.
3–5. Jane, b. 11 mo. 23, 1735-6, d. 5 mo. 16, 1795. COATES.
3–6. Ann, b. 11 mo. 3, 1737-8, d. 6 mo. 26, 1824. COATES.
3–7. John, b 8 mo 25, 1739, d. 4 mo. 16, 1817; *m.*
3–8. Elizabeth, b. 3 mo. 15, 1741, d. 6 mo. 28, 1813. STARR.
3–9. Isaac, b. 12 mo. 16, 1742-3, d. 12 mo. 4, 1817; *m.*
3–10. Joseph, b. 10 mo. 11, 1744, d. 1798 or 1803; *m.*
3–11. Benjamin, b. 7 mo. 17, 1746, d. 8 mo. 4, 1802; *m.*

After remaining a widow nearly four years, Ann Longstreth m. 2d, 6 mo. 7, 1753, ROBERT TOMKINS, who resided in War-

[1] Daniel Longstreth's letter book, 1831.

[2] It is to be borne in mind that March, the third month of the year, according to present computation, was formerly reckoned the first month. These dates of birth (of the children of Bartholomew and Ann Longstreth), designating the months by numerals, are from authentic records (the family Bible, original entries by Ann and Bartholomew L.), but in substituting the names of the months for numerals, allowance must be made for the change from old to new style. The following is an extract from a letter of Daniel Longstreth (3-3) to his "loving cousins" in England, written 20th March, 1752, in which year the change from old to new style was made. He states that his "parents had eleven children, as followeth: Sarah was born January ye 8th, 1728-9, John was born June ye 10th, 1730, and lived till he was seven years old, Daniel, born April ye 28th, 1732, Jane, born March ye 18th, 1733-4, died [aged] 1 year and 8 months, Jane, born January ye 23d, 1735-6, Ann, born January ye 3d, 1737-8, John born October ye 25th, 1739, Elizabeth, born May ye 15th, 1741,

rington township, Bucks county.[1] He is said to have wasted her fortune, and to have subjected her to personal ill usage, in consequence of which she left him, and returned to her son Daniel's, at the old homestead. Thence she removed to Charleston, in Chester county (now Phenixville), where her daughters Jane and Ann Coates resided. Here she built a house for herself, "on the hill by Mason's tavern," [2] and made her home until 1775, when she returned to her son Daniel's, on the death of his wife Grace. About the time of his second marriage (1779) she removed again to Chester county, where she d. 3 mo. 18, 1783, aged 78.[3]

2-3. Daniel Dawson, hatter, of Abington, m. at Abington, 8 mo. 26, 1730, *Elizabeth Hallowell*, b. 12 mo., 14, 1711.[4] They removed from Abington to Philadelphia, taking certificate from former to latter meeting, dated May 31, 1742, for themselves and dau. Deborah. [5] He made a will dated Nov. 23d, 1744, and proved March 3, 1745, disposing of a good estate in houses, etc. The record is that he d. 1 mo. 1, 1746, which was 1st March, 1745, new style. They had seven children:

3-12. Mary, d. 6 mo. 25, 1740.
3-13. Daniel, d. 1 mo. 6, 1738.

Isaac, born February ye 16th, 1742-3, Joseph, born Dec. ye 11th, 1744, Benjamin, born Sept. ye 17th, 1749." These dates agree with the above except as to the year of Benjamin's birth. In the original draft of his letter it appears that he wrote 1746. These figures were crossed out and 1749 inserted by another hand. The date in the old Bible of Bartholomew and Ann Longstreth, in the handwriting of Bartholomew, is 7 mo. 17, 1746.

[1] They "passed meeting" at Abington, 4 mo. 30, 1753, but the marriage was celebrated at the meeting house in Horsham. The name of "Dorothy Dawson, widow," was signed at the head of the list of witnesses. The Quakers at Hatboro mostly belonged to Abington meeting. The fact of the change of name of Ann Dawson Longstreth to Tomkins was probably not known to the writer of the letter quoted in the following note (note 3).

[2] See p. 413, note 1.

[3] "Both Dorothy Dawson and Ann Dawson Longstreth lie buried in a neglected grave yard near Kimberton, Chester county, Pa. [belonging to Pikeland monthly meeting.] The graves are nameless, as is customary in Quaker burying grounds, and but few persons except my sister, Mrs. R. L. Fussell, and myself, are left who could identify the spot. This was pointed out to us by our mother, Esther Fussell Lewis." — Grace Anne Lewis, Media, Pa., 1873.

[4] Dau. of Thomas (b. in England, d. 12 mo. 14, 1734), and *Rosamond Till* (d. 6 mo. 13, 1745), Hallowell, m. at Darby, Pa., 1702, lived at Abington; gr. dau. of John and Mary Hallowell, who emigrated to Darby from Hucknow, parish of Sutton, Nottinghamshire, England, bringing a Quaker certificate, dated 12 mo. 19, 1682.

[5] Abington records, as copied for the Penna. Historical Society, say John Dawson, w. and dau. Deborah, but Philadelphia meeting records show that it was Daniel who was received on this certificate.

3–14. Deborah, b. 6 mo. 22, 1742.
3–15. James ; *m.*
3–16. Daniel, m. Sarah ——— : d. in Philadelphia without issue.
3–17. Rosamond. GREEN.
3–18. Mary. THOMSON.

2–4. *Sarah Dawson*, m. in Abington, 9 mo. 24, 1729, WILLIAM HANCOCK, who d. 1787, son of William Hancock, of Horsham, Pa. They had:

3–19. John, d. before 1787 ; *m.*
3–20. Isaac, living 1787.
3–21. James, b. 9 mo. 2, 1730, living 1787 ; *m.*

2–5. ISAAC DAWSON, of Abington, removed to Philadelphia, taking certificate from Abington meeting, dated 2 mo. 24, 1738 : was with w. Jane in Philadelphia, 1748. She brought a certificate, dated 8 mo. 3, 1752, from Burlington, N. J., meeting, to Philadelphia, being then a wid., as her husband had d. 9 mo. 12, 1748. They had:

3–22. William, d. 6 mo. 4. 1742.
3–23. John, d. 12 mo. 6, 1742.
3–24. Jane, d. 1 mo. 30, 1749.
3–25. Elizabeth, d. 4 mo. 4, 1749.
3–26. Isaac, d. 6 mo. 21, 1749.
3–27. Mary, b. 1 mo. 17, 1742-3, lived in Philadelphia. SERMON.

Jane Dawson (widow of Isaac Dawson, and dau. of Richard and Mary Blackham, of Burlington, N. J.), m. in Philadelphia, 11 mo. 9, 1752, ROBERT WORRELL, of Abington, Pa., son of Richard Worrell, of Lower Dublin. After her first husband's death, she appears to have gone back to her father's home in New Jersey, from which she returned to Philadelphia only a few weeks before her second marriage.

2–6. BENJAMIN DAWSON, b. abt. 1718, m. in Philadelphia, 5 mo. 19, 1744,[1] *Elizabeth Fussell*, b. abt. 1727. They lived

[1] Of the witnesses present were Dorothy, mother of the groom, and Daniel, Isaac and James Dawson, probably brothers; also, Jane Dawson, supposed w. of Isaac, but perhaps sister. Elizabeth Fussell was dau. of Solomon Fussell, (b. in Yorkshire, Eng., 1704, emigrated to Pa., and settled in Philadelphia, abt. 1721, where he was a merchant, son of William and Elizabeth Fussell) and wife Susannah Coney, (dau. of Jacob Coney and wife Barbara, dau. of "William Clinkenbeard). William Clinkenbeard d. abt 1753, in the 104th year of his age. On the birth of his gt. gt. gr. dau., Susannah Dawson, he said to his dau. Barbara Coney, 'Arise daughter, go see thy daughter, for thy daughter's daughter has a daughter.' This Susannah Dawson, afterwards Susannah Smedley, was b. the 3d of the 9th mo. 1746, and having seen her gt. gt.

at Smyrna, Del., and were respected members of the Society of Friends. He d. 12 mo. 5, 1793, in his 75th year, and she d. 9 mo. 8, 1792, in her 66th year, both at Smyrna. They had twelve children, all b. at Smyrna:

3–28. John, b. 4 mo. 3, 1745, d. 10 mo. 10, 1767.
3–29. Susannah, b. 7 mo. 2, 1746, d. in Delaware Co., Pa., 11 mo. 29, 1834, aged 89. COWGILL; SMEDLEY.
3–30. Dorothy, b. 1 mo. 1, 1748, was living 1788. [1]
3–31. Solomon, b. 2 mo 13, 1749, was living 1788; *m.*
3–32. Sarah, b. 2 mo. 5, 1751, d. 12 mo. 8, 1766.
3–33. Benjamin, b. 1 mo. 13, 1753, was living, 1788.
3–34. William, b. 3 mo. 15, 1756, was living, 1788; *m.*
3–35. Elizabeth, b. 11 mo. 24, 1760, d. 9 mo. 8, 1763.
3–36. Isaac, b. 7 mo. 18, 1763, d. in Queen Anne Co., Md., abt. 1825; *m.*
3–37. Jacob, b. 12 mo. 8, 1765, d. an infant.
3–38. James, b. 4 mo. 23, 1767, d. in Chestertown, Md., 6 mo. 4, 1823; *m.*
3–39. Elizabeth, b. 3 mo. 5, 1769, d. 8 mo. 15, 1778.

3-1. *Sarah Longstreth*, b. 11 mo. 8, 1728-9, d. 9 mo. 21, 1800, (bur. Pikeland) m. at Abington, 8 mo. 10, 1751, WILLIAM FUSSELL, [2] b. 1728-9, d. 1803, or 1804, at Phenixville, Pa. (bur. Pikeland). He was enrolled a member of 5th Bat. 6th Artillery company of Chester Co., but being a Quaker, it is presumed he rendered no service. [3] They had three children:

4–1. Susannah, b. 1 mo. 29, 1753, d. 7 mo. 26, 1819. DUNKIN.
4–2. Bartholomew, b. in Philadelphia, 9 mo 28, 1754, d. near Yellow Springs, Chester Co., Pa., 10 mo. 17, 1838; *m.*
4–3. Solomon, b. 12 mo. 20, 1755, d. 10 mo. 22, 1793; *unm.*

3-3. DANIEL LONGSTRETH was b. in Warminister township, Bucks Co., Pa., on the 28th of April (then called 2d mo).

---

gr. father, lived to see her gt. gt. gr. children. She d. 29th of 11th mo., 1834, in the 89th year of her age." — Extract from a family record in possession of Mrs. Martha M. Lewis, of Huntsville, Indiana. The date of birth of Susannah Dawson, here given differs from that stated in the above record, which is from the meeting records.

[1] Mentioned with Solomon, Benjamin and William, in their father's will of that date.

[2] Son of Solomon, and *Susannah Coney* Fussell, and brother of Elizabeth, w. of Benjamin Dawson. (2-6).

[3] He was mulcted in "excise fines" in 1777-1780, in the sums of £2. 12. 6, and £19. 10. 9. Other "excise fines" levied and collected were as follows: Joseph Starr jr. £45. 18. 9, and £3. 5. 0; Moses Coates jr., £55. 2. 6, and £3. 5. 0; Benjamin Longstreth, £50. 5. 0, £3. 5. 0, and £19. 10. 0; Benjamin Coates, £10. 10. 8; Isaac Starr, £3. 5. 0. — Pennypacker's *History of Phenixville*, p. 122.

1732. When he was in his eighteenth year his father died, leaving him the care of a large family of brothers and sisters, to whom he supplied, as far as possible, a father's place, fulfilling his trust with good judgment and strict fidelity. He was a man of fine presence and great firmness of mind; a Friend in principle as well as by profession; a peace maker, often being called upon to settle differences arising between his acquaintances and neighbors; a man of benevolent and sympathetic nature, frequently interesting himself in behalf of the helpless and friendless; a man of integrity, possessing the public confidence, being often selected as executor and administrator in the settlement of estates, also at one time collector of the Provincial tax and attending to a variety of public affairs. He was a member of the Pennsylvania society for the abolition of slavery, and for bettering the condition of people of color, his diploma bearing date the 25th of 3 mo., 1793.[1] He adhered to peace principles during the Revolutionary war, notwithstanding the difficulties of his situation, being sometimes summoned to the head quarters of the army in his neighborhood, but receiving respectful treatment from the commanding officers. A company of soldiers was at one time quartered on him, and the battle of the Crooked Billet was fought along the road in front of his homestead.[2] For a time his capacious garret became a place of safe keeping for the Hatboro Library, a library which, though one of the oldest in the country, has still a flourishing existence. He maintained a correspondence with relatives in England, as late at least, as 1769. He m. 1st, at Abington meeting, 5 mo. 22, 1753, *Grace Michener*, who was b. in Moreland township (now Montgomery Co., Pa.), 3 mo. 22, 1729, and d. at the homestead, in Warminister, 4 mo. 16, 1775.[3] They had nine children:

---

[1] He inherited slaves with his father's estate, and probably employed slave labor the greater part of his life. He is referred to in the following: "Grandfather had a burying ground for slaves alongside of a lane running from the barn near the chestnut tree along Jesse Cleaver's lane. When I was small father took the fence away, and ploughed down the graves."—*Anna T. Raab* daughter of Joseph Longstreth, son of Daniel.

[2] He built a very commodious and substantial house, enlarging one erected by his father, and had what was then considered the most elegantly finished house in that part of the country. It bore on one end the initials of himself and wife, and a date, "D. L. G., 1766."

[3] Sister to Jane Michenor who m. John Hancock (3-19 of this record); dau. of John and *Martha Harker* Michenor; gr. dau. of John and Sarah Michenor, who were living in Philadelphia as early as 1686, removed to Abington 1715, and had one son

4-4. [LONGSTRETH.] John, b 4 mo. 14, 1754, d. 5 mo. 7, 1819; *m.*
4-5. Martha, b. 12 mo. 4, 1755, d 5 mo. 15, 1815. MICHENER.
4-6. Rachel, b. 8 mo. 22, 1757, d. 5 mo. 30, 1782. ROSS.
4-7. Joseph, b. 3 mo. 11, 1760, d. 5 mo. 13, 1760.
4-8. Jonathan, b. 6 mo. 1, 1761, m. at Hopewell, Va., 8 mo. 16, 1792, *Phebe Rees*, dau. of Morris and Sarah Rees. [1]
4-9. Isaac, b. 10 mo. 17, 1763, d. 2 mo. 8, 1846; *m.*
4-10. Joseph, b. 5 mo. 31, 1765, d. in Bucks Co., 4 mo. 23, 1840; *m.*
4-11. Benjamin, b. 9 mo. 10, 1767, went to Kentucky as a surveyor, with John Fitch, where he d. 6 mo. 3, 1790. He was deputy surveyor of Madison Co., in that territory.
4-12. Jane, b. 10 mo. 6, 1770, d. 2 mo. 29, 1770.

Daniel Longstreth, m. 2d, 2 mo. 2, 1779, *Martha Bye*, b. in Buckingham, Pa., 9 mo. 23, 1735, d. in Philadelphia, 3 mo. 7, 1833, aged 98, dau. of Thomas and Elizabeth Bye. She had no children. She d. at the house of Rachel Maris, her husband's grand dau., whom she had raised from infancy. Daniel Longstreth d. at the homestead in Warminster, 11 mo. 19, 1803.

3-5. *Jane Longstreth*, b. 11 mo. 23, 1735-6, d. 5 mo. 16, 1795 (bur. Friends' ground, Baltimore), m. 4 mo. 22, 1755, JONATHAN COATES, of Phenixville, who was b. 11 mo. 17, 1728, son of Moses and Susannah Coates.[2] They had eleven children:

4-13. Ann, b. 5 mo. 12, 1757.
4-14. James, b. 5 mo 22, 1759.
4-15. Hannah, b. 7 mo. 5, 1761.
4-16. Jonathan, b. 5 mo. 28, 1764, d. 9 mo. 30, 1793.
4-17. Susannah, b. 7 mo. 23, 1766.
4-18 Phebe, *twin sister of Susannah.*
5-19. Keziah, b, 2 mo. 24, 1769.
4-20. Grace, b. 7 mo. 16, 1771, m. REYNOLDS KNOX, and d. a widow in Baltimore, 3 mo. 24, 1844.
4-21. Isaac, b. 2 mo. 8, 1774.
4-22. Jane, b. 8 mo. 28, 1776.
4-23. Elizabeth, b. 9 mo. 8, 1779.

(John, above named), and five daus. Martha Harker, was dau. of Adam and Grace Harker, who came to Bucks Co. Pa., in 1699, with a certificate from the Richmond monthly meeting of Friends, at Leburne, Yorkshire, England, dated 12 mo. 10, 1698.

[1] In 1796, or '97 he made a voyage down the Ohio and Mississippi rivers to New Orleans, and thence to the West Indies. He was captured by the British, and held a prisoner, because he sailed from a Spanish port. Later, he ascended the Mississippi, to Baton Rouge, and went thence to Pinckneyville, where he d. in 1812 after 15 or 16 years' absence from home.

[2] The ancestor of Moses Coates is said to have come to Pennsylvania before the arrival of William Penn, 1682. Others of that name in Pa. are descended from one who arrived in 1686.

3-6. *Ann Longstreth*, b. 11 mo. 3, 1737-8, d. 6 mo. 26, 1824, m. 9 mo. 22, 1756, BENJAMIN COATES, son of Moses and Susannah Coates, and brother of Jonathan Coates (3-5). They lived at Phenixville, in Chester Co., and were buried at Pikeland. Children:

4–24. Jane, m.—— STEWARD, and d. 1834.
4–25. Susannah, b. 3 mo., 1772.
4–26. Benjamin, b. 9 mo. 18, 1780.
4–27. Tacy (daughter) d. 7 mo. 22, 1851.

3-7. JOHN LONGSTRETH, b. in October (then called 8th mo.) 25, 1739, d. 4 mo. 16, 1817 (buried Pikeland), m. 1762, *Jane Minshall*, b. 1 mo. 5, 1743, d. 2 mo. 9, 1813, daughter of John and Sarah Minshall.[1] He was a justice of the peace and a man of considerable influence. They lived at Phenixville, and had seven children:

4–28. Daniel, b. 1767, d. 1769.
4–29. Hannah, b. 10 mo. 9, 1768, d. at Phenixville, 1 mo. 8, 1851. COATES.
4–30. John b. 2 mo. 10, 1771, d. at Charlestown, Pa., 1 mo. 6, 1822; *m.*
4–31. Sarah, b. 10 mo. 18, 1773, d. 6 mo. 5, 1839, aged 65; *unm.*
4–32. Anne, b. 1777, d. 1777.
4–33. Moses, b. 6 mo. 18, 1780, d. 2 mo. 10, 1819; *m.*
4–34. Jane, b. 7 mo. 14, 1784, d. 5 mo. 26, 1834. JOHN.

3-8. *Elizabeth Longstreth*, b. 3 mo. 15, 1741, d. 6 mo. 28, 1813 (buried Phenixville), m. at Pikeland meeting, 6 mo. 21, 1763,[2] JOSEPH STARR, b. 7 mo. 6, 1741, d. 10 mo. 1, 1821, son of Joseph and Rebecca Starr. They lived at Charlestown, Chester Co., Pa., and had ten children:

4–35. Rebecca, b. 7 mo. 11, 1764.
4–36. Ann, b. 9 mo. 7, 1765, d. *unm.*
4–37. Elizabeth, b. 4 mo. 27, 1767, d. 12 mo. 14, 1799.
4–38. Isaac, b. 8 mo. 8, 1768.
4–39. Joseph, b. 10 mo. 5, 1769.
4–40. Sarah, b. 11 mo. 21, 1777.

---

[1] Descended from Thomas and Margaret Minshall, who came to Pa., in 1682. A genealogy of the family was printed in 1867.

[2] The original certificate of this marriage, now in possession of S. W. Pennypacker, of Philadelphia, contains the signatures as witnesses of Ann Tomkins, mother of the bride, Joseph and Rebecca Starr, the groom's parents, Daniel and Grace Longstreth, (3-3 of this record), Sarah Fussell (3-1), John Longstreth (3-7), Isaac Longstreth (3-9), Joseph Longstreth (3-10), Benjamin Longstreth (3-11), Sarah Hancock (2-4), etc.

4–41. [STARR.] John, b. 7 mo. 27, 1774.
4–42. Benjamin, b. 2 mo. 5, 1776.
4–43. Amy, b. 5 mo. 29, 1778, d. 2 mo. 5, 1837 ; *unm.*
4–44. William, b. 8 mo., 1781, d. 1786.

3–9. ISAAC LONGSTRETH, b. 12 mo. 16, 1742-3, d. 4 mo. 12, 1817 (buried Pikeland), m. 11 mo. 15, 1770, *Martha Thomas*, b. 5 mo. 20, 1748, d. at Hatboro, 12 mo. 4, 1790 (buried Horsham).[1] He was a Capt. in the Rev. army, and commanded a company at the battle of the Crooked Billet. They lived at Darby, Pa. ; and had besides four children who died young:

4–45. Susannah, b. at Hatboro, 8 mo. 10, 1771, d. near Philadelphia, 3 mo. 15, 1856.[2]
4–46. Elizabeth, b. at Hatboro, 2 mo. 2, 1783, d. at Miami, Ohio, 2 mo. 22, 1845. MATHER.
4–47. Isaac Thomas, b. at Hatboro, 2 mo. 26, 1785, d. 10 mo. 6, 1849 ; *m.*
4–48. David, b. at Hatboro, 11 mo. 16, 1786, d. 11 mo. 24, 1859 ; *m.*
4–49. Charles, b. in Mahoning Valley, Pa., 4 mo. 3, 1788, d. 1 mo. 2, 1861 ; *m.*

3–10. JOSEPH LONGSTRETH, b. 10 mo. 11, 1744, d. 5 mo. 18, 1803 (buried at Horsham), m. 4 mo. 16, 1772, *Susannah*

[1] Dau. of Daniel Thomas (b. 1711, d. 1766), and w. Susannah (?) Livezey, dau. of Thomas Livezey; gr. dau. of Daniel Thomas, (from Wales, 1700), and wife Catharine Morris.

[2] She removed to Philadelphia in 1795, and in 1797 entered into the wholesale dry goods business with two of her cousins. It is said she was the first woman who imported dry goods into that city. "While she continued in business, a period of about fifteen years, her sound judgment, kind disposition, and perfect uprightness, secured the esteem of a large circle of friends. In 1815 she removed to Greenway Farm, which she had purchased a few years before, and resided there until her decease, enjoying the simple pleasures of the country, superintending the business of the farm, and dispensing the hospitalities of a large heart, until prevented by the infirmities of age. Although her affections centred with uncommon force and ardor upon the members of her family, even to cousins of the third and fourth degree, they were by no means limited to those who were connected with her by the ties of consanguinity. Her love and interest took a much wider range, embracing, indeed, the whole human family. She felt especial sympathy for those who were in danger of being overlooked. She was a striking example of watchfulness in conversation, being rarely heard to speak of the faults of others, and when these were mentioned in her presence she generally had something to say of the irgood qualities, or, if nothing could be said in extenuation, she would turn the conversation into another channel, possessing that cahrity which 'thinketh no evil, and hopeth all things.' She was remarkable for a happy, cheerful spirit, which diffused its influence like genial sunshine upon all around her, and a thankful heart induced her frequently to number her blessings. She was in the daily practice of reading the Holy Scriptures, which shem uch enjoyed, and was diligent in her attendance of our religious meetings as long as health permitted." *Friends' Intelligencer.*

Morris, b. 7 mo. 23, 1746, d. 8 mo. 28, 1814, dau. of Joshua and Mary Morris, of Abington. They settled in Southampton township, Bucks Co., near the old homestead. It was on his premises that Fitch, the inventor, first tried his steamboat.[1] They had nine children:

4–50. [LONGSTRETH.] Josiah, b. 8 mo. 1, 1772, d. at Abington, 3 mo. 6, 1834; *m.*
4–51. Charles, b. 12 mo. 30, 1773.
4–52. Joshua, b. 6 mo. 20, 1775, d. near Philadelphia, 1 mo. 27, 1869; *m.*
4–53. Mary, b. 2 mo. 28, 1777.
4–54. William, b. 7 mo. 24, 1778, d. Philadelphia, 11 mo. 16, 1814; *m.*
4–55. Morris, b. 8 mo. 7, 1780, d. Philadelphia, 12 mo. 5, 1803.
4–56. Ann, b. 2 mo. 12, 1784, d. 5 mo. 26, 1868. HALLOWELL.
4–57. Samuel, b. 9 mo. 28, 1787, d. near New Orleans, 4 mo. 7, 1826; *m.*
4–58. Thomas Mifflin, b. 9 mo. 17, 1790, d. Philadelphia, abt. 1848; *m.*

3–11. BENJAMIN LONGSTRETH, b. September (then called 7 mo.) 17, 1746, d. 8 mo. 4, 1802,[2] (buried Friends' ground, Valley, Montgomery Co., Pa.), m. *Sarah Fussell*, who d. 4 mo. 23, 1797 (buried Pikeland), daughter of Solomon Fussell, and his second w. Mary Wilson, b. 10 mo. 12, 1751.[3] They lived at Phenixville, Pa., of which place he was the founder. He built the first iron-works erected there.[4] They had twelve children:

4–59. Joseph, b. 11 mo 25, 1773, d 3 mo. 9, 1807; *m.*
4–60. William Wilson, b. 9 mo. 1, 1775, d. 11 mo. 2, 1805; *m.*
4–61. Benjamin, b. 2 mo. 1, 1777, d. 9 mo. 5, 1851; *m.*
4–62. Mary, b. 1 mo. 7, 1779, d. 9 mo. 7, 1850. TEA.
4–63. Ann, b. 1 mo. 27, 1781, d. 5 mo. 31, 1840. PARRISH; KEEN.
4–64. Sarah, b. 2 mo. 11, 1783, d. 12 mo. 19, 1807 (buried Arch St., Philadelphia); *unm.*

---

[1] See Westcott's *Life of John Fitch.*

[2] There seems to be a doubt as to the correctness of this date of B. L.'s death. The following is a copy of a memorandum made by Daniel Longstreth, 1841, of information from his uncle Isaac Longstreth: "Benjamin d. in 1798, of yellow fever, near the Valley meeting house, where he was buried. He took the fever in Philadelphia, and was on his way home, on French Creek, now Phenixville, Chester Co., Pa. He was 50 or 51 years old." In another place he makes a memorandum taken from a record of graves in Valley Meeting Cemetery, of a charge for digging Benjamin Longstreth's grave, 8 mo. 18, 1802.

[3] See 2-6, note 1. One correspondent writes that B. L. married *Sarah Wilson*, who d. 1797. If so, probably dau. of second w. of Solomon Fussell, by a former husband. She is said to have been a widow at the time of her marriage to S. F., but the record does not so describe her.

[4] See Pennypacker's *History of Phenixville*, for account of B. L. Jonathan and Benjamin Coates purchased the mill tract in 1760, and sold to John Longstreth, who in 1785 rebuilt the mill, and sold to Benjamin Longstreth. The latter commenced a series of improvements, and to him Phenixville owes its origin.

4-65. [LONGSTRETH.] Samuel, b. 2 mo. 19, 1785, went west when a young man, and was never heard from afterward by his family.
4-66. Elizabeth, b. 7 mo. 9, 1787. PAXSON.
4-67. Rachel Wilson, b. 7 mo. 10, 1789. ORUM.
4-68. Hannah, b. 7 mo. 26, 1791, d. 4 mo. 30, 1838. WILSON.
4-69. Jacob, b. 9 mo. 27, 1793 ; *m.*
4-70. George Field, b. 4 mo. 26, 1796, res. Ohio ; *m.*

3-15. JAMES DAWSON, m. Oct. 29, 1762, *Mary Hamilton.* They had :

4-71. Rosamond. MURRAY.

3-17. *Rosamond Dawson* (dau. of Daniel, 2-3), m. May 18, 1752, CHARLES GREEN. They had :

4-72. Charles ; *m.*
4-73. Mary. HILL.
4-74. Sarah. JONES.

3-18. *Mary Dawson*, m. 11 mo. 14, 1758, JOHN THOMSON, son of Peter Thomson, of Marple, Chester Co., Pa. They had :

4-75. Elizabeth. FISHER.

3-19. JOHN HANCOCK, d. in Philadelphia, before 1787, m. 11 mo. 25, 1754, *Jane Michener*, dau. of John and *Martha Harker* Michener, of Abington. She d. 1758, and her husband administered on her estate.[1] (William Hancock, 2-4 of this record, who d. 1787, had a grand dau. Jane Hancock, who was his executrix, — supposed dau. of John, and *Jane Michener* Hancock.)

4-76. Jane, m. ——— RICHARDSON.

3-21. JAMES HANCOCK, b. 9 mo. 2, 1730, living 1787, m. 3 mo. 26, 1752, *Elizabeth Randall*, b. 5 mo. 11, 1725, d. before 1787, dau. of Joseph and Rebecca Randall. They lived in Bucks Co., and had ten children :

4-77. Joseph, b. 2 mo. 11, 1753.
4-78. William, b. 10 mo. 14, 1754, d. 2 mo., 1755.
4-79. Sarah, b. 6 mo. 13, 1756, d. 10 mo., 1758.
4-80. Rebecca, b. 10 mo. 22, 1757, d. 3 mo., 1758.
4-81. Elizabeth, b. 2 mo. 2, 1759.
4-82. James, b. 12 mo. 21, 1760.

---

[1] See 3-3, note 3.

4–83. [HANCOCK.] John, b. 11 mo. 9, 1762.
4–84. Sarah, b. 11 mo. 4, 1764.
4–85. Benjamin, b. 5 mo. 10, 1767.
4–86. Joel, b. 4 mo. 26, 1769.

3–27. *Mary Dawson*, b. 1 mo. 17, 1742-3 (dau. of Isaac, 2-5), m. 1 mo. 12, 1764, JOSEPH SERMON, of Philadelphia, whitesmith, d. 1790, son of Richard Sermon, of Lower Dublin. They had five children:

4–87. Richard.
4–88. Isaac.
4–89. Robert.
4–90. Jane, m. 1796, GEORGE WORRELL.
4–91. Hannah.

3–29. *Susannah Dawson*, b. in Smyrna, Del., 7 mo. 2, 1746,[1] d. in Radnor township, Delaware Co., Pa., 11 mo. 29, 1834, aged 89. She m. 1st, 1765, THOMAS COWGILL, who died 1766. They had:

4–92. Sarah, b. 2 mo. 24, 1766, who m.—— Cox, before 1781, and was mentioned that year in the will of her grandfather, Benjamin Dawson (2–6).

Susannah (3–29), m. 2d, 1772, JOHN SMEDLEY, b. 1716, who d. 1793, aged 77. She survived him many years.[2] They had nine children:

4–93. Elizabeth, b. 7 mo. 4, 1773.
4–94. Thomas, b. 10 mo. 24, 1774, m. 3 mo. 17, 1796, *Lydia Hoopes;* no issue.
4–95. Esther, b. 1 mo. 18, 1776, m. 2 mo. 22, 1797, JACOB ROGERS, son of James and Priscilla Rogers.
4–96. John, b. 9 mo. 7, 1777, d. 10 mo. 15, 1825; *m.*
4–97. Susannah, b. 11 mo. 11, 1779, d. 12 mo. 18, 1858. HOOD.
4–98. Benjamin, b. 1 mo. 13, 1782.

---

[1] The place and date of her birth, as above, from Mr. James William Dawson, Wilmington, Del. The following from Daniel Longstreth's memoranda: "Susannah Smedley, b. opposite Christ's Church, in Second St. (Philadelphia), on 13th of 9 mo., or 2d of 9 mo. new style, 1746. She m. Thomas Cowgill, and buried him, and having remained a widow six years, she m. John Smedley, aged 56, and she aged 26. He d. when turned of 77, and left her with seven children, and one she had by Cowgill. They had also buried one."

[2] "Her gt. gt. grandfather, William Clinkenbeard, who was 108 years old when he died, and owned a small farm in Plymouth, was seen by her when an infant; and she has now seen her great great grand children, making in all nine generations which her eyes have beheld. She still retains her memory in a most surprising manner, though turned of 85 years of age. But few persons can ever say as much as this."—Daniel Longstreth, 12 mo., 1831.

4–99. [SMEDLEY.] Mary, b. 11 mo. 7, 1783, d. [in Jefferson Co., Ohio, 1 mo. 10, 1857. LAMBORN.
4–100. Jacob, b. 12 mo. 27, 1784, lived in Philadelphia; *m.*[1]
4–101. Isaac, b. 12 mo. 14, 1786, lived in Philadelphia; *m.*

3–31. SOLOMON DAWSON, b. 2 mo. 13, 1749, was living 1788, m. *Mary* ——; both lived and d. at Smyrna, Del. Their only child was:

4–102. Benjamin, who d. at 45; *unm.*

3–34. WILLIAM DAWSON, b. 3 mo. 15, 1756, living 1788, m. 1st, —— *Corse.* They lived in Caroline Co., Md., and had:

4–103. Sarah.

He afterwards moved to Redstone, Pa., and m. 2d, —— *Cadwalader.*

3–36. ISAAC DAWSON, b. 7 mo. 18, 1763, hatter, d. in Queen Anne's county, Md., about 1825; m. 1st, —— *Cox*; no issue. 2d, *Rachel Lamb*, of Kent county, Md. They had eight children:

4–104. Thomas, d. in infancy.
4–105. Mary, m. DANIEL LAMB, res. Baltimore; 2 children.
4–106. Sarah, m. ISAAC COX, of Easton, Md.; 3 children.
4–107. Eliza, m, BENJAMIN HOWARD, of Kent county, Md.; 4 children.
4–108. Susannah, m. PAUL JONES, of Baltimore, moved west; 2 children.
4–109. Isaac, b. 10 mo. 25, 1802, res. Balto., Md.; *unm.*
4–110. Rebecca, d. young.
4–111. George, d. in infancy.

3–38. JAMES DAWSON, tanner, b. in Smyrna, Delaware, 4 mo. 23, 1767, m. 9 mo. 6, 1790, *Ann Lamborn*, who was b. in London Grove township, Chester county, Pa., 8 mo. 22, 1766.[2] They were members of the Society of Friends, and lived first at Third Haven (otherwise Easton), Talbot Co., Md., removing thence in 1801 to Chestertown, Kent Co., Md., where they d.,

---

[1] Another list of John and Susannah Smedley's children, had *Isaac*, b. 12 mo. 4, 1786, *Jacob*, b. 12 mo. 27, 1789.

[2] Eleventh child of Robert Lamborn (b. Chester county, Pa., 6 mo. 3, 1723, d. 12 mo., 1801), and w. Ann Browne (d. 6 mo. 6, 1790, dau. of Jesse and Olive Browne, of Calvert Co., Md.), m. 1747; gr. dau. of Robert Lamborn, who emigrated from Berkshire, England, to America, 1713, purchased land at London Grove, Chester Co., Pa., 1716, and m. there, 1722, Sarah Swayne, dau. of Francis Swayne, of that place. Robert and *Sarah Swayne* Lamborn had ten children, of whom Robert who m. Ann Browne, was eldest. Robert Lamborn sen., was son of Josiah and Ann Lamborn, of East Hampstead, Berkshire.

she 10 mo. 23, 1815, and he 6 mo. 4, 1823. They had eight children:

4–112. Elizabeth, b. at Third Haven, 4 mo. 21, 1792, d. in Wilmington, Del., 3 mo. 7, 1836; *unm.*
4–113. Ann, b. at Third Haven, 11 mo. 11, 1793, d. 10 mo. 11, 1794.
4–114. Mary, b. at Third Haven, 11 mo. 10, 1795, d. 11 mo. 11, 1795.
4–115. Lydia, b. at Third Haven, 12 mo. 8, 1796, d. at Wilmington, 5 mo. 28, 1866; *unm.*
4–116. Sarah, b. at Tuckahoe, Talbot Co., Md., 1 mo. 1, 1799, res. 1873, Wilmington. DAVIS.
4–117. Mary Ann, b. at Chestertown, 8 mo. 14, 1802, res. 1873, Wilmington; *unm.*
4–118. Martha Susannah, b. at Chestertown, 11 mo. 8, 1805, d. 10 mo. 27, 1806.
4–119. James William, b. at Chestertown, 8 mo. 22, 1808, res. 1873, Wilmington; *unm.*

4–1. *Susannah Fussell*, b. 1 mo. 29, 1753, d. 7 mo. 26, 1819, m. 9 mo. 14, 1775, AARON DUNKIN. They had eight chn.:

5–1. Lydia, b. 1776, d. 1776.
5–2. Ann, b. 1777, d. 1777.
5–3. Sarah, b. 8 mo. 30, 1778. DILLIN; LONGSTRETH.
5–4. Ann, b. 2 mo. 5, 1781.
5–5. Susannah, b. 5 mo. 11, 1782, d. 4 mo. 25, 1814. WEBSTER.
5–6. Martha, b. 4 mo. 5, 1784. WATSON.
5–7. Gulielma, b. 7 mo. 30, 1787.
5–8. Elizabeth, b. 5 mo. 23, 1789.

4–2. BARTHOLOMEW FUSSELL, b. in Philadelphia, 9 mo. 28, 1754, d. near Yellow Springs, Chester Co., Pa., 10 mo. 17, 1838, "*young*," as it was remarked of him, "*at* 84." In his youth he removed with, his parents, to near Phenixville, Chester Co., Pa.; lived also in Montgomery Co.; and afterwards removed to Maryland, and became a member of Little Falls (now Fallston) monthly meeting of Friends. In old age he returned with his w. to Chester Co. He was for many years a highly esteemed minister of the Society, and at the time of his death a member of the Uwchlan monthly meeting in Chester county, which meeting published a *Testimonial* concerning him.[1] He m. 6 mo. 6, 1781, *Rebecca Bond*,[2] b. 10 mo. 9, 1751, d. near Kimberton, in

[1] See *A Memorial*, published by direction of the Yearly Meeting of Friends., (Hickites). S. B. Chapman & Co., Philadelphia, 1841.

[2] Dau. of Joseph and *Esther Jeanes* Bond; gr. dau. of Richard and Charity Bond. Esther Jeanes was dau. of William Jeanes and w. *Esther Brewer*, and is said to have been the first white child b. in Philadelphia.

Chester county, 3 mo. 4, 1851, having reached the age of nearly 100 years. They had eight children:

5–9. [FUSSELL.] Esther, b. at Hatboro, Pa., 3 mo. 18, 1782, d. in Chester Co., Pa., 2 mo. 8, 1848. LEWIS.
5–10. William, b. 6 mo. 30, 1783, d. 6 mo. 4, 1856; *m.*
5–11. Sarah, b. 9 mo. 10, 1784, d. 8 mo. 11, 1860. JACOBS.
5–12. Joseph, b. 4 mo. 26, 1787, d. at Fall Creek, Ind., 10 mo. 15, 1855; *m.*
5–13. Solomon, b. 6 mo. 28, 1789, d. —— ; *m.*
5–14. Jacob, b. 2 mo. 7, 1792, d. in Philadelphia, 8 mo. 7, 1855; *m.*
5–15. Bartholomew, b. 1 mo. 9, 1794, d. in Chester Springs, Pa., 1 mo. 14, 1871; *m.*
5–16. Rebecca, b. 4 mo. 21, 1796, res. 1873, Radnor, Delaware Co., Pa. TRIMBLE.

4–4. JOHN LONGSTRETH, farmer, b. 4 mo. 14, 1754, d. (Groveville, N. J.), 5 mo. 7, 1819, m. 1778, *Esther Kirkbride*, b. 10 mo. 24, 1761, d. 1 mo. 15, 1844, dau. of Robert and Hannah Kirkbride. When a widow she lived in Philadelphia. They had eight children:

5–17. Mahlon, b. 1779, d. in Philadelphia, 1 mo. 8, 1837; *m.*
5–18. Martha. SPENCER.
5–19. Daniel, d. 5 mo. 25, 1832; *m.*
5–20. Hannah L., b. 1788, d. 10 mo. 1, 1843, m. Dr. GAUNT, bur. 12 mo. 22, 1822, Groveville, N. J.; no issue.
5–21. Rachel, res. in Philadelphia. MILNER.
5–22. Sarah, b. 1791, res. Philadelphia; *unm.*
5–23. Esther L., res. Bristol, Pa. HAYWARD.
5–24. John Kirkbride; *m.*

4–5. *Martha Longstreth*, b. 12 mo. 4, 1755, d. 5 mo. 15, 1815, m. 1779, JOHN MICHENER, b. 12 mo. 21, 1750, d. in Ohio, 2 mo. 8, 1837, son of Mordecai and *Sarah Fisher* Michener.[1] They had ten children:

5–25. Daniel, b. 12 mo. 21, 1780; *m.*
5–26. Mordecai, b. 6 mo. 9, 1782, d. 8 mo. 15, 1836; *m.*
5–27. Benjamin, b. 10 mo. 26, 1783; *m.*
5–28. Grace, b. 4 mo. 21, 1785, d. 7 mo. 25, 1832. HOBSON.
5–29. Jonathan, b. 11 mo. 29, 1787; *m.*

---

[1] Mordecai Michener, above named, was son of William and *Mary Kuster* Michener; gr. son of John and Sarah Michener, who lived in Phila., 1686, and removed to Abington, 1715. (See 3–3, note 1, and 3–19). John Michener, above named (4–5), had a brother Mordecai, who m. Alice Dunn, and had besides other children, Ezra, b. 11 mo. 24, 1794, res. 1873, in Chester Co., Pa., author of Michener's *Retrospect of Early Quakerism*, and is an industrious genealogist. The compiler is indebted to him for a list of the descendants of John and *Martha Longstreth* Michener, embracing 227 names.

5–30. [MICHENER.] Sarah, b. 10 mo. 1, 1789, d. 8 mo. 15, 1836. MARTIN.
5–31. Rachel, b. 9 mo. 22, 1791. HAINES.
5–32. Martha, b. 2 mo. 15, 1794.
5–33. Hannah, b. 2 mo. 1, 1796. CLARKE.
5–34. Barak, b. 11 mo. 8, 1799; *m.*

4–6. *Rachel Longstreth*, b. 8 mo. 22, 1757, d. 5 mo. 30, 1782, m. at Abington meeting, 3 mo. 30, 1781, THOMAS ROSS, junior. They had:

5–35. Rachel, b. 3, mo. 23, 1782, res. Phila. MARIS.

4–9. ISAAC LONGSTRETH, b. 10 mo. 17, 1763, d. 2 mo. 8, 1846,[1] m. at Horsham meeting, 2 mo. 1789, *Jane Van Dearen*, (or *Van Deren*), b. 7 mo. 17, 1764, d. 12 mo. 6, 1825,[2] They had eight children:

5–36. Martha, b. 10 mo. 20, 1789. SHOEMAKER.
5–37. Benjamin, b. 4 mo. 29, 1792, d. 1795.
5–38. Charlotte, b. 12 mo. 17, 1793, d. 4 mo. 1, 1830.
5–39. Benjamin, b. 1 mo. 17, 1797, d. in Phila., 1 mo. 10, 1872; *m.*
5–40. Edith, b. 12 mo. 18, 1798, d. in Phila., 1 mo. 5, 1868. SHOEMAKER.
5–41. Daniel, b. 3 mo. 19, 1801, d. 6 mo. 23, 1856; *m.*
5–42. Esther, b. 4 mo. 20, 1803, d. 5 mo. 11, 1837, having been her father's housekeeper since the death of her mother.
5–43. John, b. 11 mo. 19, 1804, res. Phila.; *m.*

4–10. JOSEPH LONGSTRETH, b. 5 mo. 31, 1765, d. in Bucks county, 4 mo. 23, 1840, removed when in his 13th year (1778) to learn the trade of a hatter with Joseph Budd, with whom he remained most of the time until his 22d year. He afterwards carried on the hatting business for some years at Hatboro. He m. at Providence meeting, Montgomery Co., 9 mo. 9, 1797, *Sarah Thomas*, b. 11 mo. 3, 1769, d. in Bucks Co., 3 mo. 10, 1829, dau of David and *Mary Richardson* Thomas, [3] of Upper Providence, Montgomery Co., Pa. She was a woman of firm

---

[1] "His disease was dropsy of the chest. His sufferings, which for several weeks prior to his dissolution, were very severe, were borne with great patience, and truly Christian resignation. He was an indulgent parent, faithful, sincere friend, and kind neighbor." — D.L.

[2] Dau. of Godfrey Van Dearen and w. *Charity Van Horn*, of Abington; gr. dau. of Rev. John Van Dearen.

[3] David Thomas, above named, was son of David Thomas m. 1731 (blacksmith, b. in Wales, an early settler in Pennsylvania), and w. Anna Noble, dau. of Abel Noble. Mary Richardson, was dau. of Edward Richardson; gr. dau. of Joseph; gt gr. dau. of Samuel Richardson who was b. in England, came to Pa. from Jamaica, W. I. Sarah Thomas had a brother David, who settled near Auburn, N. Y., and

religious principles and unaffected piety. Both were very kind to the poor, and held in high esteem. They had six children :

5–44. [LONGSTRETH.] Edward Thomas, b. 8 mo. 30, 1798, d. 1 mo. 22, 1802.
5–45. Daniel, b. 11 mo. 25, 1809, d. 3 mo. 30, 1846 ; *m.*
5–46. Anna Thomas, b. 10 mo. 8, 1800, res. Highland P. O., Bradford Co., Pa. THOMSON ; RAAB.
5–47. Susannah, b. 11 mo. 28, 1804, d. 2 mo. 7, 1835. CLEAVER.
5–48. Mary Thomas, b. 12 mo. 20, 1807, res. Mt. Holly, N. J. WORRELL.
5–49. Martha Michener, b. 2 mo. 28, 1811, d. 1 mo. 5, 1862 ; *unm.*

4–29. *Hannah Longstreth*, b. 10 mo. 9, 1768 (dau. of John, 3-7), d. a widow, at Phenixville, Pa., 1 mo. 8, 1851, m. 6 mo. 22, 1770, JOHN HUTCHINSON COATES, b. 7 mo. 9, 1761, d. 4 mo. 21, 1804, son of Moses and Priscilla Coates. They lived at Phenixville, and had five children :

5–50. Sarah, b. 4 mo. 8, 1791, d. 11 mo. 5, 1863 ; *unm.*
5–51. Jane, b. 12 mo. 27, 1793, d. 1864. HEACOCK.
5–52. Cyrus, b. 2 mo. 25, 1795, d. 1832 ; *unm.*
5–53. Charles, b. 3 mo. 15, 1797, d. ; *unm.*
5–54. Aquila, b. 10 mo. 30, 1799 ; *m.*

4–30. JOHN LONGSTRETH, b. 2 mo. 10, 1771, d. at Charlestown, Pa., 1 mo. 6, 1822, m. *Ann Stewart*, who res. 1873, at Muscatine, Iowa. They had :

5–55. John, b. 11 mo. 7, 1810, res. Trappe, Pa., ; *m.*
5–56. Jane, m. —— HENCKER, res. Muscatine, Iowa ; 11 children.
5–57. Elizabeth, m. —— DOBBS, res. Melpine, Muscatine Co., Iowa ; 5 children.
5–58. Isaac, m. ————, res. Muscatine, Iowa ; 4 children.

4–33. MOSES LONGSTRETH, b. 6 mo. 18, 1780, d. 2 mo. 10, 1819, m. *Rebecca Williams*, b. 1786. They lived in Chester Co., Pa., and had two children :

5–59. Samuel Preston, b. 1808, d. 2 mo. 9, 1825.
5–60. Mary, b. 1810, res. Chester Co., Pa. RHOADES.

4–34. *Jane Longstreth*, b. 7 mo. 14, 1784, d. 5 mo. 26,

was a civil engineer on the Erie canal, in the time of Gov. DeWitt Clinton. He was also a distinguished florist, pomologist, and writer on agriculture. Born, 1776, d. 1859. His son, Dr. Joseph Thomas, is the compiler of *Lippincott's Biographical Dictionary*, and *Lippincott's Gazetteer of the World*. This family is distinct from that of Martha Thomas, w. of Isaac Longstreth (3–9). For an account of Samuel Richardson, "*A Councilor, Judge and Legislator of the Olden Time*," see S. W. Pennypacker's article with this title in *Lippincott's Magazine*, vol. xiii, No. 76, pp. 501–507.

1834, m. SAMUEL PRESTON JOHN, b. 1784, d. 1808. They lived at Phenixville, Pa. They had one dau.:

5-61. Hannah Minshall, b. 1808, res. Phenixville. JONES.

4-46. *Elizabeth Longstreth*, b. at Hatboro, Pa., 2 mo. 2, 1783, d. at Miama, O., 2 mo. 22, 1845, m. at Arch St. meeting, Phila., 4 mo. 6, 1809, RICHARD MATHER, son of Benjamin Mather, of Abington. They moved from Darby, Pa., in 1815, to Miama, O., where he still lives. Nine children:

5-62. David, b. at Neave Hall, near Germantown, Pa., 1 mo. 11, 1810, res. Little Miama, O.; *m.*
5-63. Martha Longstreth, b. at Greenway farm, Kingsessing, Pa., 1 mo. 3, 1812, d. in Ohio. JONES.
5-64. Ann, b. at Greenway farm, 2 mo. 8, 1814, res. Ohio. HORNEY.
5-65. Charles L., b. at Little Miama Mills, Warren Co., O., 1 mo. 30, 1816, res. Mt. Holly, N. J.; *m.*
5-66. Phineas Ross, b. at Little Miama Mills, 2 mo. 11, 1818, res. Richmond, Ind.; *m.*
5-67. Susannah L., b. at Little Miama Mills, 5 mo. 29, 1820, res. Richmond, Ind. HORNEY.
5-68. Benjamin, b. at Little Miama Mills, 11 mo. 5, 1822, m. *Ruth Brown.*
5-69. Susan Bacon, b. at Little Miama Mills, 3 mo. 5, 1825, res. Richmond, Ind. HORNEY.
5-70. Joseph, b. at Little Miama Mills, 11 mo. 29, 1827, res. Ohio; *m.*

4-47. ISAAC THOMAS LONGSTRETH, b. at Hatboro, Pa., 2 mo. 26, 1785, d. 10 mo. 6, 1849, m. at Burlington, N. J., meeting, 10 mo. 27, 1808, *Mary Collins*, d. 7 mo. 7, 1865, dau. of Isaac and Rachel Collins. They had five children:

5-71. Mary Ann, b. in Phila., 2 mo. 9, 1811, res. Phila.; *unm.*
5-72. Susannah, b. in Phila., 1 mo. 4, 1813, res. Phila.; *unm.*
5-73. Henry, b. in Burlington, N. J., 7 mo. 11, 1814, res. Phila.; *unm.*
5-74. Elizabeth, b. in Burlington, N. J., 6 mo. 28, 1817, res. Phila. MORRIS.
5-75. William C., b. in Philadelphia, 3 mo. 12, 1821, res. Phila.; *m.*

4-48. DAVID LONGSTRETH, b. at Hatboro, Pa., 11 mo. 16, 1786, d. 11 mo. 24, 1859, m. in Springfield meeting, Delaware Co., Pa., 5 mo. 9, 1811, *Martha Ogden*, b. 11 mo. 12, 1783, dau. of John and *Sarah Crozier* Ogden, of Abington.[1]

[1] John Ogden, above named, was son of Stephen and *Hannah Sermon* Ogden; gr. son of David Ogden and w. Mary, dau. of John Houlston, m. 1686. David Ogden was from Worcestershire, England, came to America in the ship "Welcome," with William Penn, 1682, and settled near the site of the present town of Media, Delaware Co., Pa. Sarah Crozier was dau. of James Crozier.

JOSHUA LONGSTRETH.

She is still living, aged 90. They had three children, all b. in Philadelphia:

5–76. [LONGSTRETH.] John Ogden, b. 8 mo. 31, 1812, d. at Clifton, Delaware Co., Pa., 2 mo. 29, 1871; *m.*
5–77. Anna, b. 9 mo. 11, 1816, d. in Phila., 3 mo. 28, 1823.
5–78. Sarah Anna, b. 10 mo. 10, 1823, res. Clifton, Pa. LEVIS.

4–49. CHARLES LONGSTRETH, b. in Mahoning Valley, Northampton Co., Pa., 4 mo. 3, 1788, d. 1 mo. 2, 1861, m. at Darby meeting, Pa., 10 mo. 29, 1818, *Rachel Hunt*, b. 1794, d. 10 mo., 1846, dau. of John and Rachel Hunt. They had four children, all b. in Phila.:

5–79. John Hunt, b. 1 mo. 2, 1820, res. Phila., Pa.; *m.*
5–80. Rachel Hunt, b. 11 mo. 24, 1822, res. Phila. BOLDIN.
5–81. Charles, b. 10 mo. 19, 1825, res. Brooklyn, N. Y.; *m.*
5–82. Samuel, b. 11 mo. 20, 1828; *unm.*

4–50. JOSIAH LONGSTRETH, b. 8 mo. 1, 1772, d. 3 mo. 6, 1834, m. *Sarah Dillin*, widow of Isaac Dillin (or Dillon), dau. of Aaron and *Susannah Fussell* Dunkin (4–1 of this record). She d. 1 mo. 28, 1845. They lived at Abington, Pa., where both d. Two children:

5–83. Joshua, b. 4 mo. 4, 1818, res. Philadelphia Co., Pa.; *m.*
5–84. Joseph, b. 2 mo. 24, 1820, d. 8 mo. 20, 1873; *m.*

4–52. JOSHUA LONGSTRETH, b. 6 mo. 20, 1775, d. at Barclay Hall, near Phila., 1 mo. 27, 1869, m. 11 mo. 9, 1800, *Sarah Williams*, b. 1781, d. at Barclay Hall, 3 mo. 16, 1848, dau. of Jesse and Elizabeth Williams. Mr. Longstreth was for many years a prominent dry goods merchant in Philadelphia, and was also a director of the Philadelphia Bank, and of other moneyed institutions. They had three children:

5–85. Lydia, b. 1801, d. in Philadelphia, 7 mo. 5, 1843. PRICE.
5–86. Elizabeth, b. 3 mo. 4, 1810, d. 7 mo. 8, 1865, m. GEORGE ABBOTT, b. 2 mo. 26, 1803, d. ——, son of George and Mary Abbott. No issue.
5–87. Susan Morris, d. in England abt. 1860. THOMPSON.

4–54. WILLIAM LONGSTRETH, b. 7 mo. 24, 1778, d. 11 mo. 16, 1814 (buried Arch St., Philadelphia), m. *Sarah Rudolph*. Three children: (She m. 2d, —— HAMPTON. Res. Phila.).

5–88. John Rudolph, m. Julia ——; widow res. Philadelphia.
5–89. Catharine, m. 1, DR. SPACKMAN; 2, JOSEPH BRIGGS.
5–90. George.

4-56. *Ann Longstreth*, b. 2 mo. 12, 1784, d. 5 mo. 26, 1868, m. at Abington, 10 mo. 9, 1806, CHARLES TYSON HALLOWELL, b. 4 mo. 28, 1780, d. 7 mo. 7, 1829.[1] They had nine children:

5–91. Priscilla, b. 9 mo. 18, 1807, d. 5 mo. 8, 1808.
5–92. Morris Longstreth, b. 8 mo. 14, 1809, res. Philadelphia; *m.*
5–93. Caleb, b. 5 mo. 31, 1811, d. *unm.*
5–94. Susan Morris, b. 3 mo. 18, 1813, d. 9 mo. 25, 1846. WALTON.
5–95. Maria, b. 7 mo. 28, 1815, d. 3 mo., 1816.
5–96. Samuel Longstreth, b. 1 mo. 10, 1817, d. 4 mo. 27, 1864, m. 1845, *Elizabeth Chase*; res. San Francisco, Cal., ; 3 children.
5–97. Joshua Longstreth, b. 3 mo. 31, 1819, d. 7 mo. 25, 1873; *m.*
5–98. Charles, b. 7 mo. 31, 1821, d. 1 mo. 2, 1864, m. *Almira R. Stephens.*
5–99. Ann, b. 2 mo. 23, 1824, d. 10 mo., 1824.

4-57. SAMUEL LONGSTRETH, merchant, b. 9 mo. 28, 1787, d. near New Orleans, La., 4 mo. 7, 1826, m. at Abington, Pa., 11 mo. 14, 1811, *Sarah Redwood Fisher*, b. 1791, d. 11 mo. 18, 1827, dau. of Miers and Sarah Fisher.[2] They had seven children:

5–100. Esther Fisher, b. 11 mo. 10, 1812, d. 9 mo. 24, 1829.
5–101. Sarah Redwood, b. 12 mo. 19, 1814. PARRISH.
5–102. Helen G., b. 12 mo. 14, 1816; *unm.*
5–103. Miers Fisher, b. 3 mo. 15, 1819, res. Darby, Pa.; *m.*
5–104. Anna, b. 2 mo, 6, 1821, d. 12 mo., 1843; *m.* ROBERT K. WRIGHT, son of Peter; res. Phila. No issue.
5–105. Lydia W., b. 3 mo. 29, 1823. WILMER.
5–106. Sidney Elizabeth, b. 5 mo. 16, 1825, res. Phila.; *unm.*

4-58. THOMAS MIFFLIN LONGSTRETH, b. 9 mo. 17, 1790, d. in Philadelphia, 11 mo. 10, 1845, m. *Deborah M. Dempsey*, b. 12 mo. 18, 1798, d. in Philadelphia, 8 mo. 10, 1873. They had three children:

5–107. Lydia Price, b. 1 mo. 4, 1837, m. 2 mo. 24, 1859, NICHOLAS BAGGS, b. 6 mo. 6, 1835, res. Philadelphia; four children.
5–108. Thomas Miffln, b. 5 mo. 7, 1839, res. Philadelphia; *unm.*
5–109. Elizabeth Abbott, b. 6 mo. 12, 1844, m. 6 mo. 3, 1869, Rev. LEIGHTON W. ECKARD, res. Chefoo, China; two children.

---

[1] Son of Caleb Hallowell (b. 11 mo. 21, 1756, d. 1 mo. 6, 1829), and 1st wife *Priscilla Tyson*, m. in Abington, 1778; gr. son of William Hallowell (b. 6 mo. 1, 1707, d 8 mo. 23, 1794), and 2d w. *Agnes Shoemaker* (b. 1716, d. 1782), m. at Abington, 1754. William Hallowell was brother of Elizabeth, who m. Daniel Dawson. (See 2-3, note 4). Agnes Shoemaker was dau. of Richard (b. 1707), and *Agnes Cleaver* Shoemaker, m. 1732; gr. dau. of George Shoemaker and w. Sarah Waln (dau. of Richard Waln, of Fair Hill), m. 1694; gt. gr. dau. of Jacob Shoemaker, who came from Cresheim, Germany, and settled at Germantown, Pa., 1683.

[2] Miers Fisher was a prominent lawyer of his day. He is mentioned in Westcott's *Life of John Fitch*, p. 263.

4-59. Joseph Longstreth, dry goods merchant, b. in Chester Co., Pa., 11 mo. 25, 1773, d. 3 mo. 9, 1807, (bur. Arch St., Phila.), m. *Margaret Mc Kee*, dau. of Robert and Sarah McKee. They had five children, all b. in Phila. (She m. 2d, Gabriel Middleton, of Phila.):

5-110. Thomas Bedford, b. 12 mo. 10, 1797, d. 9 mo. 6, 1867 ; *m.*
5-111. Mira, b. 4 mo. 25, 1799, d. 12 mo. 23, 1801.
5-112. Morris, b. 12 mo. 3 1800, d. 4 mo. 26, 1855 ; *m.*
5-113. William Wilson, b. 11 mo. 14, 1802 ; *m.*
5-114. Joshua, b. 11 mo. 10, 1805, d. 1 mo. 5, 1812.

4-60. William Wilson Longstreth, b. 9 mo. 1, 1775, d. 11 mo. 2, 1805, (bur. Arch St., Phila.), m. 3 mo. 10, 1803, *Elizabeth Howell*, d. 4 mo. 13, 1818, dau. of Hugh and Hannah Howell. They lived in Chester Co., Pa. One son :

5-115. Howell, b. 6 mo. 10, 1804.

4-61. Benjamin Longstreth, b. 2 mo. 1, 1777, m. 1st, at Lambertsville, N. J., Dec. 31, 1801, *Isabella Dennis*, who d. June 26, 1836. They lived near Prall's Mills, Hunterdon Co., N. J., and had eleven children :

5-116. George, b. July 20, 1802, res. Columbus, O. ; *m.*
5-117. Hannah, b. April 14, 1804.
5-118. Clemence, b. May 29, 1805, d. Aug. 13, 1855.
5-119. Sarah, b. Aug. 21, 1807.
5-120. William, b. June 26, 1809, m. *Martha Coates.*
5-121. Amelia, b. April 8, 1811, d. May 18, 1817.
5-122. John Lambert, b. May 10, 1813, bur. Aug. 6, 1813.
5-123. Thomas, b. July 7, 1814, m. *Hannah Burdsall.*
5-124. Achsah, *twin sister of Thomas*, m. —— Bauty.
5-125. Benjamin D., b. Oct. 5, 1817, m. Oct. 21, 1847, *Caroline Brinley* ; five children.
5-126. Jerusha, b. June 17, 1819, m. Harvey Thomas.

Benj. Longstreth m. 2d, May 5, 1837, *Mary Brinley*, and d. near Monmouth, N. J., Sept. 5, 1851.

4-62. *Mary Longstreth*, b. 1 mo. 7, 1779, d. a widow in Ohio, 9 mo. 7, 1850, m. Jan. 18, 1800, Robert Tea. They had nine children :

5-127. Benjamin L., d. near Lafayette, Ind., since 1850, m. Sept. 18, 1831, *Emily Roach.*
5-128. Mark, lived in Illinois.
5-129. Theodore, m. Oct., 1860, wid. Isabel Andrews, formerly *Isabel Mc Intosh.* She d. Oct., 1871. He res. 1873, Morrow, Warren Co., Ohio.

5–130. [TEA.] Sarah Ann, d. before 1850.
5–131. Elizabeth, m. Sept., 1834, ALFRED NOBLE. She d. before 1850; two children.
5–132. Mary, m. June 9, 1836, THOMAS ROACH, res. Oregon; six children.
5–133. Richard, d. since 1850, in Indiana, leaving seven children; a son, Richard, in U. S. army.
5–134. Ann, m. ——— COUDEN, res. near Morrow, Ohio; 8 children.
5–135. Oscar, went to California, 1854, not heard from some years past.

4–63. *Ann Longstreth*, b. 1 mo. 27, 1781, m. 1st, WILLIAM PARRISH. They had one child:

5–136. Benjamin, d. in infancy.

She married 2d, JOSEPH SIDNEY KEEN, and d. in West Phila., 5 mo. 31, 1840. They had five children:

5–137. John Sidney; *m.*
5–138. Morris, res. Phila.; *unm.*
5–139. Joseph, m. *Elizabeth Watt*; res. W. Philadelphia.
5–140. Caroline, m. JOHN SELLERS; res. Phila.
5–141. Jason F., m. —————, res. Phila.

4–66. *Elizabeth Longstreth*, b. 7 mo. 9, 1787, m. 5 mo. 15, 1811, ISAIAH PAXSON, b. 2 mo. 8, 1785, d. 8 mo. 29, 1827, son of Jacob and Mary Paxson. Six children:

5–142. Jacob Longstreth, b. 6 mo. 17, 1812, res. Philadelphia; *m.*
5–143. Sarah, b. 9 mo. 13, 1815, res. Bucks Co., Pa. BEDFORD.
5–144. William Longstreth, b. 8 mo. 5, 1817, res. Bucks Co., Pa.; *m.*
5–145. Elizabeth, b. 8 mo. 18, 1821, res. Philadelphia; *unm.*
5–146. Mary, *twin sister of Elizabeth*, res. Phildelphia. FURMAN.
5–147. Benjamin, b. 3 mo. 15, 1825, d. 10 mo. 15, 1828.

4–67. *Rachel Wilson Longstreth*, b. 7 mo. 10, 1789, d. in Philadelphia, 5 mo. 16, 1865, m. DAVIS ORUM. They had five children:

5–148. Mira, m. CHARLES S. RENSHAW. Res. Mass.; five children.
5–149. Charles Longstreth, m. 1st, *Keturah Hammer*, five children; 2d, *Sarah Holt*, res. Phila.; two children.
5–150. Elizabeth, m. THOMAS TYSON BUTCHER, res. Phila.; eight children.
5–151. Morris, m. *Harriet Carter;* three children.
5–152. Margaret, b. 3 mo. 11, 1822, d. 10 mo. 31, 1855. HOOPES.

4–68. *Hannah Longstreth*, b. 7 mo. 26, 1791, d. 6 mo. 26, 1837, m. at Abington, Pa., 11 mo. 11, 1813, SAMUEL WILSON, b. 6 mo. 5, 1786, d. 1 mo. 28, 1839, son of Stephen and Sarah Wilson.[1] Eight children:

---

[1] The dates in above record of family of Samuel and *Hannah Longstreth* Wilson

5–153. [WILSON.] Charles L., b. 5 mo. 25, 1816, d. about 3 mo., 1863.
5–154. Sarah L., b. 12 mo. 5, 1817.
5–155. Rebecca, b. 9 mo. 27, 1820, d. 10 mo. 3, 1840.
5–156. Oliver, b. 10 mo. 5, 1822, d. in Sussex Co., Del., 6 mo. 19, 1866.
5–157. Samuel, b. 7 mo. 9, 1824.
5–158. Elias, b. 1 mo. 29, 1827, d. 5 mo. 13, 1837.
5–159. Margaret O., b. 8 mo. 3, 1830.
5–160. Davis, b. 5 mo. 22, 1837, d. 5 mo. 25, 1838.

4–69. JACOB LONGSTRETH, b. 9 mo. 27, 1793, m. in Ohio, *Margaret Ditto.* Four children:

5–161. Milton.
5–162. William, res. Philadelphia.
5–163. Susan, m. Dr. NOBLE, res. Ohio.
5–164. Julia.

4–70. GEORGE FIELD LONGSTRETH, b. in Pa., 4 mo. 26, 1796, removed to Miama, Ohio, 1817, walking the whole way. He m. 1st, in Ohio, 12 mo. 17, 1818, *Sarah Wilkerson*, b. 3 mo. 28, 1799, d. 8 mo. 13, 1842. They had eleven children:

5–165. James W., b. 8 mo. 23, 1819; *m.*
5–166. Sarah, b. 2 mo. 27, 1821, m. WLLIAM MAYDOLE; no issue.
5–167. Benjamin, b. 9 mo. 11, 1822; *m.*
5–168. Elizabeth, b. 9 mo. 11, 1824. McCRAY.
5–169. Almira, b. 10 mo. 13, 1826. CRANE.
5–170. George, b. 7 mo. 12, 1830, d. 8 mo. 3, 1830.
5–171. William Morris, b. 9 mo. 24, 1831, d. in Vermillion Co., Ill., from disease contracted in the war, 1864; *unm.*
5–172. Ann, b. 12 mo. 4, 1833. HARLAN.
5–173. Mary, b. 1 mo. 11, 1836. LAMBERT.
5–174. Almeda, b. 5 mo. 21, 1836, d. 9 mo. 3, 1839.
5–175. Davis Orum, b. 3 mo. 19, 1841, m. 1866 ——— ; 2 children.

Geo. F. Longstreth m. 2d, 12 mo. 3, 1843, widow Elizabeth Harlan (maiden name *Young*), b. in Ohio, 1 mo. 7, 1806. They res. at Miama, and have had three children:

---

supplied by Elias E. Paxson, of Solesbury, Pa., from whom also the following, *too late for insertion in proper order.*

OLIVER WILSON (5-156) m. 7 mo. 25, 1861, *Margaret J. Shoemaker.* They had, Samuel Allen, b. 5 mo. 23, 1862, Mary T., b. 1 mo. 20, 1864, Oliver, b. 1 mo. 6, 1866, d. 1 mo. 19, 1867.

SAMUEL WILSON (5-157) m. 8 mo. 25, 1853, *Maria Webster.* They had Samuel Howard, b. 12 mo. 23, 1854, William E., b. 10 mo. 23, 1856, Mary Elizabeth, b. 10 mo. 11, 1859.

Margaret O. Wilson (5-159) m. 3 mo. 20, 1861, ELIAS E. PAXSON. They had Samuel W., b. 8 mo. 25, 1863, Sarah W., b. 12 mo. 31, 1864, Deborah, b. 2 mo. 25, 1868, d. 5 mo. 27, 1873, Hannah, b. 1 mo. 21, 1871.

5–176. [LONGSTRETH.] Rachel Orum, b. 1 mo. 10, 1845, d. 4 mo. 4, 1847.
5–177. Amelia, b. 9 mo. 21, 1846. LAMBERT.
5–178. Giles D., b. 9 mo. 6, 1851, m. 5 mo. 28, 1873, *Florence Hathaway.*

4–71. *Rosamond Dawson* (dau. of James, 3-15), m. ——— MURRAY. Said to have settled in North Carolina. They had:

5–179. Joseph Dawson.

4–72. CHARLES GREEN m. 1st —————, and had two children:

5–180. William.
5–181. Sarah.

He m. 2d, —————. They had three children:

5–182. Hannah.
5–183. Daniel Dawson, a potter, d.
5–184. Jane.

He m. 3d, —— *Squibb.* They had two children:

5–185. Mary Ann.
5–186. Charles.

4–73. *Mary Green* m. GEORGE HILL. They had three children:

5–187. Elizabeth, m. BENJAMIN ROBERTS.
5–188. Alice.
5–189. Mary Ann, res. 703 King St., Wilmington, Del.

4–74. *Sarah Green* m. JOHN JONES, brewer. They lived in Wilmington, Del., and had eight children:

5–190. Mary, m. JOHN ELY, of Pa. no issue.
5–191. Elizabeth, d. *unm.*
5–192. Jane, d. *nnm.*
5–193. Priscilla, d. *unm.*
5–194. Sarah, res. 704 Green St., Philadelphia. WEBB.
5–195. Israel Dawson, brewer, Wilmington, m. *Caroline Chandler,* one dau.; all d.
5–196. Charles, d. young.

4–75. *Elizabeth Thompson* m. in Philadelphia, 6 mo. 16, 1789, THOMAS FISHER, of Brandywine, b. 11 mo. 1, 1765.[1] They had three children:

---

[1] Sixth child of Thomas Fisher (son of Thomas and Elizabeth Fisher), and w. Elizabeth Lamborn, who was dau. of Robert and *Sarah Swayne* Lamborn. (See 3-38, n. 1.)

5–197. [FISHER.] Elizabeth.
5–198. Rebecca, m. THOMAS ATKINSON.
5–199. Thomas Dawson.

4–96. JOHN SMEDLEY, b. 9 mo. 7, 1779, d. 10 mo. 15, 1825, m. 10 mo. 23, 1800, *Rebecca Cope*, who d. 1 mo. 24, 1846, dau. of Nathan and Amy Cope. They lived in Chester Co., Pa., and had eleven children :

5–200. Nathan, b. 9 mo. 12, 1801, d. 2 mo. 23, 1802.
5–201. Benjamin, b. 1 mo. 21, 1803, res. Willistown, Chester Co., Pa. ; *m.*
5–202. Enos, b. 5 mo. 18, 1805, res. Easttown township, Chester Co., Pa. ; *m.*
5–203. Jeffrey, b. 6 mo. 21, 1807, d. 9 mo. 15, 1854 ; *m.*
5–204. Nathan, b. 2 mo. 23, 1810, res. Kenderton, near Philadelphia, Pa. ; *m.*
5–205. Ezra, b. 4 mo. 21, 1812, res. West Bradford, Chester Co., Pa. ; *m.*
5–206. John, b. 1 mo. 11, 1814, d. 3 mo. 20, 1855 ; *m.*
5–207. Thomas, b. 1 mo. 12, 1816, d. 8 mo. 6, 1840.
5–208. Amy C., b. 3 mo. 21, 1818, res. West Bradford, Pa. PRATT.
5–209. Elwood, b. 11 mo, 11, 1820, res. Willistown, Pa. ; *m.*
5–210. Chalkley, b. 5 mo. 26, 1824, d. 11 mo. 18, 1825.

4–97. *Susannah Smedley*, b. 11 mo. 11, 1779, d. 12 mo. 18, 1858, m. JONATHAN HOOD, b. 9 mo. 17, 1777, d. 5 mo. 15, 1861. They lived at Newtown, Pa. Five children :

5–211. Mary, m. 12 mo. 3, 1828, AZARIAH LEWIS WILLIAMSON, b. 12 mo. 23, 1802, son of Enos and Sarah Williamson.
5–212. Lydia. THOMAS.
5–213. Susannah, b. 3 mo. 10, 1817.
5–214. Edmund, b. 7 mo. 22, 1819.
5–215. Jonathan, b. 11 mo. 6, 1821.

4–99. *Mary Smedley*, b. 11 mo. 7, 1783, m. 1 mo. 14, 1806, GEORGE LAMBORN, who was b. in Chester Co., Pa., 12 mo. 23, 1768.[1] They removed from Chester Co., about 1809, to Drumore, Lancaster Co., Pa., where they lived until 1829 ; thence to Jefferson Co., Ohio, where they resided a few years ; and finally to Knox Co., in that state, where he d. 9 mo. 19, 1856, and she d. 1 mo. 10, 1857. They were buried at Millwood. They had ten children :

---

[1] She was his 2d wife. By former marriage he had seven children. He was twelfth child of Robert and *Ann Browne* Lamborn ; brother of Ann Lamborn, w. of James Dawson, (see 3-38, and note).

5–216. [LAMBORN.] Smedley, b. 1 mo. 6, 1807, d. in Lancaster Co., Pa., 9 mo. 26, 1851 ; *m.*
5–217. Susan, b. 8 mo. 10, 1808, m. DAVID FRAZIER, and removed to the West.
5–218. John, b. 10 mo. 9, 1810, res. 1873, Henry Co., Iowa ; *m.*
5–219. Esther, b. 4 mo. 11, 1812, m. —— KENNEY, res. Kanzas.
5–220. Jacob, b. 4 mo. 11, 1822, d. in Mahaska Co., Iowa, 5 mo. 8, 1858 ; *m.*
5–221. Lindley, b. 12 mo. 28, 1824, res. 1873, California ; *m.*
5–222. Martha, b. 12 mo. 28, 1828, res. 1873, Oskaloosa, Iowa. HOLLISTER.
5–223. Robert, d. in infancy.
5–224. Mary, d. in infancy.
5–225. Philena, d. in infancy.

4–100. JACOB SMEDLEY, b. 12 mo. 27, 1784, m. *Rebecca Jones.* They lived in Philadelphia. One daughter :

5–226. Elizabeth Jones, b. 2 mo. 9, 1824.

4–101. ISAAC SMEDLEY, b. 12 mo. 14, 1786, m. 11 mo. 15, 1810, *Amy Cox*, who d. 4 mo. 20, 1847. They lived in Philadelphia, and had three children :

5–227. Jeffrey, b. 12 mo. 1, 1811.
5–228. Mary Ann, b. 8 mo. 1, 1813, m. 11 mo. 15, 1846, GEO. R. MCCLUEN.
5–229. Kersey, b. 10 mo. 17, 1816.

4–116. *Sarah Dawson*, b. at Tuckahoe, Talbot Co., Md., 1 mo. 1, 1799, m. JAMES DAVIS, of Kent Co., Md., who d.——. She res. 1873, Wilmington, Del. Two children :

5–230. George.
5–231. Edward, d.

5–3. *Sarah Dunkin*, b. 8 mo. 30, 1778, m. 1st, 4 mo. 12, 1803, ISAIAH DILLIN (or DILLON), b. 12 mo. 26, 1781, son of William and Sarah. They had one child :

6–1. Elizabeth, b. 11 mo. 11, 1811.

She m. 2d, JOSIAH LONGSTRETH, and d. at Abington, Pa., 1 mo. 28, 1845. They had two children, 5-83 and 5-84 of this record.

5–5. *Susannah Dunkin*, b. 5 mo. 11, 1782, d. 4 mo. 25, 1814, m. 3 mo. 11, 1807, JOSEPH WEBSTER, son of Joseph and Rebecca Webster. They had six children :

6–2. [WEBSTER.] Charles, b. 11 mo. 11, 1808.
6–3. Rebecca, b. 1 mo. 14, 1809.
6–4. Aaron Dunkin, b. 9 mo. 8, 1810, m. 5 mo. 6, 1856, *Isabella Evard*, dau. of Andrew and Rebecca Evard.
6–5. Susannah, b. 10 mo. 20, 1811.
6–6. Lydia, b. 2 mo. 13, 1813.
6–7. Joseph, b. 4 mo. 14, 1814.

5-6. *Martha Dunkin*, b. 4 mo. 5, 1784, m. 12 mo. 31, 1817, JOHN WATSON, son of John and Mary Watson, of Bucks Co., Pa. They had:

6–8. Richard.
6–9. Martha, m. —— HART.

5-9. *Esther Fussell*, b. at Hatboro, Pa., 3 mo. 18, 1782, d. in Chester Co., Pa., 2 mo. 8, 1848, m. at Little Falls meeting, Md., 9 mo. 10, 1818. JOHN LEWIS Jun., b. 3 mo. 29, 1781, d. 2 mo. 5, 1824, son of John and *Grace Meredith* Lewis, both of whom d. in Chester Co. Esther Fussell Lewis was a woman of remarkable solidity of character, and she exercised a commanding and beneficent influence commensurate with her rare ability and intelligence. In the community in which she lived her well balanced judgment caused her advice to be sought and accepted by brothers, sisters, friends, neighbors and dependants. Her life was one of distinguished usefulness and worth. It was she who so powerfully influenced her brother, Dr. Bartholmew Fussell, in his determination to secure the medical education of women. After her marriage she returned to the home of her husband, in West Vincent, Chester Co., Pa.[1] They had five children, all b. in Chester Co.[2]

6–10. Mariann, b. 6 mo. 6, 1819, d. at West Vincent, 1866; *unm.*[3]
6–11. Rebecca, b 6 mo. 10, 1820, res. Media, Delaware Co., Pa., m. EDWIN FUSSELL. (See forward, 6–16.)

[1] They occupied a farm which was part of a large tract purchased during the early settlement of Pennsylvania by his maternal ancestors of the Meredith family. Henry Lewis, the first of the family of that name who came to Pennsylvania, was a friend and correspondent of William Penn.

[2] Mrs. Lewis is said to have been "one of the most careful and accurate of women." Her papers are an invaluable source of information respecting the family history. Before her death she sent copies of such family records as she possessed, which were quite extensive, to several of her nieces. She seems to have diffused her spirit through the family. It is remarkable for the interest which its members generally display in preserving its records and traditions.

[3] See sketch of Mariann, Grace Anna and Elizabeth R. Lewis, with portrait of Grace Anna, in William Still's *The Underground Railroad*, pp. 748-753. It is said

6–12. [LEWIS.] Grace Anna, b. 8 mo. 3, 1821, res. Media, *unm.*; an accomplished ornithologist, holding an acknowledged position among Naturalists.
6–13. Charles, b. 9 mo. 11, 1822, d. 10 mo. 18, 1823.
6–14. Elizabeth R., b. 1 mo. 15, 1824, d. at West Vincent, 10 mo. 10, 1863; *unm.*

5–10. WILLIAM FUSSELL, b. 6 mo. 30, 1783, d. 6 mo. 4, 1856, m. 9 mo. 28, 1809, *Jane Foulke*, b. 8 mo. 20, 1782, d. 5 mo. 9, 1857, dau. of Edward and Elizabeth R. Foulke. They had five children:

6–15. Elizabeth R., b. 7 mo. 31, 1810, res. Pendleton, Ind. HARDY.
6–16. Edwin, b. 6 mo. 14, 1813, res. Media, Delaware Co., Pa.; *m.*
6–17. Esther Ann, b. 2 mo. 22, 1818, m. CHARLES PENNELL JACOBS. (See forward, 6–21).
6–18. Joseph, b. 8 mo. 7, 1820, res. Philadelphia; *m.*
6–19. Milton, b. 6 mo. 11, 1823, res. Radnor, Delaware Co., Pa.; *m.*

5–11. *Sarah Fussell*, b. 9 mo. 10, 1784, d. 8 mo. 11, 1860, m. 12 mo. 8, 1812, THOMAS P. JACOBS, b. 4 mo. 25, 1789, d. 3 mo. 10, 1861, son of Thomas and Lydia Jacobs. They had three children:

6–20. Rebecca Fussell, b. 4 mo. 30, 1815, d. 4 mo., 1871. BROWN.
6–21. Charles Pennell, b. 10 mo. 6, 1816, res. Pendleton, Ind.; *m.*
6–22. Lydia Pennell, b. 3 mo. 11, 1821, res. Vineland, N. J., m. ORSON S. MURRAY; no issue.

5–12. JOSEPH FUSSELL, b. in Chester Co., Pa., 4 mo. 26, 1787, d. 10 mo. 15, 1855, m. in Gwynedd meeting, Montgomery Co., Pa., 6 mo. 14, 1814, *Elizabeth Moore*, b. 2 mo. 19, 1790, d. 2 mo. 19, 1865, dau. of Henry and Priscilla Moore.

About three years after their marriage they removed to Baltimore county, Md., where they remained nearly twelve years.[1] In 1828 they removed to Pennsylvania, near Philadelphia, where

of these ladies in that work, that they "were among the most faithful, devoted, and quietly efficient workers in the Anti-slavery cause, including that department of it which is the subject of this [that] volume." . . . . "Mariann and Elizabeth having lived to see the triumph of the Right, in the Presidential Proclamation of Freedom to the slaves, have gone from their earthly to their heavenly rest."............... "Grace Anna still continues here, working for human welfare in such fields as still demand the laborer's toil, and finding mental profit and delight in the pursuit of natural science." (The dates of birth of Mariann and Rebecca have also been reported as follows: Mariann, 6 mo. 1, 1819; Rebecca, 10 mo. 6, 1821. — M. M. L.)

[1] "Their experience of slavery impressed them deeply with a sense of its evils, and they bore a testimony against it, even in that early day, by abstaining as far as possible from the use of its products. Thus they infused into the minds of their children a spirit of anti-slavery, which prepared them all to join the ranks of abolitionism in its earliest days."— Mrs. M. M. Lewis, Huntsville, Ind., 1873.

they lived until the year 1846, when they removed to Indiana, and settled at Fall Creek, Madison Co., in that state, where they d. "beloved of all who knew them well." They had nine children:

6–23. [FUSSELL.] Henry Bartholomew, b. 3 mo. 15, 1815, res. Media, Pa.; *m.*
6–24. Priscilla, d. in infancy.
6–25. Rebecca Bond, b. 7 mo. 14, 1818, res. Fall Creek, Ind. ROGERS.
6–26. Samuel, b. 7 mo. 31, 1819, res. Pendleton, Ind.; *m.*
6–27. Mary Jane, b. 11 mo. 21, 1821, d. in Ind., 8 mo. 20, 1854. HODGES.
6–28. Elizabeth Moore, b. 11 mo. 21, 1821, res. Fall Creek, Ind. LEWIS.
6–29. Solomon, d. aged 14 mos.
6–30. Solomon 2d, d. aged 2 weeks.
6–31. John Lewis, b. 8 mo. 8, 1830, res. Pendleton, Ind.; *m.*

5–13. SOLOMON FUSSELL, farmer, was born near Phenixville, Chester Co., Pa., 6 mo. 28, 1789. He removed with his parents when a child to Baltimore county, Md., but returned to Pa. when a young man. He m. 1st, at Gwynedd meeting, Montgomery Co., Pa., 2 mo. 6, 1816, *Milcah Martha Moore*, b. 1 mo. 20, 1792, sister of Elizabeth Moore, wife of Joseph Fussell (5-12). In 1830, or '31, he went west, to seek a home for himself and family, and traveled as far as Milton, in Wayne Co., Ind., beyond which place the roads were at that time almost impassable. In the fall of 1832 he removed with his wife and five children from Chester Co., Pa., to Fall Creek, Madison Co., Ind., the journey being accomplished in a two horse wagon, and occupying an entire month. The next year was one of great mortality in his family. His wife died 8 mo. 16, 1833. Three of the children died within a single week, he at the same time being too sick to be conscious of his loss. As soon as he was sufficiently recovered, leaving his two only remaining children with a relative, he returned to the East, performing the long journey, though still in feeble health, on horseback. In the fall of 1836 he returned to Indiana *on foot*, taking with him a herd of fine cattle, a cow carrying his luggage in a pair of saddle bags. He m. 2d, at Fall Creek meeting, Ind., 12 mo. 1, 1836, *Hannah Lewis*, daughter of Joseph and Lydia Lewis, formerly of Willistown, Chester Co., Pa. He d. at Fall Creek, 3 mo. 1, 1849, greatly esteemed. His character was that of the strictest integrity. He had been all his life a conscientious anti-slavery and temperance man, abstaining as far as possible from the use of all articles produced by slave labor, and being among the first in his neighborhood, it is said, to refuse to give liquor in harvest, yet never lacking help, although his experiment was one which at that time few ventured to try, for fear their grain would be left to rot in the fields. Solomon and *Milcah Martha Moore* Fussell had 11 children:

6–32. Bartholomew Bond, b. 1 mo. 19, 1817, d. 1818.
6–33. Priscilla Moore, b. 9 mo. 25, 1818, res. Fall Creek, Ind. THOMAS.
6–34. Sarah Jacobs, b. 8 mo. 15, 1820, d. 1833.
6–35. Bartholomew Bond, b. 10 mo. 16, 1822, d. 1833.
6–36. Henry Moore, b. 11 mo. 23, 1823, d. 1825.
6–37. Milcah Martha, b. 10 mo. 16, 1825, res. Huntsville, Ind. LEWIS.
6–38. Mary Fussell, b. 11 mo. 16, 1827, d. young.
6–39. Esther Lewis, b. 3 mo. 5, 1829, d. 1833.
6–40. Solomon, b. 11 mo. 26, 1830, d. 7 mo. 1, 1831.
6–41. Rebecca Jane, b. 1 mo. 19, 1832, d. young.
6–42. Marion W., d. young.

Solomon and *Hannah Lewis* Fussell had two children:

6–43. Lydia J., b. 8 mo. 9, 1838, d. in Indiana, Feb. 28, 1872. SHARP.
6–44. Anna Wood, b. 11 mo. 17, 1841, res. Indiana; *unm.*

5–14. JACOB FUSSELL, b. in Chester Co., Pa., 2 mo. 7, 1792, d. near Phila., 8 mo. 7, 1855 (bur. Frankfort), m. 12 mo. 4, 1814, *Clarissa Whitaker*, b. 7 mo. 5, 1789, d. 4 mo. 28, 1863, dau. of Joshua and Ruth Whitaker. They lived in Baltimore Co., Md., and had ten children, all b. in Baltimore:

6–45. William W., b. 10 mo. 5, 1815, d. aged 19.
6–46. Joshua W., b. 10 mo. 26, 1817.
6–47. Jacob, b. 2 mo. 24, 1819, res. New York city; *m.*
6–48. Ruthanna, b. 1 mo. 20, 1820, res. Baltimore, Md. GORSUCH.
6–49. Hannah E., res. Baltimore. HOPKINS.
6–50. Bartholomew Howard, b. 12 mo. 16, 1823, d. in Baltimore, 12 mo. 23, 1860; *m.*
6–51. Joseph B., b. 1 mo. 15, 1826, d. ———; *m.*
6–52. Philena, b. 6 mo. 13, 1828, res. Baltimore. MARTINETT.
6–53. Clarissa, b. 2 mo. 22, 1832, res. Baltimore. DAVIS.
6–54. Mary, b. 10 mo. 20, 1833, d. 1835.

5–15. Dr. BARTHOLOMEW FUSSELL, was b. in Chester Co., Pa., 1 mo. 9, 1794. He removed in early life to Maryland, where he taught school, and read medicine, and where he found means to give Sabbath and private instruction to great numbers

Dr. BARTHOLOMEW FUSSELL.

of slaves, many of whom, with hundreds of other fugitives of their class, he afterwards protected and assisted at his home in Pennsylvania, while on their way to freedom. He was one of the signers of the "Declaration of Sentiments" issued by the American Anti-Slavery Society in 1833, and he had the gratification of attending the last meeting of the Pennsylvania Anti-Slavery Society, called to celebrate the downfall of slavery in America, and for the dissolution of an organization whose purpose was effected. He was also well known as an advocate of common school education, of temperance, and of every other interest, which, in his view, pertained to the welfare of man. He became early convinced of the peculiar fitness of woman for the practice of medicine. "In the year 1840 he first gave regular instructions to a class of women, and it was through one of these pupils that the first graduate in America was interested in the study of medicine. In 1846 he communicated to a few liberal-minded professional men a plan for the medical education of women. Others, with indominable zeal, took up the work, and finally, after a succession of disappointments and discouragements, from causes within and without, the Woman's College, on North College avenue, Philadelphia, starting from the germ of his thought, entered on the career of prosperity it is so well entitled to enjoy. Though never, at any time, connected officially with the college, he regarded its success with the most affectionate interest, considering its proposition as one of the most important results of his life." [1]

Dr. FUSSELL m. 1st, 5 mo. 26, 1826, *Lydia Morris*, b. at Fox Chase, Montgomery Co., Pa., 7 mo. 13, 1804, d. 7 mo. 3, 1840, dau. of Morris and *Jerusha Whitton* Morris. They had five children :

6–55. Joshua Longstreth, b. in Kennett, Pa., 6 mo. 9, 1827, res. Fall Creek, Ind. ; *m.*

6–56. Morris, b. in Kennett, 6 mo. 27, 1829, res. near Chester Springs, Chester Co., Pa. ; *m.*

6–57. Susan, b. in Kennett, 4 mo. 7, 1832, res. Knightstown, Ind. ; *unm.* [2]

---

[1] William Still's *The Underground Railroad*, p. 697. See extended biographical notice, and portrait, in that work.

[2] Shortly after the outbreak of the civil war she volunteered as a nurse, and served during nearly three years in the hospitals of Memphis, Tenn., Louisville, Ky., and Jeffersonville, Ind. Since that time she has had charge of a home for soldiers'

6–58. [FUSSELL.] Lydia Ada, b. in Kennett, 6 mo. 24, 1837, res. near Chester Springs, Pa.: teacher; *unm.*

6–59. Benjamin Lundy, b. in Vincent, Pa., 3 mo. 17, 1840, res. Markleville, Madison Co., Indiana,: physician; *unm.*

Dr. Fussell m. 2d, 2 mo. 9, 1841, wid. Rebecca C. Hewes, dau. of Edward and Rebecca Churchman, and d. at the res. of his son, Dr. Morris Fussell, near Chester Springs, Pa., 2 mo. 14, 1871, aged 76. Issue of second marriage, two sons:

6–60. Edward C., b. York, Pa., 3 mo. 23, 1843, d. in Vincent, 3 mo. 22, 1844.

6–61. Edward C., b. in Kennett, 11 mo. 30, 1845, d. at Fall Creek, Ind., 9 mo. 17, 1865.

5–16. *Rebecca Fussell*, b. 4 mo. 21, 1796, m. 3 mo. 21, 1837, JOSEPH TRIMBLE, who d. 9 mo. 14, 1839, son of Joseph and Mary Trimble. They res. in Chester Co., Pa. One child:

6–62. Esther Jane, b. 3 mo. 2, 1838, instructor in English literature, rhetoric, and elocution (1873), at Swarthmore College, Delaware Co., Pa.; *unm.*

5–17. MAHLON LONGSTRETH, b. 1779, d. in Philadelphia, 1 mo. 8, 1837, m. *Elizabeth Wooley*. They lived at Crosswicks, N. J., and had one child:

6–63. Mary, d. at Bordentown, N. J., 4 mo. 6, 1833, aged 30. HAMILTON.

5–18. *Martha Longstreth* (dau. of John, 4-4), m. SAMUEL SPENCER. Five children:

6–64. John Longstreth; *m.*

6–65. Mahlon; *m.*

6–66. Lewis, res. Oldbridge, Middlesex Co., N. J.; *m.*

6–67. Sarah, m. I. NEWTON BAILEY.

6–68. Ferdinand; *unm.*

5–19. DANIEL LONGSTRETH, d. 5 mo. 25, 1832, m. *Letitia Milner*. Five children:

6–69. John Milner, m. *Eleanor* —— ; she d. 8 mo. 24, 1844, Centreville, Bucks Co., Pa.; 3 children.

6–70. Phebe.

---

orphans, at Knightstown, Henry Co., Ind. This was at first a private enterprise, endowed through the liberality of George Merritt, of Ind., but since has received aid from the State. The inmates consist of ten children, brought up as a private family, under Miss Fussell's entire control, as a mother would bring up her family. As one child leaves, another takes its place, but the number is limited to ten.

6–71. [LONGSTRETH.] Maria.
6–72. Robert.
6–73. Ann, m. —— BROWN.

5-21. *Rachel Longstreth* (dau. of John, 4-4), m. JOHN M. MILNER; d. at Groveville, N. J., 1 mo. 14, 1827. Six chn.:

6–74. Hetty; *unm.*
6–75. Julia, buried 2 mo. 7, 1836, aged 21.
6–76. Phebe; *unm.*
6–77. Mahlon; *m.*
6–78. Sarah Matilda, m. B. FRANKLIN MENDENHALL.
6–79. Emma.

5-23. *Esther L. Longstreth* (dau. of John, 4-4), m. 5 mo. 14, 1818, JOHN L. HAYWARD, of Baltimore, d. 4 mo., 1838, son of William and Keziah Hayward. They lived at Bristol, Pa. Five children:

6–80. Lewis W., b. 2 mo. 20, 1819, d. Dec. 6, 1872; *unm.*
6–81. Arthur, b. 6 mo. 3, 1821, m. Elizabeth Evans (b. *Dodson*). He d. at Philadelphia, March 21, 1871. No issue.
6–82. Henry E., b. 9 mo. 29, 1823, d. 5 mo. 23, 1830.
6–83. Julia, b. 1 mo. 24, 1827, res. Bristol, Pa. SLACK.
6–84. Henry E., b. 7 mo. 14, 1834, res. Philadelphia; *m.*

5-24. JOHN KIRKBRIDE LONGSTRETH m. *Elizabeth Rowland.* Two daughters:

6–85. Emma, m. —— STRAUB; res. Pottsville, Pa.
6–86. Ellen, m. —— MILNOR.

5-25. DANIEL MICHENER, b. 12 mo. 21, 1780, m. 1804, *Anna Kinsey.* They lived near Mt. Pleasant, Ohio, 1831; at Smyrna, O., 1838. One son:

6–87. John, b. 1 mo. 14, 1820; *m.*

5-26. MORDECAI MICHENER, b. 6 mo. 9, 1782, d. 8 mo. 15, 1836, m. 1804, *Susannah Shaw*, who d. 5 mo. 4, 1834. They had twelve children:

6–88. Martha, b. 9 mo. 16, 1805. KEESE.
6–89. Elizabeth, b. 10 mo. 30, 1807, d. 8 mo. 15, 1844. MEEKER.
6–90. Sarah. DANIELS.
6–91. John, b. 4 mo. 18, 1812; *m.*
6–92. Grace, b. 11 mo. 28, 1813, d. ——. BENEDICT.
6–93. Anna, d. young.
6–94. Ruth, b. 10 mo. 10, 1818. CAMP.

6–95. [MICHENER.] Jane, b. 7 mo. 9, 1820. MILLS.
6–96. Daniel, b. 3 mo. 18, 1822, d. 8 mo. 26, 1846; *m.*
6–97. Mordecai, d. young.
6–98. Susannah, d. young.
6–99. David B., b. 10 mo. 23, 1825, m. 1849, *Emeline Benedict*, b. 3 mo. 21, 1829.

5–27. BENJAMIN MICHENER, b. 10 mo. 26, 1783, m. 1808, *Abigail Stanton*, b. 3 mo. 23, 1786, d. 5 mo. 29, 1839. They had ten children:

6–100. Levi, b. 1 mo. 9, 1809, d. 7 mo. 11, 1832; *unm.*
6–101. Susanna, b. 5 mo. 6, 1810, m. 1837, JOHN BROWN, b. 7 mo. 25, 1799. No issue.
6–102. John J., b 3 mo. 10, 1812; *m.*
6–103. Lydia, b. 1 mo. 18, 1814. GRAVE.
6–104. Henry, b. 2 mo. 12, 1816; *m.*
6–105. David, b. 3 mo. 15, 1818; *m.*
6–106. Isaac, b. 7 mo. 10, 1820; *m.*
6–107. Edwin, 10 mo. 12, 1822, d. 1810; *m.*
6–108. Martha, b. 3 mo. 14, 1825. TAYLOR; WILLIAMS.
6–109. Elma, b. 1 mo. 31, 1828, d. 11 mo. 9, 1842.

Benjamin Michener m. 2d, 1840, *Sarah Canby*, b. 1 mo. 20, 1786.

5–28. *Grace Michener*, b. 4 mo. 21, 1785, d. 7 mo. 25, 1832, m. FRANCIS HOBSON, b. 4 mo. 15, 1781, d. 8 mo. 21, 1821. They had five children:

6–110. Ann M., b. 11 mo. 8, 1808, d. 11 mo. 4, 1840. WATSON.
6–111. John, b. 6 mo. 4, 1811; *m.*
6–112. Martha, b. 2 mo. 21, 1814, d. young.
6–113. Esther, b. 5 mo. 17, 1817, d. 10 mo. 19, 1836.
6–114. Rebecca, b. 3 mo. 21, 1820, d. 1 mo. 29, 1849. SCOTT.

5–29. JONATHAN MICHENER, b. 11 mo. 29, 1787, m. 1st, *Jane Hobson*. They had eight children:

6–115. Joseph; *m.*
6–116. John; *m.*
6–117. Ann. JACKSON.
6–118. James; *m.*
6–119. Barak, d. young.
6–120. Daniel, d. young.
6–121. Esther, d. young.
6–122. Jonathan, d. young.

Jonathan Michener m. 2d, *Margaret Garwood.* Two chn.:

6–123. Hannah.
6–124. Jane.

5-30. *Sarah Michener*, b. 10 mo. 1, 1789, d. 8 mo. 15, 1836, m. 1810, JOHN S. MARTIN. They had nine children:

6–125. John M., b. 2 mo. 1, 1811 ; *m.*
6–126. Paul A., b. 2 mo. 1, 1813 ; *m.*
6–127. Elizabeth A., b. 1 mo. 23, 1815. STANLEY.
6–128. Hannah, b. 3 mo. 22, 1817. WILKINSON.
6–129. Daniel.
6–130. Byers B., b. 1 mo. 3, 1822 ; *m.*
6–131. Mary, b. 5 mo. 2, 1825. CRAMER.
6–132. Susan M., b. 3 mo. 4, 1828. POORMAN.
6–133. Kinsey.

5-31. *Rachel Michener*, b. 9 mo. 22, 1791, m. 1812, ISAAC HAINES, b. 2 mo. 18, 1781. They had seven children:

6–134. Rebecca, b. 7 mo. 2, 1813. STEWART.
6–135. Edwin, b. 7 mo. 24, 1815 ; *m.*
6–136. Ruth, b. 12 mo. 13, 1821.
6–137. Daniel L., b. 11 mo. 16, 1825.
6–138. Martha M., b. 11 mo. 10, 1828.
6–139. Grace Ann, b. 4 mo. 28, 1831.
6–140. Isaac, b. 11 mo. 2, 1834.

5-33. *Hannah Michener*, b. 2 mo. 1, 1796, d. before 1833, m. 1819, SAMUEL CLARKE. They had one daughter:

6–141. Hannah, b. 8 mo. 4, 1820. MCCAUGHEY.

5-34. BARAK MICHENER, b. 11 mo. 8, 1799, m. 1st, 1823, *Harriet Comly*, who d. 8 mo. 20, 1834. He m. 2d, ———; lived in 1827, at Canton, Ohio. Four children, by first marriage:

6–142. James C.
6–143. Martha S., b. 5 mo. 4, 1827. BIGGER.
6–144. Robert O., d. young.
6–145. Lavinia, d. young.

5-35. *Rachel Ross*, b. 3 mo. 23, 1782, res. 1873, Philadelphia, m. RICHARD P. MARIS, who d. 2 mo. 5, 1817. They had four children:

6–146. Thomas Ross, m. —— *Cooch*, res Philadelphia; no issue.
6–147. Richard, graduated University Pa., 1825, m. —— *Ellmaker*, res. Philadelphia ; children all d.
6–148. George G., m. 2 mo. 13, 1833, —— *Buckman*, dau. of John Buckman ; res. Bucks Co., Pa. ; no issue.
6–149. William, m. —— *Stevens*, res. Philadelphia; 6 children.

5-36. *Martha Longstreth*, b. 10 mo. 20, 1789, m. 11 mo. 24, 1809, JOHN SHOEMAKER, b. 9 mo. 8, 1786, d. 11 mo. 2, 1865.[1] She res. 1873, at Norristown, Pa. They had three chn.:

6-150. James, b. 8 mo. 24, 1811, d. 12 mo. 21, 1811.
6-151. Isaac L., b. 6 mo. 14, 1814; *m.*
6-152. Jane L., b. 10 mo. 23, 1817. THOMAS.

5-39. BENJAMIN LONGSTRETH, b. 1 mo. 17, 1797, d. in Philadelphia, 1 mo. 10, 1872, m. 11 mo. 5, 1820, *Susannah Jarrett.*[2] They had seven children:

6-153. Joseph Jarrett, b. 1822, d. 1823.
6-154. Isaac, b. 7 mo. 6, 1824, d. 12 mo. 19, 1857; *m.*
6-155. Charles J., b. 5 mo. 9, 1827, d. 9 mo. 27, 1847.
6-156. Martha S., b. 7 mo. 13, 1830. DOUGLASS.
6-157. Lydia Ann, b. 1 mo. 29, 1833, res. Philadelphia; *unm.*
6-158. Rachel J., b. 1 mo 25, 1836, d. 1860.
6-159. Rebecca R., b. 5 mo. 8, 1838, res. Philadelphia. WATSON.

5-40. *Edith Longstreth*, b. 12 mo. 18, 1798, d. a wid. in Philadelphia, 1 mo. 5, 1868, m. 3 mo. 8, 1821, JESSE SHOEMAKER, farmer, b. 4 mo. 17, 1791, bro. of John (5-36). They lived at Upper Dublin, Pa.; had three children:

6-160. James, b. 8 mo. 20, 1822; *m.*
6-161. Charlotte L., b. 8 mo. 3, 1828, d. 1 mo. 9, 1831.
6-162. John Longstreth, b. 10 mo. 7, 1832; *m.*

5-41. DANIEL LONGSTRETH, real estate agent, b. 3 mo. 19, 1801, d. in Philadelphia, 6 mo. 23, 1856 (son of Isaac, 4-9), m. 11 mo. 17, 1825, *Hannah Kenderdine.* Four children:

6-163. Joseph K., b. 1826, d. 5 mo. 18, 1853.
6-164. Morris, res. 1873, Horsham, Pa.
6-165. Edward, d. young.
6-166. Jane, d. young.

5-43. JOHN LONGSTRETH, conveyancer, b. 11 mo. 19, 1804, m. 6 mo. 3, 1827, *Ann W. Thorne*, dau. of Isaac and Mary Thorne. They res. in Philadelphia. Nine children:

[1] Son of James (b. 1756), and *Phebe Walton* Shoemaker, m. June, 1781; gr. son of Isaac (b. Jan. 15, 1711, d. 1793); gt. gr. son of Peter Shoemaker, a friend and associate of William Penn, settled in Germantown, near Philadelphia, where, in 1686, he built what is said to have been the first house there, a picture of which can be seen in Watson's *Annals of Philadelphia.*

[2] "Susannah Longstreth, d. 3 mo. 15, 1856." — W. F. C.'s notes. Qy.: w. of Benj.?

6–167. [LONGSTRETH.] Emeline, b. 10 mo. 3, 1827 ; *unm.*
6–168. Ellis, b. 10 mo. 1, 1829, d. young.
6–169. Alfred, b. 3 mo. 6, 1831, res. Phila. ; *m.*
6–170. Mary W., b. 11 mo. 10, 1832, res. Williamsport, Pa. BRASTOW.
6–171. Edwin, d. young.
6–172. Edgar T., d. 1868.
6–173. Charlotte, d. young.
6–174. Anna, b. 3 mo. 28, 1847 ; *unm.*
6–175. Sarah Ann, b. 9 mo. 18, 1849 ; *unm.*

5-45. DANIEL LONGSTRETH, b. 11 mo. 25, 1800 (son of Joseph, 4-10), resided at the old homestead of his family, in Warminster township, Bucks Co., Pa., which he inherited from his father. In youth he received a good English education, but, possessing a fondness for mathematics and the natural sciences, he was a diligent student through life, and was thus, to a great extent, self educated. He had an inquiring mind, a retentive memory, and a pleasure in the acquisition of new and curious information which seemed in itself a reward for the greatest pains taken to acquire it. He was in the habit of noting in a common-place book or diary the facts and discoveries which especially interested him, and such as he deemed sufficiently important he communicated to the public through the medium of the newspapers and magazines of his day. He was, besides, much devoted to genealogical and antiquarian researches, and left copious memoranda of the results of his inquiries, which have been largely drawn from for the purposes of this record. His own opinion of the value of such studies is worthy of preservation. "These pursuits," he remarks, "have afforded me great amusement in spare moments. Many wiseacres may think them puerile and trifling. Be it so ; but I am of opinion that anecdotes which disclose the virtuous actions of our worthy ancestors should be preserved and held up for the example of their descendants when about forming their character in youth and early manhood."[1] His love of local history, regard for scientific pursuits, and sympathy for an unfortunate man of genius whose merits seemed to have been overlooked and forgotten, if not designedly concealed, all combined to excite in him a deep interest in the facts relating to the life of "poor John Fitch, of steamboat memory," who had made the model of his first boat

[1] Letter to a friend, 1831.

in that township in 1785. In 1833 Mr. Longstreth was actively engaged in collecting materials for a memoir of Fitch. He published a series of articles concerning him in the Bucks county newspaper, and corresponded on the subject with Watson, author of the *Annals of Philadelphia*, furnishing most of the facts which the latter used in his notice of the inventor in that work. Subsequently, Mr. Westcott wrote his *Life of John Fitch*, obtaining a part of his materials from Mr. Longstreth's papers, but poorly repaying the favor by inserting a very erroneous notice of Mr. L. (who was then dead) in that book.

Mr. Longstreth was a consistent member of the Society of Friends, and was for a number of years (1829 to 1836), clerk of the Horsham monthly meeting, and he was also clerk of the Abington quarterly meeting. In 1840 he opened, at Warminster, a boarding school for boys, which he conducted for some time in connection with his farm. The confinement proving injurious to his health, he closed his school, and afterwards acquired a knowledge of dentistry, which he practiced very successfully. He was also a surveyor, and attended to conveyancing, and the settlement of estates, and to a variety of public affairs. He m. 1st, in Green St. meeting, Philadelphia, 1 mo. 4, 1827, *Elizabeth Lancaster*, who was b. in Phila., 1803, and d. in Warminster township, 9 mo. 19, 1829.[1] They had two sons :

6–176. John Lancaster, b. 11 mo. 10, 1827, res. 1873, Philadelphia ; *m.*
6–177. Elizabeth Lancaster, b. 9 mo. 14, 1829, d. 4 mo. 23, 1848 ; *unm.*

Mr. Longstreth m. 2d, in Green St. meeting, Philadelphia, 10 mo. 25, 1832, *Hannah Townsend*, who was born in Philadelphia, 11 mo. 6, 1801, and d. a wid. in Philadelphia, 8 mo. 6, 1865.[2] She was a highly educated and accomplished lady ; for some years prior to her marriage, clerk of Green St. monthly meeting of Friends in Philadelphia. After her marriage, clerk of

---

[1] Daughter of John Lancaster, b. in Philadelphia, lumber merchant, d. 1834, and wife Elizabeth Rakestraw ; granddaughter of John and *Ann Knowles* Lancaster. The last named John son of Thomas and *Sarah Buckman* Lancaster, grandson of Thomas and *Phebe Wardell* Lancaster ; great grandson of John and Sarah Lancaster, who came from Ireland to Pa., in 1711. Sarah Buckman was granddaughter of William Buckman who came in ship "Welcome" with William Penn, in 1682.

[2] Dau. of Joseph (b. in Philadelphia, 1772, d. in Philadelphia, 8 mo. 18, 1840), and *Elizabeth Clark* Townsend, m. 5 mo. 21, 1800 ; gr. dau. of John Townsend (cabinet-maker, b. in Philadelphia), and w. Hannah Cox, b. 1751, dau. of Joseph (d. 1814) and *Catharine Watson* Cox. John Townsend was son of Charles and

Abington quarterly meeting a number of years, until her removal to Philadelphia, in 1860.[1] Daniel Longstreth d. at Warminster, 3 mo. 30, 1846, after nearly three months' illness, borne with patience and resignation. They had seven children:

6–178. Joseph T., b. 8 mo. 7, 1833, d. 7 mo. 12, 1834.
6–179. Sarah, b. 9 mo. 4, 1834, res. Fallston, Harford Co., Md. HOLLINGSWORTH.
6–180. Moses Robinson, b. 2 mo. 8, 1836, d. 4 mo. 2, 1838.
6–181. Samuel Townsend, b. 8 mo. 2, 1837, res. Philadelphia; *m.*
6–182. Edward, b. 6 mo. 22, 1839, res. Philadelphia; *m.*
6–183. Anna R., b. 4 mo. 2, 1841, res. Philadelphia; *unm.*
6–184 David T., b. 10 mo. 26, 1844, d. 7 mo. 9, 1845.

5-46. *Anna Thomas Longstreth*, b. 10 mo. 8, 1802 (dau. of Joseph, 4-10), m. 1st, at Horsham meeting, Montgomery Co., Pa., 10 mo. 13, 1825, JOHN THOMSON, b. 1795, d. 3 mo. 25, 1826, son of John Thomson, b. 1762, d. 1846. They had one son:

6–185. John Longstreth, b. in Warminster township, Bucks Co., Pa., 6 mo. 7, 1826, res. 1873, Horsham, Pa.; *m.*

Anna T. (5-46) m. 2d, 1 mo. 7, 1836, at Horsham, CHARLES JARRETT RAAB, of Abington, son of John W. and Sarah Raab. They had four children, all born in Warminster:

6–186. Joseph Longstreth, b. 4 mo. 18, 1838, res. Weston, Pa.; *m.*
6–187. Sarah L., m. RUSSELL HOLLENBACK; res. Weston.
6–188. Mary Anna, d. 9 mo. 1, 1840, aged 5 months.
6–189. Mary Anna, d.

5-47. *Susannah Longstreth*, b. 11 mo. 28, 1804, d. 2 mo. 17, 1833,[2] m. at Horsham meeting, Montgomery Co., Pa., 3 mo. 9, 1826, ELLIS CLEAVER, tailor, b. 4 mo. 15, 1801, d. 2

Abigail Townsend; gr. son of John and Elizabeth Townsend, who were of Kent Co., Pa. (now Kent Co, Del.), as early as 1690. Elizabeth Clark, b. 9 mo. 18, 1773, d. in Warminster, 1854, was dau. of Joseph Clark, b. 4 mo. 12, 1745, d. 6 mo. 27, 1833, from Bethnal Green, England, silk weaver (son of Richard and Ann Clark), and w. Elizabeth Wyer, b. 7 mo. 5, 1746, d. 6 mo. 22, 1788, from Spitalfield, England, dau. of Michael and Elizabeth Wyer.

[1] She was interested in the early anti-slavery movement, and assisted Benj. Lundy in the preparation of his *Memoirs of Elizabeth Margaret Chandler*, a poetess deeply interested in the cause of the slave.

[2] The date of her death as communicated was 2 mo. 7, 1835, which *probably* was date of her husband's death. This from Daniel Longstreth's letter-book, under date of 3 mo. 17, 1833: "My dear sister Susan L. Cleaver lingered for nearly a year and closed in peace on the 17th of 2d mo. She was fully resigned to the change, which she hailed with joy. Her eldest son died 22d of the previous month."

mo. 7, 1835, son of Ellis and Elizabeth Cleaver, of Gwynedd, Montgomery Co. Two children, both born in Montgomery Co:

6–190. [CLEAVER.] Joseph L., b. 5 mo. 25, 1827, d. 1 mo. 22, 1833.
6–191. Ellwood, b. 2 mo. 7, 1830, res. 1873, Iowa; *m.*

5–48. *Mary Thomas Longstreth*, b. 12 mo. 20, 1807, m. at Abington, Pa., 10 mo. 13, 1831, DEMAS COMLY WORRELL, of Byberry, b. in Frankford, 11 mo. 9, 1803, d. in Philadelphia, 5 mo. 29, 1870, son of Demas and Alice Worrell. He was a "recommended minister" among Friends. His widow res. 1873, at Byberry. They had five children:

6–192. Joseph Longstreth, b. at Byberry, Pa., 6 mo. 24, 1833, res. Mt. Holly, N. J.; *m.*
6–193. Sarah Longstreth, b. at Johnsville, Pa., 10 mo. 15, 1835, res. Mt. Holly, N. J. DUBELL.
6–194. Demas Comly, b. at Upper Dublin, Pa., 1 mo. 31, 1839, res. Philadelphia; *unm.*
6–195. Martha L., b. in Warminster township, Bucks Co., 5 mo. 27, 1842, d. at Mt. Holly, N. J., 12 mo. 17, 1872. CARSON.
6–196. Daniel Longstreth, b. at Hatboro, Pa., 4 mo. 29, 1845, d. 6 mo. 24, 1869; *unm.*

5–51. *Jane Coates*, b. 12 mo. 27, 1793, d. 1864 or '5 (dau. of John H., 4-29), m. 1827, B. FRANKLIN HEACOCK. They lived in Delaware Co., Ind., and had four children:

6–197. Thomas E., res. Harrison Co., Iowa; *m.*
6–198. Hannah, res. Harrison Co., Iowa. BECK.
6–199. Amelia. JACOBS.
6–200. Ellen.

5–54. AQUILA COATES, b. 10 mo. 30, 1799, m. *Rachel Pidgeon.* They had seven children:

6–201. Isaac.
6–202. John, b. 1826, d. 1852.
6–203. Benjamin.
6–204. William.
6–205. Cyrus.
6–206. Sarah.
6–207. Mary.

5–55. JOHN LONGSTRETH, b. 11 mo. 7, 1810, m. May 7, 1835, *Catharine Kline.* They res. at Trappe, Montgomery Co., Pa. Eight children:

6–208. James, b. Aug. 1, 1836, d. March 28, 1837
6–209. Henry, b. Jan. 6, 1838, d. Aug. 25, 1871; *m.*

6–210. [LONGSTRETH.] Rebecca L., b. Feb. 14, 1840. RHOADES.
6–211. Anna, b. Oct. 6, 1841, d. Jan. 10, 1863.
6–212. Morris, b. Nov. 8, 1843.
6–213. Samuel, b. Dec. 29, 1845.
6–214. Isaac, b. April 20, 1848, res. Philadelphia.
6–215. Horace, b. Jan. 21, 1853, d. Nov. 25, 1854.

5-60. *Mary Longstreth*, b. in Chester Co., Pa., 1810 (dau. of Moses, 4-33), m. SAMUEL D. RHOADES, who was b. 1808, and d. 1859. They had eleven children:

6–216. Moses, b. 1833, d. 1858.
6–217. Charles Preston, b. 1834, d. 1836.
6–218. William Franklin, b. 1836; *m.*
6–219. Samuel Preston, b. 1839; *m.*
6–220. John, b. 1841, d. 1841.
6–221. Joseph, b. 1842.
6–222. Isaac, b. 1844, d. 1873.
6–223. Robert Jones, b. 1846.
6–224. Rebecca, b. 1849. WALKER.
6–225. George Morris, b. 1851, d. 1853.
6–226. Hannah Mary, b. 1853.

5-61. *Hannah Minshall John*, b. 1808 (daughter of Samuel P., 4-34), m. ROBERT JONES, b. 1796, d. 1868. She res. at Phenixville, Pa. They had five children:

6–227. Samuel Preston, b. 1832, res. 1873, W. Philadelphia, Pa.; *m.*
6–228. Sarah Longstreth, b. 1834.
6–229. Thomas, b. 1836, d. 1841.
6–230. Henrietta Deville, b. 1838. BROWN.
6–231. Mary Jane, b. 1842.

5-62. DAVID MATHER, b. at Neave Hall, near Germantown, Pa., 1 mo. 11, 1810, m. 1st, in Ohio, 2 mo. 1, 1838, *Luranna Stedham*, d. at Little Miami, O., 10 mo. 21, 1852 (buried at Turtle Creek meeting ground). They had seven children:

6–232. Susannah, b. at Little Miami, 11 mo. 9, 1838, drowned in Little Miami river, 9 mo. 14, 1842.
6–233. Charles, b. at Little Miami Mills, O., 10 mo. 11, 1840, d. 10 mo. 21, 1845.
6–234. Susannah, b. at Little Miami, 9 mo. 29, 1842.
6–235. Elizabeth, b. at Little Miami, 11 mo. 20, 1844, res. Lebanon, O. KELSEY.
6–236. Henry, b. at Little Miami, 1 mo. 4, 1847.
6–237. Samuel, b. 1 mo. 22, 1850.
6–238. David Lindley, b. Miami river, 6 mo. 20, 1852.

David Mather m. 2d, *Laura* ——; res. Little Miami, O.

5-63. *Martha Longstreth Mather*, b. at Greenway farm, Kingsessing, Pa., 1 mo. 3, 1812, d. near Waynesville, O., 3 mo. 28, 1849, m. 5 mo. 1, 1834, SAMUEL JONES. They had seven children:

6–239. Susan L., b. at Waynesville, 2 mo. 12, 1835, d. 2 mo. 24, 1848.
6–240. Elizabeth, b. at Waynesville, 2 mo. 24, 1837.
6–241. David, b. at Waynesville, 4 mo. 9, 1839, d. 4 mo. 6, 1840.
6–242. Mary Price, b. at Little Miami, 12 mo. 21, 1840.
6–243. Richard Mather, b. at Little Miami, 4 mo. 29, 1843, d. 6 mo. 29, 1844.
6–244. Anna, b. 9 mo. 7, 1845.
6–245. Sarah M., b. 2 mo. 24, 1848.

5-64. *Ann Mather*, b. at Greenway farm, Kingsessing, Pa., 2 mo. 8, 1814, m. at Turtle Creek meeting, Little Miami, O., 9 mo. 26, 1844, DAVID SAUNDERS HORNEY, son of Solomon Horney , of Richmond, Ind. Three chn., all b. at Richmond:

6–246. Elizabeth, b. 7 mo. 13, 1846.
6–247. Martha, b. 6 mo. 6, 1849.
6–248. Susannah, b. 9 mo. 19, 1851.

5-65. CHARLES L. MATHER, b. at Little Miami Mills, Warren Co., O., 1 mo. 30, 1816, m. 5 mo. 1, 1845, *Naomi P. McIlvain*, dau. of Hugh and Hannah McIlvain. They res. at Mt. Holly, N. J. Five children:

6–249. Elizabeth L., b. at Kingsessing, Pa., 2 mo. 14, 1846, d. 9 mo. 29, 1863.
6–250. Lydia McIlvain, b. at Kingsessing, 5 mo. 18, 1848.
6–251. Charles Sidney, b. at Kingsessing, 4 mo. 19, 1850.
6–252. Susannah L., b. at Kingsessing, 7 mo. 5, 1853.
6–253. Naomi.

5-66. PHINEAS ROSS MATHER, b. at Little Miami Mills, O., 2 mo. 11, 1818, m. 8 mo. 29, 1844, *Ruth Ann Pool*, of Richmond, Ind. They res. at Richmond. Four children:

6–254. John, b. at Little Miami Mills, O., 3 mo. 5, 1846.
6–255. Elizabeth C., b. at Little Miami Mills, 11 mo. 27, 1847, m. Dr. WILLIAM HAUGHTON.
6–256. Susannah, b. at Richmond, Ind, 7 mo. 9, 1849.
6–257. Mary Anna.

5-67. *Susannah L. Mather*, b. at Little Miami Mills, O., 5 mo. 29, 1820, m. at Turtle Creek meeting, O., 9 mo. 26, 1844,

JONATHAN HORNEY, who d. at Richmond, Ind., 4 mo. 25, 1849, bro. of David S. Horney (5-64). They had two children:

6–258. Richard Mather, b. near Richmond, Ind., 6 mo. 26, 1845, d. 12 mo. 23, 1845.
6–259. Charles L., b. Richmond, 1 mo. 6, 1847.

5-69. *Susan Bacon Mather*, b. at Little Miami Mills, O., 3 mo. 5, 1825, m. at Turtle Creek meeting, O., 11 mo. 4, 1852, JOEL HORNEY, of Richmond, Ind. Two children:

6–260. Albert, b. 10 mo. 28, 1853.
6–261. Helen, b. 12 mo. 24, 1854.

5-70. JOSEPH MATHER, b. at Little Miami Mills, O., 11 mo. 29, 1827, m. at Springfield meeting, O., 1 mo., 1852, *Louisa Hadley*, who d. 11 mo. 7, 1859. They had one child:

6–262. Albert Hadley, b. Little Miami, 11 mo. 30, 1852.

5-74. *Elizabeth Longstreth*, b. in Burlington, N. J., 6 mo. 28, 1817, m. at Twelfth street meeting, Philadelphia, 9 mo. 25, 1839, ISRAEL MORRIS, son of Israel and Sarah Morris. Four children, all born in Philadelphia:

6–263. Theodore Hollingsworth, b. 10 mo. 10, 1840; *m.*
6–264. Frederick Wister, b. 3 mo. 8, 1842; *m.*
6–265. Anna M., b. 11 mo. 20, 1844; *unm.*
6–266. William H., b. 3 mo. 25, 1846; *m.*

5-75. WILLIAM COLLINS LONGSTRETH, formerly farmer, now, 1873, vice president of the Providence Life Ins. and Trust Co., of Phila., b. in Philadelphia, 3 mo. 12, 1821, m. at Mt. Holly, N. J., 11 mo. 16, 1848, *Abby Ann Taylor*, dau. of Benjamin and Sarah Taylor. They res. 1873, at Darby, Pa. Nine children:

6–267. Benjamin Taylor, b. at Locust Grove, Delaware Co., Pa., 8 mo. 18, 1849; *unm.*
6–268. Thomas Kimber, b. at Locust Grove, 8 mo. 30, 1851; *unm.*
6–269. William Morris, b. at Locust Grove, 7 mo. 7, 1853; *unm.*
6–270. Henry, b. at Locust Grove, 6 mo. 27, 1855.
6–271. Charles Albert, b. 5 mo. 20, 1857.
6–272. Mary, b. 6 mo. 20, 1859.
6–273. Sarah M., b. 2 mo. 4, 1865.
6–274. Anna, b. 2 mo. 9, 1868, d. 9 mo. 10, 1868.
6–275. Edward Rhoades, b. 1 mo. 31, 1871.

5-76. JOHN OGDEN LONGSTRETH, b. in Phila., 8 mo. 31, 1812, d. at Clifton, Delaware Co., Pa., 2 mo. 29, 1871, m. at Kingsessing, Pa., 8 mo. 16, 1845, *Elizabeth H. Gessner*, b. 3 mo. 2, 1823, d. 4 mo. 21, 1862, dau. of George and Rebecca Gessner. Two children :

6–276. Charles Gessner, b. 7 mo. 17, 1846, d. 1 mo. 16, 1860.
6–277. Anna R., b. at Upper Darby, Pa., 9 mo. 30, 1854 ; *unm.*

5-78. *Sarah Anna Longstreth*, b. in Philadelphia, 10 mo. 10, 1823, m. by the mayor in Philadelphia, 3 mo. 23, 1853, T. HARRISON LEVIS, b. 9 mo. 18, 1822, son of Garrett and Catharine Levis. They res. near Clifton, Delaware Co., Pa. Three children:

6–278. Frank, b. 2 mo. 20, 1854, d. 5 mo. 21, 1865.
6–279. Garrett H., b. 12 mo. 11, 1855.
6–280. Hannah B., b. 9 mo. 23, 1859.

5-79. JOHN HUNT LONGSTRETH, b. in Philadelphia, 1 mo. 2, 1820, m. 9 mo. 9, 1844, *Emily Burling*, dau. of Benjamin and Catharine Burling. They res. in Philadelphia, and have four children, all born in that city :

6–281. Kate, m. HENRY SAYER.
6–282. Benjamin Burling.
6–283. Anna Richardson.
6–284. Rachel B.

5-80. *Rachel Hunt Longstreth*, b. in Philadelphia, 11 mo. 24, 1822, m. 8 mo. 9, 1841, GEORGE BOLDIN. They res. in Philadelphia, and have four children, all b. in that city :

6–285. Anna Longstreth, res. Philadelphia. EVERLY.
6–286. Charles Longstreth ; *unm.*
6–287. Emily Longstreth ; *unm.*
6–288. George Longstreth ; *unm.*

5-81. CHARLES LONGSTRETH, b. in Philadelphia, 10 mo. 19, 1825, m. in Baltimore, Md., Dec. 6, 1853, *Virginia Dunham*, dau. of Thornton C. Dunham, of Baltimore. They res. 1873, in Brooklyn, N. Y., and have had five children, all b. in Philadelphia :

6–289. Thornton Dunham, b. Dec. 17, 1854.
6–290. Helen, b. May 24, 1856, d. Aug., 1856.
6–291. Louise, *twin sister of Helen*, d. Aug., 1856.
6–292. Charles Howard, b. March 27, 1858.
6–293. Lilian Verda, b. Dec. 11, 1862.

5-83. Joshua Longstreth, farmer, b. 4 mo. 4, 1818, m. *Hannah Rudolph*, dau. of Thomas Rudolph. They res. on the old Morris estate, at Fox Chase, near Philadelphia. Nine children:

6–294. Hannah, b. 10 mo. 26, 1849, d. 9 mo. 23, 1853.
6–295. Joshua, b. 7 mo. 19, 1851.
6–296. Abram, b. 5 mo. 30, 1853.
6–297. Josiah, b. 5 mo. 1, 1856.
6–298. Sarah, b. 6 mo. 29, 1858, d. 11 mo. 20, 1867.
6–299. Susannah, b. 7 mo. 29, 1860.
6–300. William Penn, b. 10 mo. 23, 1864.
6–301. Mary, b. 3 mo. 10, 1868.
6–302. Elizabeth, b. 7 mo. 5, 1872.

5-84. Joseph Longstreth, farmer, b. 2 mo. 24, 1820, d. at Fox Chase, near Philadelphia, 8 mo. 20, 1873, m. *Sarah Rudolph*, sister of Hannah, wife of Joshua Longstreth (5-83). Six children:

6–303. William Rudolph, b. 2 mo. 22, 1854.
6–304. Joseph, b. 12 mo. 30, 1855.
6–305. Thomas Rudolph, b. 8 mo. 29, 1858.
6–306. Morris, b. 3 mo. 8, 1863.
6–307. Ellwood, b. 5 mo. 5, 1865.
6–308. Sallie Elizabeth, b. 6 mo. 2, 1872.

5-85. *Lydia Longstreth*, b. 1801 (dau. of Joshua, 4–52), m. 9 mo. 30, 1819, Richard Price, a prominent merchant of Philadelphia, b. 7 mo. 21, 1754, d. ———, son of Joseph and Ann Price. They lived in Phila., where she d. 7 mo. 5, 1843, leaving six children:

6–309. Joshua Longstreth, b. 8 mo. 24, 1820, d. 3 mo. 10, 1867; *m.*
6–310. Eliz. Williams, b. 8 mo. 8, 1822, d. Parrish.
6–311. Anna C., b. 8 mo. 2, 1824. Richardson.
6–312. Sarah Longstreth, b. 9 mo. 4, 1829. Parrish.
6–313. Margaret Simmons, b. 8 mo. 15, 1832. Price.
6–314. Rebecca Thompson, b. 9 mo. 16, 1854. Hunt.

5-87. *Susan Morris Longstreth* (dau. of Joshua, 4-52), m. 9 mo. 3, 1824, Francis Thompson, son of Richard and Hannah Thompson, of Rawdon, Yorkshire, England. They had four children:

6–315. Joshua Longstreth, b. 1 mo. 17, 1826, m. *Hetty Ann Newlin*, dau. of Nathaniel and Rachel Newlin, res. New York city; no issue.

6–316. [THOMPSON.] Sarah L., b. 12 mo. 16, 1828.
6–317. Hannah, b. 10 mo. 7, 1831.
6–318. Francis, b. 10 mo. 4, 1837, in England, where the parents reside in 1873.

5–92. MORRIS LONGSTRETH HALLOWELL, formerly merchant, now, 1873, banker, b. 8 mo. 14, 1809, m. 1 mo. 5, 1831, *Hannah Smith Penrose*, b. 2 mo. 2, 1812, dau. of William and *Annah Norwood* Penrose. They res. Phila. Eight children:

6–319. Anna, b. 11 mo. 1, 1831; *unm.*
6–320. William Penrose, b. 5 mo. 18, 1833, res. Cheltenham, Pa.; *m.*
6–321. Richard Price, b. 12 mo. 16, 1835, res. Boston, Mass.; *m.*
6–322. Edward Needles, b. 11 mo. 3, 1836, d. July 26, 1871; *m.*
6–323. Norwood Penrose, b. 4 mo. 13, 1839, res. Boston; *m.*
6–324. Emily, b. 1 mo. 18, 1842; *unm.*
6–325. Susan Morris, b. 6 mo. 17, 1845; *unm.*
6–326. Morris Longstreth, b. 1 mo. 13, 1847, d. 2 mo. 13, 1847.

5–94. *Susan Morris Hallowell*, b. 3 mo. 18, 1813, d. 9 mo. 25, 1846, m. 2 mo. 2, 1831, WILLIAM WALTON, merchant, b. 3 mo. 27, 1808, d. 3 mo. 23, 1844, son of James and Achsah Walton. They had six children:

6–327. Charles M., b. 11 mo. 15, 1831, d. 1871; *unm.*
6–328. Lydia, b. 8 mo. 7, 1833, d.
6–329. Francis, b. 7 mo. 14, 1835, d.
6–330. James M., b. 7 mo. 12, 1838, m. *Mary F. Collins*, dau. of Isaac and Rebecca Collins, res. New York city.
6–331. Annie H., b. 1 mo. 24, 1841, d.
6–332. Elizabeth, b. 4 mo. 24, 1843, d.

5–97. JOSHUA LONGSTRETH HALLOWELL, merchant, b. 3 mo. 31, 1819, d. 7 mo. 25, 1873, m. 1st, 10 mo. 28, 1841, *Teresa J. Kimber*, b. 9 mo. 19, 1819, d. 2 mo. 7, 1851, dau. of Emmor and Lydia Kimber. They had three children:

6–333. Charles, b. 8 mo. 13, 1842; *m.*
6–334. Edward D., b. 5 mo. 8, 1845, d. 3 mo. 6, 1865.
6–335. Walter, b. 9 mo. 30, 1850, d. 4 mo. 21, 1851.

He m. 2d, 2 mo. 21, 1855, *Sarah C. Fraley*, b. 7 mo. 8, 1833, dau. of Frederick and Jane Fraley. She res. in Philadelphia. They had four children:

6–336. Catharine, b. 4 mo. 12, 1855.
6–337. Jennie Fraley, b. 2 mo. 9, 1857.
6–338. Frederick Fraley, b. 3 mo. 8, 1859.
6–339. Cresson, b. 4 mo. 19, 1861, d. 7 mo. 23, 1868.

5-101. *Sarah Redwood Longstreth*, b. 10 mo. 10, 1812, m. 6 mo. 24, 1835, Dr. ISAAC PARRISH, a prominent physician of Philadelphia, b. 3 mo. 19, 1811, d. in Phila., 7 mo. 31, 1852.[1] They had eight chn:

6-340. Hetty L., b. 6 mo. 20, 1836, res. Phila.; *unm.*
6-341. Joshua Longstreth, b. 9 mo. 20, 1838, d. 7 mo. 31, 1852.
6-342. James Cresson, b. 8 mo. 10, 1840, res. Phila.; *unm.*
6-343. Helen, b. 10 mo. 9, 1842, m. DR. LEE, res. New York city.
6-344. Sarah R., b. 10 mo. 28, 1844, res. Phila.; *unm.*
6-345. Isaac, b. 11 mo. 6, 1846, d. ——.
6-346. Samuel L., b. 2 mo. 28, 1849, res. Phila.; *unm.*
6-347. Miers Fisher, b. 11 mo. 26, 1852, res. Phila.; *unm.*

5-103. MIERS FISHER LONGSTRETH, formerly hardware merchant, in Phila., now physician, b. 3 mo. 15, 1819, m. 1 mo. 25, 1843, *Mary F. Clapp*, dau. of Enoch and Mary Clapp. They res. in Darby, Pa. Seven children:

6-348. Helen, b. 1844, d. 5 mo. 16, 1845.
6-349. Rebecca C., b. 7 mo. 10, 1845.
6-350. Mary C., b. 6 mo. 19, 1848.
6-351. Sarah R., b. 7 mo. 23, 1850, d. 1 mo. 3, 1854.
6-352. Samuel F., b. 2 mo. 12, 1852, d. 7 mo. 11, 1863.
6-353. Elizabeth T., b. 5 mo. 29, 1855.
6-354. Anna, b. 5 mo. 10, 1857, d. 7 mo. 12, 1858.

5-105. *Lydia W. Longstreth*, b. 3 mo. 29, 1823, m. JOHN WILMER, res. Phila. Two children:

6-355. Craig.
6-356. John.

5-110. THOMAS BEDFORD LONGSTRETH, b., 12 mo. 10, 1797, d. 9 mo. 6, 1867, was by trade a bricklayer, and carried on business as a contracting builder, from which, however, he had retired many years before his death. He was esteemed a consistent member of the Society of Friends, and accomplished much good in an unostentatious way, being of a kind and charitable disposition, and especially helpful to young beginners in business, as an adviser, etc. He m. 12 mo. 29, 1825, *Lydia Noble*,[2] b.

---

[1] Son of Dr. Joseph Parrish and w. Susannah Cox, dau. of John Cox, of Burilngton, N. J., an esteemed minister among Friends. Dr. J. P., b. in Phila., 9 mo. 2, 1779, d. 3 mo. 18, 1840, was a distinguished physician and surgeon, noted also as a scholar and philanthropist. — See *Lippincott's Biog. Dict.*; Janney's *History of Friends*, IV, 126-129.

[2] Dau. of Samuel and *Elizabeth Tomkins* Noble, m. 1792; gr. dau. of Samuel and *Lydia Cooper* Noble, m. 1746; gt. gr. dau. of Joseph and Mary Noble of Philadelphia, m. abt. 1720. Lydia Cooper was dau. of Isaac and *Hannah Coate* Cooper; gr.

10 mo. 20, 1803, res. 1873, Germantown. Nine children, all b. in Philadelphia :

6–357. [LONGSTRETH.] Elizabeth Tomkins, b. 11 mo. 21, 1826, res. Philadelphia. TAYLOR.

6–358. Sarah Noble, b. 1 mo. 11, 1829, m. CHARLES COOKE LONGSTRETH (son of Morris, 5–112).

6–359. Margaret Middleton, b. 8 mo. 6, 1831, d. 1 mo. 31, 1835.

6–360. Lydia Noble, b. 1 mo. 11, 1834. ROWLETT.

6–361. Rachel Orum, b. 12 mo. 13, 1835 ; *m.* JOHN LANCASTER LONGSTRETH (6-176 of this record).

6–362. Margaret Middleton, b. 2 mo. 11, 1838. SHOENBERGER.

6–363. Mary Bringhurst, b. 7 mo. 15, 1840, m .4 mo., 1873, BENJAMIN STARR, res. in Richmond, Ind.

6–364. Samuel Noble, b. 2 mo. 25, 1843, res. Philadelphia ; *unm.*

6–365. Morris (M. D., Pa. Hospital, grad. Harvard College, and Med. Dept. Univ. of Pa.), b. 2 mo. 24, 1846, m. *Mary Hastings*, of Cambridge, Mass.

5–112. MORRIS LONGSTRETH, b. 12 mo. 3, 1800, merchant and farmer, was a prominent and influential man, a democrat in politics, and at his death a member of the Catholic church. As a farmer, he was celebrated for the fine stock upon his farm. In 1836 he was a candidate for Congress in Philadelphia, but was defeated, and in March, 1841, he was appointed by Governor Porter, an associate judge of the courts of the county of Montgomery, which office he resigned Jan. 1, 1848, having been, in the October preceding, elected to the office of canal commissioner. On the resignation of Gov. Shunk, in 1848, Mr. Longstreth was nominated by the democrats as candidate for governor of Pa., and was defeated by a few votes only. He d. in Whitemarsh township, Montgomery Co., Pa., April 26, 1855. His death was much lamented, and marked respect was paid to him throughout the state.[1] He m. 3 mo. 22, 1827, *Mary Elizabeth Cooke*, dau. of John and Elizabeth Cooke. Four chn :

6–366. George C., b. 8 mo. 6, 1833, d.

6–367. John Cooke, b. 9 mo. 26, 1836, res. Philadelphia ; *m.*

6–368. Charles Cooke, d. 1869 ; *m.*

6–369. Lydia C., m. JESSE R. TOMLINSON.

5–113. WILLIAM WILSON LONGSTRETH, formerly hardware merchant, and afterwards president of Beaver Meadow R. R. and of the Lehigh Valley R. R., of which he is now

---

dau. of Joseph and *Lydia Riggs* Cooper ; gt. gr. dau. of William Cooper, who settled at Pine Point, now Camden, N. J., abt. 1679.

[1] See Henry Simpson's *Lives of Eminent Philadelphians, now Deceased*, 1859, p. 668.

(1873) a director, was b. 11 mo. 14, 1802, m. 1st, 10 mo., 1827, *Mary Bringhurst*, b. 1806, d. in Philadelphia, 9 mo. 26, 1835, dau. of James Bringhurst. Four chn., all b. in Philadelphia:

6–370. [LONGSTRETH.] Joseph, b. 1828, d. 12 mo. 24, 1850, m. 11 mo. 29, 1849, *Sarah Atlee*, dau. of Edwin and Margaret Atlee. No issue.
6–371. James, b. 1830, d. infant.
6–372. William, b. 4 mo. 1832; *m.*
6–373. Margaret, b. 1 mo. 12, 1835. SMITH.

William Wilson Longstreth m. 2d, 2 mo., 1841, Margaret Atlee, widow of Dr. Edwin P. Atlee (maiden name *Bullock*), b. 1800, d. 4 mo. 3, 1861. He was a clerk of Abington meeting, and she a recommended minister, and a most estimable woman. They had one child:

6–374. Hannah, res. Germantown, Pa. CARPENTER.

Mr. Longstreth m. 3d, 12 mo. 22, 1863, Ann W. Mather, daughter of John and Catharine Moore.

5–116. GEORGE LONGSTRETH, b. near Prall's Mills, Hunterdon Co., N. J., July 20, 1802, m. 1st, near Lebanon, O., June 16, 1831, *Elizabeth Sellers*. She d. Aug. 20, 1852. They had eleven children:

6–375. Henrietta, b. May 14, 1832, d. Aug. 28, 1833.
6–376. Amanda Jane, b. Sept. 20, 1833, res. Columbus, O.; *unm.*
6–377. Isabella, b. Jan. 2, 1835, d. Sept. 24, 1863, m. JAMES O'NEAL.
6–378. John S., b. Sept. 12, 1836, d. Nov. 7, 1840.
6–379. Morris O., b. July 28, 1838, d. Sept. 21, 1852.
6–380. Cornelia, b. June 19, 1840, m. June 11, 1872, JOHN W. LITTLE.
6–381. Mary, b. Feb. 28, 1842, m. Nov. 15, 1862. PHILO FINCH.
6–382. Thaddeus, b. Dec. 15, 1843, m. in Lebanon, O., May 24, 1870, *Julia M. Bown*; one child.
6–383. Addison, b. Feb. 13, 1846, m. in Franklin, O., Sept. 15, 1872, *Rachel Barkalow.*
6–384. Margaret A., b. Oct. 18, 1848, d. Nov. 13, 1849.
6–385. Clemence, b. July 5, 1851.

George Longstreth m. 2d, Nov. 7, 1854, *Elizabeth Little.* They lived many years at Lebanon, but removed to Columbus, Ohio, in Oct., 1872, where they now reside (1873).

5–137. JOHN SIDNEY KEEN m. 6 mo. 10, 1841, *Hannah McIlvain*, b. 12 mo. 22, 1817, dau. of Hugh and Hannah McIlvain. Five children:

6–386. [KEEN.] Mary H., b. 8 mo. 8, 1842. SELLERS.
6–387. Joseph S., b. 1 mo. 24, 1845; *m.*
6–388. Emily, b. 6 mo. 16, 1849, d. 12 mo. 4, 1849.
6–389. Lucinda A., b. 2 mo. 28, 1851. WOOLMAN.
6–390. Caroline Sellers, b. 4 mo. 20, 1859.

5–142. JACOB LONGSTRETH PAXSON, b. 6 mo. 17, 1812, m. at Green street meeting, Philadelphia, 12 mo. 31, 1835, *Emma Shoemaker.* They res. in Philadelphia. Four children:

6–391. Lydia, b. 5 mo. 21, 1837, m. at Norristown, Pa., 4 mo. 7, 1858, GEORGE F. NORTH, son of Abel North.
6–392. Isaiah, b. 9 mo. 25, 1838; *m.*
6–393. Charles, b. 9 mo. 25, 1840.
6–394. Mary S., b. 1 mo. 17, 1843. HOFFMAN.

5–143. *Sarah Paxson,* b. 9 mo. 13, 1815, m. in Philadelphia, by Friends' ceremony, 6 mo. 28, 1837, ISAAC T. BEDFORD. Res. Philadelphia. Four children:

6–395. William P., b. 7 mo. 22, 1838, d. 9 mo. 25, 1866; *m.*
6–396. Henry L., b. 6 mo. 9, 1846, d. 12 mo. 15, 1846.
6–397. Thomas L., b. 11 mo. 10, 1850, d. 4 mo, 21, 1870.
6–398. Morris L., b. 7 mo. 10, 1855, d. 10 mo. 18, 1855.

5–144. WILLIAM LONGSTRETH PAXSON, b. 8 mo. 5, 1817, m. in Norristown, Pa., 11 mo. 25, 1841, *Sarah A. Kirk.* They res. in Bucks Co., Pa. Four children:

6–399. Ellwood T., b. 3 mo. 3, 1843; *m.*
6–400. Susannah K., b. 3 mo. 26, 1845.
6–401. Elizabeth L., b. 3 mo. 30, 1848.
6–402. William L., b. 1 mo. 30, 1852.

5–146. *Mary Paxson,* b. 8 mo. 18, 1821, m. in Cherry St. meeting, Philadelphia, 2 mo. 2, 1842, DAVID FURMAN. They res. in Philadelphia. Six children:

6–403. Elizabeth P., b. 12 mo. 10, 1842. SMITH.
6–404. Isaiah P., b. 4 mo. 12, 1844, d. same day.
6–405. Margaret L., b. 11 mo. 22, 1846. TRUMP.
6–406. Sidney Keen, b. 6 mo. 24, 1850.
6–407. Mary P., b. 7 mo. 21, 1855.
6–408. David K., b. 12 mo. 17, 1859.

5–152. *Margaret Orum* (dau. of Davis, 4-67), m. JOSEPH HOOPES, res. Philadelphia. One dau.

6–409. Clara, res. Philadelphia. ATLEE.

5-165. James W. Longstreth, b. in Ohio, 8 mo. 23, 1819, m. *Jane McCray*. Res. Ohio. Three children:

6-410. Sarah.
6-411. Samantha.
6-412. Eva.

5-167. Benjamin Longstreth, b. in Ohio, 9 mo. 11, 1822, m. 1st, *Elizabeth Lee*. Res. Ohio. One child:

6-413. William.

B. L. m. 2d, *Elizabeth* ———. Several children.

5-168. *Elizabeth Longstreth*, b. in Ohio, 9 mo. 11, 1824, m. Richard McCray. Res. Ohio. Two children:

6-414. George.
6-415. Daniel.

5-169. *Almira Longstreth*, b. in Ohio, 10 mo. 13, 1826, m. Joel Crane. Res. Ohio. Two children:

6-416. Samantha.
6-417. Orilla.

5-172. *Ann Longstreth*, b. in Ohio, 12 mo. 4, 1833, m. 1856, Alexander Harlan. Res. Ohio. Two children:

6-418. Isabella.
6-419. Mary Amelia.

5-173. *Mary Longstreth*, b. in Ohio, 1 mo. 11, 1836, m. 1858, Harvey Lambert. Res. Ohio. Four children:

6-420. Alice.
6-421. Anna.
6-422. Irena, d.
6-423. Sarah.

5-177. *Amelia Longstreth*, b. in Ohio, 9 mo. 21, 1846, m. 1868, J. Newton Lambert. Res. Ohio. One child:

6-424. Clifford Longstreth, b. 7 mo. 4, 1869.

5-194. *Sarah Jones* (daughter of John, 4-74), m. Reuben Webb, d.——. She res. 1873, in Philadelphia. They had five children:

6-425. John, d.
6-426. Elizabeth, res. Philadelphia.
6-427. James, d.
6-428. Sarah Ann, d.
6-429. Harriet, res. Philadelphia.

5-201. Benjamin Smedley, b. in Chester Co., Pa., 1 mo. 21, 1803, m. 11 mo. 15, 1827, *Jane Williams*, daughter of Ellis and Jane Williams. They res. 1873, at Willistown, Chester Co. Two children:

6–430. Rebecca, b. 8 mo. 17, 1829, d.——, m. 3 mo. 25, 1858, Bennett Cox, son of Thomas and Mary Cox. No issue.
6–431. Chalkley, b. 12 mo. 20, 1831, res. Chester Co., Pa.; *m.*

5-202. Enos Smedley, b. in Chester Co., Pa., 5 mo. 18, 1805, m. 4 mo. 10, 1834, *Hannah H. Sharpless*, daughter of Isaac and Ann Sharpless. They res. in Easttown township, Chester Co. Three children:

6–432. Amy Mary, b. 2 mo. 11, 1836, m. 11 mo. 4, 1858, James S. Jones, son of Isaac Jones; res. Germantown, Pa.
6–433. Philena S., b. 4 mo. 13, 1840.
6–434. Rebecca, b. 4 mo. 19, 1846.

5-203. Jeffrey Smedley, b. 6 mo. 21, 1807, d. 9 mo. 15, 1854, m. 10 mo. 28, 1828, *Susannah Llewellyn*, b. 9 mo. 30, 1836, d. 7 mo. 23, 1850. They lived in Chester Co., Pa. Ten children:

6–435. Mary Ann, b. 9 mo. 5, 1829, d. 2 mo. 7, 1859, m. 10 mo. 7, 1851, Henry L. Brandt, of Columbia, Pa.
6–436. John, b. 2 mo. 19, 1831, d. 4 mo. 2, 1831.
6–437. Esther R., b. 2 mo. 23, 1832.
6–438. Ann L., b. 9 mo. 3, 1833.
6–439. David L., b. 8 mo. 9, 1835, m. 10 mo. 28, 1858, *Ann Conway*, res. Baltimore, Md.
6–440. Jonathan H., b. 9 mo. 30, 1837, m. 11 mo. 13, 1856, *Christiana Goldsborough*; res. Baltimore.
6–441. Theodore M., b. 12 mo. 28, 1839.
6–442. Stephen L., b. 7 mo. 1, 1841.
6–443. Jeffrey, b. 6 mo. 7, 1844.
6–444. Lorenzo, b. 5 mo. 20, 1846, d. 8 mo. 22, 1846.

5-204. Nathan Smedley, b. 2 mo. 23, 1810, m. 1st, 7 mo. 3, 1834, *Mary F. Matlock*, b. 1815, d. 5 mo. 26, 1845, dau. of Joseph and Dorothy Matlock. Three children:

6–445. Alban M., b. 4 mo. 13, 1835, m. 1 mo. 2, 1865, *Anna Lukens*.
6–446. Nathan G., b. 2 mo. 13, 1840.
6–447. Sarah Elizabeth, b. 3 mo. 30, 1845, d. 6 mo. 9, 1845.

He m. 2d, 12 mo. 23, 1846, *Sarah Matlock*, sister to first wife. They res. at Kenderton, near Philadelphia. Two chn.:

6–448. Mary Dorothea, b. 10 mo. 9, 1847.
6–449. Anna Frances, b. 10 mo. 21, 185–.

5-205. EZRA SMEDLEY, b. 4 mo. 21, 1812, m. 11 mo. 3, 1842, *Esther Ann Pratt*, dau. of Joseph and Mary Pratt. They res. at West Bradford, Chester Co., Pa. Four children:

6-450. Mary P., b. 8 mo. 3, 1843.
6-451. Elma H., b. 10 mo. 5, 1845, d. 8 mo. 19, 1847.
6-452. Joseph Franklin, b, 10 mo. 8, 1850.
6-453. Ella Esther Ann, b. 1 mo. 5, 1859.

5-206. JOHN SMEDLEY, b. 1 mo. 11, 1814, d. 3 mo. 20, 1855, m. 4 mo. 5, 1838, *Sarah Lewis*, dau. of Elijah and Esther Lewis. They lived in Chester Co., Pa., and had eight children:

6-454. Alfred, b. 3 mo. 29, 1839.
6-455. Elijah L., b. 1 mo. 10, 1841.
6-456. Thomas D., b. 9 mo. 15, 1842.
6-457. Anna L., b. 9 mo. 3, 1844.
6-458. Esther M., b. 10 mo. 4, 1846.
6-459. Mary S., b. 2 mo. 2, 1849.
6-460. John H., b. 5 mo. 21, 1851.
6-461. Jane, b. 11 mo. 25, 1853.

5-208. *Amy C. Smedley*, b. 3 mo. 21, 1818, m. 12 mo. 1, 1841, HENRY L. PRATT, b. 9 mo. 24, 1813, son of Joseph and Mary Pratt. They res. at West Bradford, Chester Co., Pa. Six children:

6-462. Rebecca S., b. 11 mo. 18, 1842.
6-463. Henrietta, b. 6 mo. 6, 1844, d. 1 mo. 21, 1858.
6-464. William L., b. 3 mo. 5, 1846, d. 7 mo. 15, 1851.
6-465. Davis Henry, b. 12 mo. 30, 1848, d. 7 mo. 20, 1851.
6-466. Mary Elma, b. 5 mo. 11, 1852.
6-467. Anna E., b. 11 mo. 31, 1857.

5-209. ELWOOD SMEDLEY, b. 11 mo. 11, 1820, m. *Mary Ann Massey*, dau. of Joseph and Rosanna Massey. They res. at Willistown, Chester Co., Pa. Four children:

6-468. Thomas D., b. 11 mo. 7, 1847.
6-469. Lewis Vail, b. 7 mo. 22, 1850.
6-470. Lydia, b. 7 mo. 5, 1853.
6-471. Wilbur E., b. 12 mo. 22, 1859.

5-212. *Lydia Hood* (dau. of Jonathan, 4-91), m. 12 mo. 9, 1829, ISAAC PRESTON THOMAS, b. 11 mo. 11, 1804, son of Reece and Elizabeth Thomas. Res. Chester Co., Pa. One son:

6-472. Isaac Preston, b 4 mo. 29, 1830.

5-216. Smedley Lamborn, b. in Chester Co., Pa., 1 mo. 6, 1807, m. 1829, *Margaret Bolton.* They lived in Martic township, Lancaster Co., Pa., where he d. 9 mo. 26, 1851. They had eleven children :

6-473. George S., b. 9 mo. 22, 1831, res. 1873, Martic township, Lancaster Co., Pa.; *m.*
6-474. Aquila B., b. 2 mo. 22, 1833, res. 1873, Drumore, Lancaster Co. ; *m.*
6-475. Emeline, b. 9 mo. 29, 1834, res. 1873, Drumore. Shoemaker.
6-476. Elwood, b. 8 mo. 4, 1836, res. Drumore ; *m.*
6-477. William L., b. 1 mo. 6, 1839, res. Steel Works, Dauphin Co., Pa. ; *m.*
6-478. Mary Elizabeth, b. 6 mo. 22, 1840, res. Drumore. Hambleton.
6-479. Sarah Ellen, b. 11 mo. 8, 1842, res. Drumore; *unm.*
6-480. Priscilla, b. 1 mo. 19, 1845, d. 2 mo. 27, 1847.
6-481. Alice A., b. 4 mo. 14, 1847, res. Drumore. Shoemaker.
6-482. Lucinda, b. 8 mo. 22, 1850, res. Drumore. Teunis.
6-483. Lydia S., b. 10 mo. 31, 1851, m. 1871, Amos G. Smith, res. Drumore.

5-218. John Lamborn, b. Chester Co., Pa., 10 mo. 9, 1810, m. 1st, *Harriet Cummings*, and had :

6-484. Mary Elizabeth, b. 3 mo. 11, 1857.

He m. 2d, 9 mo. 20, 1860, *Helen Michel.* They res. 1873, in Henry Co., Iowa. One child :

6-485. Emma Jane, b. 5 mo. 18, 1864.

5-220. Jacob Lamborn, b. in Chester Co., Pa., b. 4 mo. 11, 1822, m. 12 mo. 2, 1849, *Polly Hollister.* They lived in Mahaska Co., Iowa, where he d. 5 mo. 8, 1858. Seven children :

6-486. Orange Jay, b. 11 mo. 29, 1848.
6-487. Harriet M., b. 3 mo. 6, 1850.
6-488. Lemon O., b. 8 mo. 16, 1851.
6-489. John J., b. 3 mo. 21, 1853.
6-490. Thomas L., b. 6 mo. 13, 1854.
6-491. Emma L., b. 1 mo. 19, 1856.
6-492. Melinda, b. 8 mo. 9, 1858.

5-221. Lindley Lamborn, b. in Chester Co., Pa., 12 mo. 28, 1824, m. 1850, *Margaretta Jane Remminghuff.* They lived in Iowa, but removed, 1873, to California. Seven children :

6–493. [Lamborn]. Angeline, b. 4 mo. 6, 1854.
6–494. Arabella, b. 10 mo. 11, 1857.
6–495. John E., b. 10 mo. 13, 1859.
6–496. George M., b. 6 mo. 9, 1862.
6–497. Mary E., b. 6 mo. 20, 1864.
6–498. William L., b. 5 mo. 5, 1866.
6–499. Franklin S., b. 10 mo. 8, 1868.

5-222. *Martha Lamborn*, b. 12 mo. 28, 1828, m. Orange Jay Hollister. They res. at Oskaloosa, Mahaska Co., Iowa. Three children:

6–500. Ella.
6–501. Elwood.
6–502. Alice.

6-15. *Elizabeth R. Fussell*, b. 7 mo. 31, 1810 (dau. of William, 5-10), m. 1833, Neal Hardy, farmer. They res. at Pendleton, Madison Co., Ind.. and have had eight children:

7–1. Mary Jane, b. 6 mo. 19, 1834, m. John Lewis Fussell, (6-31 of this record).
7–2. William F., b. 2 mo. 7, 1836, res. at Fall Creek, Ind.; *m.*
7–3. Solomon F., b. 10 mo. 19, 1839, res. at Markleville, Ind.; *m.*
7–4. Thomas Morris, b. 2 mo. 4, 18—, farmer, m. *Margaret Wilson*, dau. of William and Margaret Wilson, of Va., res. at Fall Creek, Ind; no issue.
7–5. Eliza Ann, b. 10 mo. 13, ——, res. at Fall Creek, Ind. Knickerbocker; Boston.
7–6. Emily, b. 12 mo. 5, ——, res. at Markleville, Ind. Lewis.
7–7. Sarah, res. Fall Creek, Ind. Kinnard.
7–8. Margaret, d. aged 8 years.

6-16. Dr. Edwin Fussell, b. 6 mo. 14, 1813, m. 1 mo. 20, 1838, *Rebecca Lewis* (6–11 of this record), b. 6 mo. 10, 1820. They res. 1873, at Media, Delaware Co., Pa. Seven children:

7–9. Emma Jane, b. in Pendleton, Ind., June 7, 1839, d. in Philadelphia, July 30, 1862, from illness induced by devotion to sick and wounded soldiers in hospitals at Philadelphia.
7–10. Charles Lewis, b. in Philadelphia, Oct. 25, 1840; artist, res. Phila.
7–11. Linnaeus, b. at Pendleton, Ind., Sept. 2, 1842; surgeon U. S. Army.
7–12. Anna Esther, b. near Kimberton, Chester Co., Pa., May 1, 1847.
7–13. Mary Townsend, b. in Phila., Oct. 23, 1849, m. Henry M. Fussell, (son of Henry B., 6–23).
7–14. Horace, b. in Phila., 1 mo. 3, 1853, d. 1853.
7–15. Edwin Neal, b. in Phila., March 17, 1863.

6-18. JOSEPH FUSSELL, b. 8 mo. 7, 1820, m. 9 mo. 20, 1849, *Sarah Emily Roberts*, dau. of Lewis and Harriet B. Roberts. They res. 1873, in Philadelphia. The compiler is indebted to Mr. Fussell for extended records of the families of his name. Five children:

7–16. Florence, b. 7 mo. 4, 1850, d. 7 mo. 6, 1850.
7–17. William Lewis, b. 9 mo. 14, 1851.
7–18. Marion, b. 8 mo. 18, 1854, d. 2 mo. 8, 1866.
7–19. Emily Roberts, b. 4 mo. 25, 1859.
7–20. Harriet Jane, b. .12 mo. 21, 1865.

6-19. MILTON FUSSELL, b. 6 mo. 11, 1823, m. *Tamar J. Haldeman*, dau. of Henry and Tamar Haldeman. They res. at Radnor, Del. Co., Pa. Four children:

7–21. William Henry, b. 1 mo. 18, 1850.
7–22. Annie W., b. 7 mo. 16, 1852.
7–23. Milton Howard, b. 11 mo. 24, 1855.
7–24. Elizabeth H., b. 6 mo. 22, 1864.

6-20. *Rebecca Fussell Jacobs*, b. 4 mo. 30, 1815, m. JOSHUA P. BROWN, d. ———, son of William and Ann Brown. They had six children:

7–25. Anna Mary, d. 1863, aged 23.
7–26. Sarah Emma, b. 8 mo. 19, 1839. ANDERSON.
7–27. Emily Ann, b. 4 mo. 14, 1841.
7–28. Valeria S., b. 4 mo. 4, 1843, m. FRANK LISTER, of Wilmington, Del.
7–29. William Thomas, b. 5 mo. 10, 1845, m. ——— *Richardson*.
7–30. Joshua, b. 8 mo. 13, 1849, d.

Rebecca F. (6–20) m. 2d, DANIEL TYSON, of Linn Co., Iowa, and d. 4 mo. 9, 1871.

6-21. CHARLES PENNELL JACOBS, b. 10 mo. 6, 1816, m. 1841, *Esther Ann Fussell*, b. 2 mo. 22, 1818 (6–17 of this record). They res. at Pendleton, Madison Co., Ind., and have had two children:

7–31. Elmira, b. 9 mo. 17, 1843, d. 1865.
7–32. Cassius Clay, b. 9 mo. 1, 1845, m. 4 mo., 1873, *Sarah Vernon*, dau. of Edward and Hannah Vernon.

6-23. HENRY BARTHOLOMEW FUSSELL, b. in Pa., 3 mo. 15, 1815, m. 5 mo. 5, 1842, *Maria Douglass*, of Philadelphia. They res. 1873, at Media, Delaware Co., Pa. Seven children:

7–33. [FUSSELL.] Elwood G., d. aged 13.
7–34. Henry M., b. 9 mo. 14, 1845, res. near Media ; *m.*
7–35. Anna Catharine, b. 1 mo. 20, 1848, d.
7–36. Maria Louisa, d.
7–37. Adaline W., d.
7–38. Helen.
7–39. Theodora.

6–24. *Rebecca Bond Fussell*, b. in Md., 7 mo. 14, 1818, m. at Fall Creek meeting, Indiana, 11 mo. 22, 1849, CHARLES J. ROGERS, of Fall Creek, where they now res. (1873). Four children:

7–40. Charles Henry, b. 1 mo. 21, 1853, d. 4 mo. 15, 1854.
7–41. Solomon Fussell, b. 5 mo. 12, 1855, d. same day.
7–42. Charles Fussell, *twin bro. of Solomon F.*, d. 5 mo. 24, 1855.
7–43. Sarah D., b. 11 mo. 19, 1859.

6–26. SAMUEL FUSSELL, b. in Md., 7 mo. 31, 1819, m. 1st, in Philadelphia, *Mary Matilda Lee*, who d. in Indiana. They had four children:

7–44. Elizabeth L., m. JOHN BUNKER, res. Kansas, one child.
7–45. Joseph B., m. *Mary Crosley*, res. Iowa, three children.
7–46. Mary Matilda, d.
7–47. Laura, d.

He m. 2d, 1861, at Fall Creek meeting, Ind., *Annie E. Rogers*, daughter of Charles J. Rogers (6-24). They res. at Pendleton, Madison Co., Ind. Four children:

7–48. Charles Rogers, b. 10 mo. 15, 1862.
7–49. Mary Matilda, b. 2 mo. 9, 1865.
7–50. Sarah Rebecca, b. 7 mo. 21, 1868.
7–51. Solomon H., b. 1 mo. 31, 1873.

6–27. *Mary Jane Fussell*, b. in Md., 11 mo. 21, 1821, d. 8 mo. 20, 1854, m. at Indianapolis, Ind., 10 mo. 15, 1848, RICHARD HODGES. One child:

7–52. Edward W., b. 10 mo. 17, 1849.

6–30. *Elizabeth Moore Fussell*, b. in Md., 11 mo. 21, 1821, m. 12 mo. 2, 1853, JOSEPH B. LEWIS, of Fall Creek, Ind., son of John and Rebecca Lewis. They res. at Huntsville, Ind.: Four children:

7–53. Mary Jane, b. 12 mo. 19, 1855, d. same day.
7–54. John Joseph, b. 2 mo. 10, 1857.
7–55. Maud Mary, b. 10 mo. 1, 1859.
7–56. Evangeline Elizabeth, b. 4 mo. 27, 1865.

6-31. JOHN LEWIS FUSSELL, b. in Pa., 8 mo. 8, 1830, m. *Mary Jane Hardy* (7-1 of this record). They res. at Pendleton, Madison Co., Ind. Three children:

7-57. Ella Jane, b. 11 mo. 28, 1856.
7-58. Ernest, b. 9 mo. 13, 1861, d. 8 mo. 11, 1862.
7-59. Mary Elizabeth, b. 2 mo. 5, 1865.

6-33. *Priscilla Moore Fussell*, b. in Montgomery Co., Pa., 9 mo. 25, 1818, m. at Fall Creek meeting, Ind., 2 mo. 23, 1837, LEWIS W. THOMAS, b. in Chester Co., Pa., son of Jonathan and Ann Thomas. Eleven children:

7-60. John Lewis, b. 11 mo. 20, 1837, res. Fall Creek, Ind.; *m.*
7-61. Martha Moore, b. 2 mo. 3, 1839, res. Fall Creek, Ind. MORRIS.
7-62. Anna Lewis, b. 11 mo. 4, 1842, res. Pendleton, Ind. ROGERS.
7-63. Lucretia Mott, b. 7 mo. 6, 1844.
7-64. Jonathan, b. 1 mo. 25, 1846.
7-65. Esther Lewis, b. 7 mo. 4, 1848.
7-66. Mary Swain, b. 1 mo. 8, 1850, m. Jan. 16, 1873, WILLIAM KINNARD, farmer, son of John and Elizabeth Kinnard, formerly of Chester Co., Pa.
7-67. Solomon Fussell, b. 9 mo. 28, 1852.
7-68. Rebecca Lewis, b. 7 mo. 30, 1854, d.
7-69. Priscilla Moore, b. 11 mo. 6, 1856, d.
7-70. Alice Grace, b. 8 mo. 23, 1857.

6-37. *Milcah Martha Fussell*, b. in Montgomery Co., Pa., 10 mo. 16, 1825, m. at Fall Creek, Ind., July 7, 1847, SIMEON M. LEWIS, son of Abner and Susannah Lewis, of Radnor township, Delaware Co., Pa. They res. 1873, at Huntsville, Ind.[1] Three children:

7-71. Walter Hibbard, b. Dec. 25, 1849, graduated Pennsylvania Medical College (University of Pa.), 1873, res. Huntsville, Ind.; *unm.*
7-72. Horace Fussell, b. Feb. 25, 1852, res. Huntsville, merchant; *unm.*
7-73. Susan M., d.

6-43. *Lydia J. Fussell*, b. near Fall Creek, Ind., 8 mo. 9, 1838, m. JOHN L. SHARP, and d. in Indiana, Feb. 28, 1872, leaving one child:

7-74. Walter Lewis, b. 4 mo. 25, 1870.

6-47. JACOB FUSSELL, b. in Baltimore, Md., 2 mo. 24, 1819, m. 1st, at Philadelphia, Pa., 2 mo. 24, 1848, *Anna*

[1] The compiler is indebted to Mrs. Lewis for much assistance in the compilation of these records.

E. Taylor, daughter of Mordecai Taylor. They had five children:

7–75. [Fussell.] Edwin M., b. in Baltimore, 1 mo. 16, 1849, d. 7 mo. 19, 1851.
7–76. Richard Thomas, b. 4 mo. 6, 1850.
7–77. Mordecai T., b. 6 mo. 11, 1852, res. N. Y. city; *unm.*
7–78. Francis, b. 5 mo. 12, 1856.
7–79. Jacob, b. 5 mo. 21, 1858, d. 6 mo. 22, 1862.

Mr. Fussell m. 2d, *Caroline Kraft*. They res. in New York city. Three children:

7–80. William, b. in Washington, D. C., 10 mo. 7, 1862.
7–81. Carrie, b. 5 mo. 14, 1868.
7–82. Mary K., b. 8 mo. 3, 1870.

6–48. *Ruthanna Fussell*, b. in Baltimore, Md., 1 mo. 20, 1820 (daughter of Jacob, 5-14), m. 12 mo. 2, 1847, Joseph Gorsuch, son of Charles Gorsuch. They res. in Baltimore. Seven children:

7–83. John R., b. 9 mo. 30, 1848.
7–84. Mary Frances, b. 10 mo. 31, 1849. Bowen.
7–85. Clarissa F., b. 10 mo. 25, 1851.
7–86. Ruthanna, b. 5 mo. 21, 1853.
7–87. Ethel Jane, b. 9 mo. 23, 1855.
7–88. Joseph Franklin, b. 6 mo. 7, 1858, d. 3 mo. 3, 1859.
7–89. Alice Eliza, b. 7 mo. 24, 1860.

6–49. *Hannah E. Fussell* (daughter of Jacob, 5-14), m. 1845, Thomas C. Hopkins, son of John Hopkins. Res. Baltimore. Nine children:

7–90. John, b. 6 mo. 25, 1846.
7–91. Thomas, b. 5 mo. 19, 1847, d. 1 mo. 11, 1854.
7–92. Clarissa, b. 9 mo. 7, 1849, d. 1 mo. 15, 1854.
7–93. William, b. 8 mo. 12, 1851, d. 1 mo. 17, 1854.
7–94. George, b. 11 mo. 29, 1853.
7–95. Jesse, b. 6 mo. 27, 1856.
7–96. Edward, b. 2 mo. 27, 1858.
7–97. Rebecca, b. 5 mo. 7, 1860.
7–98. Howard, b. 5 mo. 3, 1865.

6–50. Bartholomew Howard Fussell, b. in Baltimore, Md., 12 mo. 16, 1823, d. in Baltimore, 12 mo. 23, 1860, m. in Philadelphia, Pa., 9 mo. 13, 1847, *Rebecca H. Taylor*, of Philadelphia, b. 10 mo. 18, 1818. They had seven children:

7–99. William Howard, b. 7 mo. 28, 1848; *m.*
7–100. Mary Philena, b. 5 mo. 1, 1850. Dunnington.

7–101. [FUSSELL.] Clarissa, b. 1852, d. 1852.
7–102. Elizabeth, *twin with Clarissa*, d. 1852.
7–103. Josephine, b. 11 mo. 22, 1853.
7–104. John T., b. 7 mo. 22, 1855.
7–105. Albert Fisher, b. 1 mo. 14, 1860.

6–51. JOSEPH B. FUSSELL, b. 1 mo. 15, 1826, d. —— (son of Jacob, 5-14), m. 1855, *Louisa Gordon*, dau. of Archibald Gordon. Six children:

7–106. Louis Norris, b. 7 mo. 5, 1856, d. 1 mo. 23, 1870.
7–107. Edgar, b. 12 mo. 6, 1857, d. 9 mo. 10, 1858.
7–108. Clarissa, b. 2 mo. 3, 1858.
7–109. Mary Zalinda, b. 4 mo. 22, 1859.
7–110. Joseph Edgar, b. 12 mo. 8, 1861.
7–111. Mary Philena, b. 8 mo. 7, 1862.

6–52. *Philena Fussell*, b. in Baltimore, Md., 6 mo. 13, 1828 (dau. of Jacob, 5-14), m. 1854, SIMON MARTINETT, surveyor. Res. Baltimore, Md. Nine children, all b. in Baltimore:

7–112. Jefferson, b. 5 mo. 15, 1855.
7–113. Simon Jones, b. 8 mo. 23, 1856.
7–114. Jacob Fussell, b. 7 mo. 10, 1858.
7–115. William Howard, b. 8 mo. 8, 1861.
7–116. Clarissa F., b. 1 mo. 28, 1863.
7–117. Charles Joseph, b. 7 mo. 19, 1866, d. 1 mo. 18, 1869.
7–118. John Gilbert, b. 2 mo. 19, 1868, d. 6 mo. 30, 1869.
7–119. George Oscar, b. 8 mo. 24, 1870, d. 4 mo. 15, 1871.
7–120. Philena, b. 1872, d. 1872.

6–53. *Clarissa Fussell*, b. in Baltimore, Md., 2 mo. 22, 1832 (dau. of Jacob, 5-14), m. 12 mo. 11, 1866, CHARLES W. DAVIS, son of John Davis. Res. Baltimore. Three children, all born in that city:

7–121. Charles J., b. 12 mo. 23, 1867.
7–122. Francis Howard, b. 6 mo. 20, 1870.
7–123. Mary Clarissa, b. 4 mo. 1, 1873.

6–55. JOSHUA LONGSTRETH FUSSELL, farmer b. at Kennett, Pa., 6 mo. 9, 1827, m. 5 mo. 10, 1855, *Jane Busby*, dau. of Isaac and *Sarah Willets* Busby, formerly of Va. He was Capt. of the 34th Regt. Ind. Vols. during the civil war, and engineer of the mining operations at the siege of Vicksburg, under General Grant. They res. in Fall Creek township, Madison Co., Ind. Four children:

7–124. [FUSSELL.] Morris Fremont, b. 6 mo. 4, 1856.
7–125. Jesse Leroy, b. 7 mo. 24, 1858.
7–126. Joshua Longstreth, b. 1 mo. 25, 1862.
7–127. Edward.

6–56. DR. MORRIS FUSSELL, b. in Kennett, Pa., 6 mo. 27, 1829, m. 3 mo. 6, 1860, Sarah Ann Middleton b. in Philadelphia, 10 mo. 29, 1825, wid. of R. Hamilton Middleton, and dau. of John and *Mary Phillips* Tustin. They res. near Chester Springs, Chester Co., Pa. Two children:

7–128. Susan Morris, b. 4 mo. 5, 1861.
7–129. Helen Augusta, b. 2 mo. 9, 1863.

6–63. *Mary Longstreth* (dau. of Mahlon, 5-17), d. a wid. at Bordentown, N. J., 4 mo. 6, 1833, aged 30, m. Dr. ——— HAMILTON. They had one dau.:

7–130. Caroline, b. 1825. WALLACE.

6–64. JOHN LONGSTRETH SPENCER (son of Samuel, 5-18), m. *Sarah* ——, d. 9 mo. 12, 1822. Children:

7–131. Helen.
7–132. Amanda.
7–133. Ann, bur. 1 mo. 22, 1821, aged 18.
7–134. Mary, d. 7 mo. 6, 1829.

6–65. MAHLON SPENCER (son of Samuel, 5-18), m. —— *Little*. Children:

7–135. Samuel.
7–136. Lewis.
7–137. Newton.
7–138. Flora.
7–139. Mary Ann, m. ——.
7–140. Martha.

6–66. LEWIS SPENCER (son of Samuel, 5-18), m. ——. Res. Old Bridge, Middlesex Co., N. J. Children:

7–141. Alexander.
7–142. Samuel.
7–143. John, m. ——.

6–77. MAHLON MILNER (son of John M., 5-21), m. *Elizabeth Willson*. Two children:

7–144. Lizzie.
7–145. George.

6-83. *Julia Hayward*, b. 1 mo. 24, 1827, m. JAMES M. SLACK. Res. Bristol, Pa. Three children:

7-146. Louis Hayward, b. Dec. 31, 1867, d. in Philadelphia, July 18, 1868.
7-147. Julia Hayward, b. March 10, 1869.
7-148. Lewis James, b. May 17, 1872, d. at Bristol, Dec. 10, 1873.

6-84. HENRY E. HAYWARD, b. 7 mo. 14, 1834, m. July 7, 1870, *Bessie Irvine*, daughter of William C. and Anna P. Irvine. They res. in Philadelphia. One son:

7-149. Henry E., b. April 29, 1872.

6-87. JOHN MICHENER, b. 1 mo. 14, 1820, m. 1840, *Mary Blackledge*, b. 11 mo. 24, 1813. Three children:

7-150. Rachel A.
7-151. Charles R.
7-152. Daniel.

6-88. *Martha Michener*, b. 9 mo. 16, 1805, m. 1826, TITUS KEESE, b. 10 mo. 18, 1805, d. 1 mo. 29, 1849. Four children:

7-153. Lydia, b. 4 mo. 6, 1828.
7-154. Mary S., b. 10 mo. 4, 1831.
7-155. Sarah Ann, b. 12 mo. 9, 1832.
7-156. Gulielma, b. 9 mo. 21, 1837.

6-89. *Elizabeth Michener*, b. 10 mo. 30, 1807, d. 8 mo. 15, 1844, m. 1831, DAVID MEEKER, b. 1807. Six children:

7-157. Mordecai, b. 10 mo. 30, 1832.
7-158. Dorothy, b. 1834, d. 1835.
7-159. Nathan, b. 1836.
7-160. Robert, b. 2 mo. 14, 1838.
7-161. Benjamin J., b. 11 mo., 1842.
7-162. Daniel C., b. 5 mo., 1843.

6-90. *Sarah Michener*, m. 1828, EBENEZER C. DANIELS, b. 1800, d. 3 mo., 1846. Children:

7-163. Anna, b. 12 mo., 1828.
7-164. John C., b. 11 mo., 1835.
7-165. Lindley, b. 1 mo., 1842, d. 8 mo., 1842.

6-91. JOHN MICHENER, b. 4 mo. 18, 1812, m. 1837, *Susan P. Pearson*, b. 8 mo. 4, 1817. Seven children:

7-166. William P., b. 3 mo. 18, 1838.
7-167. Charles, b. 7 mo. 26, 1839.

7–168. [MICHENER.] Enoch, b. 3 mo. 8, 1841.
7–169. Esther E., b. 12 mo. 3, 1842.
7–170. Rebecca Ann, b. 7 mo. 16, 1844.
7–171. Henry P., b. 9 mo. 3, 1846.
7–172. Martha, b. 4 mo. 27, 1849.

6–92. *Grace Michener*, b. 11 mo. 28, 1813, m. 1837, DANIEL BENEDICT, b. 3 mo. 29, 1807. Six children:

7–173. Deborah, b. 12 mo. 7, 1837.
7–174. Phebe A., b. 8 mo. 12, 1839.
7–175. Dorcas, b. 1 mo. 15, 1841.
7–176. Lavinia, b. 7 mo. 31, 1843.
7–177. Mordecai M., b. 6 mo. 26, 1845.
7–178. William, b. 10 mo. 8, 1847, d. 3 mo. 17, 1850.

6–94. *Ruth Michener*, b. 10 mo. 10, 1818, m. 1840, TRUMAN CAMP, b. 6 mo. 23, 1807. Five children:

7–179. Joseph, b. 4 mo. 15, 1840.
7–180. Sarah A., b. 3 mo. 15, 1843.
7–181. Emily, b. 8 mo. 16, 1845.
7–182. Celestia, b. 1 mo. 23, 1848.
7–183. Eliza D., b. 10 mo. 2, 1849.

6–95. *Jane Michener*, b. 7 mo. 9, 1820, m. 1842, JOSEPH MILLS, b. 12 mo. 28, 1819. Three children:

7–184. Francis, b. 1843.
7–185. Zantha A., b. 1848.
7–186. Ermina R., b. 1848.

6–96. DANIEL MICHENER, b. 3 mo. 18, 1822, d. 8 mo. 26, 1846, m. 1840, *Mary Mills*, b. 8 mo. 9, 1812. Three chn.:

7–187. Virgil A., b. 1841.
7–188. Samantha, b. 10 mo., 1842.
7–189. Angelina, b. 1844.

6–102. JOHN J. MICHENER, b. 3 mo. 10, 1812, m. 1836, *Mary Ann Brown*, b. 11 mo. 21, 1815. Seven children:

7–190. Alonzo, b. 4 mo. 19, 1837.
7–191. Mary Ann, b. 2 mo. 24, 1839, d. young.
7–192. Caroline, b. 10 mo. 6, 1841, d. young.
9–193. Ezra, b. 9 mo. 17, 1843, d. young.
7–194. Elma, b. 9 mo. 1, 1845.
7–195. Susanna, b. 1 mo. 17, 1848, d. young.
7–196. Daniel B., b. 7 mo. 8, 1849.

6-103. *Lydia Michener*, b. 1 mo. 18, 1814, m. 1845, KERSEY GRAVE, b. 11 mo. 21, 1813. Several children, two of whom were :

7-197. Benjamin, b. 3 mo. 1, 1847.
7-198. Sarah E., b. 7 mo. 19, 1849.

6-104. HENRY MICHENER, b. 2 mo. 12, 1816, m. 1840, *Lydia W. Warner*, b. 9 mo. 10, 1819. Seven children, of whom were :

7-199. Woodrow.
7-200. Elizabeth W.
7-201. Benjamin, b. 5 mo. 23, 1846, d. 8 mo. 19, 1846.
7-202. Elma Ann.

6-105. DAVID MICHENER, b. 3 mo. 15, 1818, m. 1842, *Lucetta Smith*, b. 11 mo. 27, 1823. Eight children :

7-203. Edwin R., b. 3 mo. 9, 1844.
7-204. Abigail, b. 9 mo. 30, 1846.
7-205. Amanda, b. 5 mo. 2, 1848.
7-205*b*. Earl S., b. 9 mo. 13, 1849.
7-206. William.
7-207. Avis.
7-208. Benjamin D.
7-209. Lester.

6-106. ISAAC MICHENER, b. 7 mo. 10, 1820, m. 1842, *Martha P. Gause*, b. 3 mo. 5, 1821. Children :

7-210. Casron, b. 11 mo. 30, 1844, d. 7 mo. 15, 1845.
7-211. Mary Ann, b. 6 mo. 12, 1847.
7-212. Edwin.
7-213. Samuel.
7-214. Richard.

6-107. EDWIN MICHENER, b. 10 mo. 12, 1822, d. 1850, m. 1844, *Eliza Smith*, b. 11 mo. 11, 1825. Children :

7-215. Mary F.
7-216. Samuel C.

6-108. *Martha Michener*, b. 3 mo. 14, 1825, m. 1844, WILLIAM N. TAYLOR, who d. 2 mo. 6, 1845. One child :

7-217. Mary Elma, b. 10 mo. 17, 1845.

She m. 2d, 1847, ALLAN WILLIAMS. Children :

7-218. Laura, b. 1848.
7-219. Lydia.

7–220. [Williams.] D. Hubert.
7–221. Edwin J.
7–222. Bell.
7–223. Benjamin S.
7–224. William A.
7–225. S. Anne.

6–110. *Ann M. Hobson*, b. 11 mo. 8, 1808, d. 11 mo. 4, 1840, m. Matthew Watson, b. 3 mo. 8, 1804. Seven chn.:
7–226. Grace, b. 4 mo. 30, 1826, d. 5 mo. 30, 1833.
7–227. Ann Jane, b. 12 mo. 26, 1827, d. 10 mo. 30, 1830.
7–228. John, b. 12 mo 30, 1829.
7–229. Phebe, b. 6 mo. 27, 1832.
7–230. Ann Jane, b. 1 mo. 12, 1835.
7–231. Esther H., b. 10 mo. 30, 1836.
7–232. Deborah, b. 4 mo. 24, 1839.

6–111. John Hobson, b. 6 mo. 4, 1811, m. *Christiana Graham.* Four children:
7–233 Keziah A., d. 9 mo., 1845.
7–234. Francis A.
7–235. James A.
7–236. Adaline M.

6–114. *Rebecca Hobson*, b. 3 mo. 21, 1820, d. 1 mo. 29, 1849, m. John Scott, b. 7 mo. 27, 1817. Three children:
7–237. Francis H., b. 8 mo. 25, 1842.
7–238. John F., b. 12 mo. 20, 1844.
7–239. James W., b. 6 mo. 1, 1847.

6–115. Joseph Michener m. 1842, *Olive Allen.* Two children:
7–240. Mitchell W., b. 2 mo. 9, 1843.
7–241. John F., b. 3 mo. 17, 1845.

6–116. John Michener m. 1847, *Elizabeth Beaty.* Two children:
7–242. Mary Ann, b. 5 mo. 30, 1848.
7–243. John B., b. 6 mo. 29, 1849.

6–117. *Ann Michener* m. Robert Jackson. One son:
7–244. James, b. 1848.

6–118. James Michener m. 1844, *Eliza Simmerman.* Two children:
7–245. William Henry, b. 2 mo. 7, 1846.
7–246. Joseph W., b. 7 mo. 8, 1858.

6-125. John M. Martin, b. 2 mo. 1, 1811, m. 1830, ———. Six children:

7-247. Andrew.
7-248. Susannah.
7-249. George.
7-250. Maria.
7-251. Margaret.
7-252. Sarah J.

6-126. Paul A. Martin, b. 2 mo. 1, 1813, m. 1832, *Mary Welsh*, b. 1813. Five children:

7-253. Isaac, b. 4 mo. 14, 1833, d. 8 mo. 3, 1833.
7-254. Elizabeth, b. 9 mo. 10, 1835, d. 9 mo. 15, 1836.
7-255. Eliza J., b. 12 mo. 21, 1836.
7-256. Sarah A., b. 5 mo. 23, 1840.
7-257. Laura E., b. 10 mo. 19, 1846.

6-127. *Elizabeth A. Martin*, b. 1 mo. 23, 1815, m. 1836, Milton A. Stanley. Five children:

7-258. Robert, b. 3 mo. 24, 1837.
7-259. Mary J., b. 10 mo. 24, 1839.
7-260. James, b. 2 mo. 24, 1842.
7-261. Hannah C., b. 10 mo. 22, 1844.
7-262. Samuel O., b. 1 mo. 11, 1847.

6-128. *Hannah Martin*, b. 3 mo. 22, 1817, m. 1836, Samuel Wilkinson. Six children:

7-263. Samuel, b. 12 mo. 29, 1836.
7-264. Sarah J., b. 8 mo. 11, 1838.
7-265. Catharine E., b. 3 mo. 17, 1840.
7-266. Thomas J., b. 4 mo. 29, 1842.
7-267. Daniel J., b. 11 mo. 14, 1845.
7-268. Mary M., b. 5 mo. 25, 1848.

6-130. Byers B. Martin, b. 1 mo. 3, 1822, had three children:

7-269. Francis.
7-270. Eugene.
7-271. Sarah.

6-131. *Mary Martin*, b. 5 mo. 2, 1825, m. 1841, Daniel J. Cramer, b. 5 mo. 4, 1820. Three children:

7-272. Margaret E., b. 6 mo. 8, 1843.
7-273. Benjamin W., b. 3 mo. 26, 1846.
7-274. Sarah C., b. 1 mo. 15, 1848.

6-132. *Susan M. Martin*, b. 3 mo. 4, 1828, m. 1847, PHINEAS POORMAN, b. 7 mo. 25, 1824. One son:

7-275. Henry C., b. 2 mo. 11, 1848.

6-134. *Rebecca Haines*, b. 7 mo. 2, 1813, m. 1831, JESSE STEWART. Eight children:

7-276. James, b. 7 mo. 27, 1832.
7-277. Rachel, b. 9 mo. 11, 1834.
7-278. Susannah, b. 4 mo. 26, 1836.
7-279. Juliann, b, 4 mo. 15, 1838.
7-280. Hannah, b. 3 mo. 10, 1840.
7-281. Isaac, b. 5 mo. 29, 1842.
7-282. Rebecca, b. 6 mo. 27, 1844.
7-283. Alonzo, b. 6 mo. 11, 1846.

6-135. EDWIN HAINES, b. 7 mo. 24, 1815, m. 1837, *Rebecca Hale.* Five children:

7-284. Eliz. C., b. 5 mo. 28, 1840.
7-285. Timothy H., b. 7 mo. 27, 1842.
7-286. Rachel Ann, b. 5 mo. 21, 1844.
7-287. Edwin G., b. 12 mo. 10, 1846.
7-288. Hannah Rebecca, b. 11 mo. 20, 1848.

6-141. *Hannah Clarke*, b. 8 mo. 4, 1820, m. 1837, ROBERT McCAUGHEY. Five children:

7-289. John C., b. 2 mo. 29, 1840, d. 8 mo. 7, 1841.
7-290. Hannah Jane, b. 11 mo. 23, 1841.
7-291. Elizabeth Ann, b. 10 mo. 31, 1843.
7-292. Martha L., b. 8 mo. 29, 1845.
7-293. Mary A., b. 9 mo. 25, 1847.

6-143. *Martha S. Michener*, b. 5 mo. 4, 1827, m. 1843, DANIEL J. BIGGER. Three children:

7-294. J. Camby, b. 4 mo. 13, 1844.
7-295. Harriet L., b. 12 mo. 6, 1846.
7-296. James M., b. 1 mo. 5, 1849.

6-151. ISAAC L. SHOEMAKER, b. 6 mo. 14, 1814, m. 10 mo. 27, 1836, *Jane McLean*, b. 2 mo. 2, 1815, dau. of Moses and Elizabeth McLean. Nine children:

7-297. Anna H., b. 7 mo. 25, 1837, d. 3 mo., 1838.
7-298. Emma, b. 5 mo. 27, 1839, m. CHARLES COTMAN.
7-299. Mary, b. 1 mo. 2, 1842, d. young.
7-300. John, m.——— ; res. Philadelphia.
7-301. William, res. Philadelphia.

7–302. [SHOEMAKER] Martha L., d. young.
7–303. Francis, d. young.
7–304. Anna, d. young.
7–305. Morris L.

6–152. *Jane L. Shoemaker*, b. 10 mo. 23, 1817, m. 4 mo. 13, 1845, ELIJAH THOMAS, son of William and Lydia Thomas. Two children:

7–306. Maria S., b. 3 mo. 3, 1846, m. —— HAWKSHURST; one child.
7–307. John S., b. 9 mo. 25, 1849.

6–154. ISAAC LONGSTRETH, b. 7 mo. 6, 1824, d. 12 mo. 19, 1857, m. 3 mo. 28, 1849, *Hannah Jennett.* Four chn.:

7–308. Anna, b. 6 mo. 23, 1850, m. ELWOOD GILBERT, res. Parkesburg, Pa.
7–309. Emma.
7–310. Charles, d.
7–311. Daniel, d.

6–156. *Martha S. Longstreth*, b. 7 mo. 13, 1830, m. 6 mo. 13, 1865, JAMES DOUGLASS. One son:

7–312. Charles L., b. 1 mo. 12, 1867.

6–159. *Rebecca R. Longstreth*, b. 5 mo. 8, 1838, m. 11 mo. 15, 1866, JAMES M. WATSON. They res. in Philadelphia. Two children:

7–313. Ellen L., b. 8 mo., 1867, d.
7–314. Grace.

6–160. JAMES SHOEMAKER, b. 8 mo. 20, 1822, m. 3 mo. 14, 1849, *Phebe Shoemaker*, b. 7 mo. 10, 1827, dau. of Jonathan and Margaret Shoemaker. Eight children:

7–315. Isabella F., b. 12 mo. 7, 1849.
7–316. Adeline B.
7–317. Jesse, b. 1 mo. 21, 1854, d. 5 mo. 13, 1855.
7–318. Henry.
7–319. Abram Brock.
7–320. Charlotte.
7–321. Emily.
7–322. Mary.

6–162. JOHN LONGSTRETH SHOEMAKER, b. in Upper Dublin township, Montgomery Co., Pa., 10 mo. 7, 1832, m. 12 mo. 24, 1863, *Emily R. Pierce*, dau. of Charles W. and

Elizabeth Pierce. Mr. Shoemaker is a prominent lawyer of Philadelphia, a member of the select council of that city, and counselor and solicitor of the U. S. Centennial Commission.[1] They have had three children:

7–323. Edith, b. 10 mo. 9, 1865, d. 9 mo. 12, 1866.
7–324. Anna Pierce, b. 1 mo. 1, 1867.
7–325. Charles Pierce, b. 2 mo. 22, 1870.

6–169. ALFRED LONGSTRETH, conveyancer, b. 3 mo. 6, 1831, m. 11 mo. 16, 1865, *Louisa C. Shott*, b. 1 mo. 24, 1842, dau. of Augustus H. and Anna Mary Shott. They res. in Philadelphia. Two children:

7–326. Alouise Clifton, b. 8 mo. 15, 1867.
7–327. Edwin Shott, b. 7 mo. 6, 1869, d. 3 mo. 8, 1870.

6–170. *Mary W. Longstreth*, b. 11 mo. 10, 1832, m. LOUIS C. BRASTOW. Res. Williamsport, Pa. Four children:

7–328. Louis Cornett, b. 3 mo, 23, 1860.
7–329. Frank Addison, b. 8 mo. 7, 1865.
7–330. Anna, b. 3 mo. 3, 1867.
7–331. John Longstreth, b. 1872.

6–176. JOHN LANCASTER LONGSTRETH, b. in Warminster township, Bucks Co., Pa., 11 mo. 10, 1827, m. 10 mo. 25, 1870, *Rachel O. Longstreth*, b. in Philadelphia, 12 mo. 13, 1835, dau. of Thomas B. Longstreth (5-110 of this record). They res. in Philadelphia. One child:

7–332. Edward Thomas, b. 9 mo. 20, 1872.

6–179. *Sarah Longstreth*, b. in Warminster township, Bucks Co., Pa., 9 mo. 4, 1834, m. 5 mo. 29, 1856, CHARLES ROBERT HOLLINGSWORTH, b. in Md., 3 mo. 1, 1833, son of Robert and *Elizabeth West* Hollingsworth, of Belair District, Harford Co., Md.[2] They res. at Fallston, Harford Co., and have six children:

7–333. Annie Turner, b. 3 mo. 12, 1857.
7–334. John Longstreth, b. 6 mo. 9, 1858.

---

[1] See *Sketch* and portrait in *The Centennial* for Oct., 1873.

[2] Robert Hollingsworth, above named, was son of Nathaniel and *Abigail Green* Hollingsworth, m. 1783; grandson of Thomas and *Jane Smith* Hollingsworth, m. 1754; great grandson of Thomas and *Judith Lampley* Hollingsworth, m. 1723. Thomas Hollingsworth, last named, was son of Thomas and *Grace Cook* Hollingsworth, m. 1692, who came from England.

7–335. [HOLLINGSWORTH.] William, b. 4 mo. 18, 1861.
7–336. Walter, b. 8 mo. 29, 1863.
7–337. Robert, b. 12 mo. 23, 1865.
7–338. Martha Townsend, b. 2 mo. 27, 1873.

6–181. SAMUEL TOWNSEND LONGSTRETH, b. in Warminster township, Bucks Co., Pa.,[1] 8 mo. 2, 1837, m. 6 mo. 10, 1869, *Jane Lukens Jones*, b. in Philadelphia, 9 mo. 24, 1855, dau. of William and *Elizabeth Lukens* Jones.[2] They res. in Philadelphia, and have had two children, both b. in that city :

7–339. Elizabeth Jones, b. 11 mo. 17, 1870, d. 2 mo. 24, 1872.
7–340. Emily Suplee, b. 12 mo. 9, 1872.

6–182. *Edward Longstreth*, b. in Warminster township, Bucks Co., Pa., 6 mo. 22, 1839, m. 6 mo. 7, 1865, *Annie Wise*, b. in Philadelphia, 11 mo. 7, 1840, dau. of Charles and *Lydia Pusey* Wise.[3] Mr. L. is one of the proprietors of the Baldwin Locomotive Works of Philadelphia. Two children, both b. in Philadelphia :

7–341. Charles, b. 4 mo. 11, 1868.
7–342. Ella Wise, b. 12 mo. 22, 1869.

6–185. JOHN LONGSTRETH THOMSON, b. in Warminster township, Bucks Co., Pa., 6 mo. 7, 1826, m. 4 mo. 10, 1856, *Martha Kenderdine*, b. 4 mo. 24, 1836.[4] They res. 1873, near Horsham, Montgomery Co., Pa. Three children :

---

[1] Samuel T. (6-181) and John L. (6-176) Longstreth, have furnished extended records for this work.

[2] Wm. Jones, above named, was son of Isaac and *Elizabeth Yerkes* Jones; grandson of Jonathan and *Susannah Ashton* Jones, m. 1771; great grandson of Jonathan and Sarah Jones, m. 1741. Jonathan Jones, last named, was son of Jonathan and *Gainor Owen* Jones, m. 1706; grandson of Edward Jones, "chirurgeon," who came from Bala, Wales, with wife Mary, to America, about 1683, and d. 1737. Elizabeth Lukens was daughter of Joseph and *Ann Webster* Lukens; granddaughter of Joseph and *Elizabeth Spencer* Lukens, m. 1751. Joseph Lukens, last named, was son of Peter (b. 1689) and *Gainor Evans* Lukens, m. 1719; grandson of Jan Lucken and wife Mary, who emigrated from Germany, 1683, and were of the first settlers of Germantown, Pa.

[3] Charles Wise, above named, was grandson of John Wise, miller, who emigrated from Germany. Lydia Pusey was dau. of Jonas and *Hannah Pennock* Pusey; gr. dau. of John and Hannah (wid Canby) Pusey; gt. gr. dau. of Joshua and *Mary Lewis* Pusey. Joshua, last named, was son of William Pusey, an early settler in Philadelphia, whose father, John Pusey, was of London, Eng. Hannah Pennock was dau. of John and *Rachel Starr* Pennock; gr. dau. of Joseph and *Hannah Buckingham* Pennock; gt. gr. dau. of William and *Alice Mendenhall* Pennock. William was son of Joseph Pennock, who emigrated from England to Pa.; gr. son of Christopher Pennock, a soldier under Cromwell.

[4] Daughter of Isaacher Kenderdine (b. 9 mo. 29, 1800) and w. Priscilla Shoemaker (b. 7 mo. 27, 1809, d. 12 mo. 6, 1846), m. 11 mo. 17, 1831.

7–343. [THOMSON.] Anna Mary, b. 1 mo. 24, 1857.
7–344. Priscilla Kenderdine, b. 11 mo. 8, 1858.
7–345. Chalkley John, b. 12 mo. 14, 1864.

6–186. JOSEPH LONGSTRETH RAAB, b. in Warminster township, Bucks Co., Pa., 4 mo. 18, 1838, m. in Bucyrus, Ohio, 5 mo. 21, 1861, *Elizabeth Boorom*, b. in Castalia, Erie Co., Ohio, 9 mo. 15, 1840.[1] They res. in Weston, Pa. Two children:

7–346. Charles Boorom, b. in Highland township, Bradford Co., Pa., 4 mo. 10, 1862.
7–347. William Longstreth, b. in Waterford, Ct., 8 mo. 28, 1867.

6–191. ELLWOOD CLEAVER, b. 2 mo. 7, 1830, m. 10 mo. 9, 1851, *Martha Ann Lukens*, b. 2 mo. 27, 1830, dau. of Jonathan and Elizabeth Lukens. Mr. Cleaver removed with his family to Montgomery Co., Iowa, in 1871. Eight children:

7–348. Jonathan, b. 7 mo. 21, 1852.
7–349. Ellis, b. 2 mo. 4, 1854.
7–350. Susan L., b. 10 mo. 19, 1855, d. 2 mo. 19, 1861.
7–351. Joseph A., b. 3 mo. 18, 1858, d. 3 mo. 2, 1861.
7–352. Walter L., b. 2 mo. 3, 1862.
7–353. Elizabeth, b. 4 mo. 5, 1864.
7–354. Ellwood, b. 2 mo. 15, 1867, d. 7 mo. 24, 1867.
7–355. Anna Mary, b. 2 mo. 1, 1869.

6–192. JOSEPH LONGSTRETH WORRELL, b. at Byberry, Pa., 6 mo. 24, 1833, m. 1st, in Philadelphia, 8 mo. 4, 1855, *Ellen T. Brian*, who d. 12 mo. 11, 1863, leaving three chn:

7–356. J. Edward, b. 8 mo. 6, 1856.
7–357. Mary Longstreth, b. 4 mo. 2, 1858, d. 1 mo. 30, 1865.
7–358. William Richard, b. 10 mo. 4, 1861.

Mr. Worrell m. 2d, 1865, *Elizabeth A. Carson*, who d. 1866. One child:

7–359. Laura, b. and d. 1866.

Mr. Worrell m. 3d, 1868, *Rachel McClosky*. They res. 1873, at Mt. Holly, N. J. Three children:

7–360. Mary Ella, b. 1 mo. 9, 1869.
7–361. Samuel Longstreth, b. 3 mo. 25, 1871.
7–362. George W., b. 2 mo., 1873, d. aged 4 days.

---

[1] Daughter of Abram Boorom (b. in New York, 1806, d. in Buffalo, N. Y., 1848), and wife Mary Davis (b. in Canandaigua, N. Y., 1819).

6-193. *Sarah Longstreth Worrell*, b. at Johnsville, Pa., 10 mo. 15, 1835, m. in Burlington, N. J., 11 mo. 16, 1863, JACOB K. DUBELL. They res. at Mt. Holly, N. J. Four children:

7-363. Harvey C., b. 3 mo. 23, 1865, d. 8 mo. 10, 1865.
7-364. Howard Kemble, b. 1 mo. 8, 1867, d. 7 mo. 26, 1867.
7-365. Anna Longstreth, *twin to Howard K.*
7-366. Edward Comly, b. 11 mo. 23, 1871.

6-195. *Martha L. Worrell*, b. in Warminster township, Bucks Co., Pa., 5 mo. 27, 1842, d. at Mt. Holly, N. J., 12 mo. 17, 1872, m. in Mt. Holly, 6 mo. 1866, ABRAM CARSON, Jr. Two children:

7-367. Mary, b. 5 mo. 3, 1867.
7-368. Elizabeth Gebhard, b. 10 mo. 21, 1870.

6-197. THOMAS E. HEACOCK (son of B. Franklin, 5-51), m. ———; res. Harrison Co., Iowa. Four children:

7-369. James.
7-370. Amelia Melvina.
7-371. B. Franklin.
7-372. Carrie Louisa.

6-198. *Hannah Heacock* (dau. of B. Franklin, 5-51), m. JACOB BECK. Res. Harrison Co., Iowa. Three children:

7-373. Amelia Jane.
7-374. Walter K.
7-375. Jesse Bell.

6-209. HENRY LONGSTRETH, b. Jan. 6, 1838, d. Aug. 25, 1871, m. Jan. 14, 1865, *Sarah Hunsicker*. Two children:

7-376. Ernest, b. Aug. 22, 1866.
7-377. Mayne, b. Feb. 27, 1869.

6-210. *Rebecca L. Longstreth*, b. Feb. 14, 1840, m. March 26, 1868, ISAAC P. RHOADES. Two children:

7-378. Clara Irene, b. Feb. 9, 1869.
7-379. Sterling L., b. Nov. 21, 1872.

6-218. WILLIAM FRANKLIN RHOADES, b. 1836, (son of Samuel D., 5-60), m. *Mary Ann Morgan*, b. 1833. Seven children:

7-380. Samuel, b. 1859.
7-381. Morgan, b. 1861.

7–382. [RHOADES.] Preston, b. 1863.
7–383. William, b. 1865.
7–384. Mary Elizabeth, b. 1867, d. 1867.
7–385. Harry, b. 1869.
7–386. Ida May, b. 1871.

6–219. SAMUEL PRESTON RHOADES, b. 1839, m. *Rachel Roberts.* They had five children:

7–387. Franklin Longstreth, b. 1867.
7–388. Sarah Adele, b. 1869, d. 1869.
7–389. Albert, b. 1870.
7–390. Mary, b. 1871, d. 1872.
7–391. Kate, b. 1873.

6–224. *Rebecca Rhoades*, b. 1849, m. J. GARRETT WALKER. Four children:

7–392. Charles Abbott, b. 1868.
7–393. William, b. 1869.
7–394. Ella Morrison, b. 1871.
7–395. John Peddie, b. 1873, d. 1873.

6–227. Dr. SAMUEL PRESTON JONES, b. 1832 (son of Robert, 5-61), m. *Mary Pritchard*, res. West Philadelphia. Dr. Jones is physician in charge of the Pennsylvania Hospital for the Insane. Two children:

7–396. Ellen Chapman, b. 1870.
7–397. Robert Preston, b. 1873.

6–230. *Henrietta Deville Jones*, b. 1838 (dau. of Robert, 5-61), m. THOMAS YARDLEY BROWN, b. 1834. They had three children:

7–398. Jennie, b. 1863.
7–399. Sarah L., b. 1864, d. 1870.
7–400. Lydia Townsend, b. 1867.

6–235. *Elizabeth Mather*, b. at Little Miama, Ohio, 11 mo. 20, 1844, m. ALBERT H. KELSEY. They res. at Lebanon, O. One child:

7–401. Henry.

6–263. THEODORE HOLLINGSWORTH MORRIS, b. in Philadelphia, 10 mo. 10, 1840, m. 9 mo. 3, 1863, *Mary L. Paul.* Eight children:

7–402. Elizabeth, b. 1864.
7–403. Paul Jones, b. 1865.

7–404. [MORRIS.] Israel, b. 1867.
7–405. William, *twin of Israel.*
7–406. Ellen, b. 1868.
7–407. Theodore, b. 1869.
7–408. Samuel, b. 1871, d.
7–409. Sarah, b. 1873.

6–264. FREDERICK WISTER MORRIS, b. in Philadelphia, 3 mo. 8, 1842, m. 9 mo. 3, 1866, *Elizabeth F. Paul.* Three children:

7–410. Frederick, b. 1867.
7–411. Margaret, b. 1869.
7–412. Marion, b. 1872.

6–266. WILLIAM H. MORRIS, b. in Philadelphia, 3 mo. 25, 1846, m. 12 mo. 3, 1868, *Sarah W. Paul*, sister to Mary and Elizabeth (6-263 and 6-264). Two children:

7–413. Richard Jones, b. 1869.
7–414. Mary, b. 1871.

6–285. *Anna Longstreth Boldin*, m. 12 mo. 3, 1862, ADAM EVERLY, son of William and Anna Maria Everly. They res. in Philadelphia. Two children:

7–415. Anna Geisse, b. 6 mo. 27, 1864.
7–416. Mary, b. 12 mo. 31, 1866.

6–309. JOSHUA LONGSTRETH PRICE, b. 8 mo. 24, 1820, d. 3 mo. 10, 1867, m. 8 mo. 8, 1844, *Maria Wilson*, of Philadelphia. Six children:

7–417. Harry W., b. 5 mo. 23, 1845.
7–418. Marion, b. 7 mo. 14, 1847.
7–419. Elizabeth P., b. 11 mo. 3, 1848, d. 7 mo. 13, 1860.
7–420. Fanny, b. 11 mo. 2, 1849.
7–421. Callender, b. 7 mo. 16, 1851, d. 1 mo. 7, 1852.
7–422. Mary, b. 12 mo. 22, 1852.

6-310. *Elizabeth Williams Price*, b. 8 mo. 8, 1822, d.——, m. 11 mo. 2, 1842, GEORGE D. PARRISH, b. 8 mo. 23, 1820, d. 187–, son of Joseph and Susannah Parrish. She was his first wife. They had one child:

7–423. Lydia Williams, b. 1 mo. 5, 1844; *unm.*

Mr. PARRISH m. 2d, 2 mo. 28, 1850, *Sarah Longstreth Price*, b. 9 mo. 4, 1829, sister to his first wife (6-312). They had seven children:

7–424. [Parrish.] Anna Richardson, b. 9 mo. 21, 1853, d.
7–425. Elizabeth Williams, b. 9 mo. 29, 1855, d.
7–426. Margaret Callender, b. 9 mo. 22, 1857, d.
7–427. Helen Longstreth, b. 3 mo. 15, 1859.
7–428. Hugh Roberts, b. 6 mo. 9, 1861.
7–429. Richard Price, b. 3 mo. 8, 1863.
7–430. Joseph George, b. 1 mo. 29, 1866.

6–311. *Anna C. Price*, b. 8 mo. 2, 1824, m. Thomas Richardson, who d. in Philadelphia. They had five children :
7–431. Frederick.
7–432. Chesley.
7–433. Harry, d.
7–434. Edward.
7–435. Anna P.

6–313. *Margaret Simmons Price*, b. 8 mo. 15, 1832, m. 1 mo. 8, 1857, Stephen S. Price, b. 11 mo. 27, 1830, son of Joseph and Elizabeth Price. One child :
7–436. Lilly W.

6–314. *Rebecca Thompson Price*, b. 9 mo. 16, 1834, m. 6 mo. 3, 1856, Dr. William H. Hunt, son of Uriah and Elizabeth Hunt. Three children :
7–437. William.
7–438. George W.
7–439. Margaret P.

6–320. William Penrose Hallowell, b. 5 mo. 18, 1833, m. in Philadelphia, 5 mo. 29, 1856, *Elizabeth Corbit Davis.*[1] Res. Cheltenham, Pa. Three children :
7–440. Morris Longstreth, b. 5 mo. 1, 1857.
7–441. Isaac R. Davis, b. 8 mo. 7, 1859.
7–442. William Penrose, b. 11 mo. 30, 1863.

6–321. Richard Price Hallowell, b. 12 mo. 16, 1835, m. 10 mo. 26, 1859, *Anna Coffin Davis*, b. April 21, 1838, daughter of Edward M. and Maria M. Davis. They res. 1873, Boston, Mass. Five children :
7–443. Maria, b. 8 mo. 22, 1860.
7–444. Penrose, b. 10 mo. 28, 1862, d. young.
7–445. James Mott, b. 2 mo. 13, 1865.
7–446. Lucretia Mott, b. 12 mo. 8, 1867.
7–447. Francis Walton, b. 8 mo. 12, 1870.

---

[1] Dau. of Isaac R. Davis and wife Lydia Corbit, dau. of Joseph and Elizabeth Corbit.

6-322. Edward Needles Hallowell, b. 11 mo. 3, 1836, d. July 26, 1871 (Bvt. Gen. U. S. Vols.), m. in Boston, 2 mo. 2, 1869, *Charlotte Bartlett Wilhelmina Swett*, b. Feb. 8, 1843, daughter of William Gray and *Charlotte Bartlett Phinney* Swett. Two children:

7-448. Charlotte Bartlett, b. Jan. 22, 1870.
7-449. Emily, b. June 5, 1871.

6-324. Norwood Penrose Hallowell, b. 4 mo. 13, 1839, m. Jan. 27, 1868, *Sarah Wharton Haydock*, b. Jan. 22, 1846.[1] They res. in Boston. Two children:

7-450. Anna Norwood, b. March 30, 1871.
7-451. Robert Haydock, b. June 30, 1873.

6-333. Charles Hallowell, b. 8 mo. 13, 1842, m. *Belle Jewett*, daughter of Thomas L. Jewett. One child:

7-452. Thomas Jewett, b. 12 mo. 29, 1869.

6-357. *Elizabeth Tomkins Longstreth*, b. 11 mo. 21, 1826 (dau. of Thomas B., 5-110), m. 11 mo. 21, 1849, William Curtis Taylor, b. 5 mo. 14, 1825, son of Curtis and Ann Taylor, of Philadelphia. Res. Philadelphia. Five children:

7-453. Caroline Justice, b. 12 mo. 31, 1850.
7-454. Helen Longstreth, b. 6 mo. 17, 1853, d. 1 mo. 2, 1857.
7-455. Rodney Longstreth, b. 10 mo. 15, 1857.
7-456. Norton Longstreth, b. 2 mo. 9, 1861.
7-457. Agnes Longstreth, b. 5 mo. 9, 1865.

6-360. *Lydia Noble Longstreth*, b. 1 mo. 11, 1834, m. in Philadelphia, 6 mo. 6, 1855, Thomas Phipps Rowlett.[2] They res. in Philadelphia. Three children:

7-458. Morris Longstreth, b. 5 mo. 16, 1856.
7-459. Howard Longstreth, b. 9 mo. 7, 1859, d. 3 mo. 5, 1860.
7-460. Helen Longstreth, b. 2 mo. 2, 1865.

6-362. *Margaret Middleton Longstreth*, b. 2 mo. 11, 1838, m. 6 mo. 10, 1863, Edwin Frederick Shoenberger, son of

---

[1] Daughter of Robert Haydock (b. in Philadelphia, 12 mo. 2, 1807, son of Samuel and Sarah) and wife Hannah Wharton (b. in Philadelphia, 3 mo. 6, 1818, daughter of William and Deborah F.), m. 1 mo. 26, 1843.

[2] Son of John and *Drusilla Phipps* Rowlett; gr. son of John Rowlett, who was of Philadelphia, author of Rowlett's *Tables of Interest and Discount*, a celebrated work for the use of banks, etc.

Dr. Peter and *Sarah Krug* Shoenberger. Res. Philadelphia. Four children:

7–461. Lydia L., b. 3 mo. 27, 1864.
7–462. Frederick, d.
7–463. Mary, b. 3 mo. 2, 1868.
7–464. Carl, b. 2 mo. 21, 1871.

6-367. John Cooke Longstreth, lawyer, b. 9 mo. 26, 1836, m. *Susan W. Lee*, dau. of Dr. Ralph and *Rebecca Richardson* Lee, of Newtown, Pa. Res. Philadelphia. Five children, all b. in Philadelphia:

7–465. Rebecca Lee, b. 12 mo. 5, 1853.
7–466. Mary Elizabeth, b. 10 mo. 2, 1855.
7–467. Richard Henry, b. 4 mo. 26, 1859, d. 8 mo., 1859.
7–468. Walter Brooks, b. 10 mo. 20, 1861.
7–469. Susan Lee, b. 6 mo. 13, 1863.

6-368. Charles Cooke Longstreth, secretary and treasurer of the Lehigh Valley R. R., d. 1869, m. *Sarah N. Longstreth*, b. 1 mo. 11, 1829 (6-358 of this record). Res. Philadelphia. Five children:

7–470. Helen T., b. 6 mo. 17, 1854.
7–471. Emily, b. 3 mo. 28, 1856, d. 1 mo. 5, 1862.
7–472. Morris, b. 2 mo. 7, 1858.
7–473. Sidney E., b. 7 mo. 23, 1861, d. 8 mo. 20, 1862.
7–474. Joseph, b. 1 mo. 29, 1866.

6-372. William Longstreth, b. 4 mo. 1832 (son of William W., 5-113), m. 11 mo. 13, 1866, *Ada Smith*, dau. of J. T. and H. K. Smith. One child:

7–475. William Wilson.

6-373 *Margaret Longstreth*, b. 1 mo. 12, 1835, m. Horace J. Smith, farmer. Four children:

7–476. Albanus Logan, b. 1859.
7–477. Mary B., b. 1863.
7–478. Wilson L., b. 1867.
7–479. Margaret L.

-374. *Hannah Longstreth* (dau. of William W., 5-113), m. Emlen Carpenter. Res. Germantown, Pa. Two children:

7–480. Samuel F.
7–481. Ellen.

6-385. *Mary H. Keen*, b. 8 mo. 8, 1842, m. NATHAN SELLERS, son of John Sellers sen. Two children:

7-482. Sydney.
7-483. Norman P.

6-387. JOSEPH S. KEEN, b. 1 mo. 24, 1845, m. *Charlotte Perot*, daughter of Sansom Perot. One child:

7-484. Harold.

6-389. *Lucinda A. Keen*, b. 2 mo. 28, 1851, m. SAMUEL WOOLMAN. One child:

7-485. Helen E.

6-392. ISAIAH PAXSON, b. 9 mo. 25, 1838, m. Dec. 5, 1859, *Hannah McCarter*. Three children:

7-486. Charles, b. 1860.
7-487. Emma S., b. April 14, 1863.
7-488. Mary E., b. Jan. 5, 1865.

6-394. *Mary S. Paxson*, b. 1 mo. 17, 1843, m. in Philadelphia, 2 mo. 15, 1872, GEORGE HOFFMAN. One child:

7-489. Emma S., b. Feb. 26, 1873.

6-395. WILLIAM P. BEDFORD, b. 7 mo. 22, 1838, d. 9 mo. 25, 1866, m. *Anna Rogers*, who d. in Dowingtown, 2 mo. 18, 1864. One child:

7-490. Sarah, b. 5 mo. 12, 1865.

6-399. ELLWOOD T. PAXSON, b. 3 mo. 3, 1843, m. in Philadelphia, 5 mo. 18, 1871, *Mary N. Wallace*. One child:

7-491. Ellena Wallace, b. 11 mo. 6, 1872, d. 1 mo. 7, 1873.

6-403. *Elizabeth P. Furman*, b. 12 mo. 10, 1842, m. in Philadelphia, 2 mo. 2, 1864, SAMUEL S. SMITH. One child:

7-492. Margaret F., b. 8 mo. 7, 1866.

6-405. *Margaret L. Furman*, b. 11 mo. 22, 1846, m. in Philadelphia, 11 mo. 17, 1867, WATSON M. TRUMP. Three children:

7-493. Mary Elizabeth, b. 3 mo. 15, 1869.
7-494. Howard Watson, b. 6 mo. 28, 1871.
7-495. David Furman, b. 10 mo. 7, 1873.

6-409. *Clara Hoopes* (dau. of Joseph, 5-152), m. Sept. 21, 1865, GEORGE B. ATLEE. Res. Philadelphia. Three chn.:

7-496. [Atlee.] Joshua W., b. Feb. 1, 1867.
7-497. Elizabeth, b. Feb. 24, 1869.
7-498. Clara, b. April 15, 1871.

6-431. Chalkley Smedley, b. 12 mo. 20, 1831, m. *Mary Jane* ——, and res. in Chester Co., Pa. Two children:

7-499. Rebecca, b. 2 mo. 5, 1864.
7-500. Howard, b. 6 mo. 5, 1865.

6-473. George S. Lamborn, b. in Lancaster Co., Pa., 9 mo. 22, 1831, m. 5 mo. 8, 1856, *Sarah W. Coates*, and res. 1873, Martic township, same county. They have had seven children:

7-501. Margaret C., d.
7-502. Mary, d.
7-503. Priscilla.
7-504. Comly, d.
7-505. Linnaeus.
7-506. Anna.
7-507. Lucretia.

6-474. Aquila D. Lamborn, b. in Lancaster Co., Pa., 2 mo. 22, 1833, m. 2 mo. 22, 1862, *Ann Ambler*. They res. 1873, Drumore, same Co. Two children:

7-508. Alice.
7-509. William.

6-475. *Emeline Lamborn*, b. in Lancaster Co., Pa., 9 mo. 29, 1834, m. 3 mo., 1854, Joseph Shoemaker. They res. 1873, Drumore, in same Co. Six children:

7-510. Cynthia.
7-511. Charles.
7-512. Allison.
7-513. Leander.
7-514. Lewis.
7-515. Edgar.

6-476. Elwood Lamborn, b. in Lancaster Co., Pa., 8 mo. 4, 1836, m. 9 mo. 13, 1866, *Elmira Moore*. Res. 1873, Drumore, in same county. One child:

7-516. Edgar.

6-477. William L. Lamborn, b. in Lancaster Co., Pa., 1 mo. 6, 1839, m. 1 mo. 6, 1864, *Phebe M. Barnard*, res. 1873, Penna. Steel Works, Dauphin Co., Pa. Two children:

7-517. [LAMBORN.] Ilena B., d.
7-518. Jessie Wynona.

6-478. *Mary Elizabeth Lamborn*, b. in Lancaster Co., Pa., 6 mo. 22, 1840, m. 9 mo. 19, 1870, THOMAS B. HAMBLETON, They res. 1873, Drumore, same county.

6-486. *Alice A. Lamborn*, b. in Lancaster Co., Pa., 4 mo. 14, 1847, m. 1 mo. 1869, WILLIAM SHOEMAKER. Res. 1873, Drumore, same county. One child:

7-519. Wynona.

6-482. *Lucinda Lamborn*, b. in Lancaster Co., Pa., 8 mo. 22, 1850, m. 12 mo. 1868, FRANKLIN L. TEUNIS. They res. 1873, Drumore, same county. One child:

7-520. Cynthia.

7-2. WILLIAM F. HARDY, farmer, b. 2 mo. 7, 1836 (son of Neal, 6-15[1]), m. *Maria Thomas*, dau. of Henry and Mary Thomas of Chester Co., Pa. They res. at Fall Creek, Indiana. Six children.

8-1. Sumner.
8-2. Henry.
8-3. Nina.
8-4. Arthur.
8-5. Anna.
8-6. Neal.

7-3. SOLOMON F. HARDY, merchant, b. 10 mo. 19, 1839, (son of Neal, 6-15), m. in Indiana, *Rebecca James*, dau. of Joshua P. and Sarah Ann James. They res. at Markleville, Madison Co., Indiana. Two children:

8-7. Charles.
8-8. John.

7-5. *Eliza Ann Hardy* (dau. of Neal, 6-15), m. 1st, MARTIN KINCKERBOCKER, of Michigan, d ——; no issue. 2d, JOHN BOSTON, son of Jesse Boston, of Baltimore, Md. Res. Fall Creek, Ind. One child:

8-9. Mary.

---

[1] This concerning Neal Hardy received too late for insertion on page 471. He was b. in Philadelphia, Nov. 26, 1803, and d. in Madison Co., Ind., Nov. 16, 1869. He was a man of excellent character, and a valuable citizen. It was said of him: "No clearer brain, no more open hand, no warmer and kinder heart, has death ever chilled among us."

7-6. *Emily Hardy* (dau. of Neal, 6-15), m. in Indiana, ALBERT LEWIS, merchant, son of John and Rebecca T. Lewis, formerly of Chester Co., Pa. Res. Markleville, Madison Co., Ind. Two children:

8-10. Edward.
8-11. Alice.

7-7. *Sarah Hardy* (dau. of Neal, 6-15), m. in Indiana, JOSEPH KINNARD, son of John and Elizabeth Kinnard, formerly of Chester Co., Pa. One child:

8-12. Frank.

7-26. *Sarah Emma Brown*, b. 8 mo. 19, 1839 (daughter of Joshua P., 6-20), m. ALFRED A. ANDERSON, dentist. Res. Kennett Square, Chester Co., Pa. Two children:

8-13. Hermon or Hermann.
8-14. Frederick.

7-34. HENRY M. FUSSELL, b. 9 mo. 14, 1845 (son of Henry B., 6-23), m. *Mary Townsend Fussell*, b. in Philadelphia, Pa., Oct. 23, 1849, daughter of Dr. Edwin Fussell (6-16). Res. near Media, Delaware Co., Pa. One child:

8-15. Alice.

7-60. JOHN LEWIS THOMAS, farmer, b. in Indiana, 11 mo. 20, 1837 (son of Lewis W., 6-33), m. at Fall Creek meeting, Ind., 9 mo. 18, 1862, *Caroline Swain*, b. at Bristol, Pa., daughter of Charles and Sarah Ann Swain. Res. Fall Creek, Ind. Three children:

8-16. Emma Fussell, b. 11 mo. 21, 1864.
8-17. Lewis W., d.
8-18. Charles Swain, b. 12 mo. 29, 1868.

7-61. *Mary Moore Thomas*, b. 2 mo. 3, 1839 (daughter of Lewis W., 6-33), m. at Fall Creek, Ind., AARON MORRIS, manufacturer of agricultural implements, son of George and Rhoda Morris. Res. Fall Creek, Ind. Two children:

8-19. Louella.
8-20. William F.

7-62. *Anna Lewis Thomas*, b. 11 mo. 4, 1842 (daughter of Lewis W., 6-33), m. at Fall Creek meeting, Ind., Aug.

17, 1865, BENJAMIN ROGERS, druggist, son of Jonathan and *Hannah Weeks* Rogers. They res. at Pendleton, Madison Co., Ind. Two children:

8–21. Jonathan J., b. Oct., 1867.
8–22. Mary Thomas, b. June, 1869.

7–84. *Mary Frances Gorsuch*, b. 10 mo. 31, 1849 (dau. of Joseph, 6-48), m. 5 mo. 3, 1870, GEORGE V. BOWEN. Three children:

8–23. Charles B., b. 6 mo. 11, 1871.
8–24. Clara Bell, b. 7 mo. 22, 1872, d. 1873.
8–25. John Franklin, b. 10 mo. 31, 1873.

7–99. WILLIAM HOWARD FUSSELL, b. 7 mo. 28, 1848 (son of Bartholomew H., 6-50), m. 9 mo. 3, 1870, *Fannie Fields*, of Philadelphia. One child:

8–26. Eugene Dunnington, b. 8 mo., 1871.

7–600. *Mary Philena Fussell*, b. 5 mo. 1, 1850 (dau. of Bartholomew H., 6-50), m. 9 mo. 24, 1867, STEPHEN A. DUNNINGTON, of New York. Two children:

8–27. Carrie Howard, b. 7 mo. 18, 1869.
8–28. Stephen A., b. 11 mo. 22, 1870, d. 3 mo. 23, 1873.

7–630. *Caroline Hamilton*, b. 1825 (dau. of Mary, 6-63), m. ——— WALLACE. One son:

8–29. William.

The following received too late for insertion in regular order:

4–4. John and *Esther Kirkbride* Longstreth had eleven children:

5–17. Mahlon, b. 10 mo. 14, 1779, d. in Philadelphia, 1 mo. 8, 1837; *m.*
5–18. Martha, b. 7 mo. 11, 1781. SPENCER.
5–19. Daniel, b. 12 mo. 23, 1785, d. 5 mo. 25, 1832; *m.*
5–19*b*. Robert Kirkbride, b. 10 mo. 22, 1787, d. 4 mo. 23, 1788.
5–20. Hannah, b. 7 mo. 18, 1789, d. 10 mo. 1, 1843, m. 1 mo. 14, 1817, Dr. GAUNTT, buried 12 mo. 22, 1822, Groveville, N. J.; no issue.
5–21. Rachel, b. 5 mo. 6, 1791, res. in Philadelphia. MILNOR.
5–22. Sarah, b. 8 mo. 6, 1793, res. Philadelphia; *unm.*
5–23. Esther, b. 2 mo. 22, 1796, res. Bristol, Pa. HAYWARD.
5–23*b*. Robert, b. 3 mo. 22, 1798, d. 3 mo. 23, 1800.
5–23*c*. John, b. 3 mo. 28, 1801, d. 4 mo. 3, 1801.
5–24. John Kirkbride, b. 4 mo. 23, 1803, d. ——; *m.*

Substitute the above for record of John Longstreth's children, page 431.

5–98. CHARLES HALLOWELL, b. 7 mo. 31, 1821, d. 1 mo. 2, 1864 (son of Charles T., 4-56), m. *Elmira Rebecca Stephens*, b. April 4, 1826, dau. of William and Mary S. Stephens, of Philadelphia. Six children, all b. in Philadelphia:

6–503. William Henry, b. March 7, 1848, d. Sept. 12, 1848.
6–504. Horatio Stephens, b. Nov. 11, 1849, d. July 7, 1864.
6–505. Charles Eugene, b. Jan. 13, 1852.
6–506. Louis Stephens, b. Nov. 11, 1854.
6–507. Henry Howell, b. Feb. 28, 1857.
6–508. Samuel Williams, b. Jan. 30, 1860.

NOTES. I. WILLIAM FUSSELL (5–10) m. at Quakertown meeting, Bucks Co., Pa., *Jane Foulke*, dau. of Edward and *Elizabeth Roberts* Foulke. Their two elder children were b. near Chester Springs, Chester Co., Pa.; their three younger children, were b. in West Fallowfield township, same county. Concerning him the following from his son Joseph (6–18). "In consequence of the inflation and collapse which followed the peace of 1815, he found himself in debt, and to better his condition he removed in 1827, from Chester county, to the neighborhood of Philadelphia. Prospering here, he returned after a few years to his former neighborhood, and paid his old debts, *principal and interest.* His home was a station on the underground railway from which many a fugitive from slavery was speeded on his way to freedom. Himself and wife both d. at Fall Creek, Indiana."

II. Dr. BARTHOLOMEW FUSSELL (5–15) was an acquaintance and life long friend of William Lloyd Garrison and John G. Whittier. "It was during the residence of the poet in Philadelphia in 1838–40 that his stirring poem 'The Response' was written. It was addressed to the politicians clamorous for the suppression of the abolitionists, and Whittier bade them:

'Go, hunt sedition — search for that
In every pedler's cart of rags;
Pry into every Quaker's hat,
And Dr. Fussell's saddle-bags;
Lest treason wrap, with all its ills,
Around his powders and his pills.'

"Mr. Whittier speaks of 'the beloved physician of Kennett Square, Dr. Bartholomew Fussell' in his reminiscences of the Convention of 1833, in a recent number of the *Atlantic*." — J. F.

FAMILY OF JOHN DAWSON,

OF NORTHUMBERLAND CO., PA., b. about 1750.

From W. F. Corbit, Esq., of Philadelphia, the following:[1]

1. JOHN DAWSON, b. about 1750, lived in Northumberland Co., Pa., m. *Prudence Martin*, and had children:

2–1. Edward, b. 1779, d. 1848; *m.*
2–2. Daniel, b. 1780, d. 1821 (drowned in Susquehanna river, at Selinsgrove), m. 1810, *Christiana Brown;* no issue.
2–3. Mary, b. 1782, d. 1852; *unm.*

2–1. EDWARD DAWSON, b. 1779, d. 1848, m. 1805, *Mary Y. Ostheimer*. They had thirteen children:

3–1. Jacob, b. 1807, d. 1872; *m.*
3–2. Henry, b. 1809, d. 1852; *m.*
3–3. Huldah, b. 1811, d. 1834. MANN.
3–4. Daniel, b. 1813, d. 1850; *m.*
3–5. Catharine, b. 1815, res. Sunbury, Pa. FOULKE.
3–6. Thomas, b. 1817, d. 1843; *m.*
3–7. Sarah, b. 1818, d. 1848; *unm.*
3–8. Mary, b. 1820, d. 1828.
3–9. Isaac, b. 1822, res. Warren, O.; *m.*
3–10. Margaret, b. 1823, d. 1829.
3–11. Edward, b. 1825, res. St. Louis, Mo.; *m.*
3–12. Joseph, b. 1827, res. Peru, S. Am.; *m.*
3–13. Mary, b. 1829, res. Iowa. OBERDORF.

3–1. JACOB DAWSON, b. 1807, d. 1872, m. *Anna Martin*, who res. 1873, in Philadelphia. Eight children:

4–1. Wilbur Fisk, b. June 27, 1840, res. Philadelphia, bookkeeper in office of *Evening Telegraph;* five children.
4–2. William Henry.
4–3. Charles Wesley, d.
4–4. Erastus Buck, d.
4–5. Samuel Martin.
4–6. Margaret Elizabeth, m. EDWARD BRYSON, res. Phila.; three chn.
4–7. Walter Scott, d. young.
4–8. ———, d. young.

[1] The materials for this record were gathered by Mr. C. while in pursuit of information concerning the family of John Dawson, of Abington. (See preceding record). The personal history of John Dawson, of Northumberland Co., is, unfortunately, almost a blank. The account of his descendants was furnished chiefly by Mr. Uriah Foulke, of Sunbury, Pa.

3-2. HENRY DAWSON, b. 1809, d. 1852, m. 1829, *Jane Walters*. Six children, all res. in Illinois:

4-9. Mary Ann, b. 1830.
4-10. Rachel, b. 1831.
4-11. Alice, b. 1833.
4-12. Jane, b. 1835.
4-13. Sarah, b. 1837.
4-14. Maggie, b. 1841.

3-3. *Huldah Dawson*, b. 1811, d. 1834, m. 1832, SAMUEL MANN, who res. 1873, in Lancaster, Pa. One child:

4-15. Mary Ann, b. 1835.

3-4. DANIEL DAWSON, b. 1813, d. 1850, m. 1839, *Maria Keim*, res. Northumberland Co., Pa. Children:

4-16. Lucy Ann, b. 1840.
4-17. John, b. 1843, d. 1864.
4-18. Isaiah, b. 1845.
4-19. Jackson, b. 1849.

3-5. *Catharine Dawson*, b. 1815, m. 1835, HENRY FOULKE, son of Joseph and Margaret Foulke, of Bucks Co., Pa. They res. 1873, in Sunbury, Pa. Four children:

4-20. Lucetta, b. 1836, d. 1871.
4-21. Isaiah, b. 1838, d. 1865.
4-22. Uriah, b. 1840, res. Sunbury.
4-23. Harietta, b. 1842.

3-6. THOMAS DAWSON, b. 1817, d. 1843, m. 1838, *Jerusha Trayer*. Two children:

4-24. Mary Ann, b. 1841, m. HIRAM CONRAD, preacher of Evangelical Association.
4-25. Isaac, b. 1842; *unm.*

3-9. ISAAC DAWSON, b. 1822, m. 1854, *Nancy Laurel Reeves*. Res. 1873, Warren, Ohio. Three children:

4-26. William, b. 1855.
4-27. Levis, b. 1856.
4-28. Lizzie, b. 1858.

3-11. EDWARD DAWSON, b. 1825, m. 1848, *Hester Harlocher*. Res. 1873, St. Louis, Mo. Three children:

4-29. William, b. 1849.
4-30. Alice, b. 1850.
4-31. Elmira, b. 1858.

3-12. JOSEPH DAWSON, b. 1827, m. 1856, *Nelly Kitchen*. Res. 1873, Peru, South America. One child:

4-32. William, b. 1858.

3-13. *Mary Dawson*, b. 1829, m. 1849, PHILIP OBERDORF. Res. 1873, Iowa. Four children:

4-33. Mary Alice, b. 1850.
4-34. Lewis, b. 1852.
4-35. Daniel, b. 1854.
4-36. Rosa, b. 1856.

4-1. WILBUR FISK DAWSON, b. June 27, 1840, m. Res. in Philadelphia, bookkeeper in office of *Evening Telegraph*. Five children:

5-1.
5-2.
5-3.
5-4.
5-5.

4-6. *Margaret Elizabeth Dawson*, m. EDWARD BRYSON, printer. Res. Philadelphia. Three children:

5-6.
5-7.
5-8.

NOTES. I. GEORGE B. DAWSON, said to have been an officer in the British army during the Revolutionary war, a member of Tarleton's Legion, resided in Philadelphia after the close of the struggle. Among his descendants is understood to be DAWSON COLEMAN, Esq., a well known public man of Pa. (See pp. 147 and 368.)

II. Prior to the Revolution, JOHN DAWSON BUSCH, a native of Germany (perhaps of mixed English and German parentage), emigrated to this country, and settled in Gloucester Co., N. J. He was known here as JOHN DAWSON, and numerous children and grand children claim the family name of Dawson; but a brother, who settled in Pa., retained the name of Busch, which is still borne by his descendants. John Dawson (Busch) served as a soldier in the Am. army. (See p. 186, *note*.) He was twice m., and had by 1st wife, a son William, whose son, of same name, now res. near Glassboro, N. J. By second wife he had, besides daughters, Aaron, hatter, who res. 1873, Washington, D. C., and has a family, and Job, b. about 1800, dry-goods merchant, 422 South Second street, Philadelphia (1873). The last named has sons John C. and George Dawson, of the banking house of Brown Brothers, 211 Chestnut street, Philadelphia (1873).

III. PAUL DAWSON, tailor, Philadelphia (1873), b. in Ireland, 1826, came to America, 1848. He m. *Mary Anstis*, and has had ten children, of whom three are living. He is the youngest son of John (d. about 1861), and *Mary Dawson* Dawson, cousins; grandson of Paul Dawson, who m. —— *Whelply*, and d. at an advanced age, about 1829.

MARYLAND.

"Nicholas Dawson, of Talbot county." Since the record beginning on page 302 was printed the following information has been received from Mr. James N. Dawson, of Connersville, Md.

1. Ralph Dawson, the father of Nicholas of the record above referred to, "came from England,"[1] and had children as follows:

2–1. Nicholas; *m.*[2]
2–2. Thomas.
2–3. Joseph; *m.*
2–4. Impy; *m.*
2–5. James.
2–6. Elizabeth. Sewell.

2–1. Nicholas Dawson, farmer, d. aged 89,[2] m. *Mary Cook*, and had children:

3–1. Thomas Cook; *m.*[3]
3–2. Margaret. Fairbank.
3–3. Nicholas Lurty.
3–4. Elizabeth. Nevitt.
3–5. Levin; *m.*
3–6. James, d. young.
3–7. Ann. Sears.
3–8. William; *m.*
3–9. Hugh, d. aged 25; *unm.*
3–10. Mary, m. Richard Lawrence; no issue.
3–11. Richard, d. aged about 19.

2–3. Joseph Dawson m. Miss *Hadaway*, and had chn.:

3–12. William H.
3–13. James.
3–14. Ralph.

---

[1] So states Mr. J. N. D., but see page 221; was not this the Ralph Dawson, 3-3 of that record?
[2] See page 302, No. 1, of that record.
[3] See page 302, No. 2-1, of that record.

3–15. John.
3–16. Aryann.
3–17. Elizabeth.

2–4. Impy Dawson m. *Fannie Auld*, and had children :

3–18. Deborah.
3–19. Stephen.
3–20. Thomas.
3–21. Edward.
3–22. Francis.
3–23. Sallie.

2–6. *Elizabeth Dawson* m. Basel Sewell. They had chn. :

3–24. James.
3–25. Clem.
3–26. Basel.
3–27. Elizabeth.
3–28. Thomas.

3–1. Thomas Cook Dawson, farmer, d. aged 61, m. 1st, *Elizabeth Barnett*. They had :

4–1. Mary Elizabeth. Larrimore.
4–2. Emily. Tucker.
4–3. Thomas B. ; *m.*

He m. 2d, *Harriet Linthicum.*[1] They had :

4–4. James M., d. aged 2 years.
4–5. James Nicholas ; *m.*[2]

He m. 3d, Mrs. Ann M. Fountain.[3] They had :

4–6. Richard L., d. in his 22d year ; *unm.*
4–7. John Francis ; *m.*[4]

3–2. *Margaret Dawson* m. Capt. David Fairbank. They had one child :

4–8. Dawson.

3–4. *Elizabeth Dawson* m. —— Nevitt, and had one ch. :

4–9. Mary Ann, d. aged 30 ; *unm.*

3–5. Levin Dawson m. *Jane Armor.* They had :

4–10. Mary Jane, m. Dr. Hays.
4–11. Lewis E. ; *m.*

---

1 See p. 302, 2–1. The name is there spelled *Linchicum.*
2 See p. 302, 3–1 of that record.
3 See p. 302, 2–1. The maiden name only is there given, *Ann Maria Coursey.*
4 See p. 302, 3–2 of that record.

3-7. *Ann Dawson* m. Capt. EDWARD SEARS. They had:

4-12. Ann Maria.
4-13. Theresa.
4-14. Mary Jane.
4-15. George.
4-16. John.
4-17. Margaret.

3-8. WILLIAM DAWSON m. *Sallie Smith.* They had:

4-18. Charles, d. young.
4-19. Thomas.
4-20. Mary Elizabeth.
4-21. Hugh.
4-22. Sallie.
4-23. Charles.
4-24. Rachel.

4-1. *Mary Elizabeth Dawson* m. ROBERT LARRIMORE, and had:

5-1. Mary Elizabeth.
5-2. Martha.
5-3. Robert.
5-4. John.

4-2. *Emily Dawson* m. ALFRED TUCKER, and had:

5-5. John T., physician.
5-6. Alfred.
5-7. Susan.
5-8. William.
5-9. Emma.
5-10. George.

4-3. THOMAS B. DAWSON m. 1st, *Catharine Spedden*, who d. without issue. 2d, *Sallie Lowe:* no issue. He d. aged 50.

4-5. JAMES NICHOLAS DAWSON m. *Catharine S. Muir.* They had:

5-11. John T., physician, m. *Sallie E. Mitchell*, res. Cornersville, Dorchester Co., Md.
5-12. Ida M., d. in infancy.
5-13. James M., d. in infancy.
5-14. Kate Muir, res. Dorchester Co., *unm.*

4-7. JOHN FRANCIS DAWSON m. 1st, *Sarah Josephine Delahay.* They had:

5-15. William, d. aged 5 years.

He m. 2d, *Emma Augusta Delahay.* They had:
5–16. James N., d. young.

4–11. Lewis E. Dawson m. *Kate Hayslett.* They had:
5–17. Lewis, d. aged 9 years.

Notes. I. Alcade Dawson was a prominent man in Eastern Md. a few years since: a member of the state legislature. His wid. res. 1873, at Seaford, Del.

II. Dr. James Dawson (see p. 225, 6–6), d. in Talbot Co., Md., Feb. 21, 1874. The following from an Easton paper: "*Death of Dr. James Dawson.* It becomes our duty to announce the death of our highly respectable and useful fellow citizen, Dr. James Dawson. This sad event occurred at his home in Bayside, near St. Michaels, on Saturday the 21st inst., [Feb. 1874] when he was in the 68th year of his age. His demise was not unexpected by either his friends or himself, for his health had for some months past indicated an early departure, and yet when death was at hand it was hardly less painful to those who loved or revered him, because it had been anticipated, while it found in him, who had long been fitting himself for this supreme event, hardly any better preparedness because of its having been foreseen and imminent.

"James Dawson was the son of Major John Dawson, of this county, and was born near the Royal Oak, in the year 1806 [1805.] After receiving in the common schools of the neighborhood such instruction as they afforded, he was placed at the Academy in Easton, then under most excellent direction and tuition. At a proper age he was matriculated at the University of Maryland, from which he graduated Doctor of Medicine in the year 1828. He commenced the practice of medicine immediately after receiving his diploma, at York, Penn., but returned to his native county and settled in St. Michaels. From this town he removed to Easton, where he united the business of an apothecary with his practice. He remained in Easton but a short time. Dr. John Barnett, of Bayside, being about to abandon his practice, by reason of his age, Dr. Dawson saw that an opening was made for him, and he again returned to St. Michaels, and there settled. Here he soon acquired a large and lucrative country practice, which he enjoyed for many years. But in 1843 or '44 he removed from the village to his farm just below, where he continued to exercise his profession with undiminished success and acceptance, at the same time giving attention to agricultural pursuits. Here he continued to live until his final departure, enjoying the confidence, respect and affection of the whole of that community in the midst of which he spent the greater part of his long life.

"Of his mental qualities it may be said he was endowed with great perspicacity, a quick apprehension, and sound judgment. Without pretending to extensive learning, he was well informed upon all subjects that belong to general culture, and particularly upon those relating to his profession. Justly regarding medicine as an empirical science, he naturally relied more upon experience than upon professional dogma, and as a man of independent thought and acute perceptivity, he depended more upon the results of his own observations, than upon the deductions of others. Eminently conservative in his opinions and practice, he nevertheless was not disdainful of novelties in doctrine, nor unreasonably tenacious in his adherence to ancient usage. Belonging to the 'old school' of medicine, he, who was ever youthful in his feelings, could not but be in sympathy with modern progress in therapeutic art.

"He was blessed with great cheerfulness of disposition, and buoyancy of spirits. Life seemed to present to him, like the moon to earth, its bright side only. His humor was inexhaustible and literally irrepressible. It was so ebullient that upon the most inopportune occasions it would, as it were against his will, bubble over. His wit, however, was never bitter or acrimonious, and though it sometimes irritated it inflicted no festering wound.

"Of his moral qualities, all who knew him are able to testify that he was honorable in his impulses and upright in his actions. In his youth a great exuberance of vitality may have betrayed itself in a manner which strict propriety might not approve; but for many years previous to his death religion had been a pervasive influence in his life, sanctifying motives which even without it were not unworthy, and consecrating conduct which even without it was never anything but respectable. He was warm and constant in his attachments. If nature had endowed him with strong antipathies and repugnances, she had also gifted him with a generous tolerance of the infirmities of others, while religion taught him to harbor no resentments or animosities. He was an affectionate parent, a kind friend, an obliging neighbor and a considerate master. He was always ready to obey the call of the poor for the discharge of his offices as a physician, but his charities were not confined to the gratuitous performance of his professional services. For many years he was an active and consistent member of the Methodist Episcopal church, of whose doctrine and polity he was ever an able defender, and of whose salutary influence, in amending the life and purifying the heart, he was a most conspicuous and worthy example.

"In politics he was an early Whig, and in the latter part of his life an earnest Republican. During the war of the Rebellion he warmly espoused the cause of the government, and he was one of those who, in his section, and at that dark time, were instrumental in keeping alive the sacred flame of patriotism.

"He married the daughter of the late Wm. Hambleton, of Emerson's Point, by whom there was born to him a large family. His domestic relations were of the happiest kind.

"He was buried at Emerson's Point, on Monday last, a large concourse of people following him to the grave, and ministers of different denominations participating in the funeral services."

CANADA.

JOHN WILLIAM DAWSON, LL.D., F.R.S., F.G.S., principal and vice-chancellor of McGill University, Montreal, and author of "Archaia," "Acadian Geology,"[1] "The Story of the Earth and Man," etc., is well known in the United States, not only by his published works, but as an eminent and popular lecturer on scientific subjects. He was born in Pictou, Nova Scotia, October, 1820. His father, James Dawson, publisher and bookseller at Pictou, was the son of John Dawson, of Ordiquhill, Banffshire, Scotland, who belonged to a family long settled there, and believed to have originally immigrated to Scotland from Ireland in the interest of James II, when the latter was struggling with William of Orange. They were a Roman Catholic family, but Dr. Dawson's branch of it became Protestants, and has connections scattered over England, Scotland, British America and Australia. The late Mr. R. Dawson, of Cruden, Aberdeenshire, Scotland, well known as a zoölogist, was of this family, and Mr. George Dawson, lecturer in photographic chemistry, King's College, London, is a branch of it.

Dr. Dawson's early academic training was received in the College of Pictou, Nova Scotia, under the principalship of the Rev. Dr. McCulloch, a graduate of Glasgow. After completing a course of four years in that institution, and spending some time in the study of the Natural History of his native province, he matriculated in the University of Edinburgh, session of 1840-1, and studied during the winter under Prof. Jameson. He then returned to Nova Scotia and renewed his geological researches. In 1842 he accompanied Sir Charles Lyell in his tour of that province. He returned to Edinburgh in the autumn of 1846, and again entered the University, devoting his time principally to the study of practical chemistry. At this time he contributed two papers to the Royal Society of Edinburgh and one to the Wernerian Society, and subsequently received from the University the honorary degree of Master of

[1] J. Dawson & Sons, publishers, Pictou, N. S., 1855; publishers, also, of Dawson's *Map of Nova Scotia and Prince Edward's Island*, 1851, and of *A Handbook of Geography and Natural History of the Province of Nova Scotia, for the use of Schools and Families*, by the subject of this notice. Dr. Dawson's portrait has been published in the *New Dominion Magazine;* also in a work on the medals of McGill College, by Mr. Landham.

Arts. In 1850 he was appointed superintendent of education for Nova Scotia, which office he held for three years. He afterwards served on various educational commissions, and in 1855 he was offered and accepted the office of Principal and Professor of Natural History in the McGill College and University, the oldest, and in many respects the most considerable university in Canada. This office, together with that of vice-chancellor, which has been since added, he now holds. During his connection with it the University has been extremely prosperous, and in respect to its course of study, and in public estimation and support, it may challenge comparison with most of the older universities.

Dr. Dawson is a Fellow of the Royal Society of London, of the Geological Society of London, and of the Academy of Arts and Sciences of Boston ; a Foreign Corresponding Fellow of the Edinburgh Geological Society ; a Member of the American Philosophical Society ; an Honorary Member of the Natural History Society of Boston, and a Corresponding Member of the Academy of Natural Sciences of Philadelphia, and of several other societies. He has also been several times elected President of the Natural History Society of Montreal. Among his contributions to the literature of Natural Science may be mentioned twenty-five papers published in the *Proceedings of the Geological Society of London ;* a work entitled "Acadian Geology," on the geology of the eastern provinces of British North America ; a work entitled "Archaia, or Studies of the Cosmogony and Natural History of the Hebrew Scriptures ;" "The Story of the Earth and Man," a popular scientific work illustrating the aspects of successive stages in the earth's history, as disclosed by geology ; besides several educational and scientific works of a more local nature, and numerous contributions to the *Canadian Naturalist* and other periodicals. All of these have been favorably received by the public. As a lecturer on scientific subjects Dr. Dawson is exceedingly popular. He is regarded as one of the most eminent and able opponents of the Darwinian theory of evolution. He unites the characters of a Christian and a man of science, and in his addresses and published works he seeks to emancipate his favorite study "from the control of the bald metaphysical speculations so rife in our time," and especially to deliver it "from that materialistic infidelity, which, by robbing nature of the spiritual elements and of its presiding Divinity, makes science dry, barren and repulsive, diminishes its educational value, and even renders it less efficient for purposes of practical research."

Hon. JOHN A. DAWSON, of Pictou, N. S., cousin of the above named, is a member of the House of Commons of Canada.

S. J. DAWSON, C. E., commanded the Canadian "Red River Expedition" of 1858, and is the author of *A Report on the Exploration of the Country between Lake Superior and the Red River Settlement, and between the latter place and the Assiniboine and Saskatchewan*, printed by order of the [Canadian] Legislative Assembly, 4to., Toronto, 1859.[1]

Rev. ENEAS McD. DAWSON, a Catholic clergyman, of Three Rivers, Canada, translator of the Count De Maistre's *The Pope*, is said to be a brother of the explorer, above named.

Hon. WILLIAM McD. DAWSON, a member of the Legislative Assembly of Canada, 1862-3, res. at Ottawa.

DAWSON BROTHERS, Montreal, booksellers, publishers of many educational and scientific works, and of the *Canadian Medical Journal* and *Canadian Naturalist*; SIDDONS & DAWSON, editors and publishers of the *Educator* and *Herald and Prototype*, and DAWSON & BROTHERS, publishers, at London, Province of Ontario; and MIDDLETON & DAWSON, booksellers and publishers of the *Quebec Gazette*, at Quebec, are well known Canadian names.[2]

---

[1] Mr. Dawson spent several days and nights, on Manitoba, a small Island in the middle of one of the larger lakes to the northwest of Lake Superior, which the Indians shun as haunted ground.

"On no condition will they approach it, much less land on it, for it is the home of *Manitoba* — the Speaking God — whose voice they hear nightly as they camp by the lake or guide their fishing boats over its surface. The 'voice' is no myth. It assails not the Indian's ear alone, but the white man's as well. Whence comes it? The superstitious Ojibway hears and keeps away, piously pronouncing the name of God. The Englishman hears and examines. Not the inquisitive investigator, but the divinity of the place perishes by the invasion. Touched by the wand of science, the mystery of the place is resolved into a simple natural phenomenon — the beating of the waves on a peculiarly sonorous shingle. Along the northern shore of the island runs a low cliff of compact, fine grained limestone, which clinks like steel under the stroke of a hammer. When the wind blows from the north, the waves beating at the foot of the cliff dash the fragments of stone against each other, causing them to give forth a sound which resembles the ringing of distant church bells. So strong is this resemblance that the explorer was more than once awakened in the night with the impression that he was listening to chimes. When the breeze subsides and the waves play gently on the shore, low wailing sounds — spirit voices to the awe-stricken Ojibway — come up from the beach. And as the explorer lay on his bed of moss-covered rock at night and experienced their peculiarly impressive effect, he found it very easy, he says, to understand why the credulous natives should avoid the place."

[2] See page 152, note 14.

ROLL OF HONOR.

Under this title the U. S. Government has recently caused to be published lists of the Union soldiers who died during the war, interred in the various national cemeteries and elsewhere, so far as their names and places of burial could be ascertained. The lists comprise many thousands of names and cover hundreds of closely printed pages. The following names are from these lists :

DAWSON, M. M., Lt. Col., 100th Pa., d. June 30, 1864, Nat. Cem., Arlington, Va.

" D., private, Co. D., 17th Mich. Cav., d. Aug. 8, 1864, Andersonville Cem., Ga.

" Lewis B., " " K., 58th Pa., d. Nov. 22, 1864, Nat. Cem., Hampton, Va.

" William, " " G., 2d. W. Va. Cav., d. April 24, 1865, Nat. Cem., Hampton, Va.

" Alphonzo, " " F., 12th U. S., d. March 31, 1865, Annapolis, Md.

" John, " " C., 62d Ill., d. June 8, 1864, Pine Bluffs, Arkansas.

" N. C., " 3d Ohio Battery, d. July 17, 1862, Cincinnati, O.

" James, " Co. D., 155th Pa., d. Jan. 6, 1863, Point Look Out, Md.

" William, " " G., 48th Mo. Cav., d. Jan. 31, 1865, Jefferson City, Mo.

" Wm. H., " " H., 14th Ill., d. March 18, 1862, St. Louis, Mo.

" Zadock, " " K., 24th Iowa, d. Feb. 9, 1863, St. Louis, Mo.

" Jeremiah, " " B., 13th Iowa, d. Oct. 11, 1863, Jefferson Barracks, St. Louis, Mo.

" Stephen, " " K., 79th Penn., d. May 7, 1865, New Cem., Newbern, N. C.

" John F., " " E., 31st Ind. Inft., d. June 25, 1864, Chattanooga, Tenn.

" James, " " B., 13th Iowa, d. Jan. 12, 1865, Chattanooga, Tenn.

" August, " " G., 1st Wis. Cav., d. Dec. 15, 1863, Chattanooga, Tenn.

DAWSON, Abraham, priv., Co. K., 20th Ind., d. Sept. 2, 1862, Philadelphia, Pa.
" William S., " " E., 21st Ind., d. Dec. 22, 1864, Philadelphia, Pa.
" Robert, " " D., 5th N. Y., d. March 30, 1865, Cypress Hill Cem., L. I., N. Y.
" John, " " G., 48th N. Y., d. Aug. 13, 1864, Richmond, Va.
" J. M., " " M., 6th Ky. Cav., d. Feb. 18, 1864, Richmond, Va.
" George, " " E., 8th N. Y. Heavy Art., d. Nov. 9, 1864, Salisbury, N. C.
" Smiley C., " " I., 113th Ill., d. Sept. 9, 1863, Cahaba, Ala.
" William, sergeant, Co. D., 24th Ohio Inf., d. March 10, 1864, Chattanooga, Tenn.
" C. H., " " H., 18th U. S. Inf., Chattanooga, Tenn.
" John M., private, Co. H., 76th N. Y. S. M., Nat. Cem., Gettysburg, Pa.
" Thomas, " " A., 78th N. Y., Nat. Cem., Gettysburg.
" S., " " E., 93d Ind., Millen, Ga.
" Noah, Indianapolis, Ind.

ADDITIONS AND CORRECTIONS.

1874.

Notice. The compiler solicits the aid of all interested for the correction of any errors or omissions which may be discovered in this volume, and to this end requests the communication of corrected and additional records.

He has reason to suppose that in many more instances than those in which the result has been communicated to him the collection and arrangement of family records has been undertaken as suggested and urged by his various circular letters. Not only more attention has thus been paid to the preservation of such records, as a result of his labors, but more will be paid in future; and he will be greatly obliged for the communication of any such additional records as may be sent him. He will undertake to arrange and carefully preserve the same for future use, and if they should not be printed by him they will be deposited in some proper public collection, and thus be made available to any future enquirer.

The additions and corrections following are, mainly, the result of a distribution of the proofs of the foregoing pages among the families interested.

Address,

CHARLES C. DAWSON,

Plainfield, N. J.

Page 3, note 4. For *Etyomological* read *Etymological.*

Page 10, lines 15 and 16. For Cumberland read Camberwell. Peter Dawson, vicar of Camberwell, m. Feb. 7, 1621, Mrs. Dorothy Martin. *Collectanea Gen.*, vol. 3, p. 162.

Page 13. Add to list of localities: Dawson Co., Ter. of Wyoming; Dawson's (P.O.), Hopkins Co., Ky.; Dawson's Cross Roads (P.O.), Halifax Co., N. C.; Dawson's Landing (P.O.), Bladen Co., N. C.

Page 18. Add to note 8: One Dawson, a loyalist, commanding a brig called the "Hope," planned an attack on Machias, Me., 1777. See Kidder's *Eastern Maine and Nova Scotia*, p. 43.

Page 43. W. of Titus Dawson (4-9). For *Sybil Dennison* read *Sybil Denison.*

Page 46. Children of John Daniel Smith (5-6). After 6-10, add 6-10*b*. Mary, b. July 6, 1817, m. March 6, 1838, John R. Downer, b. June 20, 1805. Two children: I. James R., b. Feb. 1, 1839, m. Dec. 22, 1864, Margaret Ann Herrick, and has three children, Frank H., b. Oct. 6, 1865, Edgar I., b. June 27, 1867, George Herbert, b. Aug. 29, 1873. II. Charles, b. May 14, 1844, m. Feb. 19, 1861, Helen Witman.

Page 55. *Mary Diane Dawson* (6-77) m. in Springfield, Mass., Jan. 1, 1874, Charles D. Pease. Res. Springfield.

Page 56. Children of John Dawson (5-21). Mary Ann (6-85), after b., for May read March. Milton (6-86), after b., for March 28, read March 1.

Page 61. Children of Joel Dawson Smith (6-10). John Daniel (7-12) m. at Castleton, Dec. 21, 1863, Maggie Hudson; child, Joel D., 2d, b. Oct. 28, 1866.

William Peck (7-13), m. at Castleton, June 24, 1868, Georgiana Knowlton; child, William K., b. March 25, 1870. Charles Hyde (7-14), m. at Castleton, Sept. 23, 1869, Hester J. Callanan; child Mary Grace, b. Sept. 15, 1871.

Page 62. Children of T. REILY VAN HOESEN. For two read three, and add: 7-21*b*. Raymond, b. May 19, 1873.

Page 62, note 2. For ELISHA FOWLER read ELIHU FOWLER.

Page 64. W. of WILLIAM HOLT DAWSON (6-33). For *Martha Wilmot* read *Martha C. Wilmot.*

Page 65. Child of WILLIAM HOLT DAWSON (6-33). For Frances Emma (7-50), read Frances Ermina.

Page 66. Children of HENRY SHEPARD DAWSON (6-34). For Henry Shepard (7-56), read Henry Smith. Florence Irene (7-63), for b. Nov. 10, read b. Nov. 15.

Page 68. For FULLAGER (7-74), read FULLAGAR.

Page 70. Children of FREDERICK WILLIAM MELOY (6-41). Anna (7-86), for res. Great Valley, read res. Ellicottville. Charles Frederick (7-87), for res. Cuba read res. Attica.

Page 70. Rev. JUDAH L. RICHMOND (6-42). For graduate of Hamilton College read graduate of Madison University, Hamilton, N. Y., 1833. He was in the Baptist ministry thirty-five years.

Page 71. RICHMOND. Frederick William (7-95), for res. Cleveland read res. Ai, Fulton Co. Katherine (7-96), for res. Goshen, Ind., read res. Brighton, Lorain Co., O.

Page 71, note 1, line 4. Res. of Lewis Keeler. For Greene read Union.

Page 74. KINNEY. For Kate Eugenia (7-132) read Kate Luthera.

Page 77. OLIVER WINSTON DAWSON (6-57). In consequence of impaired health, Mr. Dawson resigned, in Nov., 1873, his clerkship in the General Ticket office of the Michigan Southern and Northern Indiana Railway Co. In accepting his resignation the officers of that company testified in flattering terms to the fidelity and efficiency with which, during a clerkship of nearly twenty years, Mr. D. had discharged the duties of his office.

Page 77. TIMOTHY JOHN DAWSON (7-144), m. in Middletown, N. Y., April 28, 1874, Miss *Helen Dann.* They res. in Toledo, O.

Page 78. EDWARD SEBRIED DAWSON (6-58). For Robinson (first line) read Robison. For E. S. Dawson & Co. (eighth line) read Dawson & Co. *Strike out* (lines 17 and 18) is the oldest institution of the kind in Syracuse, and *and insert* was chartered in 1855, and is.

Page 78. Edward Seymour Dawson (7-149), graduated, March 12, 1874, in the College of Pharmacy, at Philadelphia, Pa., receiving the Alumni gold medal for superior scholarship.

Page 82. TRUMAN ROWLEY COLMAN (6-61), for b. Nov. 9, read b. Nov. 13; for twelve (ninth line) read thirteen.

Page 85. Children of MOSES BEECHER (6 67). Jessie Cumming (7-174), for res. 1873, in Warren, read d. in Ellicottville, Aug. 30, 1853. Harry Downer (7-178), for b. 1844 read b. 1864.

Page 86. For RICHARD CARY (6-70), read RICHARD L. CARY.

Page 87. W. of ROLLIN LAUREAT DAWSON (6-72). *Jane Elizabeth Lewis.* For b. Oct. 6, read b. March 2.

Page 87, note 1. PIERCE. For stone mason (1st line) read mason. For Ebenezer (2d line) read Eber. For Ebenezer (3d line), read Eber, and erase words in parenthesis.

Page 90. MILTON DAWSON (6-86). For b. March 28, read b. March 1. After *Mary Ann Schofield*, b. in Spencer, 1826, *erase* where she res. 1873, and add *note*: She m. Oct. 6, 1872, Samuel Miller, of Wolcott, Wayne Co., N. Y.

Page 93. Children of JOEL CAROLUS DOOLITTLE (6-107). Sylvester Legrand (7-271), for b Jan. 21, read b. Jan. 31. Emma Elizabeth (7-274), for b. April 15, read b. April 22.

Page 94. *Julia Josephine Doolittle* (7–283), m. April 14, 1872, NEWTON C. ABBOTT; res. 1873, Dover, Fayette Co., Iowa.

Page 98. CHARLES CLAPP FULLER (6-140). For res. Cumberland township, Greene Co., Pa., read res. Brownsville, Union Co., Pa.

Page 99. Children of BENAJAH HERVEY DOUGLASS (7-25). John Francis (8-9), m. Sept. 11, 1873, Annie Leffingwell Blake, b. Aug. 14, 1850, dau. of Philos Howard Blake and w. Mary Woodbridge Hudson. For Benajah Holt (8-12), read Benajah Hervey.

Page 99. VINUS ALLING (7-26). For b. 1819, read b. 1809.

Page 99. CHESTER HOLT DOUGLASS (7-28). For b. Dec. 12, read b. Dec. 10.

Page 100. BENJAMIN HULBERT ROBERTS (7-29), b. Jan. 27, 1828.

Page 100. W. of WILLIAM BRADLEY DOUGLASS (7-30). For *Martha Horton*, read *Martha Lodema Horton*.

Page 100. Rev. SOLOMON JOHNSON DOUGLASS (7-31). For Samuel H. Eliot read Samuel H. Elliot. For Eliot Chester (8-24), read Elliot Chester.

Page 104. Child of EDWARD WALTER DAWSON (7-51). For Mary Lilia (8-51) read Mary Leila.

Page 105. W. of THEODORE SIMEON ROGERS (7-73). For *Harriet Nacissa Johnson* read *Harriet Narcissa Johnson*.

Page 106. For LANGLEY FULLAGER (7-74), read LANGLEY FULLAGAR.

Page 108. Children of THEODORE RICHMOND (7-91). After 9-96 add 9-96*b*. Chester Dawson, b. in Chattanooga, Tenn., March 15, 1874.

Page 118. SAMUEL JAMES GIFFORD (7-162). Erase insurance agent.

Page 119. After DAVID GIBBS ALLING (7-167), erase the words one child : also erase the line following.

Page 122. Child of MYRON HAVILLAH DAWSON (7-221). For Sidney (8-168), read Sidney Myron.

Page 122. Erase note 1.

Page 123. Child of WALLACE ADELBERT MORSE (7-236). For Hattie Viola (8-176), read Hattie Estella, b. Jan. 4, 1872.

Page 125. SYLVESTER LEGRAND DOOLITTLE (7-271.) For b. Jan. 21, read b. Jan. 31. For *Adelle Horrey* read *Adelle Harvey*. For Hattie Horrey read Hattie Harvey.

Page 126. Child of EDWIN GARRIT DOUD (7-291). Jane Sperry (8-200), for res. Freedom read res. Nelson.

Page 127. Rev. ISAAC MILLS ELY (8-61). For Presbyterian church at Chenango Forks read Congregational church at Chenango Forks.

Page 128. Child of ROBERT D. JILLSON (8-63). After 9-8 read Robert Falkner.

Page 134. HENRY DAWSON (3-7), m. April 16, 1848, *Sarah A. Ward*, b. in Newtown, March 8, 1826. Child, Catharine (4-23), b. June 7, 1849.

Page 138. JOHN SELKIRK DAWSON (2-6), b. in Barnet, Vt., Sept. 24, 1811, m. 1st, at Bangor, Me., Jan. 25, 1838, *Salome Emerson*. They had one dau. (see p. 138, 3-22). He m. 2d, Jan. 18, 1870, Mrs. Abby E. Sharpe, and res. 1873, Putnam, Ct. Mr. Dawson began railroad building on the Boston and Lowell R. R. in 1831-32, and has been most of his life since engaged in similar enterprises. He enlisted, Sept. 12, 1862, at Davenport, Iowa, in Co. K., 37th Iowa Vols., composed of patriotic youths of over 45, and well known as the Grey-beard Regiment, in which he served until the organization was disbanded at the close of the war, in May, 1865.

Page 142. W. of HENRY DAWSON (3-1). For *Alice Wostenholme*, dau. of John Wostenholme, read *Alice Wolstenholme*, b. Oct. 12, 1804, dau. of John Wolstenholme. Their son George (4-4), for res. Blair, Neb. read res. Grant, Neb.

Page 143. Children of JAMES CROMPTON (3-2). Substitute the following for list as printed : 4-16. Margaret, m. ——— JOHNSON, res. Amesbury, Mass., five children ; 4-17. Thomas, res. Hartford, Ct., m. no issue ; 4-18. Ellen, m. ——— NESBITT, res. Amesbury, Mass. ; 4-19. Ann, *unm* ; 4-20. Rachel, m. ——— TATE, res. Ill., twelve children ; 4-21. James, res. Windsor Locks, m., several children ; 4-21*b*. Matilda, *unm*. 4-22. Alice, m. ——— JOHNSON, several children ; 4-23. Mary, *unm*.

Page 143. Child of WILLIAM CROMPTON (3-4). Mariana (4-26), m. May 10, 1855, her cousin Thomas Crompton. They res. in Windsor, Ct. ; no issue.

Page 144. Children of JOHN DAWSON (4-1). After four children read living, and add to list two children d. as follows: Esther Caroline, b. in Wallingford, Ct., Aug. 11, 1850, d. in Thompsonville, Ct., Sept. 11, 1851; Charles Robert, b. in Thompsonville, Ct., July 20, 1853, drowned at Worcester, Mass., June 22, 1859.

Page 145. Child of CHARLES DAWSON (4-7). Alida A. (5-20), m. in Holden, Mass., Jan. 1, 1874, Henry C. Chenery.

Page 146. Rev. REUEL HOTCHKISS TUTTLE (4-28). For b. in Old Town, Me., read b. in Hartford, Ct.; for He is rector read He was until recently rector. For five children read four children, and *erase line beginning* 5-34. Also, change place of birth of Annie Elizabeth (5-33) from Hartford, Ct., to Old Town, Me.

Page 150. Add to note 1, as follows: Folkert or Volkert Dawson bap. at Schenectady Sept. 26, 1731, was son of William Daasen, cooper, and w. Ariaantje, dau. of Volkert Veeder, m. Feb. 22, 1729. Folkert m. Geertruy, dau. of Ryckert Hilton, of Albany. Their son Richard was bap. Dec. 11, 1763. William Dawson, of Schenectady, m. Gennet McArthur; child, Gennet, b. Nov. 2, 1789. Pearson's *Genealogies of the First Settlers of Schenectady.*

Page 152, line 23. DAWSON. For T. W. (Rev.) read T. M. (Rev).

Page 166. Children of JAMES DAWSON (2-1). For James (3-1) read James W.; for Mary (3-5) read Mary A.; and *see page* 180.

Page 168. Child of GEORGE DAWSON (2-2). For Burritt S. (3-7) read Burret S.; for *unm.* read *m.*, and *see page* 181.

Page 173. HENRY BARTON DAWSON (2-1). For Company (1st line) read Society. For (10th line) *Manual* of the common council of New York city, for 1855, read *Manual of the Common Council of New York city for* 1855.

Page 175. Child of HENRY BARTON DAWSON (2-1). After George Cooley (3-5) read telegraph operator.

Page 183. Child of RICHARD DAWSON (2-2). For Zedediah (3-6) read Jedediah.

Page 184. Children of FRANCIS DAWSON (3-1). Deborah (4-10), for res. Gloucester Co., read Woodstown, Salem Co. Rebecca (4-13), for CASTLE read COSTLE.

Page 184. Children of FRANCIS DAWSON (4-8). For list as printed read as follows: Samuel, Jonathan, Mary Ann (m. —— CALAHAN), George, John, Elizabeth, Francis.

Page 185. Child of ISRAEL APPLEGATE (4-12). Mary (5-20) m. —— KIRKBRIDE.

Page 185. For MAHLON CASTLE (4-13) read MAHLON COSTLE.

Page 185. Child of JOHN E. TOZER (5-15). For Rachel (6-3) read Rachel C.

Page 186. Rev. THOMAS M. DAWSON (5-16). *After* from (5th line) *erase* the.

Page 187. John and Dorothy Dawson. For of Abington, Pa. (8th line), read of Hatboro and Philadelphia, Pa. After fifth paragraph read Jane Dawson w. of Emanuel Dawson. d. in Philadelphia, 1 mo. 30, 1698. Qy.: 1st w.?

Page 188. After second line read, Ann Dawson made a will dated June 16, 1755, but for some reason it was set aside, and letters of administration were granted to one of her creditors. The witnesses to the will were Robert Worrell, Jane Worrell, late Jane Dawson, Joseph Sermon, and Mary Dawson, dau. of Isaac Dawson. *See page* 420 (2-5).

Page 189. Erase first and second lines of note 3.

Page 191. Child of WILLIAM DAWSON (3-6). William Lewis (4-1), for d. young, read d. in U. S. Marine Corps.

Page 191, note 1. Add: For notice of Josiah Dawson (3-10) see Henry Simpson's *Lives of Eminent Philadelphians now deceased*, 1859.

Page 191. MORDECAI LEWIS DAWSON (4-3). *Between* the *and* monthly (4th line) *insert* Twelfth street.

Page 192. For STEPHEN P. MORRIS (5-3) read STEPHEN MORRIS. He was son of Henry and Caroline Morris.

Page 194. Child of THOMAS SCOTT DAWSON (3-1). Ella Groome (4-1), for m. PHILEMON T. KENNER, read m. PHILEMON T. KENNARD.

Page 203. Children of ROBERT DAWSON (3-10). Insert full names as follows: Elizabeth Ballantyne, Joseph Hamilton, Andrew Rea Z., Luther Gailey, John Pinkerton.

Page 204. Child of JAMES DAWSON (3-11). Martha S. (4-14), m. Dr. ADAIR.

Page 204. *Mary Dawson*, w. of MATTHEW NELSON (3-12), d. 1873.

Page 204. JOHN DAWSON and w. (3-14) res. Washington, Iowa.

Page 207. For *Elizabeth B. Dawson* (4-5) read *Elizabeth Ballantyne Dawson.*

Page 207. For LUTHER G. DAWSON (4-8) read LUTHER GAILEY DAWSON. Mr. D. was acting judge of the Washington, D. C., Police Court, 1873.

Page 207. For JOHN P. DAWSON (4-9) read JOHN PINKERTON DAWSON.

Page 225. Dr. JAMES DAWSON (6-6) d. at St. Michaels, Md., Feb. 20, 1874. *See page* 506.

Page 226. Children of Dr. JAMES DAWSON (6-6). John Alvan (7-8), after res. Talbot Co., read physician. For Douglass Hambleton (7-9) read Douglas Hambleton.

Page 228. Children of THOMAS RUSSELL DAWSON (6-20). Henry Anstice (7-34) d. June 8, 1871 ; Mary Saltonstall, b. in Philadelphia, March 26, 1874.

Page 229. Throughout the record beginning on this page, for Prince George county read Prince George's county.

Page 233. NICHOLAS DAWSON (3-2). For d. about 1800 read d. 1789. On the authority of his son, Hon. John Dawson, it is now stated (1874) that N. D. was m. in Fayette county, Pa. (*see note* 3), and had, besides two sons, two daughters, one of whom, the eldest child, was b. 1781. In last line of note 3, for child read son.

Page 233. JOHN DAWSON (3-4). He m. *Elizabeth Harrison.* They had, besides the four sons named in record, another son whose name was Benjamin.

Page 236. Child of ROBERT DOYNE DAWSON (3-17). Verlinda H., (4-34), for d. about 1864, read b. 1785, d. 1856.

Page 238. GEORGE DAWSON (4-2). His w. *Mary Kennedy*, was b. at Charleston, S. C., about 1794, only child of Samuel and Mary Kennedy. Her father d. at Charleston, and she was brought up by her grandparents, who resided at York, Pa. Her grandfather, Dr. Robert Kennedy, a Scotch Presbyterian, was an eminent physician, and one of the early settlers of York. The children of George and *Mary Kennedy* Dawson are now named in the order of birth, as follows : Sarah Ann, John Littleton, Louisa, Samuel Kennedy, Ellen, George Nicholas, Mary Kennedy, Elizabeth Jennings, Catharine Harrison, George Fielding.

Page 239. Children of ADDISON RUBY (5–12). Dawson, L. H., Edward A.

Page 239. Children of Dr. WILLIAM STURGEON (5–13). John D., Daniel, Mary E., Kate B., Ellen B.

Page 239. Children of HENRY BALDWIN (5-14). John D., Henry, Richard D., Ann B., Louisa B.

Page 239. Child of A. K. JOHNSON (5-16). Charles Dawson, b. Dec. 13, 1872.

Page 239. Children of JOHN M. BERRY (5-17). John, Bailey, Lizzie, Evie.

Page 239. Children of JOHN NICHOLAS DAWSON (5-18). J. Evans, Richard W., Ann Bailey.

Page 239. Capt. HENRY CLAY DAWSON (5-15). Erase two lines except name, also erase note 1, and read as follows : Born at Uniontown, Pa., Feb. 1, 1834, graduated at Madison College, June, 1854, and was admitted to practice law, June, 1857. He entered the Army of the Potomac on its first organization, in the 8th Reg't. Pa. Reserves, and was captain of Co. G. ; was wounded at the first battle of Fredericksburgh, Va., Dec. 13, 1862. He is now engaged in farming and stock raising. He m. April 26, 1867, *Mary Agnes McCloskey*, eldest dau. of John McCloskey, proprietor of the Port Perry Coal Mines, Alleghany Co., Pa. They res. 1874, at Lynchburg, Highland Co., Ohio, and have two children : Anne Louisa, b. May 28, 1868, Bailey, b. Dec. 22, 1871.

Page 240. BENONI DAWSON (4-18). His w. a dau. of Daniel and Katherine D. McKennon.

Page 243. DANIEL ALLNUTT (4-34). See substitute for this record, page 261, *note.*

Page 244. Child of STEPHEN N. DAWSON (4-36). Thomas J. (5-114), for res. near Russellville, read d. near Russellville, May 3, 1869.

Page 245. SAMUEL BLACKMORE (5-128). After son of Benoni, for 5-81 read 5-82.

Page 246. ASHMAN. For *Sarah Dawson* (5-1) read *Sarah Ann Dawson.*

Page 249, note, last line of first paragraph. For John Taylor of Carolina read John Taylor of Caroline.

Page 252. Hon. JOHN LITTLETON DAWSON (5-2). For *Whaley* read *Whirley*. His w. dau. of Robert Clarke, b. near Wilmington, Del., and w. Sarah Whirley, b. at Hagerstown, Md.; m. at Brownsville, Pa.

Page 252. For FRANK N. HUTCHINSON (6-8), read FRANK M. HUTCHINSON.

Page 252. CASS. *Ellen Dawson* (5-8). For youngest read third.

Page 252. HOWELL. For *Elizabeth Dawson* (5-5), read *Elizabeth Jennings Dawson*.

Pase 253. Gen. SAMUEL KENNEDY DAWSON (5-9). For m. *Jeannette Weston* read m. *Jean Weston*. After 6-18, for Jeannette read Jean.

Page 264. CHARLES E. SPEER (6-4). Add note: Son of Dr. James R. and Hetty Morrow Speer; gr. son of Rev. Dr. Speer, an eminent Presbyterian divine.

Page 264. HENRY WHITELEY PATTERSON (6-6). Add note: Alfred Patterson, b. Fayette Co., Pa., son of John Patterson, farmer; Caroline Whiteley, b. at Newark, Del., dau. of Col. Henry and Caroline Whiteley.

Page 279. SHADRACH H. DAWSON (2-9). He d. in Philadelphia.

Page 282. DANIEL DAWSON (3-14), m. at Wilmington meeting, Del.; Warner Dawson signed certificate as witness. Qy. As to latter: son of Wm. Dawson of Philadelphia? *See page* 190 (3-8).

Page 282. WILLIAM DAWSON (3-17), m. *Elizabeth* ———. Elizabeth Dawson d. 3 mo. 7, 1836. *Wilmington, Del., Meeting Records.*

Page 308. Capt. William Francis Dawson (2–2). Capt. Dawson is honorably mentioned in Bennett's *Ceylon and its Capabilities*, p. 301. He visited the island in 1826.

Page 310. Commander William Dawson (3-1). For b. 1832, read b. 1833.

Page 310. Lieut. Llewellyn Styles Dawson (3-4). For new Guinea read New Guinea.

Page 310. For Sidney Pace Dawson (3-7), read Sidney P. Dawson.

Page 312, *note*. GEORGE FRANCIS DAWSON (3-2). For fiancially (2d line) read financially; for world's (6th line) read Nation's.

Page 314, sixth line. For Commissary Dawson married read Commissary William Dawson married Mary, dau. of William and *Mary Randolph* Stith, and add note: It is said that they had a son who m. —— *Johnson*, of North Carolina, and had issue William Johnson Dawson, M. of C. from that state, 1793-5. This from a MS. Mem. Book of John Randolph of Roanoke. See Wynne's *Historical Documents from the Old Dominion*, No. V. (Vestry Book of Henrico Parish, Va.), p. 180. But see also, p. 238, *ante*.

Page 314. Hon. JOHN DAWSON, M. C. *After* served in one of the state conventions of Virginia, *add note*: This was the constitutional convention of Va., held 1788, to which he was a delegate with James Monroe for Spottsylvania (including Fredericksburg). See Reeves's *Life and Times of James Madison*, vol. 2, 553.

Page 315. Add to note 3 as follows: One Martin Dawson d. in Albemarle county, Va., May, 1835, aged 55. By his will he set free sixty slaves and provided for their removal to Liberia; and he also gave $40,000 to schools in Virginia. Allen's *American Biographical Dictionary*.

Page 316. Second line of *italics*. For *Elisha Dawson* read *Elijah Dawson*.

Page 318. Children of JAMES DAWSON (3-11). John Dabney (4-15), for Medway read Midway; Josephine (4-16) m. JAMES STRONG; son William, atty., res. St. Joseph, Mo.; James Wade (4-18) d. 1853.

Page 319. JAMES WADE DAWSON (4-18). For m. Miss *Van Pelt* read m. *Maria Van Pelt*. He d. 1853. His son (5-5), for Joseph K. read Joseph Wade, b. 1845, res. 1874, Louisville, Ky., *unm.*

Page 323. JOHN DAWSON (1), of Stafford Co., Va., removed to Jacksonville, Ill., 1831, d. 1839. His children: Bailey (2-2) d. in Jefferson Co., Ky., 1856, leaving several children, one of whom, Coleman, a Baptist minister, res. at Westfield, Clark Co., Ill. John (2-3) d. in Iowa, 1846, *unm.* Bernard (2-4), *erase* Barnett or. Elijah (2-5) d. in Iowa, 1848; children, all living in Iowa, Lindsay, Peyton (farmer and preacher, near Mt. Pleasant), John Wallace, Williamson, Lucinda, Eliza. Barton (2-7), was killed by being thrown from a cart when a young man in Ky.

Page 324. 2-4 and 3-11. Erase three lines, and read as follows: BERNARD DAWSON, blacksmith and farmer, b. at Dumfries, Prince William county, Va., 1788, d. in Jacksonville, Ill., April 13, 1853, m. *Elizabeth Low*, b. in Prince William county, 1789, d. in Jacksonville, 1854, dau. of John Low, a Rev. officer. They had eight children, viz.: I. John Thomas, blacksmith, b. in Va., 1813, res. Jacksonville, Ill., m. 1839, *Harriet Thorpe*, of Springfield, Ill.; children, Josiah, m. and res. Verdon, Ill., Charles David res. Jacksonville, *unm.*, Newton, res. Texas, *unm.*, Robert, Melissa, John, Urelius, Hattie, Minnie, all *unm.* II. Edward Logan, blacksmith, b. in Va., 1815, m. 1839, *Olive Yeamons*, res. Jacksonville, children, Nathan E. Y., m. and res. at Yatesville, Ill., William H. H., m. and res. at Nicholasville, Ky., Charles Bernard, res. Arizona, *unm.*, Sarah, m. —— BUCKINGHAM, res. Jacksonville, Susan F., m. WILLIAM WATSON, res. Jacksonville, and Olive, John Samuel, Mary J., Bailey B., all *unm.* III. Sarah Elizabeth, b. in Va., 1817, m. SAMUEL COBB, res. Jacksonville; children, Elizabeth J., d. 1873, w. of HENRY W. HUNT, Jacksonville, Mary Ann, m. —— ERVIN, res. Jacksonville, John Samuel, d., Martin Henry, *unm.*, Bailey B., *unm.*, Jennie D., d. IV. Charles Henry, blacksmith, inventor of the gang plow, cultivator, and other agricultural implements, b. in Va., 1820, d. in Sangamon county, Ill., 1870, m. *Julia A. Meachum*, who res. Laomi, Sangamon Co.; children living, Richard Henry, m. and res. in Springfield, Ill., George Ellis, teacher, res. Buffalo, N. Y., *unm.*, Lydia, m. J. E. COLEMAN, res. Springfield, Ill., Ollie, m. ROBERT SHORT, res. Laomi, Andrew and Walter, *unm.*, res. Laomi. V. Mary Ann, b. in Va., d. young. VI. Richard William, lawyer, b. in Shelby county, Ky., 1826, res. Olathe, Kansas, m. in Charleston, Ill., June 1, 1850, *Phebe Parker*, dau. of Hon. Nathaniel Parker, formerly state senator of Illinois: children, Nathaniel Bernard, lawyer, and Jennie Adelle, teacher, both res. Olathe. VII. Samuel Demanuel, b. in Shelby county, Ky., 1828, d. 1845, *unm.* VIII. Bailey Dividual, b. in Oldham county, Ky., July 7, 1830, studied at Illinois College, Jacksonville, 1849-53, read law at Jacksonville, with Yates, Brown and McClure, 1855-56, admitted to the Bar, Jan. 1, 1857. He was, in 1863-64, acting provost marshal of the Seventh District of Illinois; engrossing clerk of the Senate of Illinois, 1867; supervising special agent of the United States Treasury Department for the Ninth Customs District (the state of Texas) with headquarters at Galveston, 1869. Mr. Dawson has held various newspaper connections, and in May, 1865, as Washington correspondent of the *Chicago Tribune*, sent to that paper, over the signature of "Junius," a lengthy report of an interview with President Johnson which contained the president's first utterances on the subject of Reconstruction. This is said to have been the first instance of the now prevalent fashion of reportorial interviewing, and Mr. Dawson must have the credit of originating a new branch of industry. In 1870, Mr. D. was engaged in the real estate business at Chicago, and he now res. at Jacksonville, *unm.*

Page 324. Erase two lines (2-6 and 3-12) and read as follows: LEMUEL DAWSON, d. in Springfield, Ill., April 5, 1853, m. in Shelby county, Ky., *Mary Garrison*, who was b. in Va. She now res. in Mo. They had seven children: I. James, m. in Morgan Co., Ill., *Maradie Bozarth*, res. Mt. Pleasant, Iowa; children, Henry and Elias, both m. and res. at Council Bluffs, Iowa, Mary Jane, d. II. Benjamin, m. and res. at Decatur, Ill., five children. III. Elias, m. *Ann Bozarth* (sister to w. of James). He d. in Springfield, Ill., 1855, leaving one child, Marietta. IV. John Allen, m. and res. St. Louis, Mo. V. Barton. VI. Calvin, m. and res. in Missouri, newspaper publisher.

Pages 323-326. For Davies Co., Ky., read Daviess Co., Ky.

Page 328. BENJAMIN DAWSON (1) was son of John Dawson, of Va. He had brothers Robert and Stephen, besides those mentioned on p. 328. His bro. Capt. ARMSTRONG DAWSON m. Miss *McKinley*, dau. of John McKinley, first clerk of Fayette county, Ky. They settled at Clintonville, Bourbon Co., Ky., where he d. Aug., 1854. He was a man of considerable influence in his county, and much respected. They had twelve children: I. John, d. *unm.* II. James, d. young. III.

Thomas, d. young. IV. Benjamin, d. young. V. George, m. *Georgia McCann*, dau. of Pleasant McCann, of Mo., res. near Plattsburg, Mo. VI. Rebecca, m. GRANVILLE CRUTCHER, of Frankfort, Ky.; their son, George W. Crutcher, res. at Cynthiana, Ky. VII. Martha, m. —— DAVIS. VIII. Mary, d. *unm.* IX. Sarah, m. WILLIAM REED, Carlisle, Ky. X. Fanny, m. J. J. PIPER. XI. Sena, d. young. XII. Lucinda, m. WILLIAM SQUIRES.

Page 336. Note the following additional Virginia record. *From Thomas W. Dawson, Los Angelos, Cal.*, 1874. THOMAS DAWSON, b. and d. in Va., had brothers Abraham, Isaac (lived near Chillicothe, O.), Jacob, Nathaniel, William (lived near Cincinnati, O.), David (lived in Ky.), and John. Thomas Dawson had by first w. three children, John, Esau and Margaret. By third w. he had William, Moses and Sarah. By second w. he had eight children, as follows: I. Isaac, lived and d. in Hampshire Co., W. Va.; had sons, Daniel S. and George, res. near Salt Lake, Utah, and John T., Milton, and Horatio, who res. Hampshire Co., W. Va. II. Ephraim, m. in Va. about 1814, *Eleanor Buckingham*, and a few years after they removed to Ohio, living for a time at Washington, in Fayette county, and afterwards at London, in Madison county, where both d. about 1827. They had six children, Delilah (m. F. FAGAN, and d. in Iowa, about 1860), Eleanor (m. JAMES F. FREEMAN, of London, O., both d. about 1857), Thomas W. (see below), Lavinia (m. 1st, DAVIS, 2d, HENSLEY, lived in Mo.), Caroline (m. JOHN GREGORY, and d. in Sangamon Co., Ill., about 1855), and Charles (see below). III. Mary, m. ——— CHRISTY, res. near Washington, O. IV. Abraham, res. near Washington, O. V. Rachel, m. ——— CHRISTY, res. near Washington, O. VI. Jacob, res. near Terre Haute, Ind. VII. David. VIII. Benoni, res. near Wapello, Iowa........ THOMAS W. DAWSON (son of Ephraim, II, above), was elected clerk of Newton county, Mo., in 1846, where he m. in Oct. of that year, *Mary Rankin*, dau. of Sinnet Rankin, formerly of Fayette Co., O. They removed to Shasta county, Cal., in 1850, where he was also elected to the county clerkship. In 1856 they returned to Missouri, and settled near Carthage, Jackson county, where he was extensively engaged in farming; remaining there until the outbreak of the civil war, when he removed his family to the Brazos country, in Texas, and himself enlisted in the Confederate service. In the fall of 1868 he returned to the Pacific coast, and now res. (1874) at Los Nietos, Los Angelos Co., Cal. Mr. Dawson is 6 ft. 8 in. in height, and is familiarly called "The Long Tom of the West." Several of his family have been remarkable for their great stature and physical power. He has five children living, as follows: Eleanor (b. 1848, m. JOSEPH L. POWELL, res. Los Angelos Co., Cal.), Sue H., Sarah Elma, Lillie, Joseph W......... CHARLES DAWSON (son of Ephraim, II, above), m. 1st in Wisconsin, about 1847, Miss *Hopkins*, who d. leaving two sons, both now living, John M., Robert W. He m. 2d, Miss *McFarland*. She d. at Carthage, Mo., leaving several children, three now living, Frank, Mary, Elma. He m. 3d, Miss *Stevenson*. They res. 1874, in Los Angelos Co., Cal., and have one dau. Concerning Mr. Charles Dawson, Mr. T. W. D. writes as follows: "My brother is a fair type of the old stock; a man of fine natural abilities, not having enjoyed the advantages of an early education, yet a man of fine sense and unflinching integrity; and he has on several occasions ignored and rejected proffered popularity and pecuniary gain in order that he might have the satisfaction of feeling that he stood for the right even when moral integrity seemed to be at a discount."

Page 336. Note, also, the following additional record. *From Mr. Bertrand Dawson, Dawson, Sangamon Co., Ill.*, 1874. 1. WILLIAM DAWSON moved from Fairfax Co., Va., where he was b. and raised, to Bracken Co., Ky., in the year 1805, where he lived until his death, which occurred about 1855, at the age of 82 years. It is said that his gt. gr. father was from Ireland. He raised a family of ten children, five sons, of whom were, 2-1. John, the eldest child; 2-2. Reuben; and 2-3. Thomas, who d. *unm.* REUBEN DAWSON (2-2) was, in the early days of steamboating, a steamboat engineer on the Ohio and Mississippi rivers; afterwards, until his death in 1872, a government inspector of steamboat machinery at Louisville, Ky. He left one son, John (3-1) res. Louisville. JOHN DAWSON (2-1), was b. in Va., 1791, and removed with his father into Ky., in 1805. He was a volunteer in the war of 1812–14, was wounded and taken prisoner at the battle of the River Raisin, and taken by the Indians to Canada, where he was exchanged. He m. 1817, Miss *Cary R. Jones*, of Harrison Co., Ky., and in 1827 removed to Sangamon Co., where he d. in 1850. He was three times a representative of this county in the state Legislature, was a member of the constitutional convention of 1847, and for a number of years United States Pension Agent at Springfield. He was a farmer, laboring with his own hands, and was loved and respected by his neighbors, who honor his memory. He raised a family of ten children, seven of whom now live in Sangamon Co. Mr. Bertrand Dawson (3-1) above named, is of this number. In the Legislature of 1836-7, the delegation of Sangamon county was composed of two senators and seven representatives (two of the latter being JOHN DAWSON and ABRAHAM LINCOLN), noted then and since as the Long Nine. Their average height was exactly six feet, and they were not less remarkable for their talents and influence than for their stature.

Page 338. WILLIAM JOHNSON DAWSON (2-3). *See note for page 314, above.*

Page 338. JOHN B. DAWSON, M. C., from La. For 2-1 read 3-1. Add: He had repeatedly served in the Legislature of Louisiana; was a militia general of the state, and was judge of the parish court of the parish (West Feliciana), in which he resided before his election to Congress.

Page 344. JOHN DAWSON, of Wilmington, N. C. For b. about 1802, emigrated to this country about 1818, read b. June 23, 1803, came to America, 1821.

Page 344. JAMES DAWSON, of Wilmington, N. C. For b. about 1817, emigrated to Wilmington about 1838, read b. Nov. 8, 1813, emigrated to Wilmington, 1831, revisited Ireland and returned to America, 1838. Mr. Dawson resided for some years in Columbus, Ga., and m. at Greensboro, in that state, Aug. 5, 1847, *Missouri S. Martin*, dau. of Robert and *Edna Sandford* Martin. They have had three children: Robert Martin, b. in Columbus, Ga., Aug. 24, 1848, d. Aug., 1853, Fanny Gray, b. in Wilmington, N. C., Sept. 26, 1858, James, b. in Wilmington, April 25, 1861.

Page 345. JOHN DAWSON (1), of Charleston, S. C. His w. d. in Charleston, for 1859, read 1819. As answer to inquiry in note 1, suggesting a relationship to this family of one Thomas Dawson, a loyalist, of Charleston, N. H. R. Dawson, Esq., of Selena, Ala., sends an emphatic NO. The Thomas Dawson here mentioned may have been the clergyman of the church of England mentioned in note 1, page 367. See, also, page 392, note 2.

Page 346. JOHN DAWSON (2-3). For Cashier of the Bank of Charleston, read Cashier of the State Bank of Charleston.

Page 348. JOHN LAWRENCE DAWSON (3-24). For b. at Milton plantation, read b. at Mitton plantation.

Page 350. LAWRENCE EDWIN DAWSON (3-6). For He was several times a member of the South Carolina Legislature, read He was at one time, etc.

Page 352. For *Henry Ingraham* (3-13), read HENRY INGRAHAM.

Page 352. Children of Hon. FRANCIS BURT (3-14). For Francis St. Julien (4-32), read Francis. For George Ann Catharine (4-33), read George Ann.

Page 354. Dau. of WILLIAM ALFRED DAWSON (3-10). Catharine Cordes (4-55), for m. 1872, —— WILKINSON, read m. Dec. 26, 1872, CHAUNCEY WILKINSON.

Page 355. Dr. JOHN LAWRENCE DAWSON (3-24). For b. at Milton, read b. at Mitton. His children: Jane (4-70), for m. —— PINKNEY, read m. DOUGLASS B. PINKNEY, res. Charleston. Hester (4-71), for m. —— WARING, read m. HAYNE WARING, res. near Summerville, S. C.

Page 359. For *John Huger Dawson* (4-11), read JOHN HUGER DAWSON.

Page 359. HALL. *Harriet Dawson* (4-15). For m. 1870, read m 1871.

Page 359. WILLIAM HENRY DAWSON (4-19). For m. *George Ann Catharine Burt*, read m. *George Ann Burt.*

Page 360. *Frances Burt Dawson* (5-40), m. Oct. 29, 1873, AUGUSTUS FITCH, of Charleston.

Page 367, note 2. For Cornwalls read Cornwallis.

Page 370, first and second lines. For *Edgar E. Dawson*, read *Edgar G. Dawson.*

Page 375, note 2. For ollowing (5th line), read following.

Page 381. Dr. Thomas H. Dawson (3-3). His w. *Annie Snider;* for b. 1827, read b. 1828.

Page 382. William Curran Dawson (3-8), erase all after Alabama State Legislature, 1855, and read: also in 1856; m. Aug. 2, 1841, *Martha M. Colbert,* b. in Morgan county, Ga., May 6, 1824, dau. of Maj. John G., and *Frances Wingfield* Colbert, of Morgan county. Four children: I. Anna Wingfield, b. in Covington, Ga., July 7, 1842, m. June 10, 1863, John Tyler Howard, of Ala.; five children, three living: William Colbert, b. April 18, 1864, Robert Milton, b. June 10, 1866, Florence Dawson, b. Jan. 30, 1873. II. Thomas Colbert, b. in Russell county, Ala., July 23, 1847, res. Glenville, Ala., *unm.* III. Susan Amaret, b. in Russell Co., Ala., Dec. 17, 1849, m. Dec. 4, 1866, Crawford Brigges Griffiths, of Ala., who d. Sept. 28, 1867. She res. in Glenville; one child, Crawford Brigges, b. Sept. 27, 1867. IV. Florence, b. in Russell Co., Ala., July 11, 1853, res Glenville, *unm.*

Page 384. Henry H. Dawson (4-3). His children: Henry H., b. Nov. 14, 1869, Archie Griffith, b. April 20, 1871, Mattie Montieg, b. April 4, 1873.

Page 386. Dawson. Mary Frances (2-3). For La Grange, Ala., read La Grange, Ga.

Page 386. W. of Sidney Cook (2-1). For *Anna Burwell Dawson* read *Ann Burwell Dawson.* Their dau., Anna S. (3-2) m. Erastus Lyman Ellsworth.

Page 389. Dawson. For Alexander A. (3-10) read Alexander, b. in Madison Co., Ga. After note 4 read Mr. Dawson m. 1st, in Twiggs Co., Ga., Jan. 2, 1856, *Addie McCallum,* dau. of Archibald McCallum. She d. Dec. 20, 1866. Five children: McCallum, Homer, John Edmonds, Alexander, James S. Mr. D. m. 2d, in Twiggs Co., Nov. 15, 1871, *Margaret Horne,* dau. of Rev. William D. Horne. Two children: Cornelia, Leanna.

Page 389. *Mary McKennie Cook* (3-12) m. Fort Hargrove.

Page 390. *Mary R. Hill* (3-23) m. David A. Walker.

Page 394. John Dawson (1) was made a master mason in the Lodge of Honor and Generosity, Holborn, London, 1794. He had a bro. Thomas, who lived at Boston, Eng., and d. abt. 1810, leaving seven children; also a bro. William who was in the army, and d. in 1805. He had, also, a sister who m. a Mr. Bonner, and lived in 1811 at Langton, having then nine children. Before he came to America his mother, whose maiden name was *Mansfield Hill,* b. 1733, had m. a second husband, Mr. Gunness, who d. in 1799. Numerous letters from her to the son in London and New Orleans, dated at Horncastle, 1798 to 1812 are in possession of his son Mr. John Dawson now of New Orleans. At the time of the elder Dawson's emigration to New Orleans it was a Spanish territory under Governor Manuel Gayoso De Lemos.

Page 396. Add to note 1: Hon. John Dawson, of Uniontown, Pa., 1874 (son of Nicholas), states that his father was not a Rev. soldier. Henry, bro. of Nicholas, was, however, in the army.

Page 405. For William Dawson (2-1) read James William Dawson.

Page 407. John Dawson (1). For Bucks county read Philadelphia county.

Page 411. After Family of John Dawson for Of Bucks Co., Pa. read Of Hatboro. Same page, *second line from bottom,* for Bucks county read Philadelphia county. Moreland township is here erroneously described as formerly in Bucks county, now Montgomery. It was never in Bucks county, but was originally in Philadelphia county, though now forming a part of Montgomery.

Page 413. Add to note 5: The Longstreth arms are described in Burke's *General Armory of England* as follows: "Argent. A chevron gules, between three escolop shells sable. Crest, two rose bushes, the flowers white and red intertwined." The red rose was the emblem of the house of Lancaster, the white of the house of York. After the wars of the Roses, the intertwining of the flowers was indicative of the union of these houses. Adherents of the house of York, among whom was the ancestor of the Longstreths (Longstroder or Longstrother), bore the white rose.

Page 415. For Bucks county (10th line), read Philadelphia county.

Page 421. William Fussell (3-1). For d. 1803 or 1804, read d. 2 mo. 5, 1804. His son, Bartholomew (4-2). For d. near Yellow Springs, read d. near Kimberton.

Page 422, note 3. For Michenor, read Michener.

Page 424. John Longstreth (3-7). For m. 1762, read m. 7 mo. 17, 1766.

Page 430. Bartholomew Fussell (4-2). For d. near Yellow Springs, read d. near Kimberton. (B. F. and w. both d. on the same farm). Erase comma after with (4th line).

Page 431. John Longstreth (4-4). Erase entire record and substitute one on page 498.

Page 433. Longstreth, Susanna (5-47). For d. 2 mo. 7, 1835, read d. 2 mo. 17, 1833.

Page 434, *lines* 5, 8, 10, 14, 16, 18, 20, 22 *and* 24. For Miama read Miami.

Page 434. Mather. For Susan Bacon (5-69), read Sarah Bacon.

Page 434. Isaac Thomas Longstreth (4-47). After *Mary Collins*, read b. 7 mo. 27, 1789, d. in Philadelphia. Their children: For Mary Ann (5-71), read Mary Anna. For Susannah (5-72), read Susanna. For William C. (5-75), read William Collins. Add *note:* Mary Anna and Susanna Longstreth conducted for many years a noted "finishing school" for young ladies in Philadelphia, which is still under the direction of the former. Isaac Collins (father of *Mary Collins*), was a noted printer of Burlington, N. J. He printed much of the Continental money, also the first quarto Bible printed in America. He was b. 1746, d. 1817, m. 1771, Rachel Budd (dau. of Thomas and Rebecca Budd), and was son of Charles and Sarah Collins, who lived in New Castle county, now state of Delaware. Charles Collins came from Bristol, Eng., about the year 1700.

Page 434. David Longstreth (4-48). For Ogden, of Abington, read Ogden, of Springfield, Pa.

Page 436. Children of Nicholas Baggs (5-107). Mary Nichols, b. 7 mo. 23, 1860, Louise Dilworth, b. 5 mo. 29, 1862, Edward Colwell, b. 8 mo. 16, 1864, Albert Nicholas, b. 8 mo. 28, 1870.

Page 436. Children of Rev. Leighton W. Eckard (5-109). James Macintosh Longstreth, b. 1870, Esther Longstreth, b. 1872.

Page 437. Children of Benjamin D. Longstreth (5-125). I. William, m. July 20, 1871, *Mellie Freeze*, children: Walter, b. April 19, 1872, Earl, b. Aug. 9, 1873. II. Mary Belle, m. May 30, 1870, Howard Leever. III. Charles. IV. Albert, d. Aug. 17, 1858. V. Carrie May.

Page 437. Children of Theodore Tea (5-129). Benjamin, d. aged 2½ years, Jennie, b. in Lafayette, Ind., 1865.

Page 438. Children of Charles S. Renshaw (5-148). Fanny, Charles, James, Mira, William.

Page 438. Children of Charles Longstreth Orum (5-149). By 1st w.: Rachel, Julia, Mira, Morris, Ellen. By 2d. w.: Margaret, Gertrude.

Page 438. Children of Thomas Tyson Butcher (5-150). Frank, Amos, Thomas, Ellen (m. Robert Glendenning Jr., res. Phila., children Robert, Elizabeth), Morris, Alfred, Catharine M., Margaret.

Page 438. Children of Morris Orum (5-151). William, Frederick, Mary.

Page 439, lines 17 and 24. For Miama, read Miami.

Page 440, note 1, last line. For 3-38, n. 1, read 3-38, n. 2.

Page 443. Watson. For Richard (6-8) read Richard C., attorney at law, and associate judge of Bucks county, Pa., 1873.

Page 443. Lewis. Mariann (6-10). For d. 1866 read d. 9 mo. 3, 1866.

Page 444. William Fussell (5-10). See page 499, note 1.

Page 445. Solomon Fussell (5-13). For second sentence read, He removed with his parents about 1810 to Baltimore county, Md., but returned to Pa. while yet a young man.

Page 446. Jacob Fussell (5-14). For bur. Frankfort read bur. Frankford. His children: For William W. (6-45) read William. Ruthanna (6-48), for b. 1820, read b. 1821.

Page 448. Joseph Trimble (5-16), b. 1810, d. near Philadelphia, son of Joseph and *Mary Trimble* Trimble, cousins. His wid. res. in Chester Co., Pa.

Page 448. Mahlon Longstreth (5-17). For b. 1779 read b. 10 mo. 14, 1779.

Page 448. SAMUEL SPENCER (5-18). His w. *Martha Longstreth*, b. 7 mo. 11, 1781, d. They lived in Ohio and St. Louis, Mo.

Page 448. DANIEL LONGSTRETH (5-19), b. 12 mo. 23, 1789, d. Fallsington, Pa.

Page 449. For JOHN M. MILNER (5-21) read JOHN M. MILNOR. His w. *Rachel Longstreth*, b. 5 mo. 6, 1791, res. Philadelphia.

Page 449. JOHN L. HAYWARD (5-23). For *Esther L. Longstreth* read *Esther Longstreth*, b, 2 mo. 22, 1796.

Page 449. JOHN KIRKBRIDE LONGSTRETH (5-24), b. 4 mo. 23, 1803, d. near Long Branch, N. J.

Page 452. BENJAMIN LONGSTRETH (5-39). *Erase note* 2. Susannah, wid. of B. L., resides in Philadelphia.

Page 452. *Edith Longstreth* (5-40), w. of JESSE SHOEMAKER. For d. a wid. in Philadelphia, read d. in Philadelphia.

Page 454. DANIEL LONGSTRETH (5.45), and 1st w. *Elizabeth Lancaster.* For had two sons read had two children.

Page 455. Children of DANIEL LONGSTRETH (5-45), and 2d w. *Hannah Townsend.* For Joseph T. (6-178) read Joseph Townsend; for Anna R. (6-183) read Anna Robinson; for David T. (6-184) read David Thomas.

Page 455. Children of CHARLES JARRETT RAAB (5-46). Joseph Longstreth (6-186), for res. Weston, Pa. read res. Nevada, O. For Sarah L. (6-187), read Susan Longstreth; for m. RUSSELL HOLLENBACK, res. Weston, read m. 6 mo. 6, 1863, RUSSELL HOLLENBACK, res. Highland P. O., Bradford Co., Pa.

Page 455. *Susannah Longstreth* (5-47). In note 2, erase, which *probably* was date of her husband's death. After ELLIS CLEAVER, tailor, read and farmer; for d. 2 mo. 7, 1835, read d. 5 mo. 26, 1874.

Page 456. DEMAS COMLY WORRELL (5-48). After his widow res. 1873, for at Byberry read at Mt. Holly, N. J.

Page 459. WILLIAM COLLINS LONGSTRETH (5-75). For Providence Life Ins. read Provident Life Ins.

Page 460. LONGSTRETH. Kate (6-281). For m. HENRY SAYER read m. HENRY SAYEN.

Page 461. RICHARD PRICE (5-85). For b. 1754 read b. 1794.

Page 462. James M. Watson (6-330) d. at his res. in Pittsfield, Mass., May 25, 1874.

Page 463. Dr. ISAAC PARRISH (5-101). His w. *Sarah Redwood Longstreth;* for b. 10 mo. 10, 1812, read b. 12 mo. 9, 1814. Children: For Hetty L. (6-340) read Hetty Longstreth. Helen (6-343), for m. Dr. LEE read m. Dr. CHARLES CARROLL LEE; children: Richard Henry, Thomas Sim, James Parrish, Charles Carroll. For Sarah R. (6-344) read Sarah Redwood. Isaac (6-345) d. 2 mo. 21, 1865. For Samuel L. (6-346) read Samuel Longstreth. *Note* 1. For Burilngton read Burlington.

Page 464. LONGSTRETH. Morris (6-365). After M. D. read consulting physician; for m. *Mary Hastings* read m. *Mary O. Hastings.*

Page 464. Children of MORRIS LONGSTRETH (5-112). For Four read Five; after 6-369 read 6-369*b*. Joseph Cooke, d.

Page 465. LONGSTRETH. Thaddeus (6-382). For m. *Julia M. Bown* read m. *Julia M. Brown.*

Page 466. Erase last three lines, and read: 5-152. *Margaret Orum*, b. 3 mo. 11, 1822, d. 10 mo. 31, 1855 (dau. of Davis, 4-67), m. JOSEPH HOOPES, b, 11 mo. 3, 1814, d. 11 mo. 6, 1852. They lived in Philadelphia, and had three children: 6-409, Clara, b. 8 mo. 27, 1845, res. Philadelphia. ATLEE. 6-409*b*. Morris, b. 3 mo. 20, 1847, d. 11 mo. 17, 1868, *unm.* 6-409*c*. Elizabeth, b. 10 mo. 6, 1851, d. 3 mo. 19, 1865.

Page 467. Children of REUBEN WEBB (5-194). Elizabeth (6-426) res. Philadelphia, wid. of THOMAS HOBSON, M. D.; children, William, m. and res. Kansas City, Mo.; Jane Johnson, res. Phila., *unm.* James (6-427) m. *Susan Graeff*, dau. of Daniel Graeff. She res. in Burlington, N. J.; children, Anna, d. unm., Minnie, m. JAMES KITCHEN, res. Phila., Harriet, Benjamin Coffin and Charles, *unm.* Harriet (6-429) res. Phila., w. of MAHLON K. PAIST, coal merchant. She is a graduate of the Female Medical College of Philadelphia, and in Feb. 1874, was elected a school director from the 13th ward, being the first woman ever elected to a school directorship in Philadelphia.

Page 468. ENOS SMEDLEY (5-202). For res. Easttown township read res. Westchester. His children: For Amy Mary (6-432) read Anna Mary; her husband, JAMES S. JONES, son of Isaac and *Ann Comfort* Jones. Philena S. (6-433), m. 10 mo. 17, 1872, SAMUEL JONES, bro. of James S.

Page 471. NEAL HARDY (6-15). After farmer, read d. in Madison Co., Ind., Nov. 16, 1869. For They res. read She res.; for and have had read They had. *See p.* 496, *note.*

Page 477. For MAHLON MILNER (6-77), read MAHLON MILNOR.

Page 485. ALFRED LONGSTRETH (6-169). For conveyancer read lawyer and conveyancer.

Page 486. SAMUEL TOWNSEND LONGSTRETH'S w. *Jane Lukens Jones* (6-181). For b. 9 mo. 24, 1855, read b. 9 mo. 24, 1835.

Page 486. For *Edward Longstreth* (6-182), read EDWARD LONGSTRETH. For m. *Annie Wise*, read m. *Annie Pusey Wise.*

Page 487. JOSEPH LONGSTRETH RAAB (6-186). For res. Weston, Pa. read res. Nevada, O.

Page 488. *Martha L. Worrell* and ABRAM CORSON (6-195). For m. 6 mo., 1866, read m. 6 mo. 7, 1866.

Page 489. For Little Miama (6-235) read Little Miami.

Page 493. After WILLIAM LONGSTRETH (6-372), read wholesale tea merchant, Philadelphia.

Page 494. After *Clara Hoopes* (6-409) read b. 8 mo. 27, 1845. After GEORGE B. ATLEE, read b. in Philadelphia, 6 mo. 5, 1836, son of Dr. Edwin P. and Margaret Atlee.

Page 495. ATLEE. For Joshua W. (7-496) read Joshua Woolston.

Page 500. JACOB DAWSON (3-1). For d. 1872 read d. in Philadelphia, Sept. 7, 1872. Erase record of children, and read as follows:

4–1. William Henry, b. Sept. 25, 1833, res. New York.
4–2. Charles Wesley, b. Oct. 18, 1835, d. Dec. 1, 1861.
4–3. Erastus Buck, b. April 9, 1838, d. March 8, 1866.
4–4. Wilbur Fisk, b. June 27, 1840, res. Philadelphia; *m.*
4–5. Samuel Martin Walker, b. June 29, 1843, res. Philadelphia.
4–6. Ann Elizabeth, b. Jan. 17, 1846, d. Feb. 21, 1846.
4–7. Margaret Martin, b. April 15, 1848, res. Philadelphia. BRYSON.
4–8. Walter Scott, b. Sept. 6, 1853, d. June 7, 1855.

Page 500, note 1. For John Dawson, of Abington, read John Dawson, of Hatboro.

Page 502. WILBUR FISK DAWSON. For 4-1 read 4-4. After m. read Sept. 10, 1862, *Amanda Collins Simpson.* For five children read six children, as follows:

5–1. Mary Martin, b. Jan. 15, 1864, d. July 4, 1864.
5–2. Henry Light, b. July 17, 1865, d. Aug. 14, 1865.
5–3. Annie Meredith, b. July 5, 1866.
5–4. Carrie Lee, b. March 10, 1868.
5–5. Joseph Henry, b Aug. 17, 1871, d. April 1, 1872.
5–6. Lillian, b. July 30, 1873.

Page 502. For 4-6 read 4-7. For *Margaret Elizabeth Dawson* m. EDWARD BRYSON read *Margaret Martin Dawson* m. May 17, 1868, EDWARD E. BRYSON. Their children:

5–7. Archibald Bingham, b. April 10, 1869.
5–8. Clara Virginia, b. Dec. 27, 1870, d. March 4, 1874.
5–9. Edward Eugene, b. Dec. 12, 1872.

Page 502. Add to Pennsylvania NOTES the following copies of papers in the possession of the Historical Society of Pennsylvania.

IV. "Philadelphia, 3 mo. 2, 1719. Loving Frd. Is. Taylor. The bearer hereof JAMES DAWSON, has agreed with me for 200 acres of Land near Conestoga, whodesires to have it laid out to him next to Thomas Simmons line. He sayes there is a small Improvement on it which he had paid somewhat for to a Mulatto who has since left it. If thou canst comply with his desire please to lay it out to him as soon as may be, because he has paid me almost one half of the money. With sincere respect to thyself and spouse remain thy real Frd. JAMES STEEL." [*Endorsed,* "Warr't, JAMES DAWSON, 200 a. at Conestoga."]

V. Pennsylvania, L. S. By the Commissioners of Property. At the request of THOMAS DAWSON, of the county of Chester, that we will grant him to take up three hundred acres of Land in the said county for which he agrees to pay to the Proprietors use Thirty Pounds for the whole and the usual yearly quit rent of one shilling for each hundred acres. These are to authorize and require thee to survey or cause to be surveyed unto the said THOMAS DAWSON in the aforesaid county of Chester near the land surveyed to Francis Worley, or elsewhere at a sufficient distance from the Indians at Conestogoe, according to the methods of Townships appointed the said quantity of Three hundred acres of Land that has not been already surveyed nor appropriated, nor is seated by the Indians, and make a return thereof unto ye Secretaries office, which survey in case the said Thomas fulfil the agreement within three months shall be valid, otherwise the same to be void as if it had never been made nor this Warr't ever granted. Given under our hands and seal of the Province at Philadelphia the 18th day of February, A.D. 171$\frac{6}{7}$. (signed) ISAAC NORRIS, JAMES LOGAN. To Jacob Taylor, Survr Gen.ll *A true copy.* I desire thee to execute ye above warrt. and make a return unto my office. (signed, JACOB TAYLOR. To Isaac Taylor, surveyor, etc. [Endorsed, "THOMAS DAWSON, 300 a warrant."]

THOS. C. DAWSON OF RENFREW, ONT.
A LUMBERER AND FARMER
HE MOVED FROM ONTARIO TO N.Y.S.
HAD 3 BOYS AND 2 GIRLS
Edward - Charles - Clarence
EMMA and BELLE

Edward - a FARMER IN N.Y.
CLARENCE - a REALTOR IN DETROIT
CHARLES - a FARMER IN N.Y. died in 1915.

INDEXES.

I. Of Dawsons.

Where there are two or more individuals of the same Christian name they are distinguished by their residences, or, if married women, by the names acquired by marriage, such names being printed in CAPITALS.

INDEX II. Names other than Dawson.

Christian names are given only of heads *of* families.

www.ingramcontent.com/pod-product-compliance
Lightning Source LLC
LaVergne TN
LVHW021103110826
845150LV00001B/156

* 9 7 8 1 4 2 5 5 6 5 6 6 4 *